WORLD TRADE ORGANIZATION

Dispute Settlement Reports

2005

Volume XI

Pages 5119-5660

CAMBRIDGE UNIVERSITY PRESS

CAMBRIDGE UNIVERSITY PRESS
Cambridge, New York, Melbourne, Madrid, Cape Town, Singapore, São Paulo

Cambridge University Press
The Edinburgh Building, Cambridge, CB2 8RU, UK

Published in the United States of America by Cambridge University Press, New York

www.cambridge.org
Information on this title: www.cambridge.org/9780521885539

First published 2007

Printed in the United Kingdom at the University Press, Cambridge

A catalogue record for this publication is available from the British Library

ISBN 978-0521-88553-9 hardback

THE WTO DISPUTE SETTLEMENT REPORTS

The *Dispute Settlement Reports* of the World Trade Organization (the "WTO") include panel and Appellate Body reports, as well as arbitration awards, in disputes concerning the rights and obligations of WTO Members under the provisions of the *Marrakesh Agreement Establishing the World Trade Organization*. The *Dispute Settlement Reports* are available in English. Volumes comprising one or more complete cases contain a cumulative list of published disputes. The cumulative list for cases that cover more than one volume is to be found in the first volume for that case.

This volume may be cited as DSR 2005:XI

TABLE OF CONTENTS

Page

European Communities – Protection of Trademarks and Geographical Indications for Agricultural Products and Foodstuffs, Complaint by Australia (WT/DS290)

TABLE OF ANNEXES

ANNEX B

SUBMISSIONS BY THE EUROPEAN COMMUNITIES

Contents

ANNEX C

ARGUMENTS OF THE THIRD PARTIES

ANNEX D

MISCELLANEOUS

Contents

ANNEX B

SUBMISSIONS BY THE EUROPEAN COMMUNITIES

ANNEX B-1

EUROPEAN COMMUNITIES' REQUEST FOR A PRELIMINARY RULING

(24 February 2004)

TABLE OF CONTENTS

Page

Short Title	Full Case Title and Citation of Case
Canada – Wheat	Preliminary Ruling of the Panel, *Canada – Measures Relating to Exports of Wheat and Treatment of Imported Grain*, WT/DS276/12, circulated on 21 July 2003
EC – Bananas III	Appellate Body Report, *European Communities – Regime for the Importation, Sale and Distribution of Bananas*, WT/DS27/AB/R, adopted 25 September 1997
Guatemala – Cement I	Appellate Body Report, *Guatemala – Anti-Dumping Investigation Regarding Portland Cement from Mexico*, WT/DS60/AB/R, adopted 25 November 1998
Korea – Dairy	Appellate Body Report, *Korea – Definitive Safeguard Measure on Imports of Certain Dairy Products*, WT/DS98/AB/R, adopted 12 January 2000
Thailand – H-Beams	Appellate Body Report, *Thailand – Anti-Dumping Duties on Angles, Shapes and Sections of Iron or Non-Alloy Steel and H-Beams from Poland*, WT/DS122/AB/R, adopted 5 April 2001
US – Carbon Steel from Germany	Panel Report, *United States – Countervailing Duties on Certain Corrosion-Resistant Carbon Steel Flat Products from Germany*, WT/DS213/R and Corr.1, adopted 19 December 2002 Appellate Body Report, *United States – Countervailing Duties on Certain Corrosion-Resistant Carbon Steel Flat Products from Germany*, WT/DS213/AB/R, adopted 28 November 2002
US – FSC	Appellate Body Report, *United States – Tax Treatment for "Foreign Sales Corporations"*, WT/DS108/AB/R, adopted 20 March 2000
US – Lamb	Panel Report, *United States – Safeguard Measures on Imports of Fresh, Chilled or Frozen Lamb Meat from New Zealand and Australia*, WT/DS177/R, WT/DS178/R, adopted 16 May 2001

I. INTRODUCTION

1. The European Communities (hereinafter "the EC") is of the view that the requests for the establishment of the Panel made by Australia (hereinafter: Australian request)[1] and by the United States (hereinafter: United States request)[2] do not meet the requirements of Article 6.2 of the Dispute Settlement Understanding (DSU).

2. The Panel requests fail to identify the specific measure at issue in the present dispute. Moreover, the Panel requests do not provide a brief summary of the legal basis of the complaint sufficient to present the problem clearly.

3. The respect of the requirements of Article 6.2 DSU is an essential precondition for the jurisdiction of a Panel. Where a complaining party has failed to clearly set out its claim in accordance with Article 6.2 DSU, the Panel does not have jurisdiction.

4. Moreover, the deficiencies of the Panel requests seriously prejudice the due process rights of the EC as a defending party. As a defending party, the EC is entitled to know the case it has to answer. The Panel requests in the present case do not meet the minimum requirements necessary for ensuring a fair and orderly conduct of the dispute settlement proceedings.

5. Given these fundamental concerns, the EC requests that the Panel issue a preliminary ruling regarding Article 6.2 DSU.

II. THE REQUIREMENTS OF ARTICLE 6.2 DSU

6. Article 6.2 DSU sets out the following minimum requirements with which any Panel request must comply:

> The request for the establishment of a panel shall be made in writing. It shall indicate whether consultations were held, identify the specific measures at issue and provide a brief summary of the legal basis of the complaint sufficient to present the problem clearly.

A. The content and purpose of Article 6.2 DSU

7. In *Korea – Dairy*, the Appellate Body held that Article 6.2 of the DSU imposes four separate requirements:[3]

> When parsed into its constituent parts, Article 6.2 may be seen to impose the following requirements. The request must: (i) be in writing; (ii) indicate whether consultations were held; (iii) identify the specific measures at issue; and (iv) provide a brief summary of

---

1 Request of 18 August 2003, WT/DS290/18.

2 Request of 18 August 2003, WT/DS174/20.

3 Appellate Body Report, *Korea –Dairy*, para. 120.

> the legal basis of the complaint sufficient to present the problem clearly. In its fourth requirement, Article 6.2 demands only a summary – and it may be a brief one – of the legal basis of the complaint; but the summary must, in any event, be one that is "sufficient to present the problem clearly". It is not enough, in other words, that "the legal basis of the complaint" is summarily identified; the identification must "present the problem clearly".

8. The objective and purpose of Article 6.2 of the DSU is to guarantee a minimum measure of procedural fairness throughout the proceedings. This is of particular importance to the defendant, who must rely on the Panel request in order to begin preparing its defense. Similarly, WTO Members who intend to participate as third parties must be informed of the subject-matter of the dispute. This underlying rationale of Article 6.2 DSU has been explained by the Appellate Body in *Thailand - H-Beams*:[4]

> Article 6.2 of the DSU calls for sufficient clarity with respect to the legal basis of the complaint, that is, with respect to the "claims" that are being asserted by the complaining party. *A defending party is entitled to know what case it has to answer, and what violations have been alleged so that it can begin preparing its defence.* Likewise, those Members of the WTO who intend to participate as third parties in panel proceedings must be informed of the legal basis of the complaint. This requirement of due process is fundamental to ensuring a fair and orderly conduct of dispute settlement proceedings.

B. The Panel must not assume jurisdiction in respect of claims that have not been established in accordance with Article 6.2 DSU

9. Moreover, the respect of the requirements of Article 6.2 DSU is of crucial importance for properly establishing the jurisdiction of the Panel. As the Appellate Body has confirmed in *US – Carbon Steel*, the panel request forms the basis of the panel's terms of reference under Article 7.1 of the DSU:[5]

> There are, therefore, two distinct requirements, namely identification of *the specific measures at issue*, and the provision of a *brief summary of the legal basis of the complaint* (or the *claims*). Together, they comprise the "matter referred to the DSB", which forms the basis for a panel's terms of reference under Article 7.1 of the DSU.

10. For this reason, a strict respect of the requirements of Article 6.2 DSU is essential for the orderly conduct of dispute settlement proceedings under the

[4] Appellate Body Report, *Thailand – H Beams*, para. 88 (emphasis added). Similarly Appellate Body Report, *US – Carbon Steel*, para. 126.

[5] Appellate Body Report, *US – Carbon Steel*, para. 125. Similarly, Appellate Body Report, *Guatemala – Cement*, para. 72.

DSU. As the Appellate Body has clearly stated in *EC – Bananas*, Panels must therefore verify carefully that the conditions or Article 6.2 DSU are fulfilled:[6]

> As a panel request is normally not subjected to detailed scrutiny by the DSB, it is incumbent upon a panel to examine the request for the establishment of the panel very carefully to ensure its compliance with both the letter and the spirit of Article 6.2 of the DSU. It is important that a panel request be sufficiently precise for two reasons: first, it often forms the basis for the terms of reference of the panel pursuant to Article 7 of the DSU; and, second, it informs the defending party and the third parties of the legal basis of the complaint.

11. Accordingly, the present Panel must verify carefully that the Panel request meet the requirements of Article 6.2 DSU. The Panel must not assume jurisdiction over any claim that has not been set out in accordance with Article 6.2 DSU.

C. The requirements of Article 6.2 DSU must be evaluated on the face of the Panel request

12. In *EC – Bananas*, the Appellate Body has clarified that the claims, which are set out in the panel request, must be distinguished from the subsequent arguments of the parties in support of their claim. Consequently, the Appellate Body has held that a faulty Panel request cannot be subsequently "cured" by the written submission of the parties:[7]

> We do not agree with the Panel that "even if there was some uncertainty whether the panel request had met the requirements of Article 6.2, the first written submissions of the Complainants 'cured' that uncertainty because their submissions were sufficiently detailed to present all the factual and legal issues clearly". Article 6.2 of the DSU requires that the *claims*, but not the *arguments*, must all be specified sufficiently in the request for the establishment of a panel in order to allow the defending party and any third parties to know the legal basis of the complaint. If a *claim* is not specified in the request for the establishment of a panel, then a faulty request cannot be subsequently "cured" by a complaining party's argumentation in its first written submission to the panel or in any other submission or statement made later in the panel proceeding.

13. As a consequence, the only basis on which to establish whether a Panel request is in conformity with the requirements of Article 6.2 is the text of the

---

[6] Appellate Body Report, *EC – Bananas III*, para. 142 (emphasis added). Similarly also Appellate Body Report, *US – Carbon Steel*, para. 126.

[7] Appellate Body Report, *EC – Bananas III*, para. 143.

request itself. This has been confirmed by the Appellate Body in *United States - Carbon Steel*:[8]

> As we have said previously, compliance with the requirements of Article 6.2 must be demonstrated *on the face of the request* for the establishment of a panel. Defects in the request for the establishment of a panel cannot be "cured" in the subsequent submissions of the parties during the panel proceedings.

III. THE PANEL REQUESTS FAIL TO IDENTIFY THE "SPECIFIC MEASURE AT ISSUE"

14. Both Panel requests identify the measure at issue as Council Regulation (EEC) No. 2081/92 on the protection of geographical indications and designations of origin for agricultural products and foodstuffs, as amended (hereinafter: Regulation 2081/92). Moreover, the Australian request, in its fourth paragraph, defines the "EC measure" as also including "related implementing and enforcement measures". In the view of the EC, these references are insufficient in order to define the "specific measure at issue", as required by Article 6.2 DSU.

A. The references to Regulation 2081/92 are not sufficiently specific

15. The EC considers that the references to Regulation 2081/92 are not sufficiently specific to permit an identification of the "specific measure at issue" in the present dispute.

16. The EC would like to stress that Article 6.2 DSU requires not only the identification of a "measure", but of the "*specific* measure at issue". The wording of Article 6.2 DSU is different from that of Article 4.4 DSU, which provides that consultation requests must identify "the measures at issue". As the Panel in *Canada – Wheat* has convincingly explained, this difference in wording is intentional, and must be given meaning:[9]

> Having regard to the relevant context of Article 6.2 of the DSU, we note Article 4.4 of the DSU, which deals with the contents of requests for consultations. It states in relevant part that "any request for consultations shall give the reasons for the request, including identification of the measures at issue". Notably, Article 4.4 omits the term "specific" in referring to the "measures at issue". We believe that this difference in language is not inadvertent and must be given meaning. Indeed, in our view, this difference in language supports the view that requests for consultations need not be as specific and as detailed as requests for

[8] Appellate Body Report, *United States –Carbon Steel*, para. 127 (emphasis added).
[9] Preliminary Ruling by the Panel, *Canada – Wheat*, para. 15.

> establishment of a panel under Article 6.2 of the DSU. As a corollary, in our view, this relevant context bears out the importance of the term "specific" as it appears in Article 6.2.

17. In the view of the EC, what can be considered a "specific measure" will depend on the circumstances of the particular case, and in particular on the characteristics of the measure in question. Where a measure is of a relatively simple character, or where it is clear from the circumstances of the case which aspect of the measure is contested, it may be sufficient to refer to the measure as a whole and identify it by name, number, or date of adoption.

18. However, such a reference to a "measure" as a whole may not always be sufficient to establish the "specific measure at issue". This is the case, in particular, where the measure in question is a complex legislative text. For instance, it would not seem conceivable to the EC that a WTO member would refer, in a request for the establishment of a Panel, simply to the Civil Code of another member, without specifying which specific provision is at issue in the dispute. Accordingly, in the case of complex legislative measures, it will not be sufficient to refer to the measure as a whole, but it will be necessary to identify the specific provisions or sections of the measure which are at issue.

19. In the present case, Regulation 2081/92 is a measure with establishes the legal framework for the protection of geographical indications and designations of origin for agricultural products and foodstuffs in the European Community. The text of Regulation 2081/92, as most recently amended by Council Regulation (EC) no. 806/2003 of 14 April 2003, is attached as Exhibit EC–1.

20. The EC does not propose to describe in detail the content of Regulation 2081/92 in the context of the present request for a preliminary ruling. However, the EC believes that even a cursory study of Regulation 2081/92 will confirm that this regulation is a complex piece of legislation in the field of the protection of intellectual property. As is typical for such legislation, Regulation 2081/92 deals with a host of issues relating to all aspects of the protection of geographical indications and designations of origin for agricultural products and foodstuffs.

21. The text of Regulation 2081/92 extends over 15 pages, including two annexes. The operational provisions of Regulation 2081/92 are contained in 22 Articles, each of which in turn is subdivided into numerous further paragraphs and sections. These articles deal with a host of widely differing issues. Purely for illustrative purposes, and without any claim to being exhaustive or particularly detailed, the following topics are dealt with in Regulation 2081/92:

- The objective and scope of application of the regulation (Article 1);
- definitions (Article 2);
- exclusion from registration of names, and in particular the issue of generic names (Article 3);
- product specifications (Article 4);

- the right to apply for registrations and the procedure for applications (Article 5);
- the procedures for registration of geographical indications and related issues; the issue of homonymous names (Article 6);
- objections to registrations (Article 7);
- conditions for the use of geographical indications and designations of origin (Article 8);
- the amendment of product specifications (Article 9);
- inspection procedures (Article 10);
- procedures in case product specifications are not respected (Article 11);
- cancellation of protected names (Article 11a);
- the application of the regulation to agricultural products and foodstuffs from third countries (Article 12);
- the application procedure for the protection of third country geographical indications (Article 12a);
- the registration procedure for the protection of third country geographical indications (Article 12b);
- the amendment of the product specifications for third country geographical indications (Article 12c);
- objections to the registration of geographical indications emanating from third countries (Article 12d);
- the protection of registered names (Article 13);
- certain questions regarding the relationship between geographical indications and trademarks (Article 14);
- the Committee assisting the Commission (Article 15);
- implementing rules (Article 16);
- entry into force (Article 18).

22. The unspecific reference to "Regulation 2081/92" made in the Panel requests does not permit the EC to understand which specific aspects among those covered by Regulation 2081/92 the complainants intend to raise in the context of the present proceedings. This appears particularly objectionable given the fact that it would have been easily possible for the complainants to provide more specific references to individual provisions of Regulation 2081/92.

23. For these reasons, the EC submits that the references to "Regulation 2081/92" do not meet the requirement of the identification of the "specific measure at issue" in Article 6.2 DSU.

B. The References to "related implementing and enforcement measures" are not sufficiently specific

24. In the fourth paragraph of its Panel request, Australia has referred to "related implementing and enforcement measures" as part of the "EC measure".[10] The EC is of the view that this blanket reference to "related implementing and enforcement measures" falls short of the requirement to identify the "specific measure at issue" in Article 6.2 DSU.

25. The requirement to identify the "specific measure at issue" means that if the measure is not already identified beyond reasonable doubt through elements such as name, number, or date of adoption of the act, then the Panel request must at the very least contain the necessary information which enables the Panel, the defendant, and the third parties to establish *with full certainty* which is the specific measure at issue in the present dispute. This has been convincingly stated by the Panel in *Canada – Wheat*:[11]

> We consider that in the absence of an explicit identification of a measure of general application by name, as in the present case, sufficient information must be provided in the request for establishment of a panel itself that effectively identifies the precise measures at issue. Whether sufficient information is provided on the face of the panel request will depend, as noted above, on whether the information provided serves the purposes of Article 6.2, and in particular its due process objective, as well as the specific circumstances of each case, including the type of measure that is at issue.

26. As the Panel in *Canada – Wheat* also explained, due process does not allow the complainant to shift the burden of identifying the specific measures under challenge to the defendant:[12]

> Due process requires that the complaining party fully assume the burden of identifying the specific measures under challenge. In the present case, the panel request effectively shifts part of that burden onto Canada as the responding party, inasmuch as it leaves Canada little choice, if it wants to begin preparing its defence, but to undertake legal research and exercise judgement in order to establish the precise identity of the laws and regulations implicated by the panel request.

27. The Australian request falls entirely short of these requirements. The Australian request contains no elements to identify the "measures" at issue, other

---

[10] In this context, the EC notes that whereas the United States amended request for consultations (WT/DS174/1/Add.1), in its second paragraph, included a reference to "related implementing and enforcement measures", such a reference no longer appears in the Panel request, which, in its third and fourth paragraph, refers exclusively to "Regulation 2081/92". Accordingly, the EC understands that the United States Panel request extends only to Regulation 2081/92.

[11] Preliminary Ruling by the Panel, *Canada – Wheat*, para. 20.

[12] Preliminary Ruling by the Panel, *Canada – Wheat*, para. 24.

than they are "related" and that they are supposed to be "enforcement or implementing measures".

28. The statement that thc measures are "related" is so vague that it does not permit any meaningful narrowing-down of the measures in question. In fact, a whole range of legislative and other measures might be considered to be "related" in some way to the present dispute, including trademark and other intellectual property legislation, unfair competition laws, law on food labelling and food marketing, or consumer protection laws. Moreover, such laws may exist at the level of both the European Community and its Member States.

29. Similarly, the reference to "enforcement or implementing measures" does not provide the required precision with respect to the definition of the specific measure at issue. Since Regulation 2081/92 is a complex piece of intellectual property legislation, there is very large number of different measures that are necessary for its implementation and enforcement.

30. First of all, implementation may occur through legislative measures, for instance through the adoption of "detailed rules" on the basis of Article 16 of Regulation 2081/92. More importantly, implementation and enforcement may require measures of the executive, for instance concerning the transmission of applications or objections, the decision to register or to cancel geographical indications, or to amend specifications, etc. Finally, implementation and enforcement is also a responsibility of the judiciary, which is responsible for the judicial review of the actions of the Community and Member States authorities in the application of Regulation 2081/92.

31. Moreover, it should be noted that the implementation of Regulation 2081/92 is not only the responsibility of the Community, but also that of its Member States, who, for instance, are responsible for the transmission of applications and objections regarding the registration of geographical indications to the Commission. Therefore, Member States also may have to adopt implementing rules, and take decisions which are subject to judicial review by national courts.

32. Finally, it should be noted that the measures which have been taken for implementing or enforcing Regulation 2081/92 are of a very high number. To take only one figure, the EC has by now registered 640 geographical indications or designations of origin. The EC would consider it inconceivable that each one of these registrations would be the subject of the present dispute settlement proceedings simply because of the blanket reference to "implementing and enforcement measures".

33. For these reasons, the EC submits that the reference to "related implementing and enforcement measures" in the Australian request fails to identify the "specific measure at issue".

IV. THE PANEL REQUESTS DO NOT CONTAIN A BRIEF SUMMARY OF THE LEGAL BASIS OF THE COMPLAINT

34. The Panel requests in the present case do not only fail to identify the specific measure at issue. They also fail to include a brief summary of the legal basis of the complaint.

A. The brief summary of the legal basis of the complaint

35. Article 6.2 DSU requires that a request for the establishment of a Panel must contain a "brief summary of the legal basis of the complaint sufficient to present the problem clearly".

36. As the Appellate Body has stated in *EC – Bananas*, there is a distinction between the claims, which must be contained in the Panel request, and the arguments supporting these claims, which are set out in the subsequent submissions of the Parties.[13] However, in *Korea – Dairy*, the Appellate Body has also clarified that the mere listing of provisions claimed to have been violated may not be sufficient for the purposes of Article 6.2 DSU:[14]

> Identification of the treaty provisions claimed to have been violated by the respondent is always necessary both for purposes of defining the terms of reference of a panel and for informing the respondent and the third parties of the claims made by the complainant; such identification is a minimum prerequisite if the legal basis of the complaint is to be presented at all. But it may not always be enough. There may be situations where the simple listing of the articles of the agreement or agreements involved may, in the light of attendant circumstances, suffice to meet the standard of *clarity* in the statement of the legal basis of the complaint. However, there may also be situations in which the circumstances are such that the mere listing of treaty articles would not satisfy the standard of Article 6.2. This may be the case, for instance, where the articles listed establish not one single, distinct obligation, but rather multiple obligations. In such a situation, the listing of articles of an agreement, in and of itself, may fall short of the standard of Article 6.2.

37. In the concrete case, the Appellate Body was primarily concerned with the question of whether a reference to a provision in a WTO agreement may be sufficient when such provision contains multiple obligations. However, the findings of the Appellate Body are of a more general importance. First, the Appellate Body held that the precise identification of the WTO provisions alleged to have been violated is always required under Article 6.2 DSU. Second, the Appellate Body has also stated that the identification of treaty provisions *may not be enough* to state the problem clearly. In other words, the identification of

---

[13] Appellate Body Report, *EC – Bananas III*, para. 141.
[14] Appellate Body Report, *Korea – Dairy*, para. 124.

the treaty provisions alleged to have been violated *is a necessary, but not a sufficient condition* under Article 6.2 DSU.

38. It is this second element which is of particular interest in the present case. Article 6.2 DSU does not require complainants to "to list the treaty provisions alleged to have been violated". Rather, it obliges complainants to provide a "brief summary of the legal basis of the complaint sufficient to present the problem clearly". The reference to treaty provisions is only one element of the "legal basis of the complaint", which must also include other factual and legal elements necessary to present the problem clearly.

B. The Panel requests fail to "present the problem clearly"

39. In the view of the EC, the Panel requests do not establish the problem clearly in accordance with Article 6.2 DSU. Even a cursory examination of the Panel requests will show that the "summary of the legal basis of the complaint" provided in them is in fact limited to vague listings of articles and some narrative text which, in general, is limited to restating the language of the treaty provision in question. As the EC will show, by adopting such a minimalist approach, both the United States and the Australian request fail to present the problem clearly in accordance with Article 6.2 DSU.

1. The United States request

40. The United States request is drafted in an extremely minimalist way. The "claims" of the United States seem to be contained in the third paragraph of the United States request. In this short paragraph, the United States appears to raise seven claims with respect to Regulation 2081/92. In particular, the United States claims that Regulation 2081/92:

- does not provide the same treatment to other nationals and products originating outside the EC that it provides to the EC's own nationals and products (**claim 1**);
- does not accord immediately and unconditionally to the nationals and products of each WTO Member any advantage, favour, privilege or immunity granted to the nationals and products of other WTO Members (**claim 2**);
- diminishes the legal protection for trademarks (including to prevent the use of an identical or similar sign that is likely to confuse and adequate protection against invalidation) (**claim 3**);
- does not provide legal means for interested parties to prevent the misleading use of a geographical indication (**claim 4**);
- does not define a geographical indication in a manner that is consistent with the definition provided in the TRIPS Agreement (**claim 5**);

- is not sufficiently transparent (**claim 6**);
- and does not provide adequate enforcement procedures (**claim 7**).

(a) The United States request does not indicate the legal bases of the claims

41. The United States request does not provide any indication of a legal basis for each of these claims. The only reference to substantive WTO provisions is contained in the fourth paragraph of the Panel request, which states that Regulation 2081/92 appears to be inconsistent with "TRIPS Agreement Articles 1.1, 2.1 (incorporating by reference Article 2 of the *Paris Convention for the Protection of Industrial Property* (Paris Convention (1967)), 3.1, 4, 16.1, 20, 22.1, 22.2, 24.5, 41.1, 41.2, 41.4, 42, 44.1, 63.1, 63.3, 65.1" as well as "Articles I and III:4 of the GATT 1994".

42. This long list of WTO provisions, however, is in no way correlated with the individual claims raised in the third paragraph of the United States request. On the other hand, it is not conceivable that each of the claims of the United States would be based on all the provisions mentioned in the fourth paragraph of the United States request. The result is a total lack of clarity regarding the legal bases of the United States' claims. By not even identifying the provisions of the WTO agreements which it considers to underlie each of its claims, the US falls short of the minimum requirements for the brief summary as established by the Appellate Body in *Korea – Dairy*.[15]

(b) The United States claims are unclear

43. The absence of a sufficient summary of the legal bases of the United States claims can also be demonstrated for each of the claims set out in the third paragraph of the United States request.

44. As regards the **first claim**, the United States is alleging that Regulation 2081/92 "does not provide the same treatment to other nationals and products originating outside the EC that it provides to the EC's own nationals and products". This claim would appear to be a reference to the principle of national treatment, as contained in Article 3 TRIPS and Article III:4 GATT. However, the US claim is limited to a paraphrasing of the treaty language of these two provisions. The US claim does not permit to understand which provision or aspect of Regulation 2081/92 is supposed to violate the national treatment principle, and in which way such a violation is deemed to occur. This does not constitue a summary of the legal basis of the claim sufficient to present the problem clearly.

45. In its **second claim**, the United States claims that Regulation 2081/92 "does not accord immediately and unconditionally to the nationals and products of each WTO Member any advantage, favour, privilege or immunity granted to the nationals and products of other WTO Members". This claim seems to be a

[15] *Ibid.*

reference to the principle of most favoured nation treatment, as contained in Article 4 TRIPS and Article I:1 GATT. However, as the first claim, this claim is limited to the paraphrasing of the language of treaty provisions, without any indication of which provision of Regulation 2081/92 is supposed to constitute the violation, and how such a violation occurs. More specifically, the United States request does not indicate which are the "other WTO members" who are supposed to enjoy more favourable treatment, what constitutes this "more favourable treatment", and how it is conferred.

46. As regards the **third claim**, the United States alleges that Regulation 2081/92 "diminishes the legal protection for trademarks". Unfortunately, the United States does not provide any further explanation as to why it considers that Regulation 2081/92 diminishes the "legal protection of trademarks". In the view of the EC, this does not constitute a meaningful description of the claim. The claim is made no clearer by the cryptic parenthesis "including to prevent the use of an identical or similar sign that is likely to confuse and adequate protection against invalidation", which the United States has added to its claim. Moreover, this parenthesis would seems to indicate that there might be other aspects diminishing the legal protection for trademarks, without however indicating what these aspects are.

47. The absence of a brief summary of the third claim is further compounded by the absence of any specific references to the provisions of Regulation 2081/92. It is certainly correct that Regulation 2081/92 contains various provisions also concerning trademarks. For instance, Article 14.1 of the Regulation concerns the conditions under which the registration of a trademark conflicting with a geographical indication will be refused or invalidated. Article 14.2 deals with situations of coexistence between trademarks and geographical indications. Article 14.3 provides for situations where, in the light of a trademark's reputation, renown, and length of time of use, registration of a geographical indication shall be refused. Finally, the existence of trademarks is mentioned as a possible ground for objection in Article 7 (4) of Regulation 2081/92.

48. In other words, Regulation 2081/92 deals with conflicts between trademarks and geographical indications in a number of different constellations, and provides for specific solutions for each of these. The United States request, by merely referring to the "legal protection of trademarks", does not enable the EC to understand which specific problems the United States wishes to raise in this respect.

49. In its **fourth claim**, the United States alleges that Regulation 2081/92 "does not provide legal means for interested parties to prevent the misleading use of a geographical indication". This claim is not comprehensible to the EC. In its Article 13, Regulation 2081/92 contains detailed provisions regarding the protection of registered geographical indications. These provisions provide interested parties with the legal means to prevent the misleading use of a geographical indication. In the absence of further explanations, the EC fails to comprehend what is the claim that the United States is intending to establish.

50. In its **fifth claim**, the United States claims that Regulation 2081/92 does not define a geographical indication in a manner that is consistent with the definition provided in the TRIPS Agreement. First of all, the United States does not explain what are the differences in the definition of geographical indications between the TRIPS Agreement and Regulation 2081/92. Moreover, there is no conceivable legal basis for the US claim. It is certainly true that Article 22.1 TRIPS contains a definition of geographical indications. However, this definition is explicitly made "for the purposes of this Agreement", and in particular for the subsequent provisions setting out the substantive obligations with respect to the protection of geographic indications. In contrast, Article 22.1 does not contain any independent obligation to "define" a geographical indication in any particular way. It is therefore irrelevant under the TRIPS Agreement how the legislation of a WTO Member "defines" a geographical indication, provided that the Member affords geographical indications the necessary protection as required in the provisions of the TRIPS Agreement. In the view of the EC, the United States fails therefore to set out a claim in this respect.

51. In its **sixth claim**, the United States pretends that Regulation 2081/92 "is not sufficiently transparent". Once again, this claim is incomprehensible to the EC. Regulation 2081/92 is a legislative measure adopted by the Council of the European Union, and published in the Official Journal of the European Union. The EC notes that unlike Australia, the United States refers to the transparency of the Regulation, rather than that of its application. The EC does not understand, however, how a legislative measure such as Regulation 2081/92 can be said not to be "sufficiently transparent". In any case, the US request fails to state in which respect Regulation 2081/92 is supposed not to be "sufficiently transparent".

52. Finally, in its **seventh claim**, the United States claims that Regulation 2081/92 "does not provide adequate enforcement procedures". In the view of the EC, this claim is devoid of all clarity. The United States request neither indicates what, in its view, would be "adequate enforcement procedures", nor in which way Regulation 2081/92 falls short of providing such procedures. Moreover, the United States request does not identify what is the right to be enforced, an in particular whether it is talking about the enforcement of geographical indications or of trademarks.

53. Overall, the EC considers that the United States request fails both to identify the specific measure at issue, and to set out the claims of the United States. The compounded effect of these deficiencies is a Panel request of such vagueness and ambiguity that the EC is not capable to understand which is the case that the United States would like it to answer. For these reasons, the Panel must reject the US request as being incompatible with Article 6.2 DSU.

2. *The Australian request*

54. The Australian request is marked by deficiencies similar to those of the United States request.

55. The claims of Australia appear to be contained in the fifth paragraph of the Australian request. In this paragraph, Australia claims that Regulation 2081/92 (which, according to Australia, also includes its "related measures"):

- diminishes the legal protection for trademarks under the TRIPS Agreement, contrary to Articles 1, 2 (incorporating by reference Articles 6*quinques*(B), 10, 10*bis* and 10*ter* of the Paris Convention (1967)), 16, 20, 24.5, 41 and/or 42 of the TRIPS Agreement (**claim 1**);
- does not accord immediately and unconditionally to the nationals and/or products of each WTO Member any advantage, favour privilege or immunity granted to the nationals of any other WTO Member, contrary to Articles 1 and 4 of the TRIPS Agreement and/or Article I:1 of GATT 1994 (**claim 2**);
- does not accord to nationals and/or products of each WTO Member treatment no less favourable than that it accords to its own nationals and/or like products of national origin, contrary to Articles 1, 2 (incorporating by reference Article 2 of the Paris Convention (1967)) and 3.1 of the TRIPS Agreement and/or Article III:4 of GATT 1994 (**claim 3**);
- does not provide the legal means for interested parties to prevent misleading use of a geographical indication and/or to prevent any use of a geographical indication which constitutes an act of unfair competition within the meaning of Article 10*bis* of the Paris Convention (1967), contrary to Articles 1 and 22.2 of the TRIPS Agreement (**claim 4**);
- is not applied in a transparent manner, contrary to Articles 1, and 63.1 and 63.3 of the TRIPS Agreement (**claim 5**);
- is a technical regulation within the meaning of Annex 1 to the TBT Agreement, does not accord to products imported from the territory of any WTO Member treatment no less favourable than that accorded to like products of national origin and/or to like products originating in any other country, and/or has been prepared, adopted and/or applied with the effect of creating unnecessary obstacles to trade, being more trade-restrictive than necessary to fulfil a legitimate objective, taking account of the risks non-fulfilment would create, contrary to Articles 2.1 and 2.2 of the TBT Agreement (**claim 6**).

(a) The legal bases of the claims indicated in the Australian request are in some cases unclear

56. The structure of the Australian request differs from that of the United States in that Australia does indicate, for each of the claims it makes, the provision of the WTO agreements which it considers violated. However, even

these listings lack, in some instances, the precision required by the Appellate Body in *Korea – Dairy*.[16]

57. In its first claim, Australia is referring to "Article 41 and/or 42 of the TRIPS Agreement. However, Article 41 TRIPS Agreement is a complex provision subdivided into a number of paragraphs, which contains a number of different obligations.[17] The same also applies for Article 42 TRIPS Agreement, which, although set out in one paragraph, also comprises several sentences establishing distinct obligations for WTO Members. Finally, the EC does not understand the "and/or" which seems to indicate that Articles 41 and 42 TRIPS are somehow alternative obligations.

58. Also in its first claim, Australia refers, in conjunction with Article 2 TRIPS Agreement, to Articles 10, 10*bis* and 10*ter* of the Paris Convention. Once again, these articles of the Paris Convention are complex provisions subdivided into various paragraphs, and imposing numerous distinct obligations.

59. Accordingly, the EC considers that the references to Articles 41 and 42 TRIPS Agreement, and to Articles 10, 10*bis* and 10*ter* of the Paris Convention do not meet the minimum requirements of specificity under Article 6.2 DSU.

(b) The Australian claims are unclear

60. However, even where the Australian request lists correctly the provisions of the WTO agreements, this indication of treaty provisions is not sufficient for the purposes of Article 6.2 DSU. This is due to the fact that the narrative description of the claims, as in the case of the United States request, is limited to the paraphrasing of the text of treaty provisions, or is so excessively vague that it does not permit to understand the substance of Australia's claims.

61. Since most of Australia's claims are similar to those of the United States, reference can be made to what has been said about the United States request. Australia's **claim 1** is almost identical to the United States claim 3,[18] and similarly fails to meet the requirements of Article 6.2 DSU.[19] Australia's **claim 2** is similar to US claim 2, and Australia's **claim 3** is similar to US claim 1. Like the US claims, Australia's claims 2 and 3 are limited to the restatement of language already contained in treaty provisions, and therefore encounter the same objections.[20] Australia's **claim 4** corresponds to the fourth claim of the United States, so that reference can be made to what has been said in this respect.[21] Finally, **claim 5** corresponds to United States claim 6, with the sole difference that Australia refers to the transparency of the "application of Regulation 2081/92", rather than that of the Regulation itself. However, since Australia fails to explain in which way Regulation 2081/92 is not applied in a

---

[16] Appellate Body Report, *Korea – Dairy*, para. 124. For the full quotation, see above para. 36.

[17] It is useful to note that the United States request refers only to Articles 41.2 and 41.4 TRIPS.

[18] The only difference is that the Australian request does not contain the cryptic parenthesis included in the United States request.

[19] Supra para. 46 to 48.

[20] Supra para. 44 to 45.

[21] Supra para. 49.

transparent way, its claim fails to meet the requirements of Article 6.2 DSU for the same reasons as the United States claim.[22]

62. The only claim of Australia which finds no equivalent in the United States request is **claim 6**, by which Australia raises certain claims under the TBT Agreement, namely that Regulation 2081/92 "is a technical regulation within the meaning of Annex 1 to the TBT Agreement, does not accord to products imported from the territory of any WTO Member treatment no less favourable than that accorded to like products of national origin and/or to like products originating in any other country, and/or has been prepared, adopted and/or applied with the effect of creating unnecessary obstacles to trade, being more trade-restrictive than necessary to fulfil a legitimate objective, taking account of the risks non-fulfilment would create, contrary to Articles 2.1 and 2.2 of the TBT Agreement".

63. As to the first element of this claim, namely whether Regulation 2081/92 is a "technical regulation" within the meaning of Annex 1 to the TBT Agreement, the EC considers that this cannot constitute an admissible claim, since Point 1 of Annex 1 to the TBT Agreement, which defines the term "technical regulation" for the purposes of the TBT Agreement, does not impose any obligations which could have been violated by the EC.[23]

64. As regards the claims that Regulation 2081/92 does not accord to products imported from the territory of any WTO Member treatment no less favourable than that accorded to like products of national origin and/or to like products originating in any other country, and/or has been prepared, adopted and/or applied with the effect of creating unnecessary obstacles to trade, these claims merely seem to restate language which is contained in Article 2.1 and 2.2 of the TBT Agreement, without however providing any indication of how Regulation 2081/92, and which provision thereof, violates these obligations. For the same reasons as Australia's claims 2 and 3, claim 6 therefore fails to meet the requirements of Article 6.2 DSU.

65. In conclusion, both the United States and the US request fail to contain a brief summary of the legal basis of the claims, as required by Article 6.2 DSU. Both request do not "present the problem clearly". For the reasons set out above, the EC considers that both the Australian and the US Panel requests fail to meet the requirements of Article 6.2 DSU.

V. THE DEFICIENCIES OF THE PANEL REQUESTS RESULT IN SERIOUS PREJUDICE FOR THE EUROPEAN COMMUNITY AS A DEFENDANT

66. As has been stated above, the requirements of Article 6.2 DSU also serve to protect the due process rights of the defending party in dispute settlement

[22] Supra para. 51.
[23] Cf. also the discussion of United States claim 5 (supra para. 50).

proceedings under the DSU.[24] As a consequence, the Appellate Body has, when considering the requirements of Article 6.2 DSU, attached importance to the question of whether the defending party has suffered prejudice as a result of the deficiencies of a panel request.[25]

67. In the present case, the EC considers it clear that it is prejudiced by the lack of clarity of the United States and Australian request. As a defending party, the EC has a right to know what the case is which it will have to defend. This information must be contained in the Panel request.

68. In the present case, the ambiguity of the Panel request is such that the EC is, to this date, not sure of the case which the United States and Australia are bringing before the Panel. As a consequence, the EC has been seriously hampered in its efforts to prepare its defence.

69. This situation is not acceptable from the point of view of the due process rights of the EC. Dispute settlement proceedings under the DSU are subject to very strict deadlines. As a consequence, the EC cannot be expected to wait for the first written submission of the complainants to start preparing its defence. Rather, the time between the submission of the panel request and the constitution of the Panel is used by both complaining and defending parties for the preparation of their case.

70. The strict respect of Article 6.2 DSU is also necessary to ensure a level playing field for the complaining and defending parties. Since the complainants have the initiative in dispute settlement, they can take all the time necessary to prepare their case before the introduction of the panel request. In contrast, the defendant can begin preparing its case only once he has received a notice of the case in accordance with Article 6.2 DSU.

71. The EC notes that the United States has, as a defending party, frequently criticised Panel requests for not respecting the requirements of Article 6.2 DSU, and has requested preliminary rulings on this question.[26] In the present context, the EC considers it useful to quote from the United States' submissions before the Panel in *US – Lamb*:[27]

> The insufficiency of the Panel requests has seriously prejudiced the United States in the preparation of its defense. It prevented the United States from knowing the true nature of the claims being made against the U.S. measure and placed the United States in the position of merely guessing which of the many obligations in these several articles might be at issue in this review. This severely limited the ability of the United States to begin the task of preparing its defense. The dispute resolution process is intended to

---

[24] Supra note 4.

[25] Appellate Body Report, *Korea – Dairy*, para. 131; Appellate Body Report, *Thailand – H Beams*, para. 95. The EC does consider it necessary, in the present case, to take a position as to whether the requirement of prejudice in Article 6.2 DSU constitutes an additional requirement to those set out in Article 6.2 DSU.

[26] Panel Report, *US – Lamb*, para. 5.5; Panel Report, *US – Carbon Steel*, para. 4.1-4.2.

[27] Panel Report, *US – Lamb*, para. 5.5

> be a relatively speedy process. Central to such a speedy process is the requirement that claims be clearly stated at the required time. The failure of a complaining party to do so prejudices the responding party and undercuts the fairness of the entire process. It effectively stacks the deck against the responding party.

72. The EC does not consider that different standards should be applied in the present case. The EC would also like to recall that Article 3.10 DSU requires Members to engage in dispute settlement procedures in good faith. As the Appellate Body has underlined in *US – FSC*, this obligations applies also to the complainants:[28]

> This pervasive principle requires both complaining and responding Members to comply with the requirements of the DSU (and related requirements in other covered agreements) in good faith. By good faith compliance, complaining Members accord to the responding Members the full measure of protection and opportunity to defend, contemplated by the letter and spirit of the procedural rules.

73. The EC does not wish to speculate about what are the reasons for the deficient drafting of the Panel requests. In particular, the EC does not know whether this drafting reflects a conscious choice on the side of the complainants to leave the EC in the dark about their prospective case, or whether the complainants simply were unsure of the case that they were intending to bring. Whatever the explanation may be, the Panel requests in their current form would provide the complainants with a maximum flexibility in terms of their subsequent litigation strategy, and oblige the EC to defend itself against a moving target. This is not in accordance with the requirement of due process underlying Article 6.2 DSU.

74. By keeping their panel requests excessively vague, the United States and Australia have prevented the EC from preparing its defence in a timely manner. They have thereby caused serious prejudice to the EC.

VI. THE DEFICIENCIES OF THE PANEL REQUESTS HAVE BEEN RAISED BY THE EC IN A TIMELY MANNER, AND MUST BE ADDRESSED WITHOUT DELAY

75. In considering the requirements of Article 6.2 DSU, the Appellate Body has held that the respect of the conditions of this provision is of a fundamental nature, and may be examined at any stage in the proceedings.[29]

76. At the same time, the Appellate Body has attached importance to the fact that the parties should bring procedural deficiencies to the attention of the Panel at the earliest possible opportunity.[30] This requirement was justified by the

---

[28] Appellate Body Report, *US – FSC*, para. 166.

[29] Appellate Body Report, *US – Carbon Steel*, para. 123.

[30] Appellate Body Report, *Thailand – H Beams*, para. 95; Appellate Body Report, *US – Carbon Steel*, para. 123.

Appellate Body in *US – FSC* on the basis of the principle of good faith, which pervades dispute settlement proceedings under the DSU:[31]

> Article 3.10 of the DSU commits Members of the WTO, if a dispute arises, to engage in dispute settlement procedures "in good faith in an effort to resolve the dispute". This is another specific manifestation of the principle of good faith which, we have pointed out, is at once a general principle of law and a principle of general international law. This pervasive principle requires both complaining and responding Members to comply with the requirements of the DSU (and related requirements in other covered agreements) in good faith. By good faith compliance, complaining Members accord to the responding Members the full measure of protection and opportunity to defend, contemplated by the letter and spirit of the procedural rules. The same principle of good faith requires that responding Members seasonably and promptly bring claimed procedural deficiencies to the attention of the complaining Member, and to the DSB or the Panel, so that corrections, if needed, can be made to resolve disputes. The procedural rules of WTO dispute settlement are designed to promote, not the development of litigation techniques, but simply the fair, prompt and effective resolution of trade disputes.

77. The present request for a preliminary ruling is in full accordance with these requirements established by the Appellate Body. The EC has raised the objection regarding the compatibility of the Panel requests with Article 6.2 DSU at the first possible occasion, namely at the meeting of the Dispute Settlement Body (DSB) on 29 August 2003, at which the requests were discussed for the first time.[32] At this meeting, the EC explicitly called upon the United States and Australia to submit new panel requests compatible with Article 6.2 DSU. Since the complainants failed to do so, the EC repeated its concerns at the second meeting of the DSB on 2 October 2003, and reserved its rights to raise the issue during the Panel proceedings.[33]

78. In the view of the EC, the deficiencies of the Panel requests are such that they will affect the entire subsequent proceedings. In particular, if the Panel requests are not amended, the scope of the present dispute will remain entirely unclear. This will have as an inevitable consequence that the submissions of the parties will have to deal not only with issues of substance, but also with the scope of the claims of the complainants. Moreover, it would be regrettable for the Parties to engage in pleadings on the substance of the dispute, only for the Panel requests to be found insufficient in the Panel report or by the Appellate Body. For these reasons, and in order to safeguard the proper conduct of the

---

[31] Appellate Body Report, *US – FSC*, para. 166.

[32] Minutes of the Meeting of the Dispute Settlement Body of 29 August 2003, WT/DSB/M/155, para. 75 (Exhibit EC-2).

[33] Minutes of the Meeting of the Dispute Settlement Body of 2 October 2003, WT/DSB/M/156, para. 32 (Exhibit EC-3).

present dispute settlement proceedings, the EC considers it appropriate for the Panel to issue a preliminary ruling regarding Article 6.2 DSU.

79. This would also be in line with the ruling of the Appellate Body has *EC – Bananas,* in which the Appellate Body held that questions regarding the respect of Article 6.2 DSU should be decided early in panel proceedings, without causing prejudice or unfairness to any party or third party.[34]

80. The EC would like to clarify that it remains committed to a speedy resolution of the present dispute. For this reason, the EC would not consider it inappropriate for the Panel to suggest to the complaining parties to introduce a new Panel request in full compliance with Article 6.2 DSU. The EC would like to note that such a course of action has recently been taken by a Panel in another dispute.[35]

VII. CONCLUSION

81. For the reasons set out above, the EC respectfully requests that the Panel find that the panel requests do not meet the requirements of Article 6.2 DSU.

82. Given the importance of the jurisdictional issues raised in the present request, the EC considers it appropriate that the Panel issue a preliminary ruling on this matter before the first written submissions of the Parties are due.

---

[34] Appellate Body Report, *EC – Bananas III*, para. 144.

[35] Cf. Preliminary Ruling by the Panel, *Canada – Wheat*, para. 65. In this case, the United States indeed introduced a new Panel request (WT/DS276/9). The dispute then continued to be heard before the Panel originally established after the first Panel request.

ANNEX B-2

FIRST WRITTEN SUBMISSION OF
THE EUROPEAN COMMUNITIES

(25 May 2004)

TABLE OF CONTENTS

Page

TABLE OF WTO AND GATT CASES REFERRED TO IN THIS SUBMISSION

Short Title	Full Case Title and Citation of Case
Argentina – Textiles and Apparel	Panel Report, *Argentina – Measures Affecting Imports of Footwear, Textiles, Apparel and Other Items*, WT/DS56/R, adopted 22 April 1998, as modified by the Appellate Body Report, WT/DS56/AB/R, DSR 1998:III, 1033
Australia – Automotive Leather	Panel Report, *Australia – Subsidies Provided to Producers and Exporters of Automotive Leather*, WT/DS126/R, adopted 16 June 1999, DSR 1999:III, 951
Belgian Family Allowances	GATT 1947 Panel Report, *Belgian Family Allowances*, adopted on 7 November 1952, 1S/59
Canada – Autos	Panel Report, *Canada – Certain Measures Affecting the Automotive Industry*, WT/DS139/R, WT/DS142/R, adopted 19 June 2000, as modified by the Appellate Body Report, WT/DS139/AB/R, WT/DS142/AB/R, DSR 2000:VII, 3043
EEC – Beef from Canada	GATT 1947 Panel Report, *European Economic Community – Imports of Beef from Canada*, adopted on 10 March 1981, 28S/92
EC – Asbestos	Appellate Body Report, *European Communities – Measures Affecting Asbestos and Asbestos-Containing Products*, WT/DS135/AB/R, adopted 5 April 2001
EC – Sardines	Appellate Body Report, *European Communities – Trade Description of Sardines*, WT/DS231/AB/R, adopted 23 October 2002
India – Autos	Panel Report, *India – Measures Affecting the Automotive Sector*, WT/DS146/R, WT/DS175/R and Corr.1, adopted 5 April 2002
India – Patents (US)	Appellate Body Report, *India – Patent Protection for Pharmaceutical and Agricultural Chemical Products*, WT/DS50/AB/R, adopted 16 January 1998, DSR 1998:I, 9
Indonesia – Autos	Panel Report, *Indonesia – Certain Measures Affecting the Automobile Industry*, WT/DS54/R, WT/DS55/R, WT/DS59/R, WT/DS64/R and Corr.1, 2, 3, and 4, adopted 23 July 1998, DSR 1998:VI, 2201
Japan – Film	Panel Report, *Japan – Measures Affecting Consumer Photographic Film and Paper*, WT/DS44/R, adopted 22 April 1998, DSR 1998:IV, 1179
Korea – Dairy	Appellate Body Report, *Korea – Definitive Safeguard Measure on Imports of Certain Dairy Products*, WT/DS98/AB/R, adopted 12 January 2000, DSR 2000:I, 3

Short Title	Full Case Title and Citation of Case
Korea – Various Measures on Beef	Appellate Body Report, *Korea – Measures Affecting Imports of Fresh, Chilled and Frozen Beef*, WT/DS161/AB/R, WT/DS169/AB/R, adopted 10 January 2001
Norway – Trondheim Bridge	Panel report under the 1979 Agreement on Government Procurement, *Norway –Procurement of Toll Collection Equipment for the City of Trondheim*, GPR/DS.2/R, adopted 13 May 1992
US – Tuna	GATT 1947 Panel Report, *United States – Restrictions on Imports of Tuna*, DS21/R, 3 September 1991, 39S/155, not adopted
US – Certain EC Products	Appellate Body Report, *United States – Import Measures on Certain Products from the European Communities*, WT/DS165/AB/R, adopted 10 January 2001
US – Gasoline	Panel Report, *United States – Standards for Reformulated and Conventional Gasoline*, WT/DS2/R, adopted 20 May 1996, as modified by the Appellate Body Report, WT/DS2/AB/R, DSR 1996:I, 29
US – Section 211 Appropriations Act	Appellate Body Report, *United States – Section 211 Omnibus Appropriations Act of 1998*, WT/DS176/AB/R, adopted 1 February 2002
US – Wool Shirts and Blouses	Appellate Body Report, *United States – Measure Affecting Imports of Woven Wool Shirts and Blouses from India*, WT/DS33/AB/R and Corr.1, adopted 23 May 1997, DSR 1997:I, 323

GLOSSARY

Commission, EC Commission	Commission of the European Communities
Committee	Committee of representatives of the Member States referred to in Article 15 of Council Regulation 2081/92
Community Trademark Regulation	Council Regulation (EC) No 40/94, of 20 December 1993, on the Community Trademark, as amended on the date of establishment of the Panel
Council, EC Council	Council of the European Union
Court of Justice, European Court of Justice	Court of Justice of the European Communities
DSU	Understanding on Rules and Procedures Governing the Settlement of Disputes
EC	European Communities
GATT	General Agreement on Tariffs and Trade 1994
FWS	First Written Submission
GI	Geographical indication
Member States, EC Member States	Member States of the European Union
Official Journal	Official Journal of the European Union
Paris Convention	Stockholm Act of the Paris Convention for the protection of Industrial property, of 14 July 1967
Regulation 2081/92, Regulation	Council Regulation (EEC) No 2081/92 of 14 July 1992 on the protection of geographical indications and designations of origin for agricultural products and foodstuffs, as amended on the date of establishment of the Panel
SCM Agreement, SCM	Agreement on Subsidies and Countervailing Duties

Trademarks Directive	First Council Directive 89/104, of 20 December, on the Community Trademark, as amended on the date of establishment of the Panel
TBT Agreement, TBT	Agreement on Technical Barriers to Trade
TRIPS Agreement, TRIPS	Agreement on Trade-Related Aspects of Intellectual Property Rights
US	United States
WTO	World Trade Organization
WTO Agreement	Marrakesh Agreement Establishing the World Trade Organization

I. INTRODUCTION

1. This submission provides the response of the European Communities to the first written submissions filed by Australia and the United States on 25 May 2004.

2. Section II raises a number of issues in connection with the terms of reference of the Panel.

3. Section III sets out the content of Regulation 2081/1992 to the extent relevant for the present dispute and corrects a number of errors and misrepresentations made by the complainants in their first written submissions.

4. Section IV addresses the various claims submitted by the complainants to the effect that certain requirements of Regulation 2081/92 are incompatible with the national treatment obligations under Article 3.1 of the TRIPS Agreement, Article 2.1 of the Paris Convention and Article III:4 of the GATT, as well as with the prohibition on requirements of domicile or establishment in Article 2.2 of the Paris Convention.

5. Section V addresses the United States' claims that some of those requirements are incompatible with the most-favoured-nation obligations under Article 4 of the TRIPS Agreement and Article I:1 of the GATT.

6. Section VI deals with the complainants' various claims to the effect that Regulation 2081/92 diminishes the legal protection of trademarks, thereby violating Articles 16.1, 20 and 24.5 of the TRIPS Agreement, as well as certain provisions of Part III of that Agreement, and Articles 10*bis* and 10*ter* of the Paris Convention.

7. Section VII responds to the claims that the EC does not comply with the obligation to provide protection to geographical indications under Article 22.2 of the TRIPS Agreement.

8. Finally, Section VIII deals with the claims raised by Australia that Regulation 2081/92 is incompatible with certain provisions of the TBT Agreement.

9. For ease of reference, the EC has grouped and numbered sequentially the claims submitted by the complainants. In each case, the EC has indicated which of the complainants has made the claim, and referred to the paragraphs of the first submission where the claim is made.

II. TERMS OF REFERENCE

10. The present Panel has been established by the DSB on 2 October 2003 with standard terms of reference in accordance with Article 7.1 of the DSU.[1] These terms of reference define the Panel's scope of jurisdiction. As the Appellate Body has explained in *India – Patents (US)*, a panel cannot consider claims which are not within its terms of reference:[2]

> The jurisdiction of a panel is established by that panel's terms of reference, which are governed by Article 7 of the DSU. A panel may consider only those claims that it has the authority to consider under its terms of reference. A panel cannot assume jurisdiction that it does not have. In this case, Article 63 was not within the Panel's jurisdiction, as defined by its terms of reference. Therefore, the Panel had no authority to consider the alternative claim by the United States under Article 63.

11. In its first written submission, Australia is referring to versions of Regulation 2081/92 which were no longer in force at the time the Panel's terms of reference were established. Moreover, the complainants have referred to a number of measures that were not yet in existence at the time the Panel was established. In the view of the EC, only measures which were in force at the time that the Panel was established are within the terms of reference of the Panel.

12. Moreover, Australia and the United States raise a number of claims which are not identified in their requests for the establishment of the Panel. Such claims not identified in the panel requests are not within the jurisdiction of the Panel.

A. The measure at issue

1. Versions of Regulation 2081/92 no longer in force at the time the Panel was established

13. In its first written submission, Australia (but not the United States)[3] has referred to several versions of Regulation 2081/92 no longer in force. It has

[1] Cf. WT/DS174/21, WT/DS290/19, para. 2. As the EC has set out in its request for a preliminary ruling made on 24 February 2004, it considers that the panel requests of the United States and of Australia are not in compliance with the requirements of Article 6.2 DSU. The EC reserves the right to raise this issue in the context of an appeal.

[2] Appellate Body Report, *India – Patents (US)*, para. 92.

[3] The United States has referred to Regulation 2081/92 "as most recently amended" (US FWS, footnote 1).

numbered these versions #1 to #3, reflecting various subsequent amendments of Regulation 2081/92.[4]

14. Throughout its submission, Australia refers repeatedly to these different versions of Regulation 2081/92. In particular, Australia claims that no right of objection was available to persons not resident or established in the EC "until Article 12d (1) of *Regulation No 2081/92#3* changed the situation".[5] Similarly, Australia refers to the fact that "Article 17.1 of Regulation *No 2081/92#1 and #2* provided for a simplified registration process for certain names which were already legally protected or established by usage in the Member States".[6]

15. These references to versions of Regulation No. 2081/92 which were no longer in force at the time the present Panel was established are not within the scope of the Panel's terms of reference. This already flows from Australia's request for the establishment of the Panel,[7] which is the basis for the Panel's terms of reference. In its Panel request, Australia referred to "Council Regulation (EEC) No 2081/92 of 14 July 1992 [...] and any amendments thereto" as "the EC measure". Australia's request did not make it clear that Australia intended to challenge as the "EC measure" several versions of the same measure resulting from subsequent amendments over time.

16. Moreover, as the Panel in *India – Autos* recalled, a " WTO Panel is generally competent to consider measures in existence at the time of its establishment".[8] Accordingly, in WTO practice, Panels have declined to examine measures which were no longer in force at the time the Panel was established. In *US – Gasoline*, the Panel explained the legal situation as follows:[9]

> The Panel observed that it had not been the usual practice of a panel established under the General Agreement to rule on measures that, at the time the panel's terms of reference were fixed, were not and would not become effective. In the 1978 *Animal Feed Protein* case, the Panel ruled on a discontinued measure, but one that had terminated after agreement on the panel's terms of reference. In the 1980 *Chile Apples* case, the panel ruled on a measure terminated before agreement on the panel's terms of reference; however, the terms of reference in that case specifically included the terminated measure and, it being a seasonal measure, there remained the prospect of its reintroduction. In the present case, the Panel's terms of reference were established after the 75 percent rule had ceased to have any effect, and the rule had not been specifically mentioned in the terms of reference. The Panel further noted that there was no indication by the parties that the 75

4 Australia's FWS, para. 18.

5 Australia's FWS, para. 185 (emphasis added).

6 Australia's FWS, para. 190 (emphasis added).

7 WT/DS290/18.

8 Panel Report, *India – Autos*, para. 7.26.

9 Panel Report, *US – Gasoline*, para. 6.19; similarly, Panel Report, *Japan – Film*, para. 10.58; Panel Report, *Argentina – Textiles and Apparel*, para. 6.15.

> percent rule was a measure that, although currently not in force, was likely to be renewed. Finally, the Panel considered that its findings on treatment under the baseline establishment methods under Articles III:4 and XX (b), (d) and (g) would in any case have made unnecessary the examination of the 75 percent rule under Article I:1. The Panel did not therefore proceed to examine this aspect of the Gasoline Rule under Article I:1 of the General Agreement.

17. In the present case, there are no specific reasons which could justify an examination of versions of Regulation 2081/92 no longer in force. From its adoption in 1992 to the establishment of the Panel, Regulation 2081/92 has been amended six times.[10] Australia has arbitrarily chosen certain points in time to reflect versions of Regulation 2081/92 going as far back as 1997 or 1993.

18. The same applies also with respect to Australia's reference to the version of Regulation 2081/92 as applicable before its amendment by Regulation 692/2003 of 8 April 2003.[11] In accordance with its Article 2.1, Regulation 692/2003 entered into force on 24 April 2003, i.e. before the present Panel was established. The EC has no intention to repeal Regulation 692/2003, or to remove the changes introduced by it. Therefore, Regulation 2081/92 as applicable prior to its amendment by Regulation 692/2003 is not within the scope of the Panel's terms of reference.

19. Moreover, as the Appellate Body has recalled in *US – Shirts and Blouses*, the purpose of Panel proceedings under the DSU is the settlement of concrete disputes between the parties:[12]

> Given the explicit aim of dispute settlement that permeates the *DSU*, we do not consider that Article 3.2 of the *DSU* is meant to encourage either panels or the Appellate Body to "make law" by clarifying existing provisions of the *WTO Agreement* outside the context of resolving a particular dispute. A panel need only address those claims which must be addressed in order to resolve the matter in issue in the dispute.

20. An analysis of historical versions of Regulation 2081/92 is not useful for the purposes of settling the present dispute. Accordingly, the EC submits that the measure at issue in the present dispute is Regulation 2081/92 as in force at the time the Panel was established. A consolidated version of Regulation 2081/92 as in force on 2 October 2003 is provided by the EC as Exhibit EC-1.

2. *Measures not yet adopted at the time the Panel was established*

21. The complainants have referred to a number of measures which had not yet been adopted at the time the Panel was established.

---

[10] See consolidated version of Regulation 2081/92, Exihibit EC-1, p. 1.

[11] Exhibit COMP-1i.

[12] Appellate Body Report, *US – Shirts and Blouses*, p. 22.

22. In Exhibits COMP-4b (viii) – (xvi), the complainants are referring to a number of amendments to Commission Regulation 2400/96 adopted between 11 November 2003 and 5 April 2004. These measures did not yet exist at the time the Panel was established, and are therefore outside its terms of reference.

23. Moreover, the complainants have prepared a "consolidated unofficial version" of Regulation 2081/92, which they provide as Exhibit COMP-1a. The complainants state that this consolidated unofficial version incorporates amendments made by the Act of Accession of Cyprus, Czech Republic, Estonia, Hungary, Latvia, Lithuania, Malta, Poland, Slovakia, and Slovenia. Moreover, the complainants have also provided an extract from the Act of Accession as Exhibit COMP-3c.

24. In accordance with Article 2.3 of the Treaty of Accession, of which the Act of Accession is an integral part, the Treaty of Accession had to be ratified by all Member States of the European Union and by the acceding countries. At the time the Panel was established, the process of ratification was still ongoing. The Act of Accession entered into force only on 1 May 2004. Accordingly, the Act of Accession was not yet adopted at the time the Panel was established, and is therefore not within the scope of the Panel's terms of reference.

25. Accordingly, the EC submits that measures which had not yet been adopted at the time the Panel was established are not within the Panel's terms of reference.

B. Claims

26. In its first written submission, Australia has raised claims under Article 4 of the Paris Convention, and Articles 43 to 49 of the TRIPS Agreement. None of these claims is referred to in Australia's request for the establishment of the Panel.[13]

27. Moreover, both Australia and the United States have made claims according to which the EC measure imposes a requirement of domicile or residence for the enjoyment of intellectual property rights contrary to Article 2.2 of the Paris Convention. No such claim was raised in the panel requests of the complainants.[14]

1. Australia's claim under Article 4 of the Paris Convention

28. In its first written submission, Australia alleges that Regulation 2081/92 is incompatible with Article 4 of the Paris Convention, incorporated by Article 2.1 TRIPS, which requires that a WTO member afford a right of priority of six months in respect of an application for registration of a trademark for which an application for registration had previously been filed in another WTO member.[15]

---

[13] WT/DS290/18.

[14] WT/DS290/18; WT/DS174/20.

[15] Australia's FWS, para. 85.

29. However, Australia's panel request does not refer to Article 4 of the Paris Convention. Australia can also not argue that its reference to Article 2.1 of the TRIPS Agreement, which requires Members to comply with Articles 1 through 12 and Article 19 of the Paris Convention, is sufficient to bring Article 4 of the Paris Convention within the scope of the Panel's terms of reference. The incorporated provisions of the Paris Convention contain numerous distinct obligations, which need to be referred to specifically in order to meet the requirements of Article 6.2 of the DSU.[16] In fact, Australia's panel request specifies alongside the reference to Article 2.1 of the TRIPS Agreement a number of other provisions of the Paris Convention alleged to be violated. However, Article 4 of the Paris Convention is not among the provisions alleged to have been violated in Australia's panel request.

30. Therefore, the EC considers that Australia's claim regarding Article 4 of the Paris Convention is outside the terms of reference of the Panel.

2. *Australia's claim under Articles 43 to 49 of the TRIPS*

31. In its first written submission, Australia has claimed that the EC measure has failed "to provide the judicial authorities the authority required to be conferred on them by TRIPS Articles 43, 44, 45, 46, 48 and 49 in respect of the enforcement of trademark rights vis-à-vis the proposed registration of an EC-defined GI".[17]

32. However, Articles 43 to 49 TRIPS Agreement are not mentioned in Australia's panel request. In its panel request (fifth paragraph, first bullet point), Australia has alleged that the EC measure diminishes the legal protection of trademarks, and has referred in this respect to Articles 41 and 42 TRIPS. However, Articles 43 through 49 of the TRIPS Agreement contain distinct obligations which are separate from and additional to those contained in Articles 41 and 42.

33. Australia cannot argue that a reference to the specific provisions of Articles 43 to 49 TRIPS was made redundant by its reference to Article 41 TRIPS. Article 41 is an introductory provision contained in the first section, entitled "General Obligations", of Part III. It sets out general obligations and principles to be respected by the Parties in the application of Part III.

34. More specifically, Article 41.1 is a purely introductory provision which does not create separate legal obligations. The fact that Article 41.1 TRIPS refers to the "enforcement procedures as specified in this Part" cannot mean that a reference to Article 41.1 TRIPS would be sufficient to bring all the provisions of Part III within the terms of reference of the Panel. Otherwise, it could be argued that a simple reference to Article 1.1 TRIPS is sufficient to bring all provisions of the TRIPS Agreement within the scope of a panel's jurisdiction, or that a reference to Article XVI:4 WTO would bring all provisions of the covered agreements within the scope of a panel's jurisdiction. Such an interpretation

[16] Appellate Body Report, *Korea - Dairy*, para. 124.
[17] Australia's FWS, para. 148.

would be manifestly incompatible with the requirements for panel requests contained in Article 6.2 DSU.

35. Accordingly, the EC considers that Australia's claim under Articles 43 to 49 of the TRIPS is outside the terms of reference of the Panel.

3. *The claims regarding Article 2.2 of the Paris Convention*

36. In its first written submission, the United States has argued that with respect to the registration of foreign geographical indications, Regulation 2081/92 imposes a requirement as to domicile or establishment contrary to Article 2.2 of the Paris Convention.[18] The United States has made a claim based on Article 2.2 of the Paris Convention also with respect to the conditions under which foreign nationals can object to the registration of geographical indications.[19]

37. Australia has made a similar claim based on Article 2.2 of the Paris Convention with respect to the alleged unavailability of a right of objection to foreign right holders prior to the amendment of Regulation 2081/92 by Regulation 692/2003.[20]

38. Article 2.1 and 2.2 of the Paris Convention are drafted as follows:

> (1) Nationals of any country of the Union shall, as regards the protection of industrial property, enjoy in all the other countries of the Union the advantages that their respective laws now grant, or may hereafter grant, to nationals; all without prejudice to the rights specially provided for by this Convention. Consequently, they shall have the same protection as the latter, and the same legal remedy against any infringement of their rights, provided that the conditions and formalities imposed upon nationals are complied with.
>
> (2) However, no requirement as to domicile or establishment in the country where protection is claimed may be imposed upon nationals of countries of the Union for the enjoyment of any industrial property rights.

39. Article 2.1 of the Paris Convention is concerned with national treatment. In contrast, Article 2.2 prohibits the imposition of requirements as to domicile or establishment. This obligation is different and additional to the obligations resulting from the national treatment provision of Article 2.1 Paris Convention. This is also made clear by the term "however", which indicates that Article 2.2 goes beyond what is provided in Article 2.1.

---

[18] US FWS, para. 84.

[19] US FWS, para. 89.

[20] Australia's FWS, para. 189, second bullet point; para. 194, second bullet point. As the EC has already set out above, these claims relate to a measure which is no longer in force, and are therefore in any case outside the terms of reference of the present panel.

40. This view also seems to be shared by the complainants. In its first written submission, the United States has argued that the EC measure "is directly prohibited by Article 2(2) of the Paris Convention".[21] Similarly, Australia has referred to the EC's obligations pursuant to Article 2(2) of the Paris Convention.[22]

41. However, in their panel requests, the complainants have merely referred to an alleged failure of the EC measure to provide national treatment. They have not raised any issue regarding the imposition of a requirement as to domicile or establishment contrary to Article 2.2 of the Paris Convention.

42. For this reason, the EC submits that the US and Australian claims under Article 2.2 of the Paris Convention are outside the terms of reference of the Panel.

III. FACTS

43. The measure at issue in the present dispute is Council Regulation 2081/1992 on the protection of geographical indications and designations of origin for agricultural products and foodstuffs, as in force at the date of establishment of the Panel. A consolidated version of this Regulation is provided in Exhibit EC-1.

44. In this section, the EC will set out the content of Regulation 2081/1992 relevant for the present dispute. In this context, the EC will also correct a number of errors and misrepresentations that are contained in the first written submissions of the complainants with respect to the content of Regulation 2081/1992.

A. The definition of geographic indications

45. Regulation 2081/92 lays down rules on the protection, within the European Community, of designations of origin and geographical indications for agricultural products and foodstuffs. Article 2(2) of the Regulation defines the terms "designation of origin" and "geographical indication" as follows:[23]

> (a) *designation of origin*: means the name of a region, a specific place or, in exceptional cases, a country, used to describe an agricultural product or a foodstuff:
>
> – originating in that region, specific place or country, and
>
> – the quality or characteristics of which are essentially or exclusively due to a particular geographical environment with its inherent natural and human factors, and the production, processing and preparation of which take place in the defined geographical area;

---

21 US FWS, para. 85.

22 Australia's FWS, para. 189, 194.

23 Further specific aspects of these definitions are set out in paragraphs 3 to 7 of Article 2.

(b) *geographical indication:* means the name of a region, a specific place or, in exceptional cases, a country, used to describe an agricultural product or a foodstuff:

– originating in that region, specific place or country, and

– which possesses a specific quality, reputation or other characteristics attributable to that geographical origin and the production and/or processing and/or preparation of which take place in the defined geographical area.

46. The distinction between designations of origin and geographical indications depends on how closely the product is linked to the geographical area in which it originates. However, both designations of origin and geographical indications within the meaning of Regulation 2081/92 are geographical indications as defined in Article 22.1 TRIPS Agreement.

47. Under Regulation 2081/92, designations of origin and geographical indications are subject to identical rules as regards their registration and protection. For this reason, wherever the EC, in the present submission, refers to geographical indications within the meaning of Regulation 2081/92, this reference shall also include designations of origin.

B. Product specifications

48. In accordance with Article 4 (1) of Regulation 2081/92, in order to be eligible to use a geographical indication, an agricultural product must comply with a product specification. The purpose of this requirement is to ensure that the agricultural product marketed using a particular geographical indication in fact originates in the area to which the indication is related, and possesses the specific quality, reputation or other characteristics which justify the protection of the geographical indication.

49. Regulation 2081/92 does not itself define the product specifications with which a particular product must comply. Rather, in accordance with Article 5 (3) of Regulation 2081/92, the product specifications must be contained in the application for registration of a geographical indication. Article 4 (2) of the Regulation defines the elements with which a product specification must comply:

The product specification shall include at least:

(a) the name of the agricultural product or foodstuffs, including the designation of origin or the geographical indication;

(b) a description of the agricultural product or foodstuff including the raw materials, if appropriate, and principal physical, chemical, microbiological and/or organoleptic characteristics of the product or the foodstuff;

(c) the definition of the geographical area and, if appropriate, details indicating compliance with the requirements in Article 2 (4);

> (d) evidence that the agricultural product or the foodstuff originates in the geographical area, within the meaning of Article 2(2) (a) or (b), whichever is applicable;
>
> (e) a description of the method of obtaining the agricultural product or foodstuff and, if appropriate, the authentic and unvarying local methods as well as information concerning the packaging, if the group making the request determines and justifies that the packaging must take place in the limited geographical area to safeguard quality, ensure traceability or ensure control;
>
> (f) the details bearing out the link with the geographical environment or the geographical origin within the meaning of Article 2(2)(a) or (b), whichever is applicable;
>
> (g) details of the inspection structures provided for in Article 10;
>
> (h) the specific labelling details relating to the indication PDO or PGI, whichever is applicable, or the equivalent traditional national indications;
>
> (i) any requirements laid down by Community and/or national provisions.

C. Inspection structures

50. As has been explained, each protected geographical indication has to comply with a product specification. However, a geographical indication is less reliable and informative for consumers if its proper use is not ensured by an effective inspection regime. For this reason, Article 10(1) of Regulation 2081/92 provides that EC Member States shall ensure that inspection structures are in place, the function of which shall be to ensure that agricultural products and foodstuffs bearing a protected name meet the requirements laid down in the specifications.

51. Article 10 does not regulate all details of such inspection structures. In particular, Article 10(2) provides that an inspection structure "may comprise one or more designated inspection authorities and/or private bodies". It thereby leaves the Member State a choice between public and private elements in the design of the inspection bodies.

52. Article 10(3) further provides that designated inspection authorities and/or approved private bodies "must offer adequate guarantees of objectivity and impartiality with regard to all producers or processors subject to their control and have permanently at their disposal the qualified staff and resources necessary to carry out inspection of agricultural products and foodstuffs bearing a protected name".

53. Further, the third subparagraph of Article 10(3) provides that in order to be approved by the Member States, private bodies must fulfil the requirements laid down in standard EN 45011 of 26 June 1989, which sets out general

requirements for bodies operating product certification systems. A copy of this standard, which is available from CEN/CENELEC, is provided as Exhibit EC-2.

54. It should be noted that compliance with standard EN 45011 is only required for bodies to be approved by the EC Member States. In accordance with the last subparagraph of Article 10(3), for bodies located outside the Community, compliance with equivalent international standards will be sufficient. An example for an equivalent international standard is ISO/IEC Guide 65:1996 (E), a copy of which is provided as Exhibit EC-3.

55. In accordance with Article 4(2)(g) of Regulation 2081/92, details of the inspection structure applicable must be included in the product specification, which is part of any application for registration of a geographical indication.

D. The registration of geographical indications relating to an area located in the EC

56. Articles 5 and 6 of Regulation 2081/92 set out the procedure for the registration of geographical indications which relate to a geographical area located in the European Community.

57. In accordance with Article 5(4) of Regulation 2081/92, the application shall be sent to the EC Member State in which the geographical area is located. In accordance with Article 5(5), the Member State shall check that the application is justified and, if it considers that the application fulfils the requirements of the Regulation, shall forward the application, including the product specification and all other relevant documents to the EC Commission.

58. This involvement of the Member State in the registration process is crucial for the proper implementation of the Regulation. In fact, Member States are particularly well placed to examine the admissibility of applications relating to geographical areas located on their territory.

59. Within six months of the receipt of the application, the EC Commission shall verify, by means of a formal investigation, whether the registration application includes all the particulars provided for in Article 4 of the Regulation. If, after this examination, the Commission concludes that the name qualifies for protection, it shall publish a notice in the Official Journal of the European Union containing among others the name of the applicant, the name of the product, and the main points of the application (Article 6(2) of the Regulation).

60. If no statement of objection is notified to the Commission in accordance with Article 7 of the Regulation, the name shall be entered in the register of protected names kept by the Commission (Article 6(3) of the Regulation). The name entered in the register shall be published in the Official Journal (Article 6.4 of the Regulation).

61. If, in the light of the investigation provided for in Article 6(1) of the Regulation, the Commission concludes that the name does not qualify for protection, it shall decide, in accordance with the procedure provided for in Article 15 of the Regulation, not to proceed with the registration of the name.

E. The registration of geographical indications relating to an area located outside the EC

62. Regulation 2081/92 also applies to geographical indications relating to areas located outside the EC. For this purpose, the Regulation lays down rules relating to the registration of such geographical indications from outside the EC which closely parallel the provisions applicable to geographical indications from inside the EC.

63. The purpose of these specific rules, some of which were introduced by Regulation 692/2003, is to facilitate the registration of non-EC geographical indications while at the same time ensuring that geographical indications from outside the EC correspond to the definition of a geographical indication.

64. The United States and Australia have claimed that Regulation 2081/92 allows the registration of geographical indications from other WTO members only under the condition of "reciprocity and equivalence".[24] In support of this contention, they have relied on Article 12(1) of the Regulation, which provides as follows:

> Without prejudice to international agreements, this Regulation may apply to an agricultural product or foodstuff from a third country provided that:
>
> – the third country is able to give guarantees identical or equivalent to those referred to in Article 4,
>
> – the third country concerned has inspection arrangements and a right to objection equivalent to those laid down in this Regulation,
>
> – the third country concerned is prepared to provide protection equivalent to that available in the Community to corresponding agricultural products for foodstuffs coming from the Community.

65. However, this interpretation is based on a misunderstanding of the Regulation. Article 12(1) of Regulation 2081/92 clearly provides that it applies "without prejudice to international agreements". Such international agreements include the WTO Agreements. This is made clear by the 8th recital of Regulation 692/2003,[25] which amended the procedures for the registration of non-EC geographical indications, and in this context took specific account of the provisions of the TRIPS.

66. WTO Members are obliged to provide protection to geographical indications in accordance with Section 3 of Part II and the general provisions and basic principles of the TRIPS Agreement. For this reason, Article 12(1) and (3) of Regulation 2081/92 do not apply to WTO Members. This distinction between WTO countries and other third countries is also found in other provisions of the

---

24 US FWS, para. 22; Australia's FWS, para. 170.

25 Exhibit COMP-1h.

Regulation, for instance in Article 12(2)(a) and (b) and in Article 12d(1), both concerning objections from outside the EC.

67. Accordingly, the registration of a geographical indication relating to an area located in the territory of another WTO Member does not require that the Commission examines whether the conditions set out in Article 12(1) of the Regulation are fulfilled. Rather, the procedure for the registration of third country geographical indications can be immediately applied. The applicant shall therefore send the registration application to the authorities in the country in which the geographical area is located (Article 12a(1) of the Regulation). Like applications for registration of EC geographical indications, applications must be accompanied by the specification referred to in Article 4.

68. According to Article 12a(2), if the third country deems that the requirements of the Regulation are satisfied, it shall transmit the registration application to the Commission accompanied by the following:

> (a) a description of the legal provisions and the usage on the basis of which the designation of origin or the geographical indication is protected or established in the country,
>
> (b) a declaration that the structures provided for in Article 10 are established on its territory, and
>
> (c) other documents on which it has based its assessment.

69. Article 12b regulates the further procedure for the registration of the geographical indication in a way which corresponds closely to the procedure set out in Article 6 for the registration of geographical indications from inside the EC.[26]

F. Objections from persons resident or established in the EC

70. Within six months of the date of publication of the application in the Official Journal, the Member State may object to the registration. Article 7(2) of the Regulation provides that Member States shall ensure that all persons who can demonstrate a legitimate economic interest are authorised to consult the application. Pursuant to Article 7(3) of the Regulation, any legitimately concerned natural or legal person may object to a proposed registration by sending a duly substantiated statement to the competent authority of the Member State in which he resides or is established, who shall transmit the objection to the Commission.

71. According to Article 7 (4) of the Regulation, a statement of objection shall be admissible only if it:

> either shows non-compliance with the conditions referred to in Article 2,
>
> – shows that the registration of the name proposed would jeopardize the existence of an entirely or partly identical name or

---

[26] See above paragraph 59 et seq.

> of a mark or the existence of products which have been legally on the market for at least five years preceding the date of the publication provided for in Article 6(2).
>
> – or indicates the features which demonstrate that the name whose registration is applied for is generic in nature.

72. Where a statement of objection is admissible, the Commission shall proceed in accordance with Article 7(5):

> Where an objection is admissible within the meaning of paragraph 4, the Commission shall ask the Member States concerned to seek agreement among themselves in accordance with their internal procedures within three months. If:
>
> (a) agreement is reached, the Member States in question shall communicate to the Commission all the factors which made agreement possible together with the applicant's opinion and that of the objector. Where there has been no change to the information received under Article 5, the Commission shall proceed in accordance with Article 6(4). If there has been a change, it shall again initiate the procedure laid down in Article 7;
>
> (b) no agreement is reached, the Commission shall take a decision in accordance with the procedure laid down in Article 15, having regard to traditional fair practice and of the actual likelihood of confusion. Should it decide to proceed with registration, the Commission shall carry out publication in accordance with Article 6(4).

G. *Objections from persons resident or established outside the EC*

73. Article 12d(1) of Regulation 2081/92 provides a right of objection to persons not resident or established in the EC. Article 12d(1) is drafted as follows:

> Within six months of the date of the notice in the *Official Journal of the European Union* specified in Article 6(2) relating to a registration application submitted by a Member State, any natural or legal person that has a legitimate interest and is from a WTO member country or a third country recognised under the procedure provided for in Article 12(3) may object to the proposed registration by sending a duly substantiated statement to the country in which it resides or is established, which shall transmit it, made out or translated into a Community language, to the Commission. Member States shall ensure that any person from a WTO member country or a third country recognised under the procedure provided for in Article 12(3) who can demonstrate a legitimate economic interest is authorised to consult the application.

74. Australia and the US have claimed that this right of objection is subject to the condition that the individual concerned is from a country which is recognised as fulfilling the conditions of Article 12(1) of the Regulation.[27] This is wrong. Article 12d(1) of the Regulation refers to any person that "is from a WTO Member or a third country recognised under the procedure provided for in Article 12(3)". The phrase "recognised under the procedure provided for in Article 12(3)" only refers to third countries other than WTO Members. Otherwise, the specific reference to WTO Members would be meaningless. WTO Members are therefore not subject to the procedure of Article 12(3) applicable to other third countries.

75. This is also clear in Article 12b(2) of the Regulation, which concerns objections against applications for registration of geographical indications relating to an area outside the EC. As regards WTO Members, Article 12b(2)(a) simply provides that Article 12d shall apply; whereas Article 12b(2)(b) requires for persons resident or established in third countries that the requirements of Article 12(3) must be met.

76. In accordance with Article 12d(2), the conditions for the admissibility of objections from outside the EC are those laid down in Article 7(4) for objections from inside the EC. The admissibility conditions and the further procedure with respect to objections from outside the EC do not differ from those applicable to objections from inside the EC.

77. The United States has nonetheless seen a difference in the fact that whereas under Article 7(3) of the Regulation, only persons who are "legitimately concerned" may object to an application, under Article 12d, persons from outside the EC must have a "legitimate interest".[28] According to the US, "it would appear" that the requirement to be "legitimately concerned" is a lower standard than that one has a "legitimate interest".[29]

78. This assumption of the United States is wrong. There is no substantive difference between the two expressions "legitimately concerned" and "legitimately interested". The New Shorter Oxford English Dictionary defines "concerned" as: "*interested*, involved, troubled, anxious, showing concern".[30] In other words, "interested" and "concerned" are synonyms. The terminological difference raised by the United States is therefore without any substantive relevance, and does not imply a different standard applicable to persons resident or established outside the EC.

H. Decision-making procedures under the Regulation

79. In its first written submission, Australia has consistently misrepresented the decision-making process applicable under Regulation 2081/92. In particular, it has referred to the "Committee of EC Member States representatives" as the

---

27 US FWS, para. 27, 92; Australia's FWS, para. 204.

28 US FWS, para. 26-27.

29 US FWS, para. 94.

30 New Shorter Oxford English Dictionary, 1993, Vol. 1, p. 467 (emphasis added).

"decision-making process established by Article 15 of Regulation 2081/92".[31] Consequently, it has repeatedly referred to decisions taken according to the procedure set out in Article 15 of the Regulation as decisions taken "in the Committee of EC Member States representatives".[32] Finally, Australia has referred to the Committee of EC Member States as the "ultimate decision-maker" under the Regulation.[33]

80. These statements are based on a misconception of the decision-making process under the Regulation, and have the effect of exaggerating the role of the Committee. Under the Regulation, decisions with respect to the registration of geographical indications are in principle taken by the Commission. In certain cases, for instance where a statement of objection has been received or the Commission considers that a name does not qualify for protection, the Commission must act in accordance with the procedure in Article 15 of the Regulation.[34] Article 15 provides the following:

> 1. The Commission shall be assisted by a committee.
>
> 2. Where reference is made to this Article, Articles 5 and 7 of Decision 1999/468/EC shall apply.
>
> The period laid down in Article 5(6) of Decision 1999/468/EC shall be set at three months.
>
> 3. The Committee shall adopt its Rules of Procedure.

81. Decision 1999/468[35] is a decision which lays down, on a general level, the procedures for the exercise of implementing powers which the Council may delegate to the Commission in application of Article 202 of the EC Treaty. The procedure which is applicable under Regulation 2081/92 is the regulatory procedure set out in Article 5 of Decision 1999/468.

82. According to Article 5(1) of Decision 1999/468, the Commission is assisted by a Committee composed of representatives of the Member States. In accordance with Article 5(2) of the Decision, the Commission shall submit to the Committee a draft of the measures to be taken. If the measure is in accordance with the opinion of the Committee, the Commission adopts the Measures (Article 5(3) of the Decision). Only exceptionally, if the measure is not in accordance with the opinion of the Committee, may the matter be referred to the Council of Ministers (Article 5(4) of the Decision). In this case, the following procedure applies (Article 5(5) of the Decision):

> The Council may, where appropriate in view of any such position, act by qualified majority on the proposal, within a period to be laid down in each basic instrument but which shall in no case exceed three months from the date of referral to the Council.

---

31 Australia's FWS, para. 19.

32 E.g. Australia's FWS, para. 32, 44, 46,

33 Australia's FWS, para. 94.

34 Cf. Article 6(5), 7(5), 12b(1)(b), 12d(3) of the Regulation.

35 Exhibit EC-4.

> If within that period the Council has indicated by qualified majority that it opposes the proposal, the Commission shall re-examine it. It may submit an amended proposal to the Council, re-submit its proposal or present a legislative proposal on the basis of the Treaty.
>
> If on the expiry of that period the Council has neither adopted the proposed implementing act nor indicated its opposition to the proposal for implementing measures, the proposed implementing act shall be adopted by the Commission.

83. Consequently, the decision-maker under the Regulation is the Commission, or exceptionally the Council of Ministers. The Committee assists the Commission, but does not take decisions; it may, however, achieve that a proposal is referred to the Council of Ministers.

I. The protection of geographical indications

84. According to Article 13(1) of the Regulation, a name registered under the regulation shall be protected against:

> Registered names shall be protected against:
>
> (a) any direct or indirect commercial use of a name registered in respect of products not covered by the registration in so far as those products are comparable to the products registered under that name or insofar as using the name exploits the reputation of the protected name;
>
> (b) any misuse, imitation or evocation, even if the true origin of the product is indicated or if the protected name is translated or accompanied by an expression such as 'style', 'type', 'method', 'as produced in', 'imitation' or similar;
>
> (c) any other false or misleading indication as to the provenance, origin, nature or essential qualities of the product, on the inner or outer packaging, advertising material or documents relating to the product concerned, and the packing of the product in a container liable to convey a false impression as to its origin;
>
> (d) any other practice liable to mislead the public as to the true origin of the product.

J. Indication of the country of origin for homonymous geographical indications

85. In their first written submission, the United States has claimed that Article 12(2) requires that any use of a geographical indication in connection with products of other WTO Members can be authorized only if the country of

origin "is clearly and visibly indicated on the label", and that there is no similar requirement with respect to products of EC Member States.[36]

86. This interpretation is based on a misunderstanding of Article 12(2) of the Regulation. This provision is drafted as follows:

> If a protected name of a third country is identical to a Community protected name, registration shall be granted with due regard for local and traditional usage and the practical risks of confusion.
>
> Use of such names shall be authorized only if the country of origin of the product is clearly and visibly indicated on the label.

87. It follows clearly from the structure of this provision that the reference to "such names" in the second subparagraph of Article 12(2) is a reference to the names mentioned in the first subparagraph, i.e. identical protected names from a third country and the Community. In other words, the second subparagraph does not concern third country names in general, but only homonyms.

88. Moreover, it should be noted that the reference to "such names" applies both to third country protected names and to Community protected names. In the case of identical names, the requirement to indicate the country of origin can apply both to the third country name and the Community name. In practice, this would mean that whichever indication is registered later would normally be required to indicate the country of origin. Where a Community indication is registered after an identical third country indication, the Community indication would therefore be required to indicate the country of origin.

89. Finally, it should be noted that in case of homonymous names from the EC, the last indent of Article 6(6) of the Regulation also requires "a clear distinction in practice" between the two homonyms. Where the two homonyms are from different Member States, this may in practice require the indication of the country of origin.

K. Geographical indications and trademarks

90. The relationship between geographical indications and trademarks is regulated in Article 14 of the Regulation, which is drafted as follows:

> 1. Where a designation of origin or geographical indication is registered under this Regulation, any application for registration of a trademark that is for a product of the same type and use of which will engender one of the situations indicated in Article 13 shall be refused if made after the date of submission to the Commission of the application for registration of the designation of origin or geographical indication.
>
> Trademarks registered in breach of the first subparagraph shall be invalidated.

---

[36] US FWS, para. 25. Australia rightly assumed that this provision only applies to homonyms (Australia's FWS, para. 235).

> 2. With due regard to Community law, a trademark the use of which engenders one of the situations indicated in Article 13 and which has been applied for, registered, or established by use, if that possibility is provided for by the legislation concerned, in good faith within the territory of the Community, before either the date of protection in the country of origin or the date of submission to the Commission of the application for registration of the designation of origin or geographical indication, may continue to be used notwithstanding the registration of a designation of origin or geographical indication, provided that no grounds for its invalidity or revocation exist as specified by Council Directive 89/104/EEC of 21 December 1998 to approximate the laws of the Member States relating to trade marks and/or Council Regulation (EC) No 40/94 of 20 December 1993 on the Community trade mark.
>
> 3. A designation of origin or geographical indication shall not be registered where, in the light of a trade mark's reputation and renown and the length of time it has been used, registration is liable to mislead the consumer as to the true identity of the product.

L. Simplified registration of geographical indications prior to the entry into force of Regulation 692/2003

91. In its first written submission, Australia has also made certain claims regarding the simplified registration procedure according to Article 17 of Regulation 2081/92 as applicable until the entry into force of Regulation 692/2003.

92. As the Commission has already set out, these claims relate to a measure no longer in force at the time the Panel was established, and are therefore outside the terms of reference of the present Panel.[37] However, since certain of the factual claims made by Australia in this respect are factually wrong, the EC would like to take the opportunity to correct them.

93. In its first written submission, Australia claims that under the simplified procedure, a right of objection was available to persons resident or established in the EC, which was not available to persons from outside the EC.[38] In support of its thesis, it relies in particular on a declaration of the Commission and the Council quoted in the *Feta* judgment of the European Court of Justice.[39]

94. Australia's interpretation is unfounded. Article 17, as applicable until the entry into force of Regulation 692/2003, provided as follows (emphasis added):

> Within six months of the entry into force of the Regulation, Member States shall inform the Commission which of their legally

---

[37] See above, para. 13 et seq.

[38] Australia's FWS, para. 39, 191-192.

[39] The declaration was quoted in para. 21 of the Court's judgment (Exhibit COMP-11).

protected names or, in those Member States where there is no protection system, which of their names established by usage they wish to register pursuant to this Regulation.

In accordance with the procedure laid down in Article 15, the Commission shall register the names referred to in paragraph 1 which comply with Articles 2 and 4. *Article 7 shall not apply.* However, generic names shall not be added.

95. Article 17(2) thus provided clearly that Article 7, which laid down the right of objection, did not apply in the simplified procedure. This was explicitly confirmed by the European Court of Justice in the *Feta* judgment:[40]

> Second, as the Commission itself pointed out in its defence in Case C-293/96, it must be noted that, even though Article 17(2) of the basic regulation expressly provides that Article 7 thereof is not applicable in the simplified registration procedure, a registration under that procedure also presupposes that the names conform with the substantive requirements of that regulation. In the absence of express provisions to the contrary, there is no possibility, under the simplified procedure, of names being registered which do not fulfil the substantive conditions for registration under the normal registration procedure.

96. Furthermore, the declaration of the Council and the Commission referred to by the Court of Justice did not concern the simplified procedure of Article 17. The declaration read in relevant part as follows:[41]

> The Council and the Commission further declare that where there are agriculture products or foodstuffs already being legally marketed before the making of this Regulation which may be the subject of an application for registration, it has been provided for any Member States to object to the registration under the provisions of Article 7 of the Regulation [...].

97. This declaration simply referred to the situation envisaged in the second indent of Article 7(4) of Regulation 2081/92, in which a statement of objection will be admissible. This declaration did in no way refer to the simplified procedure foreseen in Article 17. Nor did the European Court of Justice, as shown above, deduce from this declaration that a right of objection applied in the context of the simplified procedure.

98. In accordance with the clear wording of Article 17(2) of Regulation as applicable until the entry into force of Regulation 692/2003, the right of objection did not apply in the context of the simplified procedure.

---

[40] Paragraph 92 of the Judgment (Exhibit COMP-11; emphasis added).

[41] Exhibit EC-5.

IV. REGULATION 2081/92 IS COMPATIBLE WITH NATIONAL TREATMENT OBLIGATIONS, AND DOES NOT IMPOSE A REQUIREMENT OF DOMICILE OR ESTABLISHMENT

99. In their first written submissions, the complainants have claimed that Regulation 2081/92:

- is incompatible with the national treatment obligation of the TRIPS and the Paris Convention (Article 3.1 TRIPS and Article 2.1 TRIPS in conjunction with Article 2.1 Paris Convention);
- establishes a requirement of domicile or establishment prohibited by the Paris Convention (Article 2.1 TRIPS in conjunction with Article 2.2 Paris Convention);
- is incompatible with the national treatment obligation of Article III:4 GATT.

100. The EC will discuss the claims under each of these provisions in turn.

A. National treatment under the TRIPS Agreement (Article 3.1 TRIPS and Article 2.1 TRIPS in conjunction with Article 2.1 Paris Convention)

101. Under the TRIPS Agreement, the obligation to provide national treatment with regard to the protection of intellectual property is set out in two different provisions. First, Article 3.1 TRIPS provides as follows:

> Each Member shall accord to the nationals of other Members treatment no less favourable than that it accords to its own nationals with regard to the protection of intellectual property, subject to the exceptions already provided in, respectively, the Paris Convention (1967), the Berne Convention (1971), the Rome Convention or the Treaty on Intellectual Property in Respect of Integrated Circuits. In respect of performers, producers of phonograms and broadcasting organizations, this obligation only applies in respect of the rights provided under this Agreement. Any Member availing itself of the possibilities provided in Article 6 of the Berne Convention (1971) or paragraph 1(b) of Article 16 of the Rome Convention shall make a notification as foreseen in those provisions to the Council for TRIPS.

102. Moreover, Article 2.1 TRIPS integrates into the TRIPS Agreement the national treatment provision contained in Article 2.1 of the Paris Convention. Article 2.1 of the Paris Convention reads as follows:

> Nationals of any country of the Union shall, as regards the protection of industrial property, enjoy in all the other countries of the Union the advantages that their respective laws now grant, or may hereafter grant, to nationals; all without prejudice to the rights

> specially provided for by this Convention. Consequently, they shall have the same protection as the latter, and the same legal remedy against any infringement of their rights, provided that the conditions and formalities imposed upon nationals are complied with.

103. Since both obligations are expressed in similar terms, the EC shall discuss the claims made by the complainants under both provisions jointly.

1. General remarks

104. Both Article 3.1 TRIPS and Article 2.1 Paris Convention oblige WTO Members to treat nationals of other Member no less favourably than their own nationals with respect to the protection of intellectual property rights. In *US – Section 211,* the Appellate Body has underlined the fundamental significance of the national treatment obligation within the context of the TRIPS.[42] In its first written submission, the United States has recalled this fundamental importance of the national treatment obligation under the TRIPS.[43] The EC agrees.

105. However, the EC considers it equally important to understand the correct scope and meaning of the national treatment provisions of the TRIPS and the Paris Convention. Article 3.1 TRIPS provides that each Member shall accord to the *nationals* of other Members treatment no less favourable than that it accords to its own *nationals*. Similarly, Article 2.1 of the Paris Convention provides that *nationals* of any country of the Union shall, as regards the protection of industrial property, enjoy in all the other countries of the Union the advantages that their respective laws now grant, or may hereafter grant, to *nationals*. Accordingly, the national treatment obligation under the TRIPS aims at an equality of treatment between *nationals*.[44]

106. This reference to nationals is of fundamental importance in the application of the national treatment provision under the TRIPS. This is illustrated by the findings of the Panel in *Indonesia – Cars*. In this case, the United States had argued that the Indonesian system put the United States companies in a position that, if they were successful in becoming a partner in the National Car Programme, they would be unlikely to use in Indonesia the mark normally used ("global" mark) on the vehicle marketed as a "national motor vehicle" in Indonesia, for fear of creating confusion. The Panel rejected this claim referring explicitly to the fact that no evidence had been brought to support the conclusion that the Indonesian system constituted discrimination between *nationals*:[45]

---

42 Appellate Body Report, *United States – Section 211*, para. 241.

43 US FWS, para. 33.

44 Daniel Gervais, *The TRIPS Agreement, Drafting History and Analysis*, (Sweet & Maxwell, 1998), p. 48.

45 Panel Report, *Indonesia – Cars*, para. 14.271 (emphasis added). The United States is therefore wrong to claim that *US – Section 211* has been the only dispute concerning the national treatment obligation in the context of the TRIPS Agreement (US FWS, para. 34).

> We do not accept this argument for the following reasons. First, no evidence has been put forward to refute the Indonesian statement that the system, in requiring a new, albeit Indonesian-owned, trademark to be created, *applies equally to pre-existing trademarks owned by Indonesian nationals and foreign nationals*. Second, if a foreign company enters into an arrangement with a Pioneer company, it would do so voluntarily, with knowledge of any consequent implications for its ability to maintain pre-existing trademark rights [...].

107. The emphasis put by the TRIPS Agreement on nationals is not accidental. In Article 3.1 TRIPS and 2.1 Paris Convention, national treatment is provided "with regard to the protection of intellectual property". Intellectual property rights are held by natural and legal persons.[46] It is therefore entirely consistent with the object and purpose of the national treatment provision of TRIPS that national treatment be granted between *nationals*.

108. In this regard, the national treatment obligation of the TRIPS differs fundamentally from national treatment in the GATT. Article III:4 of the GATT provides that "the *products* of the territory of any contracting party imported into the territory of any other contracting party shall be accorded treatment no less favourable than that accorded to like *products* of national origin". Accordingly, unlike Article 3.1 TRIPS and 2.1 Paris Convention, Article III:4 GATT prescribes national treatment between goods, not between nationals.

109. The Panel in *Indonesia – Autos* in fact cautioned against reading Article 3.1 TRIPS so as to apply to matters not directly related to the equal treatment of nationals:[47]

> In considering this argument, we note that any customs tariff, subsidy or other governmental measure of support could have a "de facto" effect of giving such an advantage to the beneficiaries of this support. *We consider that considerable caution needs to be used in respect of "de facto" based arguments of this sort, because of the danger of reading into a provision obligations which go far beyond the letter of that provision and the objectives of the Agreement.* It would not be reasonable to construe the national treatment obligation of the TRIPS Agreement in relation to the maintenance of trademark rights as preventing the grant of tariff, subsidy or other measures of support to national companies on the grounds that this would render the maintenance of trademark rights by foreign companies wishing to export to that market relatively more difficult.

110. The United States and Australia fail to acknowledge this fundamental difference between the national treatment obligations of the TRIPS and the

---

[46] On the definition of nationality in this respect, cf. Bodenhausen, Guide to the Application of the Paris Convention for the Protection of Industrial Property, p. 27-28 (1968).

[47] Panel Report, *Indonesia – Autos*, para. 14.723 (emphasis added).

GATT.[48] In their first written submissions, they make no attempt to establish that Regulation 2081/92 discriminates between *nationals* of the EC and *nationals* of other WTO members.

111. As the EC will show, Regulation 2081/92 does not discriminate between EC nationals and nationals of other WTO members.

112. Moreover, the EC will show for each of the claims raised that, even if Regulation 2081/92 applied differently to foreign and EC nationals, it could not be considered as providing less favourable treatment.

2. *Claims 1: Non-EC nationals are accorded less favorable treatment than EC nationals with respect to the registration of geographical indications through the application of a condition of reciprocity and equivalence*

113. The US and Australia have claimed that by subjecting the registration of geographic indications from other WTO members to "conditions of reciprocity and equivalence", Regulation 2081/92 violates the national treatment provisions of Article 3.1 TRIPS and 2.1 Paris Convention.[49]

114. This claim is wrong for the following reasons:

- The EC does not apply a condition of reciprocity and equivalence for the registration of geographical indications from other WTO members;
- The conditions for the registration of individual geographical indications do not constitute less favourable treatment;
- The conditions for the registration of geographical indications do not depend on nationality.

(a) The EC does not apply a condition of reciprocity and equivalence for the registration of geographical indications from other WTO members

115. The United States and Australia have alleged that Article 12(1) of Regulation 2081/92 subjects the registration of foreign geographical indications to a condition of "reciprocity and equivalence". In particular, the United States has argued that in order to ensure the protection of geographical indications relating to areas in other WTO Members, the EC requires them to (a) reciprocally grant equivalent GI protection for agricultural products and foodstuffs coming from the EC and (b) adopt a system for protecting

---

[48] This is all the more striking since the US, when discussing the most-favored-nation obligation under the TRIPS and the GATT, did distinguish between treatment of nationals and treatment of products (US, FWS, para. 108).

[49] US FWS, para. 57 et seq. It appears that Australia has also attempted to raise the same claim, albeit in less clear form (Australia's FWS, para. 199).

geographical indications that the EC unilaterally decides is equivalent to that in the EC, including equivalent inspection and objection systems.[50]

116. As the EC has already set out previously, this claim is factually incorrect.[51] WTO Members must provide adequate protection of geographical indications in accordance with the TRIPS Agreement. For this reason, Article 12(1) of Regulation 2081/92, which applies only subject to international agreements, does not apply to other WTO Members.[52]

117. Accordingly, the EC does not condition the registration of geographical indications relating to the territory of another WTO Member to the condition that it reciprocally grant equivalent protection for agricultural products and foodstuffs coming from the EC and that it adopts a system for protecting geographical indications equivalent to that in the EC.

(b) The conditions for the registration of individual geographical indications do not constitute less favourable treatment

118. However, the EC would like to clarify that whereas it does not require equivalence as regards the system of protection of geographical indications, it does require that the product specifications and inspection regimes with regard to specific geographical indications from third countries meet the conditions of Regulation 2081/92. For this reason, any application for a geographical indication relating to an area in a third country must be accompanied by a product specification, and must indicate that the necessary inspection procedures exist.[53]

119. It is not entirely clear to the EC whether the complainants are also challenging these GI-specific requirements. The EC notes, however, that in its submission, the United States has frequently referred to the notion of "equivalence" without any further qualification, and has claimed that the national treatment obligation was specifically intended to prohibit such a condition.[54]

120. In case the complainants should also challenge these GI-specific requirements, the EC would like to clarify that it considers that this interpretation would be erroneous. Article 3.1 TRIPS and 2.1 Paris Convention oblige WTO Members to provide "treatment no less favourable" to the nationals of other WTO Members; they do no oblige WTO Members to provide treatment more favourable.

121. As the EC has also explained, the objective of the product specification and the inspection regimes foreseen in Regulation 2081/92 is to ensure that the products meet the requirements that can be expected from products marketed

50 US FWS, para. 59.
51 Above para. 62 et seq.
52 *Ibid.*
53 Cf. above para. 68.
54 Cf. e.g. US FWS, para. 57.

using the protected name.[55] These considerations apply to protected names from the EC and from third countries alike. Therefore, the requirement in Regulation 2081/92 of an assurance that the product specifications regarding a foreign geographical indication are respected is not less favourable treatment, but equal treatment.

122. Accordingly, any claim regarding a violation of the national treatment provisions of Article 3.1 TRIPS and 2.1 Paris Convention through the conditions for the registration of individual geographic indications would be unfounded.

(c) The conditions for the registration of geographical indications do not depend on nationality

123. As the EC has set out, Article 3.1 TRIPS and 2.1 Paris Convention require equal treatment, as regards the protection of intellectual property, between *nationals*. However, the conditions and procedures contained in Regulation 2081/92 for the registration of geographical indications do not depend on nationality.

124. As the EC has explained above, the conditions and procedures for the registration of geographical indications relating to an area located in the EC are set out in Article 5 and 6 of Regulation 2081/92.[56] In contrast, the conditions and procedures for the registration of geographical indications relating to an area located in another WTO Member are contained in Article 12a and 12b of the Regulation.[57]

125. Whether the area to which a geographic indication is related is located inside the EC or outside is in no way linked to the question of the nationality of the producers of the product concerned. Protection of a geographical indication relating to an area located in the EC is obtained in accordance with Article 5 and 6 of the Regulation, even if the producers in question are foreign nationals. Inversely, protection for a geographical indication located outside the EC must be obtained in accordance with Articles 12a and 12b of Regulation 2081/92, even if the producers in question are EC nationals. In both situations, the same also applies if certain producers are EC nationals, and others are not.

126. Accordingly, Regulation 2081/92 does not distinguish between EC nationals and other nationals. For this reason also, the claim must fail.

[55] Above para. 48 et seq., 50 et seq.
[56] See above para. 56 et seq.
[57] See above para. 62.

3. *Claim 2: Regulation 2081/92 violates the national treatment obligations under the TRIPS and the Paris Convention by requiring that applications must be transmitted by the country in which the geographical area is located*

127. The United States (but not Australia) has claimed that Regulation 2081/92 violates the national treatment obligations under the TRIPS and the Paris Convention by requiring that applications must be transmitted by the country in which the geographical area is located.[58] The United States has argued that this requirement implies an "extra hurdle" for foreign nationals which is not faced by EC nationals. In particular, the United States has invoked the possibility that the third country concerned might have "neither the infrastructure nor the inclination" to process and transmit the application.

128. The EC submits that this claim must fail. First, the question which government must transmit the application in accordance with Article 6 or Article 12a of the Regulation does not depend on nationality, but on the question where the geographic area in question is located.[59] Accordingly, Regulation 2081/92 does not differentiate on the basis of nationality.

129. Second, the Regulation does not constitute less favourable treatment for third country nationals. The role of third country governments provided for in Article 12a of the Regulation corresponds exactly to that of EC Member States where geographical indications relating to an area located in the EC are concerned. As the EC has set out above, this involvement of the Member State or third country concerned in the registration process is crucial, as the government of the country concerned is particularly well placed to examine the admissibility of applications relating to geographical areas located on its territory. Accordingly, the condition that an application relating to an area located in a third country is transmitted by the government in question does not amount to "less favourable treatment", but in fact ensures equal treatment.

130. The references by the US to an absence of "infrastructure" or "inclination" on the part of the third country are not convincing. The verification and transmission of an application for registration of a geographical indication are not overly burdensome for another WTO Member. As regards "inclination", the EC finds it remarkable that the United States would invoke its own unwillingness to cooperate in the registration process in order to demonstrate a national treatment violation on the part of the EC.

131. Accordingly, the claim that Regulation 2081/92 violates the national treatment obligations under the TRIPS and the Paris Convention by requiring that applications must be transmitted by the country in which the geographical area is located is unfounded.

---

58 US FWS, para. 81.

59 Cf. above para. 123 et seq.

4. *Claim 3: Non-EC nationals are accorded less favorable treatment than EC nationals with respect to the requirement to indicate the country of origin for homonymous geographical indications*

132. The United States (but not Australia) has claimed that the requirement contained in Article 12(2) of Regulation 2081/92 to indicate the country of origin constitutes a violation of national treatment provisions under the TRIPS and the Paris Convention.[60] This claim is unfounded for the following reasons:

- Article 12(2) of Regulation 2081/92 does not apply to all geographical indications, but only to homonyms;
- the requirement to indicate the country of origin for homonymous geographical indications from the EC and third countries does not constitute less favourable treatment;
- Article 12(2) of Regulation 2081/92 does not discriminate between nationals.

(a) Article 12(2) of Regulation 2081/92 does not apply to all geographical indications, but only to homonyms

133. The United States has claimed that Article 12(2) of Regulation 2081/92 provides that use of all foreign geographical indications require the indication of the country of origin. As the EC has already clarified,[61] this claim of the United States is based on a misunderstanding. The second subparagraph of Article 12(2) only relates to the situation of the first subparagraph where "a protected name of a third country is identical to a Community protected name". Accordingly, there is no need to examine whether a requirement to indicate the country of origin for all foreign geographical indications would be compatible with national treatment obligations.

(b) The requirement to indicate the country of origin for homonymous geographical indications from the EC and third countries does not constitute less favourable treatment

134. Since it has misunderstood the meaning of Article 12(2) of the Regulation 2081/92, the United States has not indicated whether it considers the requirement to indicate the country of origin discriminatory also when only applying to homonymous names from the EC and a third country. Should the United States have intended to make such an argument, then it would be manifestly unfounded.

135. Article 12(2) in fact does not only apply to third country names, but also to Community names. As the EC has explained, it therefore may require the

---

[60] US FWS, para. 68. Australia has made a similar claim under Article 2.1 of the TBT Agreement, which will be discussed below (cf. Australia's FWS, para. 234).

[61] Above para. 85.

indication of the country of origin for both EC and third country names, depending on which geographical indication has been protected earlier.[62] Accordingly, Article 12(2) of Regulations treats geographical indications from the EC and third countries alike.

136. Accordingly, Article 12(2) of Regulation 2081/92 is entirely compatible with the national treatment obligations of the TRIPS and the Paris Convention.

(c) Article 12(2) of Regulation 2081/92 does not discriminate between nationals

137. The second subparagraph of Article 12(2) of Regulation 2081/92 provides that the use of "such names" is authorized only if the country of origin is clearly and visibly indicated on the label. As the EC has set out above,[63] "such names" is a reference to the first subparagraph of Article 12(2). Accordingly, the requirement to indicate the country of origin applies where "a protected name of a third country is identical to a Community protected name".

138. As the EC has already set out in response to Claim 1, whether a protected name is a "Community name" or a "third country name" within the meaning of Regulation 2081/92 depends on where the geographical area to which the geographical indication is related is located. It has nothing to do with nationality. Accordingly, Article 12(2) does not imply any discrimination between nationals.[64]

139. For all these reasons, the claim should be rejected.

5. Claim 4: Regulation 2081/92 accords less favourable treatment to non-EC nationals by subjecting the right to object to the registration of geographical indications to conditions of reciprocity and equivalence

140. The United States and Australia have claimed that only nationals from WTO member countries recognised in accordance with Article 12(3) of Regulation 2081/92 as fulfilling the conditions of reciprocity and equivalence may object to registrations of geographical indications in accordance with Article 12d of the Regulation.[65]

141. This is factually wrong. As the EC has already set out,[66] Article 12d(1) of Regulation 2081/92 gives a right to object to any person that "is from a WTO Member or a third country recognised under the procedure provided for in Article 12(3)". It is clear from this explicit reference to WTO Members that

[62] Above para. 88.
[63] Above para. 87.
[64] The EC would point out that if national treatment under the TRIPS were considered as applying also to discrimination between goods, then the relationship between the provisions of the TRIPS on national treatment and Article IX:1 of the GATT would become an issue (on the relationship between Article III:4 and IX:1 GATT, see below para. 213 et seq.).
[65] United States FWS, para. 92; Australia's FWS, para. 204.
[66] Above para. 73 et seq.

WTO Members are not subject to the procedure of Article 12(3) applicable to other third countries. The same applies also under Article 12.b.2 with respect to objections against the registration of geographical indications from outside the EC.

142. The claim is also legally unfounded. Article 3.1 TRIPS and 2.1 of the Paris Convention relate only to equal treatment between *nationals*. However, Article 7(3) of Regulation 2081/92 refers to persons which are resident or established in the EC, regardless of their nationality. Similarly, Article 12d(1) refers to persons resident or established outside the EC, regardless of their nationality. It should also be noted that conditions regarding domicile or establishment are the subject of Article 2.2 Paris Convention, on the basis of which the complainants have formulated separate claims.[67]

143. Accordingly, this claim should be dismissed.

6. *Claim 5: Regulation 2081/92 accords less favourable treatment to non-EC nationals by requiring their own country to transmit the objection*

144. The United States and Australia have claimed that Regulation 2081/92 accords less favourable treatment to non-EC nationals by requiring their own country to transmit the objection.[68]

145. First, it must once again be remarked that Article 12d(2) applies not to nationals, but to persons resident or established in a third country. Accordingly, Regulation 2081/92 does not accord different treatment on the basis of nationality.

146. Second, the treatment accorded to persons resident or established in the Community and persons resident or established in the EC is exactly identical. For persons resident or established in the Community, Article 7 requires that the statement of objection shall be submitted to the EC Member State where the person is resident or established, who shall transmit the objection to the Commission. For persons resident or established in a third country, Article 12d(1) provides that the statement shall be submitted to the third country of residence or establishment, which shall transmit it to the Commission. Accordingly, Regulation 2081/92 does not apply unequal, but equal treatment.

147. The United States has argued that the third country might not have "the appropriate mechanism to process the objection, or may or may not be inclined to transmit the objection, for its own political reasons".[69] Similarly, Australia has argued that third countries "have no legally defined relationship" regarding such objections.[70]

---

[67] See above Section II.B.3 and below Section IV.B.

[68] US, FWS, para. 90; Australia's FWS, para. 205.

[69] US, FWS, para. 90.

[70] Australia's FWS, para. 205.

148. These objections are unconvincing. First, it does not appear that a particularly demanding infrastructure is required for processing and transmitting a statement of objection. Second, the complainants cannot rely on their own unwillingness to cooperate in the transmission of a statement of objection in order to demonstrate a violation of national treatment obligations on the part of the EC.

149. Accordingly, Regulation 2081/92 does not accord less favourable treatment to non-EC nationals by requiring their own country to transmit the objection.

7. Claim 6: Regulation 2081/92 accords less favourable treatment to non-EC nationals by requiring non-EC national to have a "legitimate interest" to object to the registration of geographical indications

150. The United States (but not Australia) has claimed that Article 12d(1) Regulation 2081/92 accords less favourable treatment to non-EC nationals by requiring non-EC nationals to have a "legitimate interest" to object to the registration of geographical indications.[71]

151. As the EC has shown, there is no substantive difference between the term "legitimate interest" used in Article 12d(1) of Regulation 2081/92 and the term "legitimately concerned" in Article 7(3). Rather, "legitimately concerned" and "legitimately concerned" are synonymous expressions.

152. Since the claim is based on a misunderstanding of the Regulation, it does not need to be discussed any further.

8. Claim 7: Regulation 2081/92 accords less favourable treatment because a non-EC rightholder has no "representative" in the regulatory committee to "speak for him"

153. Australia (but not the United States) has argued that Regulation 2081/92 accords less favourable treatment because a non-EC rightholder has no "representative" in the regulatory committee to "speak for him".[72]

154. This claim is manifestly unfounded. First, Australia has not correctly understood the decision-making process under the Regulation. As the EC has set out,[73] the decision-maker under the Regulation is the Commission, or exceptionally the Council. The Committee merely assists the Commission, and may exceptionally achieve that a proposal is referred to the Council. In no case does it take decisions itself. Moreover, Member States representatives on the Committee do not speak for particular rightholders, but represent the respective EC Member State.

---

71 US, FWS, para. 93-94.

72 Australia's FWS, para. 203.

73 Above, para. 79 et seq.

155. Secondly, Australia's claim to have a representative on the regulatory committee is not reasonable. The public authorities of a WTO Member must be presumed to administer their duties properly and fairly. This is independent of the nationality of the civil servants and employees working for such authorities. The EC also notes that there are no "EC representatives" in the public authorities and agencies of Australia. The EC does not assume that Australia would want to suggest that for this reason, Australian authorities cannot be assumed to correctly implement their WTO obligations with respect to the EC.

9. Claim 8: A right of objection was available to persons resident or established in an EC Member State that was not available to other WTO Member nationals in respect of the registration of more than 120 geographical indications under the normal registration process

156. Australia has claimed that there is a violation of national treatment in the fact that a right of objection was available to persons resident or established in an EC Member State that was not available to other WTO Member nationals in respect of the registration of more than 120 geographical indications under the normal registration process.[74] This claim must fail for the following reasons:

- Australia's claim relates to a measure which was no longer in force at the time of establishment of the Panel, and which is therefore not within the terms of reference of the Panel;
- the individual registrations are not in violation of national treatment obligations;
- Australia is seeking to obtain a retroactive remedy it could not have obtained had it attacked the measure while it was still in force.

(a) Australia's claim relates to a measure which was no longer in force at the time of establishment of the Panel, and which is therefore not within the terms of reference of the Panel

157. Australia's claim relates to Regulation 2081/92 as in force until 8 April 2003, when Regulation 692/2003 entered into force. It therefore relates to a measure which was no longer in force at the time of establishment of the Panel. Accordingly, as the EC has set out above, this measure is therefore not within the terms of reference of the Panel.[75]

---

[74] Australia's FWS, para. 184 et seq.

[75] See above Section II.A.1.

(b) The individual registrations are not in violation of national treatment obligations

158. In its submission, Australia has also argued that "in respect to the registration under the normal registration process of more than 120 EC-defined GIs" before Regulation 2081/92 was amended by Regulation 692/2003, the "EC measure" accorded less favourable treatment to foreign nationals. With this claim, Australia seems to suggest that the individual registrations of geographical indications which were carried out prior to the entry into force of Regulation 692/2003 somehow violate the national treatment obligations under the TRIPS and the Paris Convention.

159. This claim of Australia's is unfounded. Australia has made no plausible case that the 120 registrations in question in any way violate the national treatment obligations under the TRIPS and the Paris Convention.

160. Australia's claim is based exclusively on the argument that no right of objection was available to third country-nationals under Regulation 2081/92 before its amendment by Regulation 692/2003. However, this claim relates to Regulation 2081/92 as applicable before its amendment, and the procedure it prescribed for the registration of geographical indications. The rules governing the procedure leading up to the adoption of a measure are not the same as the measure itself.

161. In contrast, Australia has advanced no arguments in support of its claim that the individual registrations are incompatible with national treatment obligations. It is submitted that Australia is unable to do so. Each individual registration grants protection to a specific geographical indication relating to a specific geographical area. It is not clear to the European Community how such a registration could be considered to grant less favourable treatment to third-country nationals.

(c) Australia is seeking to obtain a retroactive remedy it could not have obtained had it attacked the measure while it was still in force.

162. In addition, the EC considers it important to remark that Australia's claim, if directed against the individual registrations, has considerable implications for the dispute settlement system set up by the DSU. In fact, with its claim, Australia is seeking to obtain a retroactive remedy that it could not even have obtained had it attacked Regulation 2081/92 before it was amended by Regulation 692/2003.

163. According to Article 19.1 DSU, where a panel or the Appellate Body concludes that a measure is inconsistent with a covered agreement, it shall recommend that the Member concerned "bring the measure into conformity with that agreement". It is universally accepted that this signifies that recommendations of panels and the Appellate Body are prospective, not

retrospective in nature.[76] This has also been confirmed by the Appellate Body in *US – Certain EC Products*:[77]

> We note, though, that there is an obvious inconsistency between the finding of the Panel that "the 3 March Measure is no longer in existence" and the subsequent recommendation of the Panel that the DSB request that the United States bring its 3 March Measure into conformity with its WTO obligations. The Panel erred in recommending that the DSB request the United States to bring into conformity with its WTO obligations a measure which the Panel has found no longer exists.

164. Reference can also be made to the findings of the GATT Panel in *Norway – Trondheim Bridge*, which clearly stated that GATT remedies were not retroactive:[78]

> The Panel then turned its attention to the recommendations that the United States had requested it to make. In regard to the United States' request that the Panel recommend that Norway take the necessary measures to bring its practices into compliance with the Agreement with regard to the Trondheim procurement, the Panel noted that all the acts of non-compliance alleged by the United States were acts that had taken place in the past. The only way mentioned during the Panel's proceedings that Norway could bring the Trondheim procurement into line with its obligations under the Agreement would be by annulling the contract and recommencing the procurement process. The Panel did not consider it appropriate to make such a recommendation. Recommendations of this nature had not been within customary practice in dispute settlement under the GATT system and the drafters of the Agreement on Government Procurement had not made specific provision that such recommendations be within the task assigned to panels under standard terms of reference. Moreover, the Panel considered that in the case under examination such a recommendation might be disproportionate, involving waste of resources and possible damage to the interests of third parties.

165. The Panel went on to emphasise that these considerations were in no way specific to government procurement, but were of a general nature:[79]

> In considering this argument, the Panel was of the view that situations of the type described by the United States were not unique to government procurement. Considerable trade damage could be caused in other areas by an administrative decision

---

[76] Australia itself has argued in favour of the prospective character of WTO remedies even in regard to Article 4.7 SCM Agreement; cf. Panel Report, *Australia – Automotive Leather (Article 21.5 – US)*, para. 6.14.

[77] Appellate Body, *US – Certain EC Products*, para. 81.

[78] Panel Report, *Norway – Trondheim Bridge*, para. 4.17.

[79] Panel Report, *Norway – Trondheim Bridge*, para. 4.23.

without there necessarily being any GATT inconsistent legislation, for example in the areas of discretionary licensing, technical regulations, sanitary and phytosanitary measures and subsidies. Moreover, there had been cases where a temporary measure contested before the GATT had been lifted before a Panel had been able to report.

166. In the present case, even if Australia had challenged a violation of national treatment before Regulation 2081/92 was amended by Regulation 692/2003, it could therefore not have claimed that the EC undo all the registrations already carried out, or that it reopen a possibility of objection against such registrations.

167. Australia has also argued that when Regulation 692/2003 entered into force, it should have reopened a full objection period in respect to all geographical indications for which applications were pending.[80] This argument shows even more clearly the retroactive character of Australia's claims. If the period of objection had already fully or partially run out for EC residents, then claims based on national treatment would not have given a retroactive right to reopen an objection period for non-EC residents.

168. By formulating its claim not against the terminated measure but against the acts which are derived from it, Australia is effectively trying to circumvent the principle that WTO remedies are not retroactive in nature. For this reason also, Australia's claim must be rejected.

169. For all the reasons set out above, Australia's claim must be rejected.

10. Claim 9: A right of objection was available to persons resident or established in an EC Member State that was not available to other WTO Member nationals in respect of the registration of more than 480 EC-defined GIs under the simplified registration process

170. Finally, Australia also claims that a right of objection was available to persons resident or established in an EC Member State that was not available to other WTO Member nationals in respect of the registration of more than 480 EC-defined GIs under the simplified registration procedure.[81] In this respect, Australia refers to the simplified registration procedure provided for in Article 17 of Regulation 2082/92 until its amendment through Regulation 2081/92.

171. With this claim, Australia is once again trying to obtain a retrospective remedy for a measure which is not within the terms of reference of the Panel, and which it did no challenge while it was still in force. All arguments that have been set out in respect of the Claim 8 therefore apply here as well.

172. Moreover, Australia's claim is factually wrong. As the EC has already set out, there was no right of objection for EC residents under the simplified

[80] Australia's FWS, para. 188.
[81] Australia's FWS, para. 190 et seq.

procedure.[82] The fact that there was no right of objection for third-country residents therefore did not constitute a violation of national treatment obligations.

173. Australia's claims must therefore be rejected.

B. Prohibited requirement of domicile or establishment(Article 2.1 TRIPS in conjunction with Article 2.2 Paris Convention)

174. The complainants have also raised certain claims under Article 2.1 TRIPS in conjunction with Article 2.2 Paris Convention. Article 2.2 Paris Convention, which prohibits subjecting the enjoyment of intellectual property rights to a condition of domicile or establishment, is a separate and distinct obligation from Article 2.1 of the Paris Convention.

175. As the EC has set out, the complainant's claims under Article 2.2 Paris Convention are not within the Panel's terms of reference.[83] This notwithstanding, the EC will hereafter briefly refute certain erroneous arguments made in this respect by the complainants.

1. Claim 10: Regulation 2081/92 requires non-EC nationals to become established in the EC as a condition for registering geographical indications

176. The United States (but not Australia) has argued that Regulation 2081/92 requires non-EC nationals to become established in the EC as a condition for registering geographical indications.[84] This claim is unfounded for the following reasons:

- Geographical indications relating to an area located in a WTO country can be registered under Regulation 2081/92;
- The right to register a geographical indication does not depend on domicile or establishment;
- Article 2.2 Paris Convention does not exclude measures which ensure that a product originates in the geographical to which a protected geographical indication area is related.

(a) Geographical indications relating to an area located in a WTO country can be registered under Regulation 2081/92

177. The United States has based its claim on the assumption that a US national cannot register a geographical indication relating to an area in the United States.[85] The United States claim therefore seems to be based on its

[82] Supra para. 91 et seq.
[83] See above Section II.B.3.
[84] US FWS, para. 84.
[85] US FWS, para. 85.

assumption that the registration of geographical indications relating to an area outside the EC is possible only if conditions of reciprocity and equivalence of protection systems are fulfilled.

178. As the EC has already explained, the registration of geographical indications relating to an area located in anther WTO Member does not depend on the fulfilment of such conditions.[86] Any geographical indication relating to an area in another WTO Member can be registered if it fulfils the conditions set out in the Regulation.

179. Accordingly, there is no requirement as to domicile or establishment for the registration of geographical indications relating to an area located in a third country. Already for this reason, the United States claim must fail.

(b) The right to register a geographical indication does not depend on domicile or establishment

180. The United States has argued further that a US national could not register a geographical indication relating to an area located in the EC without "having some form of investment or business establishment in the EC".[87]

181. This assumption of the United States is wrong. First of all, not any form of investment or "business establishment" would appear to constitute "an establishment" within the meaning of Article 2.2 of the Paris Convention.

182. Second, in order for a name to qualify as a geographical indication under Regulation 2081/92, it must "possess a specific quality, reputation or other characteristics attributable to that geographical origin *and the production and/or processing and/or preparation of which take place in the defined geographical area*".[88]

183. Accordingly, the Regulation does not require that a producer be domiciled or established in the EC. It merely requires that the production, processing or preparation, alternatively or cumulatively, must take place in the defined geographical area. What specific activities of production, processing, or preparation must take place in the specific area will depend on the specifications for the product in question. It cannot be assumed, however, that these specifications will necessarily require a producer to be domiciled or established in the geographical area in question.

---

86 Above para. 62 et seq.

87 US FWS, para. 85.

88 Article 2.2 (b) of the Regulation. As has been noted above para. 46, a closer link with the geographical area is required for designations of origin. However, since the procedures for registration and protection of designations of origin are identical to those for geographical indications, the EC will refer only to the latter.

(c) Article 2.2 Paris Convention does not exclude measures which ensure that a product originates in the geographical area to which a protected geographical indication is related

184. Moreover, if the argument of the United States were accepted, it would have the effect of rendering the protection of geographical indications as defined in the TRIPS impossible.

185. According to Article 22.1 TRIPS, a geographical indication identifies "a good as *originating* in the territory of a Member, or a region or locality in that territory, where a given quality, reputation or other characteristic of the good is essentially attributable to its geographical *origin*". Thus, the definition of a geographical indication in the TRIPS presupposes that the good in question has an identifiable geographical *origin*.

186. The definition in Regulation 2081/92 that the production and/or processing and/or preparation must take place in the defined geographical area implements this requirement of an identifiable geographical origin. The argument of the United States that this constitutes a requirement of "domicile or establishment" incompatible with Article 2.2 of the Paris Convention is equivalent to saying that a geographical indication should be protected even if the products in question do not originate in the area to which the geographical indication relates.

187. Such an interpretation is incompatible with Article 22.1 TRIPS, and must also for this reason be rejected.

2. *Claim 11: Regulation 2081/92 requires non-EC nationals to become established in the EC as a condition for objecting*

188. The United States has argued that the fact that Regulation 2081/92 requires the home country of third country nationals to transmit the statement of objection constitutes a requirement of residence or domicile contrary to Article 2.2 of the Paris Convention.[89]

189. This claim is manifestly unfounded. Article 12d(1) of Regulation 2081/92 explicitly *allows* persons from other WTO countries who are resident or established in third countries to object to registrations. It merely requires that, in close parallelism with the situation for EC residents, the statement of objection be transmitted by the third country in which the person is resident. This procedural modality does not constitute a "requirement of domicile or establishment" for the enjoyment of an industrial property right. Accordingly, this claim must be rejected.

---

[89] US FWS, para. 91. Australia has raised Article 2.2 Paris Convention in the context of its claims with respect to Regulation 2081/92 as applicable before it was amended by Regulation 692/2003 (Australia's FWS, paras. 189, 194). Like the claims raised under Article 3.1 TRIPS and 2.1 Paris Convention, these claims are outside the terms of reference of the Panel, and therefore need not be considered further (cf. above Section II.A.1).

C. National Treatment under Article III:4 GATT

190. The complainants have raised a number of claims alleging that Regulation 2081/92 is incompatible with the national treatment obligation contained in Article III:4 GATT. In this section, the EC will show that Regulation 2081/92 is fully compatible with Article III:4 GATT. In the alternative, the EC considers that the EC measure is justified by Article XX (d) GATT.

1. The regulation 2081/92 is not incompatible with Article III:4 GATT

191. The national treatment obligation contained in Article III:4 GATT provides as follows:

> The products of the territory of any contracting party imported into the territory of any other contracting party shall be accorded treatment no less favourable than that accorded to like products of national origin in respect of all laws, regulations and requirements affecting their internal sale, offering for sale, purchase, transportation, distribution or use. The provisions of this paragraph shall not prevent the application of differential internal transportation charges which are based exclusively on the economic operation of the means of transport and not on the nationality of the product.

192. As the EC will show, Regulation 2081/92 is entirely compatible with this obligation.

(a) General remarks

193. In *Korea – Various Measures on Beef*, the Appellate Body explained that for a violation of Article III:4 to be established, three elements must be satisfied:[90]

> For a violation of Article III:4 to be established, three elements must be satisfied: that the imported and domestic products at issue are "like products"; that the measure at issue is a "law, regulation, or requirement affecting their internal sale, offering for sale, purchase, transportation, distribution, or use"; and that the imported products are accorded "less favourable" treatment than that accorded to like domestic products.

194. The EC does not contest that Regulation 2081/92 is a measure affecting the internal sale of products. However, it considers that some general remarks are necessary on the first and the third condition, namely that products at issue must be "like products", and that the imported products must be accorded "less favourable treatment" than like domestic products.

---

[90] Appellate Body Report, *Korea – Various Measures on Beef*, para. 133.

(i) Like products

195. The EC does not contest that products from third countries falling under the scope of Regulation 2081/92 may be "like" EC products which fall under the scope of that Regulation.

196. The EC would also like to stress, however, that the question of whether products are "like" for the purposes of Article III:4 GATT must be separated from the question of whether the conditions for the registration of individual geographic indications are fulfilled. In the following passage in its first written submission, Australia seems to be merging these two issues:[91]

> However, the products in respect of which an EC-defined GI may be registered remain subject to the provisions of Article III:4 of GATT 1994. Thus, within the meaning of GATT Article III:4, for example: imported apples and pears would be like products to "Savoie" apples and pears; imported oysters would be like products to "Whitstable" oysters; imported olive oils would be like product to the many olive oils for which an EC-defined GI has been registered; and imported trout would be like product with "Black Forest" trout.

197. Once again, the EC has no problem in accepting that apples or oysters from Australia may be "like" apples or oysters from the EC. However, the EC would like to remark that this does not mean that the EC cannot apply the conditions for the registration of geographic indications, as long as these conditions do not result in less favourable treatment for imported products.

198. The fact that a domestic measure may distinguish between "like" products without for that reason alone according less favorable treatment, was also explicitly confirmed by the Appellate Body in *EC – Asbestos*:[92]

> We recognize that, by interpreting the term "like products" in Article III:4 in this way, we give that provision a relatively broad product scope – although no broader than the product scope of Article III:2. In so doing, we observe that there is a second element that must be established before a measure can be held to be inconsistent with Article III:4. Thus, even if two products are "like", that does not mean that a measure is inconsistent with Article III:4. A complaining Member must still establish that the measure accords to the group of "like" *imported* products "less favourable treatment" than it accords to the group of "like" *domestic* products. The term "less favourable treatment" expresses the general principle, in Article III:1, that internal regulations "should not be applied … so as to afford protection to domestic production". If there is "less favourable treatment" of the group of "like" imported products, there is, conversely, "protection" of the group of "like" domestic products. However, a Member may draw

---

91 Australia's FWS, para. 162.

92 Appellate Body Report, *EC – Asbestos*, para. 100.

> distinctions between products which have been found to be "like", without, for this reason alone, according to the group of "like" *imported* products "less favourable treatment" than that accorded to the group of "like" *domestic* products. [...].

(ii) Less favourable treatment

199. In *Korea – Various Measures on Beef*, the Appellate Body has defined the meaning of "less favourable treatment" as follows:[93]

> We observe, however, that Article III:4 requires only that a measure accord treatment to imported products that is "no less favourable" than that accorded to like domestic products. A measure that provides treatment to imported products that is *different* from that accorded to like domestic products is not necessarily inconsistent with Article III:4, as long as the treatment provided by the measure is "no less favourable". According "treatment no less favourable" means, as we have previously said, according *conditions of competition* no less favourable to the imported product than to the like domestic product.

200. The Appellate Body continued as follows:[94]

> A formal difference in treatment between imported and like domestic products is thus neither necessary, nor sufficient, to show a violation of Article III:4. Whether or not imported products are treated "less favourably" than like domestic products should be assessed instead by examining whether a measure modifies the *conditions of competition* in the relevant market to the detriment of imported products.

201. As the EC will show, Regulation 2081/92 does not modify the conditions of competition to the detriment of imported products.

(b) Claim 12: Regulation 2081/92 accords less favourable treatment as regards the conditions for registration of foreign geographical indications

202. The complainants have claimed that Regulation 2081/92 accords less favourable treatment as regards the conditions for registration of foreign geographical indications by imposing conditions of reciprocity and equivalence.[95]

203. As the EC has already stated above, Regulation 2081/92 does not impose a condition of reciprocity and systemic equivalence for the registration of

---

93 Appellate Body Report, *Korea – Various Measures on Beef*, para. 135.

94 Appellate Body Report, *Korea – Various Measures on Beef*, para. 137.

95 US FWS, para. 104; Australia's FWS, para. 165 et seq.

geographical indications from other WTO Members.[96] Accordingly, it does not apply less favourable treatment to products from other WTO Members.

204. As it has already done in response to the claims under the national treatment provisions of the TRIPS and the Paris Convention,[97] the EC would like to recall, however, that whereas it does not require other WTO Members to have an equivalent system for the protection of geographical indications, it must ensure that indications from third countries comply with the conditions set out in Regulation 2081/92. However, in this respect, the EC treats products from the EC like it treats products from other WTO Members.

205. The claim that Regulation 2081/92 accords less favourable treatments as regards the conditions for registration of foreign geographical indications by imposing conditions of reciprocity and equivalence must therefore be dismissed.

(c) Claim 13: Regulation 2081/92 accords less favourable treatment as regards the requirement that the application must be transmitted by the government of the third country

206. The complainants have argued that Regulation 2081/92 accords less favourable treatment as regards the requirement that the application must be transmitted by the government of the third country.[98]

207. As the EC has already set out above with respect to the national treatment obligations under the TRIPS and the Paris Convention,[99] the role of third country governments provided for in Article 12a of the Regulation corresponds exactly to that of EC Member States where geographical indications relating to an area located in the EC are concerned. Accordingly, the condition that an application relating to an area located in a third country is transmitted by the government in question does not amount to "less favourable treatment", but in fact ensures equal treatment. Moreover, Australia and the United States cannot invoke their own unwillingness to cooperate in the application process in order to argue that Regulation 2081/92 constitutes less favourable treatment for their own nationals.

208. Accordingly, this claim is equally unfounded.

(d) Claim 14: Regulation 2081/92 accords less favourable treatment as regards the requirement to indicate the country of origin

209. The United States (but not Australia) has argued that Regulation 2081/92 accords less favourable treatments as regards the requirement to indicate the country of origin.[100]

---

96 See above, para. 62.

97 Above para. 113 et seq.

98 US FWS, para. 104(d); Australia's FWS, para. 172 et seq.

99 Above para. 127 et seq.

100 US FWS, para. 106. Australia has made a similar claim under Article 2.1 of the TBT Agreement, which will be discussed below (cf. Australia's FWS, para. 234).

210. This claim is unfounded for the following reasons:

- Article 12(2) of Regulation 2081/92 does not apply to all geographical indications, but only to homonyms;
- The requirement to indicate the country of origin for homonymous geographical indications from the EC and third countries does not constitute less favourable treatment;
- Article IX:1 of the GATT is a *lex specialis* to Article III:4 GATT; national treatment obligations therefore do not apply to requirements to mark the country of origin.

(i) Article 12(2) of Regulation 2081/92 does not apply to all geographical indications, but only to homonyms

211. As the EC has already set out in response to the United States' corresponding claim under the TRIPS Agreement, Article 12(2) of Regulation 2081/92 does not apply to all geographical indications, but only to homonyms.[101] Accordingly, there is no requirement to indicate the country of origin for all foreign geographical indications.

(ii) The requirement to indicate the country of origin for homonymous geographical indications from the EC and third countries does not constitute less favourable treatment

212. As the EC has also already explained, Article 12(2) does not only apply to third country names, but applies on equal terms to Community names.[102] Accordingly, Article 12(2) treats foreign and EC goods alike.

(iii) Article IX:1 of the GATT is a lex specialis to Article III:4 GATT; national treatment obligations therefore do not apply to requirements to mark the country of origin

213. Finally, it should be noted that marks of origin are dealt with in Article IX of the GATT. Article IX:1 provides as follows:

> Each contracting party shall accord to the products of the territories of other contracting parties treatment with regard to marking requirements no less favourable than the treatment accorded to like products of any third country.

214. It is noteworthy that Article IX GATT contains, with respect to marks of origin, exclusively an obligation to provide most-favoured nation treatment. It

[101] Above para. 133.
[102] Above para. 134.

does not contain an obligation to also provide national treatment. This has been confirmed by the GATT Panel in *US – Tuna*:[103]

> The Panel noted that the title of Article IX is 'Marks of Origin' and its text refers to marking of origin of imported products. The Panel further noted that Article IX does not contain a national-treatment but only a most-favoured-nation requirement, which indicates that this provision was intended to regulate marking of origin of imported products but not marking of products generally. The Panel therefore found that the labelling provisions of the DPCIA did not fall under Article IX:1.

215. This omission in Article IX:1 cannot be regarded as accidental. If the GATT had meant to also impose a national treatment obligation with respect to marks of origin, it would have been natural to include such an obligation in Article IX. Alternatively, Article IX could have remained silent on the issue of national and most-favoured nation treatment, in which case the general obligations contained in Articles I and III of the GATT would have applied.

216. By laying down an obligation only to provide most-favoured nation treatment and not also national treatment, Article IX implies that WTO members are free to impose country of origin marking only with respect to imported products and not to domestic products. This understanding is also confirmed by a report of a GATT working party:[104]

> The Working Party considered that the question of additional marking requirements, such as an obligation to add the name of the producer or the place of origin or the formula of the product, should not be brought within the scope of any recommendation dealing with the problem of marks of origin. The point was stressed that *requirements going beyond the obligation to indicate origin would not be consistent with the requirements of Article III, if the same requirements did not apply to domestic producers of like products*.

217. For these reasons, Article III:4 is not applicable to requirements to indicate the country of origin for an imported product.

218. For all the reasons set out, the EC submits that the United States claim must be rejected.

[103] Panel Report, *US – Import Restrictions on Tuna*, para. 5.41.
[104] L/595, adopted on 17 November 1956, 5S/102, 105-106, para. 13 (emphasis added).

(e) Claim 15: Regulation 2081/92 accords less favourable treatment due to an overall bias in the decision-making process

219. Australia has argued that Regulation 2081/92 accords less favourable treatment in that there is an overall bias in the decision-making process due to the alleged fact:[105]

> that the outcome of the application is to be determined through a process, that is, the Committee of EC Member State representatives, in which:
>
> - there is no representative or advocate for the registration of an EC-defined GI for an imported product; and
> - there is no requirement for procedural fairness, due process and/or transparency concerning that Committee's decision-making process.

220. First of all, this claim is based on a misunderstanding of the decision-making process under the Regulation. As the EC has already explained, the decision-maker under the Regulation is the Commission, or exceptionally the Council.[106] The Committee merely assists the Commission, and may exceptionally achieve that a proposal is referred to the Council.

221. Secondly, as the EC has already argued, Australia's claim to a have representative on the regulatory committee is manifestly unfounded.[107]

222. Finally, the Australian statement that there is "no requirement for procedural fairness, due process and/or transparency" concerning the decision-making process of the Committee is completely unsupported by fact.

223. For these reasons, the Australian claim must be rejected.

2. *The measure would be justified under Article XX (d) GATT*

224. As explained, it is unclear to the EC whether the complainants claim that the requirements imposed by Article 12a, in conjunction with Articles 4 and 10, of Regulation 2081/92 with respect to the registration of each specific geographical indication are as such incompatible with Article III:4 of the GATT. The EC has shown that those requirements do not provide less favourable treatment to imported like products and, therefore, are consistent with that provision.

225. In the event that the complainants were to claim that such requirements are inconsistent with Article III:4 of the GATT, and should the Panel find that they afford less favourable treatment to imported products, the EC submits in the

105 Australia's FWS, para. 177.
106 Above, para. 79.
107 Above, para. 155.

alternative that such requirements would be justified under Article XX(d) of the GATT.

226. More specifically, the EC submits that the requirements at issue are necessary in order to ensure that only those products which conform to the definition of geographical indications contained in Article 2(2) of Regulation 2081/92, which is itself fully consistent with the GATT, benefit from the protection afforded to geographical indications by Regulation 2081/92.

V. REGULATION 2081/92 IS COMPATIBLE WITH THE OBLIGATION TO PROVIDE MOST-FAVOURED-NATION TREATMENT

227. The United States (but not Australia)[108] has claimed that Regulation 2081/92 is incompatible with the obligation to provide most-favoured-nation treatment under Article 4 TRIPS and Article I:1 GATT. The EC will discuss the United States claims under both provisions separately.

A. Article 4 TRIPS

228. The United States has made two claims under the most-favoured-nation provision of Article 4 TRIPS:

- As among non-EC WTO Members, nationals from WTO Members that satisfy the EC's conditions of reciprocity and equivalency are accorded more favourable treatment than nationals from those WTO Members that do not;
- under Regulation 2081/92, an EC Member State grants more favourable treatment to nationals from other EC Member States than it accords to nationals from non-EC WTO Members.

1. Claim 16: As among non-EC WTO Members, nationals from WTO Members that satisfy the EC's conditions of reciprocity and equivalency are accorded more favourable treatment than nationals from those WTO Members that do not

229. The United States has claimed that nationals from WTO Members that satisfy the EC's conditions of reciprocity and equivalency are accorded more favourable treatment than nationals from those WTO Members that do not.[109]

230. This claim is unfounded for the following reasons:

---

[108] Australia has not made any claim in this respect, but has reserved the "right to pursue such a claim" in the event that the EC "is applying" or "begins to apply Community-wide protection to EC-defined GIs for foodstuffs and agricultural products from another WTO Member" (Australia's FWS, para. 65).

[109] US FWS, para. 119.

- the EC does not apply a condition of reciprocity and equivalence for the registration of geographical indications from other WTO members;
- the conditions for the registration of individual geographical indications from third countries are not discriminatory;
- Article 12 of Regulation 2081/92 does not grant any advantage, favour, privilege or immunity to any other country;
- the conditions for the registration of geographical indications do not depend on nationality.

(a) The EC does not apply a condition of reciprocity and equivalence for the registration of geographical indications from other WTO members

231. Article 4 TRIPS requires that "with regard to the protection of intellectual property, any advantage, favour, privilege or immunity granted by a Member to the nationals of any other country shall be accorded immediately and unconditionally to the nationals of all other Members".

232. As the EC has already explained, it does not apply a condition of reciprocity and equivalence to the registration of geographical indications from other WTO Members.[110] Accordingly, geographical indications relating to an area located in another WTO country can be registered under Regulation 2081/92 in accordance with Article 12a and 12b of Regulation 2081/92.

233. In contrast, the conditions of Article 12(1) and 12(3) are applicable for the registration of geographical indications from third countries which are not WTO Members. Moreover, it should be recalled that Article 4 TRIPS does not require that benefits are extended to third countries *which are not WTO Members*.

234. Accordingly, Regulation 2081/92 does not treat nationals of other WTO Members less favourable than those of other third countries.

(b) The conditions for the registration of individual geographical indications from third countries are not discriminatory

235. As in respect of the claims regarding national treatment, the EC is not sure whether the United States also challenges the product-specific conditions for the registration of geographical indications from third countries.

236. However, if it does, such a claim would have to be regarded as unfounded. The conditions for the registration of individual geographical indications, and in particular the requirement of a product specification and the existence of inspection structures, do not discriminate on the basis of nationality or product origin. Moreover, they are examined for each product individually.

---

[110] Above para. 62 et seq.

237. In this context, it is useful to recall the Panel report in *Canada – Autos*, which stated that most-favoured nation treatment does not exclude subjecting advantages to conditions, as long as these conditions are non-discriminatory:[111]

> In this respect, it appears to us that there is an important distinction to be made between, on the one hand, the issue of whether an advantage within the meaning of Article I:1 is subject to conditions, and on the other, whether an advantage, once it has been granted to the product of any country, is accorded "unconditionally" to the like product of other Members. An advantage can be granted subject to conditions without necessarily implying that it is not accorded "unconditionally" to the like product of other Members. More specifically, the fact that conditions attached to such an advantage are not related to the imported product itself does not necessarily imply that such conditions are discriminatory with respect to the origin of imported products. We therefore do not believe that, as argued by Japan, the word "unconditionally" in Article I:1 must be interpreted to mean that making an advantage conditional on criteria not related to the imported product itself is *per se* inconsistent with Article I:1, irrespective of whether and how such criteria relate to the origin of the imported products.

238. Accordingly, the application of the conditions for the registration of individual geographical indications from other WTO Members is not incompatible with most-favoured-nation principles.

(c) Article 12 of Regulation 2081/92 does not grant any advantage, favour, privilege or immunity to any other country

239. Second, Article 12 of Regulation 2081/92 does not involve the granting of any advantage to a third country.[112]

240. Article 12(1) of Regulation 2081/92 provides the conditions under which the Regulation may apply to a third country which is not a WTO Member. In accordance with Article 12(3) of the Regulation, the Commission must examine whether the conditions in Article 12(1) are fulfilled. The conditions set out in Article 12(1) are the same for all third countries which fall under this provision. In the absence of a decision under Article 12(3) of the Regulation, Article 12 does not confer any advantage onto a third country.

241. In support of its claim, the United States has referred to the GATT Panel Report in *Belgian Family Allowances*.[113] However, this Panel report does not

[111] Panel Report, *Canada – Autos*, para. 10.24.

[112] The EC notes that Australia seems to share this view, since it reserves to make a claim in regard to most-favoured-nation treatment only in the event that the EC "is applying" or "begins to apply Community-wide protection to EC-defined GIs for foodstuffs and agricultural products from another WTO Member" (Australia's FWS, para. 65).

[113] US FWS, para. 115.

support the proposition of the United States. In this case, Belgium had in fact granted an exception from a certain levy to a number of third countries.[114] This resembled the situation in *EEC – Imports of Beef from Canada*, where the Panel found as follows:[115]

> The Panel further found that exports of like products of other origin than that of United States were in effect denied access to the EEC market considering that the only certifying agency authorized to certify the meat described in Article 1(1)(d), listed in Annex II of the Commission Regulation, was a United States agency mandated to certify only meat from the United States.
>
> (b) The Panel further found that the mention "Beef graded USDA 'choice', or 'prime' automatically meets the definition above" could accord an advantage to products of United States' origin in so far as other like products were not mentioned in the same manner. The Panel found, however, that only the practical application of the Commission Regulation would make it possible to judge whether this mention in itself was inconsistent with Article I of the General Agreement.
>
> 4.3 The Panel concluded that Commission Regulation (EEC) No. 2972/79 and its Annex II, in their present form had the effect of preventing access of "like products" from other origin than the United States, thus being inconsistent with the most-favoured-nation principle in Article I of the General Agreement.

242. In both cases, it was the granting of concrete advantages to *specific countries* which led the Panels to find a violation of the most-favoured-nation principle. This is fundamentally different from the situation under Article 12 of Regulation 2081/92, which merely provides for the conditions under which Regulation 2081/92 may apply to geographical indications from third countries which are not WTO members.

243. The United States has also referred to a Joint Declaration of the European Community and Switzerland made on occasion of the signature of the Agreement between the European Community and Switzerland on Trade in Agricultural Products.[116] This declaration reads in full as follows:[117]

> The European Community and Switzerland (hereinafter referred to as "the Parties") hereby agree that the mutual protection of designations of origin (PDOs) and geographical indications (PGIs) is essential for the liberalisation of trade in agricultural products and foodstuffs between the Parties. The *incorporation of provisions relating thereto in the bilateral Agreement on trade in agricultural products is a necessary addition* to Annex 7 to the

114 Panel Report, *Belgian Family Allowances*, para. 3.

115 Panel Report, *EEC – Imports of Beef from Canada,* paras. 4.2–4.3.

116 US FWS, para. 119.

117 Exhibit US-6 (emphasis added).

> Agreement on trade in wine-sector products, and in particular Title II thereof, which provides for the mutual protection of the names of such products, and to Annex 8 to the Agreement on the mutual recognition and protection of names of spirit drinks and aromatised wine-based drinks.
>
> The Parties shall provide for provisions on the mutual protection of PDOs and PGIs to be incorporated in the Agreement on trade in agricultural products on the basis of equivalent legislation, as regards both the conditions governing the registration of PDOs and PGIs and the arrangements on controls. *The incorporation of those provisions should take place on a date which is acceptable to both Parties*, and not before Article 17 of Council Regulation (EEC) No 2081/92 has been fully applied as regards the Community as constituted at present. *In the meantime, the Parties shall keep each other informed of their work in this area while taking legal constraints into account.*

244. This declaration is merely a political declaration stating the intention of the parties to incorporate, at a later stage, provisions on the protection on geographical indications into the Agreement on Trade in Agricultural Products. No such provisions have so far been incorporated into the Agreement between the EC and Switzerland. This declaration is therefore irrelevant for the purposes of the present dispute.

245. Accordingly, Article 12 of Regulation 2081/92 does not grant any advantage, favour, privilege or immunity to any other country.

(d) The conditions for the registration of geographical indications do not depend on nationality

246. Finally, as the United States has recognised itself,[118] Article 4 TRIPS establishes a most-favoured-nation obligation as regards the treatment of nationals, whereas Article I:1 GATT establishes a most-favoured-nation obligation with respect to products. As the EC has set out above, this difference between the TRIPS and the GATT is not accidental, but results from the different object and purpose of both agreements.[119]

247. Furthermore, as the EC has already set out with respect to the claims regarding national treatment under the TRIPS, whether a geographical indication can be registered under Regulation 2081/92 does not depend in any way on nationality.[120] In particular, Articles 12a and 12b govern the registration of geographical indications where the area to which the indication is related is located outside the EC, and this irrespective of the nationality of producers. This means that where a geographical indication from a third country is protected

[118] US FWS, para. 108.
[119] Above para. 104.
[120] Above para. 123 et seq.

under the Regulation, this protection also extends to producers which are nationals of other third countries.

248. For all the reasons set out above, the United States claim must be rejected.

2. *Claim 17: Under Regulation 2081/92, an EC Member State grants more favourable treatment to nationals from other EC Member States than it accords to nationals from non-EC WTO Members*

249. The United States has claimed that under Regulation 2081/92, an EC Member State grants more favourable treatment to nationals from other EC Member States than it accords to nationals from non-EC WTO Members.[121]

250. In the view of the EC, this argument must fail already because under Regulation 2081/92, geographical indications from third countries which are WTO Members are protected on the same terms as geographical indications from other Member States.[122]

251. Secondly, as the EC has already set out, the conditions for the registration of geographical indications do not depend on nationality.[123] Accordingly, the EC is not discriminating between third-country nationals on the basis of nationality.

252. Finally, it should be noted that Article 4 TRIPS requires WTO Members to extend to other Members the advantages, favours, privileges or immunities that they grant to "the nationals of *any other country*". However, through Regulation 2081/92, the EC is not granting an advantage to the national of "any other country".

253. Regulation 2081/92 is a measure which the EC has adopted on the basis of its own competences, and which applies throughout the EC. In accordance with Articles IX:1 and XIV:1 of the WTO Agreement, the European Community is an original member of the WTO. Measures with which the EC harmonises the law inside the European Community can therefore not regarded as granting advantages to "other countries".

254. The fact that the EC Member States are also Members to the WTO[124] is irrelevant in this respect. The measure at issue is a Regulation adopted by the EC. It is not a measure of the Member States. Accordingly, it cannot be said that through Regulation 2081/92, Member States are granting one another "advantages".

255. Finally, since the measure at issue is an EC measure, the subject matter of the present dispute falls within the exclusive competence of the EC, and not of the Member States. The United States has accepted this by correctly bringing the present dispute settlement proceedings against the EC. It can therefore not now

---

[121] US FWS, para. 121.
[122] Above para. 134 et seq.
[123] Above, para. 137.
[124] US FWS para. 121.

raise a claim assuming a violation of most-favoured-nation-obligations on the part of the EC Member States.

256. Accordingly, this claim of the United States must be rejected.

B. Claim 18: By subjecting the registration of third-country geographical indications to conditions of reciprocity and equivalence, the EC measure is inconsistent with the most-favoured-nation obligation under the Article I:1 GATT

257. The United States has argued that by subjecting the registration of third-country geographical indications to conditions of reciprocity and equivalence, the EC measure is inconsistent with the most-favoured-nation obligation under Article I:1 GATT.[125]

1. Article I:1 GATT is not violated

258. Contrary to the claim of the United States, there is no violation of Article I:1 GATT.

259. Article I:1 GATT requires in relevant part that "[...] with respect to all matters referred to in paragraphs 2 and 4 of Article III, any advantage, favour, privilege or immunity granted by any contracting party to any product originating in or destined for any other country shall be accorded immediately and unconditionally to the like product originating in or destined for the territories of all other contracting parties".

260. As the EC has already set out with respect to Article 4 TRIPS, Regulation 2081/92 does not involve any less favourable treatment of WTO members compared to other third countries.

261. First of all, the EC does not apply a condition of reciprocity and equivalence for the registration of geographical indications from other WTO members, which can therefore be registered as geographical indications under the conditions set out in Regulation 2081/92.[126]

262. Secondly, as the EC has also explained, the conditions for the registration of geographical indications from third countries are not discriminatory.[127]

263. Finally, as the EC has also set out, Article 12 of Regulation 2081/92 does not grant any advantage, favour, privilege or immunity, but merely sets out the conditions under which geographical indications from third countries other than WTO members may be registered.[128]

264. For these reasons, Regulation 2081/92 is not incompatible with Article I:1 GATT.

---

125 US FWS para. 127 et seq.

126 Above para. 231 et seq.

127 Above para. 235 et seq.

128 Above para. 239 et seq.

2. *The EC measure would be justified under Article XX (d) GATT*

265. It is unclear to the EC whether the complainants claim that the requirements imposed by Article 12a, in conjunction with Articles 4 and 10, of Regulation 2081/92 with respect to the registration of each specific geographical indication are as such incompatible with Article I:1 of the GATT. As shown above, the EC considers that those requirements are fully consistent with Article I:1 of the GATT.

266. In the event that the complainants were to claim that such requirements are inconsistent with Article I:1 of the GATT, and should the Panel find that they are inconsistent with that provision, the EC submits in the alternative that such requirements would be justified under Article XX(d) of the GATT, for the same reasons already advanced in connection with the complainants' claim under Article III:4 of the GATT.

VI. REGULATION 2081/92 DOES NOT DIMINISH THE LEGAL PROTECTION OF TRADEMARKS

267. The complainants have raised a number of claims to the effect that Regulation 2081/92 diminishes the legal protection of trademarks. The EC will show hereunder that these claims are unfounded.

A. *Article 16.1 of the TRIPS Agreement*

1. *Claim 19: Article 14(2) of Regulation 2081/92 is inconsistent with Article 16.1 of the TRIPS Agreement in that it allows the co-existence of geographical indications and earlier registered trademarks*

268. The complainants claim that Article 14(2) of Regulation 2081/92 is inconsistent with Article 16.1 of the TRIPS Agreement in that it allows the "co-existence" of a registered geographical indication and a prior similar or identical registered trademark for similar or identical goods, which results in a likelihood of confusion. [129]

269. As will be shown in this section, this claim is unfounded for several reasons.

270. First, this claim is based on a misunderstanding of the relevant provisions of Regulation 2081/92. Contrary to the complainants' assumption, Article 14(3) of Regulation 2081/92 prevents the registration of geographical indications that would result in a likelihood of confusion with an earlier trademark. Thus, as a matter of fact, the situation alleged by the complainants does not even arise.

271. Second, the exclusivity conferred upon the trademark owners by Article 16.1 of the TRIPS Agreement is without prejudice to the protection that

[129] Australia's FWS, paras. 100-107. US FWS, paras. 130-170.

Members are entitled to accord to geographical indications in accordance with Part II, Section 3, of the TRIPS Agreement. The boundary between a Member's right to protect geographical indications and its obligation to protect trademarks is defined by Article 24.5 of the TRIPS, which provides for the co-existence of geographical indications and earlier trademarks. Article 14(2) of Regulation 2081/92 is fully consistent with Article 24.5.

272. Third, irrespective of whether the co-existence of geographical indications and earlier trademarks is permitted by Article 24.5, the EC is required to maintain such co-existence by virtue of Article 24.3 of the TRIPS Agreement, a "stand-still" provision that prohibits Members from diminishing the level of protection of GIs that existed at the time of entry into force of the WTO Agreement.

273. Finally, even assuming that Article 14(2) of Regulation 2081/92 were *prima facie* inconsistent with Article 16.1, it would be justified as a "limited exception" to the trademark owner's exclusive rights under Article 17 of the TRIPS Agreement.

(a) Regulation 2081/92 does not allow the registration of confusing trademarks

274. The exclusivity conferred by Article 16.1 of the TRIPS Agreement is not absolute. That provision does not grant to the owner of a registered trademark a right to prevent any possible use of the same or a similar sign, but only its use for identical or similar goods, "where such use would result in a likelihood of confusion".

275. As will be shown below, because of the criteria of registrability applied under EC trademark law, the risk of confusion between trademarks and geographical indications is very limited *a priori*. To the extent that those criteria do not preclude such possibility, the problem is addressed adequately by Article 14(3) of Regulation 2081/92, which provides that

> A designation of origin or geographical indication shall not be registered where, in the light of a trademark's reputation and renown and the length of time it has been used, registration is liable to mislead the consumer as to the true identity of the product.

276. The complainants have erroneously characterized Article 14(3) as a "narrow exception".[130] As explained below, the terms of Article 14(3), if properly interpreted, are sufficient to prevent the registration of any confusing geographical indications.

277. According to their own interpretation of Article 16.1 of the TRIPS Agreement, in order to establish a violation of that provision, the complainants would need to prove that Regulation 2081/92 mandates necessarily the registration of confusing geographical indications. The complainants have failed

---

[130] US FWS, para. 158.

to do so. Indeed, the complainants have not even shown that the actual application of Regulation 2081/92 has resulted occasionally in the registration of confusing geographical indications. As of the date of establishment of this Panel, the EC authorities had registered more than 600 geographical indications. The complainants have not alleged, let alone proved, that any of those geographical indications has resulted in a likelihood of confusion with any prior registered trademark. The complainant's claim is purely theoretical and, as will be shown below, unfounded.

(i) Registrability of geographical names as trademarks

278. The purpose of a trademark is to distinguish the goods or services of one undertaking from those of other undertakings. A sign that cannot fulfil this function, i.e. a sign which is not "distinctive", cannot be registered as a trademark. Thus, Article 15.1 of the TRIPS Agreement provides that

> Any sign, or any combination of signs, capable of distinguishing the goods or services of one undertaking from those of other undertakings, shall be capable of constituting a trademark.[131]

279. Geographical names are primarily "non-distinctive" and, as such, non apt for registration as trademarks.[132] For example, the name "Australia", if used as a trademark by an undertaking, would not allow to distinguish the goods of that undertaking from those of any other Australian undertaking selling the same or similar products. Moreover, the use of geographical names as trademarks may be deceptive in so far as they are used for goods which do not originate in the location designated by that name. For example, the name "Australia", if used as a trademark for US goods, could mislead the consumers as regards the origin of the goods.

280. For the above reasons, the registration of geographical names as trademarks is subject to restrictions in all countries.[133] Broadly speaking, it is permitted only in two situations: first, where consumers would not expect the goods to be produced in that place; and, second, where the name has become

---

[131] Similarly, Article 6*quinquies* B (2) of the Paris Convention (1967) provides that the registration of trademarks may be denied "when they are devoid of any distinctive character".

[132] Article 6*quinquies* B of the Paris Convention (1967) provides that trademarks may be denied registration when

> 2. ... they consist exclusively of signs or indications which may serve, in trade, to designate the ... place of origin;
>
> 3. when they are ... of such a nature as to deceive the public.

[133] Section 2 of the US Lanham Act prohibits the registration of trademarks that, when used in connection with the goods of the applicant, are "primarily geographically descriptive", unless they have become distinctive through use, or "primarily geographically deceptively misdescriptive" (15 USC. 1052 (e) and (f)). (Exhibit EC-6).

Similarly, Australia's Trade Marks Act of 1995 prohibits the registration of trademarks that are not "inherently adapted to distinguish goods or services" unless they have become distinctive through use. Trademarks that are not "inherently adapted to distinguish goods or services" include "trade marks that consist wholly of a sign that is ordinarily used to indicate: (a) the ... geographical origin... " (Section 41(6) Note 1 (a)) (Exhibit EC-7)

distinctive through use. In other words, when, as a result of its continued use by an undertaking, the geographical name acquires a "secondary meaning", so that consumers do not associate it with a geographical location but instead with the undertaking in question.[134] This possibility is expressly envisaged in the second sentence of Article 15.1 of the TRIPS Agreement, which provides that

> Where signs are not inherently capable of distinguishing the relevant goods or services, Members may make registrability depend on distinctiveness acquired through use.

281. Like in other jurisdictions, in the EC the registration of geographical names as trademarks is permitted only exceptionally. Article 3.1 of the Trademarks Directive provides that the following shall not be registered or, if registered, shall be liable to be declared invalid:

> (b) trade marks which are devoid of any distinctive character;
>
> (c) trade marks which consist exclusively of signs or indications which may serve, in trade, to designate ... the geographical origin;
>
> (g) trade marks which are of such nature as to deceive the public, for instance as to the ... geographical origin of the goods...[135]

282. The European Court of Justice has held that:

> under Article 3(1)(c) of the Directive, the competent authority must assess whether a geographical name in respect of which application for registration as a trade mark is made designates a place which is currently associated in the mind of the relevant class of persons with the category of goods concerned, or whether it is reasonable to assume that such an association may be established in the future.[136]

283. By way of exception to letters (b) and (c) of Article 3.1 (but not to letter (g)), Article 3.3 of the Trademarks Directive provides that geographical names that are primarily non-distinctive may be registered where they have become distinctive through use:

---

[134] A well known example of trademark consisting of a geographical name which has become distinctive through use in some countries is "Budweiser". After much litigation in the United States, it was deemed to have acquired secondary meaning in that country, so that it could be registered as a trademark. See Albrecht Conrad, "The Protection of Geographical Indications in the TRIPS Agreement", 86 *The Trademark Reporter*, p.43.

[135] Similarly, Article 7(1) of the Community Trademark Regulation provides that:

> The following shall not be registered:
>
> (b) trade marks which are devoid of any distinctive character;
>
> (c) trademarks which consist exclusively of signs or indications which may serve, in trade, to designate the...geographical origin of the goods or service;
>
> ...
>
> (g) trade marks which are of such a nature as to deceive the public, for instance as to the ... geographical origin of the goods or service;

[136] Judgement of the European Court of Justice of 4 May 1999, C-108/97 and C-109/97, *Chiemsee*, ECR [1999] I-2779, para. 37. (Exhibit EC-8).

> A trademark shall not be refused registration or be declared invalid in accordance with paragraph 1 (b), (c) or (d) if , before the date of application for registration and following the use which has been made of it, it has acquired a distinctive character.[137]

284. In sum, under EC law, the registration of a geographical name as a trademark is possible only in the following circumstances:

- where the geographical name is not currently associated, and it can be reasonably assumed that it will not be associated in the future, with the product concerned; or
- where the name has acquired distinctiveness through use.

285. In principle, any geographical name which qualifies, or may reasonably qualify in the future, as a "designation of origin" or a "geographical indication" within the meaning of Article 2(2) of Regulation 2081/92, will not fall within the first situation. Thus, it may be concluded that, in practice, a geographical indication, or a geographical name with the potential to become a geographical indication, may not be validly registered as a trademark unless it has become distinctive through use.

(ii) Article 14(3) of Regulation 2081/92

286. The complainants' claim is based on an unwarrantedly narrow interpretation of Article 14(3) of Regulation 2081/92. When properly interpreted, that provision allows the registering authorities to refuse the registration of any confusing geographical indications.

287. Australia does not even attempt to interpret the terms of Article 14(3). For its part, the United States declares it to be a "narrow exception" [138] after a cursory analysis. Moreover, the United States reaches that conclusion by reading into Article 14(3) additional requirements which are not stated in that provision. Thus, according to the United States, this provision would exclude the registration of a geographical indication "only where the trademark has been used for *a long time* and has a *considerable* reputation or renown".[139] Neither of those two qualifications is provided in Article 14(3).

288. Article 14(3) has been applied only once by the EC authorities since Regulation 2081/92 came into force.[140] It has never been interpreted by the European Court Justice or by the courts of the Member States. This confirms that, as explained above, the criteria for the registrability of trademarks ensure

---

[137] Similarly, Article 7 (3) of the Community Trademark Regulation provides that

> Paragraph 1(b), (c) and (d) shall not apply if the trade mark has become distinctive in relation to the goods or services for which registration is required in consequence of the use which has been made of it.

[138] US FWS, para. 158.

[139] *Ibid.*

[140] In that case, the EC Council concluded that the registration of the GI "Bayerisches Bier" was not likely to lead to confusion with the existing trademarks "Bavaria" and "Hoker Bajer"; Council Regulation (EC) No 1347, of 28 June 2001, OJ (2001) L 182. (Exhibit EC-9).

that the potential for conflicts between trademarks and geographical indications is indeed very limited.

289. The EC Commission considers that the criteria listed in Article 14(3) are not limitative. The registering authority may take into account also other relevant criteria in order to assess whether the registration of the geographical indication will result in a likelihood of confusion. For example, it is obvious that the degree of similarity between the signs or between the goods concerned is always relevant in assessing the likelihood of confusion between two signs for goods. Nevertheless, given that geographical names are primarily non-distinctive as trademarks, the two criteria specified in Article 14(3) will often be of particular relevance in practice. It is for that reason, and not because they are the only relevant criteria, that the registering authorities are directed expressly to consider those two criteria.

290. It is well-established that the more distinctive the trademark the greater the likelihood that consumers will confuse another sign with that trademark[141]. As explained above, geographical names are primarily non-distinctive. Thus, the degree of distinctiveness and, consequently, the likelihood that it may be confused with a geographical indication will depend to a large extent on the degree of distinctiveness which the trademark has acquired through use. In turn, the basic criteria to measure such acquired distinctiveness are the length of time during which the trademark has been used and the extent of the reputation or renown acquired as a result of such use.

291. Consumers are unlikely to confuse a geographical indication with a trademark that has never been used and/or has no reputation or renown simply because the signs and/or the goods concerned are similar. In fact, as explained above, a trademark consisting of a geographical indication, which has never been used or which has no reputation or renown, should not have been registered in the first place because it would lack the required distinctiveness.

(iii) Provisional conclusion

292. In order to substantiate their claim that Article 14(2) of Regulation 2081/92 is inconsistent with Article 16.1 of the TRIPS Agreement, the complainants should have established that Regulation 2081/92 mandates necessarily the registration of later confusing geographical indications. In turn, this would have required them to show that Article 14(3) cannot be interpreted in a manner which allows the registering authorities to refuse the registration of confusing geographical indications, or, at the very least, that, in practice, Article 14(3) is being interpreted and applied in a manner which results in the registration of confusing geographical indications. The complainants have proved neither.

293. Therefore, the Panel should conclude that, as a matter of fact, the complainants' claim is unfounded even on their own interpretation of

[141] Judgement of the European Court of Justice of 11 November 1997, C – 251/95, *Sabel*, para. 24. (Exhibit EC-10).

Article 16.1 of the TRIPS Agreement. In any event, as discussed below, that interpretation is incorrect.

(b) Article 24.5 envisages the co-existence of GIs and earlier trademarks

294. The complainants' claim rests on a misconception of the relationship between trademarks and geographical indications, as well as between Article 16.1 and Part II, Section 3, of the TRIPS Agreement. The TRIPS Agreement recognises geographical indications as intellectual property rights, on the same level as trademarks. It confers no superiority to trademarks over geographical indications. Nor are the provisions of Part II, Section 3, "exceptions" to Article 16.1. There is no hierarchy between them.

295. In an attempt to establish the superiority of trademarks over geographical indications, the complainants emphasise that exclusivity is an essential feature of trademarks. It is, of course, correct that trademarks are exclusive rights. But from this it does not follow that trademarks must prevail over geographical indications. Geographical indications are also exclusive rights, because their basic purpose, like that of trademarks, is to distinguish the goods from a certain source. The fact that geographical indications are collective rights does not render their exclusivity less indispensable. If any producer of cheese could use the term "Roquefort", the geographical indication "Roquefort" could not fulfil its distinctive function and would be deprived of its economic value.

296. As explained above, the criteria for the registrability of trademarks limit *a priori* the possibility of conflicts between geographical indications and trademarks. However, to the extent that geographical indications may exceptionally be validly registered as trademarks, there may arise conflicts between the exclusivity of those two types of intellectual property rights. The question before the Panel is, therefore, how to resolve those conflicts.

297. Article 16.1 does not address this issue. More specifically, and contrary to the complainants' claims, Article 16.1 contains no provision to the effect that trademarks must prevail over later geographical indications. The complainants argue that the right conferred by Article 16.1 to the trademark owner in order to prevent the confusing use of identical or similar "signs" for identical or similar goods applies also with respect to later geographical indications, because geographical indications are "signs". True, geographical indications consist of a special type of "sign": words or other signs with a geographical connotation. But they are more than mere "signs". They are a distinct intellectual property right, with a specific subject matter and a specific function, different from those of trademarks, which Members are entitled to protect under their domestic laws and which, indeed, they are required to protect under Part II, Section 3, of the TRIPS Agreement.

298. The boundary between geographical indications and trademarks is not defined in Article 16.1, but instead in Article 24.5 of the TRIPS Agreement. Therefore, the WTO consistency of Article 14(2) of Regulation 2081/92 must be determined in relation to that provision, and not with respect to Article 16.1.

299. Article 24.5 provides that

> Where a trademark has been applied for or registered in good faith, or where rights to a trademark have been acquired through use in good faith either:
>
> (a) before the date of application of these provisions in that member as defined in Part VI; or
>
> (b) before the geographical indication is protected in its country of origin;
>
> measures adopted to implement this Section shall not prejudice eligibility for or the validity of the registration of a trademark, or the right to use a trademark, on the basis that such trademark is identical with, or similar to, a geographical indication.

300. Article 24.5 must be read together with Articles 22.3[142] and 23.2[143], which require that the registration of trademarks must be refused or invalidated in certain situations. Those two provisions, however, do not exhaust the protection afforded to geographical indications vis-à-vis trademarks. Right holders of geographical indications can invoke also Articles 22.2[144] and 23.1[145] in order to prevent the use of a trademark (whether registered or non-registered) in the circumstances described in those provisions. In addition, in implementing Part II, Section 3, Members are entitled to provide more extensive protection for

---

[142] Article 22.3 of the TRIPS Agreement provides that:

> A Member shall, *ex officio* if its legislation so permits, or at the request of an interested party, refuse or invalidate the registration of a trademark which contains or consists of a geographical indication with respect to goods not originating in the territory indicated, if use of the indication in the trademark for such goods in that Member is of such nature as to mislead the public as to the true place of origin.

[143] Article 23.2 of the TRIPS Agreement provides that:

> The registration of a trademark for wines which contains or consists of a geographical indication identifying wines or for spirits which contains or consists of a geographical indication identifying spirits shall be refused or invalidated, *ex officio* if a Member's legislation so permits or at the request of an interested party, with respect to such wines or spirits not having this origin.

[144] Article 22.2 of the TRIPS Agreement provides that:

> In respect of geographical indications, Members shall provide the legal means for interested parties to prevent:
>
> (a) the use of any means in the designation or presentation of a good that indicates or suggests that the good in question originates in a geographical area other than the true place of origin in a manner which misleads the public as to the geographical origin of the good;
>
> (b) any use which constitutes an act of unfair competition within the meaning of Article 10*bis* of the Paris Convention (1967).

[145] Article 23.1 of the TRIPS Agreement provides that:

> Each Member shall provide the legal means for interested parties to prevent use of a geographical indication identifying wines for wines not originating in the place indicated by the geographical indication in question or identifying spirits for spirits not originating in the place indicated by the geographical indication in question, even where the true origin of the goods is indicated or the geographical indication is used in translation or accompanied by expressions such as "kind", "type", "style", "imitation" or the like. [footnote omitted]

geographical indications, in accordance with Article 1.1 of the TRIPS Agreement.

301. Article 24.5 has two implications:

- with respect to grandfathered trademarks (or applications for trademarks), Members are not allowed to *prejudice* the validity of the registration (or the eligibility of the application) or the "right to use the trademark", but they may *prejudice* other rights of the trademark owner, including in particular the right to prevent others from using the sign of which the trademark consists.
- with respect to other trademarks (or applications for trademarks), Members may prejudice *any* right.

302. Regulation 2081/92 implements Part II, Section 3, of the TRIPS Agreement. The rule of conflict between geographical indications and trademarks defined in Article 25.4 has been transposed by Articles 14(1) and 14(2) of Regulation 2081/92. Article 14(1) maintains the eligibility of the applications and the validity of the registrations "grandfathered" by Article 24.5. In turn, Article 14(2) preserves the right of the owners of "grandfathered" trademarks to continue to use their trademarks concurrently with the geographical indications.

303. Article 14(2) of Regulation 2081/92 is fully consistent with Article 24.5, which provides that Members shall not prejudice "the right to use a trademark". That phrase alludes to the owner's right to use the sign of which the trademark consists, which is one of the two basic rights of the trademark owner, together with the right to prevent other persons from using that sign.[146] If the drafters had meant to exclude the co-existence of trademarks and geographical indications, they would have provided instead that Members shall not prejudice "the *exclusive* right to use a trademark".

304. Furthermore, if Article 24.5 did not allow co-existence, the protection of geographical indications provided under Part II, Section 3, would become pointless whenever there is a grandfathered trademark. Indeed, why protect a geographical indication against illegitimate uses by third parties if the legitimate users cannot use it themselves? Yet, Article 24.5 assumes that Members will continue to protect geographical indications ("...measures adopted to implement this Section shall not prejudice..."), notwithstanding the existence of "grandfathered" trademarks. If the drafters' intention had been to prohibit the use of geographical indications concurrently with grandfathered trademarks, they would have excluded completely the applicability of Part II, Section 3, with respect to the geographical indications concerned, rather than providing that the

---

[146] WIPO's "Introduction to Intellectual Property, Theory and Practice" (Kluwer, 1997), aptly describes the rights arising from trademark registration as follows (para. 9.147):

> The registered owner has the exclusive right to use the trademark. This short definition of the specific subject matter of trademark right encompasses two things: the right to use the trademark and the right to exclude others from using it.

implementation of that Section shall not prejudice "the right to use the trademark".

305. Australia has suggested[147] that the phrase "the right to use a trademark" alludes exclusively to the trademark rights acquired through use, to which reference is made in the introductory phrase of Article 24.5. However, if so, it would have been more logical to say that the measures taken to implement Sections 3 "shall not prejudice ... the trademark rights acquired through use", rather than that they "shall not prejudice ... the right to use a trademark". Australia confuses the mode of acquisition of the trademark rights (use or registration) with one of the basic rights of the trademark owner (irrespective of whether the trademark rights have been acquired through use or registration), i.e. the right to use the trademark.

306. Moreover, trademark rights acquired through use are also, as a general rule, exclusive within the boundaries of the area in which they have been used. Article 16.1 of the TRIPS Agreement recognises expressly the right of Members to make available trademark rights, including exclusive rights, on the basis of use. In view of that, there is no good reason why Article 24.5 should provide for the co-existence of geographical indications and non-registered trademarks, but prohibit the co-existence of geographical indications and registered trademarks, which would be the anomalous consequence of Australia's interpretation.

307. Co-existence may not be a perfect solution to resolve conflicts between different types of intellectual property rights. But then there is no such perfect solution. Co-existence is preferable to a rigid application of the first-in-time rule, which is what the complainants are proposing. That rule is generally appropriate to resolve conflicts between trademarks, but not between trademarks and geographical indications, because they are distinct intellectual property rights, each with its own characteristics. In particular, the following differences make inappropriate the strict application of that principle to conflicts between geographical indications and trademarks:

- trademarks are much easier to create than geographical indications. Trademarks can be acquired almost instantaneously, simply by an "intent to use" or by the mere lodging of an application with a registration system. In contrast, the creation of a geographical indication requires to establish first a "link" between the name and certain product characteristics, which may require years. Indeed, as is often the case in the EC, such link is the result of centuries of tradition. Thus, the first-in-time principle would provide an unfair advantage to trademark owners;
- trademarks are arbitrary, with the consequence that there is a virtually unlimited choice of trademarks. By choosing deliberately a geographical name as a trademark, an undertaking accepts the risk that the same sign may be used concurrently as a geographical indication. In contrast, geographical indications are "necessary" in

[147] Australia's FWS, para. 74.

the sense that the range of names used to designate a certain geographical is limited *a priori* by well established usage. Right holders of geographical indications may not easily change the name given by the public to the geographical area where they are located. For that reason, it is much more difficult to find an alternative geographical indication than it is to find an alternative trademark;

- geographical indications serve to inform consumers that the product originates in a certain area and has certain characteristics linked to that origin. Trademarks only guarantee the identity of the undertaking that markets the product. Thus, in addition to having a commercial function, geographical indications serve a public interest, which deserves additional protection.
- geographical indications are the common patrimony of all the producers of a certain area, and ultimately of the entire population of that area, which may potentially qualify for the right to use the geographical indication. It would be unfair to deprive that population from the use of a geographical indication for the exclusive benefit of an individual trademark owner, who may or may not have contributed to the development of the geographical indication, simply because he happened to register that name first as a trademark.

308. The co-existence of intellectual property rights is by no means an unusual solution for resolving conflicts between intellectual property rights, including between trademarks. Indeed, several other provisions of the TRIPS Agreement provide for co-existence:

- Article 23.3 provides for co-existence between homonymous geographical indications for wines;[148]
- Article 24.4 permits, under certain circumstances, that the nationals or residents of one Member continue to use a geographical indication of another Member in co-existence with the users of that Member;[149]

---

[148] Article 23.3 of the TRIPS Agreement provides that:

> In the case of homonymous geographical indications for wines, protection shall be accorded to each indication, subject to the provisions of paragraph 4 of Article 22. Each Member shall determine the practical conditions under which the homonymous indications in questions will be differentiated from each other, taking into account the need to ensure equitable treatment of the producers concerned and that consumers are not misled.

[149] Article 24.4 of the TRIPS Agreement provides that:

> Nothing in this section shall require a Member to prevent continued and similar use of a particular geographical indication of another Member identifying wines or spirits in connection with goods or services by any of its nationals or domiciliaries who have used that geographical indication in a continuous manner with regard to the same or related goods or services in the territory of that Member either (a) for at least 10 years preceding 15 April 1994 or (b) in good faith preceding that date.

- Article 16.1 itself provides that the exclusivity of registered trademarks "shall not prejudice any existing prior rights".

309. The co-existence of different types of intellectual property rights, and in particular between geographical indications and trademarks, is provided also in the law of other Members.[150]

310. Remarkably, the United States itself provides for the co-existence of geographical indications and earlier trademarks with respect to wines. Specifically, the regulations of the US Alcohol and Tobacco Tax and Trade Board (the "TTB") provide that a brand name of viticultural significance (including the name of US approved viticultural areas) may not be used unless 1) the wine meets the appellation of origin requirements for the geographical area concerned; or 2) the brand name is used in accordance with a "certificate of label approval" issued prior to 1 July 1986.[151]

311. In other words, under the TTB Regulations, the existence of a registered trademark including a geographical name (e.g. "Rutherford Vintners") does not prevent the subsequent recognition and use of that name as a geographical indication ("Rutherford"), which is what would be required by the interpretation of Article 16.1 of the TRIPS Agreement put forward by the United States in this dispute. Quite to the contrary, the use of the earlier trademark is prohibited, subject to a very limited temporal exception, with a narrower scope than that of Article 24.5 of the TRIPS Agreement. Furthermore, grandfathered trademarks are allowed to co-exist with the later geographical indications, provided only that they are used in accordance with special labelling requirements. The United States should explain why this solution to the conflicts between geographical indications and earlier trademarks, which is undoubtedly a sensible one, must be deemed compatible with the TRIPS Agreement when US geographical indications for wines are at stake, but not in the case of EC geographical indications for other products.[152]

(c) The EC is required to maintain the co-existence of geographical indications and earlier trademarks by Article 24.3

312. Irrespective of whether the co-existence of geographical indications and earlier trademarks is consistent with Article 24.5, the EC is required to maintain such co-existence by virtue of Article 24.3 of the TRIPS Agreement, which provides that

---

[150] See "Review under Article 24.2 of the Application of the Provisions of the Section of the TRIPS Agreement on Geographical Indications – Summary of the Responses to the Checklist of Questions", IP/C/W/253/Rev.1, 24 November 2003, paras. 149-150.

[151] 27 CFR 4.39 (i). (Exhibit EC-11).

[152] The lack of consistency appears to be even more blatant in the case of Australia. The Wine and Brandy Corporation Act prohibits the use of a registered GI for wine which does not originate in the area covered by the GI. No exception is provided with respect to prior trademarks. Australia can hardly complain about the fact that the EC allows the co-existence of GIs with earlier trademarks grandfathered under Article 24.5, when it prohibits the use of those trademarks, unless the wine originates in the area designated by the GI. (Sections 40 D-F). (Exhibit EC -12).

> In implementing this Section, a Member shall not diminish the protection of geographical indications that existed in that Member immediately prior to the date of entry into force of the WTO Agreement.

313. Article 24.3 is in the nature of a "stand still" obligation. It requires Members to maintain at least the level of protection of geographical indications that they applied immediately prior to the entry into force of the WTO Agreement, where such level is higher than the level of protection required by Part II, Section 3, of the TRIPS Agreement.[153]

314. Regulation 2081/92 was adopted on 14 July 1992 and entered into force on 14 July 1993. As of 31 December 1995, i.e. the day before the entry into force of the WTO Agreement, Article 14(2) of Regulation 2081/92 provided for the co-existence of geographical indications and earlier trademarks. If the EC were to allow now the owners of prior registered trademarks to prevent the use of later geographical indications, as demanded by the complainants, it would be diminishing the protection of geographical indications, contrary to the obligation imposed upon the EC by Article 23.4

(d) In any event, the co-existence of geographical indications and earlier trademarks would be justified under Article 17 of the TRIPS Agreement

315. Assuming that 14(3) of Regulation 2081/92 did not prevent the registration of confusing geographical indications, and assuming further that the co-existence of geographical indications and earlier registered trademarks were neither consistent with Article 24.5 of the TRIPS Agreement nor, in the case of the EC, required by Article 24.3 of the TRIPS Agreement, the EC submits in the alternative that such co-existence would be justified under Article 17 of the TRIPS Agreement.

316. Article 17 states that:

> Members may provide limited exceptions to the rights conferred by a trademark, such as fair use of descriptive terms, provided that such exceptions take account of the legitimate interests of the owner of the trademark and of third parties.

317. Article 14(2) is a "limited exception" because it allows the concurrent use of the geographical name registered as a trademark only by those producers who are established in the geographical area designated by the geographical indication and who, furthermore, comply with the relevant product specifications and other requirements for using the geographical indication. The trademark owner retains the exclusive right to prevent the use of that name by any other persons.

---

[153] See e.g. Daniel Gervais, *The TRIPS Agreement, Drafting History and Analysis*, (Sweet & Maxwell, 1998), p. 135.

318. Moreover, Article 17 mentions expressly as an example of "limited exception" the "fair use of descriptive terms". Geographical indications are "descriptive terms".[154] The use of a geographical indication in order to indicate the true origin of the goods and the characteristic associated to that origin is certainly a "fair" use of that descriptive term.

319. Finally, the legitimate interests of the trademark owner and of third parties are "taken into account" in several ways:

- even if Article 14(3) of Regulation 2081/92 did not avoid completely the registration of confusing trademarks, it would at the very least prevent the most significant cases of confusion, in the interest of both the trademark owner and the consumers;
- moreover, the concurrent use of the geographical indications is subject to the generally applicable EC legislation on labelling and misleading advertising, as well as to the laws of the Member States on unfair competition;
- finally, geographical indications serve to inform consumers about the origin of the products and their characteristics and, therefore, "take account of the interests of third parties" also in that way.

2. *Claim 20: Regulation 2081/92 does not provide for a presumption of a likelihood of confusion in the case of use of an identical sign for identical goods*

320. Australia claims that Regulation 2081/1992 is inconsistent with Article 16.1 of the TRIPS Agreement because it does not "implement" the presumption of a likelihood of confusion in the case of use of an identical sign for identical goods.[155]

321. The EC's response to Claim 19 disposes also of this claim. However, for the sake of completeness, the EC would like to add the following comments.

322. First, contrary to what Australia appears to suggest, Members are not required to reproduce explicitly the presumption of Article 16.1 in their domestic law. It may be sufficient if their domestic law leaves to the registering authority,

---

[154] The trademark laws of both the United States and Australia provide that the use of a term registered as a trademark to indicate the origin of goods does not constitute an infringement of the trademark.

Section 33(b)(4) of the US Lanham Act (15 USC 115 (b) (4))(Exhibit EC-6) provides the following defence against a claim of infringement of the exclusive right of a trademark owner:

> That the use of a term … charged to be an infringement is a use, otherwise than as mark … of a term … which is descriptive and used fairly and in good faith only to describe the goods … of such party, or their geographical origin.

In turn, Section 122(1) (b)(i) of Australia's 1995 Trade Mark Law provides that a person does not infringe a registered trade mark when "the person uses a sign in good faith to indicate the … geographical origin … of goods." (Exhibit EC-7).

[155] Australia's FWS, para. 93.

or to the courts, the necessary discretion to apply the presumption and, in practice, the presumption is complied with.[156]

323. Second, it is extremely unlikely that the situation described by Australia will ever present itself in practice. In the first place, as explained above, the criteria for the registrability of trademarks limit a *priori* the possibility to register as a trademark a name which is identical to that of a geographical indication or of a potential geographical indication. Moreover, the definition of "geographical indication" in Regulation 2081/92, together with the requirement to comply with certain product specifications, would normally have the consequence that the goods covered by a registered geographical indication are not identical to other goods. In any event, should the situation arise, Article 14(3) would allow the registering authority to refuse the registration of a proposed geographical indication, if necessary to implement the presumption.

324. Finally, Australia's complaint is, once again, purely theoretical. Australia has not alleged, let alone proved that any of the more than 600 registered geographical indications is identical to any earlier registered trademark used for identical goods. The EC considers that none of the registered geographical indications falls within that situation.

3. Claim 21: Article 7(4) of Regulation 2081/92 is inconsistent with Article 16.1 of the TRIPS Agreement because it limits the grounds of objection

325. Australia (but not the United States) claims that Article 7(4) of Regulation 2081/92 is inconsistent with Article 16.1 of the TRIPS Agreement[157] because it does not allow trademark owners to object to the registration of a proposed geographical indication where there is likelihood of confusion, but only where the proposed geographical indication would "jeopardize the existence of an entirely or partly identical trademark."

326. This claim is unfounded, both as a matter of law, because Article 16.1 does not confer a right of objection, and as a matter of fact, because Article 7(4) of Regulation 2081/92 does not limit the grounds of objection in the manner alleged by Australia.

(a) Article 16.1 of the TRIPS Agreement does not confer a right of objection

327. Article 16.1 does not grant to the trademark owners a right to formulate objections in the framework of a procedure for the acquisition of another intellectual property right, whether it is a trademark or a different right such as geographical indication.

---

[156] Thus, for example, the EC understands that the US trademark laws do not restate the presumption, but the US authorities are satisfied that the criteria usually applied in order to appreciate the likelihood of confusion between trademarks are sufficient to meet the presumption.

[157] Australia's FWS, paras. 88-92.

328. Article 16.1 regulates exclusively the substantive content of the rights conferred to the trademark owners. It does not address the procedural means to exercise those rights, which are regulated elsewhere in the TRIPS Agreement. Thus, the possibility to raise objections to the registration of another intellectual property right is addressed in Article 62.4, with respect to all intellectual property rights in general, and in Article 15.5, with respect specifically to trademarks.

329. Article 62.4, which is included in Part IV of the TRIPS Agreement, dealing specifically with the "Acquisition and Maintenance of Intellectual Property Rights and Related *Inter Partes* Procedures", provides that

> Procedures concerning the acquisition or maintenance of intellectual property rights and, *where a Member's law provides for such procedures*, administrative revocation and *inter partes* procedures such as opposition, revocation and cancellation, shall be governed by the general principles set out in paragraphs 2 and 3 of Article 41.[158]

330. In turn, Article 15.5 provides that Members "*may* afford an opportunity for the registration of a trademark to be opposed".[159]

331. The above quoted provisions make it clear that Members are not required to grant a right of opposition to the trademark owners with respect to the acquisition of another intellectual property right.

332. Moreover, contrary to Australia's assertions, the right to formulate objections is not necessary to "exercise" effectively the substantive right conferred by Article 16, if final registration decisions are subject to judicial review, as they should under Article 62.5 of the TRIPS Agreement.

333. Since Article 16.1 does not confer to the trademark owners the right to formulate objections with respect to the registration of a geographical indication, the fact that Article 7(4) of Regulation 2081/92 limits the possible grounds of objection cannot be inconsistent with Article 16.1.

(b) Australia has misread Article 7(4) of Regulation 2081/92

334. In any event, Australia's claim is based on a misreading of Article 7(4) of Regulation 2081/92. The text in force of that Article provides in relevant part as follows:

> A statement of objection shall be admissible only if it:
>
> ...
>
> – shows that the registration of the name proposed would jeopardize the existence of an entirely or partly identical name or *of a* mark ...[160]

[158] Emphasis added.
[159] *Ibid.*
[160] *Ibid.*

335. The term "entirely or partially identical" qualifies only the term "name", and not the term "mark". Thus, an objection is admissible if the proposed name "would jeopardize the existence of the mark", regardless of whether the mark is "entirely or partially identical". This is confirmed by the other linguistic versions of the Regulation, including the French and the Spanish ones, which read as follows:

> Pour être recevable, toute déclaration d'opposition doit:
>
> ...
>
> – ... démontrer que l'enregistrement du nom proposé porterait préjudice a l'existence d'une dénomination totalement ou partiellement homonyme ou d'une marque ...
>
> Para que sea admitida, toda declaración de oposición deberá:
>
> ...
>
> – ...demostrar que el registro del nombre propuesto perjudicaría la existencia de una denominación total o parcialmente homónima o de una marca...

336. The ground provided in Article 7(4), i.e. that the proposed name "would jeopardize ("porterait préjudice" in French, "perjudicaría" in Spanish) the existence of a mark" is broad enough to encompass the likelihood of confusion between the proposed name and the trademark.

337. Australia appears to have been confused by the English version of the text in force until the amendment introduced by Council Regulation 806/2003, which read as follows:

> A statement of objection shall be admissible only if it:
>
> ...
>
> – shows that the registration of the name proposed would jeopardize the existence of an entirely or partly identical name or trade mark ...

338. However, no consequences can be attributed to the omission of the term "of a" before the term "trade mark", which appears to have been a translation error. Indeed, the other linguistics versions in force until the said amendment, including the French and the Spanish, were identical on this point to the text currently in force in those versions.

4. Claim 22: Regulation 2081/92 does not ensure that objections from trademark owners will be considered by the Committee

339. Australia (but not the United States) claims that Regulation 2081/92 is inconsistent with Article 16.1 because it does not ensure that an objection from

the owner of a registered trademark is considered by the Committee[161], which Australia characterizes as "the ultimate decision maker".

340. For the reasons explained in the response to Claim 3, Article 16.1 does not confer a right of objection to the trademark owners. Therefore, the procedures laid down in Regulation 2081/92 with a view to organize the exercise of such right cannot be inconsistent with Article 16.1.

341. In any event, Australia's allegations are incorrect as a matter of fact.

342. First, as explained above,[162] the Commission, or the Council, and not the Committee is "the ultimate decision-maker" under the Regulation.

343. Second, Regulation 2081/92 entrusts to the authorities of the Member States the task of receiving and examining the objections because they are generally better placed to ascertain and assess the relevant facts. While Member States are not required to transmit the statements objections, their decisions are not discretionary and may be subject to judicial review under the national law of each Member State.

344. Third, the authorities of other WTO Members enjoy complete discretion in order to decide whether or not to forward the objections to the EC Commission. Thus, Australia would be estopped from complaining that the refusal by the Australian authorities to transmit a statement of objections to the EC Commission would infringe the trademark rights of its own nationals in the EC. The same would be true of any other WTO Member.

B. Claim 23: By requiring the co-existence of a registered geographical indication and an earlier trademark, Article 14(2) encumbers unjustifiably the use of the trademark, contrary to Article 20 of the TRIPS Agreement

345. Australia (but not the United States) claims that by requiring the co-existence of a an existing trademark and a later geographical indication, Article 14(2) of Regulation 2081/92 "encumbers unjustifiably" the use of the trademark, thereby violating Article 20 of the TRIPS Agreement.[163]

346. Article 20 of the TRIPS provides that

> The use of a trademark in the course of trade shall not be unjustifiably encumbered by special requirements, such as use with another trademark, use in a special form or use in a manner detrimental to its capability to distinguish the goods or services of one undertaking from those of other undertakings. This will not preclude a requirement prescribing the use of the trademark identifying the undertaking producing the goods or services along with, but without linking it to, the trademark distinguishing the specific goods or services in question of that undertaking.

---

[161] Australia's FWS, paras. 94-99.
[162] See above Section II. H.
[163] Australia's FWS, paras. 108-112.

347. Australia has misunderstood the purpose and, as result, also the scope of Article 20. That provision is not concerned with the issue of exclusivity (i.e. *who* has the right to use a sign), which, as between trademarks, is dealt with exhaustively by Article 16. Instead, Article 20 addresses the distinct issue of which requirements may be imposed upon the trademark right holder with respect to the use of *his* own trademark (i.e, *how* to use a trademark").

348. On Australia's interpretation Article 20 would overlap, and potentially conflict, with Article 16. For example,

- Article 16.1 allows the use of a later similar trademark for similar goods, provided that it does not result in "likelihood of confusion". Yet, on Australia's theory, the use of that trademark would still be prohibited under Article 20 if it "encumbered unjustifiably" the use of the earlier trademark, for example by "diminishing its distinctiveness";
- Article 16.1 provides that the exclusivity of registered trademarks is without prejudice of existing prior rights. Yet, on Australia's interpretation, the exercise of such prior rights could still be prohibited if it "encumbered unjustifiably" the use of a later trademark;
- Article 16 allows the use of identical or similar signs for different goods, except as provided in Article 16.3. On Australia's interpretation, however, such use could be prohibited by Article 20 whenever it "encumbers unjustifiably" the use of another trademark.

349. The three examples of "special requirements" included in the first sentence confirm that Article 20 does not address the issue of exclusivity:

- the first example ("use with another trademark") refers to the requirement that an undertaking uses, in addition to its own trademark, another trademark for the same goods, and not to the use of a trademark in coexistence with another trademark used by a different undertaking for its own goods. A typical example is the requirement to use a foreign trademark together with the trademark of a domestic producer.[164]
- the second example ("use in a special from") is, by its owns terms, concerned exclusively with the *form* in which the trademark may be used, rather than with the issue of who has the right to use it. It concerns, for example, the requirements affecting the affixing of the trademark. [165]

[164] See Daniel Gervais, *The TRIPS Agreement, Drafting History and Analysis* (Sweet and Maxwell, 1998), p. 116. See also Eleanor.K. Meltzer, "TRIPS and Trademarks, or GATT got your tongue?" (1993) 83 *The Trademark Reporter*, pp. 18-37, p. 29.

[165] Daniel Gervais, *op.cit.*, p. 117.

- as regards the third example ("in *a manner* detrimental to the capability to distinguish the goods or services, etc."), on which Australia places particular emphasis, the term "in a manner" confirms that the requirement must relate to the "way", "method" or "mode"[166] in which the trademark is used by each trademark owner, rather than to the issue of exclusivity.

350. Article 14(2) of Regulation 2081/192 limits the exclusive right of the trademark right holder to prevent the use of the trademark by others, by providing for the co-existence of a geographical indication, but imposes no "requirement" with respect to *how* the trademark owner may use its own trademark. Since Article 14(2) imposes no requirements falling within the scope of Article 20 of the TRIPS Agreement, it cannot be inconsistent with that provision.

351. In any event, as shown in the response to Claim 19, co-existence is consistent with the relevant EC's obligations under the TRIPS Agreement and, therefore, would not be "unjustified".

C. Claim 24: Article 14(1) of Regulation 2081/92 is inconsistent with Article 24.5 of the TRIPS Agreement because it does not afford the right of priority provided in Article 4 of the Paris Convention

352. Australia (but not the United States) claims that Article 14(1) of Regulation 2081/92 violates Article 25.4 of the TRIPS Agreement because it does not afford the right of priority in respect of an application for registration of a trademark previously filed in another WTO Member provided in Article 4 of the Paris Convention (1967). [167]

353. As explained in Section II,[168] the EC considers that this claim is outside the terms of reference because it is entirely dependent on a supposed violation of Article 4 of the Paris Convention (1967), which was not mentioned in Australia's panel request.

354. In any event, Australia's claim is insufficiently argued and difficult to understand.

355. Australia appears to be arguing that, in accordance with Article 4 of the Paris Convention (1967), an application for a trademark that was filed in Member X up to six months prior to one of the two dates mentioned in Article 24.5 of the TRIPS Agreement would have the effect of bringing within the scope of the protection provided by Article 24.5 any subsequent application made after those dates in Member Y. That interpretation, however, would be incorrect, because it relies on the legal consequences of Article 24.5 in order to establish that certain facts fall within the scope of that provision. In other words,

---

166 New Shorter Oxford English Dictionary, 1993, Vol. I, p. 1687.

167 Australia's FWS, paras. 81-87.

168 See above paras. 28-30.

Australia's interpretation of Article 24.5 already anticipates the result of such interpretation.

356. Article 24.5 requires to afford the priority right of Article 4 of the Paris Convention (1967) to those applications that are "grandfathered" by virtue of that provision, i.e. to the applications filed before the date of entry into force of the WTO Agreement (1 January 1996) or before the date of protection of the GI in its country of origin. But Article 4 of the Paris Convention (1967) cannot be applied in order to determine whether an application is "grandfathered" in accordance with Article 25.4. For that purpose, the only relevant date is the actual date of filing in the Member applying the implementing measures. When that date is taken into account, Article 14(1) of Regulation 2081/1992 is fully consistent with Article 24.5 of the TRIPS Agreement.

D. Articles 41.1, 41.2, 41.3, 41.4, 42, 43, 44.1, 45, 46, 48 and 49 of the TRIPS Agreement

1. General Considerations

357. Australia and the United States claim that Regulation 2081/92 is inconsistent with numerous provisions of Part III of the TRIPS Agreement because it does not afford to trademark right holders the enforcement rights stipulated in those provisions.

358. The EC considers that these claims are unfounded because Part III of the TRIPS Agreement does not apply to Regulation 2081/92.

359. Regulation 2081/92 lays down an administrative procedure for the acquisition of geographical indications via a system of registration. It does not purport to regulate the procedures for enforcing trademark rights, which are provided instead in the trademark laws, and related civil and criminal procedural laws, of the EC and of its Member States. Those laws, which have been notified to the WTO, are not within the terms of reference of the Panel.

360. The TRIPS Agreement draws a clear distinction between, on the one hand, the procedures for the "enforcement" of intellectual property rights, which are provided in Part III, and, on the other hand, the "procedures for the acquisition and maintenance of intellectual rights and related *inter partes* procedures", which are addressed in Part IV. The procedures provided in Regulation 2081/92 for the registration of geographical indications at issue in this dispute fall clearly within the second category and are subject exclusively to Part IV, and not to Part III.

361. The purpose of Part III is expressed in Article 41.1 which provides that

> Members shall ensure that enforcement procedures as specified in this part are available under their law so as to permit effective action against any act of infringement of intellectual property rights covered by this Agreement, including expeditious remedies to prevent infringements and remedies which constitute a deterrent to further infringements.

362. The granting of an intellectual property right in accordance with the domestic law of each Member is not an "infringement" and, therefore, is not subject to Part III of the TRIPS Agreement. Further, the subsequent use of a validly granted intellectual property right in conformity with the domestic laws of a Member is also not an "infringement".

363. For the purposes of Part III, the existence of an "infringement" must be established with respect to the applicable domestic law implementing Part II of the TRIPS Agreement, and not in relation to Part II itself. In other words, an act which is consistent with a Member's domestic law, such as the use of a validly registered geographical indication, is not an "infringement" for the purposes of Part III, even if the domestic law is inconsistent with Part II. Indeed, requiring Members to provide "enforcement" procedures against acts that are consistent with their own domestic laws, but are inconsistent with Part II, would be as much as requiring them to give direct effect to the WTO Agreement in their domestic legal order.

364. In addition, applying the provisions of Part III to the procedures for the acquisition of intellectual property rights, such as those regulated in Regulation 2081/1992, would render redundant many of the provisions of Part IV and give rise to conflicts between Part III and Part IV.

365. Moreover, it would have unacceptable results for most Members, as illustrated by the complainants' claims. It would mean, for example, that intellectual property rights would have to be conferred always by a judicial body in accordance with judicial procedures, rather than by an administrative body in accordance with administrative procedures, as is currently the case in most Members, including Australia and the United States. The EC does not believe, for instance, that the complainants' own systems of registration of trademarks, which are operated by an administrative body, would comply with the provisions of Part III.

2. *Claim 25: Regulation 2081/92 is inconsistent with Article 41.1 of the TRIPS Agreement*

366. Both Australia and the United States claim that Regulation 2081/92 is inconsistent with Article 41.1 of the TRIPS Agreement[169].

367. Article 41.1 of the TRIPS Agreement is an introductory provision, which does not impose any obligation by itself. Australia appears to agree because it argues that the measure is inconsistent with Article 41.1 "as a consequence of"[170] the fact that it is inconsistent with Articles 41.2, 41.3, 42, 43, 44, 45, 46, 48 and 49. As explained in Section II, the EC considers that Articles 43, 44, 45, 46, 48 and 49 are outside the terms of reference of the Panel, because they were not mentioned in Australia's panel request. Australia's claims under Articles 41.2, 41.3 and 42 will be addressed here below.

---

[169] Australia's FWS 145-148. US FWS, para. 185.

[170] Australia's FWS, para. 148.

368. The United States submits no arguments in support of this claim.[171]

3. *Claim 26: Regulation 2081/92 is inconsistent with Article 41.2 of the TRIPS Agreement*

369. Both Australia and the United States claim that Regulation 2081/92 is inconsistent with Article 41.2 of the TRIPS Agreement[172] because

- it does not make available to trademark owners "fair and equitable procedures" for objecting to the registration of geographical indications;
- the objection procedures are "unnecessarily complicated" and "entail unwarranted delays".

370. For the reasons explained above, the EC considers that Article 41.2, like the rest of Part III of the TRIPS Agreement, does not apply to the procedures for the acquisition of intellectual property rights, which are instead subject exclusively to the provisions of Part IV. In the case of Article 41.2, this is made clear by Article 62.4 of the TRIPS Agreement, which provides that

> The procedures concerning the acquisition or maintenance of intellectual property rights and, where a Member's law provides for such procedures, administrative revocation and *inter partes* procedures such as opposition, revocation and cancellation, shall be governed by the general principles set out in paragraphs 2 and 3 of Article 41.

371. The cross-reference to "the *general principles* set out in paragraphs 2 and 3 of Article 41" would have been superfluous if Article 41 could be applied, as such, to the procedures for the registration of an intellectual property right.

372. Neither Australia nor the United States have claimed in their panel requests that Regulation 2081/92 is inconsistent with Article 62.4, which is, therefore, outside the terms of reference of the Panel.

373. In any event, as shown below, the complainants' allegations are unfounded as a matter of fact.

(a) The procedures provided in Regulation 2081/92 are neither inequitable nor unfair

374. The accusation that a Member acts in an "unfair and inequitable" manner is a very serious one. One could expect that such an accusation would be made against another Member only after careful consideration and on the basis of indisputable evidence.

375. Yet, the United States does not even bother to provide argument, let alone evidence, in support of its claim under Article 41.2.[173]

---

[171] US FWS, para. 185.

[172] Australia's FWS, paras. 126-136. US FWS, para. 186.

[173] US FWS, para. 186.

376. For its part, Australia alleges that the objection procedures provided for in Regulation 2081/92 are neither fair nor equitable because

- objections must be lodged with an agency "that is *likely* to have an interest in supporting and promoting the registration of EC-defined GIs";[174]
- objections must be considered by a Committee comprised of "delegates of the same EC Member States agencies which are *likely* to have an interest in supporting and promoting the proposed registration of EC Member State geographic terms as defined GIs"[175]
- "trademark right holders not resident in the EC face the additional hurdle of not having a national representative in the Committee".[176]

377. Australia concludes that "in such circumstances, the *possibility of bias* in favour of both the proposed EC-defined GI and the interests of EC Member States *cannot be seen to be excluded.*"[177]

378. At the outset, the EC would submit that the mere fact that the "possibility of bias cannot be seen to be excluded" cannot be sufficient to establish a violation of Article 41.2. Instead, it would need to be shown that the procedures at issue are positively unfair and inequitable. In any event, Australia has not met even the very low standard which it has set forth itself.

379. To begin with, Australia's allegations are fraught with factual errors. Australia repeats, once again, the mistake of considering that the Committee is the decision-making body. Moreover, it is also incorrect to describe the members of the Committee as "delegates" of the national agencies in charge of applying Regulation 2081/92.[178] The members of the Committee represent the Member States, and not specific agencies.

380. Even more crucially, Australia's allegations of "possibility of bias" are not based on actual fact, but on mere speculations about the "likely" conduct of public agencies and their officials. Those speculations are baseless and, indeed, offensive.

381. Neither the agencies of the Member States responsible for the administration of Regulation 2081/92, nor the officials employed by such agencies, are under any instructions to "promote" the registration of "their" geographical indications at the expense of the rights of trademark holders, whether they are EC nationals or foreigners. To the contrary, they are under a statutory duty to apply Regulation 2081/92 in an objective and unbiased manner. In the absence of compelling evidence, which Australia has not provided, it

---

[174] Australia's FWS, para. 130. Emphasis added.
[175] *Ibid.*, para.131. Emphasis added.
[176] *Ibid.*, para. 134.
[177] *Ibid.*, para. 135. Emphasis added.
[178] *Ibid.*, para. 131.

cannot be assumed that those agencies, or their officials, are "likely" to breach systematically those duties.

382. Surely, Australia would agree that Australia's own trademark office, and the officials of that agency, are not "likely" to be biased in favour of registering trademarks requested by Australian nationals over the objections of EC's right holders of geographical indications. Australia would also agree that the fact that the EC or its Member States are not "represented" in the decision making bodies of Australia's trade mark office does not render the procedures before that office "unfair" and "inequitable". Again, in the absence of any compelling evidence to the contrary, which Australia has not provided, it cannot be assumed that the agencies of the EC Member States, and their officials, will behave differently from Australia's own agencies and officials.

(b) The procedures provided in Regulation 2081/92 are not unnecessarily complicated and do not entail unwarranted delays

383. Again, the United States has not submitted any argument in support of this claim.[179]

384. The thrust of Australia's claim is that the requirement to lodge the statement of objection with the authorities of the Member State or the WTO member of residence "adds unjustifiable complexity and delay" to the enforcement of trademark rights.[180]

385. Australia's complaint is unfounded. As explained, Regulation 2081/92 entrusts the examination of objections to the Member States because they are closer to the facts and better equipped to ascertain and assess them. Even if objections were lodged directly with the EC Commission, it would still be necessary for the EC Commission to request the assistance of the authorities of the Member States in order to verify the relevant facts. Thus, it is very doubtful that centralising the submission of objections at the Commission level would add simplicity or speed to the procedures.

386. The same is true as regards the statements of objections filed with another WTO Member, in particular when they relate to the registration of a geographical indication from that WTO Member. Moreover, each WTO Member has complete discretion in order to decide whether or not to transmit an objection to the EC Commission. If they wished, the Australian authorities could limit themselves to forward immediately to the EC Commission any objection that they receive. This can hardly be described as an "unnecessarily complicated" formality or as an "unwarranted delay". Once again, Australia cannot plead its own unwillingness to forward the statement, or its failure to do so expeditiously, in order to claim that this requirement adds unjustified complexity or delay.

---

179 US FWS, para. 186.

180 Australia's FWS, para. 138.

4. *Claim 27: Regulation 2081/92 is inconsistent with Article 41.3 of the TRIPS Agreement*

387. Australia (but not the United States) claims that Regulation 2081/92 is inconsistent with Article 41.3 of the TRIPS Agreement in that the registration decisions are not "based only on evidence on which parties were offered the opportunity to be heard". Specifically, Australia alleges that Regulation 2081/92 does not ensure that the Committee will consider the objections lodged with the Member States. [181]

388. Like the rest of Part III of the TRIPS Agreement, Article 41.3 does not apply to the procedures for the acquisition of intellectual property rights, which are instead subject to the provisions of Part IV. This is made clear, once again, by Article 62.4 of the TRIPS Agreement, which makes a cross-reference to the *general principles* stated in paragraph 3 of Article 41. As mentioned, Australia did not state in its panel request Article 62.4, which is, therefore, outside the terms of reference of the Panel.

389. In any event, Australia's factual allegations under this heading are incorrect. (See above the responses to Claims 21 and 22)

5. *Claim 28: Regulation 2081/92 is inconsistent with Article 41.4 of the TRIPS Agreement*

390. The United States (but not Australia) claims that the measure is inconsistent with Article 41.4 because "owners of registered trademarks trying to enforce their Article 16.1 rights vis-à-vis a confusing GI or interested parties with GIs based in other territories other than the EC" are not provided an opportunity for review by a judicial authority. [182]

391. Again, the United States limits itself to assert this claim, but does not submit any argument in order to support it.

392. In any event, Article 41.4 of the TRIPS Agreement does not apply with respect to the procedures for the acquisition of intellectual property rights. As discussed below, Article 62.5 of the TRIPS Agreement provides that final administrative decisions in those procedures shall be subject to judicial review. The United States, however, has not mentioned this provision in its panel request. In any event, registration decisions under Regulation 2081/92 are subject to judicial review.

6. *Claim 29: Regulation 2081/92 is inconsistent with Article 42 of the TRIPS Agreement*

393. The complainants claim that Regulation 2081/92 is inconsistent with Article 42 because it does not provide to trademark right holders civil judicial

---

[181] Australia's FWS, paras. 141-144.
[182] US FWS, para. 187.

procedures for the enforcement of their rights vis-à-vis the registration of geographical indications.[183]

394. The valid registration of a geographical indication in accordance with Regulation 2081/92 does not constitute an "infringement" of trademark rights for purposes of Part III. Accordingly, there is no obligation under Article 42 to provide judicial procedures for "enforcing" those rights against the registration of a geographical indication.

395. As explained, Regulation 2081/92 lays down an administrative procedure for the acquisition of geographical indication rights via a system of registration As such, it is subject to Part IV of the TRIPS Agreement, and not to Part III. Unlike Part III, Part IV does not require to provide judicial procedures. In most countries, including the United States and Australia, registration procedures are administrative in nature.

396. While Part IV does not require to provide judicial procedures, it requires that final decisions in administrative procedures must be subject to judicial review. Thus, Article 62.5 states that

> Final administrative decisions in any of the procedures referred to under paragraph 4 shall be subject to review by a judicial or quasi judicial authority. However, there shall be no obligation to provide an opportunity for such review of decisions in cases of unsuccessful opposition or administrative revocation, provided that the grounds for such procedures can be the subject of invalidation.

397. Consistent with Article 62.5, the final decisions on registration reached under Regulation 2081/92 are subject to judicial review. Likewise, the decisions of the Member States authorities with regard to *inter alia* objections may be subject to judicial review under their national laws. In any event, neither the United States nor Australia have stated in their panel requests any claim under Article 65.2, which is therefore outside the terms of reference.

*E. Claim 30: Regulation 2081/92 is inconsistent with Article 10bis (1) and 10*ter *(1) of the Paris Convention*

398. Australia (but not the United States) claims that Regulation 2081/92 is inconsistent with Article 10*bis* (1) of the Paris Convention (1967)[184] because "it does not provide a Community wide system of effective protection of trademarks from acts of unfair competition arising from the later registration of EC-defined GIs under the Regulation".[185]

399. This claim is insufficiently argued and difficult to understand. Australia does not explain how the use of a registered geographical indication, which is otherwise consistent with the TRIPS Agreement, and in particular with Articles

[183] Australia's FWS, paras. 119-125. US FWS, para. 187.
[184] Australia's FWS, paras. 113-118.
[185] Australia's FWS, para. 114.

24.5 and 16, could constitute an act of unfair competition within the meaning of Article 10*bis* (1).

400. In any event, the use of registered geographical indications remains subject to the EC legislation on labelling and misleading advertising, as well as to the laws of the EC Member States on unfair competition. That legislation is not within the terms of reference of the Panel.

401. Australia suggests that the violation would arise from the fact that there is no Community wide system of protection.[186] However, there is no basis in Article 10*bis* (1), or anywhere else in the Paris Convention (1967) for the proposition that the protection against unfair competition must be provided at any given territorial level.[187]

402. Australia's claim under Article 10*ter* (1)of the Paris Convention (1967)[188] is based on the same allegations as the claim under Article10*bis* (1) and is equally unfounded for the same reasons.

F. Consequential Claims

1. Claim 31: Regulation 2081/92 is inconsistent with Article 2.1 of the TRIPS Agreement

403. Australia claims that, because Regulation 2081/92 is inconsistent with Articles 10*bis* (1) and 10*ter* (1) of the Paris Convention (1967), it is also inconsistent with Article 2.1 of the TRIPS Agreement.[189]

404. This claim is entirely dependent on the previous claims under Articles 10*bis* (1) and 10*ter* (1) of the Paris Convention. Both claims are unfounded and, as a consequence, so is this claim.

2. Claim 32: Regulation 2081/92 is inconsistent with Article 1.1 of the TRIPS Agreement

405. Australia claims that because Regulation 2081/92 is inconsistent with Articles 2.1, 16.1, 20, 24.5, 41.1, 41.2, 41.3 and/ or 42 of the TRIPS Agreement it is also inconsistent with Article 1.1 of the TRIPS Agreement. [190]

406. The EC has shown that Australia's claims under those provisions are without merit. Therefore, Australia's claim under Article 1.1 is likewise unfounded.

---

[186] *Ibid.*

[187] Australia is a federal state. Surely, Australia would agree that Article 10*bis* (1) does not require it to change the constitutional allocation of powers between the Commonwealth and the State and Territory Governments.

[188] Australia's FWS, para. 117.

[189] Australia's FWS, para. 151.

[190] Australia's FWS para. 152.

3. *Claim 33: The transitional national protection provided by the Member States is inconsistent with Articles 2.1, 16.1, 41.1, 41.2, 41.3 and/or 42 of the TRIPS Agreement*

407. Australia (but not the United States) claims that the transitional protection that Member States are entitled to provide under Article 5(5) of Regulation 2081/92 pending a registration decision is inconsistent with Articles 2.1 (incorporating Articles 10*bis* (1) and 10*ter* (1) of the Paris Convention (1967)) 16.1, 41.1, 41.2, 41.3 and/or 42 of the TRIPS Agreement. [191]

408. This claim is entirely dependent on the previous claims submitted by Australia under the above listed provisions. Since those claims are unfounded, so is this claim.

VII. THE EC MEASURE IS CONSISTENT WITH THE OBLIGATION TO PROVIDE PROTECTION TO GEOGRAPHICAL INDICATIONS UNDER ARTICLE 22.2 OF THE TRIPS AGREEMENT

409. Australia[192] and the United States[193] have submitted very different claims under this heading. The EC will address them separately here below.

1. *Claim 34: Regulation 2081/92 is inconsistent with Article 22.2 of the TRIPS Agreement*

410. Australia claims that [194]

> Regulation No. 2081/92 establishes a Community-wide regime for the registration and protection of EC-defined GIs. However, the EC measure does not provide –as concerns those same EC-defined GIs - legal channels for interested parties to prevent on a Community-wide basis any use of those EC-defined GIs which would mislead the public as to the geographical origin of a good or any use which would constitute an act of unfair competition within the meaning of Paris Article 10 *bis*.

411. Once again, this claim is insufficiently argued. Here below, the EC will provide a provisional answer based on its limited understanding of Australia's rather obscure arguments.

412. First, the EC considers that Article 22.2 of the TRIPS Agreement is concerned exclusively with the protection of geographical indications. It cannot be invoked by a trademark right holder in order to prevent the use a geographical indication which supposedly infringes its trademark right, which is what Australia appears to be suggesting.

---

191 Australia's FWS, paras. 149-150.
192 Australia's FWS, paras. 154-155.
193 US FWS, paras. 171-183.
194 *Ibid.*, para. 155.

413. Second, Regulation 2081/92 only allows the use of a geographical indication in connection with goods that originate in the geographical area designated by that geographical indication. The EC fails to see how the use of a validly registered geographical indication, which is otherwise consistent with the TRIPS Agreement, could possibly mislead the public as to the geographical origin of the goods. In fact, the registration of the geographical indication seeks to avoid precisely that result.

414. Third, the EC also fails to understand how the registration or the use of a geographical indication consistently with the EC domestic laws, as well as with all other provisions of the TRIPS Agreement, including Articles 24.5 and 16, could ever constitute an act of unfair competition within the meaning of Article 10*bis* of the Paris Convention (1967). Australia has not explained it. In any event, the use of registered geographical indications remains subject to the EC legislation on labelling and misleading advertising, as well as to the laws of the Member States on unfair competition. That legislation is not within the terms of reference of the Panel.

415. Finally, Australia suggests that the violation would arise from the fact that there is no Community-wide system of protection. However, there is no basis in Article 22.2, or anywhere else in the TRIPS Agreement, for the proposition that protection must be provided at any particular territorial level.

2. Claim 35: Regulation 2081/92 is inconsistent with Article 1.1 of the TRIPS Agreement because it is inconsistent with Article 22.2

416. Australia claims that, because Regulation 2081/92 is inconsistent with Article 22.2 of the TRIPS Agreement, it is also inconsistent with Article 1.1.[195]

417. This claim is entirely consequential on Claim 21. Since there is no violation of Article 22.2, there is also no violation of Article 1.1.

3. Claim 36: Regulation 2081/92 is inconsistent with Article 22.2 TRIPS

418. The United States claims that Regulation 2081/92 is inconsistent with Article 22.2 because it fails to provide to "interested parties" established outside the EC the means to prevent the acts specified in that provision.[196]

419. The United States cites the following reasons:

- the registration of geographical indications is subject to the conditions of equivalence and reciprocity;
- the applications for registration of geographical indications must be made by the foreign governments;

[195] Australia's FWS, para. 156.
[196] US FWS, paras. 171-183.

- the right to lodge an objection against a registration is subject to certain restrictions.

420. As shown below, the reasons mentioned by the United States are either incorrect, as a matter of EC law, or irrelevant under WTO law. Therefore, Regulation 2081/92 implements adequately the EC's obligations under Article 22.2 also with respect to the "interested parties" of other WTO Members.

421. In any event, the EC recalls that Regulation 2081/92 is not the only means made available by the EC and its Member States to the "interested parties" of other WTO Members in order to prevent the acts mentioned in Article 22.2. Therefore, even assuming that the US arguments with respect to Article 2081/92 were correct, the EC would still comply with its obligations under Article 22.2.

(a) Regulation 2081/92 provides to interested parties of other WTO Members the means to prevent the acts mentioned in Article 22.2

(i) Reciprocity and equivalence conditions

422. In support of its claim, the United States has claimed that the registration of geographical indications is subject to conditions of "reciprocity and equivalence".

423. As the EC has already stated before,[197] this claim is factually not correct. Article 12(1), to which the United States has referred, is not applicable to WTO Members. Accordingly, the United States' claim under Article 22.2 TRIPS is equally unfounded.

(ii) The requirement that the application must be transmitted by the Government

424. The United States has also referred to the fact that the application for registration of a geographical indication must be transmitted by the government of the country in which the relevant area is located.

425. As the EC has already set out, this requirement is a modality of the registration process which equally applies to applications from Member States and from third countries, i.e. concerns the procedure for the acquisition of an intellectual property right. According to Article 62.1 TRIPS, Members may require, as a condition of the acquisition or maintenance of intellectual property rights provided for under Sections 2 through 6 of Part II, compliance with reasonable procedures and formalities.

426. The United States has not shown that the requirement of transmission by the third country government is an unreasonable procedural requirement. In any event, such a claim would be a claim under Article 62.1 TRIPS. Since the United States has not referred to this provision in its Panel request, such a claim would be outside the Panel's terms of reference.

---

[197] See above paras. 62-69.

(iii) The right of objection

427. As explained above in response to Claim 21, the EC considers that the right to formulate objections to the registration of another intellectual property right is not inherent in the exclusivity rights conferred to trademark rights holders by Article 16.1. For the same reasons, the EC submits that Article 22.2 does not confer to "interested parties" a right to object to the registration of a geographical indication under Regulation 2081/92.

428. In any event, the US arguments are unfounded.

429. First, the exercise of the rights conferred by Article 22.2, like that of other intellectual property rights, can be made subject to compliance with reasonable procedures and formalities.[198] The requirement that statements of objections must be channelled through the authorities of other WTO Members is equivalent to the requirement imposed on EC residents. It is neither excessive nor unreasonable. Indeed, the authorities of other WTO Members enjoy complete discretion to decided whether or not to transmit an objection. If the US authorities wished, they could limit themselves to forward immediately any objection that they receive. Furthermore, the United States would be estopped from pleading that, because of its own willingness to forward a statement of objections to the EC Commission, US nationals are deprived from the means of protection required by Article 22.2.[199]

430. Second, as explained in the factual part, the United States has misread Article 12d of Regulation 2081/92.[200] The requirement that the country must have been recognized under Article 12(3) does not apply to WTO Members.

431. Third, Articles 12b (2) and 12d (1) of Regulation 2081/92 require a "legitimate interest" as a condition for objecting to the registration of a geographical indication. However, this term does not, in accordance with its ordinary meaning, require that the person concerned must have an economic interest "in the EC" in the sense that it must be "established" or "do business" within the EC.[201]

432. Fourth, a name which is misleading as to the origin of the product would fail to comply with the requirements of Article 2 (the first ground of objection under Article 7(4)).[202] The EC fails to see what "acts of unfair competition", in addition to those already covered by the existing grounds of objection, could arise from the valid registration of a geographical indication under Regulation 2081/92.[203] The United States has specified none.

(b) The EC and its Member States provides to interested parties of other WTO Members other

198 Cf. Articles 62.1 and 41.2 of the TRIPS Agreement.
199 US FWS, para. 179.
200 US FWS, para. 180.
201 US FWS, para. 181.
202 US FWS, para. 182.
203 *Ibid.*

means to prevent the acts mentioned in Article 22.2

433. Regulation 2081/92 is not the only means made available by the EC and its Member States to interested parties established both in the EC and in other WTO Members in order to prevent the acts mentioned in Article 22.2.

434. Specifically, additional means of protection are provided in:

- Directive 79/112 on the labelling, presentation and advertising of foodstuffs[204] and implementing legislation of the Member States;
- Directive 84/450 on misleading advertising[205] and implementing legislation of the Member States;
- the Trademarks Directive and implementing legislation of the Member States;
- the Community Trademark Regulation;
- unfair competition laws of the Member States.

435. The United States is aware of the above measures, which were specified in the responses provided by the EC and its Member States in the context of the review under Article 24.2 of the TRIPS Agreement[206] and have been notified to the WTO.

436. The means of protection provided by the above measures are sufficient to implement the EC's obligation under Article 22.2. In any event, these measures are outside the terms of reference of the Panel.

VIII. REGULATION 2081/92 IS CONSISTENT WITH OBLIGATIONS UNDER THE TBT AGREEMENT

437. Australia (but not the United States) has raised two claims under the TBT Agreement:

- that Article 12(2) of Regulation 2081/92 is incompatible with Article 2.1 of the TBT Agreement (claim 37);[207]
- that Articles 4 and 10 of Regulation 2081/92 are incompatible with Article 2.2 of the TBT Agreement (claim 38).[208]

438. Hereafter, the EC will first show that the provisions of Regulation 2081/92 referred to by Australia cannot be regarded as technical regulations within the meaning of Articles 2.1 and 2.2 TBT Agreement. Subsequently, the

---

[204] Directive 2000/13/EC of the European Parliament and of the Council, of 20 March 2000, on the approximation of the laws of the member States relating to the labelling, presentation and advertising of foodstuffs, OJ (2000) L 109/29.

[205] Council Directive 84/450/EEC of 10 September 1984 relating to the approximation of the laws, regulations and administrative provisions of the Member States concerning misleading advertising, OJ (1984) L 250/17.

[206] IP/C/W/117/Add. 10, 26 March 1999.

[207] Australia's FWS, para. 234 et seq.

[208] Australia's FWS, para. 249 et seq.

EC will show that in any event, Australia's claims under Article 2.1 and 2.2 TBT Agreement are unfounded.

A. Regulation 2081/92 is not a technical regulation

439. Australia has argued that Regulation 2081/92 is in part a technical regulation within the meaning of Annex 1 to the TBT Agreement.[209] In this respect, it has referred on the one hand to Article 12(2) of Regulation 2081/92, and on the other hand to Article 4, in particular 4 (2) (g), and 10 of Regulation 2081/92.[210] As the EC will show, none of these provisions constitutes a technical regulation within the meaning of the TBT Agreement.

1. General

440. Articles 2.1 and 2.2 of the TBT Agreement impose obligations on WTO Members with respect to "technical regulations". As the Appellate Body has explained in *EC – Asbestos*, whether the measure is a technical regulation is therefore a threshold issue which determines whether the obligations contained in Article 2 TBT Agreement are applicable.[211]

441. Point 1 of Annex 1 to the TBT Agreement defines a technical regulation as follows:

> Document which lays down product characteristics or their related processes and production methods, including the applicable administrative provisions, with which compliance is mandatory. It may also include or deal exclusively with terminology, symbols, packaging, marking or labelling requirements as they apply to a product, process or production method.

442. As the Appellate Body has stated in *EC – Sardines*, there are three criteria which must be fulfilled cumulatively in order for a measure to be considered a technical regulation:[212]

> We interpreted this definition in *EC – Asbestos*. In doing so, we set out *three criteria* that a document must meet to fall within the definition of "technical regulation" in the *TBT Agreement*. *First*, the document must apply to an identifiable product or group of products. The *identifiable* product or group of products need not, however, be expressly *identified* in the document. *Second*, the document must lay down one or more characteristics of the product. These product characteristics may be intrinsic, or they may be related to the product. They may be prescribed or imposed in either a positive or a negative form. *Third*, compliance with the

---

[209] Australia's FWS, para. 209 et seq.

[210] Australia's FWS, paras. 219–221.

[211] Appellate Body Report, *EC – Asbestos*, para. 59 ; similarly Appellate Body Report, *EC – Sardines*, para. 175.

[212] Appellate Body Report, *EC – Sardines*, para. 176.

product characteristics must be mandatory. As we stressed in *EC – Asbestos*, these three criteria are derived from the wording of the definition in Annex 1.1.

2. *Article 12(2) of Regulation 2081/92 is not a technical regulation*

443. Contrary to the view of Australia, Article 12(2) of Regulation 2081/92 is not a technical regulation within the meaning of the TBT Agreement.

(a) Article 12(2) does not apply to identifiable products

444. First of all, Article 12(2) of Regulation 2081/92 does not apply to identifiable products.

445. Australia has argued that Regulation 2081/92 applies to agricultural products and foodstuffs, and that these are identifiable products.[213] However, the EC would like to recall that the requirement to indicate the country of origin contained in the second subparagraph of Article 12(2) applies only to the names in the situation referred to in the first subparagraph of Article 12(2).[214]

446. Accordingly, the requirement of Article 12(2) does not apply to all agricultural products and foodstuffs for which a registration is obtained under Regulation 2081/92, but only to cases of homonymous protected names from the EC and a third country. Moreover, as the EC has also explained, the requirement in Article 12(2) can apply both to geographical indications from a third country or from the EC, depending on which name has been protected earlier.[215]

447. The Regulation itself does not allow to identify the products which might be affected by this requirement. Accordingly, Article 12(2) does not apply to identifiable products.

(b) Article 12(2) does not lay down product characteristics

448. Second, Article 12(2) does not lay down product characteristics. Australia has argued that Article 12(2) "sets out a specific labelling requirement" falling within the meaning of a technical regulation as defined in Annex 1 to the TBT Agreement.[216]

449. Australia overlooks that Article 12(2) does not contain a specific labelling requirement for any specific product. Article 12(2) sets out merely the conditions under which a geographical indication will be registered in a situation where there are homonyms from the EC and a third country. The requirement to

---

[213] Australia's FWS, para. 231.
[214] Above para. 85 et seq.
[215] Above, para. 88.
[216] Australia's FWS, para. 220.

indicate the country of origin will be a condition for the registration of the geographical indication for which protection is sought later.

450. However, it is not Article 12(2) TBT Agreement itself which imposes a labelling requirement. The application for the registration of any geographical indication, whether from the EC or a third country, must be accompanied by a product specification. In accordance with Article 4 (2) (h) of Regulation 2081/92, the product specification shall contain the specific labelling details relating to the geographical indication. In the situation envisaged by Article 12(2), the requirement to indicate the country of origin will be among the labelling details which must be indicated in the product specification.

451. Moreover, it must be noted that the definition of "technical regulation" in Annex 1 to the TBT Agreement encompasses labelling requirements only "as they apply to a product, process or production method". In the present case, the labelling requirement does not relate to a product, process, or its production method, but merely to its geographic origin. As the EC has already set out,[217] this question of origin marking is covered by the special disciplines of Article IX GATT.

452. Accordingly, Article 12(2) does not lay down product characteristics within the meaning of the definition of a technical regulation.

(c) Article 12(2) of Regulation 2081/92 is not mandatory

453. Finally, Article 12(2) does not impose a requirement with which compliance is mandatory.

454. Regulation 2081/92 establishes a system for the registration and protection of geographical indications. The possibility to apply for registration of a geographical indication is a right, not an obligation. In particular, registration under Regulation 2081/92 is not a precondition for the marketing of products.

455. Article 4(1) of Regulation 2081/92 provides that in order to be eligible to use a geographical indication, a product "must comply with a specification". However, it is important to note that this compliance refers only to the specifications in Article 4(2), not to the Regulation itself.

456. Similarly, Article 12(2) is a condition for the registration of a geographical indication. Since the registration process is voluntary, compliance with Article 12(2) is not a mandatory condition for the placing of products on the market.

457. For all the reasons set out above, Article 12(2) of Regulation 2081/92 is not a technical regulation within the meaning of the TBT Agreement.

---

[217] Above 213.

3. *Articles 4 and 10 of Regulation 2081/92 are not a technical regulation*

458. Contrary to the view of Australia, Articles 4 and 10 of Regulation 2081/92 are not a technical regulation within the meaning of the TBT Agreement.

(a) Articles 4 and 10 do not lay down product characteristics

459. First of all, Article 4 and 10 of Regulation 2081/92 do not lay down product characteristics.

460. Article 4(g), to which Australia has referred specifically, provides merely that the product specification shall include the details of the inspection procedures provided for in Article 10. Article 10 provides the basic criteria with which such inspection structures must comply. These provisions cannot be regarded as laying down product characteristics.

461. First, Article 10(1) defines that the function of inspection structures is "to ensure that agricultural products and foodstuffs bearing a protected name meet the requirements laid down in the specifications". Accordingly, the purpose of Article 4(g) in conjunction with Article 10 is not to lay down product characteristics, but to ensure conformity with the product specification.

462. However, the TBT Agreement makes a clear distinction between measures *laying down* product characteristics, and measures *ensuring conformity* with technical regulations. Articles 2 to 4 of the TBT Agreement deal with *technical regulations and standards*, whereas Articles 5 to 9 of the TBT Agreement are concerned with the assessment of *conformity* with technical regulations and standards. Point 3 of Annex 1 to the TBT Agreement defines a conformity assessment procedure as follows:

> Any procedure used, directly or indirectly, to determine that relevant requirements in technical regulations or standards are fulfilled.

463. Even if the product specification were to be considered a technical regulation, the inspection structure ensuring conformity with the specification would not be a technical regulation, but a conformity assessment procedure. Accordingly, Australia's claim regarding the inspection procedure does not concern a technical regulation, and accordingly does not fall under Article 2 TBT Agreement. Rather, Australia's claim would appear to fall, depending on the nature of the conformity assessment body involved, under Articles 5 to 9 of the TBT Agreement. However, since Australia did not refer to these provisions in its Panel request, any such claim would be outside the terms of reference of the present Panel.

464. Second, Article 4 of Regulation 2081/92 does not lay down product characteristics. Article 4(2) simply sets out the requirements with which a product specification must comply in order to permit the registration of a geographical indication. Article 4 (2) does not itself set out the product

characteristics for specific products; rather, these characteristics are contained in the application for registration of a geographical indication in accordance with Article 5 (3) of the Regulation.

465. Moreover, it is not exceptional that the definition of product characteristics is required as a condition for the acquisition of certain intellectual property rights. In particular, the system of certification marks which used by certain countries requires that products bearing the mark comply with certain product characteristics.[218] However, it does not appear that such trade mark laws have so far been considered as falling under the TBT Agreement.

466. Accordingly, Article 4 in conjunction with Article 10 of Regulation 2081/92 cannot be regarded as laying down product characteristics.

(b) Articles 4 and 10 are not mandatory

467. As the EC has already explained, Regulation 2081/92 establishes a system for the registration and protection of geographical indications which is voluntary. The requirement that inspection structures must exist is a necessary requirement for the registration of geographical indications. However, this registration is not a precondition for the placing of products on the market.

468. For these reasons, Articles 4 and 10 of Regulation 2081/92 are not a technical regulation within the meaning of the TBT Agreement.

B. Claim 37: Article 12(2) of Regulation 2081/92 is incompatible with Article 2.1 of the TBT Agreement

469. Australia has claimed that Article 12(2) of Regulation 2081/92 is incompatible with Article 2.1 of the TBT Agreement.[219] As the EC has already explained, Article 12(2) of the Regulation is not a technical regulation, and Article 2.2 TBT Agreement is therefore not applicable.

470. Alternatively, the EC considers that Article 12(2) is fully compatible with Article 2.1 of the TBT Agreement. In this respect, the EC can also refer to the response the EC has already given to the United States' claims 3 and 14, regarding Article 12(2) with respect to the national treatment provisions of the GATT and the TRIPS.

1. General

471. Article 2.1 TBT Agreement contains a national treatment provision applicable to goods in respect of technical regulations. The provision is drafted as follows.

> Members shall ensure that in respect of technical regulations, products imported from the territory of any Member shall be accorded treatment no less favourable than that accorded to like

---

218 Cf. e.g. US Trademark Act, 15 US § 1127 (Exhibit EC-6).

219 Australia's FWS, para. 234 et seq.

products of national origin and to like products originating in any other country.

472. There is so far no WTO jurisprudence on this provision. For the reasons set out below, the EC does not consider it necessary to define, in the present context, the meaning of each of the elements of Article 2.1 TBT Agreement.

473. However, the EC would also like to recall that each provision of a covered agreement must be interpreted within the specific context of that agreement. For this reason, the EC does not agree with Australia that the jurisprudence concerning Article III GATT can simply be transposed to Article 2.1 TBT Agreement, for instance with respect to the likeness of products.[220]

474. Such an approach would overlook that there are important structural differences between the GATT and the TBT Agreement. In particular, there is no provision corresponding to Article XX of the GATT in the TBT Agreement. These structural differences between the two agreements must be taken into account when interpreting the requirements of Article 2.1 TBT Agreement.

2. *Article 12(2) of Regulation 2081/92 does not apply to all geographical indications, but only to homonyms*

475. As the EC has already set out, Article 12(2) merely sets out the conditions under which a geographical indication will be registered in a situation where there are homonyms from the EC and a third country. The requirement to indicate the country of origin will be a condition for the registration of the geographical indication for which protection is sought later.[221]

476. Accordingly, Article 12(2) does not treat foreign and EC geographical indications differently; on the contrary, it treats them exactly alike. Accordingly, there is no violation of the national treatment obligation in Article 2.1 TBT Agreement.

3. *The requirement to indicate the country of origin for homonymous geographical indications from the EC and third countries does not constitute less favourable treatment*

477. Australia has argued that a violation of Article 2.1 exists to the extent that a requirement to indicate the country of origin does not exist in the case of two homonyms from the EC.[222]

478. This claim is equally unfounded. First of all, such a difference of treatment would also affect EC geographical indications, which are equally covered by Article 12(2), and therefore not be an issue of national treatment. In addition, the relevant point of comparison in this case would be the treatment of

---

220 Australia's FWS, para. 226.
221 Above para. 88.
222 Australia's FWS, para. 235.

two homonyms within Australia; however, this is not a question which falls within the responsibility of the EC.

479. Moreover, Article 6(6) of Regulation 2081/92 requires "a clear distinction in practice" also where conflicts between homonyms arise within the EC. As the EC has explained, where the two homonyms are from different Member States, this may in practice require the indication of the country of origin.[223] The only reason why the last indent of Article 6 (6) does not explicitly require the indication of the country of origin is that this provision deals with a wider set of conflicts than Article 12(2). In particular, Article 6(6) also applies to conflicts *between homonyms from the same EC Member State*. In such a situation, the indication of the country of origin would not be a meaningful way of achieving the necessary "clear distinction".

480. Accordingly, Article 12(2) of Regulation 2081/92 is compatible with Article 12(1) TBT Agreement.

4. National treatment obligations do not apply to requirements to mark the country of origin

481. Finally, it must be recalled that marks of origin are specifically dealt with in Article IX:1 of the GATT, which excludes the applicability of the national treatment obligation under Article III:4 GATT.[224] Should Article 12(2) of Regulation 2081/92 be considered as a technical regulation, then this should not have the effect of rendering the specific provision of Article IX:1 GATT useless. Accordingly, in this case, the national treatment obligation contained in Article 2.1 TBT Agreement could not apply to origin marking requirements.

482. In conclusion, Article 12(2) of Regulation 2081/92 is not incompatible with Article 2.1 TBT Agreement.

C. Claim 38: Articles 4, 10, and 12 (1) of Regulation 2081/92 are incompatible with Article 2.2 of the TBT Agreement

483. Australia has claimed that Articles 4, 10, and 12(1) of Regulation 2081/92 are incompatible with Article 2.2 of the TBT Agreement.[225] Article 2.2 is drafted as follows:

> Members shall ensure that technical regulations are not prepared, adopted or applied with a view to or with the effect of creating unnecessary obstacles to international trade. For this purpose, technical regulations shall not be more trade-restrictive than necessary to fulfil a legitimate objective, taking account of the risks non-fulfilment would create. Such legitimate objectives are, *inter alia:* national security requirements; the prevention of deceptive practices; protection of human health or safety, animal

[223] Above para. 89.
[224] Above para. 213.
[225] Australia's FWS, para. 249 et seq.

> or plant life or health, or the environment. In assessing such risks, relevant elements of consideration are, *inter alia:* available scientific and technical information, related processing technology or intended end-uses of products.

484. Australia has explicitly recognised that Regulation 2081/92 pursues a legitimate objective, and is capable of fulfilling its legitimate objective.[226] However, Australia argues that Article 4, 10, and 12(1) of Regulation 2081/92 read together require that another WTO Member have in place "inspection arrangements equivalent to those laid down" in the Regulation, and that this is more trade-restrictive than necessary to fulfil the legitimate objective.

485. As the EC has already explained, the provision of Regulation 2081/92 regarding inspection structures do no constitute a technical regulation, and therefore do not fall under Article 2.2 of the TBT Agreement. In any case, the EC considers that the requirements regarding inspection structures are not more trade-restrictive than necessary, and this for the following reasons:

- the existence of inspection structures is only required with respect to the specific product for which protection is sought;
- the Regulation does not determine the specific design of the inspection structures;
- the existence of inspection structures is necessary to achieve the legitimate objectives of Regulation 2081/92.

1. *The existence of inspection structures is only required with respect to the specific product for which protection is sought*

486. In support of its claim, Australia has referred also to Article 12(1) of Regulation 2081/92. However, as the EC has explained, Article 12(1) is not applicable to WTO Members.[227]

487. Accordingly, the registration of a geographical indication from another WTO country does not require the existence of equivalent inspection structures for all products in that country. Rather, Article 12a, 10 and 4(2)(g) require the existence of equivalent inspection structures only with respect to the *specific* product for which protection is sought.

2. *The Regulation does not determine the specific design of the inspection structures*

488. Australia has argued that Article 10(1) of Regulation 2081/92 sets out the "detailed requirements" for the inspection structures, and claimed that the Regulation "provides no leeway for regard to be had to the particular

---

226 Australia's FWS, paras. 247–248.

227 Above, para. 62.

circumstances or the existing arrangements of another WTO Member".[228] Similarly, Australia has argued that the Regulation imposes an "EC model", and rules out the acceptability of other types of inspection mechanisms.[229]

489. These allegations are wrong. As the EC has explained, Regulation 2081/92, and in particular Article 10 thereof, provides considerable flexibility as to the specific design of inspection structures.[230] Article 10 limits itself to setting out the basic functions and principles applicable to inspection bodies, without regulating their design in detail. Moreover, Articles 10(2) specifically allows a choice between public and private elements in the design of the inspection bodies. Finally, for bodies outside the EC, Article 10 does not mandate compliance with EC standards, but also allows compliance with equivalent international standards.

490. Accordingly, Australia's allegation that Regulation 2081/92 "leaves no leeway" for the design of inspection structures is unsupported by fact. Indeed, Australia does not explain what specific problems it has with the principles and objectives set out in Article 10 of Regulation 2081/92. Moreover, it does not give any example for "other types of inspection mechanisms" which would be excluded by Regulation 2081/92.

491. Accordingly, Australia fails to show that the requirements relating to inspection structures are more trade-restrictive than necessary.

3. *The existence of inspection structures is necessary to achieve the legitimate objectives of Regulation 2081/92*

492. Indeed, it appears from Australia's submission that its real concern is not with the specific requirements for inspection structures set out in Regulation 2081/92, but rather that it considers that no inspection structures at all should be required.[231]

493. However, this argument of Australia must be rejected. The legitimate objective of Regulation 2081/92 is the protection of geographical indications. Geographical indications within the meaning of Article 22.1 TRIPS relate to goods that have "a given quality, reputation or other characteristic" essentially attributable to their geographical origin.

494. The objective of the inspection procedures foreseen in Regulation 2081/92 is to ensure that products using a protected geographical indication do comply with the product specifications, and therefore have the "quality, reputation or other characteristic" which justifies this protection.

495. The existence of such inspection procedures is beneficial both to consumers and to producers. Through the existence of inspection regimes, consumers have a higher degree of assurance that a product using a specific

[228] Australia's FWS, paras. 249–250.
[229] Australia's FWS, para. 252.
[230] Above para. 50 et seq.
[231] Australia's FWS, para. 255 et seq.

geographic indication will indeed comply with their expectations. This in turn will increase the value of the geographical indication, and thereby benefit the producers which produce in accordance with the product specifications.

496. The EC notes that as regards certification marks, the United States has also recognised that some form of control of the proper use of the name may be necessary, and that this cannot be simply left to the user of the mark:[232]

> When a geographic term is used as a certification mark, two elements are of basic concern: first, preserving the freedom of all persons in the region to use the term and, second, preventing abuses or illegal uses of the mark which would be detrimental to all those entitled to use the mark. *Normally a private individual is not in the best position to fulfill these objectives satisfactorily.* The government of a region would be the logical authority to control the use of the name of the region. The government, either directly or through a body to which it has given authority, would have power to preserve the right of all persons and to prevent abuse or illegal use of the mark.

497. Australia has argued that inspection structures might not be necessary where there is only one producer, for instance where there is only one occupant of the geographical area where the good can be produced.[233] The EC does not agree with this argument. Even where there is only one producer, the expectations of consumers should still be protected. In fact, a monopolistic situation might require inspections even more strongly then where several producers produce a good protected by a geographical indication.

498. Australia has also argued that other systems of protection of geographical indications might achieve the same objective, and has referred in particular to the application of unfair competition law. The EC does not consider this convincing. The EC does not contest that Members are free to implement Article 22 TRIPS through different systems of protection. This follows explicitly from Article 1.1 TRIPS, according to which Members shall be free to determine the appropriate method of implementing the provisions of the Agreement within their own legal system.

499. However, Article 1.1 TRIPS also provides that Members may implement in their law more extensive protection than is required by the TRIPS, provided that such protection does not contravene the provisions of the TRIPS. By establishing a specific system for the protection of geographical indications, the EC has established a system which grants more extensive protection, in respect of geographical indications, both to consumers and producers. This discretion left to the EC under Article 1.1 TRIPS cannot be limited on the basis of Article 2.2 TBT Agreement.

---

232 IP/C/W/117/Add.3, p. 10, 1 December 1998 (emphasis added).

233 Australia's FWS, para. 254.

500. The requirements regarding inspection structure are an indispensable part of the EC system for the protection of geographical indications. It is therefore necessary to achieve the legitimate objectives of Regulation 2081/92.

501. Accordingly, Regulation 2081/92 is fully compatible with Article 2.2 TBT Agreement.

IX. CLAIM 39, 40: THE EC MEASURE IS COMPATIBLE WITH ARTICLE 65.1 TRIPS AND ARTICLE XVI:4 WTO

502. The United States has claimed that the EC has not fulfilled its obligations under Article 65.1 TRIPS.[234] Similarly, Australia has claimed that the EC has not complied with its obligations under Article XVI:4 WTO.[235]

503. Both claims are dependent on substantive claims discussed above. Since these claims are unfounded, the consequential claims under Article 65.1 TRIPS and XVI:4 WTO are equally unfounded.

X. CONCLUSION

504. For the reasons set out in this submission, the EC requests the Panel:

- to find that the claims and the measures specified in Section II are outside its terms of reference;
- to reject all the claims within its terms of reference.

[234] US FWS, para. 190.

[235] Australia's FWS, para. 267.

ANNEX B-3

ORAL STATEMENT OF THE EUROPEAN COMMUNITIES FIRST SUBSTANTIVE MEETING

(23 June 2004)

Mr Chairman, distinguished Members of the Panel,

1. The European Communities (the "EC") welcomes this opportunity to submit its views in this dispute. The EC has provided a comprehensive response to the complainants' claims in its first written submission. In this statement we will limit ourselves to outline briefly our main arguments.

2. I will first recall a number of objections raised by the EC in connection with the coverage of the terms of reference of the Panel. I will then address the complainants' claims that Regulation 2081/92 diminishes the legal protection of trademarks, contrary to Articles 16, 20, 24.5 and several provisions of Part III of the TRIPS Agreement. I will then turn to the complainants' claims that the EC measure is inconsistent with the obligation to protect geographical indications under Article 22.2 of the TRIPS Agreement.

3. Following that, my colleague, Mr Martenczuk, will discuss the claim that Regulation 2081/92 is inconsistent with the national treatment obligations under the GATT and the TRIPS Agreement. He will then respond to the US claims that Regulation 2081/92 is inconsistent with the obligation to provide most-favoured nation treatment under those two agreements. To conclude, he will address Australia's claims that Regulation 2081/92 is inconsistent with the TBT Agreement.

I. TERMS OF REFERENCE

4. At the outset, we would like to stress that the Panel should consider only those claims which are properly within its terms of reference.

5. First of all, certain claims of Australia, in particular those regarding the right of objection, concern versions of Regulation 2081/92 which had already been repealed at the time that the Panel was established. In addition, the complainants have also referred to certain measures which were not yet adopted at the time that the Panel was established. The EC has submitted that such measures which were no longer, or not yet, in existence at the time when the Panel was established are not within the terms of reference of the Panel.

6. Moreover, a number of claims raised by the complainants in their first written submissions are based on WTO provisions that were not cited in their panel requests. For this reason, the Australian claims made under Article 4 of the Paris Convention and Articles 43 to 49 of the TRIPS Agreement are outside the Panel's terms of reference. The same is true of the complainants' claims under Article 2.2 of the Paris Convention.

II. REGULATION 2081/92 DOES NOT DIMINISH THE LEGAL PROTECTION OF TRADEMARKS

7. The Complainants have raised numerous claims (we have counted as many as fourteen) to the effect that the registration of geographical indications under Regulation 2081/92 diminishes the legal protection of trademarks. The complainants' arguments could suggest to the Panel that the registration of confusing geographical indications is a frequent occurrence in the EC, which should be a cause of immediate and serious concern to all WTO Members. That suggestion is totally unfounded.

8. As of the date of establishment of this Panel, the EC authorities had registered more than 600 geographical indications. The complainants have never alleged that any of those geographical indications has resulted in a likelihood of confusion with any prior registered trademark, let alone with a trademark owned by a US or by an Australian national. The complainants' claims, all fourteen of them, are purely theoretical. They are based on supposed "systemic" concerns. Those concerns, however, have not prevented the complainants from enacting in their own statute books legislation which is less protective of the rights of trademark owners than the EC measure that they attack in this dispute.

A. Article 16.1 of the TRIPS Agreement

1. The issue of "co-existence"

9. Both Australia and the United States claim that Article 14(2) of Regulation 2081/92 is inconsistent with Article 16.1 of the TRIPS Agreement in that it allows the "co-existence" of a later confusing geographical indication and a prior registered trademark.

10. As we have shown, this claim is unfounded for several reasons.

11. *First*, this claim is wrong as a matter of fact. Because of the registrability criteria provided under EC trademark law, the risk of confusion between trademarks and geographical indications is very limited. To the extent that there subsists any such risk, the problem is addressed adequately by Article 14(3) of Regulation 2081/92. The complainants have mischaracterized that provision. Article 14(3) is not a "narrow exception". The terms of Article 14(3), if properly interpreted, are sufficient to prevent the registration of any confusing geographical indications.

12. In order to substantiate their claim, the complainants should have established that Regulation 2081/92 mandates necessarily the registration of later confusing geographical indications. In turn, this would have required them to show that Article 14(3) cannot be interpreted in a manner which allows the registering authority to refuse the registration of confusing geographical indications. At the very least, the complainants should have established that, in practice, Article 14(3) is being interpreted and applied in a manner which results in a consistent pattern of registrations of confusing geographical indications. The complainants have proved none of this. Indeed, they have not even attempted to

do so. As mentioned, their complaint is purely theoretical. The Panel, therefore, should conclude that, as a matter of fact, the complainants' claim would be unfounded even on their own interpretation of Article 16.1 of the TRIPS Agreement.

13. *Second*, in any event, the complainants' interpretation of Article 16.1 is wrong as a matter of law. The complainants' claim rests on a misconception of the relationship between trademarks and geographical indications. The TRIPS Agreement recognises geographical indications as intellectual property rights, on the same level as trademarks. It confers no superiority to trademarks over geographical indications. Nor are the provisions of Part II, Section 3, "exceptions" to Article 16.1. There is no hierarchy between them. In an attempt to establish the superiority of trademarks over geographical indications, the complainants have emphasised the exclusivity of trademarks. But from this it does not follow that trademarks must prevail over geographical indications. Geographical indications are also exclusive rights.

14. The boundary between a Member's right to protect geographical indications and its obligation to protect trademarks is not established in Article 16.1. It is defined in Article 24.5 of the TRIPS Agreement. Article 14(2) of Regulation 2081/92 is fully consistent with Article 24.5, which provides that Members shall not prejudice "the right to use a trademark". Had the drafters meant to exclude the co-existence of trademarks and later geographical indications, they would have provided instead that Members shall not prejudice "the *exclusive* right to use a trademark". Furthermore, if Article 24.5 did not allow co-existence, the protection of geographical indications would become pointless whenever there is a grandfathered trademark. Indeed, why protect a geographical indication against illegitimate uses by third parties if the legitimate users cannot use it themselves? Yet, Article 24.5 envisages such protection even in the presence of grandfathered trademarks.

15. Co-existence may not be a perfect solution, but then there is no such perfect solution. Co-existence is, nonetheless, a more reasonable solution than a rigid application of the first-in-time rule, because when comparing trademarks and geographical indications one is not comparing apples with apples. Trademarks and geographical indications are distinct intellectual property rights, each with a different subject matter and a different function. Moreover, the co-existence of intellectual property rights is by no means an unusual solution. Several other provisions of the TRIPS Agreement provide expressly for co-existence. The same is true of the law of other Members, including the United States itself.

16. The following example, drawn from the US own practice, illustrates the unreasonable consequences of the interpretation put forward by the complainants in this dispute. Napa Valley is a famous geographical indication for wine. Prior to its official recognition by the US authorities, the term "Napa" had been registered as part of several trademarks, some of which were not used for wine originating in that region. On the complainants' interpretation, the owners of those trademarks should be entitled to prevent the winemakers of Napa Valley

from using that term in order to describe the origin and the characteristics of their wine. This result would be manifestly inequitable. And, indeed, the US authorities seem to agree. The applicable regulations reserve the term "Napa Valley" exclusively for the wine originating in that region. By way of exception, prior trademarks including that name are allowed to "co-exist" with that geographical indication, subject to certain labelling requirements. This solution is similar to that provided under Regulation 2081/92. The EC, therefore, fails to understand why the United States has considered it necessary to bring this claim against Regulation 2081/92.

17. *Third*, irrespective of whether the co-existence of geographical indications and earlier trademarks is envisaged by Article 24.5 of the TRIPS Agreement, the EC is required to maintain such co-existence by virtue of Article 24.3, a "stand-still" provision that prohibits Members from diminishing the level of protection of geographical indications that existed at the time of entry into force of the WTO Agreement.

18. *Finally*, even assuming that Article 14(2) of Regulation 2081/92 were *prima facie* inconsistent with Article 16.1, it would be justified as a "limited exception" to the trademark owner's exclusive rights under Article 17 of the TRIPS Agreement.

2. *Article 16.1 does not confer a right of objection*

19. Australia (but not the United States) also claims that Regulation 2081/92 is inconsistent with Article 16.1 of the TRIPS Agreement in that it restricts the grounds on which trademark owners may object to the registration of a geographical indication and does not ensure that objections from trademark owners are considered by the Committee.

20. These claims are based on a mistaken premise. Contrary to Australia's assumption, Article 16.1 does not confer to trademark owners a right of objection. The wording of Article 15.5 and 62.4 of the TRIPS Agreement is unequivocal in this respect. Members may, but are not required to, make available opposition procedures. In any event, as a matter of fact, Article 7(4) of Regulation 2081/92 does not limit the grounds of objection in the manner alleged by Australia. Nor is it correct that the Committee is the "ultimate decision-maker" under Regulation 2081/92. Furthermore, while Member States are not required to forward all objections to the Commission, their decisions are not discretionary and may be subject to judicial review.

B. Article 20 of the TRIPS Agreement

21. Australia (but not the United States) claims that, by requiring the co-existence of an existing trademark and a later geographical indication, Article 14(2) of Regulation 2081/92 "encumbers unjustifiably" the use of the trademark, thereby violating Article 20 of the TRIPS Agreement.

22. As we have shown, Australia has misunderstood the purpose and the scope of Article 20. That provision is not concerned with the issue of exclusivity

(i.e. *who* has the right to use a sign). Instead, Article 20 addresses the distinct issue of which requirements may be imposed upon the trademark right holder with respect to the use of *his* own trademark. As described in our first written submission, on Australia's interpretation, Article 20 would overlap and conflict with Article 16. The three examples of "special requirements" included in its first sentence confirm beyond doubt that Article 20 does not address the issue of exclusivity.

C. Article 24.5 of the TRIPS Agreement

23. Australia (but, again, not the United States) claims that Article 14(1) of Regulation 2081/92 is inconsistent with Article 24.5 of the TRIPS Agreement because it does not afford the right of priority provided in Article 4 of the Paris Convention (1967).

24. As the EC has already explained, Article 4 of the Paris Convention was not identified in Australia's Panel request and is therefore outside the terms of reference. Moreover, this claim is insufficiently argued and difficult to understand. In so far as the EC understands it, Australia's claim is patently flawed. Article 24.5 requires to afford the priority right of Article 4 of the Paris Convention (1967) to those applications that are "grandfathered" by virtue of that provision. But Article 4 of the Paris Convention (1967) cannot be applied in order to determine whether an application is "grandfathered".

D. Part III of the TRIPS Agreement

25. Australia and the United States claim that Regulation 2081/92 is inconsistent with numerous provisions of Part III of the TRIPS Agreement because it does not afford to trademark right holders the enforcement rights stipulated in those provisions.

26. These claims are unfounded because Part III of the TRIPS Agreement does not apply to Regulation 2081/92.

27. Regulation 2081/92 lays down an administrative procedure for the acquisition of geographical indications via a system of registration. It does not purport to regulate the procedures for enforcing trademark rights. Those procedures are provided in the trademark laws, and related civil and criminal procedural laws, of the EC and of its Member States. Those laws are not within the terms of reference of the Panel.

28. The TRIPS Agreement draws a clear distinction between, on the one hand, the procedures for the "enforcement" of intellectual property rights, which are provided in Part III, and, on the other hand, the "procedures for the acquisition and maintenance of intellectual rights and related *inter partes* procedures", which are dealt with in Part IV. The procedures provided in Regulation 2081/92 fall clearly within the second category and are subject exclusively to Part IV, and not to Part III.

29. The granting of an intellectual property right in accordance with the domestic law of each Member is not an "infringement" and, therefore, is not

subject to Part III of the TRIPS Agreement. The subsequent use of a validly granted intellectual property right in conformity with the domestic laws of a Member is also not an "infringement". Requiring Members to provide judicial "enforcement" procedures against acts that are consistent with their own domestic laws, but are inconsistent with Part II of the TRIPS Agreement, would be as much as requiring them to give direct effect to the WTO Agreement in their domestic legal order. The EC would be surprised if the complainants agreed with that proposition.

30. Furthermore, applying the provisions of Part III to the procedures for the acquisition of intellectual property rights, such as those regulated in Regulation 2081/1992, would render redundant many of the provisions of Part IV and give rise to conflicts between Part III and Part IV.

31. Moreover, it would have unacceptable results for most Members. It would mean, for example, that intellectual property rights would have to be conferred always by a judicial body in accordance with judicial procedures, rather than by an administrative body in accordance with administrative procedures, as is currently the case in most Members, including Australia and the United States. The EC does not believe, for instance, that the complainants' own systems of registration of trademarks, which are operated by an administrative body, would comply with the provisions of Part III.

III. THE EC MEASURE IS CONSISTENT WITH THE OBLIGATION TO PROVIDE PROTECTION TO GEOGRAPHICAL INDICATIONS UNDER ARTICLE 22 OF THE TRIPS AGREEMENT

32. Australia and the United States have submitted very different claims under this heading.

33. Australia's claims are, once again, insufficiently argued and difficult to understand. Australia suggests that the alleged violation would arise from the fact that there is no "Community-wide system of protection" outside Regulation 2081/92. However, there is no basis in Article 22.2, or anywhere else in the TRIPS Agreement, for the proposition that protection must be provided at any particular territorial level. Again, the EC would be surprised if it were the considered view of Australia, a federal state, that the WTO Agreement may affect the constitutional allocation of competencies within Members.

34. For its part, the United States claims that Regulation 2081/92 is inconsistent with Article 22.2 because it fails to provide to "interested parties" established outside the EC the means to prevent the acts specified in that provision. As we have shown in our first written submission, the grounds alleged by the United States are either incorrect, as a matter of EC law, or irrelevant under WTO law.

35. In any event, Regulation 2081/92 is not the only means made available by the EC and its Member States. Additional means of protection are provided in:

- Directive 2000/13/EC on the labelling, presentation and advertising of foodstuffs and implementing legislation of the Member States;
- Directive 84/450 on misleading advertising and implementing legislation of the Member States;
- the Trademarks Directive and implementing legislation of the Member States;
- the Community Trademark Regulation; and
- the unfair competition laws of the Member States.

36. The United States was aware of the above measures, which were specified in the responses provided by the EC and its Member States in the context of the review under Article 24.2 of the TRIPS Agreement and have been notified to the WTO.

37. The means of protection provided by these measures are sufficient in themselves to implement the EC's obligation under Article 22.2. In any event, they are outside the terms of reference of the Panel.

IV. REGULATION 2081/92 IS COMPATIBLE WITH NATIONAL TREATMENT OBLIGATIONS, AND DOES NOT IMPOSE A REQUIREMENT OF DOMICILE OR ESTABLISHMENT

38. The complainants have raised a large number of claims alleging that Regulation 2081/92 is incompatible with national treatment obligations under the TRIPS Agreement or under the GATT, and with the prohibition on requirements of domicile or residence in Article 2.2 of the Paris Convention.

39. As the EC has shown in its written submission, these claims are unfounded both in fact and in law. In particular, many of the claims of the complainants seem to be based on misunderstandings of the content of Regulation 2081/92. The EC will now briefly recall its main arguments regarding the most salient of these claims.

A. National treatment under the TRIPS Agreement

1. The conditions for the registration of geographical indications from third countries

40. The complainants have argued that Regulation 2081/92 violates the national treatment obligation of the TRIPS Agreement by imposing a condition of reciprocity and equivalence for the registration of geographical indications relating to areas located outside the EC.

41. At the outset, the EC would like to point out that neither complainant has identified an example where the EC has refused to register a geographical indication from the United States or Australia – or from any other WTO Member, for that matter – on account of conditions of reciprocity and

equivalence. In fact, there has never been an application for registration of a geographical indication from the United States or Australia. Like many other claims in the present dispute, it appears therefore that this claim is purely theoretical in nature.

42. More importantly still, the claim is based on a misinterpretation of the Regulation. As the EC has set out in its first written submission, the EC does not impose conditions of reciprocity and equivalence on the registration of geographical indications from other WTO Members. Article 12 (1) of Regulation 2081/92, on which the complainants have based their arguments, clearly applies "without prejudice to international agreements", including the WTO Agreements.

43. This important element of Article 12 (1) has been completely ignored by the complainants. Under the TRIPS Agreement, WTO Members are obliged to provide protection to geographical indications. This is why the EC does not apply conditions of reciprocity and equivalence to other WTO Members. Moreover, other provisions of Regulation 2081/92, in particular those regarding the right of objection, similarly distinguish the situation of WTO Members from that of other third countries. Accordingly, it should be clear that WTO Members are not in the same situation as other third countries with respect to the registration of geographical indications relating to areas on their territory.

44. Accordingly, the registration of geographical indications from other WTO Members is subject to exactly the same conditions as the registration of geographical indications from the EC. As the EC has confirmed in its written submission, this means that geographical indications must comply with the same requirements regarding product specifications as geographical indications from the EC. Moreover, just like for EC indications, there must be inspection structures in place that ensure that the products comply with the product specifications for the specific geographical indication in question.

45. In their written submission, the complainants have not made clear whether they also consider these product-specific requirements to be in violation of national treatment obligations. In case they intended such a challenge, the EC would like to affirm that this would be manifestly unfounded. The very definition of a geographical indication is that products must have a certain quality, reputation, or other characteristics attributable to their geographical origin. The regulation simply intends to ensure that products using a protected name indeed comply with these requirements, and it does so in a way which does not distinguish between domestic and foreign products. The application of these product-specific conditions does therefore not constitute less favourable, but indeed equal treatment.

46. As a final point, the EC would like to recall that Article 3.1 TRIPS Agreement, just like Article 2.1 of the Paris Convention, requires national treatment as between *nationals*, i.e. natural or legal persons. National treatment under the TRIPS Agreement therefore differs in an important respect from Article III:4 GATT, which requires national treatment as between foreign and domestic *products*. It is striking that in their written submissions, the complainants do not acknowledge this important difference, and indeed provide

no indication of how they consider that Regulation 2081/92 discriminates between nationals.

47. Contrary to the assumption of the complainants, the conditions for registration of geographical indications do not depend on nationality. The regulation contains parallel procedures for the registration of geographical indications, depending on whether the area to which the indication is related is located inside or outside the EC. This is a question which may concern the origin of the product, but which has nothing to do with the nationality of the producer. The nationality of the producers is simply of no relevance for the registration of geographical indications. Accordingly, for this reason also, the Regulation cannot be said to discriminate between EC and non-EC nationals.

48. For all these reasons, the conditions for registration of geographical indications are fully compatible with national treatment obligations.

2. *The right of objection*

49. The complainants have also claimed that Regulation 2081/92 violates the national treatment obligation under the TRIPS Agreement by subjecting the right to object to a registration to conditions of reciprocity and equivalence.

50. Once again, this claim is based on an incorrect interpretation of Regulation 2081/92. As the EC already has set out, Article 12d (1) of Regulation 2081/92 gives a right to object to any person that "is from a WTO Member *or* a third country recognised under the procedure provided for in Article 12 (3)". It is therefore clear that WTO Members are not subject to the procedure of Article 12 (3) applicable to other third countries. The same applies also under Article 12b (2) with respect to objections against the registration of geographical indications from outside the EC.

51. Moreover, the claim is also legally unfounded. Once again, the complainants fail to establish that there is discrimination between *nationals*. Article 12d (1) of the Regulation refers to persons resident or established outside the EC, regardless of their nationality. It cannot simply be assumed that the reference to "nationals" in the national treatment provisions of the TRIPS Agreement also applies to persons who are domiciled or established abroad, regardless of their nationality. In fact, conditions regarding domicile or establishment are the subject of Article 2.2 Paris Convention, on the basis of which the complainants have formulated separate claims. It is not clear to the EC how these claims are consistent with the complainant's apparent view that Article 3.1 TRIPS Agreement and 2.1 of the Paris Convention also provide for national treatment between domestic and foreign residents.

3. *The transmission of applications and objections*

52. The complainants have argued that the requirement that applications for the registration of geographical indications must be transmitted by the government of the country where the geographical area is located, constitutes a

violation of national treatment obligations. Moreover, they have raised the same claim also with respect to the transmission of statements of objection.

53. The EC considers this claim to be unfounded. First of all, the requirement of transmission through governmental channels applies to domestic and foreign geographical indications alike. Accordingly, the Regulation cannot be said to discriminate between nationals, nor between foreign and domestic geographical indications.

54. More importantly still, governments fulfil an important role in the registration process. It is clear that the government in whose territory the geographical area is located to which a geographical indication relates, is better placed than any other to verify the admissibility of applications relating to such an area. It is rather striking to the EC that the complainants seem to consider that the protection in one country of a geographical indication related to an area located in the territory of another country could be achieved without any cooperation between the two countries concerned. Moreover, it does not appear that the responsibilities of governments in the transmission of applications and objections are unduly burdensome or difficult for another WTO Member to fulfil.

55. In fact, as the complainants themselves have indicated in their written submission, the real problem is essentially their absence of "inclination" to cooperate in the process. However, this unwillingness to cooperate is not attributable to the Community, but is the choice of the complainants. The complainants should therefore not be permitted to label as less favourable treatment by the EC a situation that would exclusively be due to their own attitude.

4. *Indication of the country of origin for homonymous names*

56. The United States has argued that Article 12 (2) of Regulation 2081/92 provides less favourable treatment to nationals because it requires in certain circumstances the indication of the country of origin.

57. Once again, this claim is theoretical in nature, and is moreover based on a misinterpretation of the Regulation. First of all, it should be relatively clear that Article 12 (2) is not a provision which requires the origin labelling of protected products generally, but is a provision which applies only in very specific circumstances, namely where there are identical protected names from the EC and a third country.

58. Secondly, the provision, when understood properly, in no way discriminates between foreign and domestic geographical indications, let alone nationals. It simply requires that the country of origin be indicated in order to avoid confusion and to achieve a clear distinction in practice. Logically, this requirement will normally be applied to whichever name is protected later, regardless of whether this is the EC or the foreign indication. Accordingly,

Article 12 (2) of the Regulation treats foreign and domestic products exactly alike.

5. *The historical claims of Australia*

59. Australia has formulated a number of claims also regarding the alleged absence of a right of objection under Regulation 2081/92 before it was amended through Regulation 692/2003, which entered into force on 8 April 2003.

60. The EC finds it astonishing to have to defend itself against claims which are formulated essentially in the past tense. The objective of WTO dispute settlement is to solve actual disputes and to achieve compliance with WTO obligations. It is not the object of WTO dispute settlement to dwell on historical grievances, whether real or perceived. As the EC has already stated, it therefore considers that Australia's claims relating to measures no longer in force at the time of the Panel's establishment are outside the Panel's terms of reference.

61. However, since Australia has raised these historical claims, the EC nonetheless would like to take the opportunity to correct the historical facts. Australia has referred to the simplified procedure which used to be provided for in Article 17 of Regulation 2081/92, and has claimed that under this procedure, a right of objection was available to EC residents which was not available to foreign residents. This claim is historically incorrect. As the EC has set out in its first written submission, under Article 17 of Regulation 2081/92, the right of objection was explicitly excluded. Therefore, there existed no possibility for objection, regardless of whether the person in question was an EC or a foreign resident. Australia's claims of unequal treatment are already for this reason deprived of any historical basis.

62. The EC notes furthermore that in its submission, Australia appears to have made its national treatment claims not just with respect to the Regulation itself, but also with respect to the over 600 registrations of individual geographical indications carried out until the entry into force of Regulation 692/2003. In the view of the EC, this apparent attempt to invalidate the individual registrations is devoid of all legal basis. The registrations of the individual indications are not in violation of national treatment obligations. In reality, Australia is simply attacking the procedure that was set out in Regulation 2081/92 until its amendment through Regulation 692/2003, but which it did not challenge when it was still in force.

63. Moreover, Australia seems to forget that WTO remedies are not retroactive. Even if it had challenged Regulation 2081/92 before it was amended through Regulation 692/2003, all it could have achieved would have been the amendment of that particular measure. It could not have claimed the cancellation of the hundreds of geographical indications already registered. It seems to the EC that not having attacked Regulation 2081/92 before it was amended, Australia can certainly not claim more now than it could have claimed then.

B. Prohibited requirement of domicile or establishment

64. The United States has claimed that the conditions for registration of geographical indications amount to a requirement of domicile or establishment prohibited by Article 2.2 of the Paris Convention. As the EC has already mentioned, this claim was not identified in the Panel requests, and is therefore outside the terms of reference of the Panel. Moreover, as the EC has also set out, this claim also fails on its merits.

65. In a first alternative, the United States has argued that Regulation 2081/92 imposes a requirement of domicile or establishment because it prevents a US national from registering a geographical indication relating to an area located in the US. Quite apart from the question of whether this has anything to do with domicile or establishment, the EC has already confirmed that geographical indications relating to areas in the US *can* be registered under Regulation 2081/92. Therefore, this claim must fail.

66. Presumably conscious of this weakness, the United States has also tried an alternative formulation of this claim. In this formulation, Regulation 2081/92 imposes a requirement of domicile or establishment because a US national could not register a geographical indication relating to an area located in the EC without some form of investment or business establishment in the EC.

67. This claim already does not do justice to the content of Regulation 2081/92. Faithful to Article 22.1 of the TRIPS Agreement, Regulation 2081/92 requires that in order to qualify for protection as a geographical indication, the product in question must possess characteristics attributable to that geographical origin and that "*the production and/or processing and/or preparation*" of the product must take place in the defined geographical area. Nowhere does the Regulation, nor indeed Article 22.1 of the TRIPS Agreement, impose a requirement of domicile or establishment.

68. Moreover, the implications of the United States claim are worth noting. The United States seems to believe that a US national should be allowed to register a geographical indication relating to an area in the EC regardless of whether this producer or his products have any link with that area. Taken to its logical consequence, this view of the United States would entirely undermine the protection of geographical indications as foreseen in the TRIPS Agreement. The EC regrets to have to say that this claim casts some doubt on how seriously the United States takes the conditions for the protection of geographical indications.

69. Finally, both complainants have also alleged that the conditions for objecting to the registration of geographical indications impose a requirement of domicile or establishment. These claims seem to be based on the assumption that residents of WTO Members cannot object under the Regulation. As the EC has already stated, that is not so. Accordingly, this claim is unfounded.

C. National Treatment under Article III:4 GATT

70. The complainants have raised a number of their national treatment claims also under the GATT, namely as regards the conditions of registration, the

transmission of applications, and the labelling of homonymous geographical indications.

71. As the EC has already set out, none of these elements of Regulation 2081/92 constitute less favourable treatment, regardless of whether one refers to nationals or to goods. The EC will therefore not restate its arguments in this respect, which equally apply to Article III:4 GATT.

72. The EC would merely signal one additional question regarding the issue of origin labelling, which the Panel would have to consider should it come to the conclusion that, contrary to the EC's submission, Article 12 (2) of the Regulation does involve discrimination between domestic and foreign products. When they argue that there is a violation of national treatment under the GATT of other agreements, the complainants seem to have forgotten the existence of Article IX GATT, which is, however, the specific provision in WTO law concerning origin marking. Remarkably, Article IX:1 GATT does specifically contain a most-favoured nation rule in respect of origin marking, but does not contain a national treatment rule. If Article IX:1 GATT is to have any useful meaning at all, then it must be that it contains a specific – and exclusive – set of disciplines for origin marking. Accordingly, national treatment obligations would not seem to apply to origin marking.

73. As a final point on national treatment under the GATT, and only in case the Panel should come to the conclusion that Regulation 2081/92 does entail a difference in treatment between domestic and foreign products, the EC considers that the challenged elements of Regulation 2081/92 are justified by Article XX (d) GATT. All relevant aspects of the Regulation, and in particular the conditions for the registration of geographical indications, are necessary to secure compliance with the conditions for the registration and protection of geographical indications.

74. In conclusion, Regulation 2081/92 is therefore compatible with national treatment obligations under the GATT.

V. REGULATION 2081/92 IS COMPATIBLE WITH THE OBLIGATION TO PROVIDE MOST-FAVOURED-NATION TREATMENT

75. The United States has also claimed that Regulation 2081/92 is incompatible with the obligation to provide most-favoured-nation treatment under the TRIPS Agreement and under the GATT. In this respect, the US has claimed that a) the EC discriminates among non-EC WTO Members by imposing conditions of reciprocity and equivalence and b) that the EC Member States grant each other more favourable treatment than they accord to non-EC WTO Members.

A. The EC does not discriminate among WTO Members

76. The first of these US MFN claims is already clearly unfounded in fact and in law.

77. First of all, the US claim is based on the assumption that the EC applies a condition of reciprocity and equivalence to WTO Members. As the EC has already stated, it does not apply such a condition to WTO members. Therefore, WTO Members are treated as well as any other in respect of the conditions of registration of geographical indications.

78. Second, the conditions which the Regulation requires to be fulfilled for registration, notably the requirement of product specifications and inspection structures, apply without discrimination to all foreign products. Accordingly, they cannot be argued to be incompatible with most-favoured-nation principles.

79. Third, even if Article 12 (1) of Regulation 2081/92 did apply to WTO Members, which it does not, it is worth pointing out that this provision does not yet confer any advantage on any third country. It merely sets out the abstract conditions for rendering the Regulation applicable to non-WTO third countries. These conditions do not distinguish between third countries, and can therefore not be said to confer an advantage on any particular country.

80. Finally, as regards most-favoured-nation treatment under the TRIPS Agreement, it should be recalled that unlike Article I:1 GATT, Article 4 TRIPS requires discrimination between nationals, not between products. However, Regulation 2081/92 does not refer to nationality, but to the question of where the geographical area is located. As the EC has said already, this may have something do with the origin of the product, but it has nothing to do with the nationality of the producer.

81. For all these reasons, this claim of the United States should be rejected.

B. Regulation 2081/92 does not involve the granting of advantages between Member States

82. The second claim of violation of Article 4 TRIPS Agreement by the United States is a rather curious one. In essence, the United States is arguing that "through Regulation 2081/92", EC Member States are granting "each other" advantages, which are not available to other WTO Members, and are thereby violating Article 4 TRIPS.

83. In the view of the EC, this claim is entirely unfounded. To begin with, as the EC has already set out, the conditions for the registration of geographical indications do not discriminate between geographical indications from the EC and from WTO countries. Accordingly, the EC does not understand which are the specific advantages which the US claims are being withheld from it.

84. Moreover, Article 4 TRIPS refers to advantages which are granted to the "nationals of another country". Regulation 2081/92 does not grant any advantage to nationals of "another country". The EC is a founding member of the WTO. When it adopts a measure which harmonises the law within the EC, it does

therefore neither grant its Member States any advantages, nor do its Member States grant each other advantages.

85. As the United States knows perfectly well, Regulation 2081/92 is a measure of the EC. This is why the United States has correctly brought this case against the EC, and not against its Member States. The US claim that "through Regulation 2081/92", Member States are granting each other advantages is therefore entirely artificial and in contradiction with the United States' own actions in the present dispute settlement proceedings.

VI. REGULATION 2081/92 IS CONSISTENT WITH OBLIGATIONS UNDER THE TBT AGREEMENT

86. Australia has alleged that Regulation 2081/92 is inconsistent with the TBT Agreement in two respects: first, it has claimed that the requirement to indicate the country of origin in Article 12 (2) of the Regulation is inconsistent with Article 2.1 TBT Agreement; and second, it has claimed that Articles 4 and 10 of Regulation 2081/92 are incompatible with Article 2.2 TBT Agreement to the extent that the require they existence of inspection structures.

A. Regulation 2081/92 is not a technical regulation

87. Article 2 of the TBT Agreement applies only to technical regulations. The claims raised by Australia under the TBT Agreement must fail already because none of the provisions of Regulation 2081/92 challenged by Australia constitutes a technical regulation within the meaning of the TBT Agreement.

1. Article 12 (2) of Regulation 2081/92 is not a technical regulation

88. As the EC has already set out in its written submission, Article 12 (2) is not a technical regulation within the meaning of the TBT Agreement.

89. First of all, Article 12 (2) does not apply to all agricultural products and foodstuffs covered by the Regulation, but only to products in the specific situation envisaged in the provision, namely where a protected name from the EC is identical to a protected name from a third country. Accordingly, Article 12 (2) does not apply to identifiable products.

90. Moreover, Article 12 (2) does not lay down product characteristics. First of all, the provision does not itself lay down how any specific product should be labelled. As the EC has set out in its written submission, where the situation envisaged in Article 12 (2) occurs, the labelling requirement will normally be part of the product specifications. In addition, the indication of the country of origin does not constitute a labelling requirement as it applies "to a product, process or production method".

91. Finally, it should also be noted that the possibility for registration under Regulation 2081/92 is a right, but is not a condition for marketing of products in

the EC. The registration process is entirely voluntary. Accordingly, Regulation 2081/92 cannot be held to lay down product characteristics with which compliance is mandatory.

2. Articles 4 and 10 of Regulation 2081/92 are not a technical regulation

92. With its claim regarding Articles 4 and 10 of Regulation 2081/92, Australia is challenging the requirement that inspection structures must exist. As follows from Article 10(1) of Regulation 2081/92, the objective of inspection structures is to ensure that agricultural products and foodstuffs bearing a protected name meet the requirements laid down in the specification.

93. As the EC has set out in its first written submission, this requirement of the existence of inspection structures cannot be regarded as constituting a technical regulation. Under the TBT Agreement, a technical regulation is a measure which *lays down product characteristics*. The TBT Agreement carefully distinguishes technical regulations from conformity assessment procedures, which are used to determine whether the requirements contained in technical regulations are met. Whereas technical regulations are dealt with in Articles 2 and 3 of the TBT Agreement, the WTO obligations regarding conformity assessment procedures are set out separately in Articles 5 to 9 of the TBT Agreement.

94. Even if the product specifications, with which the inspection structures must ensure conformity, were to be regarded as a technical regulation, then the inspection structure itself could still not be regarded as a technical regulation falling under Article 2 of the TBT Agreement. Rather, it would have to be regarded as a conformity assessment procedure falling under Articles 5 to 9 of the TBT Agreement. However, Australia has not referred to these provisions in its panel request, so that such a claim would be outside the terms of reference of the panel.

95. For this reason, Articles 4 and 10 of Regulation 2081/92 cannot be regarded as technical regulation falling under Article 2 of the TBT Agreement.

B. Article 12 (2) of Regulation 2081/92 is not incompatible with Article 2.1 of the TBT Agreement

96. Australia has claimed that the requirement to indicate the country of origin in Article 12 (2) of Regulation 2081/92 violates the national treatment provision in Article 2.1 TBT Agreement. In the view of the EC, even if the Panel came to consider that Article 12 (2) constitutes a technical regulation, this claim would have to fail.

97. As the EC has said earlier, Article 12 (2) does not treat EC and foreign geographical indications differently. It merely requires that where there are identical protected names from the EC and from a third country, the country of origin must be indicated. This requirement may affect the EC or the third country

geographical indication, whichever is registered later. There is therefore perfect equality of treatment between domestic and foreign geographic indications.

98. Australia has criticised the fact that Article 6 (6) of Regulation 2081/92 does not contain the same requirement as regards identical geographical indications from within the EC. In the view of the EC, this comparison is not pertinent. First of all, the EC does not see how Australian products can be disadvantaged by the way in which conflicts between homonyms from within the EC are being resolved. Moreover, it should be noted that Article 6 (6) deals with a larger set of potential conflicts than Article 12 (2). In particular, it also may concern conflicts between geographical indications from within the same Member State. It is therefore not surprising that the provision requires a "clear distinction in practice", rather than requiring the indication of the country of origin in all cases.

C. Articles 4, 10, and 12 (1) of Regulation 2081/92 are not incompatible with Article 2.2 of the TBT Agreement

99. Finally, even if the Panel considered that Articles 4 and 10 constituted a technical regulation, there would be no violation of Article 2.2 TBT Agreement.

100. Article 2.2 TBT Agreement provides that technical regulation must not be more trade-restrictive than necessary to fulfil a legitimate objective. The EC submits that the requirement that inspection procedures must exist to ensure that products bearing a protected name comply with the product specifications is necessary to fulfil the legitimate objectives of Regulation 2081/92.

101. The legitimate objective of the inspection procedures foreseen in Regulation 2081/92 is to ensure that products using a protected geographical indication do comply with the product specifications, and therefore have the "quality, reputation or other characteristics" which justify this protection. The existence of such inspection procedures is beneficial both to consumers and to producers.

102. The existence of such inspection structures is also in no way disproportionate to this objective. First of all, as the EC has set out in its written submission, Article 10 of Regulation 2081/92 limits itself to fixing the general principles, and leaves a maximum of flexibility as regards the specific design of the inspection procedures. Despite its complaints that Article 10 is unduly restrictive and obliges other WTO Members to follow an "EC model", Australia has not actually explained what specific type of inspection structures it envisages which would be ruled out by Article 10 of Regulation 2081/92.

103. In reality, Australia's argument seems to be that the existence of inspection structures should be required at all. However, this does not seem to be compatible with the objectives of Regulation 2081/92 regarding the protection of geographical indications. In fact, Australia does not take into account the specific nature of geographical indications, which are defined as having a specific quality, reputation, or characteristics attributable to their geographical origin. It is therefore entirely appropriate that the EC provides for mechanisms which

ensure that products marketed bearing a geographical indication do in fact comply with these requirements.

104. Whether there are also, as Australia argues, other systems of protection which may achieve the objective of protecting geographical indications in accordance with Article 22 TRIPS is not the question. Article 1.1 TRIPS explicitly allows each WTO member the freedom to determine how to implement the provisions of the Agreement within their legal system. Moreover, Article 1.1 also allows the WTO Members to provide more extensive protection than required by the Agreement. This is indeed what the EC has done in Regulation 2081/92. However, it would not be acceptable for third country geographical indications to take advantage of this extensive protection without complying with the same requirements as an EC indication. This would in fact not result in equal treatment, but in more favourable treatment for foreign products.

105. Accordingly, Australia's claim under Article 2.2 TBT Agreement must be rejected.

*

* *

106. Thank you for your attention. This concludes our statement. We look forward to answering any questions that the Panel may wish to ask.

ANNEX B-4

REPLIES BY THE EUROPEAN COMMUNITIES TO QUESTIONS POSED BY THE PANEL FOLLOWING THE FIRST SUBSTANTIVE MEETING

TABLE OF WTO CASES REFERRED TO IN THE RESPONSES

Short Title	**Full Case Title and Citation**
Canada – Autos	Appellate Body Report, *Canada – Certain Measures Affecting the Automotive Industry*, WT/DS139/AB/R, WT/DS142/AB/R, adopted 19 June 2000, DSR 2000:VI, 2995
Canada – Pharmaceutical Patents	Panel Report, *Canada – Patent Protection of Pharmaceutical Products*, WT/DS114/R, adopted 7 April 2000, DSR 2000:V, 2295
EC – Asbestos	Appellate Body Report, *European Communities – Measures Affecting Asbestos and Asbestos-Containing Products*, WT/DS135/AB/R, adopted 5 April 2001
EC – Bananas III	Appellate Body Report, *European Communities – Regime for the Importation, Sale and Distribution of Bananas*, WT/DS27/AB/R, adopted 25 September 1997, DSR 1997:II, 591
India – Patents (US)	Appellate Body Report, *India – Patent Protection for Pharmaceutical and Agricultural Chemical Products*, WT/DS50/AB/R, adopted 16 January 1998, DSR 1998:I, 9
US – Corrosion-Resistant Steel Sunset Review	Appellate Body Report, *United States – Sunset Review of Anti-Dumping Duties on Corrosion-Resistant Carbon Steel Flat Products from Japan*, WT/DS244/AB/R, adopted 9 January 2004.
US – Section 110(5) Copyright Act	Panel Report, *United States – Section 110(5) of the US Copyright Act*, WT/DS160/R, adopted 27 July 2000, DSR 2000:VIII, 3769
US – Section 211 Appropriations Act	Panel Report, *United States – Section 211 Omnibus Appropriations Act of 1998*, WT/DS176/R, adopted 1 February 2002, as modified by the Appellate Body Report, WT/DS176/AB/R
US – Section 211 Appropriations Act	Appellate Body Report, *United States – Section 211 Omnibus Appropriations Act of 1998*, WT/DS176/AB/R, adopted 1 February 2002

Short Title	Full Case Title and Citation
US – Section 301 Trade Act	Panel Report, *United States – Sections 301-310 of the Trade Act of 1974*, WT/DS152/R, adopted 27 January 2000, DSR 2000:II, 815

Question 1

To what extent is the Panel bound by the EC's interpretation of its own Regulation?

1. Regulation 2081/92, which is the measure at issue in the present proceedings, is an act of EC domestic law. As the Appellate Body has held in *India – Patents*, domestic law may constitute evidence of compliance or non-compliance with international obligations.[1] Accordingly, as the Appellate Body has held, a Panel may be required to determine the meaning of an act of domestic law in order to establish whether such act is compatible with WTO obligations.[2]

2. The Panel's approach to the interpretation of Regulation 2081/92 should therefore be governed by Article 11 of the DSU, according to which the Panel must make "an objective assessment of the facts of the case". Accordingly, the EC does not consider that the Panel is "bound" by the EC's interpretation of Regulation 2081/92.

3. However, the EC would like to underline that in making an objective assessment of the facts, and in particular of the meaning of Regulation 2081/92, the Panel must take due account of the fact that Regulation 2081/92 is a measure of EC domestic law. It can therefore not "interpret" Regulation 2081/92, but rather must establish the meaning of its provisions as factual elements. In this context, reference can be made to the approach described by the Panel in *US – Section 301*:[3]

> In this case, too, we have to examine aspects of municipal law, namely Sections 301-310 of the US Trade Act of 1974. Our mandate is to examine Sections 301-310 solely for the purpose of determining whether the US meets its WTO obligations. In doing so, we do not, as noted by the Appellate Body in *India – Patents (US)*, interpret US law "as such", the way we would, say, interpret provisions of the covered agreements. We are, instead, called upon to establish the meaning of Sections 301-310 as factual elements and to check whether these factual elements constitute conduct by the US contrary to its WTO obligations. The rules on burden of proof for the establishment of facts referred to above also apply in this respect.

---

1 Appellate Body Report, *India – Patents*, para. 65.
2 Appellate Body Report, *India – Patents*, para. 66.
3 Panel Report, *US – Section 301*, para. 7.18 (footnotes omitted).

> It follows that in making factual findings concerning the meaning of Sections 301-310 we are not bound to accept the interpretation presented by the US. That said, any Member can reasonably expect that considerable deference be given to its views on the meaning of its own law.

4. It follows from this approach that there are considerable differences between the interpretation of the WTO agreements by a Panel, and the establishment of the meaning of a challenged act of domestic law by a Panel. First of all, as a question of fact, the rules regarding the burden of proof must apply. Accordingly, the burden of proof for establishing that Regulation 2081/92 as the measure at issue has a particular meaning is on the complainants, not on the EC.

5. This is particularly important in the case of *per se* challenges against measures which have so far not been applied by the authorities of a Member. In such a case, a Member should not be held in violation of its WTO obligations unless it is established beyond doubt that the measure in fact entails the violations alleged by the complainants.

6. Second, the establishment of the meaning of an act of domestic law is not governed by the customary principles of interpretation of international law. Rather, the objective assessment of the facts requires establishing the meaning that the act will normally have within the legal order of the WTO Member in question. This means that the interpretation should be guided by the rules of interpretation customary in the legal order of such member, and taking account of the legal context of the measure in the domestic law of the Member.

7. Third, even though a Panel is not bound by the interpretation of a WTO Member of it own measure, due account must be taken of the fact that it is the authorities of this Member which must interpret and apply the measure in the domestic legal order. Therefore, as the Panel set out in *US – Section 301*, the explanations given by such Member of the meaning of its own measure must be given considerable deference.

8. This deference accorded to the author of a domestic act is also illustrated in Panel practice. When establishing the meaning of domestic measures, Panels have regularly relied on statements and explanations given by the defending party in the course of the proceedings. This is the case for instance in *US – Section 301*, where the Panel relied to an important extent on statements made by the United States as regards the interpretation and application of the challenged measure.[4] The same was also the case in *Canada – Pharmaceutical Patents*, where the Panel relied on assurances given by Canada during the proceedings.[5] Similarly, in *US – Section 211*, the Panel relied on a US response given to the Panel in order to establish the meaning of the challenged measure.[6]

---

[4] Panel Report, *US – Section 301*, para. 7.125.

[5] Panel Report, *Canada – Pharmaceutical Patents*, para. 7.99.

[6] Panel Report, *US – Section 211*, para. 8.69.

Question 2

Can the procedures under Articles 5 and 6 of Regulation (EC) No. 2081/92 apply to names of geographical areas located outside the EC?

9. The procedures set out in Articles 5 and 6 of Regulation 2081/92 in principle apply only to names related to geographical areas located inside the EC. The corresponding procedures for geographical indications related to geographical areas located outside the EC are contained in Articles 12a and 12b. However, these provisions also contain a number of references to specific sections of Articles 5 and 6, which to this extent are applicable to the registration of geographical indications from outside the EC.

Question 3

Did the phrase "[w]ithout prejudice to international agreements" in Article 12(1) of Regulation (EC) No. 2081/92 predate the TRIPS Agreement? Did it refer to any specific agreements when it was adopted? Which agreements does it refer to now? Would it cover bilateral agreements for the protection of individual geographical indications?

10. The phrase "[w]ithout prejudice to international agreements" was already contained in Article 12(1) of Regulation 2081/92 as originally adopted in 1992.

11. The phrase "without prejudice to international agreements" is not in any way limited to particular specific agreements or types of agreements. Accordingly, this phrase applies both to multilateral and to bilateral agreements. Moreover, the phrase does not just apply to agreements in force at the time the Regulation was adopted, but also to agreements which were adopted subsequently.

12. At the time that Regulation 2081/92 was adopted, the GATT was one of the agreements to which the "without prejudice" clause applied. Moreover, at the time that Regulation 2081/92 was adopted, the TRIPS Agreement was in the final phases of its negotiation. It was therefore the objective that the "without prejudice" clause should also apply to the TRIPS and other WTO agreements resulting from the Uruguay Round.

13. The importance of the WTO Agreements, and notably of the TRIPS Agreement, for the interpretation and application of Regulation 2081/92 was reconfirmed by Regulation 692/2003,[7] the 8th recital of which prominently refers to the obligations resulting from the TRIPS Agreement.

Question 4

Is it unusual that the text of Article 12(1) of Regulation (EC) No. 2081/92 covers only a small number of countries that are non-WTO Members, but the introductory phrase "[w]ithout prejudice to international agreements" covers the entire membership of the WTO? Why was this structure retained when the Regulation was amended in April 2003?

---

[7] Exhibit COMP 1h.

14. The EC does not consider this as unusual. First, the EC would like to point out that out of the 191 current Members of the United Nations, 48 are not Members of the WTO, including certain important countries such as Russia. Therefore, even though this group has been shrinking since the establishment of the WTO, the EC does not consider this number as "small".

15. It is also not surprising that the fundamental structure of Article 12 was not changed. When proposing to amend an act of the Council, it is a concern for the Commission to preserve the Council act to the extent that it does not require amendment. Therefore, the Commission proposal will frequently limit itself to those amendments which are strictly speaking necessary, and will leave those provisions the amendment of which is not necessary untouched.

Question 7

Do the last sentence of Article 12(3) of Regulation (EC) No. 2081/92 and the first clause in Article 12a "[i]n the case provided for in Article 12(3)" limit the applicability of Article 12a?

16. No. The last sentence of Article 12 (3) of Regulation 2081/92 merely provides that where the Commission decision provided for in this provision is in the affirmative, the procedure set out in Article 12a shall apply. This does not mean that the procedure in Article 12a cannot apply in other cases.

17. As regards the reference in Article 12a (1) to Article 12 (3), the EC would like to point out that Article 12 (3) refers to the conditions set out in Article 12(1). As the EC has confirmed, by virtue of the "without prejudice" clause, these conditions do not apply to WTO Members. Accordingly, since the procedure in Article 12 (3) is inapplicable to WTO Members, so is the reference to this provision in Article 12a (1).

Question 8

Which references to a "third country" in Articles 12, 12a, 12b and 12d of Regulation (EC) No. 2081/92 include all WTO Members, and which do not? What, in the context of each reference, indicates what "third country" means? Why are different terms not used?

18. Whether the term "third country" includes WTO Members or not must be established on the basis of the wording, context, and objectives of the specific provision in question. In Article 12(1) of Regulation 2081/92, this context includes the "without prejudice" clause. Accordingly, as the EC has explained, the references to "third countries" in Article 12(1) do not include WTO Members. The same applies where a provision refers to a "third country meeting the equivalence conditions of Article 12(3)" (Article 12b[2][b]) or a "third country recognised under the procedure provided for in Article 12(3)" (Article 12d[1]), or where a provision specifically distinguishes between third countries and WTO Members. Where this is not the case, as for instance in Article 12a(1) or Article 12b(1), the reference to third countries may also include WTO Members.

Question 9

Why is it that only the rights of objection in Articles 12b(2)(a) and 12d(1) of Regulation (EC) No. 2081/92 mention a "WTO Member" or "WTO member country"? Is it relevant that Regulation (EC) No. 692/2003 explained, in its 10th recital, that in the matter of objections the provisions in question apply without prejudice to international agreements but, in its 9th recital, it explained that the protection provided by registration is open to third countries' names by reciprocity and under equivalence conditions?

19. This is due to the differences in the structure of Article 12 on the one hand, and of Articles 12b and 12d, on the other. Article 12 contains the introductory clause "without prejudice to international agreements", which made it possible not to specifically single out the position of WTO Members in the text of the provision. Articles 12b and 12d do not contain such a clause, so that it was necessary to differentiate between WTO Members and other third countries.

20. The 10th recital of Regulation 692/2003 confirms this interpretation by stating that the objective of the amendment of the provisions regarding objections was "that it should be made clear that in this matter nationals of WTO member countries are covered by these arrangements and that the provisions in question apply *without prejudice to international agreements*". In order words, the distinction between WTO Members and third countries was intended to have exactly the same function as the without prejudice clause in Article 12(1) of Regulation 2081/92. Given this common objective of ensuring compatibility with WTO obligations, the differences in drafting technique between Articles 12(1) and 12b and 12d appear secondary.

21. As regards the 9th recital, this recital refers to the reciprocity and equivalence conditions "as provided for in Article 12" of Regulation 2081/92. This reference of course includes the "without prejudice" clause of Article 12(1). Accordingly, the 9th recital does not concern WTO Members.

Question 10

Has the Commission recognized any countries under the procedure set out in Article 12(3) of Regulation (EC) No. 2081/92? Have any countries requested to be recognized under that procedure?

22. No (to both questions).

Question 11

Has an application for registration under Regulation (EC) No. 2081/92 ever been made in respect of the name of a geographical area located outside the EC? If so, what happened?

23. No.

Question 13

What discretion does the Commission enjoy in the application of Regulation (EC) No. 2081/92?

24. Whether the provisions of the Regulation leave the Commission a discretion or not, and the extent of such discretion, will depend on the wording of each particular provision conferring powers on the Commission. Where such provisions provide that the Commission "shall" take a certain action, the Commission would normally be obliged to take such action. Where the Regulation provides that the Commission "may" take a certain action, then the Commission would normally enjoy a discretion as to whether to take such action or not. In any case, the Commission is bound to respect and apply the terms of the Regulation.

Question 14

Please express your view on whether and to what extent the mandatory/discretionary distinction in GATT and WTO jurisprudence applies under the TRIPS Agreement. Would the nature of those TRIPS obligations which are not prohibitions but rather oblige Members to take certain actions, affect the application of the distinction?

25. The relevance of the distinction between "mandatory" and "discretionary" measures under the TRIPS Agreement is the same as under the other WTO Agreements.

26. As clarified by the Appellate Body in *United States – Carbon Steel (Japan)*[8], panels are not required, as a preliminary jurisdictional matter, to examine whether the challenged measure is "mandatory". Rather, this issue is relevant as part of the panel's assessment of whether the measure is, as such, inconsistent with particular obligations. Accordingly, whether or not the distinction between "discretionary" and "mandatory" measures is "relevant" under the TRIPS Agreement will depend on the specific obligations imposed by each provision at issue.

27. That the distinction between "discretionary" and "mandatory" measures may be relevant also under the TRIPS Agreement is illustrated by *United States – Section 211*, where the Appellate Body recalled such distinction and concluded that the panel had applied it correctly.[9]

Question 15

What would be the most authoritative statement of the interpretation of Regulation (EC) No. 2081/92? Is a statement by the EC delegation to this Panel legally binding on the European Communities?

28. According to Article 220 (1) of the EC Treaty, it is the European Court of Justice which ensures that in the interpretation and application of the Treaty the law is observed. This judicial function of the Court of Justice also applies to acts of the Community institutions adopted on the basis of the Treaty. Accordingly, the highest judicial authority competent to interpret the meaning of Regulation 2081/92 is the European Court of Justice.

---

[8] Appellate Body Report, *United States – Carbon Steel (Japan)*, para. 89

[9] Appellate Body Report, *United States – Section 211*, para. 258.

29. The European Commission represents the European Community in the proceedings before the Panel. Accordingly, the statements made by the agents of the European Commission before the Panel commit and engage the European Communities.

30. However, it should also be noted that where the statements of the European Communities regard the interpretation of Regulation 2081/92, these statements concern an issue *of fact*. These statements are made in order to assist the Panel in its function to make an objective assessment of the facts. Their purpose is therefore to clarify the existing legal situation in European Community law. Their intention is not to create new legal obligations in public international or in Community law.

31. This being said, the EC does not consider that its statements before the Panel are without legal significance. In this context, the EC is aware that its submissions to the Panel will be public as part of the final report to the Panel. It is not conceivable to the European Commission that it would, in the interpretation or application of the Regulation, take a different approach to the one it has set out before the Panel.

32. As regards the approach to be taken by the European Court of Justice, the European Commission considers it important to underline that the European Court of Justice has shown a consistently high degree of awareness and respect for the international obligations of the European Communities.

33. According to the settled case law of the Court of Justice, Community legislation must, so far as possible, be interpreted in a manner that is consistent with international law, in particular where its provision are intended specifically to give effect to an international agreement concluded by the Community.[10]

34. As one scholar of Community law has observed in a recent book on the external relations law of the European Communities, the principle of consistent interpretation has been particularly important with respect to GATT and WTO law: "The EU Courts have never hesitated to make use of consistent interpretation for the purpose of applying GATT and WTO law".[11]

35. As regards specifically the TRIPS Agreement, the Court for instance has held as follows:[12]

> It is true that the measures envisaged by Article 99 and the relevant procedural rules are those provided for by the domestic law of the Member State concerned for the purposes of the national trade mark. However, since the Community is a party to the TRIPs Agreement and since that agreement applies to the Community trade mark, the courts referred to in Article 99 of

---

[10] Case C-61/94, *Commission/Germany*, [1996] ECR I-4006, para. 52 (Exhibit EC-13); C-341/95, *Bettati*, [1998] ECR I-4355, para. 20 (Exhibit EC-14).

[11] Piet Eeckhout, *External Relations of the European Union*, Oxford University Press, p. 315 (2004).

[12] Case C-53/96, *Hermès*, [1998] ECR I-3603, para. 28 (Exhibit EC-15); confirmed in C-300/98 and 392/98, *Dior*, [2000] ECR I-1344, para. 47 (Exhibit EC-16).

> Regulation No 40/94, when called upon to apply national rules with a view to ordering provisional measures for the protection of rights arising under a Community trade mark, are required to do so, as far as possible, in the light of the wording and purpose of Article 50 of the TRIPs Agreement.

36. The Court of Justice will be particularly prone to take into account the international obligations of the Community where the Community legislative act itself indicates that it is intended to implement obligations of international law. For instance, in a recent judgment, the Court held that, on the basis of a recital in the Community Anti-Dumping Regulation, the duty to provide an explanation contained in Article 2.4.2 of the AD Agreement had to apply also in the context of the application of the Community Regulation:[13]

> However, where the Community intended to implement a particular obligation assumed in the context of the WTO, or where the Community measure refers expressly to precise provisions of the agreements and understandings contained in the annexes to the WTO Agreement, it is for the Court to review the legality of the Community measure in question in the light of the WTO rules (see, in particular, Portugal v Council, paragraph 49).
>
> The preamble to the basic regulation, and more specifically the fifth recital therein, shows that the purpose of that regulation is, inter alia, to transpose into Community law as far as possible the new and detailed rules contained in the 1994 Anti-dumping Code, which include, in particular, those relating to the calculation of dumping, so as to ensure a proper and transparent application of those rules.
>
> It is therefore established that the Community adopted the basic regulation in order to satisfy its obligations arising from the 1994 Anti-dumping Code and that, by means of Article 2(11) of that regulation, it intended to implement the particular obligations laid down by Article 2.4.2 of that code. To that extent, as is clear from the case-law cited in paragraph 54 of the present judgment, it is for the Court to review the legality of the Community measure in question in the light of the last-mentioned provision.
>
> In that regard, it should be recalled that Community legislation must, so far as possible, be interpreted in a manner that is consistent with international law, in particular where its provisions are intended specifically to give effect to an international agreement concluded by the Community (see, in particular, Case C-341/95 Bettati [1998] ECR I-4355, paragraph 20).

37. The interpretation of Article 12 of Regulation 2081/92 which the EC has set out before the Panel is therefore in full accordance with the principles of interpretation applied on a constant basis by the European Court of Justice.

---

[13] Case C-76/00 P, *Petrotub*, [2003] ECR I-79, para. 54–57 (Exhibit EC-17).

38. In addition, it also useful to know that the Court of Justice may take account of statements which the Commission has made on behalf of the European Community in the WTO. For instance, in the judgement just cited, the Court of Justice referred in support of its interpretation to a assurances given by the European Commission to the secretariat of the WTO Committee on Anti-Dumping Practices:[14]

> Such an interpretation coincides in essence with the international assurances given in the communication of 15 February 1996 from the Commission to the secretariat of the WTO Committee on Anti-Dumping Practices, according to which the explanation referred to in Article 2.4.2 of the 1994 Anti-dumping Code will be given directly to the parties and in regulations imposing anti-dumping duties.

Question 16

Can the EC provide the Panel with any official statement predating its first written submission that names of geographical areas located in all WTO Members could be registered under Regulation (EC) No. 2081/92 without satisfying its equivalence and reciprocity conditions?

39. In the context of the review under Article 24.2 TRIPS, the EC explained that the reciprocity requirement applied without prejudice to international agreements.[15] Moreover, in the meeting of the TRIPS Council of 16 June 2004, the EC was asked to clarify whether it applied conditions of reciprocity and equivalence to other WTO Members. The EC provided the following response to this question:[16]

> EC Regulation No 2081/92 applies to geographical indications relating to areas located inside as well as outside the EC. For this purpose, the Regulation lays down rules relating to the registration of geographical indications from outside the EC which closely parallel the provisions applicable to geographical indications from inside the EC. The purpose of these specific rules, some of which were recently introduced by Regulation No. 692/2003, is to facilitate the registration of non-EC geographical indications while at the same time ensuring that geographical indications from outside the EC correspond to the definition of a geographical indication.
>
> As to the conditions which must be fulfilled for registration to take place, some WTO Members have considered, on the basis of Article 12(1) of Regulation No 2081/92, that registration of geographical indications from outside the EC is possible in only under conditions of "reciprocity and equivalence". However,

---

[14] Case C-76/00 P, *Petrotub*, [2003] ECR I-79, para. 59 (Exhibit EC-17).

[15] IP/C/W/253/Rev.1, p. 27 (Exhibit EC-18).

[16] The EC's statement should be reflected in due course in the minutes of the TRIPS Council.

Article 12(1) of Regulation No. 2081/92 provides that it applies "without prejudice to international agreements" including the TRIPs Agreement. Since WTO Members are obliged to provide protection to geographical indications in accordance with the TRIPS Agreement, the reciprocity and equivalence conditions mentioned in Article 12(1) of Regulation 2081/92 do not apply to WTO Members.

In other words, the EC GI register is open to GIs from other WTO Members, and registration of such GIs may take place on the same substantive conditions which apply to registration of GIs from EC Member States.

40. Moreover, the EC would like to remark that this question concerns evidence regarding the interpretation of Regulation 2081/92 as in force at the time of establishment of the Panel. Regarding a question of admissible evidence, the EC does not consider that only evidence which predates the date of its first written submission in the present proceedings is relevant. For this reason, for instance, the statements made by the EC in the course of the Panel proceedings should also be taken into account.

Question 17

Is the EC's explanation of the availability of registration of foreign GIs under its system, set out in its written statement to the Council for TRIPS in September 2002, (IP/C/M/37/Add.1, para. 142 and Annex, pp. 77-85) consistent with the text of Articles 12-12c of the Regulation? Why did that written statement not qualify the position that the Regulation's equivalence and reciprocity conditions apply to foreign GIs, if they did not apply to WTO Members, to whom the statement was addressed?

41. The EC considers that the written statement to the TRIPS Council is not incompatible with the text of Regulation 2081/92 as in force at the time it was made or with the statements of the EC in the present case.

42. The EC would like to remark, however, that this statement is of limited relevance for the present case. It was made in the context of the negotiations for the extension of protection under Article 23 TRIPS to products other than wines and spirits. The intention of the statement was therefore not primarily to explain the EC system for the protection of geographical indications. In addition, the statement was made in 2002, and therefore does not take into account the amendments made by Regulation 692/2003.

Question 18

Did the EC member States agree with the Commission's written statement to the Council for TRIPS in September 2002 with respect to the conditions attached to the registration of foreign GIs? How can the Commission ensure that the Council of Ministers will not prevent registration under the Regulation of the name of a geographical area located in a third country WTO Member because that Member does not satisfy the equivalence and reciprocity conditions of Article 12(1)?

43. It is the European Commission which represents the European Communities within the WTO. Where appropriate, the European Commission consults with the competent instances of the Council. The position of individual Member States is therefore of no relevance in the present proceedings.

44. Like the Commission, the Council of Ministers is bound to apply the terms of Regulation 2081/92. Like the Commission, it is bound to give effect to the wording "without prejudice to international agreements", and to take account of the Community's international obligations under the WTO Agreements.

Question 19

Has a judicial authority ever ruled on the availability of protection provided by registration for third countries under Regulation (EC) No. 2081/92? If the Commission registered the name of a geographical area located in a third country WTO Member, could that registration be subject to judicial review because the area was located in a WTO Member that did not fulfil the equivalence and reciprocity conditions of Article 12(1) of the Regulation?

45. Community courts can only rule on an issue when concrete cases are brought before them. Since no request for registration has ever been made in respect of a geographical indication from a third country, no judicial authority has ever had the occasion to rule on the availability of protection provided by registration for third countries under Regulation 2081/92.

46. The registration of the name of a geographical indication, whether from a third country or from within the EC, takes the form of a regulation of the Commission. The condition under which such a regulation can be challenged before the European Court of Justice are set out in Article 230 of the EC Treaty, which reads as follows:

> The Court of Justice shall review the legality of acts adopted jointly by the European Parliament and the Council, of acts of the Council, of the Commission and of the ECB, other than recommendations and opinions, and of acts of the European Parliament intended to produce legal effects vis-à-vis third parties.
>
> It shall for this purpose have jurisdiction in actions brought by a Member State, the European Parliament, the Council or the Commission on grounds of lack of competence, infringement of an essential procedural requirement, infringement of this Treaty or of any rule of law relating to its application, or misuse of powers.
>
> The Court of Justice shall have jurisdiction under the same conditions in actions brought by the Court of Auditors and by the ECB for the purpose of protecting their prerogatives.
>
> Any natural or legal person may, under the same conditions, institute proceedings against a decision addressed to that person or against a decision which, although in the form of a regulation or a

> decision addressed to another person, is of direct and individual concern to the former.
>
> The proceedings provided for in this Article shall be instituted within two months of the publication of the measure, or of its notification to the plaintiff, or, in the absence thereof, of the day on which it came to the knowledge of the latter, as the case may be.

47. The question of the validity of EC regulations may also become an issue in proceedings before the courts of the Member States. According to Article 234 of the EC Treaty, national courts are obliged to refer questions concerning the validity of EC regulations to the European Court of Justice for a preliminary ruling. Such preliminary rulings are legally binding upon the national courts. Article 234 of the EC Treaty provides:

> The Court of Justice shall have jurisdiction to give preliminary rulings concerning:
>
> (a) the interpretation of this Treaty;
>
> (b) the validity and interpretation of acts of the institutions of the Community and of the [European Central Bank];
>
> (c) the interpretation of the statutes of bodies established by an act of the Council, where those statutes so provide.
>
> Where such a question is raised before any court or tribunal of a Member State, that court or tribunal may, if it considers that a decision on the question is necessary to enable it to give judgment, request the Court of Justice to give a ruling thereon.
>
> Where any such question is raised in a case pending before a court or tribunal of a Member State against whose decisions there is no judicial remedy under national law, that court or tribunal shall bring the matter before the Court of Justice.

Question 20

With reference to paragraph 43 of the EC's oral statement, does the EC contest that equivalence and reciprocity conditions such as those under Article 12(1) and (3) of Regulation (EC) No. 2081/92, if applied to other WTO Members, would be inconsistent with the national treatment obligations in the TRIPS Agreement and/or Article III:4 of the GATT 1994?

48. First of all, the EC considers that this question may be too broad to be answered in abstract terms. Since different things may be understood by "conditions of reciprocity and equivalence", an answer can only be given on a case by case basis. This is aptly illustrated by the United States' reference to the EC's requirement of inspection structures as "equivalence by another name".[17] As the EC has already indicated during the first meeting with the Panel, it emphatically considers that this requirement is not inconsistent with the national treatment obligations of the TRIPS Agreement or the GATT.

---

[17] Oral Statement of the US at the first substantive meeting of the Panel, para. 17.

49. As regards the specific conditions contained in Article 12(1) of Regulation 2081/92, the EC has already confirmed that it does not apply these to WTO Members. For this reason, the EC considers that the question whether these conditions are inconsistent with the national treatment obligations of the TRIPS Agreement and the GATT does not arise.

Question 21

If Switzerland, as a WTO Member, can apply for registration of its GIs under Regulation (EC) No. 2081/92 without satisfying equivalence and reciprocity conditions, what was the purpose of its joint declaration with the EC concerning GIs set out in Exhibit US-6 and mentioned in paragraph 119 of the US first written submission and paragraphs 243-244 of the EC's first written submission?

50. The bilateral agreement envisaged in the declaration represents an alternative approach to the protection of geographical indications to the direct registration under Regulation 2081/92. Compared to the registration on a case-by-case basis, a bilateral agreement would have the advantage that protection of the parties' geographical indications would be obtained in one single act. Moreover, possible controversial issues, for instance regarding generic names, homonyms, or registrations concerning cross-border areas, could be resolved in a non-contentious way.

51. However, the declaration is without prejudice to the possibility of applying for protection of Swiss geographical indications under Regulation 2081/92. Accordingly, the envisaged agreement merely represents an alternative approach to protection which does not exclude direct applications under Regulation 2081.

52. Finally, as the EC has already said in its first written submission, it would like to recall that the declaration is merely a political text, and that so far no such agreement has been concluded.

Question 22

Are there any legal requirements or other provisions in EC or national laws which ensure that groups or persons entitled to apply for registration under Article 5 of Regulation (EC) No. 2081/92 are always, or usually, EC citizens or legal persons organized under the laws of the EC or an EC member State? What conditions have been laid down for natural or legal persons to be entitled to apply for registration pursuant to Article 5(1)?

53. There are no such requirements.

54. The conditions subject to which a natural or legal person shall be entitled to apply for registration are set out in Article 1 of Commission Regulation 2037/93,[18] which reads as follows:

> Applications for registration pursuant to Article 5 of Regulation (EEC) No 2081/92, may be submitted by a natural or

[18] Exhibit COMP-2.

> legal person not complying with the definition laid down in the second subparagraph of paragraph 1 of that Article in exceptional, duly substantiated cases where the person concerned is the only producer in the geographical area defined at the time the application is submitted.
>
> The application may be accepted only where:
>
> (a) the said single person engages in authentic and unvarying local methods; and
>
> (b) the geographical area defined possesses characteristics which differ appreciably from those of neighbouring areas and/or the characteristics of the product are different.
>
> 2. In the case referred to in paragraph 1, the single natural or legal person who has submitted the application for registration shall be deemed to constitute a group within the meaning of Article 5 of Regulation (EEC) No 2081/92.

55. These conditions define only the conditions under which a natural or legal person, as opposed to a group as defined in the second subparagraph of Article 5 (1) of Regulation 2081/92, may apply for registration. As can be seen, these conditions have nothing to do with nationality.

Question 23

How do you interpret the term "nationals" as used in Article 1.3, including footnote 1, and Articles 3.1 and 4 of the TRIPS Agreement and Article 2 of the Paris Convention (1967) in relation to this dispute? Do a Member's nationals necessarily include natural persons who are domiciled, or legal persons who have a real and effective industrial and commercial establishment, in that Member?

56. As regards the definition of nationals in Article 3.1 and 4 of the TRIPS Agreement and Article 2.1 of the Paris Convention, a distinction must be made between natural and legal persons. For natural persons, a national is any person who holds the nationality of the State in question in conformity with the legislation of such state. As regards legal persons, the question of nationality depends on the law of the state in question, which may use criteria such as the law of incorporation, headquarters, or other criteria. The legal situation has been summed up by Bodenhausen in his commentary to Article 2.1 of the Paris Convention as follows:[19]

> In deciding the question who are such nationals, account has to be taken of the fact that the Convention can also apply to *legal persons or entities*, so that a distinction must be made between the nationality of *natural* and *legal* persons, respectively.

[19] Bodenhausen, Guide to the Application of the Paris Convention for the Protection of Industrial Property, p. 27-28 (1968).

> With respect to *natural* persons, nationality is a quality accorded or withdrawn by the legislation of the State whose nationality is claimed. Therefore it is only the legislation of that State which can define the said nationality and which must be applied also in other countries where it is invoked.
>
> With respect to *legal* persons, the question is more complicated because generally no "nationality" as such is granted to legal persons by existing legislations. Where these legal persons are the States themselves, or State enterprises, or other bodies of *public status*, it would be logical to accord to them the nationality of their country. With regard to corporate bodies of *private status*, such as companies and associations, the authorities of the countries where application of the Convention is sought will have to decide on the criterion of "nationality" which they will employ. This "nationality" can be made dependent upon the law according to which these legal persons have been constituted, or upon the law of their actual headquarters, or even on other criteria. Such law will also decide whether a legal person or entity really exists.

57. Natural persons who are merely domiciled in a State, but are not nationals of that state, are not "nationals" within the meaning of the national treatment provisions of the TRIPS Agreement and the Paris Convention. Similarly, legal persons who have a real and effective industrial and commercial establishment in a State, but do not fulfil the conditions for nationality of such state, are not nationals of such state. Domicile and establishment can therefore not simply be equated with "nationality" within the meaning of the national treatment provisions of the TRIPS Agreement and the Paris Convention.

58. That nationality on the one hand, and domicile or establishment on the other hand, are not identical concepts also follows from the context of the Paris Convention. First of all, if all persons domiciled or established in a particular State were its nationals, then the separate prohibition on conditions of domicile or establishment in Article 2.2 of the Paris Convention would be devoid of all useful purpose.

59. More importantly still, Article 3 of the Paris Convention enlarges the national treatment obligation to "nationals of countries outside the Union who are domiciled or who have real and effective industrial or commercial establishments in the territory of one of the countries of the Union". This provision would be completely unnecessary if all residents of a member of the Union were in any event to be considered as its nationals, and therefore benefited from national treatment under Article 2.1 of the Paris Convention. Article 3 of the Paris Convention therefore clearly illustrates that the Paris Convention, and similarly also the corresponding provisions of the TRIPS Agreement, regard nationality as a concept different from domicile or residence.

60. Finally, this is also illustrated by footnote 1 to Article 1.3 of the TRIPS Agreement. This footnote defines nationals, *in the case of a separate customs territory which is a WTO Member*, to mean persons natural or legal who are

domiciled or who have a real and effective industrial or commercial establishment in that customs territory. This definition was necessary since separate customs territories are not states, and therefore normally do not have "nationals". Thus, the criterion of residence or establishment is used here as a replacement for the criterion of nationality, which cannot apply to separate customs territories. In turn, this special definition for custom territories would have been unnecessary had this been already the normal meaning of "nationality". Once more, footnote 1 to Article 1.3 proves that nationality and residence or establishment are not identical concepts under Articles 3.1 and 4 TRIPS and 2.1 Paris Convention.

Question 24

In your view, which natural or legal persons can be considered "interested parties" in the sense of Article 22.2 of the TRIPS Agreement? Is Article 10(2) of the Paris Convention (1967) relevant?

61. The notion of "interested parties" must be defined in relation to the intellectual property rights that Article 22.2 seeks to protect. Article 22.2 is included in Section 3 of Part II of the TRIPS Agreement dealing with "Geographical Indications" and is entitled "Protection of geographical indications". Moreover, the introductory phrase of Article 22.2 provides that the obligation set out in that provision apply "in respect of geographical indications". Accordingly, for purposes of Article 22.2, "interested parties" are those which can claim an interest in the protection of a geographical indication, and not of other intellectual property rights, such as, for example, a conflicting trademark.

62. The definition of "interested parties" in Article 10(2) of the Paris Convention does not apply to Article 10*bis*, which is the only provision of the Paris Convention referred to in Article 22.2 of the TRIPS Agreement. Nor should Article 10*bis* be extrapolated by way of contextual interpretation to Article 22.2. Article 10*bis* is concerned with false "indications of source", a notion which is much broader than that of geographical indications, as defined in Article 22.1 of the TRIPS Agreement.

63. Without prejudice to the above, the EC recalls that Regulation 2081/92 grants to "any legitimately concerned legal or natural person"[20] the right to object to the registration of a geographical indication. The EC considers that this wording is broad enough to encompass all "interested parties", as defined in Article 10*bis* of the Paris Convention.

Question 25

Is it appropriate to compare nationals who are interested in GIs that refer to areas located in different WTO Members in order to examine national treatment under the TRIPS Agreement? Why or why not?

---

[20] Cf. Article 7(4). Equivalent wording is used in Articles 12b(2) and 12d(1), which confer a right of objection to any legal or natural person with a "legitimate interest".

64. The EC is not entirely certain that it understands the meaning of the phrase "nationals who are interested in GIs that refer to areas located in different WTO Members" in the present context. However, the EC would like to recall that national treatment under the TRIPS requires a comparison as between domestic and foreign *nationals* who are otherwise in the same situation.

Question 26

If national treatment can be examined in relation to GIs in terms of the location of the geographical area to the territory of a Member, is it appropriate to examine national treatment in relation to any other intellectual property rights in terms of an attachment to a Member besides the nationality of the right holder? Why or why not?

65. The EC would once again like to stress that the term "nationality" in Articles 3.1 and 4 TRIPS and 2.1 Paris Convention is not linked to an attachment to the territory of a Member.

66. Moreover, the EC would like to stress that the term "national" must be given a uniform meeting regardless of which intellectual property right is concerned. It is incontestable that in accordance with Article 22.1 TRIPS, geographical indications are characterised by a link with a particular geographical area. However, this link, which is an inherent part of the definition of a geographical indication, provides no justification for defining the term "national" in Articles 3.1 and 4 TRIPS and 2.1 Paris Convention differently when geographical indications are concerned.

Question 29

The Japan - Alcoholic Beverages II, Korea - Alcoholic Beverages and Chile - Alcoholic Beverages disputes show that measures which are origin-neutral on their face can be inconsistent with Article III of GATT 1994. Is Regulation (EC) No. 2081/92 also open to challenge under Article 3.1 of the TRIPS Agreement despite its apparently national-neutral text?

67. The EC notes that the disputes *Japan - Alcoholic Beverages II*, *Korea - Alcoholic Beverages* and *Chile - Alcoholic Beverages* all concerned tax measures which were found to be incompatible with Article III:2 of the GATT.

68. The EC considers that this jurisprudence concerning the interpretation of Article III:2 of the GATT is not relevant for the present dispute. Article III:2 GATT is a provision dealing specifically with national treatment as regards internal taxes or other internal charges. As the Appellate Body has stated in *EC – Asbestos*, there are important textual and structural differences between Articles III:2 and III:4 of the GATT. Accordingly, the Appellate Body found for instance that the term "like products" in Article III:4 GATT could not be interpreted in the same way as the same term in the first sentence of Article III:2 GATT.[21]

---

[21] Appellate Body Report, *EC – Asbestos*, para. 94-96.

69. These findings of the Appellate Body confirm that national treatment provisions cannot simply be assumed to have the same scope and meaning, but must be interpreted on the basis of their specific wording and context. If this already applies between two paragraphs of Article III GATT, even more caution is necessary when attempting to transpose national treatment principles from one agreement to another.

70. As the Panel in *Canada – Pharmaceutical Patents* has convincingly explained, there is therefore no general concept of discrimination which would be common to all WTO Agreements. Rather, the meaning of each provision prescribing equal treatment must be established on the basis of the precise legal text in issue:[22]

> In considering how to address these conflicting claims of discrimination, the Panel recalled that various claims of discrimination, *de jure* and de facto, have been the subject of legal rulings under GATT or the WTO. These rulings have addressed the question whether measures were in conflict with various GATT or WTO provisions prohibiting variously defined forms of discrimination. As the Appellate Body has repeatedly made clear, each of these rulings has necessarily been based on the precise legal text in issue, so that it is not possible to treat them as applications of a general concept of discrimination. Given the very broad range of issues that might be involved in defining the word "discrimination" in Article 27.1 of the TRIPS Agreement, the Panel decided that it would be better to defer attempting to define that term at the outset, but instead to determine which issues were raised by the record before the Panel, and to define the concept of discrimination to the extent necessary to resolve those issues.

71. The EC would suggest that such a case-specific approach would also be appropriate in the present case. In this context, the EC would not exclude entirely that under certain circumstances, measures which are neutral on their face may nonetheless constitute less favourable treatment of foreign nationals. However, the EC would suggest that when considering whether Regulation 2081/92 involves discrimination as between nationals within the meaning of Article 3.1 TRIPS and 2.1 of the Paris Convention, the Panel should also take account of the following considerations:

72. First, Article 3 TRIPS refers to nationals. This specific reference, which differs from Art III:4 GATT, must be given meaning. For this reason, it should not be argued that because a measure involves discrimination on the basis of the origin of a good, or of domicile and establishment, it also constitutes de facto discrimination of nationals, since such discrimination is already covered by Article III:4 GATT, or Article 2.2 of the Paris Convention.

73. Second, the Appellate Body has held repeatedly that *de facto* discrimination is a notion intended to prevent circumvention of national

---

22 Panel Report, *Canada - Pharmaceutical Patents*, para. 7.98 (footnotes omitted).

treatment obligations.[23] Such a risk does not exist if a specific issue is already dealt with in other national treatment provisions, such as those of the GATT.

74. Third, the national treatment provisions of the TRIPS and the GATT should not systematically overlap. The Panel must also take account the different legal context of the provisions, which are contained in different agreements. For example, the Panel would have to consider whether Articles XX and XXIV GATT, which are available as defenses against national treatment claims under the GATT, could also apply under the TRIPS Agreement. This is an issue of major systemic implications, which should be taken into account in the interpretation of the national treatment provisions of the TRIPS Agreement.

Question 30

In Article 2(1) of the Paris Convention (1967) as incorporated in the TRIPS Agreement by its Article 2.1, should the words "country of the Union" be read mutatis mutandis to refer to "WTO Member"?

75. Yes.

Question 31

What is the respective scope of the national treatment obligations in Article 2(1) of the Paris Convention (1967) and Article 3.1 of the TRIPS Agreement? Do they overlap?

76. The scope of the national treatment obligations in Article 2(1) of the Paris Convention (1967) and Article 3.1 of the TRIPS Agreement must be derived from the precise wording of those provisions. Given the closely parallel wording of the two provisions, it appears to the EC that they overlap to a considerable extent.

Question 33

Is there a public policy requirement specific to GIs which underlies the requirement that a group or person must send a registration application under Regulation (EC) No. 2081/92 to the EC Member State or authorities of a third country in which the geographical area is located, rather than directly to the Commission?

77. The requirement that a group or person must send a registration application to the EC Member State or authorities of a third country in which the geographical area is located reflects the important role that Member States or third country authorities play in the registration process under Regulation 2081/92.

78. According to Article 5 (5) of Regulation 2081/92, the Member State shall check that the application is justified and shall forward the application, including the product specification referred to in Article 4 and other documents on which it

[23] Cf. Appellate Body Report, *EC – Bananas III*, para. 233; Appellate Body Report, *Canada – Autos*, para. 142.

has based its decision, to the Commission. In a recent judgment, the European Court of Justice has explained that this role of Member States is due in particular to the detailed knowledge of Member States in respect of geographic indications relating to their territory:[24]

> It follows that the decision to register a designation as a PDO or as a PGI may only be taken by the Commission if the Member State concerned has submitted to it an application for that purpose and that such an application may only be made if the Member State has checked that it is justified. That system of division of powers is attributable particularly to the fact that registration assumes that it has been verified that a certain number of conditions have been met, which requires, to a great extent, detailed knowledge of matters particular to the Member State concerned, matters which the competent authorities of that State are best placed to check.

79. These same considerations are also underlying the requirement in Article 12a (2) of the Regulation, according to which the third country must verify that the requirements of the Regulation are verified before it transmits the application. Indeed, the need for an involvement of the national authorities appears even more compelling when the application concerns a geographical indication from a third country rather than from a Member State.

80. First, the evaluation of whether a name fulfils the conditions for protection as a geographical indication requires familiarity with a host of geographical, natural, climatic and cultural factors specific to the geographical area in question. Moreover, knowledge of the market conditions in the country of origin may also be required, e.g. in order to establish whether the product in question has a particular reputation. Like in the case of applications from Member State, it is the third country's authorities which are best placed to evaluate such factors. In contrast, the European Commission is less likely to be familiar with such factors than in the case of an area in a Member State. Moreover, the evaluation may also require knowledge of the language of the third country in question, which the authorities of the European Community may not have.

81. Second, the evaluation of the application may require the assessment of legal questions arising under the law of the country where the area is located. In particular, Article 12a of the Regulation requires the application to be accompanied by a description of the legal provisions and the usage on the basis of which the geographical indication is protected or established in the third country. The Commission cannot unilaterally resolve such issues pertaining to the law of a third country, which therefore necessarily require the implication of the authorities of the third country.

82. Third, the involvement of the third country government appears called for also out of respect for the sovereignty of the third country. The assessment of whether an application meets the requirements of the Regulation, in particular

---

[24] Case C-269/99, *Karl Kühne*, [2001] ECR I-9517, para. 53 (Exhibit EC-19).

concerning the link with the geographical area, requires in-depth knowledge of the conditions related to this area, as well as the possibility to verify on the spot the relevant claims made in the application. It would not be possible for the European Commission to carry out such inspections on the territory of the third country without the agreement or involvement of the third country.

83. Fourth, the involvement of the third country government also facilitates the cooperation of the authorities of the Community and of the third country throughout the registration process. If doubts or question arise during the registration process, the European Commission may need a contact point in the third country to which it can address itself. Moreover, the Regulation foresees that the third country which has transmitted the application must be consulted at certain stages of the procedure before the Commission can take a decision (cf. Articles 12b [1] [b]; 12b [3]).

84. Fifth, the involvement of the third country authorities should also be beneficial to the applicant. Regulation 2081/92 effectively enables the applicant to discuss, prepare, file, and where necessary refine and amend his application directly with the authorities where the geographical area is located. Since these authorities are more familiar with the area in question, this should help speed up the registration process. Moreover, frequently these authorities may be geographically closer to the applicant and may speak the applicant's language, which may also be a further benefit to the applicant.

Question 34

Is there a public policy requirement specific to GIs which underlies the requirement that a person wishing to object to a registration under Regulation (EC) No. 2081/92 must send an objection to the EC Member State or authorities of a third country in which he resides or is established, rather than directly to the Commission?

85. Article 12d(1) requires any natural or legal person that has a legitimate interest and is from a WTO Member Country to transmit a duly substantiated statement to the country in which it resides or is established, which shall transmit it to the Commission.

86. It is to be noted that under this provision, the third country is not required to verify the admissibility of the objection on the basis of the criteria laid down in Article 7(4) of the Regulation. Accordingly, the transmission of such applications does not require the same degree of verification as the transmission of applications for registration, and should therefore not be particularly burdensome for third countries.

87. Despite this somewhat less important role of third countries in the transmission of statements of objection, some degree of involvement of the third country government remains necessary. First, it is necessary to verify whether the person objecting is indeed resident or established in the third country, which is only possible for the authorities of that country. Second, it is not excluded that in the further procedure, questions relating to the territory of the third country might arise, in which case it is useful for there to be an official contact point in

the third country. Third, it should also be beneficial to the person making the objection to be able to deal directly with an authority in the country where it is resident or established. Finally, if a statement of objection is admissible, Article 12d (3) provides that the third country which has transmitted the statement of objection is to be consulted before the Commission takes its decision.

Question 35

Has an objection to the registration of a name under Regulation (EC) No. 2081/92 ever been filed by a person from a third country? If so, what happened?

88. No.

Question 37

Please indicate examples of other international arrangements, such as the Madrid Protocol, under which national governments cooperate by acting as agents or intermediaries in the protection of private rights. Which of these arrangements are established under international treaties and which under the legislation of one of the parties to the arrangement? Which are relevant to the matter before the Panel?

89. There are a large number of examples in international law and practice in which national governments cooperate by acting as agents or intermediaries in the protection of private rights. Given the limited time available, the EC will limit itself to providing some examples drawn from a number of different sectors.

90. As referred to by the Panel, a first example is already provided by Article 2 (2) of the Protocol to the Madrid Agreement concerning the international registration of trademarks (Exhibit EC-20), which reads as follows:

> The application for international registration (hereinafter referred to as "the international application") shall be filed with the International Bureau through the intermediary of the Office with which the basic application was filed or by which the basic registration was made (hereinafter referred to as "the Office of origin"), as the case may be.

91. Similar examples where the protection of an intellectual property right requires action of the home country of the right holder can also be found in other agreements. For instance, Article 6 quinquies A (1) of the Paris Convention provides that Members of the Union may require, before registering a trademark duly registered in the country of origin, a certificate of registration in the country of origin, issued by the competent authority.

92. Similarly, Article 5(1) of the Lisbon Agreement for the Protection of Appellations of Origin (Exhibit EC-21) provides that applications for the registration of appellations of origin must be requested by the offices of the countries of the Special Union:

> The registration of appellations of origin shall be effected at the International Bureau, at the request of the Offices of the countries of the Special Union, in the name of any natural persons or legal entities, public or private, having, according to their national legislation, a right to use such appellations.

93. Such examples for requirements for cooperation between governmental authorities can also be found outside the area of intellectual property protection. For instance, the Specific Annex on Origin to the International Convention on the Simplification and Harmonisation of Customs Procedures (Kyoto Convention) provides that in certain cases, a certificate of origin issued by the competent authorities of the country of origin may be required.[25] Moreover, the Specific Annex also provides that in certain cases, the customs authorities of the importing party may request the competent authorities of the party where the certificate of origin has been established to carry out controls.[26]

94. Further examples can be found in the field of technical standards and conformity assessment. For instance, the EC has concluded mutual recognition agreements with both the United States and Australia. Under these agreements, the parties mutually recognize the results of conformity assessment carried out by conformity assessment bodies recognized under the agreement. Each party designates its conformity assessment bodies to be recognized under the agreement.[27] Moreover, each party remains responsible for monitoring the conformity assessment bodies which it has designated.[28]

95. Similar arrangements can be found in the field of transport. According to Article 31 of the Chicago Convention on International Civil Aviation (Exhibit EC-25), every aircraft engaged in international navigation shall be provided with a certificate of airworthiness issued or rendered valid by the State in which it is registered. Similarly, according to Article 32 of the Chicago Convention, the pilot of every aircraft and the other members of the crew of every aircraft engaged in international civil aviation shall be provided with certificates of competency and licences issued or rendered valid by the State in which the aircraft is registered.

96. Another example can be drawn from the field of fisheries. In accordance with Article 62 of the UN Convention on the Law of the Sea, bilateral agreements may give other states access to fishing resources in the exclusive economic zone of a coastal state. However, the applications for fishing licenses must usually be transmitted by the authorities of the fishing state to those of the coastal state. By way of example, reference can be made to the Annex of the bilateral fisheries agreement between the European Community and Mozambique (Exhibit EC-26), which provides the following:

---

25 Specific Annex K to the Kyoto Convention, pts. 2 to 5, 9-12 (Exhibit EC-22).

26 Appendix III to Specific Annex K to the Kyoto Convention, pt. 3 (Exhibit EC-22).

27 Cf. Article 7 of the Agreement with the United States (Exhibit EC-23); Article 5 of the Agreement with Australia (Exhibit EC-24).

28 Cf. Article 10 of the Agreement with the United States (Exhibit EC-23); cf. also Article 8 of the Agreement with Australia (Exhibit EC-24).

> The procedure to be followed in applying for and issuing licences authorising Community vessels to fish in Mozambican waters shall be as follows:
>
> (a) for each vessel, the European Commission, acting via its representative in Mozambique and through the agency of its delegation in that country, shall submit to the Mozambican authorities a licence application drawn up by the vessel owner wishing to carry on fishing activities under this Agreement; the application shall be submitted no later than 25 days before the start of the validity period mentioned therein. Applications shall be made using the forms provided for this purpose by Mozambique, specimens of which are given in Appendix 1 for tuna seiners and longliners, and in Appendices 1 and 2 for freezer bottom trawlers. They shall be accompanied by proof of payment of the advance payable by the vessel owner;

97. Finally, examples can also be found in the field of judicial cooperation in civil and commercial matters. For instance, Article 3 of the Hague Convention on the Service Abroad of Judicial and Extrajudicial Documents in Civil or Commercial Matters (Exhibit EC-27) provides as follows:

> The authority or judicial officer competent under the law of the State in which the documents originate shall forward to the Central Authority of the State addressed a request conforming to the model annexed to the present Convention, without any requirement of legalisation or other equivalent formality.

98. Finally, the EC would like to recall that it is a common feature of customary international law that states act on behalf of their nationals and their rights and interest. This is most clearly recognized in the institution of diplomatic protection, on the basis of which states may raise claims against other states on the basis of injury suffered by the national of the claiming state.[29]

99. That fact that most of the examples above are drawn from international agreements does not diminish their relevance for the present case. Rather, these examples illustrate that in an increasingly interdependent world, the effective protection of individual rights in cross-border situations inevitable engenders a need for cross-border cooperation.

100. The EC considers that the examples quoted above are merely a fraction of the cases where intergovernmental cooperation occurs in the cross-border protection of individual rights. The EC reserves the right to elaborate further on this question in the later stages of the procedure. However, at this stage, the EC would like to remark that the Panel should be mindful that the claims of the complainants may have implications that go far beyond the present case.

---

[29] Cf. Diplomatic Protection of Foreign Nationals, in: Encyclopaedia of Public International Law, Vol. 1, p. 1067 (1992).

Question 39

Does an EC member State participate in decision-making on a proposed registration either in the Committee established under Article 15 of Regulation (EC) No. 2081/92 or in the Council of Ministers, where that EC member State transmitted the application or an objection to it to the Commission? Is the EC member State identified with the applicant or person raising the objection in any way? Are there any limits on the participation of the EC member State - for instance, can it object to an application which it transmitted?

101. The Committee assisting the Commission in accordance with Article 15(1) of Regulation 2081/92 is composed of representatives of all Member States. This includes also the Member State which has transmitted the application or the statement of objection.

102. As the EC has already explained in its first written submission,[30] the constitution of regulatory committees is a typical modality under which the Council of Ministers delegates regulatory powers to the European Commission. Regulatory committees such as the one foreseen in Article 15(1) of Regulation 2081/92 are therefore an integral part of the Community's constitutional system.

103. When fulfilling their functions under Regulation 2081/92, a Member State is in no way identified with the applicant or the person raising the objection. In verifying the applications or statements of objection, the Member State must correctly, impartially and objectively apply the terms of the Regulation. Similarly, when exercising its role in the Committee, the Member States must be guided by the terms of the Regulation, and not act as a representative of any individual applicant or objecting person.

104. It should be noted that already when examining the admissibility of an application, the Member State must take into account all objections from within its own country, and resolve these before transmitting the application. The situation envisaged in the last sentence of the question can therefore not occur. This has been clarified in a recent judgment of the European Court of Justice:[31]

> In this connection, it should be observed that it follows from the wording and the scheme of Article 7 of Regulation No 2081/92 that a statement of objection to a registration cannot come from the Member State which has applied for the registration and that the objection procedure established by Article 7 of that regulation is not therefore intended to settle disputes between the competent authority of the Member State which has applied for registration of a designation and a natural or legal person resident or established in that Member State.

---

30 EC, FWS, paras. 79 to 83.

31 Case C-269/99, *Karl Kühne*, [2001] ECR I-9517, para. 55 (Exhibit EC-19).

Question 40

How many applications to register names under Regulation (EC) No. 2081/92 have been considered by the Committee established under Article 15 of the Regulation or the Council of Ministers?

105. Under the simplified procedure foreseen in Article 17 of Regulation 2081/92 as applicable until its amendment through Regulation 692/2003, the consultation of the Committee was required in all cases. A number of these applications were also, for various reasons, referred to the Council.

106. As regards the normal procedure, out of 171 applications, only a small number (10) have been considered by the Committee. Non of these cases was referred to the Council.

107. For the convenience of the Panel, the EC submits as Exhibit EC-28 a table which sets out in more detail the different cases of consultation of the Committee and referral to the Council.

Question 41

In paragraph 137 of your first written submission, you indicate that the term "such names" in the second suparagraph of Article 12(2) of Regulation (EC) No. 2081/92 is a reference to the first suparagraph of Article 12(2), and that this means that the requirement to indicate the country of origin applies where "a protected name of a third country is identical to a Community protected name". Please clarify the meaning of the following terms, as used in Article 12(2) of Regulation (EC) No. 2081/92:

> *(a)* *what is the meaning of the term "protected" in the phrase "a protected name of a third country"?*

108. Both in "protected name of a third country" and in "Community protected name", "protected" in principle means "protected under Regulation 2081/92". However, the provision also applies where protection under Regulation 2081/92 is sought for a protected name from a third country.

> *(b)* *does the phrase "a Community protected name" cover both names of geographical areas located in the EC as well as in third countries, registered under the Regulation?*

109. No. "Community protected name" covers only protected names of areas located in the EC.

> *(c)* *does the requirement to indicate the country of origin apply also where a name of a geographical area located in the EC is identical to a Community protected name (irrespective of whether this Community protected name is the name of a geographical area located in the EC or in a third country).*

110. No. "Community protected name" covers only protected names of areas located in the EC. Moreover, the provision applies only to protected names.

Question 42

If Article 12(2) of Regulation (EC) No. 2081/92 applies to the registration of a name of a geographical area located in the EC that is identical to a name, already registered in the EC, of an area located in a third country, what is the difference in its scope compared to Article 6(6) of the Regulation? Why is it necessary to cover this situation in both provisions?

111. Article 12(2) is a specific provision dealing with certain cases of conflicts between homonyms which may arise between Community and third country protected names. Article 6(6) is a more general provision dealing with a wider set of conflicts, and notably conflicts between homonyms from within the Community, but including also conflicts involving third country names not yet resolved by Article 12(2), for instance between names from within the same third country, or between third countries.

Question 43

Where does Regulation (EC) No. 2081/92 provide for the registration of a name of a geographical area located in a third country WTO Member which is a homonym of an already registered name? Where does it provide for the registration of a name which is a homonym of an already registered name of a geographical area located in a third country WTO Member?

112. As regards the first question, if the already registered name is a name from the Community, this situation would be covered by Article 12(2) of Regulation 2081/92. As regards the second question, if the name to be registered is from the Community, this situation would equally be covered by Article 12(2).

Question 44

Can the EC provide the Panel with any official statement predating its first written submission that Article 12(2) of Regulation (EC) No. 2081/92 applies to names of geographical areas located in the EC and that Article 12(2) will be applied on the basis of the date of registration?

113. No. The EC would like to remark that since there have been no cases of application of Article 12(2) so far, the EC has not felt a need to make official statements as regards the application of this provision.

Question 45

With respect to paragraph 135 of the EC's first written submission, could the Council of Ministers prevent a registration because the Commission applied Article 12(2) to names of geographical areas located in the EC on the basis of the date of registration?

114. No. As the Commission, the Council is bound by law to apply the terms of Regulation 2081/92.

Question 46

Has a judicial authority ever ruled on the applicability of Article 12(2) of Regulation (EC) No. 2081/92? If the Commission applied Article 12(2) to the name of a geographical area located in the EC on the basis of the date of registration, could that action be subject to judicial review due to the fact that the area was located in the EC?

115. Since Article 12(2) has never been applied, no judicial authority has ever had the occasion to interpret this provision.

116. Any Commission decision regarding the registration of a geographical indication can be the subject of judicial review under the conditions to which the EC has referred in its response to Question 19.[32]

Question 49

Do you seek separate rulings on the procedural aspects of Regulation (EC) No. 2081/92 or a ruling on the Regulation as a whole? For example, should the provision in Article 12(2) be examined in isolation, or would it be appropriate to adopt an approach like the Panel in Korea – Beef, which only examined a display sign requirement within its findings related to a system as a whole?

117. In accordance with Article 3.7 of the DSU, the purpose of the present proceedings is to secure a positive solution to the dispute. In the view of the EC, securing a positive solution to the dispute requires the Panel to address all the claims which have been raised by the complainants with respect to particular aspects of Regulation 2081/92.

118. Moreover, Article 19.1 of the DSU provides that where a Panel concludes that a measure is inconsistent with a covered agreement, it shall recommend the Member concerned to bring the measure in conformity. The Panel's recommendations are the basis for implementation in accordance with Article 21 of the DSU. In order to enable the Member to properly implement the Panel's recommendations, it is therefore essential that a Panel's recommendation be as specific and clear as possible.

119. For this reason, if the Panel came to the conclusion that certain aspects of Regulation 2081/92 are inconsistent with a covered agreement, it would be necessary that these aspects be specifically identified in the Panel's conclusions and recommendations in order to enable the EC to duly implement the report.

Question 50

In paragraph 451 of its first written submission, the EC argues that labels which address the geographical origin of a product cannot be considered a technical regulation under the TBT Agreement, since they do not apply to a "product, process or production method". Why in the EC's view is the geographical origin of a product not related to that product or its process or production method?

---

[32] Above para. 46 et seq.

Does the coverage of the TBT Agreement with respect to labels depend on the content of the labels?

120. First of all, the EC would like to recall that Article 12(2) is not a labelling requirement, but merely sets out the conditions under which geographical indications can be registered in the case of homonymous protected names from the EC and from a third country.

121. Second, it is clear that the origin of a product is not a "process or production method". The question can therefore only be whether the indication of the country of origin is a labelling requirement as it relates to a product. However, it seems to the EC that the origin of a product is different from the product itself.

122. Of course, the origin of a product may confer specific characteristics or a reputation on it, which may entitle it for protection as a geographical indication. However, these issues are already covered in the TRIPS, and do therefore not need to be addressed by the TBT Agreement. Moreover, as the EC has already remarked, the question of origin marking is already covered by the special disciplines of Article IX GATT.[33]

Question 51

How should the term "like products" be interpreted under Article 2.1 of the TBT Agreement? If the labelling requirement in Article 12(2) of Regulation (EC) No. 2081/92 applies to situations where identical names arise between imported products and EC products, but does not apply to situations where identical names arise between two EC products, to what extent would this be a distinction between "like situations" rather than a distinction between "like products"?

123. The EC agrees that Article 2.1 TBT Agreement requires a comparison between like products, not between "like situations". In the view of the EC, Australia has not shown that homonymous products from within the EC covered by Article 6 (6) of the Regulation would in any sense be "like" a third country product which is covered by Article 12(2) of the Regulation. Accordingly, Australia has failed to establish any claim under Article 2.1 TBT Agreement.

124. Moreover, the EC considers that under Australia's argument, the two situations are not even like. In fact, the comparable situation to two homonymous EC GIs protected under Regulation 2081/92 would be that of two homonymous Australian GI's protected under Australian law. This is obviously not a situation which can give rise to discrimination between Australian and EC products. In fact, as the EC has already stated, it does not understand how Australian products could be affected by the way in which conflicts between homonymous names from within the EC are resolved.

125. Since Australia has in any case failed to establish a case under Article 2.1 TBT Agreement, the EC considers that the Panel does not need to resolve the meaning of the expression "like products" in Article 2.1 TBT Agreement. As the

[33] EC FWS, paras. 450-451.

EC has already said in its first written submission, this is an issue of considerable legal complexity, which could not be resolved simply through transposition of jurisprudence on Article III:4 GATT, but rather would also have to take the structural differences between the TBT Agreement and the GATT into account.[34]

Question 54

Article 12(2) of Regulation (EC) No. 2081/92 is designed to avoid "practical risks of confusion". How would the application of the country of origin label on the basis of a product's date of registration help avoid those risks of confusion?

126. Typically, the geographical indication which is registered first will have been marketed under that name longer, and will therefore already be known by consumers. Inversely, the geographical indication which is registered later will have been used less long, and will be less known by consumers. It is therefore in line with consumer expectations to require appropriate labelling for the indication registered later. This solution also takes into account the fact that the older geographical indication is already registered, and that the terms of its protection can therefore no longer easily be amended.

Question 55

Does the TRIPS Agreement apply as lex specialis as regards GATT 1994 and the TBT Agreement, with respect to a practical condition to differentiate homonymous or identical GIs on a label? Please comment in the light of Article 23.3 of the TRIPS Agreement, which is applicable to homonymous GIs for wines, and the national treatment obligation, which is applicable to GIs for other products.

127. The EC would agree that Article 23.3 TRIPS must be considered as a *lex specialis* with respect to the practical conditions to differentiate homonymous or identical GIs on a label. Under this provision, the practical conditions for differentiation of homonymous indications will be determined by each Member, taking into account the need to ensure equitable treatment of the producers concerned and that consumers are not misled. This constitutes an exhaustive set of disciplines for this issue, which exclude the application of the national treatment provisions of the GATT and the TBT Agreement.

128. It is noteworthy that the TRIPS Agreement does not contain a corresponding provision for homonymous geographical indications for products other than wines. Therefore Members must decide whether and how to accord protection to homonymous geographical indications on the basis of the general provisions of Section 3, and notably of Article 22.4 of the TRIPS Agreement. This indicates that Member enjoy a greater degree of discretion as to how to resolve conflicts between homonyms for products other than wines. This further confirms the view of the EC that the national treatment provisions of the GATT, the TRIPS and the TBT Agreement should not be held to apply to Article 2(2) of Regulation 2081/92.

---

34 EC FWS, para. 474.

Question 57

Does the EC consider that it may apply equivalence and reciprocity conditions to WTO Members under Article 12a(2) or any other provision of Regulation (EC) No. 2081/92, even if Article 12(1) does not apply to them?

129. No. The EC merely requires that the conditions of Regulation 2081/92 regarding product specifications and inspections are met as regards the specific product for which protection is sought.

Question 59

Under what circumstances would the Commission consider the holder of a GI certification mark registered in another WTO Member to meet the requirements for inspection structures under Article 10 of Regulation (EC) 2081/92 (read together with Article 12a of that Regulation)?

130. The EC understands that the question of the Panel relates to a certification mark which protects the use of a name which would qualify for protection as a geographical indication under Regulation 2081/92.

131. Any inspection structure must comply with the conditions set out in Article 10 of Regulation 2081/92. According to Article 10 (2) of Regulation 2081/92, the inspection structures must offer adequate guarantees of objectivity and impartiality with regard to all producers or processors subject to their control. The answer to the question would therefore depend on how the holder of the certification mark is related to the producers or processors in question. If the holder is not itself a producer or processor, and is independent of them, then it would not seem excluded that it could also function as an inspection structure. Otherwise, it would be necessary to establish an independent inspection structure which offers the necessary guarantees of independence and impartiality.

Question 60

Australia argues that the EC's inspection structures requirements are a technical regulation under the TBT Agreement (paragraphs 209-224 of its first written submission). Is there a dividing line lies under the TBT Agreement between a technical regulation and a conformity assessment procedure? If so, where does it lie?

132. In the view of the EC, the dividing line follows clearly from the definitions in points 1 and 3 of Annex 1 to the TBT Agreement. According to point 1 of Annex 1, a technical regulation "lays down product characteristics". According to point 3, a conformity assessment procedure ensures that "relevant requirements in technical regulations [...] are fulfilled".

133. In other words, technical regulation set down product characteristics in general and abstract terms. Conformity assessment procedures verify the compliance of concrete products with such requirements. In yet other words, the difference is the one between abstract regulation and the enforcement of regulations in concrete cases.

134. In accordance with Article 10(1) of Regulation 2081/92, inspection structures ensure that agricultural products and foodstuffs bearing a protected name meet the requirements laid down in the specifications. In other words, inspection procedures ensure the compliance of concrete products with the abstract specifications. On the basis of the definitions set out above, there should therefore be no doubt that the requirements regarding inspection structures concern a conformity assessment procedure.

Question 61

If the inspection structures are conformity assessment procedures, are the eligibility criteria for registration under Regulation (EC) No. 2081/92, against which conformity is assessed, technical regulations?

135. As a preliminary point, the EC would like to remark that the only claim which Australia has raised with respect to the eligibility criteria for registration under Regulation 2081/92 concerns Article 12(2), i.e. the provision regarding homonymous protected names from the EC and third countries. The Panel does therefore not need to the address the question of whether other eligibility criteria contained in the Regulation might constitute technical regulations.

136. Furthermore, the EC notes that it is wrong to suggest that "conformity is assessed against" the eligibility criteria for registration. The existence of inspection structures constitutes a condition for registration. Accordingly, inspection structures do not ensure that the criteria for the eligibility of registration are met; they ensure that concrete products bearing a protected name comply with the product specifications.

137. In reality, the eligibility criteria for registration have nothing to do with technical regulations. They do not lay down characteristics for specific products, but apply for all geographical indications for which protection is sought under the Regulation. Accordingly, the Regulation, and in particular its eligibility criteria for registration, do no lay down product characteristics. Rather, they require the definition of product specifications as part of the application process. However, "requiring the definition of product characteristics" (by the applicant) is not the same thing as "laying down product characteristics".

138. Quite remarkably, Australia has characterised Regulation 2081/92 as "establishing a process related to product characteristics".[35] However, as the EC has already had the occasion to remark at the first meeting with the Panel, a measure "establishing a process related to product characteristics" is not the same thing as a measure actually laying down product characteristics.

139. Are the very most, the question could therefore be asked whether the individual product specifications for specific protected names constitute technical regulations. However, the EC notes that Australia has made no claims with respect to any particular specifications, and that this issue is therefore outside the terms of reference of the Panel.

---

[35] Oral Statement by Australia at the First Panel hearing, para. 43.

Question 63

What does Article 14(2) of Regulation (EC) No. 2081/92 mean where it provides that a prior trademark "may continue to be used"?

140. Article 14(2) of Regulation 2081/92 is an exception to Article 13(1) of the same regulation, which provides that registered geographical indications shall be protected against certain practices, including certain uses of trademarks. Article 14(2) allows trademark owners to continue to use their trademarks in relation to goods which do not comply with the requirements of the geographical indication, in circumstances where such use would be prohibited by Article 13(1).

Can a trademark owner invoke the rights conferred by the trademark registration against the user of a GI used in accordance with its GI registration?

141. Article 14(2) of Regulation 2081/92 does not confer to a trademark owner the right to prevent the use of the name, as such, that has been registered as a geographical indication by the right holders of such indication. That would render meaningless the registration of that name as a geographical indication and the protection attached to such registration by Article 13(1).

142. On the other hand, and contrary to what is erroneously assumed by the United States[36], a trademark owner may use its trademark rights in order to prevent the right holders of a geographical indication from using confusingly any other names or other signs (e.g. graphic signs) in conjunction with, or in place of, the name registered as a geographical indication, which are not covered by such registration. In other words, the right holders of a geographical indication only have a positive right to use the name registered as a geographical indication. That right does not extend to other names or signs which have been not been registered. If the use of such unregistered names or signs leads to likelihood of confusion with the same or a similar sign which is the subject of a valid trademark it may be prevented by the owner of that trademark.

143. Furthermore, while the right holders of a geographical indication have a positive right to use the registered name, this does not mean that they are allowed to use it in any possible manner. As explained[37], the name registered as a geographical indication must be used in accordance with the generally applicable provisions of Directive 2000/13 on the labelling, presentation and advertising of foodstuffs[38] and of Directive 84/450 on misleading advertising[39], as well as with the unfair competition laws of the Member States.[40]

---

[36] US Oral Statement paras. 54-55.

[37] EC's First Submission, para. 319. See also the responses of the EC and its Member States to the review under Article 24.2 of the TRIPS Agreement contained in document IP/C/W/117/Add10 (Exhibit EC-29).

[38] Exhibit EC-30. See in particular Article 2.1, which provides that

> The labelling and methods used must not: (a) be such as could mislead the purchaser to a material degree, particularly: (i) as to the characteristics of the foodstuff and, in particular, as to its … origin or provenance …

[39] Exhibit EC-31. Article 2.2 of the Directive defines "misleading advertising" as

Question 64

Does Article 14(2) of Regulation (EC) No. 2081/92 implement the provision in Article 24.5 of the TRIPS Agreement that measures adopted to implement the Section on GIs shall not prejudice "eligibility for or validity of the registration of a trademark, or the right to use a trademark" or does it only implement the provision that such measures shall not prejudice "the right to use a trademark"?

144. As explained in the EC's First Written Submission (paragraph 302), Article 14(1) of Regulation 2081/92 maintains the eligibility of the applications and the validity of the registrations grandfathered by Article 24.5 of the TRIPS Agreement, while Article 14(2) preserves the right of the owners of grandfathered trademarks to continue to use their trademarks concurrently with a registered geographical indication.

Question 65

Does the scope of Article 14(2) of Regulation (EC) No. 2081/92, as drafted, include trademarks applied for or registered, or to which rights have been acquired, subsequent to both dates set out in Article 24.5(a) and (b) of the TRIPS Agreement?

145. This question does not appear to be relevant to resolve the issues before the Panel, since the complainants have not made any claim to the effect that the temporal criteria laid down in Article 14(2) of Regulation 2081/92 would be somehow inconsistent with those of Article 24.5 of the TRIPS Agreement. Were the complainants to raise any such claim at this stage of the proceedings, it would have to be considered outside the terms of reference of the Panel.

146. In any event, Article 14(2) is fully consistent with Article 24.5 of the TRIPS Agreement. Any trademark applied for, or established by use, before 1 January 1996, but after the date of application for a registered geographical indication, could not be deemed to have been so "in good faith".

147. Furthermore, the complainants have not alleged, let alone proved, that the registration of any of the geographical indications that were applied for before 1 January 1996, which constitute a closed category, has resulted or will result in a likelihood of confusion with any of the trademarks that were applied for, registered, or established by use before 1 January 1996, but after the date of the application for the geographical indication, which also constitute a closed category.

> "any advertising which in any way, including presentation, deceives or is likely to deceive the person to whom it is addressed or whom it reaches and which, by reason of its deceptive nature, is likely yoto affect their economic behaviour or which, for those reasons, injures or is likely to injure a competitor".

Article 3 provides that in determining whether advertising is misleading account shall be taken *inter alia* of information concerning the geographic or commercial origin of the goods and of the rights of the advertiser, including ownership of commercial, industrial and intellectual property rights.

[40] References to the relevant laws of the Member States are found in their responses to the review under Article 24.2 of the TRIPS Agreement. (Exhibit EC-29)

Question 66

Has Article 14(2) of Regulation (EC) No. 2081/92 ever been applied in a specific case? For example, what did the national courts finally decide in the Gorgonzola case, referred to in Exhibit US-17 and in footnote 140 to paragraph 163 of the US first written submission, after the order of the European Court of Justice?

148. Article 14(2) of Regulation 2081/92 does not have to be "applied" by the registering authorities. Rather, it sets out the legal consequences that follow from a decision providing for the registration of a proposed geographical indication.

149. The "Cambozola"[41] case mentioned in the question remains so far the only instance where Article 14(2) has been interpreted by the European Court of Justice. In essence, the issues in dispute in that case were whether the use of the trademark "Cambozola" fell within one of the situations listed under Article 13(1) and, if so, whether the conditions laid down in Article 14(2) for allowing the continued use of that trademark were met.

150. The European Court of Justice concluded that the use of the trademark "Cambozola" might be deemed to evoke the registered geographical indication "Gorgonzola" and, therefore, fall within the scope of Article 13(1)(b), even if the true origin was indicated in the package. As regards the question of whether the trademark "Cambozola" could continue to be used in accordance with Article 14(2) the Court ruled that

> ... It is for the national court to decide whether, on the facts, the conditions laid down in Article 14(2) of Regulation No 2081/92 allow use of an earlier trademark to continue notwithstanding the registration of the protected designation of origin 'Gorgonzola', having regard in particular to the law in force at the time of registration of the trade mark, in order to determine whether such registration could have been made in good faith, on the basis that use of a name such as 'Cambozola' does not, per se, constitute an attempt to deceive the consumer.

151. Following the Judgement of the European Court of Justice, the Supreme Court of Austria ruled that the trademark "Cambozola" had been registered in good faith and was not affected by any ground of invalidity and, therefore, in accordance with Article 14(2), could continue to be used concurrently with the registered geographical indication "Gorgonzola".[42]

152. The EC Commission is not aware of any other decisions of the courts of the Member States where Article 14(2) has been interpreted.

---

[41] Judgement of the European Court of Justice of 4 March 1999, Case C- 87/97, *Consorzio per la tutela del Fromaggio Gorgonzola v. Kaeserai Champignon Hofmeister GmbH & Co. KG, Eduard Bracharz GMbH.* (Exhibit EC-32).

[42] Austrian Supreme Court (Oberster Gerichtshof), Case 40625/01 G, Judgement of 7 October 2001.

Question 67

Does Article 14(3) of Regulation (EC) No. 2081/92 affect the possibility of coexistence of GIs already on the register with prior trademarks, such as Gorgonzola? In these cases, is Article 14(3) relevant to the applicability of Article 14(2)?

153. Article 14(3) remains relevant even after a geographical indication has been formally registered. The owner of a concurrent trademark (e.g. "Cambozola") could challenge before the courts the decision to register the geographical indication by claiming that the decision is inconsistent with Article 14(3).

Question 68

Article 14(3) of Regulation (EC) No. 2081/92 mentions certain criteria. If these are not exhaustive, why does is it not expressly stated as in Articles 3(1), 4(2) and 6(6) of the Regulation?

154. At the outset, it is useful to recall the wording of Article 14(3) of Regulation 2081/92:

> A designation of origin or geographical indication shall not be registered where, in the light of trade mark's reputation and renown and the length of time it has been used, registration is liable to mislead the consumer as to the true origin of the product.

155. Thus, contrary to what has been claimed by the complainants, Article 14(3) does not say that the registering authority shall refuse the registration of a geographical indication only if it gives rise to a likelihood of confusion with a trademark which is famous and has been used for a long period of time. Rather, Article 14(3) says that the registration of a geographical indication shall be refused if it is likely to lead to confusion with a trademark, "in light of" the trademark's reputation and renown and the length of time that it has been used.

156. In other words, the length of use and reputation/renown of the trademark are not separate "requirements"[43], additional to the likelihood of confusion, for the application of Article 14(3). Rather, they are criteria for establishing the existence of a likelihood of confusion. From the fact that the Commission must consider those two criteria when assessing the likelihood of confusion, it does not follow *a contrario* that it cannot consider also other criteria. Indeed, as explained below, in practice it would be impossible to evaluate the likelihood of confusion on the basis of only those two criteria.

157. As explained[44], Article 14(3) directs expressly the registering authority to consider the length of use and the reputation and renown of earlier trademarks because those criteria will generally be decisive in order to establish the likelihood of confusion, given that geographical names are primarily non-

---

43 US Oral Statement, para. 53.
44 EC's FWS, paras. 278-291.

distinctive, and not because only the likelihood of confusion with famous marks that have been used for a long time is deemed relevant.

158. If Article 14(3) does not mention expressly the similarity of goods and signs, it is simply because those criteria are always relevant to establish the likelihood of confusion between two signs and must necessarily be taken into account. Indeed, as discussed below, neither the length of use nor the reputation and renown of a trademark can be assessed meaningfully without taking into account the degree of similarity of the goods and signs. Moreover, it must be recalled that the application of Article 14(3) presupposes the applicability of Article 13(1) and that, in order to determine whether the use of a trademark falls within one of the situations listed under Article 13(1), it is necessary to consider the similarity of goods and signs.

159. Furthermore, the interpretation of Article 14(3) made by the complainants would lead to a result which conflicts and cannot be reconciled with the obligations imposed upon the EC institutions by Articles 7(4) and 7(5)(b).

160. Article 7(4) provides that a statement of objection shall be admissible, *inter alia*, if it shows that "the registration of the name proposed would jeopardize the existence of a mark".[45] This language encompasses any instance of likelihood of confusion between the proposed geographical indication and an earlier trademark. If Article 14(3) only required the refusal of a proposed geographical indication where it gives rise to likelihood of confusion with a famous trademark used for a long time, as claimed by the complainants, the admissible grounds of objection would have been limited to the cases where one such mark is likely to be jeopardized. Article 7(4), however, refers to all trademarks, without any distinction or qualification. It would be pointless to admit an objection on certain grounds if, in any event, it were not possible to reject the application on such grounds.

161. Further confirmation is provided by Article 7(5)(b), which provides that where an objection is admissible, and no agreement is reached among the Member States concerned,

> the Commission shall take a decision in accordance with the procedure laid down in Article 15, having regard to traditional fair practice and likelihood of confusion.[46]

162. Thus, Article 7(5)(b) requires the Commission to adopt a decision having regard to the "likelihood of confusion" between the proposed geographical indication and *any* other marks. There is no basis in Article 7(5)(b) for the proposition that only the likelihood of confusion with famous marks used for a long time must be taken into account by the Commission.

---

[45] Articles 12b(3) and 12d(2) provide, respectively, that the criteria of Article 7(4) shall apply also with respect to the admissibility of objections to the registration of foreign geographical indications and of objections from outside the EC to EC geographical indications.

[46] Similar language is found in Articles 12b(3) and12d(3) with regard to the registration of geographical indications from other WTO Members and third countries and to the registration of EC geographical indications, following an objection from outside the EC, respectively.

Do other criteria, such as similarity of signs and goods fall within "reputation and renown"?

163. As suggested by the question, the criteria mentioned expressly in Article 14(3) cannot be applied without taking into account at the same time the degree of similarity between the goods and signs concerned, which must, therefore, be deemed implicit in Article 14(3).

164. The mere fact that a trademark enjoys reputation and renown and that it has been used for a long time is not sufficient to establish that a geographical indication will be confused with that trademark, if the two signs are not similar. For example, it is beyond dispute that "Coca-Cola" is a trademark that enjoys a formidable reputation and renown and has been used for a long time. Yet, it would be absurd to pretend that, as a result, the EC public is likely to confuse the geographical indication "Jijona" with the trademark "Coca-Cola", given the lack of similarity between the two signs.

165. Similar considerations can be made with respect to the similarity of goods. For example, a geographical indication for cheese may be less likely to be confused with a trademark that enjoys great reputation and renown with respect to shoes than with a trademark for cheese even if it has less renown and reputation. Similarly, the length of time during which a trademark has been used must be determined in relation to a given category of goods. To continue with the same example, a geographical indication for cheese may be less likely to be confused with a trademark for shoes that has been used for decades than with a relatively recent trademark for cheese.

166. The above examples illustrate that the likelihood of confusion between two signs cannot be properly established by considering only the length of use and the reputation/renown of one of them, but must take into account necessarily the similarity of the goods and signs concerned. An interpretation of Article 14(3) which prevented the registering authority from considering the similarity of goods and signs would be neither reasonable, nor workable, and cannot be correct. It must be concluded, therefore, that the criteria mentioned in Article 14(3) do not purport to be exhaustive.

Is the criterion of "length of time [a trade mark] has been used" relevant to its liability to mislead if the trademark has not been used for a significant, or considerable, length of time?

167. Article 14(3) requires the registering authority to consider the length of time during which a trademark has been used. The reason why this criterion must be considered is because, as a general rule, the longer a trademark has been used, the more distinctive it will be, and, as result, the more likely that a proposed geographical indication may be confused with it.

168. However, contrary to what has been argued by the complainants, Article 14(3) does not say that the registering authority must refuse the registration of a geographical indication only if it has been shown that the trademark has been used for a long time. It is conceivable that a trademark which has been used for a relatively short period of time may, nevertheless, have

become strongly distinctive through other means (e.g. publicity), so as to make it likely that the proposed geographical will be confused with it.

Question 69

Can the EC provide the Panel with any official statement predating its first written submission that application of the grounds for registration, invalidity or revocation of trademarks and Article 14(3) of Regulation (EC) No. 2081/92 will or should be applied in such a way as to render Article 14(2) inapplicable?

169. The EC institutions have not issued any general interpretative "statement" of Article 14(3) of Regulation 2081/92. The same is true of all the other provisions of Regulation 2081/92. Indeed, unlike in other jurisdictions, it is relatively unusual for the EC authorities to issue any such general interpretative statements with respect to the EC legislative acts.

170. As mentioned in the EC's First Written Submission[47], Article 14(3) of Regulation 2081/92 has been applied only once by the EC institutions. The interpretation made in that case is consistent with the interpretation advanced by the EC in this dispute. The Council concluded that there was no likelihood of confusion with earlier trademarks "in view of the facts and information available". There is no suggestion in the Council decision that it was considered that there was no likelihood of confusion because the trademarks concerned were not famous enough or had not been used for a sufficiently long time.

171. The EC wishes to clarify that it is not the EC's position that its trademark legislation, together with Article 14(3) of Regulation 2081/92, "render Article 14(2) inapplicable". Rather, the EC's position is that its trademark legislation, together with Article 14(3), prevent the registration of geographical indications that result in a likelihood of confusion with pre-existing trademarks, which is the only type of confusion envisaged in Article 16.1 of the TRIPS Agreement. Article 14(2) applies to other situations not involving that type of confusion where, in accordance with Article 13(1) of Regulation 2081/92, the right holders of a registered geographical indication would be entitled, in principle, to prevent the use of an earlier trademark.

Question 70

Do the EC member States agree with the Commission's submission to this Panel that the terms of Article 14(3) of Regulation (EC) No. 2081/92, if properly interpreted, are sufficient to prevent the registration of any confusing GIs?

172. The EC recalls that the submissions to the Panel are made on behalf of the European Communities, and not of the EC Commission.

173. The EC also recalls that Regulation 2081/92 is a measure of the European Community and not of its Member States. Therefore, in principle, only the views of the EC institutions, and not the individual views of the EC Members States, are relevant for the interpretation of Regulation 2081/92.

---

[47] EC's FWS, para. 288.

174. In any event, the Member States of the EC are aware of the legal interpretations stated in the EC submission. They have expressed no objections or reservations.

Could the EC member States apply national trademark laws in a way that made this impossible?

175. This question is unclear to the EC. The EC fails to see how the Member States could, through the application of their national trademark laws, prevent a correct application of Article 14(3) of Regulation 2081/92.

176. In any event, the EC Member States are required under EC law to apply their trademark laws consistently with all the relevant provisions of EC law, including in particular the Trademark Directive. For the reasons explained by the EC in its First Written Submission, the registrability criteria provided in the Trademark Directive limit *a priori* the risk of conflicts between trademarks and geographical indications. The complainants have not been able to identify one single case where a registered geographical indication has resulted in a likelihood of confusion with a trademark registered by the authorities of the Member States under their national trademark laws. This confirms that, in practice, Member States apply those laws consistently with the interpretation advanced by the EC in this dispute.

Could the Council of Ministers prevent the application of Article 14(3) of the Regulation if proposed by the Commission in a specific case and apply Article 14(2)?

177. In principle, the Commission is not required to submit proposals to the Council. Rather, the Commission must request the opinion of the Committee in accordance with Article 15 of Regulation 2081/92 before adopting a decision granting or refusing a registration. If the Committee gives a negative opinion, the Commission must submit a proposal to the Council, which may, acting by qualified majority, adopt it or indicate its opposition within a certain period of time. The Council could oppose a proposal from the Commission to refuse a registration on the basis of Article 14(3) if it considers that the conditions provided in that Article are not met.

Question 71

Has a judicial authority ever ruled on the interpretation of Article 14(3) of Regulation (EC) No. 2081/92?

178. As noted in the EC's First Written Submission (para. 288) Article 14(3) of Regulation (EC) No. 2081/92 has never been interpreted by the European Court of Justice or by the courts of the Member States. Once again, this confirms that, as explained by the EC, the criteria for the registrability of trademarks ensure that the potential for conflicts between trademarks and geographical indications is very limited.

179. As explained above[48], according to well-established case law of the European Court of Justice, EC law must be interpreted, to the extent possible, in a manner that ensures its consistency with the WTO Agreement, in particular where it is intended specifically to give effect to that agreement. This principle of interpretation must be observed also by the other EC institutions and by the courts of the Member States when interpreting EC law.

180. Moreover, as also explained[49], the European Court of Justice takes account of the assurances regarding the interpretation of EC law given by the EC Commission on behalf of the European Communities in international fora, such as the WTO.

If Article 14(3) of the Regulation, the Community trademark regulation and national trademark laws were applied in such a way as to prevent the registration of GIs that were confusing with a prior trademark, could this be subject to judicial review?

181. A decision refusing the registration of a proposed geographical indication on the grounds provided in Article 14(3) of Regulation 2081/92 can be challenged before the courts, just like any other decision refusing or granting the registration of a proposed geographical indication.

182. Likewise, the decisions of the trademark authorities of the Member States or of the Office for Harmonisation in the Internal Market to refuse the registration of a trademark on the grounds provided in letters (b), (c) or (g) of Article 3.1 of the Trademarks Directive, or in letters (b), (c) or (g) of Article 7.1 of the Community Trademark Regulation, respectively, are also subject to judicial review.

Question 73

Please supply a copy of the wine regulations referred to in paragraph 16 of the EC oral statement.

183. The wine regulations referred to in paragraph 16 of the EC's First Oral Statement are the same mentioned in paragraphs 310-311 of the EC's First Written Submission. A copy of the relevant provisions of those regulations has been supplied as Exhibit EC-11, together with the EC's First Written Submission.

Question 74

Which particular GIs did the EC protect under Regulation (EC) No. 2081/92 prior to 1 January 1995?

184. The registration of a geographical indication under Regulation 2081/92 produces effects vis-à-vis concurrent trademarks from the date of application (cf. Article 14(1) of Regulation 2081/92). Of the 658 geographical indications currently registered, 487 were applied for prior to 1 January 1995.

---

48 Response to Question 15.

49 *Ibid.*

185. Furthermore, many of the geographical indications registered or applied for under Regulation 2081/92 were already protected at the Member State level prior to 1 January 1995.

Is Article 24.3 of the TRIPS Agreement relevant to any other GIs?

186. Yes. Article 24.3 requires to maintain the level of protection of geographical indications available on 1 January 1995, rather than the protection of the particular geographical indications that were registered, or applied for on that date.

187. On the interpretation suggested in the question, Article 24.3 would impose obligations only upon those Members which protect geographical indications via a system of registration, or another system involving the recognition *ex ante* of geographical indications, but not where protection is provided through other systems (e.g. unfair competition laws or generally applicable consumer protection regulations that apply indistinctly to any geographical indications).

188. For example, assume that, before 1 January 1995, a Member had legislation in place prohibiting the use of *any* geographical indications for products of a different origin, even when the geographical indication is used together with terms such as "type", "kind", etc. On the interpretation suggested in the question, after 1 January 1995, that Member would be free to repeal such legislation with respect to products other than wine and spirits, even though this would clearly "diminish the protection of geographical indications".

189. Moreover, the above result would be at odds with the principle established in Article 1.1 of the TRIPS Agreement, according to which Members are free to determine the appropriate method of implementation of their WTO obligations. Members cannot be said to be "free" to choose the method of implementation of Section 3 of Part II, if choosing a certain method has the consequence of subjecting them to stricter obligations under Article 24.3.

190. The United States has argued that the meaning of Article 24.3 is that "the protection provided to those GIs should not diminish the protections (sic) for the GIs that existed when the TRIPS Agreement came into force."[50]

191. This proposition is difficult to understand. Providing protection to geographical indications cannot, as a matter of simple logic, "diminish" such protection. Rather the existing protection of geographical indications may be "diminished" as a result of the implementation of the limitations to the protection of geographical indications provided in Section 3 of Part II, including in particular those stipulated in Article 24.5 in order to maintain certain rights of the owners of grandfathered trademarks.

192. Moreover, the US interpretation has no textual basis in the wording of Article 24.3, which reads as follows:

> In implementing this section, a Member shall not diminish the protection of geographical indications that existed in that Member

50 US Oral Statement, para. 70.

> immediately prior to the date of entry into force of the WTO Agreement.

193. First, Article 24.3 alludes to the "protection of geographical indications", and not to the "protections" in the plural form, as argued by the United States. Moreover, the term "geographical indications" is not preceded by the word "the". This indicates that the drafters had in mind the general level of protection available in each Member. Second, the term "existed" refers to the word "protection" and not to the "geographical indications". It is not required, therefore, that the geographical indications "existed", or *a fortiori* that they had been specifically recognised as such, as of the date of entry into force of the WTO Agreement. This is made clear by the Spanish and the French versions, which read as follows, respectively:

> Al aplicar esta Sección, ningún Miembro reducirá la protección de las indicaciones geográficas que **existía** en él inmediatamente antes de la fecha de entrada en vigor del Acuerdo sobre la OMC. [emphasis added]

> Lorsqu'il mettra en oeuvre la présente section, un Membre ne diminuera pas la protection des indications géographiques qui **existait** dans ce Membre immédiatement avant la date d'entrée en vigueur de l'Accord sur l'OMC. [emphasis added]

194. The United States also argues that Article 24.3 is an "exception" with respect to the "implementation of the GI Section of the TRIPS Agreement" and not an "exception to the implementation of the trademark obligations".[51] This argument is specious. In the first place, Article 24.3 is not an "exception" to the protection of geographical indications, because it does not exempt Members from the obligations provided under Section 3 of Part II. Rather, it adds a supplementary obligation. Second, the "protection" of geographical indications includes "protection" vis-à-vis the exercise of trademark rights. Indeed, Section 3 of Part II provides expressly for such type of protection in Articles 22.3, 23.2 and 24.5. Those provisions operate as limitations to the "trademark obligations" under Article 16.1. Article 24.3 provides for another limitation to those "trademarks obligations".

195. The objective of Article 24.3 is to maintain the balance between the protection of geographical indications and that of trademarks that existed in each Member at the entry into force of the WTO Agreement. If, prior to that date, a Member provided protection vis-à-vis trademarks going beyond that required by Section 3 of Part II, it is required to continue do so after that date. For example, if prior to 1 January 1995 a Member provided generally the type of protection required by Article 23.2 for wines and spirits with respect to all products, it must continue to do so after that date, whether or not a certain geographical indication had been specifically recognised as such before that date.

---

[51] *Ibid.*

196. Finally, the United States argues that the EC interpretation would allow Members to derogate from "*any* WTO provision".[52] This is simply not true. Article 24.3 requires Members to depart from other WTO provisions only to the extent necessary to maintain the existing "protection" of geographical indications. In order to "protect" geographical indications it is not necessary, for example, to limit patent rights or copyrights.[53] On the other hand, as mentioned, it is beyond question that "protecting" geographical indications may require to limit trademark rights.

Question 75

Which party bears the burden of proof in relation to:

(a) Article 24.5 of the TRIPS Agreement? In particular, does this relate to the scope of the obligation in Article 16.1? Does it create an exception for measures otherwise covered by Article 16.1? Or neither?

197. Article 24.5 is not an "exception" to Article 16.1. Rather, it defines the boundary between a Member's right to implement protection for geographical indications and its obligation to protect trademarks under Article 16.1.[54] The burden of proving that a measure falls within the scope of the obligations provided in Article 16.1 is on the complainants.

198. The EC notes that, while the United States now argues that Article 24.5 is an "exception"[55], in its panel request it has stated a claim under that provision. Similarly, Australia cited Article 24.5 in its panel request and has made a claim under that provision in its First Written Submission.[56]

(b) Article 17 of the TRIPS Agreement? In particular, does this only permit exceptions to the rights conferred by a trademark, or does it also create an exception to the obligations imposed on Members?

199. Article 17 allows Members to provide limited exceptions to the rights which they are obliged to confer upon the owner of trademark by virtue of Article 16. To that extent, it is an exception to the obligations imposed upon Members by Article 16. The function of Article 17 is similar to that of Articles 13 and 30. Previous panels have taken the view that the burden of invoking those provisions and of proving that the relevant conditions for their applicability were met was on the defendant.[57]

---

[52] *Ibid.*, para. 72.

[53] *Ibid.*

[54] Australia's FWS, para. 105.

[55] US Oral Statement, para. 58.

[56] Australia's FWS, paras. 81-87.

[57] See Panel Report, *United States – Section 110(5) of the Copyright Act*, paras. 6.9-6.16; and Panel Report, *Canada – Patent Protection of Pharmaceutical Products*, para. 7.16.

Question 76

Article 24.5 of the TRIPS Agreement uses the phrases "validity of the registration of a trademark" and "the right to use a trademark". Please set out your interpretation of these phrases, in accordance with the general rule of treaty interpretation in Article 31 of the Vienna Convention on the Law of Treaties and, if appropriate, the supplementary means in Article 32. Please explain how you determine what is the relevant context.

The ordinary meaning

200. A "trademark" is not a right. It is a sign which may be the subject of a right. Thus, Article 15.1 of the TRIPS Agreement provides in relevant part that

> Any sign, or any combination of signs, capable of distinguishing the goods or services of one undertaking from those of other undertakings, shall be capable of constituting a trademark.

201. Therefore, the "right to use a trademark" is the right to use a sign. That right is different from, and does not include the right to prevent others from using the same or a similar sign. According to WIPO[58], typically the owner of a registered trademark has an "exclusive right to use the trademark", which "encompasses two things":

- the "right to use the trademark" and
- the "right to exclude others from using the mark".

202. In turn, according to WIPO the "right to use a trademark" means the following:[59]

> It means first the right of the owner of the mark to affix it on goods, contains, packaging, labels, etc. or to use it in any other way in relation to the goods for which it is registered.
>
> It means also the right to introduce the goods to the market under the trademark.

203. The term "validity" alludes to something which is "valid", which in turn means something "having legal strength or force, executed with proper formalities, incapable of being rightfully overthrown or set aside."[60] The opposite of "valid" is "invalid", which means "having no force, efficacy, or cogency, esp. in law".[61]

204. In order to be "valid", the registration of a trademark does not necessarily have to confer exclusive rights vis-à-vis all third parties. The fact that the owner of a registered trademark cannot prevent the use of the same or a similar sign by the right holders of a geographical indication does not mean that the registration

---

[58] WIPO, *Introduction to Trademark Law & Practice, The Basic Concepts, a WTO Training Manual*, Geneva 1993, p.51

[59] *Ibid.*

[60] Black's Law Dictionary, West Publishing Co., St. Paul, Minn., 1990.

[61] The New Shorter Oxford English Dictionary, Ed. Lesley Brown, Clarendon Press, Oxford 1993.

of the trademark is, for that reason alone, "set aside", or "overthrown" or that it is without "legal strength" or "efficacy".

205. The US interpretation of Article 24.5 fails to give meaning to the phrase "the right to use the trademark". If the exclusive right to use a trademark were already inherent in the term "validity of the registration", it would have been superfluous to provide in Article 24.5 that the implementation of Section 3 of Part II shall not prejudice "the right to use the trademark".

206. The United States asserts that the phrase "the right to use a trademark" *clarifies* and *adds* to the protection of grandfathered trademarks already provided by the other terms of Article 24.5.[62] However, as a matter of simple of logic, that phrase cannot do both things simultaneously. Either it *adds* an obligation, or it *clarifies* those obligations already provided by the other terms of Article 24.5.

207. If the phrase "the right to use a trademark" *adds* new obligations, it would mean that, as argued by the EC, the "validity" of a registration does not confer *per se* the exclusive right to use a trademark. Moreover, the United States does not explain how it can reconcile its position that Article 24.5 is an "exception" with the view that Article 24.5 confers to the trademark owners *additional* rights which they do not have under Article 16.

208. On the other hand, if the purpose of the phrase "the right to use a trademark" is to *clarify* the obligations provided by the other terms of Article 24.5, then why did the drafters not use *clear* wording to that effect, such as, for example, that the implementation of Section 3 of Part II is without prejudice to "the *exclusive* right to use the trademark" or to "the rights conferred by Article 16.1"?

209. The United States also argues that the EC's interpretation would allow to "deny all the rights connected with registration" and would render it "meaningless".[63] This is simply not true. It must be emphasised, once again, that, on the EC's interpretation, the trademark owner retains the right to prevent all others parties from using the trademark.

210. For its part, Australia has suggested[64] that the phrase "the right to use a trademark" alludes exclusively to the trademark rights acquired through use, to which reference is made in the introductory phrase of Article 24.5. However, if so, it would have been more logical to say that the measures taken to implement Sections 3 "shall not prejudice ... the trademark rights acquired through use", rather than that they "shall not prejudice ... the right to use a trademark". Australia confuses the mode of acquisition of the trademark rights (use or registration) with one of the basic rights of the trademark owner (irrespective of whether the trademark rights have been acquired through use or registration), i.e. the right to use the trademark.

211. Moreover, trademark rights acquired through use are also, as a general rule, exclusive within the boundaries of the area in which they have been used.

---

[62] US Oral Statement, para. 64.

[63] *Ibid.*

[64] Australia's FWS, para. 74.

Article 16.1 of the TRIPS Agreement recognises expressly the right of Members to make available exclusive trademark rights on the basis of use. In view of that, there is no good reason why Article 24.5 should provide for the co-existence of geographical indications and non-registered trademarks, but prohibit the co-existence of geographical indications and registered trademarks, which would be the anomalous but necessary consequence of the complainants' interpretation.

The context

212. Article 24.5 is included in Section 3 of Part II, the purpose of which is to provide a minimum of protection to geographical indications. Such protection is subject to limitations in order to accommodate other intellectual property rights. However, it would be a paradoxical result if Article 24.5 were interpreted in such a way that, far from providing any protection to the legitimate right holders of a geographical indication, it prohibited them from even using that indication.

213. As already explained by the EC, co-existence is by no means an unusual solution. It is envisaged by several other provisions of Section 3, of Part II, and not just by Article 23.3, contrary to what is argued by the United States. Furthermore, co-existence is envisaged even where it may lead to some confusion. For example:

- Article 23.2 allows co-existence of a geographical indication for wines or spirits and a trademark consisting or including such geographical indication if used for wines and spirits originating in the area to which the geographical indication relates. *A priori*, the risk that consumers may confuse that geographical indication with the trademark may be the same as when the products covered by the trademark do not originate in that area. Nevertheless, co-existence is allowed because it does not mislead consumers as to the true geographical origin of the products;
- Co-existence may arise as well from Article 24.3, when the protection of geographical indications existing before the date of entry into force of the WTO Agreement provided for such co-existence (see the response to Question 74 above);
- Finally, co-existence is envisaged also by Article 24.4, which provides that a Member may allow "continued and similar" use of a geographical indication for wines or spirits of another Member by its nationals or domiciliaries who have used it before 1 April 1994 in good faith or for at least 10 years preceding that date, regardless of whether this gives rise to confusion with the products of the other Member that are entitled to use that geographical indication.

Object and purpose

214. In its First Written Submission, the United States stressed that Article 16.1 had to be interpreted "in the light of the object and purpose of the

TRIPS Agreement, and specifically with respect to Article 16.1 and its grant of exclusive rights".[65]

215. It must be recalled, however, that, under Article 31 of the *Vienna Convention*, only the object and purpose of the treaty as a whole is relevant. To the extent that granting exclusivity to trademark owners is one of the objects and purposes of the TRIPS Agreement, so is affording exclusivity to the right holders of geographical indications. As explained, exclusivity is as essential to geographical indications as to trademarks. Indeed, it could be argued that exclusivity is even more important in the case of geographical indications because the choice of geographical indications, unlike the choice of trademarks, is not arbitrary, and because it takes longer to establish a geographical indication.[66]

Drafting history

216. The United States has argued that the predecessor to the current Article 24.5 included in the so-called Brussels Draft made no reference to the right to use the trademark.[67] However, such reference was included in the predecessor to the current Article 24.4, which provided as follows:[68]

> Where a geographical indication of a PARTY has been used with regard to goods originating outside the territory of the PARTY in good faith and in a widespread and continuous manner by nationals or domiciliaries of another PARTY, **including as a trademark**, before the date of application of these provisions in the other PARTY as defined in Article [65] below, nothing in this Agreement shall prevent such continued use of the geographical indication by those nationals or domiciliaries of the said other PARTY. [emphasis added]

217. The scope of the above draft provision overlapped, as far as trademarks are concerned, with the predecessor to Article 24.5, which read as follows:[69]

> A PARTY shall not take action to refuse or invalidate registration of a trademark first applied for or registered:
>
> (a) before the date of application of those provisions in that PARTY as defined in Article [65] below;
>
> (b) before the geographical indication is protected in its country of origin;
>
> on the basis that the trademark is identical with, or similar to, a geographical indication.

---

65 US FWS, para. 145.

66 EC's FWS, paras. 295 and 307.

67 US Oral Statement, para. 64.

68 Reproduced in Daniel Gervais, "The TRIPS Agreement, Drafting History and Analysis", Sweet and Maxwell, 1998, p. 133.

69 *Ibid.*

218. The reference in the predecessor to Article 24.4 to the continued use of the geographical indications as trademarks indicates that the authors of the Brussels Draft envisaged the co-existence of trademarks and geographical indications of other Members. Such co-existence, however, would be rendered impossible by the US reading of the predecessor to Article 24.5, which would confer to the owners of the trademarks covered by the predecessor to Article 24.4 an exclusive right to use the geographical indication.

219. In the final text of the agreement, the reference to the "use of trademarks" was deleted from the predecessor to Article 24.4 and added to Article 24.5, but it has the same meaning and purpose as when it was included in Article 24.4.[70]

Question 77

Article 24.5 of the TRIPS Agreement uses the phrase "right to use" a trademark. Why did the drafters not choose to state, for example, "exclusive rights" or "rights under Article 16.1"? Is that fact relevant to interpretation of the phrase "right to use" a trademark?

220. As suggested in the question, if the drafters had intended to preserve the right of the owners of the grandfathered trademarks to prevent the use of the geographical indication, they would have used express language to that effect.

221. Furthermore, if Article 24.5 did not allow co-existence, the protection of geographical indications provided under Part II, Section 3, would become pointless whenever there is a grandfathered trademark. Indeed, why protect the intellectual property rights of the holders of geographical indications against illegitimate uses by third parties if the right holders cannot use it themselves? Yet, Article 24.5 assumes that Members will continue to protect geographical indications ("...measures adopted to implement this Section shall not prejudice..."), notwithstanding the existence of "grandfathered" trademarks. If the drafters' intention had been to prohibit the use of geographical indications concurrently with grandfathered trademarks, they would have excluded completely the applicability of Part II, Section 3, with respect to the geographical indications concerned, rather than providing that the implementation of that Section shall not prejudice "the right to use the trademark".

Question 86

Article 4 the Paris Convention (1967) creates no right of priority for indications of source. Does this indicate that they are irrelevant for the purposes of the right of priority?

---

[70] Several reasons may explain why the reference to the use of trademarks was deleted from Article 24.4 and added to Article 24.5. First, unlike its predecessor in the Brussels Draft, Article 24.4 applies to wines and spirits only. Second, the temporal criteria for the application of Article 24.4 were changed and differ from those of Article 24.5. Third, unlike its predecessor in the Brussels Draft, Article 24.4 applies only to the use of geographical indications by nationals and domiciliaries of the Member concerned. Finally, from a systematic point of view, it is more logic to group in the same Article all the provisions concerning the relationship between geographical indications and earlier trademarks.

222. The fact that the Paris Convention does not provide for a right of priority in respect of indications of source (including appellations of origin) suggests that the parties to the Paris Convention were of the view that conflicts between indications of source and other industrial property rights should not be resolved according to the first-in-time principle.

Question 87

What is the significance of the EC's statement that the complainants' claims are "theoretical"? Does the EC suggest that this affects the Panel's mandate or function in any way?

223. The fact that the claims raised by the complainants are purely theoretical cast doubts on whether the complainants have a genuine interest in bringing this dispute. The EC, nevertheless, is not suggesting that the Panel's jurisdiction is affected by the complainants' apparent lack of genuine interest. In particular the EC does not consider it necessary to request the Panel to rule on whether the complainants have acted consistently with Article 3.7 of the DSU.

224. If the EC has insisted that the complainants' claims are often theoretical it is because this has implications for the Panel's assessment of whether such claims are well-founded. In particular, in some cases the fact that the complainants' claims are theoretical confirms that they are based on a misinterpretation of the measures in dispute.

225. For example, the fact that the complainants have not been able to identify any single registered geographical indication which gives rise to likelihood of confusion with any prior trademark confirms that, as argued by the EC, the criteria for registrability of trademarks, together with Article 14(3) of Regulation 2081/92, prevent the registration of confusing geographical indications.

226. Similarly, to mention but another example, the fact that Australia has not been able to provide any evidence that the EC authorities have rejected statements of objection for the reasons mentioned by Australia under Claim 21[71] confirms that Article 7(4) does not provide for the limitation of the grounds of objection alleged by Australia.

Question 89

Is there a notion of estoppel in WTO dispute settlement which applies where a Member refrains from raising claims in relation to a measure until after it is amended?

227. According to Article 3.10 of the DSU, the participants in dispute settlement procedures under the DSU are bound by an obligation of good faith. The principle of estoppel is similarly based on the notion of good faith. Accordingly, the EC considers that the notion of estoppel is applicable in the context of WTO dispute settlement.

---

[71] Australia's FWS, paras. 89-92.

228. However, the EC considers that the Panel may not have to rely on the notion of estoppel in the present case. As the EC has set out already in its first written submission, it considers that the Panel does not have jurisdiction to hear claims which are directed at measures which were no longer in force at the time the Panel was established.[72] Similarly, as regards the individual registrations, even if these were considered to be within the terms of reference of the Panel, the EC has already set out that these registrations in now way violate the principle of national treatment.[73]

229. Since the claims which Australia has raised are either manifestly inadmissible or unfounded, the EC does not consider it necessary to rely on the notion of estoppel at this stage. However, the EC is ready to return to this issue at a later stage should the Panel consider it necessary.

[72] EC FWS, para. 13 et seq.
[73] EC FWS, para. 156 et seq.

ANNEX B-5

TABLE OF CONTENTS

SECOND WRITTEN SUBMISSION OF THE EUROPEAN COMMUNITIES

(22 July 2004)

TABLE OF WTO CASES REFERRED TO IN THIS SUBMISSION

Short Title	Full Case Title and Citation of Case
Canada – Autos	Panel Report, *Canada – Certain Measures Affecting the Automotive Industry*, WT/DS139/R, WT/DS142/R, adopted 19 June 2000, as modified by the Appellate Body Report, WT/DS139/AB/R, WT/DS142/AB/R, DSR 2000:VII, 3043
EC – Sardines	Appellate Body Report, *European Communities – Trade Description of Sardines*, WT/DS231/AB/R, adopted 23 October 2002
EC – Hormones	Appellate Body Report, *EC Measures Concerning Meat and Meat Products (Hormones)*, WT/DS26/AB/R, WT/DS48/AB/R, adopted 13 February 1998, DSR 1998:I, 135
Korea – Various Measures on Beef	Appellate Body Report, *Korea – Measures Affecting Imports of Fresh, Chilled and Frozen Beef*, WT/DS161/AB/R, WT/DS169/AB/R, adopted 10 January 2001
US – Gasoline	Appellate Body Report, *United States – Standards for Reformulated and Conventional Gasoline*, WT/DS2/AB/R, adopted 20 May 1996, DSR 1996:I, 3
US – Section 301 Trade Act	Panel Report, *United States – Sections 301-310 of the Trade Act of 1974*, WT/DS152/R, adopted 27 January 2000, DSR 2000:II, 815

GLOSSARY

Commission, EC Commission	Commission of the European Communities
Committee	Committee of representatives of the Member States referred to in Article 15 of Council Regulation 2081/92
Community Trademark Regulation	Council Regulation (EC) No 40/94, of 20 December 1993, on the Community Trademark, as amended
Council, EC Council	Council of the European Union
Court of Justice, European Court of Justice	Court of Justice of the European Communities
DSU	Understanding on Rules and Procedures Governing the Settlement of Disputes
EC	European Communities
GATT	General Agreement on Tariffs and Trade 1994
FOS	First Oral Statement
FWS	First Written Submission
GI	Geographical indication
Member States, EC Member States	Member States of the European Union
Official Journal	Official Journal of the European Union
Paris Convention	Stockholm Act of the Paris Convention for the protection of Industrial property, of 14 July 1967
Regulation 2081/92, Regulation	Council Regulation (EEC) No 2081/92 of 14 July 1992 on the protection of geographical indications and designations of origin for agricultural products and foodstuffs, as amended on the date of establishment of the Panel
SCM Agreement, SCM	Agreement on Subsidies and Countervailing Duties
Trademarks Directive	First Council Directive 89/104, of 20 December, on the Community Trademark, as amended
TBT Agreement, TBT	Agreement on Technical Barriers to Trade

TRIPS Agreement, TRIPS	Agreement on Trade-Related Aspects of Intellectual Property Rights
US	United States
WTO Agreement	Marrakesh Agreement Establishing the World Trade Organization

I. INTRODUCTION

1. This submission provides the rebuttal of the European Communities to the arguments made by the complainants at the first meeting with the Panel of 23-24 June 2004, as well as in their responses to the questions from the Panel and from the EC of 8 July 2004. The EC has addressed some of those arguments as part of its own responses to the Panel's questions. In order to avoid unnecessary repetitions, the EC will refer to those responses where appropriate.

2. In the following section, the EC will first discuss some horizontal issues concerning the objective assessment of the content of Regulation 2081/92. In the following sections, the EC will comment on the arguments of the complainants claim by claim, following the structure already used in the EC's first written submission.

II. THE OBJECTIVE ASSESSMENT OF THE CONTENT OF REGULATION 2081/92

3. The EC has already set out the content of Regulation 2081/92 in its first written submission.[1] In the present submission, the EC refers to this general presentation. Where the complainants have contested the interpretation of particular provisions of Regulation 2081/92, the EC will respond to these arguments in the discussion of the specific claims raised by the complainants.

4. In the present section, the EC would like to address two horizontal issues which are essential for the objective assessment of the content of Regulation 2081/92 by the Panel:

- the proper approach to the interpretation of Regulation 2081/92 as a measure of EC domestic law;
- the importance of WTO law and obligations for the interpretation of Regulation 2081/92 in the EC legal order.

---

[1] EC FWS, para. 43 et seq.

A. The proper approach to the interpretation of Regulation 2081/92 as a measure of EC domestic law

5. In its response to the first question asked by the Panel after the first substantive hearing, the EC has set out how it believes the Panel should approach the interpretation of Regulation 2081/92.[2]

6. As the EC has already stated, the meaning of Regulation 2081/92 is, for the purposes of the present dispute, a question of fact. Accordingly, the burden of proof for establishing that Regulation 2081/92 has a particular meaning rests on the complainants. This means that it is the complainants, not the EC, who must show that Regulation 2081/92 has in fact the meaning which they allege it has.

7. Since the interpretation of Regulation 2081/92 as a measure of EC domestic law is a question of fact, it follows that Panel must not "interpret" the meaning of Regulation 2081/92 as it would interpret provisions of the WTO Agreement. Rather, the Panel must, accordance with Article 11 DSU, proceed to an objective assessment of the meaning of this Regulation within the legal order of the EC.

8. For the purposes of this objective assessment, it is essential that the Panel take into account the legal context of the measure within the legal order of the Member concerned. For this reason, due account must also be taken of the meaning which is given to the measure in question by the authorities of the Member concerned. As the Panel in *US – Section 301* has held, for this reason, considerable deference must be given to the explanations given by the Member concerned as to the meaning of its own measure.[3]

9. In their responses to the questions of the Panel, the United States and Australia have failed to correctly appreciate these principles. First of all, it appears that the United States attempts to shift the burden of proof as regards the content of Regulation 2081/92 to the EC.[4] However, this burden of proof is on the complainants; and as the EC will set out in its discussion of the individual claims Australia and the United States do not provide sufficient evidence to demonstrate that the provisions of the Regulation do indeed have the meaning which they allege.

10. More importantly still, the United States and Australia fail to give due weight to the fact that Regulation 2081/92 is a measure of EC domestic law. This is illustrated by the incorrect statements of the United States and Australia as regards the interpretation of the Regulation 2081/92 by the Court of Justice. As the EC will set out in greater detail in the next section, these statements entirely fail to appreciate the relevance of WTO law and obligations for the interpretation of Regulation 2081/92 in the EC legal order.

---

[2] EC Response to Panel's Question No. 1, para. 1 et seq.

[3] Panel Report, *US – Section 301*, para. 7.18. Full quotation cf. EC Response to Panel's Question No. 1, para. 3.

[4] US Response to Panel's Question No. 1, para. 1.

11. Particularly striking in this context is the contention of the United States that the "Commission's interpretation" before the Panel should not be granted "any particular deference".[5] First of all, the EC would like to stress that the US is incorrect to refer to the "Commission's" statements or interpretations. As the US is well aware, the European Communities as a Member of the WTO is represented by the European Commission. Accordingly, the statements made by the EC representatives before the Panel are made on behalf of the European Communities as a whole, and not on behalf of the European Commission or any other institution of the EC.

12. For this reason, the US comments regarding the weight of the Commission's opinions with respect to other institutions within the EC legal order[6] are without any relevance for evaluating the statements made by the EC before the Panel. In addition, the US statements in this regard are partially incorrect, and give a tilted picture of the institutional system of the EC.

13. For instance, the United States refers to the practice of complaint letters in the field of competition law.[7] The EC does not see the relevance of this example for the present dispute. That the Commission's comfort letters, which are not intended to be binding, are not binding on national courts, is not particularly surprising. What the US fails to mention, in contrast, is that despite their not being binding, such letters are usually respected. As one author has put it in a recent publication on competition law: "Furthermore, it is likely that a national court, although not formally bound by a comfort letter, would be strongly influenced by it".[8]

14. Similarly, the EC wonders what is the basis for the US statement that before the Court of Justice, the Commission's brief "carries no greater weight than a brief submitted by a private party", and that "in many cases, the ECJ does not even accept the Commission's interpretation".[9] This statement already disregards that in accordance with Article 211 EC Treaty, the Commission is responsible "to ensure that the provision of this Treaty and the measures taken by the institutions pursuant thereto are applied". In other words, the EC is not just "any other private party", but is the guardian of the EC Treaty.

15. This is also reflected by the fact that unlike a private party, the Commission may intervene in any proceedings pending before the Court of Justice to which it is not itself a party.[10] Similarly, it may present observations with respect to all requests for preliminary rulings.[11] The Commission exercises this right to intervene and present observations systematically, and in the great majority of cases, its observations are followed by the Court.

---

5 US Response to Panel's Question No. 1, para. 18.
6 US Response to Panel's Question No. 1, para. 8 et seq.
7 Cf. US Response to Panel's Question No. 1, para. 10.
8 R. Whish, *Competition Law*, 5th edition (2003), p. 167 (Exhibit EC-33).
9 US Response to Panel's Question No. 1, para. 11.
10 Article 40 (1) of the Statute of the European Court of Justice.
11 Article 23 (2) of the Statute of the European Court of Justice.

16. Finally, the complainants fail to accord a reasonable degree of deference to the statements of the EC as regards its own measure. In its oral statement in the first hearing, the United States has stated that a clarification that the EC does not apply conditions of reciprocity and equivalence to other WTO Members "will be welcome".[12] However, its comments give the opposite impression. Indeed, the EC is wondering from whom the US is hoping to receive the desired clarification, if not from the representatives of the European Communities.[13]

17. In conclusion, the Panel should, in its approach to Regulation 2081/92, take due of account of the character of this measure as a measure of EC domestic law, and give due weight to the explanation which are furnished by the European Communities in this respect.

B. *The importance of WTO law and obligations for the interpretation of Regulation 2081/92 in the EC legal order*

18. A particular point with respect to which the United States and Australia fail to appreciate the proper legal context of Regulation 2081/92 is the importance of WTO law and obligations for the interpretation of the Regulation. This issue is of particular importance regarding the claims that the EC applies conditions of "reciprocity and equivalence" to the registration of geographical indications from other WTO Members, and the EC will return to it in this context. However, it is also a horizontal question, on which the EC would therefore offer a number of general observations.

19. In its response to Question 15 of the Panel, the EC has already set out in detail, citing concrete examples from the case law, how the European Court of Justice takes into account the obligations arising from international agreements, in particular the WTO Agreements, in the interpretation and application of acts of Community law.[14]

20. The United States and Australia have entirely ignored this case law, and have rather superficially limited themselves to stating that according to the European Court of Justice, the WTO Agreements do not have direct effect, and are not in principle among the rules in the light of which the Court of Justice is to review the legality of measures adopted by the Community institutions.[15] In support of this statement, the complainants have relied on two judgements of the Court of Justice, namely the judgements in case C-149/96, *Portugal/Council*, and in Case C-93/02 P, *Biret*.[16]

---

[12] US FOS, para. 16.

[13] The EC also notes that in its comments on the Panel's draft letter to WIPO, which it transmitted by e-mail to the Secretariat on 9 July 2004, Australia warns against "inappropriate interpretative analysis on the part of the International Bureau of WIPO of those countries' legislation and intentions". The EC wonders why Australia insists on deference as regards the legislation of WIPO Members, but would not want the Panel to afford any deference as regards the interpretation of EC legislation.

[14] EC Response to Panel's Question No. 15, para. 28 et seq.

[15] US Response to Panel's Question No. 1, para. 15–16; Australian response to Question 6.

[16] Exhibits US-31 and US-32.

21. This presentation of the importance of WTO law within the EC legal order is incorrect. First of all, the cases referred to by the complainants are not relevant for the present context. Both judgments concerned the conditions under which the legality of a Community measure could be challenged under EC law because of incompatibilities with WTO law. This question has nothing to do with the present case. In the present case, the question is not whether Regulation 2081/92 could be challenged before the European Court of Justice for alleged inconsistencies with WTO law; the question is how Regulation 2081/92 must be interpreted taking into account the international obligations of the EC, and given the references to these international obligations which it contains.

22. In fact, the complainants fail to appreciate that WTO law is important in more than one way in the EC legal order. As one scholar of Community law has observed, one of the most important openings for WTO law in the legal order of the EC is the principle of that EC law must be interpreted in line with the EC's international obligations:[17]

> As a consequence, WTO compliant interpretation could result in the most effective means to judicially enforce, in the absence of specific measures of transformation, WTO law into the Community legal order. This is not the least reinforced by the weight the Panel in its Report on Section 301 on the US Trade Act has put on the option of WTO conform interpretation.

23. In fact, the European Court of Justice consistently strives to interpret EC legal measures in accordance with the EC's international obligations. As the EC has already set out, there are numerous examples where the European Court of Justice has taken account of and applied international obligations, including the WTO agreements, in the interpretation of EC law.[18]

24. As one commentator, now a Judge of the European Court of Justice, has observed, the judgement in case C-149/96, *Portugal/Council*, does not have the effect of rendering WTO law irrelevant under Community law:[19]

> The judgment in *Portugal v. Council* does not render the WTO Agreements irrelevant under Community law. First of all, they may have what has been called "indirect" effect, implying an obligation for domestic courts to *interpret* national law in the light of WTO law. In *Hermès*, the Court of Justice made the following finding:
>
> > "It should be stressed at the outset that, although the issue of the direct effect of Article 50 of the TRIPs Agreement has been argued, the Court is not required to give a ruling on that question, but only to answer the question of *interpretation* submitted to it by the national court so as to

[17] Stefan Griller, *Enforcement and Implementation of WTO Law in the European Union*, in Breuss/Griller/Vranes (ed.), The Banana Dispute, p. 247, 270 (2003) (Exhibit EC-34).

[18] EC Response to Panel's Question No. 15, para. 33–38.

[19] Allan Rosas, Case note, 37 CMLR 797, 814 (2000) (Exhibit EC-35).

> enable that court to *interpret Netherlands procedural rules in the light of that article*". (emphasis added)

Apart from this "indirect" effect, the Court in an infringement case has held that, because of the "primacy" of international agreements over provisions of secondary Community legislation, such provisions "must", so far as is possible, be interpreted in a manner that is consistent with those agreements" (the agreement in question was a GATT Agreement). In the same case, the Court confirmed that EU Member States are called upon to respect the GATT Agreements and can in the interest of uniform application of these Agreements throughout the EU be brought before the Court of Justice in infringement proceedings.

25. Accordingly, the misgivings that the complainants voice regarding the approach which the European Court of Justice, or other institutions of the EC, might take to the interpretation of Regulation 2081/92 are misplaced. This is particularly so where, as in the case of Article 12(1) of Regulation 2081/92, the EC measure specifically provides that it applies "without prejudice to international agreements".

26. For these reasons, the Panel should not assume that the institutions of the EC, and in particular the European Court of Justice, will ignore WTO obligations in the interpretation and application of Regulation 2081/92.

III. REGULATION 2081/92 IS COMPATIBLE WITH NATIONAL TREATMENT OBLIGATIONS, AND DOES NOT IMPOSE A REQUIREMENT OF DOMICILE OR ESTABLISHMENT

27. The EC has already responded in its first written submission to the claims raised by the complainants as regards the alleged violation of the national treatment provisions of the TRIPS and the GATT, as well as the prohibition on conditions of residence and domicile in Article 2.2 of the Paris Convention.[20] Hereunder, the EC will add a number of further observations on these claims in response to the statements made by the complainants during the first hearing and in their responses to the Panel's questions.

A. National treatment under the TRIPS Agreement (Article 3.1 TRIPS and Article 2.1 TRIPS in conjunction with Article 2.1 Paris Convention)

28. As in its first written submission, the EC will first turn to the claims made in respect of the national treatment provisions of the TRIPS and the Paris Convention.

[20] EC FWS, para. 101 et seq.

1. The Meaning and Scope of National Treatment under the TRIPS Agreement

29. Already in its first written submission, the EC has pointed out the importance of giving a proper interpretation to the national treatment provisions of Article 3.1 TRIPS Agreement, and similarly of Article 2.1 of the Paris Convention. In particular, the EC has stressed that unlike national treatment under the GATT, which concerns products, national treatment under the TRIPS Agreement is concerned with the treatment of nationals.[21]

30. In their responses to the questions of the Panel, the complainants offer interpretations of Article 3.1 TRIPS Agreement which do not correspond to the wording of the provision. Since this is a horizontal question underlying all the claims brought by the complainants under the national treatment provisions of the TRIPS and the Paris Convention, the EC will offer here some general remarks on the interpretations made by the complainants.

(a) The meaning of "national"

31. In its response to Question 23 of the Panel, the EC has explained that for natural persons, a national is any person who holds the nationality of the State in question in conformity with the legislation of such state. As regards legal persons, the question of nationality similarly depends on the law of the state in question, which may use criteria such as the law of incorporation, headquarters, or other criteria.[22] In the view of the EC, nationality is a distinct concept from domicile or establishment. Accordingly, the EC is of the view that it cannot be assumed that a Members State's nationals necessarily include natural persons who are domiciled, or legal persons who have a real and effective industrial and commercial establishment, in that Member.

32. In their responses to the Panel, the United States and Australia have argued the contrary. However, the legal grounds on which they base this view are unclear to the EC.

33. In its responses, the United States seems to have relied primarily on footnote 1 to Article 1.3 of the TRIPS Agreement, which defines the notion of national for the purposes of a "separate customs territory". This reliance by the US on footnote 1 is misplaced.

34. In its response to Question 52, the United States alleges that "footnote 1 to Article 1.3 of the TRIPS Agreement defines 'national' throughout the Agreement not in terms of nationality, but in terms of where a person is domiciled or where a person has a real and effective industrial or commercial establishment".[23] This statement is misleading. Footnote 1 does not define the term "national" for all purposes of the Agreement, but only as regards separate customs territories. As the EC has already remarked, this definition in fact

---

[21] EC FWS, para. 104 et seq.

[22] EC Response to Panel's Question No. 23, para. 56 et seq.

[23] US Response to Panel's Question No. 26, para. 52.

demonstrates that for all cases other than separate customs territories, nationality does not depend on domicile or establishment.[24]

35. Attempting another variant of its argument, the United States seems to suggest that the EC is a separate customs territory, to which footnote 1 to Article 1.3 of the TRIPS Agreement should apply.[25] The EC is not quite sure whether this is a drafting error, or meant to be a serious argument. In the latter case, the EC would be interested to know from what other customs territory the EC is supposed to be "separate".[26] It seems that if the EC is a separate customs territory, so are the United States, Australia, and in fact all WTO Members. Obviously this cannot be the correct meaning of "separate customs territory" in footnote 1 to Article 1.3 TRIPS Agreement.

36. Australia's responses on this point are no less unclear. In its responses, Australia first states that nationals are in the case of natural persons, "persons who possess the nationality of a State", and in regard to legal persons, persons "who are domiciled or established in that WTO Member in accordance with the laws of the WTO Member of which nationality is claimed". However, then Australia goes on to conclude that "nationals *normally* include natural persons who are domiciled or legal persons who have a real and effective industrial and commercial establishment in that Member". Australia notes further "that these categories of person would not always qualify as nationals".

37. In the view of the EC, these responses obscure the question. The question is not who is "normally" included among nationals, but the question who is a national. Contrary to the views of the complainants, "nationality" is a distinct concept, which is different from questions of domicile or establishment.

38. This is particularly obvious in the case of natural persons. National laws do not "normally" confer nationality simply on the basis of residence or establishment. Similarly, a national does not normally lose his or her nationality simply because of residence abroad.

39. The situation in this respect is not fundamentally different for legal persons. Even if the criteria which national laws use may vary, typically nationality is not simply attributed on the basis that a legal person is established in a particular country. The EC would note that if this criterion were sufficient, this could lead to situation where e.g. multinationals companies would be nationals of a very large number of countries.

40. In the view of the EC, this would not be a reasonable definition of nationality. This is why other criteria, such as notably the law of incorporation,

---

[24] EC Response to Panel's Question No. 23, para. 60.

[25] US Response to Panel's Question No. 23, para. 49 (referring to "a separate customs territory, such as the EC").

[26] In passing, the EC would note that unlike in the case of a a separate customs territory, there is a citizenship of the European Union. Cf. 17 of the EC Treaty, which provides that every person holding the nationality of a Member State shall be a citizen of the Union.

are used.[27] The EC notes that its views in this respect coincide with those expressed by Canada in its responses to a Question of the Panel.[28]

41. Accordingly, the Panel should conclude that the term "national" in Article 3.1 TRIPS Agreement and Article 2.1 Paris Convention does not necessarily include persons who are domiciled or established in a particular WTO Member.

(b) The conditions for applications and objections do not depend on nationality

42. On the basis of this understanding, the EC is of the view that the claims of the complainants raised in respect of Regulation 2081/92 do not involve any difference in treatment on the basis of nationality.

43. As the EC has already set out in its first submission, the parallel procedures for the registration of geographical indications depend exclusively on where the area is located to which the geographical indication is related. The conditions for registration do not therefore depend on nationality.[29] Similarly, the procedures for objecting to the registration of a geographical indication do not distinguish between nationals, but depend on where the objecting person is domiciled or established.[30] The fact that there are different provisions setting out parallel procedures does not entail any discrimination, but simply is necessary to take account of the need to involve the governments of the Member States or of the third country, respectively.

44. The EC notes that in their responses to the Panel, the complainants seem to recognise that Regulation 2081/92 does not contain any distinctions on the basis of nationality. Rather, the complainants seem to be basing themselves on the notion that US and Australian nationals would more "likely" be affected by the alleged violations than EC nationals.[31]

45. First of all, the EC would note that the complainants do not provide any factual basis for these claims. Even though it may be true that persons producing in a specific geographical area may frequently be nationals of the state where the area is located, this is not inevitably so. Indeed, there is no reason why a US or Australian national could not produce products in accordance with the product specifications of an EC GI.

---

[27] In this respect, reference can be made to Article 48(1) of the EC Treaty, which provides as follows: "Companies or firms formed in accordance with the law of a Member State and having their registered office, central administration or principal place of business within the Community shall, for the purposes of this Chapter, be treated in the same way as natural persons who are nationals of Member States".

[28] Response of Canada to Panel's Question No. 6 to the third parties, para. 2–5.

[29] EC FWS, para. 123 et seq.

[30] EC FWS, para. 142.

[31] Cf. US Response to Panel's Question No. 27, para. 54-55, where the US refers to the possibility of an EC national being prevented by Regulation 2081/92 from registering a US GI in the EC; Australia's Response to Question 27.

46. Indeed, in the area of wines and spirits, investment by foreign nationals in protected geographic names is a common phenomenon. By way of example, the EC can refer to the story of Jens-Reidar Larsen, a Norwegian national who is the founder of the Larsen Cognac House in Cognac, France (extract from Exhibit EC-36):

> The Larsen firm was founded in 1926 by Jens-Reidar Larsen, a young Norwegian, who arrived in Bordeaux in 1919. He settled shortly afterwards in Cognac, charmed by the inimitable atmosphere of the small Charentes town and there, discovered the refinement of its famous eau-de-vie. Having become a fine connoisseur, and driven by an innate business insight, he bought the small firm of Cognac Joseph Gautier. He then launched his own "Larsen" brand which soon prospered on Scandinavian markets, particularly in Norway. Having married a native of Cognac, he had a son who took over the Larsen firm and made the brand prosper around the world.

47. Similar examples of foreign companies, including from the United States or Japan, investing in wine or spirits estates in France, Italy, or German can be seen in Exhibits EC-37 to EC-39.

48. The EC sees no reason why the example of Mr. Larsen could not be followed by a US or Australian national who devotes himself to the making of Roquefort or Stilton cheese, or of other agricultural products and foodstuffs protected under Regulation 2081/92.[32] That such examples may not yet be as common for agricultural products and foodstuffs covered by Regulation 2081/92 as they are for wines and spirits has nothing to do with any restrictions imposed by that Regulation. Rather, it is the result of the fact that wines and spirits are high-value products, which have been traded for a long time, and where international investment accordingly has a long tradition. However, the EC is convinced that with the growing appreciation and knowledge of agricultural products and foodstuffs protected by geographical indications, this may change, and foreign nationals may indeed begin to produce such products in accordance with the product specifications.

49. Moreover, as the EC has already explained in its response to Question 29 of the Panel,[33] the present case is not one which implies a "*de facto*" discrimination between nationals within the meaning of the TRIPS Agreement. As the EC has set out, *de facto* discrimination is a notion which is closely related to preventing circumvention of national treatment obligations.[34] However, the concerns that the complainants have raised, in particular the application procedure, are linked primarily to the origin of the goods. Such issues regarding

[32] As a matter of fact, the EC believes that there probably are examples of non-EC nationals who produce products in the EC bearing names protected under Regulation 2081/92. However, since nationality of the producer is not a relevant criterion for protection under Regulation 2081/92, the EC does not have specific information about the nationality of such producers.

[33] EC Response to Panel's Question No. 29, para. 67 et seq.

[34] Cf. EC Response to Panel's Question No. 29, para. 73-74.

the treatment of goods are dealt with more appropriately in the context of the GATT, and not of the TRIPS Agreement. Similarly, conditions of residence and requirement are dealt with in Article 2.2 of the Paris Convention, on the basis of which the complainants have made separate claims.

50. For the reasons set out, the claims do not fall under the scope of Article 3.1 TRIPS and 2.1 Paris Convention.

2. Claim 1: Non-EC nationals are accorded less favorable treatment than EC nationals with respect to the registration of geographical indications through the application of a condition of reciprocity and equivalence

51. The US and Australia have claimed that by subjecting the registration of geographic indications from other WTO members to "conditions of reciprocity and equivalence", Regulation 2081/92 violates the national treatment provisions of Article 3.1 TRIPS and 2.1 Paris Convention.

52. In its submissions to the Panel, the EC has repeatedly confirmed that it does not apply such conditions to other WTO Members.[35] Accordingly, this claim of the complainants is without factual basis. However, the complainants have expressed scepticism about the EC's interpretation.[36] Hereunder, the EC will show that such scepticism is unwarranted.

(a) The complainant's interpretation is incompatible with the plain wording of Regulation 2081/92

53. First of all, the interpretation given by the complainants of Regulation 2081/92 is incompatible with the plain wording of Regulation 2081/92. Article 12(1) of the Regulation states clearly that it applies only "without prejudice to international agreements". Accordingly, the conditions of reciprocity and equivalence set out in Article 12(1) are applied only without prejudice to international agreements.

54. The formula "without prejudice to" is a common occurrence in EC legislation. In a drafting manual for EC legislation, the meaning of the expression "without prejudice to ... " is defined as "without affecting ...", "independently of ...", "leaving intact ...".[37]

55. In other words, the effect of such "without prejudice" clauses is to isolate and protect the act or provision to which reference is made from the effect of the act or provision in which the reference is contained. In other words, should a conflict between the two acts or provisions occur, then the act or provision to which the "without prejudice" reference is made prevails.

---

[35] EC FWS, para. 65 et seq, 115 et seq.; EC FOS, para. 42.

[36] US FOS, para. 16; Australia's FOS, para. 19.

[37] Manual of Precedents for Acts Established within the Council of the European Communities, 3rd edition, p. 135 (1990) (Exhibit EC-40).

56. According to the submissions of the complainants, the application of conditions of reciprocity and equivalence to WTO Members conflicts with the national treatment obligations of the TRIPS Agreement and the GATT. However, Article 12(1) precisely prevents such a conflict by stating that it applies "without prejudice" to international agreements.

57. Accordingly, on the basis of the plain wording of the Regulation, the conditions of reciprocity and equivalence do not apply to WTO Members. Rather, as the EC has already explained in its response to Question 7 of the Panel, an application for registration of a geographical indication from a WTO Member may be made directly under Article 12a of Regulation 2081/92.[38]

(b) The without prejudice clause requires that the WTO Agreements be taken into account

58. The EC's interpretation of the plain meaning of Article 12(1) of the Regulation is further confirmed by the legal context of the Regulation in the EC domestic legal order.

59. As the EC has already explained, an important principle in the jurisprudence of the Court of Justice is that the legal acts of the institutions should be interpreted in line with the international obligations of the European Communities.[39] On this basis, the EC does not see how the European institutions, and in particular the European Court of Justice, could avoid taking into account the EC's obligations under the WTO agreements. The fears and doubts which the complainants have expressed in this context as regards the possible approach that could be taken by the Commission, the Council of Ministers, or the European Court of Justice, are exaggerated and based an insufficient understanding of the relationship between EC law and WTO law.

60. Quite on the contrary, the EC believes that on the basis of the wording of Regulation 2081/92, there would be a considerable risk of a successful legal challenge if the Community institutions rejected an application for the registration of a geographical indication from another WTO member with the argument that such WTO Member does not fulfil the conditions of Article 12(1) of the Regulation. The wording "without prejudice to international agreements" clearly requires the institutions to take into account and apply international agreements, including the WTO Agreements. In such a situation, the Community institutions would be violating Community law if they applied Regulation 2081/92 in a way that prejudices the WTO Agreements. This is confirmed also by the jurisprudence of the Court of Justice, which has held that where a Community measure is intended to implement a particular obligation, or where the Community measure refers explicitly to the precise provisions of the WTO Agreements, the Court may review the legality of EC measures in the light

[38] EC Response to Panel's Question No. 7, para. 16-17.

[39] Supra para. 18. Cf. also EC Response to Panel's Question No. 15, para. 32 et seq.

of WTO obligations.[40] In the case of Article 12(1) of Regulation 2081/92, the measure not only "implements" or refers" to obligations of WTO law, but provides that it shall be "without prejudice". This is a stronger formulation than the one relied on by the Court in previous cases where it reviewed the compatibility of Community measures with WTO law, and therefore requires even more strongly that WTO obligations be taken into account.

61. The plain wording of the Regulation, in particular when interpreted in the light of the principles of interpretation of Community law, clearly confirms the interpretation given by the EC.

(c) It is not uncommon for Community legal acts to apply "without prejudice to international agreements"

62. It may also be useful for the Panel to know that there is nothing unusual about the fact that a Community legal act would apply "without prejudice to international agreements". In fact, analogous provisions can be found in numerous Community legislative acts drawn from various sectors.

63. For instance, Article 22.4 of Regulation 1784/2003 on the common market organisation in cereals provides that it applies "*having regard to the obligations arising from agreements concluded in accordance with Article 300 of the Treaty*".[41] Similar provisions were introduced into a number of Regulations in the agricultural field by Council Regulation EC 3290/94 of 22 December 1994 on the adjustments and transitional arrangements required in the agricultural sector resulting from the Uruguay Round agreements.[42]

64. Article 4(2) of Regulation 2407/92 on licensing of air carriers provides as follows:[43] "*Without prejudice to agreements and conventions to which the Community is a contracting party*, the undertaking shall be owned and continue to be owned directly or through majority ownership by Member States and/or nationals of Member States."

65. Article 3 of Council Regulation 1356/96 on transport of persons and goods on Community rivers reads as follows:[44] "This Regulation shall not affect the rights of third-country operators under the Revised Convention for the Navigation of the Rhine (Mannheim Convention), the Convention on Navigation on the Danube (Belgrade Convention) *or the rights arising from the European Community's international obligations*."

66. Article 12(1) of Directive 2003/86 on the right to family reunification reads as follows:[45] "*Without prejudice to international obligations*, where family

---

[40] Case C-70/87, *Fediol*, [1989] ECR 1781, para. 19–22 (Exhibit EC-41); Case C-69/89, *Nakajima* [1991] ECR I-2069, para. 30–32 (Exhibit EC-42); Case C-93/02 P, *Biret*, Judgment of 30 September 2003, para. 53 (Exhibit US-31).

[41] Exhibit EC-43 (emphasis added).

[42] Exhibit EC-44.

[43] Exhibit EC-45 (emphasis added).

[44] Exhibit EC-46# (emphasis added).

[45] Exhibit EC-47 (emphasis added).

reunification is possible in a third country with which the sponsor and/or family member has special links, Member States may require provision of the evidence referred to in the first subparagraph".

(d) The "without prejudice" clause was not intended to apply only to bilateral agreements, or to agreements which contain "specific rules" on geographical indications

67. In its oral statement, the US has argued that the "without prejudice" clause in Article 12(1) of the Regulation applies only to bilateral, but not to multilateral agreements.[46] In response to the questions of the Panel, the complainants now seem to argue that the "without prejudice" clause covers certain "specific" agreements concerning the protection of geographical indications, but not the obligations under the WTO Agreements.[47]

68. Neither the former nor the latter distinction has any basis in the wording of Article 12(1) of the Regulation. Article 12(1) simply refers to "international agreements". It does not distinguish between bilateral and multilateral agreements. Neither does it distinguish between agreements which lay down "specific rules" for the protection of geographical indications, and others which do not.

69. The EC would note the suggestion that the "without prejudice" clause should only apply to agreements which set out specific rules by "either directly specifying GI protection for specific names or specifying procedures and requirements for protecting GIs from the parties to that agreement" is not consistent with the wording and context of Article 12(1). Whereas it is not excluded that such specific agreements might be covered by the "without prejudice" clause, there is no reason why *only* such specific agreements should be covered.

70. Similarly, the fact that in the context of the TRIPS Agreement, "there is no specific international registration regime for the Commission to apply", to quote another US argument,[48] does not prevent the application of the "without prejudice" clause to the WTO Agreements. Moreover, the EC does not understand where the US would draw the line between "specific" and "unspecific" agreements. After all, the WTO Agreements, and in particular the TRIPS Agreement, also contain rules concerning the protection of geographical indication. To the extent that they contain rules applicable to geographical indications, the EC does not see why they should not be covered by the "without prejudice" clause.

71. The EC would like to point out that the interpretation made by the complainants would largely deprive the "without prejudice" clause of its useful value. In order to counter this argument, the United States has attempted to give

46 US FOS, para. 8.
47 US Response to Panel's Question No. 5, para. 19; Australian response to Question 6.
48 US Response to Panel's Question No. 5, para. 29.

a number of examples of agreements which it believes fall under the "without prejudice" clause. However, the United States' examples prove the opposite, since not a single of the agreements to which it refers in fact fall under this clause.

72. As a first example, the United States refers to bilateral agreements in the field of wines.[49] However, it follows clearly from Article 1 (1), second subparagraph, of Regulation 2081/92, that the Regulation does not apply to wine-sector products. Since the Regulation does not apply to wines, bilateral agreements concerning geographical indications for wines are hardly a pertinent example.

73. As a second example, the United States once again refers to the joint declaration to the Agreement on Trade in Agriculture between Switzerland and the EC.[50] Similarly, the US refers to Article 46 (4) of the Cotonou Agreement, according to which the Community and the ACP countries "may consider the conclusion of agreements aimed at protecting trademarks and geographical indications, and to "ongoing negotiations between the EC and China".[51] In all these respects, the EC would simply like to remark that no such agreement has so far been negotiated with any of the parties mentioned. Political statements of intent or interest do not constitute examples of application of the "without prejudice" clause.

74. Finally, the US is also referring to agreements between the EU Member States and third countries as a possible example for the application of the "without prejudice" clause.[52] This is wrong. The reference to "international agreements" in Article 12(1) of the Regulation applies only to international agreements concluded by the Community.

75. This follows simply from the fact that there are no bilateral agreements of Member for the protection of geographical indications which could be covered by the "without prejudice" clause. Agreements concerning the protection of geographical indications fall under the exclusive competence of the EC. The only agreements which may be legally maintained by Member States in this field are such which the Member State concluded before it became an EU member, or before the EC competence became exclusive. However, this situation is explicitly covered by Article 307 of the EC Treaty, which reads as follows:

> The rights and obligations arising from agreements concluded before 1 January 1958 or, for acceding States, before the date of their accession, between one or more Member States on the one hand, and one or more third countries on the other, shall not be affected by the provisions of this Treaty.
>
> To the extent that such agreements are not compatible with this Treaty, the Member State or States concerned shall take all

[49] US Response to Panel's Question No. 5, para. 20.

[50] US Response to Panel's Question No. 5, para. 22.

[51] US Response to Panel's Question No. 5, para. 25.

[52] US Response to Panel's Question No. 5, para. 24.

> appropriate steps to eliminate the incompatibilities established. Member States shall, where necessary, assist each other to this end and shall, where appropriate, adopt a common attitude.
>
> In applying the agreements referred to in the first paragraph, Member States shall take into account the fact that the advantages accorded under this Treaty by each Member State form an integral part of the establishment of the Community and are thereby inseparably linked with the creation of common institutions, the conferring of powers upon them and the granting of the same advantages by all the other Member States.

76. Since the only possible agreements of Member States which may still remain in force are covered by Article 307 EC Treaty, there is no need to apply the "without prejudice" clause to such agreements. Contrary to the view of the United States, the recent judgment of the European Court of Justice in Case C-216/01, *Budejovicky Budvar*, proves this point. In this case, which concerned an agreement between Austria and Czechoslovakia concluded in 1976, i.e. before either country became a Member of the EU, the Court did not base itself on the "without prejudice" clause, but on Article 307 EC Treaty:[53]

> In the light of the foregoing, the answer to the third and fourth questions must be that the first paragraph of Article 307 EC is to be interpreted as permitting a court of a Member State, subject to the findings to be made by that court having regard inter alia to the criteria set out in this judgment, to apply the provisions of bilateral agreements such as those at issue in the main proceedings, concluded between that State and a non-member country and according protection to a name from the non-member country, even where those provisions prove to be contrary to the Treaty rules, on the ground that they concern an obligation resulting from agreements concluded before the date of the accession of the Member State concerned to the European Union. Pending the success of one of the methods referred to in the second paragraph of Article 307 EC in eliminating any incompatibilities between an agreement predating that accession and the Treaty, the first paragraph of that article permits that State to continue to apply such an agreement in so far as it contains obligations which remain binding on that State under international law.

77. Accordingly, one is left with the perplexing result that the US is unable to quote a single example of an agreement to which the "without prejudice" clause would apply, but at the same time denies that it applies to the Agreements to which according to its own submissions it should certainly apply, namely the WTO agreements. This is hardly an interpretation which gives its full useful meaning to the "without prejudice" clause.

---

[53] Judgment of 18 November 2003, Case C-216/01, *Budejovicky Budvar*, para. 173 (Exhibit US-36).

(e) The evidence adduced by the complainants is neither pertinent nor conclusive

78. The complainants have alleged that the interpretation made by the EC of Article 12(1) of Regulation 2081/92 in the present proceedings is not in accordance with the interpretation given by the EC previously. In support of this argument, the complainants cite a number of presentations and other documents made by officials of European Institutions.

79. As a general remark, the EC would like to recall that in principle, the content of Regulation 2081/92 must be evaluated on the face of the measure. Of course, it is not excluded to take into account authoritative statements made on behalf of the European Communities as regards the interpretation of Regulation 2081/92. In contrast, statements made by officials of the European institutions in the course of presentations or slide shows cannot be assumed to necessarily reflect the opinion of the European Communities, and to correctly represent the content of Community law.

80. With this caveat, the EC would like to offer the following comments on the "evidence" advanced by the complainants:

81. The US has referred to an EC press release concerning Regulation 2081/92.[54] It is true that this press release did not refer to the "without prejudice language", and the implications it had for WTO countries. However, this was simply due to the fact that this part of Article 12(1) of Regulation 2081/92 had not been amended. It should also be kept in mind that press releases are typically short documents, which are not intended to give a comprehensive explanation of the content of a complex legislative measure.

82. In its oral statement, the US has referred to a slide show given on 10-12 March 2004.[55] Quite apart from the evidentiary value of such a slide show, the EC would remark that this slide show simply seems to contain a literal reproduction of Article 12(1), including the "without prejudice" language. The EC does not see what conclusions the US could draw from this slide show.

83. In its responses to the Panel, Australia has similarly referred to a slide show given in Beirut in March 2003.[56] However, this presentation was made before and clearly directed at a Lebanese public. Since Lebanon is not a WTO Member, the EC does not see what should follow from this presentation for the purposes of the present dispute.

84. In its responses to the Panel, the US has referred to a "communication" which it claims to have received from the EC on January 16, 2003.[57] The corresponding exhibit consists of one single page of text, apparently taken from a longer document, and indicates neither the date, the title, the author nor the addressee of the document. Accordingly, the EC does not consider that this document is attributable to the EC, and will not comment on it any further.

---

[54] US FOS, para. 13; Exhibit US-22.

[55] Exhibit US-23.

[56] Australian response to Question 6, and Exhibit 5 thereto.

[57] US Response to Panel's Question No. 12, para. 38, and Exhibit US-40.

85. In its responses to the Panel's questions, the US has referred to complaints raised on the part of certain US industries regarding the application of Regulation 2081/92.[58] However, these industry statements are based on misperceptions of the content of Regulation 2081/92, and are not pertinent evidence as to its proper interpretation. Moreover, none of the industries concerned in fact seem to have attempted to register a geographical indication under Regulation 2081/92, so that the complaints are largely theoretical. Finally, the EC notes that the concerns expressed on behalf of the Idaho Potato Commission seem to be related, to the extent that the EC understands them, more to the protection of trademarks in the EC than to the registration of geographical indications.[59]

86. Finally, in its responses to the Panel's questions, Australia has also referred to the EC responses to the questions of Australia during the consultations.[60] In this regard, the EC would like to recall that according to Article 4.6 of the DSU, consultations are confidential, and cannot therefore be relied on as evidence in subsequent panel proceedings. Moreover, the EC did not give any answers during the consultations which are inconsistent with its submissions before the Panel.

87. In conclusion, the complainants have not adduced evidence which contradict the interpretation of Regulation 2081/92 set out by the EC in the present proceedings.

(f) The EC is not belated in having corrected the complainants' misunderstanding

88. Finally, Australia has reproached the EC for not having corrected Australia's understanding of Article 12(1) of Regulation 2081/92 at the DSB meetings of 29 August or 2 October 2003, at which the Panel requests were considered.[61]

89. The EC considers this argument to be remarkable. Quite apart form the fact that there is certainly no obligation for a defendant to present its arguments already at the meeting of the DSB, it should be recalled that the panel requests of both Australia and the United States did not contain any reference to Article 12(1) of the Regulation, nor to "conditions of reciprocity and equivalence". In fact, as the EC stated already at the meeting of the DSB, and as it still believes, the Panel requests did not set out in sufficient detail the claims of the complainants, and did therefore not comply with Article 6.2 DSU. In its response to the EC's request for a preliminary ruling on this issue, Australia argued that Article 6.2 DSU "does not require Australia to set out in its panel establishment request precisely how it believes the EC measure violates fundamental national treatment and most favoured nation principles".[62]

---

58 US Response to Panel's Question No. 12, para. 36.

59 Cf. Exhibit US-38, p. 353.

60 Australia's Response to Panel's Question No. 6.

61 *Ibid.*

62 Comments of Australia on the EC Request, para. 27.

90. The EC finds it hard to believe that Australia would first deliberately withhold its arguments from the EC until its first written submission, and then reproach the EC for not having responded to its arguments already at the meeting of the DSB. It rather appears to the EC that this is a consequence of the deficient drafting of Australia's panel request, for which it cannot blame the EC.

3. Claim 1bis: Regulation 2081/92 violates the national treatment obligations under the TRIPS Agreement by requiring the existence of inspection structures with respect to the specific product for which protection is requested

91. In its first written submission, the United States had broadly criticised the EC for applying conditions of "reciprocity and equivalence" to the registration of geographical indications from other WTO Members. As the EC has stated in its first written submission, it was not clear whether the United States also intended to challenge the conditions for the registration of individual geographical indications, and notably the requirement that inspection structures must exist with respect to the product concerned.[63]

92. In its Oral Statement before the Panel, the United States has claimed that the requirement of the existence of inspection procedures amounts to a requirement of "equivalence by another name".[64] Moreover, in its response to Question 58 of the Panel, the United States now claims that the requirement that a Member "have a particular inspection structure [...] is itself inconsistent with WTO obligations".[65]

93. The EC therefore understands that the United States is raising a separate claim as regards the compatibility of the requirement of inspection structures with national treatment obligations.[66] As the EC will show, this claim of the United States is unfounded for the following reasons:

- The requirement of inspection structures represents equal, not unequal treatment;
- The requirement of inspection structures does not require "equivalence by another name";
- Regulation 2081/92 does not impose an "EC model" of inspection structures;
- The existence of inspection structures is necessary for attaining the objectives of Regulation 2081/92.

---

63 EC FWS, para. 119.

64 US FOS, para. 17–21.

65 US Response to Panel's Question No. 58, para. 85. Cf. also US Response to Question 56, para. 83.

66 The EC recalls that Australia has not raised such a claim under the national treatment provisions of the TRIPS Agreement or of the GATT, but has made a similar claim under Article 2.2 of the TBT Agreement.

(a) The requirement of inspection structures represents equal, not unequal treatment

94. First of all, since the United States is making its claim under the national treatment provisions of the TRIPS Agreement and the GATT, the EC would like to recall that the requirement of inspection procedures in Regulation 2081/92 does not involve any less favourable treatment of foreign nationals or goods.

95. As the EC has already explained in its first written submission, the requirement of inspection structures does apply to geographical indications from the EC and from third countries alike.[67] Accordingly, it does not involve less favourable treatment of foreign nationals or products, but indeed equal treatment.

(b) The requirement of inspection structures does not require "equivalence by another name"

96. The United States has attempted to cast doubt on this conclusion by arguing that "the EC's requirement that the United States establish EC-style inspection structures to enforce GIs is simply equivalence by another name".[68] Similarly, in its response to the Question 58 of the Panel, the United States has argued that the requirement of inspection structures "is not related to the question of whether the product for which GI protection is sought in the EC qualifies for that protection". The US goes on to add that "the particular method chosen by another WTO Member to enforce GI rules in its territory is not relevant to such a determination".[69]

97. These statements are simply incorrect. As the EC has already set out in its first written submission, as regards applications for registration from other WTO Members, Regulation 2081/92 requires the existence of inspection structures only with respect to the particular product for which protection is sought.[70]

98. Article 12a(2)(b) of the Regulation requires that the application for the registration of a geographical indication from a third country be accompanied by a declaration that the inspection structures provided of in Article 10 of the Regulation are established on its territory. This requirement is part of the application process leading to the registration of the individual geographical indication. It is clear from the provision that this condition is, like those contained in Article 12a(2)(a) and (c), applied on a product-specific basis.

99. Accordingly, the United States' claim that through its requirement of inspection structures, the EC is imposing on other WTO Members "the particular method chosen by them to enforce GI rules in their territory" is without foundation. The EC recognises the freedom granted by Article 1.1 of the TRIPS Agreement to each WTO Member to decide how to implement protection of geographical indications in its legal system.

---

67 EC FWS, para. 121.

68 US FOS, para. 21.

69 US Response to Panel's Question No. 58, para. 85.

70 EC FWS, para. 118.

100. The requirement of inspection structures does not relate to the question of how geographical indications are protected in the United States. It exclusively concerns the question of how a particular geographical indication can be protected *in the EC*. Accordingly, the United States is wrong to claim that the EC's requirement of inspection structures some constitutes a condition of "equivalence by another name".

(c) Regulation 2081/92 does not impose an "EC model" of inspection structures

101. The United States has referred to "EC-style inspection structures", and has argued that the United States should not be required to adopt "the same inspection structures as are required of Member States".[71] In the same vein, Australia has referred to "the absolute requirement for an EC model 'one size fits all'".[72]

102. These statements have no basis in the text of Regulation 2081/92. Regulation 2081/92 does not prescribe a particular "EC model" of inspection structures. The Regulation merely requires that inspection structures must exist, and in its Article 10 sets out the general principles with which such inspection structures must comply.

103. The EC notes that despite the explicit questions of the Panel, both the United States and Australia have been unable to identify a single element in the requirements of Article 10 of Regulation 2081/92 that would be objectionable.[73] In the view of the EC, this is hardly surprising given the content of Article 10 of the Regulation. In fact, Article 10 is far from establishing any kind of "model" inspection structure. For instance, Article 10 (3) sets out general principles such as that inspection bodies must offer adequate guarantees of objectivity and impartiality, and must have the qualified staff and resources at their disposal to carry out their functions. The EC hardly sees what could be objectionable about these principles. For the rest, as the EC has already explained in its first written submission, Article 10 allows a considerable flexibility in the design of the actual inspection structures.[74] In particular, it leaves the choice between public and private elements in the design of the inspection structures.

104. This considerable flexibility in the design of inspection structures is also illustrated by EC practice in the application of Article 10. For the information of the Panel, the EC attaches a list of inspection structures notified by the EC Member States in accordance with Article 10 (2) of Regulation 2081/92 (Exhibit EC-48). As a cursory examination of this list will show, the practices regarding inspection structures vary considerable from Member State to Member State, and within Member States. First of all, inspection structures are almost evenly divided between public and private bodies. Whereas in some Member States,

[71] US FOS, para. 21; US Response to Panel's Question No. 56, para. 83.
[72] Australia's Response to Panel's Question No. 62.
[73] US Response to Panel's Question No. 58, para. 85; Australia's Responses to Panel's Question No. 58 and to Panel's Question No. 62.
[74] EC FWS, para. 488 et seq.

public bodies are more prevalent, other Member States seem to prefer private bodies, and some use both, depending on national traditions and other considerations.

105. As regards public bodies, there is also considerable variety. Inspection bodies can be situated at national, regional, or even local level. Frequently, they are general public administrations dealing with many public policy issues besides inspections under Regulation 2081/92. In other cases, their only task may be such inspections.

106. The same variety of designs can also be observed in respect of private bodies. Frequently, such private bodies may be commercial enterprises; however, not-for-profit bodies can also be found. Private inspection bodies may engage in a large number of activities besides inspections under Regulation 2081/92; however, in other cases, bodies may be dedicated only to carrying out such activities.

107. As regards commercial enterprises carrying out inspections under Regulation 2081/92, the EC would like to give the example of two firms which are authorised to carry out inspections for a number of geographical indications under Regulation 2081/92 (Exhibits EC-49 and EC-50). As can be seen from the descriptions attached, both firms engage, besides inspections under Regulation 2081/92, in a vast number of professional activities in the field of agriculture, food, and sanitation, including sanitary inspections, inspections under organic labelling programmes, or food safety inspections of factories, hotels and retail premises. In other words, an inspection structure may also be a service which can be procured commercially. It would appear to the EC that there must be firms which could provide comparable services in the United States or Australia, if it was decided to have recourse to private firms for the purposes of inspections under Regulation 2081/92.

108. Overall, it should have become clear that Article 10 of Regulation 2081/92 in no way imposes an "EC model". On the contrary, there are many different ways to satisfy the requirement of Regulation 2081/92 that an inspection structure must exist.

(d) The existence of inspection structures is necessary for attaining the objectives of Regulation 2081/92

109. Indeed, it seems to the EC that the real concern of the complainants, as expressed in particular by Australia, is not so much the specific "model" of inspection structure which Regulation 2081/92 requires, but rather that no inspection structures should be required at all.[75]

110. However, the existence of inspection structures is inseparably linked with the object and purpose of Regulation 2081/92. Removing the requirement of inspection structures would therefore undermine the system of protection of geographical indications established by Regulation 2081/92.

---

[75] In its Response to the Panel's Question No. 62, Australia for instance speculates about the circumstances in which an inspection structure might "not be necessary at all".

111. It should be recalled that in accordance with Article 4(1), to be eligible to use a protected geographical indication, an agricultural product or foodstuff must comply with a product specification. For the information of the Panel, and purely for purposes of illustration, the EC attaches to its submission the applications setting out the product specifications for the following products:

- Pruenaux d'Agen (Exhibit EC-51)
- Melons du Haut Poitou (Exhibit EC-52)
- Dorset Blue Cheese (Exhibit EC-53)
- Thüringer Leberwurst (Exhibit EC-54)

112. The product specifications are set out in point 4 of each application. As can be seen from the applications, which are the basis of the registrations, for each product, the specifications contain a detailed description of the raw materials and of the methods and processes according to which the product is obtained. Compliance with these specifications is essential since it is these materials, methods and processes which will confer on the product in question the specific quality, reputation or other characteristics attributable to its geographic origin which justify the protection of the geographical indication.

113. In accordance with Article 10(1) of Regulation 2081/92, it is the function of inspection structures to ensure that agricultural products and foodstuffs bearing a protected name shall meet the requirements laid down in the specifications. The inspection structures are based on continuous control, and may involve on-site inspections at the place of production. In this way, inspection structures provide a high degree of assurance that products bearing a protected name do indeed comply with the product specifications.

114. Australia has suggested that the same degree of protection might also be achieved through other systems of protection of geographical indications, and has in particular referred to the application of unfair competition law.[76] Whereas the EC does not contest that unfair competition laws may be one way of protecting geographical indications in accordance with Article 22.2 TRIPS Agreement, the EC does not believe that such laws could provide an equivalent degree of protection of geographical indications to that achieved by Regulation 2081/92.

115. This can be illustrated with the example of a producer of a protected product who wants to defend himself against unfair competition from another producer marking a similar product using the same protected name. Under a system based on unfair competition law, this producer will have to prove in court that his competitor is producing using materials, methods or processes which are not compatible with the use of the protected name, or is not producing in the required geographic area. This in turn may require knowledge about the materials, methods or processes employed by the competitor which may be difficult to ascertain.

116. In contrast, Article 10(4) of Regulation 2081/92 provides that where an inspection body establishes that a product marketed using a protected name does

[76] Australia's Response to Panel's Question No. 62.

not comply with the product specifications, it shall take the necessary steps to ensure that the specifications are complied with. Accordingly, the producer does not have to investigate the facts himself, and accept the considerable litigation risk in pursuing unfair competitors. Rather, the producer can rely on the controls carried out by the inspection body, and be thereby be assured that any competitor using the name will indeed comply with the specifications. It is clear that in this way, the Regulation provides a higher degree of protection than the simple application of unfair competition laws.

117. The requirement of inspection structures is equally beneficial to consumer. For consumers, it will, at least at the time of purchase, be very difficult to ascertain that product bearing a protected name is indeed complying with the required specifications. The only assurance that a system based on the application of unfair competition laws can provide to the consumer is the possibility that some competitor might (or might not) pursue unfair competitors through the courts. It is clear that this is a far lower degree of assurance than that provided by Regulation 2081/92. This in turn will also affect the value of the geographical indication for producers.

118. Accordingly, if a product from third countries were entitled to benefit from protection under Regulation 2081/92 without having to comply with inspection structures, this would effectively allow third country a free ride on the EC system. Third countries would be able to use the same designation and logo as EC products, and like EC producers would benefit from the possibility of excluding others from the use of the geographical indication in accordance with Article 13 of the Regulation, without however at the same time providing the same assurances as EC geographical indications. This would create two classes of protected geographical indications, and undermine confidence in the protection of geographical indications on the part of both producers and consumers.

119. The EC would like to remark that the US itself has variously recognised the need for inspection structures. The EC has already pointed out that according to the US authorities' opinion, use of certification marks may require some public involvement to insure the proper use of such a mark.[77] Another pertinent example in the present context is the US National Organic Program run by the US Department of Agriculture. The applicable US regulations (Exhibit EC-55) provide that a person wanting to obtain or maintain organic certification must be certified by a "certifying agent", to whom he must submit an annual organic production plan (Exhibit EC-55, §205.400). It is also provided that the certifying agent must conduct an initial on-site inspection, and annual inspections thereafter (Exhibit EC-55, §205.403). The conditions for accreditation of certifying agents are described in the regulations in terms not dissimilar to those of Article 10 of Regulation 2081/92. In particular, it is required that the certifying agent must have sufficient experience, adequately trained personnel, and must prevent conflicts of interest (Exhibit EC-55, § 205.501 [a] [1], [4], and [11]).

---

[77] EC FWS, para. 496.

120. The EC assumes that the objective of certification and accredited certifying agents under the US Organic Production Program is to prevent that products are marketed as organic which do not comply with the requirements of the program, and in this way to protect the expectations of producers and consumers. These objectives are comparable to those underlying the requirement of inspection structures in Regulation 2081/92. However, if the logic of the complainants were followed, it would appear that the conditions of the US National Organic Program are unnecessary, and unduly trade restrictive, because the application of unfair competition laws should be sufficient to prevent any such abuses. The EC wonders why what is acceptable in the case of the US National Organic Program should not be acceptable in the case of Regulation 2081/92.

121. In conclusion, the requirement of inspection structures is an integral part of the EC's system of protection of geographical indications. With this system, the EC obtains, in full compliance with Article 1.1 TRIPS Agreement, a higher degree of protection of geographical indications than other Members may have chosen to do. The requirement of inspection structures does not involve discrimination between EC and foreign products, let alone nationals. Accordingly, the US claim should be rejected.

4. Claim 2: Regulation 2081/92 violates the national treatment obligations under the TRIPS and the Paris Convention by requiring that applications must be transmitted by the country in which the geographical area is located

122. The United States has claimed that Regulation 2081/92 violates the national treatment obligations under the TRIPS and the Paris Convention by requiring that applications must be transmitted by the country in which the geographical area is located. Australia has made no such claim under the TRIPS Agreement, but has raised similar claims under Article III:4 GATT.

123. In the view of the EC, these claims are unfounded. As the EC has already explained in its first written submission, the requirement that applications must be transmitted by the country in which the geographical area is located does not constitute less favourable, but indeed equal treatment.[78] As the EC has also set out in its responses to the questions to the Panel, the cooperation of the country in which the geographical area is located is indispensable for the protection of the geographical indications relating to such an area.[79] Moreover, as the EC has also explained, the role of the third country government corresponds to the cooperation required from Member States in the implementation of Regulation 2081/92.[80]

---

[78] EC FWS, para. 87 et seq.

[79] EC Response to Panel's Question No. 33, para. 80 et seq.

[80] EC Response to Panel's Question No. 33, para. 77 et seq.

(a) The cooperation of the country on whose territory the area is located is indispensable for the implementation of Regulation 2081/92

124. As the EC has already set out in response to the Panel's Question 33, the cooperation of the third country on whose territory the geographical area is located is an indispensable element of the registration process. The EC considers it useful to recall here once again the basic need for cooperation between the home country of the geographical indication and the country of registration.

125. First, the evaluation of whether a name fulfils the conditions for protection as a geographical indication requires familiarity with a host of geographical, natural, climatic and cultural factors specific to the geographical area in question. Moreover, knowledge of the market conditions in the country of origin may also be required, e.g. in order to establish whether the product in question has a particular reputation. Like in the case of applications from Member States, it is the third country's authorities which are best placed to evaluate such factors. In contrast, the European Commission is less likely to be familiar with such factors than in the case of an area in a Member State. Moreover, the evaluation may also require knowledge of the language of the third country in question, which the authorities of the European Community may not have.

126. Second, the evaluation of the application may require the assessment of legal questions arising under the law of the country where the area is located. In particular, Article 12a of the Regulation requires the application to be accompanied by a description of the legal provisions and the usage on the basis of which the geographical indication is protected or established in the third country. This reflects Article 24.9 of the TRIPS Agreement, according to which there shall be no obligation to protect geographical indications which are not or cease to be protected in their country of origin, or which have fallen into disuse in that country. Clearly, the Commission cannot unilaterally resolve such issues pertaining to the law of a third country, which therefore necessarily require the implication of the authorities of the third country.

127. Third, the involvement of the third country government appears called for also out of respect for the sovereignty of the third country. The assessment of whether an application meets the requirements of the Regulation, in particular concerning the link with the geographical area, requires in-depth knowledge of the conditions related to this area, as well as the possibility to verify on the spot the relevant claims made in the application. It would not be possible for the European Commission to carry out such inspections on the territory of the third country without the agreement or involvement of the third country.

128. Fourth, the involvement of the third country government also facilitates the cooperation of the authorities of the Community and of the third country throughout the registration process. If doubts or questions arise during the registration process, the European Commission may need a contact point in the third country to which it can address itself. Moreover, the Regulation foresees that the third country which has transmitted the application must be consulted at

certain stages of the procedure before the Commission can take a decision (cf. Articles 12b [1] [b]; 12b [3]).

129. Fifth, the involvement of the third country authorities should also be beneficial to the applicant. Regulation 2081/92 effectively enables the applicant to discuss, prepare, file, and where necessary refine and amend his application directly with the authorities where the geographical area is located. Since these authorities are more familiar with the area in question, this should help speed up the registration process. Moreover, frequently these authorities may be geographically closer to the applicant and may speak the applicant's language, which may also be a further benefit to the applicant.

(b) The requirement that the application be verified by the country on whose territory the area is located is not unreasonable

130. On the basis of the considerations above, it appears indispensable that the country where the geographical area is located be involved in the verification of applications for the protection of geographical indications relating to its territory. Independent of whether the area is located in a third country or a Member State, this involvement is a necessary element of the application process.

131. Contrary to the allegations of the complainants, this has nothing to do with whether the United States and Australia are under an obligation to cooperate with the EC or not. Obviously, the EC does not pretend that it could impose obligations on the United States or Australia by adopting internal measures. However, the essential point is not that the EC wants to impose obligations on third countries, but rather that it depends on the cooperation of those third countries for the protection of geographical indications related to their territory.

132. It should be noted that this cooperation is partially mandated by the TRIPS Agreement itself. Article 22.1 TRIPS specifically requires that a good using a geographical indication must have a given quality, reputation or other characteristics essentially attributable to its geographical origin. As the EC has already explained, the verification of whether these conditions are fulfilled can be done by no one better than by the country of origin of the indication. Accordingly, the need for cooperation is not created by the EC, but results directly from the definition of a geographical indication in the TRIPS Agreement.

133. Similarly, Article 12a of the Regulation requires the application to be accompanied by a description of the legal provisions and the usage on the basis of which the geographical indication is protected or established in the third country. This directly reflects the provision of Article 24.9 of the TRIPS Agreement, according to which there is no obligation to protect geographical indications which are not protected in their country of origin. Whether this condition is fulfilled clearly depends on legal questions under the law of the country of origin of the geographical indication. It is unreasonable for the

complainants to expect that the EC should resolve such questions of US or Australian law.

134. The fact that unlike the EC, the US or Australia do not have a specific registration system for the protection of geographical indications is no counterargument. The EC appreciates that in the absence of such a dedicated registration system, it may be more difficult to determine whether a geographical protection is protected in its country of origin. However, the fact remains that Article 24.9 TRIPS Agreement requires that it must be protected, and that this is a question of US or Australian law. It is simply unreasonable for the complainants to argue that because this may be a difficult question of Australian or US law, the EC should find the answer by itself.

135. As the EC has also shown in its responses to the Panel's Question 37, there are numerous examples in international practice where cooperation between governments is necessary for the protection of private rights and interests.[81] Contrary to the views of the complainants,[82] it is not a decisive difference that these examples are drawn from international agreements. First of all, there is an agreement between the parties, namely the TRIPS Agreement. As the EC has shown, the conditions for applications in Regulation 2081/92 reflect the conditions for the protection of geographical indications in the TRIPS Agreement.

136. Moreover, it is simply a matter of fact that the protection of geographical indications related to the territory of the United States or Australia has a link to those territories, and that therefore the cooperation of those governments is inevitable. In fact, in *US – Gasoline*, the Appellate Body specifically recognised that there may be situations were cooperation between WTO Members as territorial sovereigns is necessary to facilitate trade:[83]

> There are, as the Panel Report found, established techniques for checking, verification, assessment and enforcement of data relating to imported goods, techniques which in many contexts are accepted as adequate to permit international trade - trade between territorial sovereigns - to go on and grow. The United States must have been aware that for these established techniques and procedures to work, cooperative arrangements with both foreign refiners and the foreign governments concerned would have been necessary and appropriate. At the oral hearing, in the course of responding to an enquiry as to whether the EPA could have adapted, for purposes of establishing individual refinery baselines for foreign refiners, procedures for verification of information found in US antidumping laws, the United States said that "in the absence of refinery cooperation and the possible absence of foreign government cooperation as well", it was unlikely that the

[81] EC Response to Panel's Question No. 37, para. 89 et seq.

[82] Cf. US Response to Panel's Question No. 37, para. 69, 72; Australia's Response to Panel's Question No. 37 (referring to the absence of " express consent ").

[83] Appellate Body Report, *US – Gasoline*, p. 26.

> EPA auditors would be able to conduct the on-site audit reviews necessary to establish even the overall quality of refineries' 1990 gasoline. From this statement, there arises a strong implication, it appears to the Appellate Body, that the United States had not pursued the possibility of entering into cooperative arrangements with the governments of Venezuela and Brazil or, if it had, not to the point where it encountered governments that were unwilling to cooperate.

137. In the present case, however, it is the complainants who have explicitly declared their unwillingness to cooperate in the protection of their own geographical indications. The EC considers that this is not an admissible way of showing that the EC Regulation constitutes less favourable treatment for US or Australian nationals. To the extent that Regulation 2081/92 requires cooperation from the complainants which is reasonable and necessary, it cannot be held to constitute less favourable treatment for the nationals of these countries.

(c) The requirement that the application be transmitted by the country on whose territory the area is located is not unreasonable

138. Similarly, the requirement that the application must be transmitted by the country on whose territory the area is located cannot be regarded as unreasonable, and does not constitute an extra hurdle constituting discrimination of US or Australian nationals.

139. First of all, the requirement that the application be transmitted by the third country government simply reflects the important role played by such governments in the verification process. It does not appear that for a government that has verified the application conditions, the transmission of the application would constitute a significant extra burden. Moreover, the transmission by the government also ensures that the Commission has a contact point to which it can address any questions it might have regarding the application.

140. In fact, in its response to Question 38 of the Panel, the United States has explicitly recognised that "it would probably not be difficult to designate an office in the US government to perform a purely ministerial act of transmitting registration applications and objections to the EC".[84] The EC agrees with this statement. Accordingly, the EC understands that the United States claim relates essentially to the requirement of cooperation regarding the verification of the conditions for registration, and not to the requirement of transmission by the government.

141. The EC in fact considers that it would be rather odd for the United States or Australia to argue that they are not able to designate an office to transmit an application for registration of a geographical indication. In order to escape the apparent difficulty of this argument, the US is arguing that even if it were willing and able to transmit such applications, other WTO Members might not be

[84] US Response to Panel's Question No. 38, para. 74.

similarly willing and able.[85] This argument is unfounded. First of all, the Panel is dealing with a dispute between the US and the EC. The EC does not understand why it should be of concern to the US whether and how other WTO Members cooperate with the EC in the protection of geographical indications relating to their territory. Moreover, as the US has said itself, the transmission of an application as a purely ministerial act is not one of particular difficulty. In fact, any WTO Member with a normally functioning government should be able to carry out such an act.

142. Accordingly, the claim that Regulation 2081/92 violates the national treatment obligations under the TRIPS and the Paris Convention by requiring that applications must be transmitted by the country in which the geographical area is located is unfounded.

5. *Claim 3: Non-EC nationals are accorded less favorable treatment than EC nationals with respect to the requirement to indicate the country of origin for homonymous geographical indications*

143. The United States has claimed that the requirement contained in Article 12(2) of Regulation 2081/92 to indicate the country of origin constitutes a violation of national treatment provisions under the TRIPS and the Paris Convention, whereas Australia has made a similar claim only under Article 2.1 TBT Agreement.

144. As the EC has set out in its first written submission, this claim is unfounded.[86] First of all, contrary to the view that the US still seems to maintain,[87] it is clear form the wording of the provision that the second subparagraph of Article 12(2) of Regulation 2081/92 does not apply to all geographical indications, or all foreign geographical indications, but only to the names in the specific situation of the first subparagraph, i.e. homonymous geographical indications from the EC and a third country.

145. Second, as the EC has also explained, Article 12(2) in fact does not only apply to third country names, but also to Community names. It therefore may require the indication of the country of origin for both EC and third country names, depending on which geographical indication has been protected earlier. Accordingly, Article 12(2) of Regulations treats geographical indications from the EC and third countries alike.

146. In its oral statement, Australia has contested the EC's interpretation of Article 12(2) of the Regulation, and has relied in particular on a comparison with Article 6.6 of the Regulation. However, the EC believes that such a comparison in fact shows that the EC's interpretation is correct. Unlike Article 6 (6), the first subparagraph of Article 12(2) of Regulation 2081/92 simply refers to "protected names" from the EC and a third country, without specifying which of these

---

85 *Ibid.*

86 EC FWS, para. 132 et seq.

87 US Response to Panel's Question No. 48, para. 80.

names is the one for which registration is sought, and which is the one which is already protected. Moreover, Article 12(2), second subparagraph, explicitly states that the requirement to indicate the country of origin applies to "such names". The use of the plural in this provision clearly indicates that the requirement can relate both to the EC name and to the third country name.

147. The EC would also remark that its interpretation is the only one which is feasible in the context of the registration system established by Regulation 2081/92. In order to be legally binding, the requirement to indicate the country of origin would normally be included in the product specifications, which, in accordance with Article 4(2)(h) of Regulation 2081/92, also include specific labelling details. However, once a geographical indication is registered, it not easily possible to amend this registration to impose such labelling details. For this reason, unless registration for two homonymous geographical indications is sought simultaneously, Article 12(2) will inevitably have to apply to the geographical indication which is registered later.

148. Finally, it should also be recalled that Community law is to be interpreted to the extent possible in accordance with the Community's international obligations.[88]

149. For all these reasons, the claim should be rejected.

6. *Claim 4: Regulation 2081/92 accords less favourable treatment to non-EC nationals by subjecting the right to object to the registration of geographical indications to conditions of reciprocity and equivalence*

150. The United States and Australia have claimed that only nationals from WTO member countries recognised in accordance with Article 12(3) of Regulation 2081/92 as fulfilling the conditions of reciprocity and equivalence may object to registrations of geographical indications in accordance with Article 12d of the Regulation.

151. As the EC has already set out in its first written submission,[89] and as it has further explained in its responses to the questions of the Panel,[90] the claim is based on a misunderstanding of the Regulation. Article 12d (1) of Regulation 2081/92 gives a right to object to any person that "is from a WTO Member or a third country recognised under the procedure provided for in Article 12(3)". It is clear from this explicit reference to WTO Members that WTO Members are not subject to the procedure of Article 12(3) applicable to other third countries. The same applies also under Article 12.b.2 with respect to objections against the registration of geographical indications from outside the EC.

---

88 Above Section II.B.

89 EC FWS, para. 140.

90 EC Response to Panel's Question No. 8, para. 18, 19.

152. In fact, since the entry into force of Regulation 692/2003, the publications of all applications for registration of a geographical indication specifically refer to the possibility of residents from WTO countries to object to the application. As an example, the EC can refer to the publication of the application for the registration of a geographical indication for "Lardo di Colonnata", which was published in the Official Journal on 6 June 2003. The introductory sentence of this publication reads as follows (Exhibit EC-56; emphasis added):

> This publication confers the right to object to the application pursuant to Articles 7 and 12(d) of the abovementioned Regulation. Any objection to this application must be submitted via the competent authority in a Member State, *in a WTO member country* or in a third country recognised in accordance with Article 12(3) within a time limit of six months from the date of this publication. The arguments for publication are set out below, in particular under 4.6, and are considered to justify the application within the meaning of Regulation (EEC) No 2081/92.

153. The EC notes that the complainants have not submitted any detailed arguments on this point in response to the EC's submision. Accordingly, this claim should be dismissed.

7. *Claim 5: Regulation 2081/92 accords less favourable treatment to non-EC nationals by requiring their own country to transmit the objection*

154. The United States and Australia have claimed that Regulation 2081/92 accords less favourable treatment to non-EC nationals by requiring their own country to transmit the objection. This claim is equally unfounded. As the EC has already explained, this requirement applies equally to persons resident or established in the EC or in third countries. The attempts of the complainants to show that somehow, this requirement constitutes an "extra hurdle" for third country residents amounting to less favourable treatment fail.

(a) The complainants are not required to verify the admissibility of objections, but merely to transmit the objection

155. In its responses to the questions of the Panel, the United States seems to assume that before transmitting a statement of objection, it must verify that the objection is admissible on the basis of the criteria contained in Article 7(4) of the Regulation.[91] As it has already explained in its responses to the Panel, the EC would like to confirm that this is not so.[92] In fact, the second sentence of Article 12d(2) of Regulation 2081/92 states clearly that the conditions of Article 7(4) must be assessed in relation to the territory of the Community. This is why, unlike in the case of applications for registration, which require an

---

[91] US Response to Panel's Question No. 38, para. 75.

[92] EC Response to Panel's Question No. 34, para. 86.

assessment in relation to the territory and law of a third country, the Regulation does not require that these conditions be verified by the third country concerned.

156. This having been said, and as the EC already explained in its responses to the Panel's questions,[93] some degree of involvement of the third country government remains necessary. First, it is necessary to verify whether the person objecting is indeed resident or established in the third country, which is only possible for the authorities of that country. Second, it is not excluded that in the further procedure, questions relating to the territory of the third country might arise, in which case it is useful for there to be an official contact point in the third country. Third, it should also be beneficial to the person making the objection to be able to deal directly with an authority in the country where it is resident or established. Finally, if a statement of objection is admissible, Article 12d(3) provides that the third country which has transmitted the statement of objection is to be consulted before the Commission takes its decision.

(b) The transmission of objections is not an unreasonable requirement

157. The requirement that statements of objection be transmitted by the country where the objecting person is resident or established does not appear to be an unreasonable condition which could amount to an "extra hurdle" for third country residents.

158. As the United States has itself acknowledged in its response to Question 38 of the Panel, "it would probably not be difficult to designate an office in the US government to perform a purely ministerial act of transmitting registration applications and objections to the EC".[94] If this is not particularly difficult, then the question arises why the United States would refuse to transmit such objections. However, if there is not objective reason for this refusal to cooperate, then the complainants can also not pretend that it is the EC's rules which amount to extra hurdles for their residents. Similarly, as the EC has already explained in response to the United States claim regarding the transmission of applications, the US can not invoke the attitude which other WTO Members might or might not take in respect of the requirements of Regulation 2081/92.[95]

159. Accordingly, this claim should be dismissed.

[93] EC Response to Panel's Question No. 34, para. 85 et seq.
[94] US Response to Panel's Question No. 38, para. 74.
[95] Above para. 141.

8. *Claim 6: Regulation 2081/92 accords less favourable treatment to non-EC nationals by requiring non-EC national to have a "legitimate interest" to object to the registration of geographical indications*

160. The United States (but not Australia) has claimed that Article 12d (1) of Regulation 2081/92 accords less favourable treatment to non-EC nationals by requiring non-EC nationals to have a "legitimate interest" to object to the registration of geographical indications.

161. In its first written submission,[96] the EC has shown that there is no substantive difference between the term "legitimate interest" used in Article 12d (1) of Regulation 2081/92 and the term "legitimately concerned" in Article 7 (3). Rather, it results from simple consultation of the New Shorter Oxford English Dictionary that "legitimately concerned" and "legitimately interested" are synonymous expressions.

162. In its Oral Statement, the United States has raised the question why, if the standard is the same, the Regulation uses different words, and has claimed that the EC has "failed to rebut the presumption" that this amounts to less favourable treatment.[97] First of all, the burden of proof for showing that there is a difference in standard is on the US, not on the EC. Second, the fact that words are different does not yet create a presumption that such a difference in wording entails a difference in treatment, let alone less favourable treatment. Third, the EC considers that by referring the US to a standard dictionary of English, according to which "concerned" and "interested" are synonyms, it should have been shown that there is indeed no difference in treatment. As regards finally the question why the same language was not chosen, the EC would remark that WTO dispute settlement is concerned with the enforcement of rights and obligations under the WTO Agreement. Its objective is not to criticise the legal drafting of internal measures of a Member when such drafting question have no impact on the WTO rights of any Member.

163. Accordingly, this claim should also be rejected.

9. *Claim 7: Regulation 2081/92 accords less favourable treatment because a non-EC rightholder has no "representative" in the regulatory committee to "speak for him"*

164. Australia has argued that Regulation 2081/92 accords less favourable treatment because a non-EC rightholder has no "representative" in the regulatory committee to "speak for him".

---

[96] EC FWS, para. 78, 150-152.

[97] US FOS, para. 34.

165. Already in its first written submission, the EC has set out that this claim is patently unfounded.[98] The EC notes that Australia has not so far responded to the EC's arguments.

166. However, at this stage the EC would like to add that this claim is in remarkable contradiction with Australia's claims regarding the requirements of transmission of applications and objections. As the EC has explained, these requirements also permit the Commission to take into account the views of the third country government concerned. Moreover, certain provisions of the Regulation require that the third country government which has transmitted an application or objection must be consulted before the Commission decides on such an application or objection.[99] However, Australia has argued that it does not wish to cooperate at all in the transmission of objections and applications. The EC finds it highly contradictory that Australia should on the one hand refuse any cooperation in the protection of its geographical indications in the EC, and then on the other hand complain that it is not sufficiently heard and does not have a "representative" on a Committee composed of representatives of the Member States.

167. Accordingly, not only should this claim be dismissed, but it also casts doubt on the consistency of Australia's arguments regarding its role in the protection of the geographical indications related to its territory.

10. Claim 8: A right of objection was available to persons resident or established in an EC Member State that was not available to other WTO Member nationals in respect of the registration of more than 120 geographical indications under the normal registration process

168. Australia has claimed that there is a violation of national treatment in the fact that a right of objection *was* available to persons resident or established in an EC Member State that *was* not available to other WTO Member nationals in respect of the registration of more than 120 geographical indications under the normal registration process.[100] As the EC has set out already in its first written submission, this historic claim of Australia must fail. First, it relates to a measure which was no longer in force at the time of establishment of the Panel, and which is therefore not within the terms of reference of the Panel. Second, the individual registrations, even if considered to be within the Panel's terms of reference, are not in violation of national treatment obligations.[101]

169. The EC notes that the Panel has posed a number of specific questions regarding Australia's claims relating to past versions of Regulation 2081/92 (Questions 88 and 90 to 93). In the view of the EC, Australia's responses demonstrate that its claims are unfounded.

---

[98] EC FWS, para. 153–155.

[99] Above para. 128, 156.

[100] Australia's FWS, para. 184 et seq.

[101] EC FWS, para. 156 et seq.

(a) The legal basis of Australia's claim is unclear, and keeps shifting

170. As a preliminary point, the EC would like to recall that so far, Australia had raised its claims concerning the absence of a right of objection under previous versions of Regulation 2081/92 under the national treatment provisions of the TRIPS Agreement and the Paris Convention.[102]

171. To its astonishment, the EC notes that in its response to the Panel's question 92, Australia alleges that the absence of a right of objection under previous versions of Regulation 2081/92 constitutes a violation not only of national treatment obligations under the TRIPS Agreement and the Paris Convention, but also of Article 16.1 TRIPS, Article 22.2 TRIPS in conjunction with Article 10*bis* of the Paris Convention, Articles 41.1, 41.2, 41.3, and 42 TRIPS, and Article III:4 GATT.

172. The EC considers that in its responses, Australia is raising new claims, which it did not raise in its first written submission. The EC notes also that Australia does not offer any arguments in support of its claims. The EC considers therefore that the Panel should not consider these claims.

173. In addition, the EC has already explained in its first written submission that *inter partes* procedures such as objection procedures are covered by Article 62.4 TRIPS Agreement, which makes it optional whether to provide for such procedures. Accordingly, there is no obligation on Members to provide for objection procedures.[103] Already for this reason, the claims under Articles 16.1, 22.2, 41.1, 41.2, 41.3 and 42 TRIPS are unfounded. Moreover, as regards the reference to Article III:4 GATT, the EC does not see how a provision concerning a right of objection to the registration of a geographical indication is related to the treatment of *products*.

(b) Australia's claims regarding old versions of Regulation 2081/92 are outside the terms of reference of the Panel

174. Australia's claim relates to Regulation 2081/92 as in force until 8 April 2003, when Regulation 692/2003 entered into force. In its first written submission, the EC has already pointed out that the terms of reference of the Panel include only measures which were in existence at the time that the Panel was established.[104]

175. In its oral statement, Australia has argued that that the reference in its Panel request to Regulation 2081/92 "and any amendments thereto" should not be read as Regulation 2081/92 "as amended by".[105] It appears from these statements that Australia maintains that any version of Regulation 2081/92 which applied at any point in time, even if no longer in force at the time the

---

[102] Australia's FWS, para. 184, para. 190.

[103] EC FWS, para. 327 et seq., para. 357 et seq.

[104] EC FWS, para. 13 et seq., para. 157.

[105] Australia FOS, para. 13.

Panel was established, is nonetheless within the terms of reference of the Panel. The EC does not understand what could possibly be the justification for such an approach, which condemns Panels to examine historical facts which may have no relevance for current legal dispute. In any case, the EC submits that Australia's interpretation of its Panel request is so unusual that it would have had to make its intention to also attack historical versions of the Regulation much clearer in its Panel request.

176. The EC notes that this also seems to have been the understanding of the Panel. In its preliminary ruling issued on 5 April 2004, the Panel argued that "[t]here is no doubt as to which specific measure is in issue, as the European Communities has itself demonstrated by annexing a *consolidated text* of the regulation to the request for a preliminary ruling".[106] By referring to "consolidated text", the Panel made it clear that like the EC, it understood Australia's request to refer only to Regulation 2081/92 at the time the Panel was established, and not to older versions no longer in force.

177. The EC notes that Australia does not seem to be entirely sure of its own interpretation. Already in its oral statement, Australia has indicated that "it is not seeking to analyse historical versions of Regulation 2081/92 in a vacuum".[107] In its response to Question 88 of the Panel, Australia indicates that it "seeks rulings and recommendations from the Panel in respect of earlier versions of Regulation 2081/92 to the degree necessary to establish the extent to which the EC's actions in registering those EC-defined GIs were inconsistent with the EC's obligations".[108] The EC considers that these ambiguous submissions of Australia create a total confusion as to whether in Australia's view the measures at issue are also the historical versions of Regulation 2081/92 or not.

178. Overall, the Panel should conclude that the historical versions were not identified in the Panel request, and already for this reason are not within the Panel's terms of reference.

(c) Australia's claims are moot and therefore not within the terms of reference of the Panel

179. In any event, even if the historical versions had been clearly referred to in the Panel request, it is not up to Australia to enlarge the Panel's terms of reference in a way that runs counter to the object and purpose of the DSU.

180. As the EC has already recalled in its first written submission, the object and purpose of dispute settlement in accordance with Article 3.3 DSU is the settlement of concrete disputes between the parties, and to induce compliance with WTO obligations.[109] It does not serve as a mechanism for investigating historical violations. This is why according to constant case law under the DSU,

---

106 Preliminary Ruling of 5 April 2004, para. 24.
107 Australia FOS, para. 14.
108 Australia's Response to Panel's Question No. 88.
109 EC FWS, para. 19.

Panels are competent to consider measures in force at the time of their establishment, and not measures which have already ceased to exist.[110]

181. This limitation to actual and current disputes is not unique to the DSU, but is in fact a general principle of international dispute settlement. For instance, in the case concerning *Border and Transborder Armed Actions (Nicaragua v. Honduras)*, the International Court of Justice stated that "the critical date for determining the admissibility of an application is the date on which it is filed".[111] Similarly, in the *Nuclear Tests* Case, the International Court of Justice stated that "[t]he Court, as a court of law, is called upon to resolve *existing* disputes between States."[112]

182. In the case concerning the *Northern Cameroons*, the International Court of Justice specifically refused to rule on a question regarding the interpretation of a trusteeship agreement which had expired after the application was filed, but before the Court rendered its judgment. The Court explained its decision as follows:[113]

> Moreover the Court observes that if in a declaratory judgment it expounds a rule of customary law or interprets a treaty which remains in force, its judgment has a continuing applicability. But in this case there is a dispute about the interpretation and application of a treaty – the Trusteeship Agreement – which has now been terminated, is no longer in force, and there can be no opportunity for a future act of interpretation or application of that treaty in accordance with any judgment the Court might render.

183. Interestingly, the International Court of Justice in its judgment explicitly noted that this did not mean that the trusteeship agreement could no longer have any legal effects, for instance as regards property rights which might have been obtained in accordance with the trusteeship agreement:[114]

> Looking at the situation brought about by the termination of the Trusteeship Agreement from the point of view of a Member of the United Nations, other than the Administering Authority itself, it is clear that any rights which may have been granted by the Articles of the Trusteeship Agreement to other Members of the United Nations or their nationals came to an end. This is not to say that, for example, property rights which might have been obtained in accordance with certain Articles of the Trusteeship Agreement and which might have vested before the termination of the Agreement, would have been divested by the termination.

---

[110] EC FWS, para. 16.

[111] *Border and Transborder Armed Actions (Nicaragua v. Honduras), Jurisdiction and Admissibility,* Judgment of 20 December 1988, I.C.J. Reports 1988, p. 69.

[112] *Nuclear Tests (Australia vs. France)*, Judgment of 20 September 1974, I.C.J. Reports 1974, para. 253 (emphasis added).

[113] *Northern Cameroons (Cameroon v. United Kingdom)*, Preliminary Objections, Judgment of 2 December 1963, I.C.J. Reports 1963, p. 37.

[114] *Northern Cameroons (Cameroon v. United Kingdom)*, Preliminary Objections, Judgment of 2 December 1963, I.C.J. Reports 1963, p. 34.

184. In the present case, the Australian claims did not become moot during the Panel proceedings; rather, they were already moot when Australia made its Panel request. The fact that Regulation 2081/92 before its amendment through Regulation 692/2003 did not provide for a right of objection is a fact entirely in the past. As a situation in the past, it is not possible for any dispute settlement procedures to undo this historical fact.

185. For this reason also, the Australian claim is outside the Panel's terms of reference.

(d) Australia has not shown that the individual registrations are in violation of national treatment obligations

186. Presumably aware of these difficulties, Australia has argued that the measure at issue also includes the registrations of the "600 EC-defined GIs" which were carried out until the Panel was established.

187. The EC has already indicated that it does not believe that the individual registrations were identified in sufficient detail in Australia's Panel request.[115] However, even if the Panel, on the basis of its Preliminary Ruling issued on 5 April 2004, should consider that the individual registrations are within the Panel's terms of reference, Australia still fails to make any case that these individual registrations are in violation of the national treatment obligations under the TRIPS Agreement or the Paris Convention.

188. This follows clearly from Australia's response to Question 93 of the Panel, in which Australia concedes that it is "not able to say which individual registrations may have constituted a denial of rights to trademark holders". However, if this is so, then the EC seriously wonders what is the basis of Australia's claim that there is a violation not only of national treatment obligations under the TRIPS Agreement and the Paris Convention, but also of Article 16.1 TRIPS, Article 22.2 TRIPS in conjunction with Article 10*bis* of the Paris Convention, Articles 41.1, 41.2, 41.3, and 42 TRIPS, and Article III:4 GATT.

189. In the same response, Australia continues with the statement that "nor can the EC legitimately say that its actions have not resulted in a denial of rights". In this respect, the EC would like to recall that the burden of proving its claim is on Australia, not on the EC. In the view of the EC, Australia entirely fails in discharging this burden of proof.

190. Finally, the EC would recall that Australia's claim is based on a violation of national treatment obligations. In this respect, as the EC has already said in its first written submission, even if an individual registration might conceivable violate trademark rights, it is not clear how an individual registration could violate national treatment principles.[116] Australia forgets that the individual registrations and Regulation 2081/92 are separate measures. Therefore, even if

[115] EC Request for a Preliminary Ruling, para. 32.

[116] EC FWS, para. 161.

an older version of Regulation 2081/92 had contained a violation of national treatment principles by not providing for a right of objection, this does not mean that individual registrations based on such a version also violate national treatment principles.

(e) There is no legal basis for the recommendations suggested by Australia

191. Finally, the EC would also like to comment on the recommendations suggested by Australia.

192. In its response to Question 92 of the Panel, Australia suggests that the EC might implement any recommendation e.g. by providing persons adversely affected with access to a "civil judicial proceeding", through the provision of "just compensation" for trademark owners whose rights have been infringed, or through the revocation of "a few registrations of EC-defined GIs".

193. The EC sees no legal basis for these suggestions. According to Article 19.1 of the DSU, a Panel shall recommend to the Member concerned to bring its measure into conformity with its WTO obligations. As the EC has set out in its first written submission, this implies that WTO remedies are prospective, not retrospective.[117]

194. Accordingly, if a Panel had found that Regulation 2081/92 violated national treatment obligations by not providing for objection procedures, the way to implement such a finding for the EC would have been to amend Regulation 2081/92 accordingly. The EC would not have been obliged to reopen the registration procedures for already registered geographical indications, nor would it have been obliged to provide compensation or to cancel such trademarks. Accordingly, the EC cannot be under an obligation to do so now.

195. In its Response to Question 92, Australia has also indicated that it cannot cite any precedents where a Panel has made comparable recommendation because "Australia is not aware of a similar factual situation in another dispute". The EC considers that given over 300 disputes which have been dealt with by the dispute settlement system to date, this by itself is already an indication that Australia's claim is not in line with WTO law and practice.

196. In conclusion, this claim of Australia should be rejected.

11. Claim 9: A right of objection was available to persons resident or established in an EC Member State that was not available to other WTO Member nationals in respect of the registration of more than 480 EC-defined GIs under the simplified registration process

197. Finally, Australia also claims that a right of objection was available to persons resident or established in an EC Member State that was not available to

[117] EC FWS, para. 162 et seq.

other WTO Member nationals in respect of the registration of more than 480 EC-defined GIs under the simplified registration procedure.[118] In this respect, Australia refers to the simplified registration procedure provided for in Article 17 of Regulation 2082/92 until its amendment through Regulation 692/2003.

198. With this claim, Australia is once again trying to obtain a retrospective remedy for a measure which is not within the terms of reference of the Panel, and which it did no challenge while it was still in force. All arguments that have been set out in respect of Claim 8 therefore apply here as well.

199. Moreover, Australia's claim is factually wrong. As the EC has already set out in its first written submission, there was no right of objection for EC residents under the simplified procedure.[119] The fact that there was no right of objection for third-country residents therefore did not constitute a violation of national treatment obligations.

200. Finally, Australia's claim also falls outside the temporal scope of application of the TRIPS Agreement. In accordance with Article 70.1 of the TRIPS Agreement, the Agreement does not give rise to obligations in respect of acts (or omissions) which occurred before the date of application of the Agreement for the Member in question. In accordance with Article 65.1 of the TRIPS Agreement, the date of application for the EC was 1 January 1996.

201. In accordance with Article 17.1 of Regulation 2081/92 as originally adopted, Member States had to inform the Commission of the names for which protection was sought under this provision within six months of the entry into force of the Regulation. Since the Regulation entered, in accordance with its Article 18, into force on 24 July 1993, the Member States had to request protection at the latest by 24 January 1994. If the Community had been obliged to provide objection procedures to the registration of these geographical indications, it is at this date that it should have opened them. However, at this date, the TRIPS Agreement was not yet in force, let alone applicable to the EC.

202. In its response to Question 90 of the Panel, Australia has argued that Article 70.1 TRIPS is inapplicable since the first registration under Regulation 2081/92 did not occur until the adoption of Regulation 1107/96 of 12 June 1996. This argument is erroneous. By the time the registration occurs, objection procedures are no longer meaningful. Accordingly, objection procedures have to be provided before. The natural date for opening these procedures, had there been an obligation to do so, would have been the expiration of the time limit provided for in Article 17.1 of Regulation 2081/92, i.e. at the latest on 24 January 1994. However, at this time, the TRIPS Agreement did not yet apply.

203. For all these reasons, Australia's claims must be rejected.

---

[118] Australia's FWS, para. 190 et seq.

[119] EC FWS, para. 91 et seq., para. 172.

B. Prohibited requirement of domicile or establishment (Article 2.1 TRIPS in conjunction with Article 2.2 Paris Convention)

204. The complainants have also raised certain claims under Article 2.1 TRIPS in conjunction with Article 2.2 Paris Convention. As the EC has set out in its first written submission, the complainant's claims under Article 2.2 Paris Convention are not within the Panel's terms of reference.[120] Moreover, the EC has shown in its first written submission that these claims are unfounded.

1. Claim 10: Regulation 2081/92 requires non-EC nationals to become established in the EC as a condition for registering geographical indications

205. The United States (but not Australia) has argued that Regulation 2081/92 requires non-EC nationals to become established in the EC as a condition for registering geographical indications.[121] As the EC has set out in its first written submission, this claim is unfounded for the following reasons:

- Geographical indications relating to an area located in a WTO country can be registered under Regulation 2081/92;
- The right to register a geographical indication does not depend on domicile or establishment;
- Article 2.2 Paris Convention does not exclude measures which ensure that a product originates in the geographical to which a protected geographical indication area is related.

206. So far, the United States has not responded in substance to the EC's arguments. Accordingly, the EC can refer to what it has already said in its first written submission.[122]

2. Claim 11: Regulation 2081/92 requires non-EC nationals to become established in the EC as a condition for objecting

207. The United States has argued that the fact that Regulation 2081/92 requires the home country of third country nationals to transmit the statement of objection constitutes a requirement of residence or domicile contrary to Article 2.2 of the Paris Convention.[123]

208. As the EC has explained in its first written submission, this claim is manifestly unfounded.[124] Article 12d(1) of Regulation 2081/92 explicitly *allows*

---

[120] EC FWS, para. 36 et seq.

[121] US FWS, para. 84.

[122] EC FWS, para. 176 et seq.

[123] US FWS, para. 91. Australia has raised Article 2.2 Paris Convention in the context of its claims with respect to Regulation 2081/92 as applicable before it was amended by Regulation 692/2003 (Australia's FWS, para. 189, 194), which are in any event outside the Panel's terms of reference.

[124] EC FWS, paras. 188–189.

persons from other WTO countries who are resident or established in third countries to object to registrations. Accordingly, this claim must be rejected.

C. National Treatment under Article III:4 GATT

209. The complainants have raised a number of claims alleging that Regulation 2081/92 is incompatible with the national treatment obligation contained in Article III:4 GATT. As the EC has already shown in its first written submission,[125] Regulation 2081/92 is fully compatible with Article III:4 GATT. In the alternative, the EC submits that the measure is justified by Article XX(d) GATT.

1. The regulation 2081/92 is not incompatible with Article III:4 GATT

210. So far, the complainants have not specifically responded to the EC's arguments concerning the claims under Article III:4 GATT. Accordingly, the EC can generally refer to what it has said in its first written submission. In addition, it can also refer to its remarks in the present submission regarding the parallel claims made under the national treatment provisions of the TRIPS Agreement.

(a) Claim 12: Regulation 2081/92 accords less favourable treatment as regards the conditions for registration of foreign geographical indications

211. The complainants have claimed that Regulation 2081/92 accords less favourable treatment as regards the conditions for registration of foreign geographical indications by imposing conditions of reciprocity and equivalence.[126]

212. As the EC has already stated in its first written submission,[127] and confirmed in the present submission,[128] Regulation 2081/92 does not impose a condition of reciprocity and equivalence for the registration of geographical indications from other WTO Members. Accordingly, it does not apply less favourable treatment to products from other WTO Members.

213. The claim that Regulation 2081/92 accords less favourable treatments as regards the conditions for registration of foreign geographical indications by imposing conditions of reciprocity and equivalence must therefore be dismissed.

(b) Claim 12*bis*: Regulation 2081/92 violates the national treatment obligations under the GATT by requiring the existence of inspection structures

---

[125] EC FWS, para. 190 et seq.
[126] US FWS, para. 104; Australia's FWS, para. 165 et seq.
[127] EC FWS, para. 62 et seq., 202 et seq.
[128] Above para. 51 et seq.

with respect to the specific product for which protection is requested

214. As the EC has noted above, the US has now clarified that it considers the requirement of inspection structures with respect to specific products for which protection is sought constitutes a violation of national treatment obligations. The EC assumes that the United States is raising this claim also under the national treatment provisions of the GATT.

215. The EC considers that as under the national treatment obligations of the TRIPS, this claim is also unfounded under Article III:4 GATT. In this respect, the EC can refer to its arguments regarding Claim 1*bis* under the TRIPS Agreement.[129]

216. Accordingly, this claim should also be rejected.

(c) Claim 13: Regulation 2081/92 accords less favourable treatment as regards the requirement that the application must be transmitted by the government of the third country

217. The complainants have argued that Regulation 2081/92 accords less favourable treatment as regards the requirement that the application must be transmitted by the government of the third country.[130]

218. As the EC has already set out above with respect to Claim 2, the role of third country governments provided for in Article 12a of the Regulation corresponds exactly to that of EC Member States where geographical indications relating to an area located in the EC are concerned. Accordingly, the condition that an application relating to an area located in a third country is transmitted by the government in question does not amount to "less favourable treatment", but in fact ensures equal treatment. Moreover, the EC has also explained that the cooperation of the home country of a geographical indication is indispensable for the protection of a geographical indication in the EC.[131]

219. Accordingly, this claim is equally unfounded.

(d) Claim 14: Regulation 2081/92 accords less favourable treatment as regards the requirement to indicate the country of origin

220. The United States (but not Australia) has argued that Regulation 2081/92 accords less favourable treatments as regards the requirement to indicate the country of origin.[132]

---

[129] Above, para. 91.

[130] US FWS, para. 104 (d); Australia's FWS, para. 172 et seq.

[131] Above, para. 122.

[132] US FWS, para. 106. Australia has made a similar claim under Article 2.1 of the TBT Agreement (cf. Australia's FWS, para. 234).

221. As the EC has already set out in its first written submission, this claim is unfounded for the following reasons:[133]

- Article 12(2) of Regulation 2081/92 does not apply to all geographical indications, but only to homonyms;
- The requirement to indicate the country of origin for homonymous geographical indications from the EC and third countries does not constitute less favourable treatment;
- Article IX:1 of the GATT is a *lex specialis* to Article III:4 GATT; national treatment obligations therefore do not apply to requirements to mark the country of origin.

222. To the extent that the complainants have responded to the first and second of the EC's arguments, the EC can refer to what it is replied above in respect of claim 3.[134]

223. In response to the EC's third argument relating to Article IX:1 GATT, the United States in its oral statement has argued that Article 12(2) of Regulation 2081/92 "is not a general country of origin requirement as described in Article IX of the GATT 1994".[135] The EC does not consider this objection to be justified. Article IX GATT is entitled "Marks of Origin". Article IX:1 GATT establishes a most-favoured nation rule "with regard to marking requirements". The article contains no distinction between "general requirements", which would apply to all products, and "specific requirements", which would apply only to specific products or groups of products.

224. Accordingly, Article 12(2) of Regulation 2081/92 is an origin marking requirement falling under Article IX:1 GATT. For this reason, national treatment obligations do not apply to this requirement.

225. For all the reasons set out, the EC submits that the United States claim must be rejected.

(e) Claim 15: Regulation 2081/92 accords less favourable treatment due to an overall bias in the decision-making process

226. Australia has argued that Regulation 2081/92 accords less favourable treatment in that there is an overall bias in the decision-making process.[136] As the EC has already set out in its first submission, this claim is confused and insufficiently reasoned.[137] So far, Australia has not further substantiated its claim.[138] Accordingly, the EC sees no need to discuss this claim any further.

---

[133] EC FWS, para. 209.

[134] Above, para. 143.

[135] US FOS, para. 35.

[136] Australia's FWS, para. 177.

[137] EC FWS, para. 219 et seq.

[138] In para. 24 of its FOS, Australia has argued that the EC's description of the decision-making process is "not accurate". The EC does not understand in what respect its description is "not accurate". The EC also does not understand what is the relevance of the discussion of the Community's comitology procedures for the present case.

227. For these reasons, the Australian claim must be rejected.

2. *The measure would be justified under Article XX(d) GATT*

228. The EC considers that if the Panel were to find that Regulation 2081/92 does involve less favourable treatment of foreign goods by requiring the existence of inspection structures, the transmission and verification of applications by the third country government, and the indication of the country of origin for homonymous geographical indications, this less favourable treatment would be justified by Article XX(d) GATT.

229. According to Article XX(d) GATT, a measure otherwise incompatible with the GATT will be justified under the following conditions:

> Subject to the requirement that such measures are not applied in a manner which would constitute a means of arbitrary or unjustifiable discrimination between countries where the same conditions prevail, or a disguised restriction on international trade, nothing in this Agreement shall be construed to prevent the adoption or enforcement by any contracting party of measures:
>
> [...]
>
> (*d*) necessary to secure compliance with laws or regulations which are not inconsistent with the provisions of this Agreement, including those relating to customs enforcement, the enforcement of monopolies operated under paragraph 4 of Article II and Article XVII, the protection of patents, trade marks and copyrights, and the prevention of deceptive practices;
>
> [...]

230. In *Korea – Various Measures on Beef*, the Appellate Body held that paragraph (d) of Article XX contained the following two requirements.[139]

> For a measure, otherwise inconsistent with GATT 1994, to be justified provisionally under paragraph (d) of Article XX, two elements must be shown. First, the measure must be one designed to "secure compliance" with laws or regulations that are not themselves inconsistent with some provision of the GATT 1994. Second, the measure must be "necessary" to secure such compliance. A Member who invokes Article XX(d) as a justification has the burden of demonstrating that these two requirements are met.

231. The Appellate Body continued to define the term "necessary" in Article XX(d) as follows:[140]

---

139 Appellate Body Report, *Korea – Various Measures on Beef*, para. 157.
140 Appellate Body Report, *Korea – Various Measures on Beef*, para. 161.

> We believe that, as used in the context of Article XX(d), the reach of the word "necessary" is not limited to that which is "indispensable" or "of absolute necessity" or "inevitable". Measures which are indispensable or of absolute necessity or inevitable to secure compliance certainly fulfil the requirements of Article XX(d). But other measures, too, may fall within the ambit of this exception. As used in Article XX(d), the term "necessary" refers, in our view, to a range of degrees of necessity. At one end of this continuum lies "necessary" understood as "indispensable"; at the other end, is "necessary" taken to mean as "making a contribution to." We consider that a "necessary" measure is, in this continuum, located significantly closer to the pole of "indispensable" than to the opposite pole of simply "making a contribution to".

(a) The requirement of inspection structures is justified by Article XX(d) GATT (Claim 12*bis*)

232. The EC has already explained above that the requirement of inspection structures is necessary for the attainment of the objectives of Regulation 2081/92.[141] In particular, the EC has explained that the requirement of inspection structures provides a high degree of assurance for producers and consumers that a product bearing a protected name does in fact correspond to the required product specifications.

233. Moreover, the EC has shown that a similar degree of protection could not be achieved through other means. In particular, the EC has explained that the application of unfair competition law would not result in the same degree of protection of geographical indications.[142] Moreover, the EC has also explained that the requirement of inspection structures does not go beyond what is necessary for the attainment of the objectives of the Regulation, and in particular leaves considerable flexibility in terms of the design of the concrete structures.[143]

234. Accordingly, the requirement of inspection structures is necessary to secure compliance with Regulation 2081/92, which is a measure not incompatible with the provisions of the GATT. In this context, the EC notes that the protection of intellectual property rights and the prevention of deceptive practices is an objective explicitly referred to in Article XX(d) GATT.

235. Moreover, the requirement of inspection structures is not applied in a manner which would constitute a means of arbitrary or unjustifiable discrimination between countries where the same conditions prevail. Similarly, it is not a disguised restriction on international trade.

236. Accordingly, the requirement of inspection structures is in any event justified under Article XX(d) GATT.

---

141 Above, para. 109 et seq.

142 Above, para. 114 et seq.

143 Above, para. 101 et seq.

(b) The requirement that the application must be verified and transmitted by the government where the area is located is justified by Article XX(d) GATT (Claim 13)

237. As the EC has already set out above, the cooperation of the government of the country where the geographical indication is located is indispensable for the implementation of Regulation 2081/92.[144] The EC has explained, in particular, that the registration of geographical indications requires the evaluation of factual and legal questions which only the home country of the geographical indication is in a position to carry out. Moreover, the EC has also explained that the requirements for cooperation do not go beyond what is necessary for the implementation of Regulation 2081/92.[145] As regards specifically the requirement that the application be transmitted by the government of the home country, the EC has explained that this follows naturally from the required intergovernmental cooperation, and is not particularly burdensome for any WTO Member.[146]

238. Accordingly, the requirement of verification and transmission of applications by the government of the home country of the geographical indication is necessary to secure compliance with Regulation 2081/92, which is a measure not incompatible with the provisions of the GATT. Moreover, the requirement of verification and transmission of applications by the government of the home country of the geographical indication is not applied in a manner which would constitute a means of arbitrary or unjustifiable discrimination between countries where the same conditions prevail. Similarly, it is not a disguised restriction on international trade.

239. Accordingly, the requirement of verification and transmission of applications by the government of the home country of the geographical indication is in any event justified under Article XX(d) GATT.

(c) The requirement to indicate the country of origin for homonymous geographical indications is justified by Article XX(d) GATT (Claim 14)

240. Finally, the EC has already indicated that the requirement to indicate the country of origin for homonymous geographical indications serves the purpose of achieving a clear distinction in practice between homonymous geographical indications.[147] In this way, it prevents that consumers are confused by homonymous geographical indications. As the EC has also explained, Article 12(2) achieves this in the least intrusive way by requiring that the indication which is registered later, and which is therefore typically the one less known to

---

[144] Above para. 124 et seq.
[145] Above para. 130 et seq
[146] Above para. 138 et seq
[147] EC FWS, para. 479.

the consumer, be the one for which it is required to indicate the country of origin.[148]

241. Accordingly, the requirement to indicate the country of origin for homonymous geographical indications is necessary to secure compliance with Regulation 2081/92, which is a measure not incompatible with the provisions of the GATT. Moreover, the requirement to indicate the country of origin for homonymous geographical indications is not applied in a manner which would constitute a means of arbitrary or unjustifiable discrimination between countries where the same conditions prevail. Similarly, it is not a disguised restriction on international trade.

242. Accordingly, the requirement to indicate the country of origin for homonymous geographical indications is in any event justified under Article XX(d) GATT.

IV. REGULATION 2081/92 IS COMPATIBLE WITH THE OBLIGATION TO PROVIDE MOST-FAVOURED-NATION TREATMENT

243. The United States (but not Australia) has claimed that Regulation 2081/92 is incompatible with the obligation to provide most-favoured-nation treatment under Article 4 TRIPS and Article I:1 GATT. As it has done in its first written submission, the EC will discuss the United States claims under both provisions separately.

A. Article 4 TRIPS

244. The United States has made two claims under the most-favoured-nation provision of Article 4 TRIPS:

- As among non-EC WTO Members, nationals from WTO Members that satisfy the EC's conditions of reciprocity and equivalency are accorded more favourable treatment than nationals from those WTO Members that do not;
- under Regulation 2081/92, an EC Member State grants more favourable treatment to nationals from other EC Member States than it accords to nationals from non-EC WTO Members.

---

[148] Above para. 143.

1. Claim 16: As among non-EC WTO Members, nationals from WTO Members that satisfy the EC's conditions of reciprocity and equivalency are accorded more favourable treatment than nationals from those WTO Members that do not

245. The United States has claimed that nationals from WTO Members that satisfy the EC's conditions of reciprocity and equivalency are accorded more favourable treatment than nationals from those WTO Members that do not.

246. In its first written submission, the EC has explained that this claim is unfounded for the following reasons:[149]

- the EC does not apply a condition of reciprocity and equivalence for the registration of geographical indications from other WTO members;
- the conditions for the registration of individual geographical indications from third countries are not discriminatory;
- Article 12 of Regulation 2081/92 does not grant any advantage, favour, privilege or immunity to any other country;
- the conditions for the registration of geographical indications do not depend on nationality.

247. The EC notes that the United States has made almost no arguments in defence of this claim. Accordingly, the EC can largely refer to what is has already set out in its first written submission.

248. The EC notes, however, that the United States claim appears to be parallel to its Claim 1, according to which the EC violates its national treatment obligations under the TRIPS Agreement by applying "conditions of reciprocity and equivalence" to other WTO Members.[150] As the EC has already explained in detail in response to Claim 1, it does not apply such conditions to other WTO Members.[151] Accordingly, the United States claim must fail already for this reason.

249. In its oral statement, the United States has also claimed that there is a violation of most-favoured nation treatment because Regulation 2081/92 favours nationals of countries "that have an EC-style GI protection system, *including inspection structures*".[152] The EC would like to underline that this is wrong. As the EC has already explained in response to Claim 1*bis*, as regards geographical indications from WTO Members, the requirement of inspection structures is evaluated with respect to the specific product for which protection is sought.[153] Accordingly, Regulation 2081/92 does not impose a requirement that a "WTO Member" must have particular inspection structures. Rather, the requirement of inspection structures applies purely on a product-specific basis, and without

149 EC FWS, para. 228 et seq.
150 Above para. 51.
151 *Ibid.*
152 US FOS, para. 36 (emphasis added).
153 Above, para. 96.

regard to the country of origin of the product. As the Panel in *Canada – Autos* has said, such non-discriminatory conditions are not a violation of most-favoured nation treatment.[154]

250. Finally, the United States has claimed that Regulation 2081/92 involves the granting of an advantage within the meaning of Article 4 TRIPS because Articles 12 (1) and 12a are "designed" to favour national from countries that have an EC-style protection system.[155] Even if the United States' interpretation of these provisions were correct, which it is not, then the Regulation 2081/92 would not involve the granting of an advantage to any specific country. Rather, as the EC has already explained,[156] Article 12 merely sets out the conditions under which the Regulation may apply to a third country which is not a WTO Member. Accordingly, in the absence of a decision under Article 12(3) of the Regulation, Article 12 does therefore not confer any advantage onto any specific third country.

251. For all the reasons set out, the United States claim must be rejected.

2. *Claim 17: Under Regulation 2081/92, an EC Member State grants more favourable treatment to nationals from other EC Member States than it accords to nationals from non-EC WTO Members*

252. The United States has claimed that under Regulation 2081/92, an EC Member State grants more favourable treatment to nationals from other EC Member States than it accords to nationals from non-EC WTO Members.[157]

253. In its first written submission, the EC has already explained that this claim is fundamentally flawed.[158] The EC is an original member of the WTO. Measures with which the EC harmonises the law inside the EC are not measures through which the Member States grant "each other" advantages. That Regulation 2081/92 is a measure of the Community, and not of the Member States, is also reflected in the fact that the United States has correctly brought the present dispute against the EC, and not against its Member States. Accordingly, the EC does not comprehend why, in the context of this dispute with the EC concerning an EC measure, the United States is now alleging a violation of WTO obligations by the EC Member States.

254. So far, the United States has not been able to provide an explanation for its claim. In its Oral Statement, the US has merely argued that each Member State is under the obligation to provide MFN, and argued "that the fact that they may be acting pursuant to an EC regulation does not excuse them from this obligation".

---

154 Panel Report, *Canada – Autos*, para. 10.24 (full quotation in EC FWS, para. 237).

155 US FOS, para. 36.

156 EC FWS, para. 239 et seq.

157 US FWS, para. 121.

158 EC FWS, para. 249 et seq.

255. The EC does not understand what the United States means when it says that Member States are "acting pursuant to an EC Regulation". Undoubtedly, the Member States have certain responsibilities in the implementation and execution of Regulation 2081/92. However, the EC does not see that these functions give rise to any particular MFN violation, nor has the United States identified any such violations.

256. As regards the real concern of the United States, namely the alleged application of conditions of reciprocity and equivalence and the requirement of inspection structures, these result –supposing that the erroneous interpretations of the United States of Regulation 2081/92 were correct - not from any actions of the Member States, but from the text of EC Regulation 2081/92. Accordingly, the claim that Member States are granting each other advantages, or granting other third countries advantages, is devoid of all foundation.

257. Accordingly, this claim of the United States must be rejected.

B. Claim 18: By subjecting the registration of third-country geographical indications to conditions of reciprocity and equivalence, the EC measure is inconsistent with the most-favoured-nation obligation under the Article I:1 GATT

258. The United States has argued that by subjecting the registration of third-country geographical indications to conditions of reciprocity and equivalence, the EC measure is inconsistent with the most-favoured-nation obligation under Article I:1 GATT.[159]

1. Article I:1 GATT is not violated

259. Contrary to the claim of the United States, there is no violation of Article I:1 GATT.

260. Since the United States has so far not made any specific arguments in response to the EC's first written submission, the EC can refer to what it has said in its first written submission.[160]

261. The EC can also refer to its arguments in response to Claim 16, concerning a violation of national treatment principles under the TRIPS Agreement,[161] which apply also in the present context. In particular, the EC would like to point out once more that the requirement of inspection structures applies on a product-specific basis, and does in no way involve discrimination on the basis of the origin of the product.

262. For these reasons, Regulation 2081/92 is not incompatible with Article I:1 GATT.

---

159 US FWS para. 127 et seq.

160 EC FWS, para. 258 et seq.

161 Above para. 245.

2. *The EC measure would be justified under Article XX(d) GATT*

263. For the sake of completeness, the EC would like to remark that should the Panel nonetheless come to the conclusion that the requirement of inspection structures somehow involves discrimination between third countries, the EC would consider that this requirement is justified under Article XX(d) GATT.

264. In relation to the claims regarding a violation of Article III:4 GATT, the EC has already explained that the requirement of inspection structures is necessary for the attainment of the legitimate objectives of Regulation 2081/92.[162] These considerations apply not only to the claim under Article III:4 GATT, but also to the claim under Article I:1 GATT.

265. Accordingly, the requirement of inspection structures is in any event justified by Article XX(d) GATT.

V. REGULATION 2081/92 DOES NOT DIMINISH THE LEGAL PROTECTION OF TRADEMARKS

A. *Article 16.1 of the TRIPS Agreement*

1. *Claim 19: Article 14(2) of Regulation 2081/92 is inconsistent with Article 16.1 of the TRIPS Agreement in that it allows the co-existence of geographical indications and earlier registered trademarks*

(a) Article 14(3) of Regulation 2081/92

266. The United States, but not Australia, addressed the EC's arguments based on Article 14(3) of Regulation 2081/92 in its First Oral Statement. The EC has provided a comprehensive response to the US counter-arguments as part of its replies to the Panel's questions Nos. 63 to 71, to which the Panel is referred. In this section the EC will elaborate on those replies and provide comments on the responses given by the United States to the Panel's Questions Nos. 14 and 67.

(i) Registrability of geographical names as trademarks

267. In its First Written Submission, the EC explained that geographical terms are primarily "non-distinctive" and, for that reason, their registration as trademarks is permitted only exceptionally.[163] More specifically, the EC explained that, under the Trademark Directive and the Community Trademark Regulation, as interpreted by the European Court of Justice, the registration of a geographical term is permitted only in the following circumstances:[164]

162 Above para. 232.
163 EC FWS paras. 278-285.
164 *Ibid.*, para. 284.

- where the geographical name is not currently associated, and it can be reasonably assumed that it will not be associated in the future, with the product concerned; or
- where the name has acquired distinctiveness through use.

268. The United States does not dispute this. Yet it suggests that, in practice, the registration as trademarks of geographical terms which qualify, or may potentially qualify, as geographical indications is a frequent occurrence. As discussed below, however, the United States provides no evidence of this, other than a few hypothetical examples.

269. In addition, the United States seeks to misrepresent the EC position by attributing to the EC arguments which the EC has not made. Thus, the EC has not argued that the criteria for the registrability of trademarks are sufficient in themselves to prevent the registration of later confusing geographical indications. In particular, the EC has never said that "valid registered trademarks cannot incorporate certain geographical elements."[165] Indeed, if so, it would have been unnecessary to include Article 14(3) in Regulation 2081/92. Nor is it the EC's position that the violation of Article 16.1 of the TRIPS claimed by the complainants should be tolerated because "the number of specific rights affected is small".[166] The EC is not seeking to "minimize the violation of Article 16.1".[167]

270. To be clear, the EC's position is that there is no violation of Article 16.1, even on the complainants' interpretation of that provision. First, the criteria for the registrability of trademarks limit *a priori* the possibility of conflicts between geographical indications and earlier trademarks. Second, to the extent that any such conflict arises, Article 14(3) of Regulation 2081/92 provides the necessary means to trademark owners in order to prevent or invalidate the registration of *any* confusing geographical indications. Finally, the provisions of Regulation 2081/92, together with other provisions of EC law and the unfair competition laws of the Member States, provide the necessary means to ensure that, in practice, registered geographical indications are not misused so as to create confusion.

(ii) Standard of evidence for establishing the meaning of Article 14(3)

271. The United States argues that the EC has made an improper application of the "mandatory/discretionary analysis".[168] This criticism is misplaced because the EC is not relying on that distinction. The EC is not arguing that Article 14(3) complies with Article 16.1 of the TRIPS Agreement because it gives "discretion" to the EC authorities in order to decide whether or not to refuse the registration of a confusing geographical indication. Article 14(3) is a "mandatory" provision in the sense that it imposes an unqualified obligation upon the EC authorities to

165 US FOS, para. 50.
166 *Ibid.*, para. 49.
167 US Response to Panel's Question No. 67.
168 US Response to Panel's Question No. 14.

refuse any proposed geographical indication that gives rise to the situation described in that provision.

272. The EC's statement quoted by the United States does not relate to the distinction between "mandatory" and "discretionary" legislation, but instead to the issue of what is the appropriate standard of evidence in order to establish the meaning of Article 14(3).

273. The complainants' claim is premised on a certain reading of Article 14(3), which is contested by the EC. The interpretation of Article 14(3) is a matter of EC law and must be treated as a factual issue by the Panel. The complainants bear the burden of proving that Article 14(3) has the meaning which they have asserted in this dispute. In order to do so, it is not enough for them to show that their reading of Article 14(3) is a reasonable interpretation of that provision. As explained above, the EC's own views on the meaning of Article 14(3) must be given "considerable deference". For that reason, the complainants must show not only that their interpretation is reasonable but, in addition, that the EC's interpretation of Article 14(3) is not a reasonable one.

274. Furthermore, Article 14(3) must be interpreted in accordance with the relevant rules of interpretation of EC law. This means, in particular, that, in accordance with well-established case law of the European Court of Justice, the complainants must prove that is impossible to interpret Article 14(3) in a manner that is consistent with the EC's obligations under Article 16.1 of the TRIPS Agreement, as the complainants understand such obligations.

275. Unless the complainants can show that their reading of Article 14(3) is, on the basis of the terms of that provision, the only reasonable interpretation, they would have to prove that, as a matter of fact, Article 14(3) is being applied in practice by the EC authorities in accordance with the complainants' interpretation of that provision, as demonstrated, for example, by the decisions of the EC authorities that apply Article 14(3) or by a consistent pattern of registration of confusing geographical indications.

276. As discussed below, the complainants have failed to show that their interpretation of Article 14(3) is the only reasonable interpretation of that provision. And they have not even attempted to prove that their reading of Article 14(3) is, in practice, the interpretation effectively applied by the EC authorities. Therefore, the Panel should conclude that this claim is unfounded, as a matter of fact, even on the complainants' own interpretation of Article 16.1 of the TRIPS.

(iii) The Complainants have misinterpreted Article 14(3)

277. Far from being the only reasonable interpretation of the terms of Article 14(3), the complainants' reading of that provision is unsupported by the ordinary meaning of its terms. Furthermore, the complainants' interpretation is neither workable nor reasonable in practice and cannot be reconciled with the obligations imposed upon the EC authorities by other provisions of Regulation 2081/92.

278. The complainants' claim is based on the false premise that Article 14(3) applies only to a special sub-category of trademarks, namely those which have been used "for a long time" and which, in addition, are famous. Thus, for example, the United States argues that Article 14(3) "only comes into play where there exists a trademark with reputation, renown and history of use".[169] But this is not what Article 14(3) says.

279. The length of use and reputation/renown of the trademark are not separate "requirements"[170] for the application of Article 14(3), distinct from, and additional to the likelihood of confusion. Rather, they are criteria for assessing the existence of a likelihood of confusion. From the fact that the EC Commission must consider those two criteria in order to establish the existence of a likelihood of confusion, it does not follow *a contrario* that any other criteria must be deemed irrelevant for that purpose.

280. As explained[171], Article 14(3) directs expressly the registering authority to consider the length of use and the reputation and renown of earlier trademarks because those criteria will generally be decisive in order to establish the likelihood of confusion, given that geographical names are primarily non-distinctive when used as trademarks.

281. If Article 14(3) does not mention expressly the similarity of goods and signs, it is simply because those criteria are always relevant for a determination of likelihood of confusion. The likelihood of confusion between two signs cannot be meaningfully established by considering only the length of use and the reputation/renown of one of them. The analysis must take into account necessarily the similarity of the goods and signs concerned, which must therefore be deemed implicit in Article 14(3). As shown by the EC, an interpretation of Article 14(3) which prevented the registering authority from considering the similarity of goods and signs would be neither reasonable, nor workable, and cannot be correct.[172]

282. Moreover, the interpretation of Article 14(3) made by the complainants would lead to a result which is incompatible with the terms of Articles 7(4) and 7(5)(b) of Regulation 2081/92.

283. Article 7(4) provides that a statement of objection shall be admissible, *inter alia*, if it shows that "the registration of the name proposed would jeopardize the existence of a mark".[173] This language encompasses *any* instance of likelihood of confusion between the proposed geographical indication and *any* earlier trademark. If Article 14(3) required the refusal of a proposed geographical indication only where it gives rise to a likelihood of confusion with a trademark which is famous and which has been used for a long time, as claimed by the

[169] US FOS, para. 52.
[170] US FOS, para. 53.
[171] EC FWS, paras. 278-291.
[172] EC Response to Panel's Question No. 68.
[173] Articles 12b(3) and 12d(2) provide, respectively, that the criteria of Article 7(4) shall apply also with respect to the admissibility of objections to the registration of foreign geographical indications and of objections from outside the EC to EC geographical indications.

complainants, the admissible grounds of objection would have been limited to the cases where one such trademark is likely to be jeopardized. Article 7(4), however, refers to all trademarks, without any distinction or qualification. It would be pointless to admit an objection on certain grounds if, in any event, it were not possible to reject the application on such grounds.

284. Consistent with Article 7(4), Article 7(5)(b) provides that where an objection is admissible,

> the Commission shall take a decision in accordance with the procedure laid down in Article 15, having regard to traditional fair practice and likelihood of confusion.[174]

285. Thus, Article 7(5)(b) requires the Commission to adopt a decision having regard to the "likelihood of confusion" between the proposed geographical indication and *any* trademark, and not just with those trademarks which are famous and which have been used for a long time.

(iv) There is no evidence that Article 14(3) has been applied in accordance with the complainants' interpretation

286. Since the complainants have failed to show that their reading of the terms of Article 14(3) is the only reasonable interpretation of that provision, they should prove that, *de facto*, Article 14(3) is being applied by the EC authorities in accordance with that interpretation. The complainants have not even attempted to do so.

287. Article 14(3) of Regulation 2081/92 has been applied only once by the EC institutions, in a case where it was alleged that the proposed geographical indication "Bayerisches Bier" was likely to be confused with the existing trademarks "Bavaria" and "Hoker Bajer".[175] The interpretation of Article 14(3) made in that case is consistent with the interpretation put forward by the EC in this dispute. The EC Council concluded that there was no likelihood of confusion with the trademarks in question "in view of the facts and information available". There is no suggestion in the Council decision that this conclusion was reached because the trademarks concerned were not famous enough or had not been used for a sufficiently long time.

288. The United States now suggests that the Council decision to register the geographical indication "Bayerisches Bier" was flawed because that term is likely to be confused with the trademarks at issue when used in translation.[176] This criticism is unfounded because the registration covers only the term "Bayerisches Bier" and not its translations to other languages. Moreover, even if the decision in the "Bayerisches Bier" case had been based on an erroneous

---

[174] Similar language is found in Articles 12b (3) and12d(3) with regard to the registration of geographical indications from other WTO Members and third countries and to the registration of EC geographical indications, following an objection from outside the EC, respectively.

[175] Council Regulation (EC) 1347/2001, of 28 June 2001 (Exhibit EC-9).

[176] US Response to Panel's Question No. 44.

factual assessment, that would not contradict the EC's interpretation of Article 14(3).[177]

289. In response to a question from the Panel[178], neither the complaining parties nor any of the third parties have been able to identify even one single geographical indication, of the more than 600 registered under Regulation 2081/92, which gives rise to a likelihood of confusion with an earlier trademark.

290. Instead, the United States refers to purely hypothetical examples, which have no probative value whatsoever with respect to the actual interpretation of Article 14(3) made by the EC authorities.[179]

291. The United States also refers to a case pending before the Swedish courts, where a a US company claims that the use by Czech producers of beer of the names "Budweiser Budwar", "Budweis" and "Budbräu" infringe its trademarks for the names "Budweiser", "Bud" and "Budweiser King of Beers".[180]

292. The EC understands that the United States is not raising a claim concerning the registration of the geographical indications Budějovické pivo, Českobudějovické pivo and Budějovický měšt'anský var" at this stage of the proceedings. Were the United States to raise that claim, the EC would object that the claim is clearly outside the terms of reference of the Panel, given that the process of ratification of the Treaty of Accession providing for the registration

---

[177] Furthermore, the US suggestion that *any* possible use of the term "Bayerisches Bier" would create *per se* a likelihood of confusion with the trademarks "Bavaria" and "Bajer Hoker" is difficult to reconcile with the US position, as the EC understands it, that the use of geographical indications for wines recognised in the United States such as "Rutherford" or "Santa Rita Hills" does not lead *per se* to a likelihood of confusion with virtually identical earlier trademarks such as "Rutherford Vintners" or "Santa Rita", respectively, but needs to be examined on case-by-case basis with respect to particular uses. See US Response to EC's Question No. 3.

[178] Panel's Question No. 47 to Australia and the United States and Panel's Question No. 9 to third parties.

[179] The examples cited by the United States are:

1) the hypothetical conflict between the hypothetical trademark "Luna" for cheese and the hypothetical geographical indication "Luna" for a hypothetical cheese produced in a hypothetical Spanish small town called "Luna". (US FOS, para. 50). There is no town in Spain, or in any other Spanish speaking country, whether big or small, called "Luna". For Spanish speakers, "Luna" is the name of the only satellite of the planet Earth, which is as an unlikely place for producing cheese as the planet "Mars" for producing chocolate bars. In view of that, EC trademark officials would be likely to register "Luna" as a purely fanciful name. But, for the same reason, it is unlikely that such trademark would enter into conflict with a subsequent geographical indication.

2) the hypothetical conflict between the trademark "Faro" for coffee and tea and a hypothetical geographical indication "Faro" for the hypothetical coffee and tea grown in the Portuguese town of Faro. (US Response to Panel's Question No. 47). To the best of the EC's knowledge, no tea or coffee has ever been grown in Faro. Indeed, it is doubtful that either coffee or tea can be grown commercially in Faro, given the prevailing climatic conditions. Therefore, the town of Faro is unlikely to be associated by consumers with those products. Even if, as an effect of global warming, coffee and tea became one day a speciality of the town of Faro, the registration of the hypothetical geographical indication would still have to be refused if it led to confusion with the earlier trademark "Faro" in accordance with Article 14(3).

[180] US Response to Panel's Question 47.

of those names had not been completed yet at the time of establishment of this Panel.[181]

293. In any event, the EC recalls that the registration under Regulation 2081/92 only covers the terms Budějovické pivo, Českobudějovické pivo and Budějovický měšt'anský and not any alleged translations of those terms to other languages. The EC understands that the United States is not suggesting that the use of those names is *per se* likely to result in a likelihood of confusion with the above mentioned trademarks of the US producer concerned.

(v) Article 14(3) confers enforceable rights to the trademark owners

294. The United States argues that, even if the EC's reading of Article 14(3) were correct, that provision "merely authorizes the EC to decline registration of a GI"[182], but does not accord rights to the trademark owners.

295. The United States is wrong again. The EC authorities are required, and not simply authorized, to refuse the registration of a geographical indication. Article 14(3) provides that the registration "shall not be registered" and, therefore, leaves no margin of discretion to the Commission in order to register the proposed geographical indication where the conditions set out in Article 14(3) are met.

296. Furthermore, Article 14(3) confers judicially enforceable rights to the owners of trademarks. If a trademark owner considers that the EC authorities have registered a geographical indication in violation of Article 14(3) it is entitled to challenge the validity of such registration before the courts, including in the framework of the infringement proceedings brought against the user of the geographical indication under the Community Trademark Regulation or the trademark law of the Member States.

297. The United States argues that some geographical indications have been registered in accordance with special procedures that do not provide for a right of objection, such as the so-called "fast track" procedure provided in the former Article 17 of Regulation 2081/92.[183] As explained by the EC[184], however, neither Article 16.1 nor Article 22.2 of the TRIPS Agreement requires to grant a right of objection with respect to the registration of geographical indications. All that is required by the TRIPS Agreement is that the final registration decision be subject to judicial review.[185] Trademark owners have a right to challenge the

---

181 EC FWS, paras. 21-25.

182 US FOS, para. 54. See also US Responses to Panel's Questions Nos. 14 (at para. 41) and 67 (at para. 87).

183 US Response to Questions No. 6 (at para. 68) and 67 (at para. 87).

184 EC FWS, paras. 327-333 and para. 427.

185 Cf. Article 62.5 of the TRIPS Agreement.

validity of the registrations under Regulation 2081/92 also in those cases where no right of objection has been provided as part of the registration procedure.[186]

(vi) EC law provides means to prevent confusing uses of a registered geographical indication

298. The United States goes on to argue that, even if Article 14(3) prevents the registration of confusing geographical indications, it does not provide means to prevent that a registered geographical indication will be used subsequently in a confusing manner. Specifically, the United States has argued that[187]

> ...even if Article 14(3) accorded rights to trademark owners rather than just authority to the EC, the trademark owner would not necessarily be able to tell, at the time of registration of the GI, whether the use of the GI will be confusing. For example, a registered GI may unexpectedly be used in translation, or in a manner that emphasizes certain aspects or letters of the geographical name, in a way that causes a likelihood of confusion with respect to a registered trademark.

299. These concerns are largely theoretical and, in any event, unfounded.

300. First, the product specifications to be submitted with the application for registration must include "the specific labelling details" relating to the geographical indication.[188] Those specifications may be subject to objections in accordance with Article 7(4) and are taken into account for the purposes of the determination required by Article 14(3) and of the final decision provided in Article 7(5)(b). Any change of the labelling specifications must be approved by the EC authorities.[189] Failure to comply with the specifications may lead to the cancellation of the registration.[190]

301. Second, the right holders of a geographical indication have a positive right to use the name registered as a geographical indication. But that right does

---

[186] The EC notes that, unlike Australia, the United States did not claim in its First Written Submission that the lack of an adequate right of objection with respect to the registration of a geographical indication under Regulation 2081/92 is inconsistent with Article 16.1 of the TRIPS Agreement. It is unclear to the EC whether the United States is raising this claim at this stage.

In any event, the EC would note that, under US law, trademark owners do not seem to have a right to challenge *ex post* before the courts the validity of the recognition of a geographical indication for wines on the grounds that it infringes their trademark rights, let alone a right to object in advance to such recognition. See *Sociedad Anonima Viña Santa Rita v. US Dept. of the Treasury*, 193 F. Supp. 2d 6 (D.D.C 2001) ("The Court finds that an entity with a non-geographic interest in a particular name is not empowered, under the Lanham Act, to contest the ATF's recognition of a distinct geographic region that bears that name".) (Exhibit US–48, at. p. 13). In view of this, the United States can hardly complain about the fact that trademark owners have not been recognised a right of objection with respect to the registration of some geographical indications under Regulation 2081/92.

[187] US FOS, para. 54

[188] Cf. Article 4(2)(h) of Regulation 2081/92.

[189] Cf. Article 9 of Regulation 2081/92.

[190] Cf. Articles 11(4) and 11a of Regulation 2081/92.

not extend to other names or signs which have been not been registered. If the use of such unregistered names or signs leads to a likelihood of confusion with the same or a similar sign which is the subject of a valid trademark, it can be challenged judicially by the trademark owner under the Community Trademark Regulation or the trademark laws of the Member States, as applicable.

302. Third, in so far as a right holder of a registered geographical indication were to present the registered name in a mutilated or deformed manner so as to imitate an earlier trademark, which is what the United States appears to be suggesting, a court would be entitled to find, depending on the specific circumstances of each case, that the "used sign" is different from the "registered sign" and, therefore, not protected under Regulation 2081/92.

303. Furthermore, while the right holders of a geographical indication have a positive right to use the registered name, this does not mean that they are allowed to use it in any conceivable manner. As explained[191], the use of a name registered as a geographical indication is subject to the applicable provisions of

- Directive 2000/13 on the labelling, presentation and advertising of foodstuffs[192], and in particular Article 2(1)(a), which provides that

    > the labelling and methods used must not be such as could mislead to the purchaser to a material degree, particularly:
    >
    > (i) as to the characteristics of the product and, in particular, as to ... its origin or provenance
    >
    > [...]

    For the purposes of this Directive, "labelling" is defined as:

    > any words, particulars, trade marks, brand name, pictorial matter or symbol relating to a foodstuff and placed on any packaging, document, notice, label, ring or collar accompanying or referring to such foodstuff.

    Article 2(1)(a) also applies to:

    > (a) the presentation of foodstuffs, in particular their shape, appearance or packaging, the packaging materials used, the way in which they are arranged and the setting in which they are displayed;
    >
    > (b) advertising.[193]

- Directive 84/450 on misleading advertising[194], which is defined as:

    > any advertising which in any way, including presentation, deceives or is likely to deceive the person

[191] EC's First Submission, para. 319. See also the responses of the EC and its Member States to the review under Article 24.2 of the TRIPS Agreement contained in document IP/C/W/117/Add.10 (Exhibit EC-29).

[192] Exhibit EC–30.

[193] Article 2(3).

[194] Exhibit EC–31.

> to whom it is addressed or whom it reaches and which, by reason of its deceptive nature, is likely to affect their economic behaviour or which, for those reasons, injures or is likely to injure a competitor.[195]

- the unfair competition laws of the Member States.[196]

(b) Article 24.5 of the TRIPS Agreement

304. The EC has addressed the arguments made by the United States with respect to Article 24.5 in its First Oral Statement as part of the EC's responses to the Panel's Questions Nos. 76 and 77, to which the Panel is referred. Here below, the EC will provide its comments with respect to some issues raised by the complainants' responses to the Panel's Questions Nos. 75 to 79.

(i) Relationship between Section 3 of Part II and Article 16.1

305. In response to the Panel's Question No.79, both Australia and the United States argue that there is no "conflict" between Articles 16.1 and 22.3 because Members may, in accordance with Article 15.2, refuse or invalidate the registration of any trademark that would be misleading as to the place of origin of the goods and in practice most Members do so. This is, of course, correct and has never been disputed by the EC.

306. It remains, however, that, as matter of law, neither Article 15.2 nor any other provision of Section 2 of Part II requires Members to refuse or invalidate the trademarks that are misleading as to the place of origin of the goods. Such obligation arises exclusively from Article 22.3. This shows that, contrary to what is suggested by the complainants, the provisions of Section 3 of Part II do impose restrictions on the protection of trademarks, and not just on the protection of geographical indications, and, therefore, that Section 2 of Part III cannot be applied without having regard to Section 3.

307. That Section 3 limits the protection of trademarks is made even clearer by Article 23.2, which requires Members to refuse or invalidate trademarks for wines and spirits which could, and in practice would, have been validly registered in most Members before the entry into force of the WTO Agreement. As a result, both Australia and the United States, like many other Members, had to amend their trademark laws in order to implement Article 23.2.

308. While, for the reasons explained, there is no "conflict" between Articles 16.1 and 22.3, there is a potential "conflict" between Article 16.1 and Article 22.2(a), which requires Members to provide legal means for interested parties to prevent

> the use of any means in the designation or presentation of a good that indicates or suggests that the good in question originates in a

[195] Article 2(2).

[196] References to the relevant laws of the Member States are found in their responses to the review under Article 24.2 of the TRIPS Agreement. (Exhibit EC-32).

> geographical area other than the true place of origin in a manner which misleads the public as to the geographical origin of the goods.

309. The "means" referred to in Article 22.2(a) may include the use of a geographical indication as a trademark, whether registered or established through use. Thus, Article 22.2 confers to the right holders of a geographical indication the right to prevent the use of any trademark which misleads the public as to the origin of the goods. This right may conflict with the right of the owner of a trademark under Article 16.1 to prevent the use of any sign that results in a likelihood of confusion with its trademark. The simultaneous exercise of both rights would lead to a situation where neither the trademark owner nor the right holders of the geographical indication could use the sign in question. A similar conflict may arise between Articles 16.1 and 23.1.

310. The above described conflict between Articles 16.1, on the one hand, and Article 22.2 and 23.1, on the other hand, was resolved by the drafters of the TRIPS Agreement through the application of the rules contained din Articles 22.3, 23.2 and 24.5, which together define the boundary between the protection that Members must or may provide to trademarks under Section 2 of Part III and the protection which Members must or may provide to geographical indications under Section 3 of Part III.

311. In response to the Panel's Question No. 75, the United States makes the unsupported assertion that[197]

> the EC is arguing that Article 24.5 is an affirmative defence to the US claims that the GI Regulation is inconsistent with the EC's obligations under Article 16.1 of the TRIPS Agreement (that is that Article 24.5 is an exception to Article 16.1).

312. This is a gross misrepresentation of the EC's position. The EC has never argued that Article 24.5 is an "exception" to Article 16.1, let alone an "affirmative defence".

313. Although Article 24.5 is part of Article 24, which is entitled "International Negotiations: Exceptions", it is not an exception in the same sense as, for example, Article XX of the GATT.[198] The Appellate Body has cautioned against characterizing a measure as an exception simply because it is referred as such in the agreement. This caution applies *a fortiori* in the present case, given that the term "exception" is not used in the text of Article 24.5 itself, or in another provision that refers specifically to Article 24.5, but only in the title of Article 24, an article consisting of many distinct and heterogeneous provisions, not all of which can be considered as "exceptions" or concerned with

---

[197] US Response to Question No. 75, para. 91.

[198] See Appellate Body Report, *EC – Hormones*, para. 104, where the Appellate Body held that the burden of proof with respect to Article 3.3 of the *SPS Agreement* was on the complaining party, even though that provision was described as an exception in Article 3.1. See also Appellate Body Report, *EC – Sardines*, para. 275, where the Appellate Body ruled that the last part of Article 2.4 of the *TBT Agreement* was not an affirmative defence even though it is introduced by the term "except".

"international negotiations". For example, Article 24.3 is clearly not an exception. To the contrary, it imposes additional obligations upon Members.

314. Unlike paragraphs 6 to 9 of Article 24, Article 24.5 does not provide an exemption from an obligation, of which Members may or may not avail themselves. Instead, Article 24.5 places a limit on the measures that Members must or may take in order to protect geographical indications when implementing Section 3 of Part II. As explained, by doing so, Article 25.4 defines the boundary between the protection of trademarks and the protection of geographical indications. The EC has submitted that the protection provided to geographical indications under Article 14(2) of Regulation 2081/92 is within the limits defined in Article 24.5. It is for the United States and Australia, as the complaining parties, to show that, in fact, such protection goes beyond those limits and is inconsistent with Article 16.1.

315. The US position that Article 24.5 is an "exception" to the obligations provided in Section 3 of Part II, which, therefore, cannot affect the scope of the obligations imposed by Article 16.1 is contradicted by the fact that Article 24.5 confers to the owners of trademarks established by use rights which they do not have under Article 16.1. The last sentence of Article 16.1 reserves "the possibility of Members making trademark rights available on the basis of use", but it does not require them to do so. Members are free to decide whether or not to grant such rights and, if so, to limit or withdraw them at will. Yet, one of the consequences of Article 24.5 is that, in implementing protection for geographical indications, Members must not prejudice "the right to use" a grandfathered trademark acquired through use. Thus, Article 24.5 imposes upon Members an obligation with respect to the protection of trademarks which they do not have under Article 16.1.

(ii) The meaning of "the right to use a trademark"

316. In response to the Panel's Questions Nos. 76 and 77, Australia and the United States have provided different and contradictory interpretations of the phrase "the right to use a trademark".

317. Australia says that the phrase "the right to use a trademark" applies only to the trademarks acquired through use and not to registered trademarks. Australia does not say whether "the right to use a trademark" includes also the right to prevent others from using the trademark, as claimed by the United States. Instead, Australia suggests the Panel need not reach that question.

318. Australia's reading of the phrase "the right to use a trademark" raises obvious problems. First, it cannot be reconciled with the ordinary meaning of the term "trademark", which includes all trademarks, whether registered or acquired through use. Moreover, as used throughout the TRIPS Agreement, the term "trademark" includes both types of trademarks (for example, in the title of Section 2 of Part III). When the drafters intended to distinguish between

registered trademarks and trademarks acquired through use they did so expressly, like in Article 16.1 or in Article 21.[199]

319. In its First Written Submission, Australia suggested that the phrase "the right to use a trademark" is linked to the reference made in the chapeau of Article 24.5 to the situation where "rights to a trademark have been acquired through use". But, as already noted in the EC's First Written Submission, in that case it would have been more logical to say in the chausette that implementation "shall not prejudice ... the rights to a trademark acquired through use". Australia's argument confuses the mode of acquisition of the trademark with one of the basic rights attached to any trademark, whether registered or established by use.

320. Furthermore, by arguing that the phrase "the right to use a trademark" refers exclusively to the trademarks acquired through use, and not contesting that such phrase does not include the right to prevent others from using the trademark, Australia appears to be conceding that Article 24.5 provides for the co-existence of geographical indications with earlier trademark acquired through use. Australia does not explain why co-existence should be allowed in that case, but not with respect to registered trademarks, given that Article 16.1 reserves the right of Members to grant trademark rights, including exclusive rights, on the basis of use.

321. For its part, the United States, following a contorted reasoning, concludes that the phrase "the right to use a trademark" has simultaneously three different meanings:

- first, it would be a reference to the trademarks whose rights are acquired through use;[200]
- second, it means the "the right to use *per se*" the trademark;[201]
- third, it would mean also "the right to exclude others from using similar signs".[202]

322. The EC has already commented upon the first meaning and agrees with the second meaning.

323. The view that the phrase "the right to use a trademark" includes the right to exclude others from using the trademark cannot be reconciled with the meaning of that phrase in ordinary language or in the particular context of intellectual property law.

324. For example, WIPO's Trademark Manual says that the "the registered owner has the exclusive right to use the trademark", which encompasses two

[199] Contradicting Australia's position, the United States says that (Response to Question No. 76, para. 105):

"the right to use a trademark" is not specifically linked in the text to trademarks whose rights are acquired through use (although it would appear to include such trademarks).

[200] US Response to the Panel's Question No. 76, para. 103.

[201] US Response to the Panel's Question No. 77, para. 106.

[202] US Response to the Panel's Question No. 76, para. 103.

things: "the right to use the trademark" and "the right to exclude others from using the mark".[203]

325. Similarly, to mention but another example, Section 20 of Australia's Trade Marks Act 1995 (which is entitled "Rights given by registration of trade mark") provides in relevant part that

> (1) If a trade mark is registered, the registered owner of the trademark has, subject to this Part, the *exclusive* rights:
>
> (a) to use the trade mark;
>
> (b) to authorise other persons to use the trade mark;
>
> (2) The registered owner of trade mark has *also* the right to obtain relief under this Act if the trade mark has been infringed.
>
> [...][204]

326. By implication, Australia's Trade Marks Act 1995 recognises that the right to use a trademark is not necessarily "exclusive" and that "the right to use a trademark" is different from the right to prevent others from infringing the trademark.[205]

327. The United States itself refers to what it calls "the right to use *per se*"[206], thus acknowledging implicitly that, in its ordinary meaning, the phrase "the right to use a trademark" does not include the right to exclude others from using the trademark. In spite of this, the United States seeks to stretch the meaning of the phrase "the right to use the trade mark" by resorting to an interpretation based on the "purpose" of a trademark.[207] It is beyond dispute that, as argued by the United States, the purpose of a trademark is to distinguish the goods from a certain source and that, in order to achieve that purpose, the right to use a trademark *should* be exclusive. But from this it does not follow logically that "the right to use a trademark" is inherently exclusive. In practice, the right to use a trademark is not always exclusive. Indeed, if the "right to use a trademark" were inherently exclusive, it would have been superfluous to provide in Article 16.1 that the owners of registered trademarks shall have exclusive rights. Also, on the US interpretation, any rights granted to the owners of unregistered trademarks on the basis of use would have to be exclusive. While this may be generally the case, there is no obligation under the TRIPS Agreement to do so.

328. As suggested by the Panel's Question No. 77, if the drafters had intended to preserve the right of the trademark owners to exclude all others, including the right holders of a protected geographical indication, from using the trademark, they would have used express language to that effect, such as "shall not prejudice

---

[203] WIPO, "Introduction to Trademark Law & Practice, The Basic Concepts, A WIPO Training Manual", Geneva 1993, pp. 51–52 (Exhibit EC-57).

[204] Exhibit EC -58. [Emphasis added].

[205] The term "exclusive right to use a trademark" is used also in the US Lanham Act. See e.g. Section 1115, which is entitled "Registration on principal register as evidence of exclusive right to use a mark; defenses). (Exhibit EC–6).

[206] US Response to the Panel's Question No. 77, para. 106.

[207] US Response to the Panel's Question No. 76, para. 102.

... the exclusive right to use the trademark" or "the rights conferred to the trademark owners under Article 16.1" The explanations given by the United States in its response to this question are unconvincing:

- the United States says that reference to "exclusive right to use" would have been "confusing"[208], because the "specific exclusive right in Article 16.1 is the right to exclude, not the right to use *per se*."[209] As shown above, however, the phrase "exclusive right to use" is of common usage in the intellectual property law field, including in the trademark laws of both Australia and the United States. Moreover, the right to exclude all others from using the trademarks is but the corollary of the exclusivity of the owner's right to use it. There is no contradiction or confusion.
- the United States also says that a reference to "the rights conferred under Article 16.1" would have been "confusing" because Article 16.1 describes three sets of rights.[210] Yet, the US position, as the EC understands it, is that Article 24.5 leaves unaffected each of those three sets of rights. Thus, the suggested formula would have described accurately the result sought by the United States.

329. Australia has suggested that the Panel need not concern itself with the meaning of "the right to use a trademark".[211] The EC disagrees. And apparently so does the United States. The two phrases need to be interpreted together because they are part of the same obligation and impart meaning to each other.

330. If the phrase "right to use the trademark" means what it says, rather than the "right- to-use-a-trademark-and-in-addition-to-exclude-all-others-from-using-it", as argued by the United States, it would confirm the EC's reading of the phrase "the validity of the registration". If the drafters deemed necessary to specify that the implementation of protection for geographical indications shall not prejudice one of the two basic rights of the owner of a registered trademark (the right to use it), but not the other (the right to exclude others from using it), the clear implication is that they did not intend to prevent Members from limiting the latter right in order to allow the use of a geographical indication in co-existence with a grandfathered trademark. Hence the US insistence that the phrase the "right to use a trademark" includes also the right to exclude others. Because Australia, apparently, does not share this interpretation, it is forced to argue instead that the phrase "the right to use a trademark" does not apply at all to registered trademarks and need not be considered by the Panel.

(c) Article 24.3 of the TRIPS Agreement

331. The EC has argued that, regardless of whether the co-existence of geographical indications and earlier trademarks is permitted by Article 24.5, it is

---

208 US Response to the Panel's Question No. 77, para. 106.
209 *Ibid.*
210 *Ibid.*
211 Australia's Response to the Panel's Question No. 77.

required to maintain such co-existence by virtue of the stand-still provision contained in Article 24.3.[212]

332. Australia has not responded to this argument. The United States addressed it in its Oral Statement.[213] The EC has responded comprehensively to the US arguments in its reply to the Panel's Question No. 74, to which the Panel is referred.

(d) Article 17 of the TRIPS Agreement

333. The EC has argued in the alternative that, even if Regulation 2081/92 were found to be *prima facie* inconsistent with Article 16.1 of the TRIPS Agreement in that it allows the co-existence of a registered geographical indication with an earlier trademark, such co-existence would be justified under Article 17 of the TRIPS Agreement.[214]

334. Australia has not addressed this defence. Here below, the EC will respond to the counter-arguments made by the United States in its Oral Statement[215] and in response to the Panel's Question No. 75.

(i) The scope of the exception is "limited"

335. The United States contends that Regulation 2081/92 does not provide a "limited exception" because its scope is too broad:[216]

> Further, with respect to the scope of the so-called "exception", the GI Regulation entirely eliminates the trademark holder's right to prevent confusing uses by all others, which is the core of its legitimate interest.

336. This is plainly wrong as a matter of fact. Regulation 2081/92 does not "eliminate the trademark holder's right to prevent confusing uses by *all* others". Article 14(2) of Regulation 2081/92 allows the concurrent use as a geographical indication of a name registered as a trademark only in relation to products which originate in the area designated by the registered geographical indication and which, in addition, comply with all the relevant product specifications and other requirements for using the registered geographical indication. The trademark owner retains the exclusive right to prevent the confusing use of that name by *any* person in relation to *any* products which do not qualify for the use of the registered geographical indication.

337. Moreover, Article 14(3) of Regulation 2081/92 restricts even further the scope of the exception. Even if the complainants' interpretation of Article 14(3) were correct and that provision did not prevent the registration of all confusing geographical indications, it would nonetheless prevent the registration of confusing geographical indications in those instances where the likelihood of

212 EC FWS, paras. 312-314.
213 US FOS, paras. 69-73.
214 EC FWS, paras. 315-319.
215 US FOS, paras. 74-75.
216 US FOS, para. 75.

confusion is greater, because the trademarks are particularly distinctive, and may cause a greater prejudice to the trademark owners, because of the reputation and renown of the trademark.[217]

338. Article 17 mentions expressly as an example of limited exception "the fair use of descriptive terms". The notion of "descriptive terms" includes *inter alia* any term used to indicate the place of origin of a product.[218] In other words, it includes any term used as an "indication of source" in the sense of the Paris Convention. Geographical indications are a subset of the category of indications of source. The universe of potential users of a geographical indication registered under Regulation 2081/92 is narrower than that of the universe of potential users of an indication of source which does not qualify as a geographical indication, because the products bearing a registered geographical indication must comply with certain product specifications and other requirements, while an indication of source may be used by any product of that origin. If "fair use" of an indication of source qualifies as as a "limited exception", as the United States appears to concede, so must be, *a fortiori*, the fair use of a geographical indication registered under Regulation 2081/92.[219]

---

[217] This may be contrasted with the situation under US law, where the risk of likelihood with an existing trademark is *never* considered a relevant ground for not recognising a geographical indication for wines. See *Sociedad Anonima Viña Santa Rita v. US Dept. of the Treasury*, 193 F. Supp. 2d 6 (D.D.C 2001) (Exhibit US–48). Hence the recognition of geographical indications such as "Rutherford" or "Santa Rita Hills", despite the existence of virtually identical earlier trademarks such as "Rutherford Vintners" and "Santa Rita", respectively. Instead, trademark owners are forced to bring infringement suits against each particular use of the geographical indication. Once again, EC law is more protective of the rights of trademark owners than US law.

[218] In the United States, the courts have considered that recognised geographical indications for wine are descriptive terms. See *Sociedad Anonima Viña Santa Rita v. US Dept. of the Treasury*, 193 F. Supp. 2d 6 (D.D.C 2001) (Exhibit US–48):

As the ATF aptly explains in its opposition, "AVA designations differ from trademark because a trademark is used to convey to the consumer the identity of the manufacturer or producer of the good whereas the AVA is used to describe the geographical origin of the good and can be used by many wineries". ... Thus, by approving the Santa Rita Hills AVA, the ATF has not developed any name or mark of its own. Rather, the ATF has simply taken the step of recognizing its viticultural singularity and confirming the boundaries that encompass the region.

[219] The EC finds it difficult to understand the explanation provided by Australia in its Response to the Panel's Question No. 80 to the effect that the exception provided under Section 122 of the Australian Trade Marks Act (Exhibit EC-7) with respect to the "good faith use" of a sign used "to indicate the geographic origin" of a product does not apply with respect to a "TRIPS-defined GI", because Section 6 (Exhibit EC-59) of that Act defines expressly the notion of "geographical indication". In the EC's respectful view, this is an obvious *non-sequitur*. Section 6 defines a geographical indication as follows:

> in relation to goods originating in a particular country or in a region or locality of that country, means a sign recognised in that country as a sign indicating that the goods: (a)originated in that country, region or locality; and (b)have a quality, reputation or other characteristic attributable to their geographical origin.
>
> Thus, it is plain that the term "signs used to indicate the geographical origin of goods" used in Section 122 includes any sign falling within the category of geographical indications as defined in Section 6.

Although, as noted by Australia, Section 61 (Exhibit EC-60) provides for the rejection of an application for the registration of a trademark that contains or consists of a geographical indication, this is subject to exceptions, including one which purports to implement Article 24.5 of the TRIPS Agreement. As a result, Australia's reading of Section 6 would have the manifestly absurd

(ii) The exception "takes account" of the interests of the trademark owners

339. The United States argued in its First Oral Statement that Article 14(2) of Regulation 2081 is not covered by Article 17 because[220]

> It should be possible to inform consumers about the origin of a product and its characteristics through the use of descriptive terms in a non-trademark sense without affirmatively *confusing* the consumer about the source of the goods.

340. The United States has repeated again the same argument literally in its response to the Panel's Question No. 75.[221] Its precise meaning, however, still remains unclear to the EC.

341. This argument suggests that the United States considers that an exception may not be justified under Article 17 unless it avoids any likelihood of confusion with the trademark. Thus, the United States appears to be importing into Article 17 the interpretation made by the US courts of the "fair use" exception provided under US trademark law. According to that interpretation, as restated in the US response to the Panel's Question No. 80:[222]

> The user invoking fair use must adapt and design his usage of the geographical indication so as not to cause a likelihood of consumer confusion.

342. This interpretation of the US "fair use" exception cannot be transposed to Article 17 because it would render that provision inoperative and superfluous. Article 17 is an exception to Article 16.1, which does not come into play unless there is a *prima facie* violation of the exclusive rights conferred by Article 16.1. If the use of a geographical indication does not result in a likelihood of confusion with an earlier registered trademark, there is no violation of Article 16.1 and, therefore, no need to invoke Article 17. The application of Article 17 presupposes necessarily that the excepted uses give rise to a likelihood of confusion with the trademark. Requiring as a condition for the application of Article 17 that the excepted uses must not result in a likelihood of confusion with the trademark would render that provision wholly redundant.

343. Alternatively, the US argument could be understood as meaning that, in order to be justified under Article 17, the likelihood of confusion must be confined to the strictly necessary. However, the wording of Article 17 provide no basis for such narrow interpretation. Article 17 includes no "necessity" test, unlike other exceptions in the TRIPS Agreement (for example, Articles 3.2, 27.2, 39.3 and 73(b)) or in other WTO Agreements (for example, Article XX (a), (b)

---

consequence that geographical indications, which would be entitled in principle to protection under the TRIPS Agreement, could not be used under the "good faith use" exception, while other indications of source, which are not geographical indication and are not entitled to protection under Section 3 of Part II of the TRIPS Agreement, would qualify for that exception.

220 US FOS, para. 75. Emphasis added.

221 At para. 94.

222 At para. 120.

and (d) of the GATT).[223] All that is required by Article 17 is that the exception "takes account" of the legitimate interests of the trademark owner and of third parties.

344. The language of Article 17 may be contrasted also with that of Articles 13, 26.2 and 30 of the TRIPS Agreement, which provide that exceptions "shall not unreasonably prejudice" the interests of the right holder. This is a more stringent requirement than simply "taking account"[224] of the interests of the right holders, which nevertheless falls short of a "necessity" requirement.

345. The United States also argues that the exception invoked by the EC is not justified under Article 17 because it fails to[225]

> take account of the interests of the trademark owners and of third parties on a case-by-case basis, depending on the manner in which a descriptive term is used.

346. Once again, the United States is importing into Article 17 conditions from its own trademark law which have no basis in that provision. Article 17 provides that the exception must "take account" of the interests of trademark owners and third parties. It does not prescribe any particular method to do so. Members may choose to define an exception in very broad terms and leave to their courts wide discretion in order to apply it on a case-by-case basis, as appears to be the US own preference.[226] But Members may as well choose to define in advance with greater precision the conditions for the application of an exception in its laws or regulations, in a manner which leaves less discretion to the implementing authorities. This method is arguably less flexible than the method advocated by the United States. But it has the advantage of providing greater legal certainty to all the parties involved, including the trademark owners, and is not incompatible *per se* with Article 17.

347. In any event, as a matter of fact, the US objections are unwarranted. As explained above at paragraphs 299-303 the concerns expressed by the United States with respect to certain particular misuses of a registered geographical indication are largely theoretical and can be addressed appropriately under Regulation 2081/92 and complementary legislation. Even if the remedies against those particular misuses available under EC law were not deemed sufficient in order to comply with Article 16.1, they would be sufficient to consider that the

---

[223] In *US – Gasoline*, pp. 14-19, the Appellate Body chastised the panel for reading a necessity requirement into Article XX(g) which, unlike other exceptions included in Article XX, does not use the term "necessary".

[224] Articles 26.2 and 30 of the TRIPS Agreement distinguish between the interests of the right holders, which must not be "unreasonably prejudiced" and the interests of third parties, which must be simply "taken account of".

[225] US FOS, para. 75

[226] As explained above, under US law, trademark owners may not challenge before the courts the validity of the decision recognising a geographical indication for wines on the grounds that it infringes their trademark rights. Instead, they are forced to bring individual suits against each particular infringing use. In contrast, Article 14(3) of Regulation 2081/92 allows trademark owners to prevent *a priori* the registration of any proposed geographical indication that results in a likelihood of confusion with an earlier trademark. This limits considerably the risk of subsequent infringing uses, since they are limited to the misuse of a name which is not confusing *per se*.

interests of the trademark owners and third parties are appropriately taken into account for the purposes of Article 17.

(iii) Article 17 applies to non-geographical names

348. Finally, the United States contends that "nothing in the EC's interpretation explains how the Article 17 fair use exception applies to non-geographic names".[227]

349. The EC fails to understand the pertinence of this argument. The reasoning developed by the EC applies indistinctly to all geographical indications, regardless of whether they consist of a geographical or a non-geographical names, because all of them serve identical purpose. They identify a product as originating in a certain geographical location to which consumers associate a given quality, reputation or other characteristic.[228]

350. There is nothing in Article 17 which excludes non-geographical names from its scope. In particular, the term "descriptive terms" may include any term which serves to describe the origin of goods, and the product characteristics associated to such origin, regardless of whether it is a geographical name.

2. Claim 20: Regulation 2081/92 does not provide for a presumption of a likelihood of confusion in the case of use of an identical sign for identical goods

351. Australia has submitted no further arguments.

3. Claim 21: Article 7(4) of Regulation 2081/92 is inconsistent with Article 16.1 of the TRIPS Agreement because it limits the grounds of objection

352. Australia has submitted no further arguments.

353. The EC notes that, in response to a question from the EC, Australia has been unable to identify any case where the EC authorities have limited the grounds of objection under Article 7(4) of Regulation 2081/92 in the manner alleged by Australia.[229] This confirms the EC's interpretation of that provision.

4. Claim 22: Regulation 2081/92 does not ensure that objections from trademark owners will be considered by the Committee

354. Australia has submitted no further arguments.

---

227 US Response to the Panel's Question No. 75, at para. 96.

228 Cf. Article 22.1 of the TRIPS Agreement.

229 Australia's Response to the EC's Question No. 1.

B. Claim 23: By requiring the co-existence of a registered geographical indication and an earlier trademark, Article 14(2) encumbers unjustifiably the use of the trademark, contrary to Article 20 of the TRIPS Agreement

355. Australia has submitted no further arguments.

C. Claim 24: Article 14(1) of Regulation 2081/92 is inconsistent with Article 24.5 of the TRIPS Agreement because it does not afford the right of priority provided in Article 4 of the Paris Convention

356. Australia has submitted no further arguments, even though the EC had requested Australia to clarify this claim.

357. The EC notes that, in response to a question from the EC, Australia has not been able to identify even one single application for a trademark that falls within the situation that Australia alleges under this claim.[230]

D. Articles 41.1, 41.2, 41.3, 41.4, 42, 43, 44.1, 45, 46, 48 and 49 of the TRIPS Agreement

1. General Considerations

358. In response to the Panel's Question No. 85, Australia appears to concede that Parts III and IV of the TRIPS Agreement cannot be applied cumulatively to the same procedures:

> In the event that the Panel should consider that the decision-making process provided by Article 15 of Regulation 2081/92 does provide a means for the owner of a registered trademark to enforce rights required to be granted by TRIPS Article 16.1, it is Australia's view that the decision-making process constitutes an enforcement process in respect of such trademark rights governed by Part III of the TRIPS Agreement: Part IV is not applicable.

359. The registration procedure laid down in Regulation 2081/92, including the objection procedure, is not a means to "enforce" the rights of the trademark owners. Article 16.1 of the TRIPS Agreement confers to the owner of a registered trademark the exclusive right to prevent all third parties from *using* identical or similar signs for identical or similar good where such use would result in a likelihood of confusion

360. The registration of geographical indication does not amount to the *use* of that geographical indication and does not infringe *per se* any rights of the trademarks owner.[231] Such infringement may result only from the subsequent *use*

---

[230] Australia's Response to the EC's Question No. 2.

[231] The US courts have followed a similar reasoning in order to deny to trademark owners the right to contest judicially the validity of the decision to recognise a geographical indication for wines on the grounds that it infringes their trademark rights. See *Sociedad Anonima Viña Santa Rita v. US*

of the registered geographical indication by one of the right holders. Regulation 2081/92 does not prevent trademark owners from bringing infringement proceedings under the applicable provisions of trademark law against a right holder of a geographical indication, if and when it *uses* the geographical indication, in the context of which trademark owners can invoke that the registration is invalid or that the particular use (or misuse) of the geographical indication is not covered by Regulation 2081/92.

361. The EC notes that, in response to questions posed by the EC, Australia has conceded that

- Australia's Trade Marks Office is not a judicial body;[232]
- the procedures before Australia's Trade Marks Office are not "judicial procedures" within the meaning of Article 42 of the TRIPS Agreement;[233]
- Australia's Trade Marks Office does not have the authority to order the remedies provided in Articles 44, 45 and 46.[234]

362. Despite the above, Australia maintains that the registration and opposition procedures before Australia's Trade Marks Office may be characterised as "enforcement procedures" within the meaning of Part III of the TRIPS Agreement.[235] However, if so, it would follow that Australia's registration and opposition procedures for trademarks are subject to Part III and not to Part IV. Furthermore, it would mean that those procedures are in clear violation of Part III, and in particular of Articles 42, 44, 45 and 46.

363. Australia appears to consider that there is no such violation because the decisions of the Trade Marks Office are reviewable by the Federal Court of Australia.[236] But the requirement to provide for such judicial review is contained in Part IV and not in Part III (cf. Article 62.5). Furthermore, the EC has explained repeatedly that the registration decisions under Regulation 2081/92 and the decisions of the authorities of the Member States with respect to the statements of objections are also subject to review by the courts, which can order the remedies provided in Part III. In view of that, Australia should explain why the EC's procedures for the registration of geographical indications are inconsistent with Part III, but Australia's own procedures for the registration of trademarks are not.

364. The United States does not answer to the questions whether the USPTO is a judicial body and whether the procedures before the USPTO are judicial procedures, although it seem to concede that they are not by saying that some of

---

Dept. of the Treasury, 193 F. Supp. 2d 6 (D.D.C 2001) (Exhibit US–48) ("While the Bureau has recognized an AVA under the name "Santa Rita Hills" it has not used, imitated, or copied the name at all. Because such conduct is a necessary element of an infringement claim … the Court finds that the ATF's decision does not, in and of itself, contravene Plaintiff's trademark rights").

232 Australia's Response to the EC's Question No. 6 b).

233 Australia's Response to the EC's Question No. 6 c).

234 Australia's Response to the EC's Question No. 6 d).

235 Australia's Response to the EC's Question No. 6 a).

236 *Ibid.*

them are "quasi-judicial".[237] The United States also says that "certain aspects of the procedures of the USPTO could be regarded as part of the enforcement procedures available to US right holders".[238] For example, according to the United States, a petitioner could take a cancellation decision of the USPTO to a federal court to get an injunction.[239] But the same is true of Regulation 2081/92. If a trademark owner objects successfully to the registration of a geographical indication, it could take the decision rejecting the registration to a Member State court to get an injunction against an infringing use.

365. In its First Written Submission, the EC argued that, for the purposes of Part III, the existence of an "infringement" must be determined in relation to the domestic law implementing Part II and not to Part II itself. Otherwise, Members would be required to give "direct effect" to the provisions of Part II. In connection with this argument the EC asked the following question to the complainants:[240]

> Would it be possible under domestic law for an EC national who owns an Australian/US trademark to claim before the Australia/US courts that another trademark has been registered by Australia's Trademark Office/the US PTO in violation of Article 16.1 of the TRIPS Agreement, even where it is not contested that such registration is in conformity with all the relevant provisions of your domestic trademark law?

366. The United States has responded evasively:

> ... any person likely to be damaged by the registration or continued registration of a mark at the USPTO may request cancellation of the registration at the USPTO or in a federal court and would cite grounds under US law for such request.

367. The EC understands that the "grounds under US law" mentioned in the above response do not include the violation of Article 16.1. The EC assumes, therefore, that the United States agrees that there is no obligation under Part III to provide "enforcement procedures" against the infringement of Article 16.1 as such, but only against the infringement of those provisions of domestic law that purport to implement Article 16.1, irrespective of their consistency with Article 16.1.

368. For its part, Australia answered as follows:

> A decision to register a trademark is reviewable *de novo* by the Federal Court of Australia. Thus, it would be possible for an EC national who owns an Australian trademark to claim before that court that another trademark has been registered by the Trade Marks Office of IP Australia in violation of the exclusive rights to use a trademark and to authorise other persons to use the

237 US Response to the EC's Question No. 7.
238 *Ibid.*
239 *Ibid.*
240 EC's Question to the complainants No. 8.

> trademark granted by section 20 of the Australian Trade Marks Act, which implements Australia's obligations pursuant to TRIPS Article 16.1, even where it is not contested that the latter registration is in conformity with all the relevant provisions of the Act.

369. The EC does not understand this response, which appears to be contradictory. How could the EC owner of the Australian trademark "A" claim that the registration of the Australian trademark "B" infringes section 20 without contesting that the registration of trademark "B" is in conformity "with all the relevant provisions of the Act"? In a footnote to this response Australia confirms that "the provisions of international agreements do not have direct effect in Australian law". Thus, the EC understands that the owner of trademark "A" could not claim that, although trademark "B" has been registered in conformity with section 20, the registration of trademark "B" should be cancelled because it breaches Article 16.1. The EC assumes that, in view of this, Australia would agree that the situation described in the question would not give rise *per se* to a violation of Part III of the TRIPS Agreement, irrespective of the question whether section 20 is consistent with Article 16.1 of the TRIPS Agreement.

2. *Claim 25: Regulation 2081/92 is inconsistent with Article 41.1 of the TRIPS Agreement*

370. Neither Australia nor the United States have submitted any further arguments.

3. *Claim 26: Regulation 2081/92 is inconsistent with Article 41.2 of the TRIPS Agreement*

371. Neither Australia nor the United States have submitted any further arguments.

372. The EC notes, nevertheless, that, in the context of another claim, the United States has conceded that:[241]

> in the case of the United States, it would probably not be difficult to designate an office in the US Government to perform a purely ministerial act of transmitting a registration ... objections to the EC.

373. As explained by the EC[242], the action described in the US response is all that is required from the governments of other WTO Members under the objection procedure. The US admission confirms that, contrary to Australia's allegations[243], the requirement to lodge objections with the governments of other WTO Members does not "add unjustifiable complexity and delay".

---

241 US Response to the Panel's Question No. 38, para. 74.

242 EC Response to the Panel's Question No. 34, para. 86.

243 Australia's FWS, para. 138.

4. *Claim 27: Regulation 2081/92 is inconsistent with Article 41.3 of the TRIPS Agreement*

374. Australia has submitted no further arguments.

5. *Claim 28: Regulation 2081/92 is inconsistent with Article 41.4 of the TRIPS Agreement*

375. The United States has made no further arguments.

6. *Claim 29: Regulation 2081/92 is inconsistent with Article 42 of the TRIPS Agreement*

376. See above the comments under "General Considerations".

E. *Claim 30: Regulation 2081/92 is inconsistent with Article 10bis (1) and 10*ter *(1) of the Paris Convention*

377. Australia has submitted no further arguments.

F. *Consequential Claims*

1. *Claim 31: Regulation 2081/92 is inconsistent with Article 2.1 of the TRIPS Agreement*

378. Australia has made no further arguments.

2. *Claim 32: Regulation 2081/92 is inconsistent with Article 1.1 of the TRIPS Agreement*

379. Australia has conceded that this claim is entirely dependent on other claims.[244]

3. *Claim 33: The transitional national protection provided by the Member States is inconsistent with Articles 2.1, 16.1, 41.1, 41.2, 41.3 and/or 42 of the TRIPS Agreement*

380. Australia has made no further arguments.

---

[244] Australia's Response to the Panel's Question No. 82.

VI. THE EC MEASURE IS CONSISTENT WITH THE OBLIGATION TO PROVIDE PROTECTION TO GEOGRAPHICAL INDICATIONS UNDER ARTICLE 22.2 OF THE TRIPS AGREEMENT

1. Claim 34: Regulation 2081/92 is inconsistent with Article 22.2 of the TRIPS Agreement

381. In its First Written Submission, Australia stated this claim as follows:[245]

> Regulation No. 2081/92 establishes a Community-wide regime for the registration and protection of EC-defined GIs. However, the EC measure does not provide –as concerns those same EC-defined GIs - legal channels for interested parties to prevent on a Community-wide basis any use of those EC-defined GIs which would mislead the public as to the geographical origin of a good or any use which would constitute an act of unfair competition within the meaning of Paris Article 10 *bis*.

382. The EC noted that this claim was insufficiently argued and difficult to understand. As discussed below, after one hearing and a round of questions and answers, this claim remains as obscure, if not more, as in Australia's First Written Submission.

383. The above quoted passage suggested that the alleged violation would arise from the absence of Community-wide system of protection. The EC noted in its First Written Submission that there is no basis in Article 22.2, or anywhere else in the TRIPS Agreement, for the proposition that protection must be provided at any particular territorial level. The Panel seemed to share the EC's perplexity because it asked Australia to "cite any authority for the proposition that a Member must comply with a particular WTO obligation through a single measure applicable throughout its territory". Australia has responded this question as follows:[246]

> Australia has not contended –and does not contend – that a WTO Member must comply with a particular WTO obligation though a single measure applicable throughout its territory. Rather, Australia contends that, while the EC can choose to offer more extensive protection of EC-defined GIS at the Community level, the EC must also ensure that it does not breach its TRIPS obligations in doing so. Given the legal EC system, and the terms of Regulation No. 2081/92 and of other EC and Member States law, the EC has effectively implemented a TRIPS right –at Community level- without also effectively implementing at the same level the concurrent TRIPS obligation.

384. The EC wishes to put on record that it still fails to understand the grounds for Australia's claim. In particular, the EC does not know what are the

---

245 *Ibid.*, para. 155.

246 Australia's response to the Panel's Question No. 81.

"concurrent TRIPS obligations" that the EC should have implemented at Community level, rather than at Member State level. In addition, the EC notes that Australia does not answer the Panel's question, because it does not cite any authority for the proposition that WTO rights and "concurrent obligations" should be implemented at the same level. The EC is not aware of any such authority.

385. In its First Written Submission, the EC noted that it failed to see how the use of a validly registered geographical indication, which is otherwise consistent with the TRIPS Agreement, could possibly mislead the public as to the geographical origin of the goods. The EC also observed that it failed to understand how the registration or the use of a geographical indication consistently with the EC domestic laws, as well as with all other provisions of the TRIPS Agreement, including Articles 24.5 and 16, could ever constitute an act of unfair competition within the meaning of Article 10*bis* of the Paris Convention (1967).

386. In response to the Panel's Question No. 24 concerning the meaning of the term "interested parties" in Article 22.2 Australia provides an "example" of the type of "uses" which it has in mind:

> For example, it is entirely possible that there are products which, while originally based on European processes, have subsequently come to represent the "international" trading standard for that product: to register the original geographic name under regulation No. 2081/92 in such circumstances – notwithstanding that the product qualify for registration – could well constitute misleading use or use which constitutes an act of unfair competition within the meaning of TRIPS Article 22.2 even within the EC. This type of action is clearly contemplated by the text of Article 22.2.

387. Later, in response to the Panel's Question No. 82, Australia states what appears to be a condensed version of the same "example":

> the situations covered by TRIPS Article 22.2 do not necessarily involve trademark rights: for example, a term may have become a generic product description in international trade before it was protected in its country of origin.

388. It is unclear to the EC whether these "examples" are provided simply in order to illustrate Australia's interpretation of the notion of "interested parties" or purport to be claims on their own. The EC surmises that Australia does not dare to state them more openly as claims because it realises that they are as provocative as ill-founded.

389. First, the EC does not understand, and Australia does not explain, how the use of a term which in the territory of Member "A" is not a "generic" product description but a "geographical indication" within the meaning of Article 22.1 (i.e. a term which "identifies the origin" of the product) could be deemed "misleading" for the purposes of Article 22.2(a) when used in relation to goods of the origin designated by the geographical indication, simply because the same term has become "generic" in the territory of Member "B".

390. Second, Article 22.2 is concerned with the protection of geographical indications as defined in Articled 22.1. Article 22.2(b) applies to unfair competition acts against the right holders of geographical indications and not to supposed unfair competition acts against other parties arising from the legitimate use of geographical indications.

391. Third, in any event, the conduct described by Australia cannot be deemed an act of unfair competition by any reasonable standard. Australia cites no authority for its interpretation, except a quotation from Bodenhausen's treatise to the effect that the notion of "honest practice in industrial or commercial matters" within the meaning of Article 10*bis*.2 of the Paris Convention includes "honest practices established in international trade".[247] The EC submits that the exercise of a right conferred by a WTO Member in order to comply with its obligations under the TRIPS Agreement is not a "dishonest practice" in international trade. In particular, where such right is exercised in order to avoid that the public of that WTO Member be mislead as to the origin of the products. In other words, in order to prevent a genuine act of unfair competition.

392. Moreover, Australia's interpretation would create a conflict between Article 22.2(a), which requires Members to provide means to protect the geographical indications of other Members, unless they have become "generic" in *their* own territory[248], and Article 22.2(b), which, on Australia's construction, would require them to provide means to prevent the use of geographical indications that are "generic" in the territory of *other* Members. Indeed, Australia's interpretation would create a conflict *within* Article 22.2(b) itself, because, as mentioned, the fact of using a term which is a geographical indication in the territory of one Member in relation to products that do not have that origin is an act of unfair competition.

393. Finally, Article 22.2(b) applies to "uses". The registration of a geographical indication is not a "use" and cannot be *per se* an act of unfair competition. Rather the alleged act of unfair competition would result from the subsequent use of a geographical indication. Regulation 2081/92 does not exclude the application of the laws on unfair competition of the Member States. To the extent that the conduct described by Australia could ever be considered as an act of unfair competition, the use of a registered geographical indication would be caught by those laws, which are all based on the relevant provisions of the Paris Convention. Those laws are not within the terms of reference of the Panel.

---

[247] Australia's Response to Question No. 24.
[248] Cf. Article24.9 of the TRIPS Agreement.

2. Claim 35: Regulation 2081/92 is inconsistent with Article 1.1 of the TRIPS Agreement because it is inconsistent with Article 22.2

394. Australia concedes that this claim is entirely dependent on its claim under Article 22.2 of the TRIPS.[249]

3. Claim 36: Regulation 2081/92 is inconsistent with Article 22.2 TRIPS

395. In its response to the Panel's Question No. 84, the United States argues that the fact that opposition procedures are regulated specifically in Part IV does not exclude the possibility that the lack of adequate objection procedures may be inconsistent as well with Article 22.2.

396. The United States argues that Article 62.1 envisions that the procedures for the acquisition of an intellectual property right can violate both Part IV and other provisions of the TRIPS Agreement, including Part II. This is correct. For example, it is beyond question that those procedures may violate Articles 3 and 4. In addition, some provisions of Part II lay down special procedural rules. For example, Article 15.5 provides that "Members may afford an opportunity for the registration of a trademark to be opposed".

397. Unlike Article 15.5, Article 22.2 does not regulate expressly the right of opposition. In the absence of any such express rules in Article 22.2 or elsewhere in Section 3 of Part II, it may not be assumed that the drafters' intention was to derogate from the generally applicable rules contained in Part IV.

398. Moreover, Article 22.2 requires to provide "means" to prevent certain "uses". The registration of a geographical indication is not a "use" of a geographical indication. For that reason, in order to comply with Article 22.2 it is not necessary to provide for a right of objection to the registration of a geographical indication. Article 22.2 does not even require to provide for the possibility to challenge directly before the courts the registration decision. In order to comply with Article 22.2 it may be sufficient if a Members provide for the possibility to bring infringement proceedings against a particular "use" prohibited by Article 22.2, in the context of which the plaintiff may challenge the validity of the registration, if necessary. EC law does provide for such possibility.

VII. REGULATION 2081/92 IS CONSISTENT WITH OBLIGATIONS UNDER THE TBT AGREEMENT

399. Australia (but not the United States) has raised two claims under the TBT Agreement:

[249] Australia's Response to the Panel's Question No. 82.

- that Article 12(2) of Regulation 2081/92 is incompatible with Article 2.1 of the TBT Agreement (Claim 37);[250]
- that Articles 4 and 10 of Regulation 2081/92 are incompatible with Article 2.2 of the TBT Agreement (Claim 38).[251]

400. In its first written submission, the EC has shown that the provisions of Regulation 2081/92 referred to by Australia cannot be regarded as technical regulations within the meaning of Articles 2.1 and 2.2 TBT Agreement.[252] Moreover, the EC has shown that in any event, Australia's claims under Article 2.1 and 2.2 TBT Agreement are unfounded.[253]

A. Regulation 2081/92 is not a technical regulation

401. At this stage, Australia has provided very little in response to the EC's arguments. In particular, in the view of the EC, Australia has failed to show that the provisions of Regulation 2081/92 which it challenges do indeed constitute a technical regulation falling under Article 2 of the TBT Agreement.

1. Article 12(2) of Regulation 2081/92 is not a technical regulation

402. Contrary to the view of Australia, Article 12(2) of Regulation 2081/92 is not a technical regulation within the meaning of the TBT Agreement. In its first written submission, the EC has set out that Article 12(2) does not apply to identifiable products, does not lay down product characteristics, and is not a mandatory requirement.[254] Moreover, in response to Question 50 of the Panel, the EC explained that the requirement to indicate the origin of the product is not a "labelling requirement as it applies to a product, process or production method" within the meaning of Annex 1, Point 1, to the TBT Agreement.[255]

403. For all these reasons, Article 12(2) of Regulation 2081/92 is not a technical regulation within the meaning of the TBT Agreement.

2. Articles 4 and 10 of Regulation 2081/92 are not a technical regulation

404. Contrary to the view of Australia, Articles 4 and 10 of Regulation 2081/92 are not a technical regulation within the meaning of the TBT Agreement.

405. In its first written submission, the EC has explained that by requiring the existence of inspection structures, Articles 4 and 10 of Regulation 2081/92 do not lay down product characteristics, and therefore cannot be regarded as a

[250] Australia's FWS, para. 234 et seq.
[251] Australia's FWS, para. 249 et seq.
[252] EC FWS, para. 439 et seq.
[253] EC FWS, para. 469 et seq.
[254] EC FWS, para. 443 et seq.
[255] EC Response to Panel's Question No. 50, para. 120.

technical regulation within the meaning of Point 1 of Annex 1 to the TBT Agreement.[256] The EC stressed that the objective of the requirement of inspection structures was to ensure that the product specifications are complied with. Accordingly, even if, for the sake of argument, it were accepted that these product specifications are a technical regulation or a standard, then the inspection structures would constitute a conformity assessment procedure within the meaning of Point 3 of Annex 1 to the TBT Agreement, but not a technical regulation. Accordingly the applicable provisions would be Articles 5 to 9 of the TBT Agreement, and not Articles 2 to 4 thereof.

406. In response to Question 60 of the Panel, Australia has claimed that the dividing line between a technical regulation and a conformity assessment procedure is "difficult to determine in the abstract". The EC does not agree. As the EC has set out in its response to the same question,[257] the dividing line is perfectly clear, and follows from the definitions contained in Points 1 and 3 of Annex 1 to the TBT Agreement. According to Point 1 of Annex 1, a technical regulation "lays down product characteristics". According to Point 3, a conformity assessment procedure ensures that "relevant requirements in technical regulations or standards are fulfilled". In application of these definitions, it should be clear that the requirement of inspection structures is not a technical regulation.

407. In its response to Question 60, Australia has raised the question whether the EC contends that the "product specifications requirement set out in Article 4 of the Regulation" constitutes a technical regulation. The EC certainly does not contend that the requirement that a geographical indication must correspond to certain product specifications constitutes a technical regulation. This requirement is merely a condition for the registration of geographical indications, i.e. of an intellectual property right, and does not itself constitute a technical regulation.

408. A different question would be whether individual product specifications laid down for particular geographical indications are technical regulations. The EC does not believe so. However, the Panel does not need to address this issue, since Australia has not raised any specific claims with respect to specific product specifications. It is sufficient to note that even if, for the sake of hypothesis, Australia's thesis were accepted that somehow product specifications are technical regulations, still the requirement of inspection structures would not constitute a technical regulation.

409. For these reasons, the requirement of inspection structures set out in Articles 4 and 10 of Regulation 2081/92 does not constitute a technical regulation within the meaning of the TBT Agreement.

[256] EC FWS, para. 458 et seq.

[257] EC Response to Panel's Question No. 60, para. 132-134.

B. *Claim 37: Article 12(2) of Regulation 2081/92 is incompatible with Article 2.1 of the TBT Agreement*

410. Australia has claimed that Article 12(2) of Regulation 2081/92 is incompatible with Article 2.1 of the TBT Agreement.[258]

411. As the EC has set out in its first written submission, Article 12(2) is fully compatible with Article 2.1 of the TBT Agreement.[259] In particular, the EC has explained that Article 12(2) of Regulation 2081/92 applies to domestic and foreign geographical indications in a non-discriminatory fashion, since it requires in fact the indication of the country of origin for the homonymous geographical indication which is protected later, irrespective of whether this is the EC or the third country indication.

412. The EC notes that in its response to Question 53 of the Panel, Australia has indicated that if interpreted in this way, Article 12(2) would not be incompatible with Article 2.1 TBT Agreement. However, Australia voices doubts as to whether the interpretation set out by the EC is correct. As the EC has already explained above in response to Claim 3, these doubts are unfounded.[260]

413. Accordingly, Article 12(2) of Regulation 2081/92 is not incompatible with Article 2.1 TBT Agreement.

C. *Claim 38: Articles 4, 10, and 12 (1) of Regulation 2081/92 are incompatible with Article 2.2 of the TBT Agreement*

414. Australia has claimed that Articles 4, 10, and 12 (1) of Regulation 2081/92 are incompatible with Article 2.2 of the TBT Agreement.[261]

415. Australia's claims in this respect are similar to those which the United States now is raising under the national treatment provisions of the TRIPS Agreement and the GATT (Claims 1*bis* and 12*bis*). In response to Claim 1*bis*, the EC has already set out in detail that the requirement of inspection structures is necessary for the attainment of the objectives of Regulation 2081/92, and is not more trade-restrictive than necessary for the fulfilment of these purposes. These arguments apply also to the Australian claim made under Article 2.2 TBT Agreement. Accordingly, the EC refer to its defence to Claim 1*bis* in this respect.[262]

416. Accordingly, Regulation 2081/92 is fully compatible with Article 2.2 TBT Agreement.

---

[258] Australia's FWS, para. 234 et seq.

[259] EC FWS, para. 469 et seq.

[260] Above para. 143.

[261] Australia's FWS, para. 249 et seq.

[262] Above, para. 91.

VIII. CLAIM 39, 40: THE EC MEASURE IS COMPATIBLE WITH ARTICLE 65.1 TRIPS AND ARTICLE XVI:4 WTO

417. The United States has claimed that the EC has not fulfilled its obligations under Article 65.1 TRIPS.[263] Similarly, Australia has claimed that the EC has not complied with its obligations under Article XVI:4 WTO.[264]

418. Both claims are dependent on substantive claims discussed above. Since these claims are unfounded, the consequential claims under Article 65.1 TRIPS and XVI:4 WTO are equally unfounded.

IX. CONCLUSION

419. For the above reasons, the EC reiterates the conclusions stated in its First Written Submission.

263 US FWS, para. 190.

264 Australia's FWS, para. 267.

ANNEX B-6

ORAL STATEMENT OF THE EUROPEAN COMMUNITIES SECOND SUBSTANTIVE MEETING

(12 August 2004)

TABLE OF CONTENTS

TABLE OF WTO AND GATT CASES REFERRED TO IN THIS STATEMENT

Short Title	Full Case Title and Citation of Case
Argentina – Footwear (EC)	Appellate Body Report, *Argentina – Safeguard Measures on Imports of Footwear*, WT/DS121/AB/R, adopted 12 January 2000, DSR 2000:I, 515
EC – Asbestos	Appellate Body Report, *European Communities – Measures Affecting Asbestos and Asbestos-Containing Products*, WT/DS135/AB/R, adopted 5 April 2001
Indonesia – Autos	Panel Report, *Indonesia – Certain Measures Affecting the Automobile Industry*, WT/DS54/R, WT/DS55/R, WT/DS59/R, WT/DS64/R and Corr.1, 2, 3, and 4, adopted 23 July 1998, DSR 1998:VI, 2201
Korea – Dairy	Appellate Body Report, *Korea – Definitive Safeguard Measure on Imports of Certain Dairy Products*, WT/DS98/AB/R, adopted 12 January 2000, DSR 2000:I, 3
Korea – Various Measures on Beef	Appellate Body Report, *Korea – Measures Affecting Imports of Fresh, Chilled and Frozen Beef*, WT/DS161/AB/R, WT/DS169/AB/R, adopted 10 January 2001
US – Section 337	Panel Report, *US – Section 337 of the Tariff Act of 1930*, Report by the Panel adopted on 7 November 1989 (L/6439 – 36S/345)
US – Taxes on Automobiles	Panel Report, *United State – Taxes on Automobiles*, DS31/R, 11 October 1994

GLOSSARY

Commission, EC Commission	Commission of the European Communities
Committee	Committee of representatives of the Member States referred to in Article 15 of Council Regulation 2081/92
Community Trademark Regulation	Council Regulation (EC) No 40/94, of 20 December 1993, on the Community Trademark, as amended
Council, EC Council	Council of the European Union
Court of Justice, European Courtof Justice	Court of Justice of the European Communities
DSU	Understanding on Rules and Procedures Governing the Settlement of Disputes
EC	European Communities
GATT	General Agreement on Tariffs and Trade 1994
FOS	First Oral Statement
FWS	First Written Submission
GI	Geographical indication
Member States, EC Member States	Member States of the European Union
Official Journal	Official Journal of the European Union
OHIM	Office for Harmonization in the Internal Market
Paris Convention	Stockholm Act of the Paris Convention for the protection of Industrial property, of 14 July 1967
Regulation 2081/92, Regulation	Council Regulation (EEC) No 2081/92 of 14 July 1992 on the protection of geographical indications and designations of origin for agricultural products and foodstuffs, as amended on the date of establishment of the Panel
SCM Agreement, SCM	Agreement on Subsidies and Countervailing Duties
SWS	Second Written Submission
Trademarks Directive	First Council Directive 89/104, of 20 December, on the Community Trademark, as amended

TBT Agreement, TBT	Agreement on Technical Barriers to Trade
TRIPS Agreement, TRIPS	Agreement on Trade-Related Aspects of Intellectual Property Rights
US	United States
WTO Agreement	Marrakesh Agreement Establishing the World Trade Organization

I. INTRODUCTION

1. The European Communities welcomes this opportunity to submit its views in this dispute. In our statement of this morning we will provide a response to the rebuttal submissions of the complainants. We will follow the same order of claims as in our written submissions.

2. While we have striven to avoid unnecessary repetitions, the large number of claims involved, together with the fact that the complainants often make divergent, if not contradictory arguments under each claim, have prevented us from being as concise as we would have liked at this stage of the proceedings. We trust, however, that the panel will understand that the EC cannot leave without response the numerous new arguments, and in some cases new claims, made by the complainants in their rebuttal submissions.

II. THE OBJECTIVE ASSESSMENT OF THE CONTENT OF REGULATION 2081/92

3. The complainants and the EC disagree about the interpretation which must be given to a number of the provisions of Regulation 2081/92. A central task for the Panel will therefore be to establish the proper meaning of Regulation 2081/92 as a measure of EC domestic law. The Panel must carry out this task in accordance with Article 11 of the DSU, which requires "an objective assessment of the facts of the case".

4. At this stage, the EC does not wish to repeat what it has already said in its previous submissions.[1] However, since this is a horizontal issue of some importance to a number of the claims, and since the complainants persist in interpreting several of the provisions of Regulation 2081/92 in a way which does not correspond to the meaning of the measure, the EC would like to offer some general observations about the objective assessment of Regulation 2081/92.

5. First, and maybe most obviously, it must be recalled that since the interpretation of Regulation 2081/92 is a question of fact, the burden of proof for establishing that Regulation 2081/92 has the meaning which the complainants allege is on the complainants. In their submissions, however, the complainants have repeatedly attempted to shift this burden of proof to the EC, and asked the EC to disprove their claims.[2] This is not admissible. In order to prove their case,

---

[1] EC Response to the Panel's Question No. 1, para. 1 et seq.; EC SWS, para. 3 et seq.

[2] US Response to Panel's Question No. 1, para. 1.

the complainants must do more than simply make factual assertions. They must establish that the interpretation of Regulation 2081/92 which they defend is the only correct one, taking into account the wording, objectives and context of the measure in the EC legal order.

6. Second, the assessment of the content of Regulation 2081/92 must be objective. In their submissions, the complainants are systematically defending those interpretations of Regulation 2081/92 which are the least compatible with the EC's WTO obligations. In contrast, the complainants systematically discard those interpretations of Regulation 2081/92 which do not result in a violation of WTO obligations, even where these interpretations are mandated by the wording, objectives and context of the Regulation. It is submitted that such an approach to the interpretation of Regulation 2081/92 does not constitute an objective assessment of the facts.

7. Third, as a measure of EC domestic law, Regulation 2081/92 must be interpreted in accordance with the principles of interpretation applicable in the EC domestic legal order. A particularly important element for the interpretation of Regulation 2081/92 are therefore the international obligations of the European Community, including the WTO Agreements. Contrary to what Australia continues to argue, this has nothing to do with the question of whether WTO law has "direct effect" in the EC legal order, and whether the European Court of Justice can review the legality of EC measures on the basis of their compatibility with WTO obligations.[3]

8. The European Court of Justice has held repeatedly that Community law must be interpreted in accordance with the Community's international obligations.[4] This principle is highly relevant to the present case. It seems excluded that when faced with two equally possible interpretations of a provision of Community law, the Court of Justice would simply chose the one which leads to a violation of WTO obligations rather than the one which would not.

9. As one practical example for the way in which the European Court of Justice takes into account WTO law in the interpretation of EC law, the EC has referred to the Court's judgment in the Petrotub case.[5] To the EC's surprise, the United States has found this case not only instructive, but also "worrisome".[6] In the view of the EC, the Petrotub judgment should be reassuring to the complainants, not worrisome. In this judgment, the Court gave effect to a provision of the Anti-Dumping Agreement on the basis that the EC Anti-Dumping Regulation was intended to implement this agreement. The Court of Justice reached this result despite the fact that the AD Regulation did not contain a specific reference to the provision applied, let alone a "without prejudice" clause similar to that contained in Article 12(1) of Regulation 2081/92.[7]

---

[3] Australia's SWS, para. 42.

[4] EC Response to Panel's Question No. 15, para. 32 et seq.; EC, SWS, para. 18 et seq.

[5] EC Response to the Panel's Question No. 15, para. 36.

[6] US SWS, para. 13.

[7] The US has attempted to cast doubt on this fact by pointing out that in the Petrotub judgment, the Court of Justice also referred to Article 253 EC Treaty (former Article 190 EC), which lays down the

10. The US has also referred to the fact that in the Petrotub case, the Commission had defended a contrary position in the proceedings before the Court of Justice to the one the EC had taken in a response to questions in the WTO AD Committee.[8] The EC does not consider this relevant for the present case. What is relevant is that despite the contrary position of the Commission and the Council, the Court of Justice took account of the international obligations of the Community, and of the statements of the EC in the WTO, and applied these international obligations.

11. In the case of Regulation 2081/92, the case for an interpretation in the light of the EC's WTO commitments is even clearer. Regulation 2081/92 contains clear references to international obligations, particularly in Article 12(1). In the present proceedings, the EC has unambiguously and publicly explained the interpretation to be given to the contentious provisions of the Regulation. On the basis of the case law of the European Court of Justice, there should be no doubt that the Court will take this into due account in its interpretation of the Regulation.

12. In its second submission, the United States has suggested that the explanations offered by the EC should be disregarded because they "lack legal force". Moreover, the United States has raised the concern that the Council, the "25 Member States" or individuals might contest the "Commission's" interpretation.

13. In this respect, the EC would like to recall once again that the explanations given before this Panel are given on behalf of the European Communities, not of any particular Community institution. Secondly, the question before the Panel involves the interpretation of an act of domestic law within the domestic legal order of the Member concerned. There is therefore no need to create new legal obligations, but to establish the proper meaning of the EC measure within the EC legal system. It is not sufficient for the complainants simply to refer to the risk that the interpretation of the Regulation could be contested. In a system based on the rule of law, any legal measure can in principle be contested. However, the question is whether such a challenge would realistically succeed; and this the complainants have failed to show.

14. In its second submission, the United States has also argued that "if a WTO-consistent interpretation is not possible, the ECJ will apply EC law alone".[9] The EC can agree with this statement. However, in its submission, the US is not applying its own standard correctly. It is not sufficient for the complainants to show that a WTO-inconsistent interpretation is possible; rather, they must show that a WTO-consistent interpretation is impossible. As the EC

general duty to state reasons for Community legislative acts (US SWS, para. 17-18). The EC fails to see the relevance of this distinction. Whether the Court applied the EC Anti-Dumping Regulation or Article 253 EC Treaty, the fact is that it interpreted EC law in line with the EC's WTO commitments. The fact that it did this even with respect to a provision of EC primary law should strengthen the confidence of the US, not diminish it.

[8] US SWS, para. 14.

[9] US SWS, para. 16.

will show with respect to the individual claims, the complainants do not meet this standard.

III. REGULATION 2081/92 IS COMPATIBLE WITH NATIONAL TREATMENT OBLIGATIONS, AND DOES NOT IMPOSE A REQUIREMENT OF DOMICILE OR ESTABLISHMENT

15. The EC will now address the claims that Regulation 2081/92 constitutes a violation of the national treatment provisions of the TRIPS and the GATT, as well as the prohibition on conditions of domicile and establishment in Article 2.2 of the Paris Convention.

A. National treatment under the TRIPS Agreement (Article 3.1 TRIPS and Article 2.1 TRIPS in conjunction with Article 2.1 Paris Convention)

1. The Meaning and Scope of National Treatment under the TRIPS Agreement

16. Before addressing the individuals claims of the complainants under the national treatment provisions of the TRIPS Agreement, the EC considers it necessary to comment on the following general points:

- TRIPS national treatment concerns the treatment of nationals;
- Regulation 2081/92 does not discriminate between nationals;
- Regulation 2081/92 does not involve *de facto* discrimination between nationals;
- The fact that different legal provisions apply does not prove that there is less favourable treatment.

(a) TRIPS national treatment concerns the treatment of nationals, not of goods, or of residents

17. As the EC has already set out in its previous submissions, unlike Article III:4 GATT, the national treatment provisions of the TRIPS concern discrimination as between *nationals*, not between goods, or between residents.[10]

18. In their second submission, the complainants continue to contest this essential difference between GATT and TRIPS national treatment.[11] According to the complainants, the fact that different legal provisions apply depending on the location of the area to which the geographical indication is related amounts to discrimination between nationals.[12] In the view of the EC, this interpretation is incompatible with the national treatment provisions of the TRIPS Agreement.

---

[10] EC FWS, para. 104 et seq.; EC SWS, para. 28 et seq.

[11] US SWS, para. 25 et seq. ; Australia SWS, para. 182.

[12] The complainants have made similar arguments also as regards the right of objection.

19. Article 3(1) of the TRIPS Agreement – and similarly Article 2(1) of the Paris Convention – requires WTO Members to accord to the *nationals* of other Members treatment no less favourable than to their own *nationals*. This reference to nationals in the TRIPS Agreement is intentional, and must be given meaning.

20. In their submissions, the complainants fail to provide a meaningful interpretation of this concept. Their argument is that the Regulation requires foreign nationals to become resident or established in the EC, and that because of this requirement, foreign nationals are required to become "EC nationals".[13] This argument is false in two respects. First, as the EC will set out, the Regulation 2081/92 does not contain any requirement of domicile or establishment. Second, even if a foreign national becomes domiciled or established in the EC, this does not mean he becomes an EC national.

21. Nationality on the one hand, and domicile and establishment on the other, are distinct concepts which cannot simply be equated in the way the complainants suggest. For a natural person, a national is a person who holds the nationality of a country in accordance with the laws of that country. Neither in the EC, nor in the United States or Australia, does a person acquire the nationality simply by being a resident. In the same way, the nationality of legal persons is defined using various criteria other than establishment, most importantly the law of incorporation.

22. The fact that nationality and domicile are separate concepts is also borne out in the TRIPS Agreement itself. Several provisions of the TRIPS Agreement, namely Article 24.4, 40.3 and 40.4, refer to "nationals and domiciliaries" in the alternative. If the drafters of the TRIPS Agreement had wanted to refer to both "nationals and domiciliaries" in Article 3.1 TRIPS Agreement, they could very easily have done so. That they did not indicates that TRIPS national treatment was intended to apply as between nationals, not as between domiciliaries. The same also follows from the specific prohibition of conditions of domicile and establishment in Article 2 (2) of the Paris Convention, which otherwise would have been superfluous.

23. The only text in the TRIPS Agreement to which the United States has pointed in support of its interpretation is footnote 1 to Article 1.3 of the TRIPS Agreement. In its second submission, the United States claims again that this provision "would apply to the EC, among other WTO Members".[14] This is manifestly wrong. Footnote 1 defines the term "national" only for separate customs territories, which are part of another State, and which therefore may not have a "nationality". Footnote 1 would therefore seem to apply, for instance, to Chinese Taipei, Hong Kong, China, or Macao, China. It does not apply to the EC, or to other WTO Members which are not separate customs territories.

---

[13] US SWS, para. 29.

[14] US SWS, para. 27.

24. Accordingly, the Panel should find that Article 3(1) TRIPS Agreement requires national treatment as between *nationals*, not as between domiciliaries or as between goods.

(b) Regulation 2081/92 does not discriminate between nationals

25. Once Article 3(1) TRIPS Agreement is given its proper scope, it is clear that Regulation 2081/92 does not discriminate between nationals.

26. In support of their claims, the complainants have referred in particular to the fact that Regulation 2081/92 contains separate provisions governing the registration of geographical indications, depending on where the geographical area to which the indication is related is located. The US has argued that there is "a close relationship between the geographical area that gives rise to the GI right and the nationality of the right holder".[15] Moreover, the US has argued that "any legal person producing or obtaining agricultural products and foodstuffs in a country will, as a practical *and perhaps a legal matter*, become a juridical person of that Member".[16]

27. The EC submits that these statements are unsupported by fact. Regulation 2081/92 does not contain any requirements as regards the nationality of producers which produce products bearing a protected name. It is not enough for the US to state that this is "perhaps a legal matter". It should state where, in the measure at issue, namely Regulation 2081/92, there is a requirement as to the nationality of producers.

28. In this context, it may be important to know for the Panel that there are cases where non-EC companies have become producers of products bearing a protected name under Regulation 2081/92. Some examples of which the EC is aware, but which are presumably not exhaustive, are the following:

- In 1996, Sara Lee, a large US multinational, acquired Al Ponte Prosciutti, which produces Prosciutto di Parma (Exhibit EC-61).
- From 1985 to 2003, Kraft Foods, a large US multinational, owned Invernizzi, an Italian company which produces among other products Gorgonzola and Grana Padano (Exhibit EC-62).
- Until 2000, Nestlé, a large Swiss multinational, used to own Vismara, an Italian company which produces among others Prosciutto di Parma (Exhibit EC-63).

29. These cases show clearly that non-EC companies may become producers of products bearing a protected name under Regulation 2081/92. In its second submission, the EC has also shown similar examples from the area of wines and

---

15 US, SWS para. 26.

16 US, SWS para. 32 (emphasis added). As for Australia, Australia's arguments seem to be limited to noting that 10 headlines in the EC's first submission use the word "national" (cf. Australia's SWS, para. 182). The EC would comment that this is hardly surprising, given that these headlines restated the claims of the complainants.

spirits.[17] Whether and to which extent foreign nationals become producers of such products may depend on business interests, and to some extent on coincidence. It has nothing to do with Regulation 2081/92, which is entirely neutral as to the nationality of producers.

30. The complainants might argue that even where a foreign company acquires an EC producer, or establishes itself as a producer, it is likely to do this through a European subsidiary. However, even if, as a practical matter, this were true in certain cases, it is still not attributable to Regulation 2081/92, which is the measure before this Panel.

31. Accordingly, the Panel should find that Regulation 2081/92 does not constitute discrimination between *nationals*.

(c) Regulation 2081/92 does not involve *de facto* discrimination between nationals

32. The EC would like to emphasize that if Regulation 2081/92 does not involve discrimination of nationals *de jure*, it also does not do so *de facto*.

33. As the EC has set out in its earlier submissions, *de facto* discrimination is a concept which is closely related to preventing circumvention of national treatment obligations.[18] A good complying with the product specifications of a protected geographical indication will originate in the geographical area to which the indication is related. As a consequence, any discrimination on the basis of whether the geographical indication is located in the EC or abroad would be discrimination between foreign and domestic products. The EC sees therefore no reason to extend TRIPS national treatment to a situation which by definition is covered by Article III:4 GATT.

34. In its second submission, the United States has referred to the Panel Report in *US – Section 337*, in which the Panel held that procedures in principle applying to persons can still involve a discrimination of goods of foreign origin.[19] However, this report hardly supports the US view. First, in the present case, the submission of the complainants is the reverse of the conclusions in *US – Section 337*, namely that even though covered by Article III:4 GATT, an alleged discrimination between products should also be considered discrimination between nationals. Second, *US – Section 337* was decided under the GATT 1949 at a time when the TRIPS Agreement did not yet exist. Accordingly, the question of how TRIPS and GATT national treatment relate was not an issue before that Panel.

35. In its submission, as an example for a *de facto* violation of TRIPS national treatment, the United States has constructed a case where all patents first filed abroad are subjected to higher fees.[20] Once again, this example does nothing to support the US arguments in the present case. In the US example, the

---

17 EC SWS, para. 46.
18 EC Response to Panel's Question No. 29, para. 67 et seq; EC SWS, para. 49.
19 US SWS, para. 38-39.
20 US SWS, para. 40.

fees for the registration of patents are not related to the origin of products. Accordingly, such a case would not fall under Article III:4 GATT, and a case for a *de facto* application of TRIPS national treatment might possibly be made. This is different from the present case, which clearly falls under Article III:4 GATT.

36. The US has attempted to dismiss the EC's arguments by stating that there is no reason why the national treatment obligations of the GATT and the TRIPS should not apply simultaneously.[21] At a general level, it is of course true that obligations arising under several covered agreements can apply simultaneously. Still, the US argument is too superficial. In particular, the US overlooks Article II:2 of the WTO Agreement, according to which both the TRIPS and the GATT are integral parts of the WTO Agreement, i.e. of one single international agreement. As the Appellate Body has stated repeatedly, the covered agreements must therefore be interpreted as a whole, and "in a way that gives meaning to all of them, harmoniously".[22] For the same reason, the Panel in *Indonesia – Autos* found that there is a presumption against conflict between the covered agreements.[23]

37. The interpretation of the complainants is not in line with these principles. It is not a harmonious interpretation to needlessly enlarge the scope of TRIPS national treatment to overlap with GATT national treatment. In addition, there are important structural differences between the GATT and the TRIPS. For instance, the TRIPS Agreement does not contain any provision corresponding to Article XX GATT. It would not seem appropriate that a measure discriminating between goods which is justified on the basis of Article XX GATT would nonetheless be found incompatible with the covered agreements on the simple basis of a *de facto* application of TRIPS national treatment.[24]

38. Accordingly, the Panel should not find that Regulation 2081/92 involves *de facto* discrimination between nationals.

---

[21] US SWS, para. 42.

[22] Appellate Body Report, *Argentina – Footwear (EC)*, para. 81; Appellate Body Report, *Korea – Dairy*, para. 81.

[23] Panel Report, *Indonesia – Autos*, para. 14.28. The US has argued that the report of the Panel in *Indonesia – Autos*, which cautioned against an extensive interpretation of TRIPS national treatment, is not relevant to the present case because it dealt with measure of support not relating to intellectual property (US SWS, para. 43). However, the US overstates the difference between this case and the present. The Panel in *Indonesia – Autos* was concerned with the maintenance of an intellectual property right, namely a trademark. The only difference was that the Panel did not consider specifically the relationship of TRIPS national treatment to Article III:4 GATT, but to other disciplines of the covered agreements. However, in carrying out its analysis, the Panel clearly recognised that the need for a harmonious and coherent interpretation of the covered agreements which required caution with respect to a *de facto* application of Article 3.1 TRIPS.

[24] The EC is not taking a view on the complex legal issue of whether Article XX GATT may be of relevance in connection with the TRIPS Agreement. However, the interpretation of TRIPS national treatment put forward by the complainants inevitably would raise this complex systemic question.

(d) The fact that different legal provisions apply does not prove that there is less favourable treatment

39. Throughout its submission, the United States has argued that because there are different provisions governing the registration of geographical indications depending on where the geographical area is located, the EC is applying "differential treatment", and has called on the EC to show that, despite such differences, the no less favourable standard is met.[25] The US has also made similar suggestions with respect to the right of objection.[26]

40. The EC strongly contests this attempt by the United States to shift the burden of proof. In *Korea – Various Measures on Beef*, the Appellate Body stated clearly that a formal difference in treatment is not sufficient to show that there is less favourable treatment.[27] Accordingly, the US must do more than just show that the registration of EC and foreign geographical indications is dealt with in different provisions. It must show that there is a substantive difference between these provisions, and that this difference entails less favourable treatment of foreign nationals.

41. In support of its statement, the United States[28] has referred to the Panel Report in *US – Section 337*, where the Panel stated that where "different provisions" apply, it is incumbent on the contracting party applying "differential treatment" to show that in spite of such differences, the no less favourable standard is met.[29] However, it does not appear that the Panel in this case meant to say to a formal difference in treatment would entail "differential treatment", and thus entail a reversal of the burden of proof. Moreover, if this is what it meant, then this is certainly not in line with the case law of the Appellate Body, which has not linked such consequences to a formal difference in treatment.[30]

42. It should also be noted that the United States argument is inconsistent with its own submissions on other claims. As a matter of fact, the United States does not want formally equal treatment for foreign geographical indications, but differential treatment. For instance, the United States argues that unlike EC geographical indications, foreign geographical indications should not have to satisfy the requirement of inspection structures. Similarly, the United States argues that unlike for EC geographical indications, requests for the registration of foreign geographical indications should not have to be submitted through the government of the country in which the area is located. Accordingly, the submission of the United States would appear to be that there is formally equal treatment, but that this formally equal treatment nevertheless involves less favourable treatment.

---

[25] US SWS, para. 25, 46, 70, 88.
[26] US SWS, para. 86.
[27] Appellate Body Report, *Korea – Various Measures on Beef*, para. 137.
[28] US SWS, para. 46.
[29] Panel Report, *US – Section 337*, para. 5.11.
[30] It is interesting to note that in *Korea – Various Measures on Beef*, para. 136, the Appellate Body omits from its quotation the last two sentences of para. 5.11 of the Panel Report in *US – Section 337*. It appears that this omission is deliberate.

43. Accordingly, the burden of proof that Regulation 2081/92 involves less favourable treatment is on the US, not on the EC.

2. *Claim 1: Non-EC nationals are accorded less favorable treatment than EC nationals with respect to the registration of geographical indications through the application of a condition of reciprocity and equivalence*

44. We will now turn to the individual claims of the United States and Australia regarding TRIPS national treatment. The first claim is that by subjecting the registration of geographic indications from other WTO members to "conditions of reciprocity and equivalence", Regulation 2081/92 violates the national treatment provisions of Article 3.1 TRIPS and 2.1 Paris Convention.

45. In its submissions to the Panel, the EC has already confirmed that it does not apply such conditions to the registration of geographical indications from other WTO Members.[31] The EC, in particular, has explained that the application of these conditions to WTO Members is in fact excluded by the introductory language of Article 12(1) of Regulation 2081/92, which provides that these conditions apply "without prejudice to international agreements". The EC has also explained that this reference to international agreements requires in particular that the EC's WTO obligations be taken into account. As the EC has said earlier, this is fully in line with the jurisprudence of the Court of Justice, according to which EC law must be interpreted consistently with international law.

46. In their second submissions, the complainants have not advanced many new arguments which have not already been responded to by the EC. The EC can therefore limit itself to a few additional remarks.

47. In its second submission, the United States has argued that even if Article 12(1) did not apply to WTO Members, the EC could still not register geographical indications from other WTO Members because Article 12a (1) provides for such a registration procedure "in the case provided for in Article (12)(3)".[32] The US has claimed that because of this, "there is no registration procedure at all in the EC GI Regulation for non-WTO Members".[33]

48. These US arguments do not do justice to the content and objectives of Regulation 2081/92. First of all, the US overlooks that the "without prejudice" clause in Article 12(1) applies to the conditions set out in this Article only. It does not exclude the applicability of the registration procedures set out in Article 12a. Obviously, if the conditions of Article 12(1) do not apply because they would prejudice an international agreement, then the consequence cannot be that the registration procedures of Regulation 2081/92 do not apply. This would be a nonsensical result, which would not be in accordance with the requirement to interpret the EC legislation in accordance with WTO obligations. As the EC

[31] Cf. in particular EC SWS, para. 51 et seq.
[32] US SWS, para. 8, 21.
[33] US SWS, para. 21.

has already explained in response to the Panel's questions, the reference to the procedure of Article (12)(3) is therefore relevant only where the conditions of Article 12(1) are applicable.[34]

49. In its second submission, Australia has concentrated less on the text of Regulation 2081/92, and more on the various statements that the EC is alleged to have made in the past. However, in its second written submission, the EC has already discussed most of these statements, and has shown that they are not relevant for the interpretation of Article 12(1) of Regulation 2081/92.[35]

50. Finally, it is important for the Panel to be aware that the European Commission has issued a 2nd edition of its Guide to Regulation 2081/92 (Exhibit EC-64).[36] This 2nd edition contains also a specific section on the interpretation of geographical indications related to areas located outside the EC. In this guide, it is explained that the conditions of Article 12(1) do not apply to other WTO Members.[37]

51. Accordingly, since the EC does not apply conditions of reciprocity and equivalence to the registration of geographical indications from other WTO Members, the claim should be rejected.

---

[34] EC Response to Panel's Question No. 7, para. 17.

[35] EC SWS, para. 78 et seq. About the only document on which the EC has not yet commented is the Opinion of the European Parliament's Agriculture and Rural Development Committee, to which Australia refers in its second submission (Australia's SWS, para. 36). In this respect, it should first be recalled that according to the Panel Report in *US – Taxes on Automobiles*, para. 5.12, the assessment of the aim of a legislative act should not be based only on statements of legislators or other preparatory work, but on the wording of the legislation as a whole. Second, the statement in the Committee's report, which concerned Regulation 692/2003, did not concern the "without prejudice" language, in Article 12(1), which was not the subject of the amendment. Third, Australia fails to quote the opinion of the Committee on Legal Affairs and the Internal Market, contained in the same report, which does recall that the conditions of reciprocity and equivalence apply "without prejudice to the international agreements in force" (Exhibit COMP-14, p. 23). Finally, it should be generally noted that individual committees of the Parliament do not represent the opinion of the European Parliament as a whole, and frequently give divergent opinions. Moreover, particularly where the European Parliament is only consulted, they cannot be regarded as giving an authoritative statement of the intention of the legislator.

[36] This new edition replaces the version referred to by the US as Exhibit US-24.

[37] Cf. Exhibit EC-64, p. 18: "However, the conditions in Article 12(1) of Regulation (EEC) no. 2081/92 are without prejudice to international agreements. Relevant international agreements include the WTO Agreements, in particular the TRIPS Agreement. Since under the TRIPS Agreement, WTO Members are obliged to provide protection to geographical indications, the conditions set out in Article 12(1) do not apply to WTO Members. Accordingly, an application for registration of a PGI or PDO relating to an area located in a WTO Member may be made without a prior Commission decision on the basis of Article (12)(3) of Regulation (EEC) no. 2081/92."

3. *Claim 1bis: Regulation 2081/92 violates the national treatment obligations under the TRIPS Agreement by requiring the existence of inspection structures with respect to the specific product for which protection is requested*

52. It has become clear that the United States is also claiming that the requirement that inspection structures must exist for each protected name is in violation of TRIPS national treatment obligations. Australia has made no such claim under TRIPS, but has made a similar claim under the GATT.

53. In its second submission, the EC has explained in detail that the requirement of inspection structures represents equal, not unequal treatment; that the requirement of inspection structures does not require "equivalence by another name"; that Regulation 2081/92 does not impose an "EC model" of inspection structures; and that existence of inspection structures is necessary for attaining the objectives of Regulation 2081/92.[38] In its present statement, the EC will therefore only respond to a number of erroneous arguments of the United States, and similarly, by Australia in the context of its claims under the TBT Agreement.

(a) The requirement of inspection structures does not require "equivalence by another name"

54. In its submission, the EC has already explained that the requirement of inspection structures is not "equivalence by another name", but rather is a requirement that is applied on a product-specific basis for each product for which protection is sought.[39]

55. In its second submission, the US continues to submit that the requirement of inspection structures is "a requirement for a broad inspection structure capable of performing this function for all agricultural products and foodstuffs".[40] The EC notes that Australia has explicitly not shared this view of the US.[41]

56. In fact, the United States interpretation is incompatible with both the wording and the application in practice of Regulation 2081/92. Nowhere in the Regulation does it say that when transmitting an application for registration of a geographical indication, a WTO Member must show the existence of "a broad inspection structure capable of performing this function for all agricultural products and foodstuffs". Article 12a(2) merely requires the declaration that the inspection structures by Article (10)(1) are in place.

57. Article 10(1), in turn, requires that the necessary inspection structures exist to ensure that agricultural products and foodstuffs bearing a protected name meet the requirements laid down in the specification. Article (10)(1) refers to "structures" in the plural. Nothing in Article (10)(1) therefore requires one single structure; it is entirely imaginable that in one state, several structures might co-

---

38 EC SWS, para. 91 et seq.
39 EC SWS, para. 96 et seq.
40 US SWS, para. 53.
41 Australia's SWS, para. 216.

exist. Moreover, Article (10)(1) requires inspection structures only for products "bearing a protected name", not for "all" agricultural products or foodstuffs as the US suggests.

58. Should there have been any doubt left about the interpretation of Regulation 2081/92, the practical application of the Regulation should have dispelled it. The EC has already provided the Panel with the latest publication of the inspection bodies existing in the Member States of the Community.[42] As is obvious from this publication, there is not a single Member State in which one single "broad inspection structure" exists. Rather, all Member States have a multitude of inspection bodies showing a considerable variety of designs, and mixing private and public elements.[43]

59. Accordingly, it is clear that the requirement of inspection structures is not "equivalence by another name", but is applied on a product-specific basis.[44]

(b) Regulation 2081/92 does not impose an "EC model" of inspection structures, and is not unduly prescriptive

60. Despite their frequent reference to an "EC model" of inspection structures imposed by the Regulation, the United States and Australia have so far not been able to identify clearly what aspects of the EC requirements they consider objectionable.

61. In its second submission, the United States now argues that the "pertinent issue" is not which aspects of the inspection structures are objectionable, but whether the EC can demand "the establishment of the *same particular inspection structure* that the EC has chosen for itself".[45] The EC must say that it does not understand how the United States can complain about having to adopt "the same" structures if it is not able to say in which way the structures should be different.

62. Presumably conscious of this contradiction, the US now attempts to identify certain aspects that would be objectionable. In particular, the US complains about the requirement in Article 10 (3) that inspection bodies must permanently "have at their disposal the qualified staff and resources necessary to carry out inspections".[46] A similar argument has also been made by Australia in the context of its claim under the TBT Agreement.[47] Secondly, the US questions why the inspection structure must be independent from the producers which it inspects.[48]

---

[42] Exhibit EC-48.

[43] This practice has been entirely consistent since the beginning of the implementation of the Regulation. For further information of the Panel, the EC also attaches the first publication of inspection bodies dating from 1996 (Exhibit EC-65).

[44] This is also confirmed by the Guide to Regulation 2081/92 (Exhibit EC-64, p. 23).

[45] US SWS, para. 49 (emphasis added).

[46] US SWS, para. 53.

[47] Australia's SWS.

[48] US SWS, para. 57. The US also claims that inspection bodies must comply with the European standard for inspection bodies (EN 45011 – Exhibit EC-2). However, it follows clearly from

63. As regards the requirement that inspection bodies must permanently have at their disposal the necessary qualified personnel, the EC fails to see what should be objectionable about this. In fact, the EC notes that this requirement corresponds closely to §205.501 of the Regulations of the US Organic Program (Exhibit EC-55), which require that certifying agents "must use a sufficient number of adequately trained personnel". It is obvious that inspections cannot be carried out without qualified personnel. Moreover, the Regulation does not specify how much personnel is necessary, during which periods it should be employed, and whether such employment should for instance be full-time or part-time. All that is required is that the "necessary" personnel is at the disposal of the inspection body. What this means has to be decided for each specific inspection structure in the concrete circumstances. The Regulation is thus not overly prescriptive.[49]

64. As regards the US argument that inspection bodies should not be required to be independent of producers, the EC finds this wholly unconvincing. If inspection structures are to deserve their name, they have to be objective and impartial as regards producers. It is noteworthy that in the context of its organic program, the US follows exactly the same logic by requiring that certifying agents should prevent conflicts of interest with respect to producers and handlers, and should exclude any person with a conflict of interest from the certification process (§ 205.501 (a) (10) and (11), Exhibit EC-55).

(c) The existence of inspection structures is necessary for attaining the objectives of Regulation 2081/92

65. The real issue before this Panel is therefore not the precise nature of the inspection structures, but that the EC requires such inspection structures at all.

66. In this context, the United States has referred to its system of certification marks and collective marks, and argued that the owner of the private rights are in the best position to ensure that the marks are used in manner consistent with their specifications.[50] This appears somewhat similar to the arguments made by

Article 10 (3) of Regulation 2081/92 that compliance with an equivalent international standard is sufficient. In its first written submission, the EC has already identified ISO/IEC Guide 65: 1996 as such an equivalent standard (EC FWS, para. 54 and Exhibit EC-3).

[49] Australia has argued that it in certain cases, it may not be necessary for inspection bodies to have personnel "permanently" at their disposal, for instance where there is a particular harvest season. Although this is certainly not the rule, the EC does not exclude that there might be products for which the entire production process is confined to a part of the year, and for which therefore the need for inspections arises only or primarily during that time of the year. In this case, the Regulation 2081/92 does not require unnecessary levels of staff to be maintained throughout the year. In fact, since it is presumably not economic to establish and wind down an inspection body every year, in such a case it would be reasonable to entrust the function of inspections to a body which also carries out tasks other than inspections under Regulation 2081/92. In its second submission, the EC has pointed to the existence of private firms which can carry out such tasks (EC SWS para. 107 and Exhibits EC-49 and EC-50).

[50] US SWS, para. 51.

Australia, which has argued that the application of unfair competition law may be sufficient to prevent the misuse of protected geographical indications.[51]

67. At the outset, the EC would remark that this US position contradicts earlier statements made by the US according to which "normally, a private individual is *not* in the best position" to control the use of a certification mark.[52] The EC finds it therefore surprising, and contrary to US practice, that the United States is now arguing that certification marks and collective marks can be enforced efficiently purely at the initiative of the owner of the mark.[53]

68. Moreover, in response to the arguments of Australia, the EC has already explained that the application of unfair competition law does not provide the same degree of protection and assurance to producers and consumers as the EC system.[54] These arguments apply equally if the United States now argues that geographical indications should be protected purely through the initiative of the owner of the certification mark or collective mark. As in the case of the application of unfair competition law, the enforcement of marks depends on the initiative of the owner of the mark. Accordingly, the control and monitoring is by definition intermittent and varying, and will not provide a full degree of assurance to producers and consumers.

69. The United States has put a certain emphasis on the fact that collective marks and certification marks are private rights. However, whether the rights are private is not the question. Like geographical indications, collective marks and certification marks remain collective rights, and are used by a potentially large number of producers. It cannot simply be assumed that because these collectives rights are "private", their enforcement and protection would necessarily be as efficient as the one provided through Regulation 2081/92.

70. Once again, the EC would like to emphasize that it is not contesting the right of the United States to protect geographical indications in its territory through a system of certification marks or collective marks. However, it seems that it is not the EC which is trying to "impose" its system on the US, but the US and Australia which are trying to impose their system on the EC. By requiring the EC to protect US or Australian geographical indications without requiring inspection structures, the EC would essentially have to lower its level of protection of geographical indications to that of the US and Australia. This would be incompatible with Article 1.1 TRIPS Agreement, which allows the EC to provide a higher level of protection to geographical indications than that required by the TRIPS Agreement.

71. Accordingly, this claim should be rejected.

---

51 Australia's SWS, para. 220.

52 Cf. EC FWS, para. 496.

53 In this context, the EC would like to recall that it has not ruled out that the owner of a certification mark might fulfil the requirements of Article 10 of Regulation 2081/92 (EC Response to Panel's Question No. 59, paras. 130-131. However, whether these requirements are met, and in particular whether the necessary objectivity and impartiality with regard to producers is ensured, would have to be evaluated on a case by case basis.

54 EC SWS, para. 114 et seq.

4. Claim 2: Regulation 2081/92 violates the national treatment obligations under the TRIPS and the Paris Convention by requiring that applications must be transmitted by the country in which the geographical area is located

72. In its previous submissions, the EC has responded in detail to the claim that Regulation 2081/92 violates the national treatment obligations under TRIPS and the Paris Convention by requiring that applications must be transmitted by the country in which the geographical area is located. In particular, the EC has explained that this requirement for the involvement of the country to whose territory the geographical indication is related constitutes equal, not unequal treatment, that this involvement is indispensable for the proper implementation of Regulation 2081/92, and that this requirement does not impose any undue burden on third country governments.[55]

73. In its second submission, the United States[56] fails to provide a convincing response to the EC's arguments. The United States continues to argue that the EC's requirements are unwarranted because in the United States, geographical indications are protected through collective marks and certification marks, and because the US government therefore "does not have any specialized knowledge that would render it better qualified than the rightholder or the EC".[57]

74. These arguments are remarkable. The EC would like to recall that according to Article 24.9 TRIPS, the EC is not obliged to protect geographical indications which are not protected in their country of origin. Now, whether a geographical indication relating to US territory is protected in the US is clearly a question of US law. It is not unreasonable for the EC to request the cooperation of the US on such a question of US law. In contrast, it is simply not credible for the United States to pretend that it does not have any greater experience on questions of US law than the EC, and that therefore the EC should resolve these questions for itself.

75. The United States has also argued that it is in no position to make a determination on whether a US geographical indication has a reputation *in the EC market*.[58] With due respect, this is besides the point. Obviously, the EC does not expect the US to make a determination about reputation in the EC market. However, first of all, the protection of geographical indications is not just based on reputation, but also on whether products have a particular quality or other characteristics attributable to their geographic origin. Since the geographical origin is in the United States, that question should be one which the United States is best placed to evaluate. Second, where the protection is based on

---

55 EC SWS, para. 122 et seq.

56 Australia has made no such claim under the TRIPS Agreement, but has raised similar claims under Article III:4 GATT. In its second submission, however, Australia has not provided any substantive response to the arguments of the EC on this claim (Australia's SWS, para. 177-181). Accordingly, Australia's corresponding claims should also be rejected.

57 US SWS, para. 73.

58 *Ibid.*

reputation of a geographical indication, that reputation must also be based on its geographical origin. Since this origin is in the US, one would normally expect the geographical indication to have a reputation in the US market. This, once again, is a question which the US is best placed to evaluate.

76. Finally, the United States has argued that it protects foreign geographical indications in the US as collective marks or certification marks without the intercession of foreign governments.[59] This argument is without merit. First, whether the United States protects geographical indications as marks irrespective of whether they are protected in their country of origin is a matter for the United States, but irrelevant in the present context. Second, it should be noted that even as regards the registration of marks, Article 6 (A) (a) *quinquies* of the Paris Convention explicitly permits the registering country to request a certificate of registration issued by the country of origin. Finally, at least as regards geographical indications from the EC, which has a specific registration system, the question of whether a geographical indication is protected in the EC is fairly easy to ascertain. As the United States has itself acknowledged, this is not as obvious for US geographical indications, given the absence of a specific system of protection in the US. It is unreasonable for the United States to try to devolve these difficulties on other governments.

77. Accordingly, claim 2 should be rejected.

5. *Claim 3: Non-EC nationals are accorded less favorable treatment than EC nationals with respect to the requirement to indicate the country of origin for homonymous geographical indications*

78. According to the United States, the requirement in Article 12(2) of Regulation 2081/92 to indicate the country of origin for homonymous geographical indications constitutes a violation of national treatment provisions under TRIPS and the Paris Convention.[60]

79. In its previous submissions, the EC has already explained that Article 12(2) does not apply to all foreign geographical indications, but only to the names in the specific situation of the first subparagraph, and that it requires the indication of the country of origin for both EC and third country names, depending on which geographical indication has been protected earlier. Accordingly, Article 12(2) of the Regulation treats geographical indications from the EC and third countries alike.[61]

---

[59] *Ibid.*

[60] Australia has not made such a claim under TRIPS, but has made a similar claim under Article 2.1 TBT Agreement. In its second submission, apparently unsure of this legal basis, Autralia has now raised such a claim also under Article III:4 GATT, but still not under the TRIPS Agreement (cf. Australia's SWS, para. 179).

[61] EC SWS, para. 143 et seq. This interpretation is also confirmed in the Guide to Regulation 2081/92 (Exhibit EC-64, p. 21).

80. In its second submission, the United States continues to contest even the first premise of the EC's arguments, namely that Article 12(2) applies only to homonymous geographical indications.[62] The EC is unable to understand the basis for the United States' view. The second subparagraph of Article 12(2) refers clearly to "such names", i.e. the homonymous names referred to in the first subparagraph. There is no ambiguity about this in the Regulation. Indeed, the US view seems to be inspired more by a desire to find fault with the EC measure than by the text of the EC measure.

81. As regards the second element of the EC's response, the EC's interpretation is clearly borne out by the wording of Article 12(2) of Regulation 2081/92, which refers to "protected names" both from the EC and from third countries. As its only counter-argument, the US has argued that Article (12)(2) seems to be "directed at the authorisation of third country GIs". However, there is nothing in the wording of the provision to prevent it from applying to geographical indications from both third countries and from the EC.

82. Interestingly, this point seems to have been recognised by Australia, which has argued that the expression "Community protected name" in Article (12)(2) should be read also to include names from third countries under the GI regulation.[63] This is not the interpretation of the EC. However, if indeed this were the correct interpretation, then surely the expression "protected name of a third country" should similarly be interpreted to include names protected in a third country regardless of whether they are from a third country or the EC. In this case, Article (12)(2) once again would not result in any discrimination.[64]

83. Finally, the EC would remark that it does not see in which way a requirement to truthfully indicate the origin of a product constitutes less favourable treatment. In this context, the EC also notes that the complainants have not yet provided any response as to how their claims under the TRIPS Agreement relate to Article IX:1 of the GATT, which explicitly excludes origin marking requirements for imported goods from national treatment obligations. The EC will comment on this question in more detail in response to the complainants' claims under the GATT.

84. In conclusion, this claim should be rejected.

6. *Claim 4: Regulation 2081/92 accords less favourable treatment to non-EC nationals by subjecting the right to*

[62] US SWS, para. 76.

[63] Australia's SWS, para. 65.

[64] In addition, the complainants have argued that Article 6 (6) of Regulation 2081/92 would be applicable to the registration of a geographical indication from the EC which is homonymous with an already registered geographical indication from a third country. The EC does not agree. However, even if the complainants were right, the results would be not different. As a precondition for the registration of homonymous geographical indications, Article 6(6) requires "a clear distinction in practice". Where two homonymous geographical indications are from different countries, this will require the indication of origin. Accordingly, even if Article 6(6) did apply, there still would be no difference in treatment.

object to the registration of geographical indications to conditions of reciprocity and equivalence

85. The United States has claimed that only nationals from WTO member countries recognised in accordance with Article 12(3) of Regulation 2081/92 as fulfilling the conditions of reciprocity and equivalence may object to registrations of geographical indications.

86. As the EC has set out in its previous submissions, it is clear from the explicit reference to WTO Members in Article 12d(1) and 12b(2) of the Regulation that WTO Members are not subject to the procedure of Article 12(3) applicable to other third countries.[65] Still, in its second submission, the US argues that the Regulation requires persons to reside in the EC "in order to object under Article 7 objection procedures".[66]

87. This argument is manifestly unfounded. Persons resident or established in the US can object to the registration of EC geographical indications under the procedures of Article 12d(1) or 12b(2). The US has failed to explain in which way this procedure is different from the one available to persons resident or established in the EC. As said earlier, the fact that a different legal provision applies does not show that there is differential treatment.[67] In fact, it is the US which argues that unlike for EC residents, its residents should not be required to have to transmit objections through the US government. Accordingly, it is the US which wants differential treatment, while the EC measure provides equal treatment.

88. Claim 4 is unfounded and should be rejected.

7. *Claim 5: Regulation 2081/92 accords less favourable treatment to non-EC nationals by requiring their own country to transmit the objection*

89. With claim 5, the complainants have claimed that Regulation 2081/92 accords less favourable treatment to non-EC nationals by requiring their own country to transmit the objection.

90. This claim is equally unfounded. As the EC has already explained, this requirement applies both to persons resident or established in the EC or in third countries and is neither unreasonable nor unduly burdensome for third countries.[68]

91. In their second submissions, the United States and Australia have offered almost no arguments in support of this claim.[69] In particular, they do not

---

65 EC FWS, para. 140; EC SWS, para. 150 et seq.

66 US SWS, para. 86.

67 In passing, it should be noted that objections to geographical indications from outside the EC are covered by Article 12b(2) both for EC and foreign residents.

68 EC SWS, para. 154 et seq.

69 Cf. Australia's SWS, which merely refers to a requirement for the "involvement" of another WTO Member without distinguishing between applications and objections, and without answering any of the EC's arguments.

acknowledge the difference in the requirements for the transmission and verification of applications for registration, on the one hand, and the transmission of objections, on the other.

92. In fact, the United States seems to suggest that third country governments must verify the admissibility of the statement of objection on the basis of the criteria set out in Article 7(4) of the Regulation.[70] This is not true. In its submissions, the EC has clearly explained that Articles 12b(2) and 12d(1) do *not* require the third country government to verify the admissibility of the objection.[71]

93. Accordingly, the transmission of objections is, as the US has itself acknowledged,[72] a "purely ministerial act" which should not pose any particular problem to the government of any WTO Member, including the United States and Australia. The only way in which US or Australian residents could be prejudiced would be by the unwillingness of their governments to transmit such objections. However, such a problem would not be attributable to the EC, and can therefore not be argued to constitute less favourable treatment by the EC.

94. Accordingly, claim 5 is equally unfounded.

8. Claim 6: Regulation 2081/92 accords less favourable treatment to non-EC nationals by requiring non-EC national to have a "legitimate interest" to object to the registration of geographical indications

95. In its second submission, the US continues to claim that Article 12d(1) of Regulation 2081/92 accords less favourable treatment to non-EC residents by requiring non-EC residents to have a "legitimate interest" to object to the registration of geographical indications, whereas as regards EC residents, Article 7(3) requires that they be "legitimately concerned".[73]

96. In its submissions, the EC has already shown that there is no substantive difference between the term "legitimate interest" used in Article 12d(1) of Regulation 2081/92 and the term "legitimately concerned" in Article 7(3).[74] The EC would have expected this to be obvious enough, but apparently, for the United States it is not. Therefore, the EC will make two additional remarks.

97. First, it is important to note that Article 12b(2), which concerns objections to registrations of third country geographical indications, and which applies for residents of the EC and WTO Members, also requires a "legitimate interest". If the United States were right, and "legitimate interest" were a more demanding standard than "legitimately concerned", this would mean that EC residents could object to the registration of third country geographical indications under stricter

70 US SWS, para. 66.
71 EC Response to Panel's Question No. 34, para. 86; EC SWS, para. 155.
72 US Response to Panel's Question No. 38, para. 74.
73 US SWS, para. 87-88.
74 EC FWS, para. 78, 150-152; EC SWS, para. 160 et seq.

conditions than to the registration of EC geographical indications. This would be an odd result.

98. Second, reference should also be made to the French and Spanish versions of Regulation 2081/92, which are equally authentic. In fact, in the French version, Articles 7(3), 12b(2) and 12d(1) uniformly use the expression "legitimement concerné". The Spanish version in both Articles 7(3) and 12d(1) uses the expression "legítimamente interesada", whereas Article 12b(2) uses, without any difference in meaning, the expression "legítimamente afectada".

99. In conclusion, the difference between "legitimately concerned" and "legitimately interested" is a mere difference of drafting specific to the English text of the Regulation, which does not entail any difference in meaning. Accordingly, the Panel should reject the US claim.

9. *Claim 7: Regulation 2081/92 accords less favourable treatment because a non-EC rightholder has no "representative" in the regulatory committee to "speak for him"*

100. Australia has argued that Regulation 2081/92 accords less favourable treatment because a non-EC rightholder has no "representative" in the regulatory committee to "speak for him". In its second submission, Australia has provided no further arguments to substantiate its claim.[75] Accordingly, Australia's claim should be dismissed.

10. *Claims 8 and 9: A right of objection was available to persons resident or established in an EC Member State that was not available to other WTO Member nationals*

101. Australia has claimed that there is a violation of national treatment in the fact that a right of objection *was* available to persons resident or established in an EC Member State that *was* not available to other WTO Member nationals in respect of the registration of more than 120 geographical indications under the normal registration process (Claim 8). Australia has also raised a similar claim with respect to the absence of an objection procedure under the simplified

[75] Instead, Australia has engaged, over a length of two and a half pages, in a discussion of the EC's "Article 15 decision making process", which culminates in the statement that the EC "has not disproved the factual premise informing Australia's claims" that the Committee/and or the Council "participate in the decision-making process under Regulation 2081/92" (Australia's SWS, para. 59). The EC wonders why it should "disprove" this "factual premise" given that it never contested that the Council and/or the Committee participate under certain conditions in the decision-making process under the Regulation. What the EC did have to correct was the rash statement by Australia that the Committee and/or the Council were somehow the "ultimate decision-maker" under the Regulation (EC FWS, para. 79 et seq). Cf. also EC Response to Panel's Question 40, para. 105-107, and Exhibit EC-28, which shows that only three geographical indications were ever the subject of a Regulation adopted by the Council, whereas all others were registered through Regulations of the Commission.

procedure which used to be provided for in Article 17 of Regulation 2081/92 (Claim 9).[76]

102. In its prior submissions, the EC has already explained why these claims must fail.[77] First, as regards Regulation 2081/92 itself, the claims relate to a measure which was no longer in force at the time of establishment of the Panel, and which is therefore not within the terms of reference of the Panel. Second, as regards the individual registrations, even if considered to be within the Panel's terms of reference, they are not in violation of national treatment obligations.

103. In its second written submission, Australia has not provided any coherent response to the EC's submissions.[78] In particular, Australia apparently does not appreciate that Regulation 2081/92, on the one hand, and the individual registrations, on the other, are separate measures. Accordingly, Australia does not clearly state whether its claims relate to Regulation 2081/92, or to the individual registrations. However, such a clear distinction is essential for an appraisal of whether the measures in question fall within the terms of reference of the Panel, and if they do, whether the measures are in violation of national treatment obligations.

104. As regards Regulation 2081/92, the EC has already shown in its previous submission that Australia's panel request did not clearly refer to historical versions of the Regulation as the "measure at issue" in the present dispute.[79] Even more importantly, it is not up to Australia to enlarge the terms of reference of the Panel contrary to the object and purpose of the DSU. Dispute settlement under the DSU serves the purpose of solving disputes about existing measures. Its purpose is not to provide opinions about historical grievances, in particular where it is not demonstrated what relevance such grievances are still supposed to have. This is why the present Panel, like all WTO Panel before it, should decide on the measure at issue as it existed at the time of the establishment of the Panel.

105. As regards the individual registrations, it is clear that these registrations are still in force. On the basis of the preliminary ruling issued by the Panel, and for the purposes of the present proceedings, the EC therefore bases itself on the assumption that the individual registrations are within the terms of reference of the present Panel.[80]

106. However, the issue regarding the registrations is whether these registrations are in violation of national treatment obligations. So far, Australia

---

[76] In its second submission, Australia has occasionally referred to "600 registrations", and occasionally to "120" (Australia's SWS, para. 17, 185). The EC is therefore uncertain to which extent Australia maintains its argument that the simplified procedure was incompatible with national treatment obligations. In any event, as the EC has set out in its previous submissions (EC FWS, para. 170 et seq.; EC SWS, para. 197 et seq.), Claim 9 is unfounded also because first, there was never any right of objection in the context of the simplified procedure, whether for domestic or for foreign residents; and second, because these claims fall outside the temporal scope of the temporal scope of the TRIPS Agreement as defined in Article 70.1 thereof.

[77] EC FWS, para 156 et seq.; EC SWS, para. 168 et seq.

[78] Australia's SWS, para. 15-19, 185.

[79] EC SWS, para. 174.

[80] The EC reserves the right to raise this issue in the context of a possible appeal.

has not substantiated its allegations in this respect. Indead, it has tried to shift the burden of proof to the EC by reproaching the EC for having asserted that the registrations are compatible with national treatment obligations "without any supporting argument".[81] In this context, it appears necessary to recall that the burden of showing that there is a violation is on Australia, not on the EC.

107. The EC submits that Australia has not demonstrated the existence of such a violation. Australia has brought the present claim under the national treatment obligations of the TRIPS. However, Australia fails to explain how the registration of a particular geographical indication can constitute a violation of national treatment obligations.

108. Presumably aware of this weakness, Australia has, in its responses to the Panel's questions, also referred to other WTO provisions as violated by the individual registrations, and in particular to Article 16.1 of the TRIPS Agreement.[82] However, Australia has not offered a scrap of evidence for any such violation. It has acknowledged that it is not able to identify a single Australian trade mark that would be infringed by any geographical indication registered under Regulation 2081/92.[83] Rather it has told the panel that it has "chosen" not to identify specific commercial interests potentially affected by the EC measure.[84] The EC does not know what the reasons for this choice are, but the consequences are clear: Australia has failed to establish its claim, and its claim should be rejected.

109. Australia has also argued that the EC is asking the Panel to find that "short-lived statutory frameworks" are beyond the reach of WTO dispute settlement. In this regard, it is worth pointing out that 11 years passed between the adoption of Regulation 2081/92 and its amendment by Regulation 692/2003. This can hardly be called a "short lived" statutory framework. The EC does not know why Australia did not bring its national treatment claims when Regulation 2081/92 was still in force. However, it cannot now bring these claims against the individual registrations, when it failed to bring them against the measure which allegedly constituted the violation, namely the Regulation itself.

110. In conclusion, the Panel should firmly resist Australia's attempt to revive moot claims in flagrant disregard for the law and practice of the DSU.

B. Prohibited requirement of domicile or establishment (Article 2.1 TRIPS in conjunction with Article 2.2 Paris Convention)

111. The US has also raised certain claims under Article 2.1 TRIPS in conjunction with Article 2.2 Paris Convention. The EC considers that these claims under Article 2.2 Paris Convention are not within the Panel's terms of reference. Subsidiarily, the EC will show that these claims are unfounded.

---

81 Australia's SWS, para. 185. Cf. also Australia's Response to Panel's Question No. 93.

82 Australia's Response to Panel's Question No. 92.

83 Australia's Response to Panel's Question No. 93.

84 Australia's SWS, para. 10.

1. *The claims based on Article 2(2) Paris Convention are not within the Panel's terms of reference*

112. First, the claims based on Article 2.2 of the Paris Convention are outside the Panel's terms of reference.

113. Article 2.2 of the Paris Convention contains a separate prohibition of conditions of domicile or establishment, which is independent of Article 2.1 of the Paris Convention. The complainants have argued that this is not so because the word "however" at the beginning of Article 2.2 establishes a "linkage" between the two provisions.[85] The EC does not agree. The word "however" indicates a contradiction between the provisions; rather than link, it separates. The use of the word "however" therefore clearly indicates that Article 2.2 contains an obligation going beyond Article 2.1 of the Paris Convention.

114. In fact, the US own arguments are based on the assumption that Article 2.2 is a separate legal obligation. In its first written submission, the US argued that conditions of domicile or establishment were "directly" prohibited by Article 2.2.[86] Similarly, in its second written submission, the US speaks of an obligation "under Article 2 (2) not to impose any requirement as to domicile or establishment".[87]

115. However, the US and Australian panel requests did not contain any explicit reference to Article 2(2) of the Paris Convention. Nor did they contain any claim about the application of illicit conditions of domicile or establishment by the EC.

116. In its submission, the only response of the US has been that "the EC was clearly aware of the nature of the US complaint".[88] The EC formally contests this statement. Until the US first written submission, the EC was not aware that the US intended to claim that the EC measure involved illicit conditions of domicile or establishment. Moreover, the EC also notes that the US argument is in contradiction with the United States response to the EC's request for a preliminary ruling, where the United States announced that precisely how Regulation 2081/92 is incompatible with WTO obligations would be the subject of future US submissions.[89]

117. Accordingly, the Panel should find that the claims under Article 2(2) of the Paris Convention are not within its terms of reference.

2. *Claim 10: Regulation 2081/92 requires non-EC nationals to become established in the EC as a condition for registering geographical indications*

118. The United States has argued that Regulation 2081/92 requires non-EC nationals to become established in the EC as a condition for registering

85 US SWS, para. 80; Australia's SWS, para. 27.
86 US FWS, para. 85.
87 US SWS, para. 79.
88 US SWS, para. 83.
89 Response of the United States of 15 March 2004, para. 36.

geographical indications. As the EC has set out in previous submissions,[90] this claim is unfounded because first, geographical indications relating to an area located in a WTO country can be registered under Regulation 2081/92; second, the right to register a geographical indication does not depend on domicile or establishment; and third, Article 2.2 Paris Convention cannot exclude measures which ensure that a product originates in the geographical area to which a protected geographical indication is related.

119. In its second submission, the United States has responded that it is arguing merely that the EC cannot require that the geographical area to which an indication relates be in the EC.[91]

120. However, as the EC has already said earlier in response to Claim 1, Regulation 2081/92 contains no such requirement. Geographical indications relating to an area located in another WTO Member can be registered under Regulation 2081/92. Accordingly, already for this reason, Regulation 2081/92 cannot be said to establish a requirement of domicile.[92]

121. Accordingly, the US claim should be rejected.

3. *Claim 11: Regulation 2081/92 requires non-EC nationals to become established in the EC as a condition for objecting*

122. In its second submission, the United States continues to argue that Regulation 2081/92 establishes a condition of domicile or establishment because a person "must reside or become established in the EC in order to object under the Article 7 objection procedures".[93]

123. As the EC has already said, this claim is manifestly unfounded. The point is not whether a person can object "under Article 7 objection procedures", but whether a person can object at all. Persons resident or established in WTO countries can object according to Article 12d (1) and 12b (2), and are therefore in exactly the same position as persons resident or established in the EC.

124. Accordingly, the US claim should be rejected.

---

[90] EC FWS, para. 176 et seq.

[91] US SWS, para. 85.

[92] Moreover, the EC would recall that regardless of whether EC or foreign geographical indications are concerned, Regulation 2081/92 does not establish any requirements of domicile or establishment. It merely requires that product specifications are established which ensure that the products in question in fact have a specific quality, reputation or characteristics attributable to their geographical origin (cf. EC FWS, para. 183).

[93] US SWS, para. 86.

C. National Treatment under Article III:4 GATT

1. The Regulation 2081/92 is not incompatible with Article III:4 GATT (Claims 12–15)

125. The complainants have raised a number of their claims also under Article III:4 GATT, namely with respect to the registration of foreign geographical indications, the requirement of inspection structures, the transmission and verification of applications for registration, the requirement to indicate the country of origin for homonymous geographical indications, and finally the alleged overall bias in decision making.

126. All of these claims involve allegations of less favourable treatment similar to those also made under the TRIPS Agreement. In their second submissions, the complainants have not added any specific new arguments regarding their claims under Article III:4. Accordingly, the EC can refer to what it has said already previously in respect to the complainant's arguments under the TRIPS agreement.

127. There is, however, one specific aspect arising under the GATT on which the EC would like to comment. It concerns the US claim that the requirement to indicate the country of origin for homonymous geographical indications constitutes a violation of Article III:4 GATT. The EC notes that in their second submissions, both the United States and Australia recognise that Article IX:1 GATT exempts country of origin marking requirements from the national treatment obligations of Article III:4.[94] However, the United States does not offer any convincing explanation of why this exemption would then not also apply to the labelling requirement in Article (12)(2) of Regulation 2081/92, assuming that indeed this requirement was in violation of national treatment obligations.

128. As its only argument, the US has advanced that Regulation 2081/92 is not a "general" marking requirement. However, the word "general" does not appear in Article IX:1 GATT. Article IX:1 simply refers to requirements to mark the country of origin, regardless of whether they apply to all imported products or only to some. The EC also does not understand what would be the logic of a provision that would permit subjecting all imported products to country of origin marking, but not only some of them.

129. The perverse logic of the US claim – and similarly of Australia's corresponding claim under the TBT Agreement - is also illustrated by the practice of the US and Australia with respect to origin marking. Unlike the EC, both the US and Australia require the indication of the country of origin for all imported products.[95] This is a condition for the importation of any product into the United States or Australia, with which compliance is mandatory, and which does not apply to domestic products.

---

94 US SWS, para. 99; Australia's SWS, para. 212.

95 Cf. for the US 19 CFR 134.11 (Exhibit EC-66); for Australia, cf. the Commerce (Trade Descriptions) Act (Exhibit EC-67) and Commerce (Imports) Regulations, Regulation 8 (c) (i) (Exhibit EC-68).

130. It is astonishing that the United States and Australia, while themselves applying discriminatory country of origin marking requirements of the most sweeping nature, would fault the EC for applying a targeted, entirely reasonable and non-discriminatory labelling provision allowing the distinction between two homonymous geographical indications.

131. In the view of the EC, the Panel should resist this attempt to create double standards for WTO Members, and accordingly reject the claim.

2. *The measure would be justified under Article XX(d) GATT*

132. At a subsidiary level, the EC considers that if the Panel were to find that Regulation 2081/92 does involve less favourable treatment of foreign goods by requiring the existence of inspection structures, the transmission and verification of applications by the third country government, and the indication of the country of origin for homonymous geographical indications, this less favourable treatment would be justified by Article XX(d) GATT.

133. In their second submission, the complainants have argued that the EC has not shown that the alleged inconsistencies would be justified by Article XX(d) GATT.[96] However, in its second submission, the EC has set out in detail why the requirement of inspection structures, the requirement of the transmission and verification of applications by the third country government, and the indication of the country of origin for homonymous geographical indications, are necessary to secure compliance with Regulation 2081/92.[97]

134. The United States and Australia have so far not rebutted these arguments of the EC. They have also not shown that the EC measure is applied in a manner which would constitute an arbitrary or unjustifiable discrimination between countries where the same conditions prevail, or constitute a disguised restriction on international trade.

135. Accordingly, the measures in question are justified by Article XX(d) GATT. As a consequence, the corresponding claims should be rejected.

IV. REGULATION 2081/92 IS COMPATIBLE WITH THE OBLIGATION TO PROVIDE MOST-FAVOURED-NATION TREATMENT

136. The EC will now turn to the US claims that Regulation 2081/92 is incompatible with the obligation to provide most-favoured-nation treatment under Article 4 TRIPS and Article I:1 GATT.

---

[96] US SWS, para. 100; Australia's SWS, para. 181.

[97] EC SWS, para. 228-242 (incorporating by reference the EC arguments in response to the claims under the national treatment provision of the TRIPS Agreement).

A. *Article 4 TRIPS*

1. *Claim 16: As among non-EC WTO Members, nationals from WTO Members that satisfy the EC's conditions of reciprocity and equivalency are accorded more favourable treatment than nationals from those WTO Members that do not*

137. Originally, the United States claimed that Regulation 2081/92 is incompatible with Article 4 TRIPS Agreement because nationals from WTO Members that satisfy conditions of reciprocity and equivalence are accorded more favourable treatment than nationals from those WTO Members that do not.

138. In its second submission, the United States has enlarged this claim, and is now alleging that three separate aspects of Regulation 2081/92 constitute a violation of most-favoured nation obligations, namely:[98]

- the application of conditions of "reciprocity and equivalence" (**claim 16**);
- the requirement of inspection structures (**claim 16*bis***);
- the requirement of "substantial participation" in administering and enforcing the EC Regulation (**claim 16ter**).

139. As regards the first claim, the EC has already confirmed that it does not apply conditions of reciprocity and equivalence to other WTO Members. Already for this reason, the US claim is unfounded. Moreover, the EC has also explained that even if Article 12(1) were applicable to WTO Members, this provision merely sets out the conditions under which Regulation 2081/92 may apply, but does not confer any advantage within the meaning of Article 4 TRIPS Agreement. Finally, the EC has also explained that Regulation 2081/92 does not discriminate on the basis of nationality.[99] For all these reasons, this US claim should be rejected.

140. As regards Claim 16*bis*, the EC has already set out in detail that the requirement of inspection structures is not "equivalence by another name", but rather is applied on a product-specific basis.[100] This means that the question whether appropriate inspection structures exist must be evaluated for each specific application separately. There is no rule which would imply that for certain countries, inspection structures are automatically deemed to exist, whereas for other countries they are deemed not to exist.

141. This is not just so for applications from third countries, but also for applications from the EC. In fact, each application must contain the indication of the competent inspection body.[101] If no inspection body is indicated, or if the inspection body indicated is not in compliance with the requirements of Article 10 of Regulation 2081/92, the geographical indication cannot be

98 US SWS, para. 104.
99 Cf. EC FWS, para. 228 et seq.; EC SWS, para. 245 et seq.
100 EC SWS, para. 96 et seq.; above, para. 54 et seq.
101 Cf. as examples the applications in Exhibits EC-51 to EC-54, EC-56.

registered. The requirement of inspection structures is thus applied in a completely non-discriminatory fashion. It involves discrimination neither on the basis of nationality nor on the basis of product origin. Accordingly, Claim 16*bis* should be rejected.

142. As regards Claim 16ter, which is newly raised by the United States, essentially the same objections apply. There is no rule in the Regulation 2081/92 which would define which WTO members can transmit and verify applications for registration and which cannot. In fact, the United States does not even claim this, but instead argues that some WTO Members "might not be able to prosecute" applications for registration, whereas others might be.[102] This argument is without merit. The Regulation does not require anything that would be outside the scope of any WTO Member with a normally functioning government.

143. In reality, and certainly as regards the United States itself, the issue is not ability, but willingness. The United States has stated clearly that it is unwilling to cooperate in the registration process under Regulation 2081/92. However, this is not a choice which is attributable to the EC. Accordingly, Claim 16ter should equally be rejected.

2. Claim 17: Under Regulation 2081/92, an EC Member State grants more favourable treatment to nationals from other EC Member States than it accords to nationals from non-EC WTO Members

144. The United States has claimed that under Regulation 2081/92, an EC Member State grants more favourable treatment to nationals from other EC Member States than it accords to nationals from non-EC WTO Members.

145. In its written submissions, the EC has already explained that this claim is unfounded.[103] In particular, the EC is an original member of the WTO. Measures with which the EC harmonises the law inside the EC are not measures through which the Member States grant "each other" advantages. Since Regulation 2081/92 is a measure of the EC, the United States has therefore correctly brought its claim against the EC, and not against the Member States.

146. Obvious as this seems, in its second submission, the US persists with its fallacious arguments. In particular, the US argues that the terms of reference of the Panel include also "related implementation and enforcement measures", including measures taken by the Member States. On this basis, the US asks the Panel to "review" whether the measures of the EC Member States are in accordance with MFN obligations.

147. At the outset, the EC would observe that the United States has not indicated what measures of the Member States it is talking about, and in which way such measures are supposed to be in violation of WTO obligations.

---

[102] US SWS, para. 107.
[103] EC FWS, para. 249 et seq. ; EC SWS, para. 252 et seq.

Accordingly, the United States has not provided sufficient evidence to establish the existence of a violation.

148. Moreover, the EC would remark that the present dispute relates to measures adopted by the EC. That, as in many other areas of EC law, the EC Member States have certain responsibilities in the execution of Regulation 2081/92 is irrelevant. The EC generally does not execute its laws through authorities at the EC level; rather, it has recourse to the authorities of the Member States, which in such a situation act *de facto* as organs of the Community, for which the Community would be responsible under WTO law and international law in general. In this context, it is also interesting to note that the European Court of Justice upheld EC competence for an agreement falling under the common commercial policy while holding that "it was of little importance that the obligations and financial burdens inherent in the execution of the agreement envisaged are borne directly by the Member States".[104]

149. Accordingly, where EC Member States take measures for the execution of Community law, such measures are derived from Community law, fall under the competence of the Community, and it is the Community that is responsible for them, not the Member States. Accordingly, such measures cannot be regarded as the granting of an advantage from one WTO Member to another, or as "avoiding MFN obligations" towards other WTO Members. Moreover, the fact that MFN obligations do not apply does not mean that other WTO obligations, and in particular national treatment obligations, would become inapplicable.

150. The EC would also remark that this US claim has nothing to do specifically with the protection of geographical indications, but is of a horizontal nature. The EC has adopted tens of thousands of acts harmonising the law within the EC. If the United States were right, then presumably the entire body of EC law should be applied to the US, and indeed to any other WTO Member. This cannot be right, and to the knowledge of the EC, no other Member has ever made a similar claim.

151. To conclude this point, this claim is an ill-considered attempt to undermine the integrity of the EC legal system, and the Panel should reject it as such.

B. Claim 18: By subjecting the registration of third-country geographical indications to conditions of reciprocity and equivalence, the EC measure is inconsistent with the most-favoured-nation obligation under the Article I:1 GATT

152. The United States has argued that by subjecting the registration of third-country geographical indications to conditions of reciprocity and equivalence, the EC measure is inconsistent with the most-favoured-nation obligation under Article I:1 GATT.

104 Opinion 1/75, *Local Cost Standard*, [1975] ECR 1355 (Exhibit EC-69).

153. As the EC has already set out in its written submission, Regulation 2081/92 is not incompatible with Article I:1.[105] In its second submission, the United States has not made any specific arguments on Article I:1 GATT, but simply referred to its arguments on Article 4 TRIPS.[106] Accordingly, the EC can also refer to the arguments that it has made earlier in response to the United States claim under Article 4 TRIPS.[107] Accordingly, the claim should be rejected.

V. REGULATION 2081/92 DOES NOT DIMINISH THE LEGAL PROTECTION OF TRADEMARKS

154. In this section of our statement, we will address the complainants' claims under Article 16.1 of the TRIPS Agreement and, in particular, their claims concerning the issue of "co-existence". The complainants have submitted no new arguments with respect to their other claims in their rebuttal submissions. The EC refers, with respect to those claims, to its earlier submissions to the Panel.

A. Claim 19: Article 14(2) of Regulation 2081/92 is inconsistent with Article 16.1 of the TRIPS in that it allows the co-existence of geographical indications and earlier trademarks

1. Article 14(3) of Regulation 2081/92

155. The EC has shown that the co-existence of geographical indications and earlier trademarks provided in Article 14(2) of Regulation 2081/92 would not be inconsistent with Article 16.1 of the TRIPS Agreement, even if the complainants' interpretation of that provision, and of its relationship to Section 3 of Part II, were correct:

- first, the criteria for the registrability of trademarks limit *a priori* the possibility of conflicts between geographical indications and earlier trademarks;
- second, to the extent that any such conflict arises, Article 14(3) of Regulation 2081/92 provides the necessary means to trademark owners in order to oppose or invalidate the registration of *any* confusing geographical indication;
- finally, the provisions of Regulation 2081/92, together with other provisions of EC law and the unfair competition laws of the

[105] EC SWS, para. 259.

[106] US SWS, paras. 114-115.

[107] It is not clear from the US second submission whether the United States considers also that the requirement of inspection procedures and of transmission and verification of applications by the government of the home country of the geographical indication constitutes a violation of Article I:1 GATT. To the extent that the US makes such a claim, the EC can refer to its response to the claims under Article 4 TRIPS. Moreover, subsidiarily, the EC would also consider that these measures would be justified by Article XX(d) GATT, in line with what it has already set out in response to the claims under Article III:4 GATT.

Member States, provide the necessary means to ensure that, in practice, registered geographical indications are not used in a confusing manner.

(a) Registrability of geographical names as trademarks

156. The EC has set out in detail the criteria for the registrability of trademarks because they define the legal context within which Article 14(3) must be applied. A proper understanding of those criteria is, therefore, essential in order to interpret correctly Article 14(3).

157. Contrary to the complainants' assertions, the EC has never said that "valid registered trademarks cannot incorporate certain geographical elements."[108] Indeed, if so, it would have been unnecessary to include Article 14(3) in Regulation 2081/92. Rather, the EC has explained that, under EC trademark law, terms which are, or which may reasonably qualify in the future, as geographical indications cannot be validly registered as trademarks unless they have acquired distinctiveness (a "secondary meaning") through use. Hence the express reference in Article 14(3) to the criteria that are relevant for measuring such acquired distinctiveness.

158. The facts bear out the EC's position. Neither the complainants nor the third parties have been able to identify even one single geographical indication, of the more than 600 registered by the EC, which gives rise to a likelihood of confusion with an earlier trademark. Instead, the United States cites hypothetical examples involving cheese from the Moon and tropical products from Portugal.

159. Australia argues that the registrability criteria of the Trademark Directive did not apply to trademarks registered before its adoption.[109] Australia has overlooked that, under the Trademark Directive, the grounds for refusing a registration are also grounds for invalidating existing trademarks, including trademarks pre-dating the Trademark Directive, unless the Member States have provided otherwise. Moreover, the Trademark Directive was hardly innovative on this point. Before the adoption of the Trademark Directive, the trademark laws of the Member States provided already similar registrability criteria, just like the laws of most other countries, including those of the complainants.

160. In turn, the Unites States argues that the EC's reasoning would not apply to registered geographical indications which do not consist of a place name.[110] The United States is wrong. The Trademark Directive prohibits the registration of trademarks which consist "of signs or indications which may serve, in trade, to designate ... geographical origin".[111] Terms like "Feta" or "Reblochon" operate as indirect indications of origin and, therefore, fit this description even if they are not place names. In any event, the Trademark Directive also prohibits the

---

108 US SWS, para. 169.
109 Australia's SWS, para. 91.
110 US SWS, para. 168.
111 Cf. Article 3.1(c) of the Trademark Directive.

registration of terms which serve to designate the "kind", "quality" or "other characteristics" of the goods.[112]

(b) The Complainants have misinterpreted Article 14(3)

161. The EC has shown that, far from being the only reasonable interpretation of Article 14(3), the complainants' reading of that provision is unsupported by the ordinary meaning of its terms. Furthermore, the complainants' interpretation is neither reasonable nor workable in practice and cannot be reconciled with the terms of other provisions of Regulation 2081/92.

162. Australia asserts that "the term misleading establishes a stricter evidentiary standard than confusing".[113] At most, this could be considered one possible reading of "misleading". But Australia has not proved that the EC's own interpretation of "misleading" is less reasonable, or that it is impossible to interpret the term "misleading" consistently with Article 16.1. In fact, Australia's interpretation does not even pass the dictionary test. As acknowledged by Australia, one of the ordinary meanings of "misleading" is "confusing".[114] The same is true of the other linguistic versions of Regulation 2081/92. For example, the term "mislead" has been rendered as "inducir a error" in the Spanish version. According to the Diccionario de la Real Academia Española, one of the ordinary meanings of "error" is "equivocación, confusión".[115] Furthermore, the EC's reading of "misleading" is supported contextually by Article 7 (5) (b) of Regulation 2081/92, which provides that the Commission shall decide on the objections having regard to the "likelihood of confusion".

163. For its part, the United States persists on its misguided theory that Article 14(3) applies only with respect to a certain subset of trademarks. But this is not what Article 14(3) says. Article 14(3) does not say that registration shall be refused where it leads to confusion with a trademark *provided* that such trademark has been used for a long time and *provided* that it enjoys considerable reputation and renown. Instead, Article 14(3) says that registration shall be refused where the proposed name would be misleading "*in the light of* a trademark's reputation and renown and the length of time it has been used". Thus, length of use and reputation/renown are not "threshold pre-requisites" for the application of Article 14(3). They are criteria for assessing whether the geographical indication is misleading. As explained, Article 14(3) mentions expressly those criteria because they will be particularly relevant, given that geographical terms are inherently non-distinctive as trademarks.

164. The United States notes that Article 6*bis* of the Paris Convention and Articles 16.2 and 16.3 of the TRIPS Agreement confer additional protection to so-called "well-known" marks and that reputation, renown and length of use are "factors" generally used in order to establish whether a trademark qualifies as

---

112 *Ibid.*
113 Australia's SWS, para. 104.
114 *Ibid.*
115 Diccionario de la Real Academia Española, 20th Edition, 1984. (Exhibit EC-70).

"well known".[116] But from this it does not follow logically that these factors are relevant *only* as "threshold pre-requisites" for the application of the provisions in question. Length of use and reputation/renown are relevant criteria in order to assess the likelihood of confusion with *any* trademark. In particular, regardless of whether a trademark has enough reputation/renown to qualify as a "well-known" mark under Paris Article 6*bis*, its reputation/renown (or the lack thereof) will also be relevant for the purposes of establishing the likelihood of confusion with a sign for similar goods under Article 16.1.

165. The United States also refers[117] to the so-called "anti-dilution" provisions of the Trademark Directive and the Community Trademark Regulation, which confer protection to a trademark, despite the lack of similarity between the goods concerned, "where the trademark has a reputation". In the context of those provisions, "reputation" functions as a "threshold pre-requisite". But, again, this does not mean that, under EC trademark law, reputation is relevant only for that purpose. Nor does it mean that the relatively high level of reputation required by the ECJ[118] and the OHIM[119] when applying those provisions can be extrapolated to Article 14(3). That standard is linked to the far-reaching protection afforded by the "anti-dilution" provisions and would not be justified in a situation involving signs for similar goods.

166. The tenth recital of the Trademark Directive says that the appreciation of likelihood of confusion

> depends on numerous elements and, in particular, on the recognition of the trade mark on the market, of the association which can be made with the used or registered sign, of the degree of similarity between the trade mark and the sign and between the goods or services identified.

167. Interpreting Article 4(1)(b) of the Trademark Directive, which is the equivalent of Article 16.1, the ECJ has said that[120]

> ... the more distinctive the earlier mark, the greater the risk of confusion ... Since protection of a trademark depends, in accordance with Article 4.1(b) of the Directive, on there being a likelihood of confusion, marks with a highly distinctive character, either *per se* or because of the *reputation* they possess in the market, enjoy broader protection than marks with a less distinctive character.

168. This confirms that reputation, in addition to being a "threshold pre-requisite" for the application of certain provisions providing additional protections to highly reputed marks, is also a general criterion for assessing likelihood of confusion with *any* trademark.

---

[116] US SWS, para. 146.
[117] US SWS, para. 150.
[118] US SWS, para. 151.
[119] US SWS, para. 152.
[120] Case C-39/97, *Canon Kabushiki Kaisha v Metro Goldwyn-Mayer Inc.* , ECR [1998] I-5507, para. 18 (Exhibit EC-71). Emphases added.

169. EC trademark law is by no means unique in this respect.[121] Similar criteria are applied by most other Members.[122] In the United States, the factors to be examined in determining likelihood of confusion in infringement proceedings include the so-called "strength" of the trademark.[123] Trademarks consisting of descriptive terms, such as place names, are deemed inherently "weak" and are protected only to the extent that "secondary meaning" is shown.[124] In turn, secondary meaning is measured according to criteria such as reputation, renown and length of use.[125]

170. Even less pertinent are the US references to the EC Wine Regulation.[126] Indeed, the Wine Regulation proves the opposite. The differences between Article 14(3) and the corresponding provision of the Wine Regulation underscore that the EC authorities intended to apply a different rule in the context of Regulation 2081/92.

171. The United States alleges that the EC's interpretation of Article 14(3) is a novel one which contradicts previous positions of the EC. Given the tone in which this accusation is made, one would expect that the United States has credible evidence to substantiate it. It does not.

172. The United States cites three pieces of "evidence":

- The first one is a slide included in a promotional presentation made by a low level Commission official in Tokyo, which, for pedagogical reasons, describes the requirements of Article 14(3) in

---

[121] According to WIPO's Trademark Manual:

> If the infringed trademark is being used, the extent of use can influence the test of confusing similarity. Intensive use increases distinctiveness of the mark, and confusion with well known marks is more likely if the goods on which the infringing mark is used are less similar or if the similarity of the marks is less apparent.

WIPO, *Introduction to Trademark Law & Practice, The Basic Concepts, A WIPO Training Manual*, Geneva 1993, 2nd Ed., at point. 6.2.3 in fine (Exhibit EC-72).

WIPO's Manual distinguishes the relevance of intensive use as a factor that influences the test of confusing similarity from the protection given to well known marks beyond the scope of confusing similarity. (*Ibid.*, at point 6.2.4).

[122] For example, Section 6(5) of Canada's Trade Marks Act (Exhibit EC-73) provides that (emphases added):

> In determining whether trade-marks or trade names are confusing, the court or the Registrar, as the case may be, shall have regard to all the surrounding circumstances including: (a) the inherent distinctiveness of the trade-marks or trade names and *the extent to which they have become known*; (b) *the length of time the trade-marks or trade-names have been in use*; (c) the nature of the wares, services or business; (d) the nature of the trade; and (e) the degree of resemblance between the trade-marks or trade names in appearance or sound or in the ideas suggested by them.

[123] See e.g. *Polaroid Corp. v. Polarad Elect. Corp.*, 287 F.2d 492 (2d Cir.) cert. denied, 368 U.S. 820 (1961) (Exhibit EC-74); *E.I. DuPont DeNemours & Co. Application of*, 476 F.2d 1357 (Cust. & Pat. App.1973), 261 (Exhibit EC-75).

[124] See e.g. *AMF Inc. v. Sleekcraft Boats*, 5499 F.2d 341 (9th Cir. 1979) (Exhibit EC-76).

[125] See e.g. *Zatarian's, Inc. v. Oak Grove Smokehouse*, Inc., 698 F.2d 786 (5th Cir. 1983) (Exhibit EC-77).

[126] US SWS, para. 152.

an oversimplified manner. Needless to say, that slide has no legal authority whatsoever.

- The second one is a passage from the EC Commission's Guide to Regulation 2081/92.[127] The passage in question, however, repeats verbatim the wording of Article 14(3) and, therefore, does not support the US interpretation. The United States makes much of the fact that the passage describes Article 14(3) as "the only circumstance" in which a "conflicting trademark" (i.e. a trademark that engenders one of the situations indicated in Article 13(1)) prevents the registration of the geographical indication. However, the EC's interpretation does not contradict this. Regardless of which is the correct interpretation of Article 14(3), it is beyond dispute that the situation referred to in that Article is the "only circumstance" in which the registration of a geographical indication must be refused. The reference to "other cases" in the passage quoted by the United States is an allusion to the other situations included in Article 13(1) in which a trademark "conflicts" with a geographical indication.
- The third one is a statement of "ministerial reasoning" accompanying Section 45 of Hungary's Law on the Protection of Trademarks and Geographical Indications.[128] Contrary to what is said by the United States, that provision does not implement Regulation 2081/92, which, being a directly applicable Regulation, and not a Directive, need not, and indeed must not, be implemented by the Member States. The provision in question applies to products not covered by Regulation 2081/92, in respect of which the Member States remain competent to adopt their own rules. The EC finds it rather curious that the United States considers more authoritative the interpretation of an EC Regulation made by a minister of a Member State in order to explain an amendment to a law of that Member State which, on that point, does not implement EC law, than the interpretation made by the EC authorities of an EC Regulation which those authorities have drafted and adopted themselves and which they have been interpreting and applying for more than 15 years prior to Hungary's accession to the EC. But then, of course, one should not forget that the United States speaks from the premise that the EC institutions are the only government in the world which is entitled to no deference from panels.[129]

173. The EC has pointed out that the interpretation of Article 14(3) made by the United States would lead to a result which cannot be reconciled with the terms of other provisions of Regulation 2081/92 and, in particular, with

[127] US SWS, para. 155, with reference to Exhibit US-24.
[128] US SWS, para. 148.
[129] US Response to the Panel's Question No. 1, para. 8 and para. 18.

Article 7(4).[130] In response, the United States notes that the two provisions apply cumulatively.[131] However, this still does not explain why Article 7(4) allows objections in respect of *any* trademarks, and not just in respect of "well-known" trademarks. It would be pointless to admit an objection on certain grounds if, in any event, it were not possible to reject the objection on such grounds. The United States has no answer for this.

(c) Article 14(3) confers enforceable rights to the trademark owners

174. The United States argues that, even if the EC's reading of Article 14(3) were correct, that provision "merely authorizes the EC to decline registration of a GI"[132], but does not accord rights to the trademark owners.[133]

175. The United States is wrong again. When applying Article 14(3), the EC authorities have a margin of appreciation in order to assess the relevant facts. But once they have determined, as a factual matter, that a proposed geographical indication would be misleading, they are required, and not simply authorized, to refuse the registration of that geographical indication.

176. Furthermore, Article 14(3) confers judicially enforceable rights to the owners of trademarks.

177. In accordance with Article 230 of the EC Treaty, if a trademark owner can show that it is directly and individually concerned by the decision to register a geographical indication, it may bring an action in annulment before the European Court of Justice against that decision on the grounds that it is inconsistent with Article 14(3) of Regulation 2081/92.

178. In any event, trademark owners may raise the invalidity of the registration of a geographical indication before the courts of the Member States in accordance with the procedure provided in Article 234 of the EC Treaty. For example, a trademark owner could bring infringement proceedings under the Community Trademark Regulation and/or under the trademark law of a Member State against the user of a registered geographical indication and argue that the registration of the geographical indication is invalid because it is inconsistent with Article 14(3) of Regulation 2081/92. The national court would then have to request a preliminary ruling on the validity of the registration from the European Court of Justice. That ruling would be binding upon the national court. Unlike the action in annulment, the possibility to request a preliminary ruling is not subject to any time limits.[134]

---

[130] Articles 12b(3) and 12d(2) provide, respectively, that the criteria of Article 7(4) shall apply also with respect to the admissibility of objections to the registration of foreign geographical indications and of objections from outside the EC to EC geographical indications.

[131] US SWS, para. 161.

[132] US FOS, para. 54. See also US Responses to Panel's Questions Nos. 14 (at para. 41) and 67 (at para. 87).

[133] US SWS, para. 136.

[134] US SWS, para. 138.

179. Australia has said that the decisions to register a geographical indication under Regulation 2081/92 are subject to judicial review only "on points of law".[135] This is wrong. The ECJ may review not only points of law but also the factual assessment made by the registering authorities, both in annulment proceedings under Article 230 of the EC Treaty and in the context of a preliminary ruling on the validity of the registration under Article 234 of the EC Treaty.

(d) EC law provides means to prevent confusing uses of a registered geographical indication

180. The United States goes on to argue that, even if Article 14(3) prevents the registration of confusing geographical indications, it does not provide means to prevent that a registered geographical indication is used subsequently in a confusing manner.

181. The United States is asking the EC to provide a remedy against the use of a registered geographical indication which is not required by Article 16.1 and which few Members, if any, provide against the use of a registered trademark. The registration of a trademark confers a right to use that sign.[136] For that reason, in most jurisdictions a trademark owner cannot prevent the owner of another registered trademark from using the sign covered by the registration unless it requests and obtains first the cancellation, invalidation or revocation of such registration.[137] Under EC law, the relationship between trademarks and registered geographical indications rests on the same principle. The owner of a trademark may not prevent the right holders of a registered geographical indication from using the registered name on the grounds that such name is confusing. As just explained, however, the trademark owner is entitled to request a judicial ruling to the effect that the registration of the geographical indication is invalid on those grounds.

182. The United States contends that, in practice, questions may arise as to what exactly is encompassed by the "registered name". The same kind of questions, however, may arise in connection with the scope of the registration of a trademark. Whether or not a particular sign falls within the scope of a particular registration is a factual question to be resolved by the courts on a case-

---

[135] US SWS, para. 152.

[136] For example, Section 122 of Australia's Trade Marks Act 1995 (Exhibit EC-7) provides that:

> In spite of section 120, a person does not infringe a registered trade mark when: [...] (e) the person exercises a right to use a trade mark given to the person under this Act.

Section 120 defines when a trademark is deemed infringed (Exhibit EC-78). Section 23 of Australia's Trade Marks Act 1995 (Exhibit EC-79) further clarifies that:

> If trade marks that are substantially identical or deceptively similar have been registered by more than one person (whether in respect of the same or different goods or services), the registered owner of any one of those trademarks does not have the right to prevent the registered owner of any other of those trade marks from using that trade mark except to the extent that the first mentioned owner is authorised to do so under the registration of his or her trade mark.

[137] See e.g. Article 95 of the Community Trademark Regulation.

by-case basis. In should not, and indeed cannot possibly be decided in the abstract by this Panel.

183. The United States also argues that confusion could arise if the geographical indication is used "in ways that cannot be anticipated, such as in a trademark-like manner".[138] This reflects certain pre-conceived notions as to how trademarks and geographical indications should be used which have no basis in the TRIPS Agreement and which the EC does not share. For example, the EC does not agree that the "pictorial depictions" of the packaging for four EC cheeses included in Exhibit US-52 ("Esrom", "Bra", "Bitto" and "Tomme de Savoie") demonstrate that the geographical indications are used in "trademark-like fashion".[139] Rather, they demonstrate simply that trademarks and geographical indications can be presented in similar fashion. To characterize that fashion as "trademark-like" assumes that trademarks enjoy priority in order to use certain types or styles of presentation.

184. What the United States characterizes as "trademark-like" manner is, in fact, a legitimate, ordinary and predictable manner of using a geographical indication, at least in the EC. EC consumers are familiar with the use of geographical indications for foodstuffs. They value them as much as trademarks when making their purchasing decisions, if not more, and expect them to be used in what the United States calls "trademark-like" fashion. For example, Italian consumers probably care more about whether their cheese is genuine "Bra" (rather than, say, "Bitto") than about whether it has been produced by the firm "Vittorio" or by another cheese maker, in particular since the conditions for using the geographical indication ensure that all Bra cheese has homogenous characteristics, regardless of the brand. In conducting the assessment provided in Article 14(3), the EC authorities will assume that the proposed geographical indication will be used in what the United States calls "trademark-like" manner. Accordingly, if the EC authorities reach the conclusion that a geographical indication is not "misleading", it is because they consider that such name is not "misleading" even when used in what the United States calls "trademark-like" fashion.

185. Finally, the EC recalls once again that, while the right holders of a geographical indication have a positive right to use the registered name, this does not mean that they are allowed to use it in any conceivable manner. As explained[140], the use of a name registered as a geographical indication, like the use of name registered as a trademark, is subject to the generally applicable provisions of Directive 2000/13 on the labelling, presentation and advertising of foodstuffs[141], of Directive 84/450 on misleading advertising[142] and of the unfair competition laws of the Member States.[143]

---

138 US SWS, para. 131.

139 US SWS, para. 133.

140 EC's FWS, para. 319. See also the responses of the EC and its Member States to the review under Article 24.2 of the TRIPS Agreement contained in document IP/C/W/117/Add.10 (Exhibit EC-29).

141 Exhibit EC–30.

2. *Article 24.5 of the TRIPS Agreement*

(a) The relationship between Section 3 of Part II and Article 16.1

186. The United States has argued that "it is not necessary for the Panel to even consider Article 24.5 to find a violation of Article 16.1, as Article 24.5 is an exception to GI protection, not trademark protection"[144].

187. As we have shown, this argument is specious. True, Article 24.5 limits "GI protection". But, in turn, the measures taken to implement "GI protection" under Section 3 of Part II limit "trademark protection". Thus, by defining the scope of "GI protection" Article 24.5 defines simultaneously the scope of "trademark protection". In other words, as conceded by Australia[145], together with other provisions of Section 3 of Part II, Article 24.5 defines the boundary between the right to protect geographical indications and the obligation to protect trademarks. The issue before the Panel is whether the co-existence provided in Regulation 2081/92 is within the boundary defined by Article 24.5.

188. Moreover, Article 16.1 must be read together with Article 15.2. In accordance with that provision, Members have a right to refuse (and by implication to invalidate) the registration of trademarks on a variety of grounds relating to the "form" of the trademark. That right, however, is circumscribed by Article 24.5, which provides that, in implementing protection for geographical indications, Members may not invalidate a grandfathered trademark "on the basis that such a trademark is identical with or similar to a geographical indication". Since Article 24.5 limits the right of Members under Section 2 of Part III to invalidate the registration of certain trademarks, it may, at the same time, limit some of the obligations arising from the registration of such trademarks under that section.

(b) The meaning of "the right to use a trademark"

189. By now it has become clear that the key issue before the Panel is the interpretation of the phrase "the right to use a trademark". Australia and the United States have advanced different and contradictory interpretations of that phrase.

190. Australia says that the phrase "the right to use a trademark" applies only to the trademarks acquired through use.[146] There are, however, obvious problems with this reading, which Australia has failed to address. First, it cannot be reconciled with the ordinary meaning of the term "trademark", which includes all trademarks. Moreover, as used throughout the TRIPS Agreement, the term "trademark" includes both types of trademarks. When the drafters intended to

---

[142] Exhibit EC–31.

[143] References to the relevant laws of the Member States are found in their responses to the review under Article 24.2 of the TRIPS Agreement (Exhibit EC-32).

[144] US SWS, para. 173

[145] Australia's SWS, para. 96.

[146] Australia's SWS, para. 100.

distinguish between registered trademarks and trademarks acquired through use they did so expressly, like in Article 16.1 or in Article 21.

191. Australia suggests that the phrase "the right to use a trademark" is linked to the reference made in the chapeau of Article 24.5 to the situation where "rights to a trademark have been acquired through use". But, if so, it would have been more logical to say that the implementation of protection for geographical indications "shall not prejudice ... the rights to a trademark acquired through use". Contradicting expressly Australia's position, the United States has said that "'the right to use a trademark' is not specifically linked in the text to trademarks whose rights are acquired through use".[147]

192. Furthermore, by arguing that the phrase "the right to use a trademark" refers exclusively to the trademarks acquired through use, and not contesting that this phrase does not include the right to prevent others from using the trademark, Australia concedes that Article 24.5 provides for the co-existence of geographical indications with earlier trademark acquired through use. Australia suggests that co-existence is justified in the case of non-registered trademarks, because Article 16.1 only requires to grant exclusive rights to the owners of registered trademarks.[148] However, Article 16.1 reserves expressly the right of Members to grant rights on the basis of use, including exclusive rights. Australia does not explain how Article 24.5, which Australia insists is *not* an exception to Article 16.1, can nevertheless limit the Members' right to protect non-registered trademarks under Article 16.1.

193. In turn, the United States argues that the phrase "the right to use a trademark" means in fact "the right to use a trademark and, in addition, to exclude others from using it". This reading cannot be reconciled with the ordinary meaning of that phrase. Nor with the meaning commonly given to that phrase in the context of trademark law, including in US trademark law. Contradicting expressly the US position, Australia agrees with the EC that the phrase "the right to use a trademark" does not mean the *exclusive* right to use a trademark.[149]

194. The United States attempts to stretch the meaning of the phrase "the right to use the trade mark" by resorting to what it calls a "contextual" interpretation. It is, of course, true that the purpose of a trademark is to distinguish the goods from a certain undertaking. But from this it does not follow logically that "the right to use a trademark" is inherently exclusive. In practice, the right to use a trademark is not always exclusive. Indeed, if so, it would have been superfluous to provide in Article 16.1 that registered trademarks must be exclusive. Also, on the US interpretation, any rights granted to the owners of unregistered trademarks on the basis of use would have to be exclusive. Yet, while this may be generally the case, there is no obligation under the TRIPS Agreement to grant such exclusive rights, as emphasised by Australia.[150]

---

[147] US Response to the Panel's Question No. 70, para. 105.
[148] Australia's SWS, para. 100.
[149] *Ibid.*
[150] *Ibid.*

195. The United States confuses the trademark, which is a sign, with the rights that the law may confer over that sign. That a trademark is a sign, and not a right, is confirmed by the fact that an undertaking may use a sign as a trademark even if it has acquired no rights over it. In most countries, including the majority of EC Member States, the rights over a trademark are acquired only upon registration. In other words, an undertaking has no rights over a trademark, including the right to use it, unless and until it registers it. But there is nothing that prevents an undertaking from using a non-registered trademark in order to distinguish its goods, even if it has no rights over it, provided that it does not infringe the rights of another undertaking. In other countries, including the United States, it is possible to acquire rights over a trademark on the basis of use. But even in those countries it is necessary, before any rights over the trademark are acquired, that the trademark is used for a certain period of time. This confirms that one thing is using a sign as a trademark and another thing having a right to use such trademark, let alone an exclusive right.

(c) The validity of the registration

196. While the two complainants disagree with respect to the meaning of the phrase "the right to use a trademark", both contend that the phrase "shall not prejudice ... the validity of the registration" means that the implementation of protection for geographical indications cannot prejudice the right to exclude others from using the trademark.

197. This reading confuses the registration with the exercise of one the rights that may be conferred by the registration. That the validity of the registration cannot be "prejudiced" means that Members cannot cancel the registration, or limit its scope or its duration. It does not mean that Members are prohibited from adopting any measure that may affect the exercise of the rights of the owner of the registered trademark. Moreover, on the complainants' interpretation, the phrase "the right to use a trademark" would become duplicative and superfluous. If the obligation not to prejudice the exclusive right to use a trademark were already inherent in the obligation not to prejudice the validity of the trademark, it would have been pointless to specify that the implementation of protection for geographical indications shall not prejudice "the right to use a trademark".

198. The complainants suggest[151] that while the right to exclude others is inherent in the "validity" of the registration by virtue of Article 16.1, the "right to use a trademark" is not. However, the right to use a trademark is the most basic right of the owner of a registered trademark. Indeed, even more so than the right to exclude others. Trademarks are generally exclusive, but not inherently so. Hence the obligation provided in Article 16.1. On the other hand, a registered trademark which did not confer the right to use the trademark would be meaningless. The right to use a trademark is implicit in Section 2 of Part III. It is implicit, for example, in Article 16.1. The right to prevent others from using a sign which would result in a likelihood of confusion with the registered

[151] See e.g. Australia's SWS, para. 99.

trademark presupposes that the owner of the registered trademark can use the trademark himself, since otherwise there could be no possibility of confusion. The right to use a trademark is also implicit in Article 19, which provides that, in order to maintain a registration, Members may require the use of the trademark. It is also implicit in Article 20, which provides that the use of a trademark shall not be unjustifiably encumbered.

199. If the drafters deemed necessary to specify in Article 24.5 that the implementation of protection for geographical indications shall not prejudice the most basic right of the owner of a registered trademark ("the right to use it"), but not the right to exclude others from using it, the clear implication is that they did not intend to prevent Members from limiting the exercise of the latter right in order to allow the use of a geographical indication in co-existence with a grandfathered trademark.

3. *Article 24.3 of the TRIPS Agreement*

200. The EC has argued that, regardless of whether the co-existence of geographical indications and earlier trademarks is envisaged by Article 24.5, it is required to maintain such co-existence by virtue of the stand-still obligation contained in Article 24.3.[152]

201. The complainants read Article 24.3 as if it were subject to the proviso that Members are exempted from the obligation not to diminish the protection of geographical indications, where such protection would not be consistent with the provisions of Section 2 of Part III.[153] But Article 24.3 contains no such proviso. The United States suggests that Article 24.3 is subject to Article 1.1.[154] But Article 1.1 applies only when a Member decides, voluntarily, to implement more extensive protection. Article 24.3, however, does not simply *permit* Members to implement more extensive protection. It *requires* them to do so. This obligation is not subordinated in any manner to the obligation imposed by Article 16.1. Both have equal rank. Thus, the complainants' reading of Article 24.3 would result in a genuine conflict between that provision and Article 16.1.

202. The distinction drawn by the complainants between the "implementation" of Section 2 and that of Section 3 is fallacious, because the protection of geographical indications with respect to trademarks is an essential and inseparable component of the protection of geographical indications provided in Section 3. Several provisions of Section 3 limit expressly the protection of trademarks under Section 2. There is no reason why Article 24.3 cannot impose an additional limitation.

203. The United States devotes considerable space to argue that the EC's reading of Article 24.3 would have provided "a road map to circumvent the

152 EC FWS, paras. 312-314.
153 See e.g. US SWS, paras. 189-190.
154 US SWS, para. 191.

disciplines of the TRIPS Agreement."[155] The US concerns are exaggerated and unconvincing.

204. In the first place, Article 24.3 is not an open ended provision. It applies only with respect to measures that were in force prior to the entry into force of the WTO Agreement. Those measures should have been known to the negotiators. Even if the disciplines of the TRIPS Agreement "were essentially agreed"[156] as of 1991, there was nothing that prevented the participants from reopening the negotiation of Article 24.3, had they considered that other participants were taking advantage of it in order to circumvent their future TRIPS obligations. Furthermore, the conduct described by the United States would have been manifestly contrary to the requirements of the principle of good faith. The interpretation of Article 24.3 cannot be premised on the assumption that the participants in the negotiations would have acted in bad faith.

205. Moreover, the Unites States exaggerates the opportunities for circumvention. The EC's interpretation of Article 24.3 does not extend to measures limiting copyright or patent protection. Section 3 of Part II does not address the relationship between geographical indications and those rights. Therefore, measures limiting those rights cannot be considered as "implementing" Section 3. Moreover, the United States does not explain how a limitation of patent rights or other intellectual property rights could contribute to protect geographical indications. The example provided by the United States with respect to copyrights[157] is so contrived and unrealistic that it undermines rather than supports its argument.

206. Both complainants argue that, in any event, Article 24.3 would apply only with respect to protection provided to individual geographical indications registered prior to the entry into force of the WTO Agreement.[158] The complainants, however, do not address the EC's argument that this would have the consequence that Article 24.3 would impose obligations only upon those Members that protect geographical indications via a system of registration, or another system involving the recognition *ex ante* of geographical indications.

207. Furthermore, if it were considered that, for purposes of Article 24.3, a geographical indication is not "protected" unless and until it has been registered, the same interpretation should apply to Article 24.9. Accordingly, the EC would be entitled to deny protection to any US or Australian geographical indication which has not been registered or otherwise individually recognised in those countries.

208. Finally, the United States makes much of the fact that the French and the Spanish version of Article 24.3 use the Article *des/las*, respectively, before the term "geographical indication.[159] However, as any French speaker or Spanish speaker struggling to speak English would attest, French and Spanish use

[155] US SWS, para. 192.
[156] *Ibid.*
[157] US SWS, para. 193.
[158] US SWS, paras. 196-197. Australia's SWS, para. 115.
[159] US SWS, para. 196.

liberally determinative articles in contexts where none would be required in English. For example, in Spanish it would be grossly ungrammatical to say "indicaciones geográficas deben ser protegidas", which would be the literal translation of "geographical indications must be protected". Instead, one would have to say "*las* indicaciones geográficas deben ser protegidas", even if the phrase refers to all and not just to certain geographical indications.

4. *Article 17 of the TRIPS Agreement*

209. The EC has submitted in the alternative that, even if Regulation 2081/92 were found to be *prima facie* inconsistent with Article 16.1 of the TRIPS Agreement, the co-existence of geographical indications and earlier trademarks would be justified under Article 17 of the TRIPS Agreement.[160]

210. At the outset, it is useful to recall the differences between the terms of Article 17 and those of the exceptions provided in Article 13, with respect to copyrights, in Article 26.2, with respect to industrial designs, and in Article 30, with respect to patents. Those three provisions, like Article 17, provide for "limited" exceptions. But the similarities end there:

- unlike Article 13, Article 17 does not require that the exceptions be "confined" to "certain special cases";
- unlike Articles 13, 26.2 and 30, Article 17 does not require that the exceptions "do no conflict unreasonably with the normal exploitation" of the right; and
- unlike Articles 13, 26.2 and 30, Article 17 does not require that the exceptions "do not unreasonably prejudice the legitimate interests" of the right holder.

211. All that is required by Article 17 is that the exception be "limited" and that it "take account of the legitimate interests of the owner of the trademark and of third parties". The EC has shown that the co-existence provided in Regulation 2081/92 fulfils both conditions.

(a) The exception is "limited"

212. The United States has advanced several arguments to the effect that the exception claimed by the EC is not "limited". All of them are without merit.

213. First, the United States contends that the exception is not "limited" because "there are no limits on the number of potential GI right holders for each individual GI".[161] But the same is true of other place names which do not qualify as geographical indications. Yet the United States concedes that the use of those place names may be permitted by Article 17.[162]

---

[160] EC FWS, paras. 315-319.
[161] US SWS, para. 205.
[162] US SWS, note 194.

214. The United States argues that, unlike ordinary place names, geographical indications are not "descriptive terms" because they indicate not only the origin of the product but also certain product characteristics attributable to that origin.[163] In other words, the United States appears to be saying that geographical indications are not "descriptive terms" because they are "too descriptive". The United States concedes that a place name is a "descriptive term". And we assume that it would not dispute that a term which describes a product characteristic is also a "descriptive term". Yet, inexplicably, the United States takes the view that a term which indicates both a place name and a product characteristic linked to that place is not "descriptive". The EC does not understand this logic, which would have manifestly absurd consequences. For example, it would mean that the wine makers of the Santa Rita Hills in California would have qualified for an Article 17 exception vis-à-vis the registered trademark "Santa Rita", before the place name "Santa Rita Hills" was recognised as a geographical indication by the US authorities, but would have lost the entitlement to the exception as a result of such recognition.

215. Furthermore, the US reading of the term "descriptive" in Article 17 is in contradiction with the meaning given to that term under US trademark law. The Lanham Act prohibits the registration of terms which are "primarily geographically *descriptive*" except as collective or certification marks.[164] If geographical indications were not "descriptive" terms, they would be registrable as ordinary trademark marks. Yet, as the Panel is aware, the United States purports to protect geographical indications *inter alia* through their registration as certification marks.

216. The United States also argues that the exception is not "limited" because it does not require that the geographical indication be used "otherwise than as mark".[165] However, this is a requirement of US trademark law[166], which is not provided in the trademark laws of many other Members. For example, all that is required by Australia's trademark law is that indications of origin be used "in good faith".[167]

217. As mentioned before, the requirement that geographical indications should not be used "as trademarks", as this term is interpreted by the United States, reflects certain pre-conceived notions as to how trademarks and geographical indications should be used, which have no basis in the TRIPS Agreement and which the EC does not share. When interpreting the notion of "fair use" it is necessary to take account of local factors, such as the consumers' habits and expectations, business practices or even the production and

---

163 *Ibid.*

164 15 USC 1052(e) (Exhibit EC-6).

165 US SWS, para. 199.

166 15 USC Section 1115(b)(4) (Exhibit EC-6).

167 Section 122(1)(a) of Australia's Trade Marks Act 1995 (Exhibit EC-7). To mention but another example, Section 95 of New Zealand's Trade Marks Act 2002 (Exhibit EC-80), provides that indications of origin must be used "in accordance with honest practices in industrial or commercial matters".

distribution structures prevailing in each country. The United States cannot expect to export its own notions of "fairness" together with its cheese.

218. Furthermore, if geographical indications could not be used "as trademarks", as this term is understood by the United States, the use of a geographical indication could never give rise, by definition, to a likelihood of confusion with a trademark and, therefore, would not need to be justified under Article 17. Indeed, the US courts have construed the US "fair use" exception as requiring that the use of the descriptive term must not cause a likelihood of confusion.[168] As explained in our written submission, importing that interpretation into Article 17 would render it wholly redundant.[169]

(b) The exception "takes account" of the interests of the trademark owners and third parties

219. Contrary to the complainants' assertions, EC law does take account of the legitimate interests of the trademark owners and third parties.

220. First, even if the complainants' interpretation of Article 14(3) were correct and that provision did not prevent the registration of all confusing geographical indications, it would nonetheless prevent registration in those instances where the likelihood of confusion is greater, because the trademarks are particularly distinctive, and may cause a more significant prejudice to the trademark owner, because of the reputation and renown of the trademark.

221. This may be contrasted with the situation under US law, where the risk of likelihood of confusion with an existing trademark is *never* considered a relevant ground for refusing the recognition of a geographical indication for wines.[170] Hence the recognition of geographical indications such as "Rutherford" or "Santa Rita Hills", despite the existence of virtually identical earlier trademarks such as "Rutherford Vintners" and "Santa Rita", respectively. Once again, EC law is more protective of the rights of trademark owners than US law. Indeed, last week the Supreme Court of California upheld a California statute that prohibits the use of *any* trademarks consisting of or including a recognised geographical indication for wines of a different origin, including the trademarks grandfathered by federal labelling regulations.[171]

222. The United States has described Article 14(3) as a "narrow"[172] exception for "well-known" [173] trademarks. However, the term "well-known" trademarks is not used in Article 14(3). Even if the length of use and renown/reputation of the trademark were "threshold prerequisites"[174] for the application of Article 14(3), rather than criteria for assessing the likelihood of confusion with any trademark,

---

168 US Response to the Panel's Question No. 80.
169 EC SWS, para. 342.
170 See *Sociedad Anonima Viña Santa Rita v. U.S. Dept. of the Treasury*, 193 F. Supp. 2d 6 (D.D.C 2001) (Exhibit US–48).
171 Exhibit EC-81.
172 US SWS, para. 208.
173 *Ibid.*
174 US SWS, para. 145.

there is no reason why those criteria should be construed "narrowly". Nor has the United States provided any evidence that, in practice, those criteria are being interpreted and applied "narrowly" by the EC authorities.

223. Moreover, contrary to the US assertions, it is not correct that EC law "places no limits on the manner in which a geographical indication can be used".[175]

224. First, the specific concerns with respect to certain particular uses raised by the United States do not relate to the use of the name registered as a geographical indication, but instead to the use of *other* signs in place of or in conjunction with the registered geographical indication. Regulation 2081/92 does no confer a positive right to use those other signs.

225. Furthermore, while the right holders of a geographical indication have a positive right to use the registered name, this does not mean that they are allowed to use that name in any conceivable manner. As explained[176], the use of a name registered as a geographical indication, like the use of a name registered as a trademark, is subject to the requirements of Directive 2000/13 on the labelling, presentation and advertising of foodstuffs[177], and in particular to Article 2(1)(a), which provides that "the labelling and methods used must not be such as could mislead the purchaser to a material degree". This applies *inter alia* with respect to misleading statements concerning the producer or the brand of the goods.[178] The use of registered geographical indications is subject as well to Directive 84/450 on misleading advertising[179] and the unfair competition laws of the Member States, including both specific legislation and/or case law based on general tort law.[180]

226. The United States has dismissed this legislation as irrelevant[181], but without giving any proper reason. The Directives on labelling and misleading advertising and the laws on unfair competition limit the use of geographical

---

[175] US SWS, para. 203.

[176] EC FWS, para. 319. See also the responses of the EC and its Member States to the review under Article 24.2 of the TRIPS Agreement contained in document IP/C/W/117/Add10 (Exhibit EC-29).

[177] Exhibit EC-30.

[178] See also Article 3(1) of Directive 2000/13, which requires that labels must state among other things:

> (7) the name, or business name and address of the manufacturer or packager, or of a seller established within the Community ...
>
> (8) particulars of the place of origin or provenance where failure to give such particulars might mislead the consumer as to the true origin or provenance of the foodstuff.

[179] Exhibit EC-31. Article 2(2) defines misleading advertising as:

> any advertising which in any way, including presentation, deceives or is likely to deceive the person to whom it is addressed or whom it reaches and which, by reason of its deceptive nature, is likely to affect their economic behaviour or which, for those reasons, injures or is likely to injure a competitor

[180] One of the aspects typically covered by such laws is the imitation of labels and packaging in cases where it cannot be addressed as a trademark infringement. See WIPO's *Introduction to Trademark Law & Practice, the Basic Concepts, a WIPO Training Manual*, Geneva 1993, 2nd Edition, pp. 97-100. (Exhibit EC-82).

[181] US SWS, para. 210.

indications in a manner which protects the interests of competitors (including trademark owners) and third parties and are, therefore, relevant for the purposes of Article 17. The United States appears to be suggesting that only those conditions for the use of geographical indications that are provided in Regulation 2081/92 itself or in the EC trademark laws are relevant. But, once again, Article 17 does not prescribe any particular implementation method. Whether the conditions for the use of geographical indications are found in Regulation 2081/92 or in a separate legal instrument is totally irrelevant, as long as the legitimate interests of the trademark owners and of third parties are sufficiently taken into account.

B. *Claim 20: Regulation 2081/92 does not provide for a presumption of a likelihood of confusion in the case of use of an identical sign for identical goods*

227. The EC notes that neither Australia nor the United States appear to contest that Members are not required to restate explicitly in their legislation the evidentiary presumption that the use of identical signs for identical goods will result in a likelihood of confusion.[182] Furthermore, Australia takes the view that such presumption may be rebutted.[183]

228. The terms of Article 14(3) do not prevent the EC authorities from applying the presumption. As shown by the EC, in applying Article 14(3) the authorities must take into account not only the criteria mentioned expressly therein, but also the similarity of goods and signs. And the complainants have provided no evidence that, in practice, the EC is not applying the presumption. The Complainants, therefore, have failed to meet their burden of proof with respect to this claim.

C. *Claims 21 and 22: Article 7(4) of Regulation 2081/92 is inconsistent with Article 16.1 of the TRIPS Agreement because it does not provide a right of objection*

229. The EC has shown that Article 16.1 does not require to make available a right of objection with respect to the registration of another intellectual property right and that, in any event, Regulation 2081/92 does not limit the right of objection in the manner alleged by Australia.

230. Australia argues that "the terms 'jeopardise the existence' used in Article 7(4)[184] establish a far more rigorous standard than a likelihood of confusion".[185] Once again, Australia makes an unwarrantedly narrow interpretation of the terms of the Regulation. Australia's interpretation is, at most,

---

182 See e.g. Australia's SWS, para. 137.

183 Australia's SWS, para. 137.

184 Articles 12b(3) and 12d(2) provide, respectively, that the criteria of Article 7(4) shall apply also with respect to the admissibility of objections to the registration of foreign geographical indications and of objections from outside the EC to EC geographical indications.

185 Australia's SWS, para. 133.

one possible interpretation. But this is not enough to meet Australia's burden of proof. To repeat, Australia must show that the EC's own reading is unreasonable and that it is impossible to read Article 7(4) consistently with Article 16.1. As usual, Australia omits to consider other linguistic versions of the Regulation which shed light on the intention of the EC legislator. For example, in the Spanish version the terms "jeopardise the existence" have been rendered as "perjudicar la existencia". In order to show this, it is not necessary to show that "the very being of that trademark would be threatened".[186] Also, Australia fails to take into account the relevant context and in particular Article 7(5)(b), which provides that objections shall be decided having regard to the "likelihood of confusion".[187] In view of this, there would be no good reason to read Article 7(4) as limiting the grounds of objection in the manner asserted by Australia. Furthermore, the EC recalls once again that Australia has submitted no evidence that any Member State or the Commission have ever rejected a statement of objections for the reasons alleged by Australia.

231. The EC would like to clarify that, when it said in its first submission that the decisions of the Member States rejecting a statement of objection are subject to judicial review in accordance with the national law of each Member State, it was referring to the procedural requirements provided by the administrative law of each Member State, and not to the substantive grounds that can be raised before the courts of the Member States, contrary to what appears to be assumed by Australia.[188] Regulation 2081/92 is directly applicable, like all EC regulations. This means that if, for example, the authorities of a Member States reject a statement because they consider that the objecting party has failed to show that the proposed name does not meet the definition of geographical indication in Regulation 2081/92, the national courts are required to apply the relevant provisions of that Regulation, if necessary after requesting a preliminary ruling from the ECJ.

VI. THE EC MEASURE IS CONSISTENT WITH THE OBLIGATION TO PROVIDE PROTECTION TO GEOGRAPHICAL INDICATIONS UNDER ARTICLE 22.2 OF THE TRIPS AGREEMENT

232. The complainants have not submitted any new arguments with respect to their claims under Article 22.2. The EC would like, nevertheless, to correct some incorrect factual assertions by the complainants regarding the relationship between Regulation 2081/92 and the other means of protection of geographical indications provided in EC law.

---

186 *Ibid.*

187 Similar language is found in Articles 12b(3) and 12d(3) with regard to the registration of geographical indications from other WTO Members and third countries and to the registration of EC geographical indications, following an objection from outside the EC, respectively.

188 Australia's SWS, para. 134.

233. Australia has argued that the Directives on labelling and misleading advertising "are not Community 'law' in the sense of a Regulation with Community level effect in relation to labelling and misleading advertising in any case".[189] Australia goes on to suggest that Regulation 2081/92 would prevail over the measures of the Member States implementing those Directives by virtue of the principle of supremacy of Community law. Australia's arguments evidence once again a crass ignorance of the most basic principles of EC law.

234. First, a Directive is no less "Community law" than a Regulation. Further, there is no hierarchy between a Regulation and a Directive. Second, Community law prevails over the law of the Member States only where there is a conflict between them. Since the laws of the Member States implement the Directives on labelling and misleading advertising, which are themselves Community law, they cannot be said to "conflict" with EC law. To the extent that there was a conflict between the Directives and Regulation 2081/92, *quod non*, it could not be resolved by applying the principle of primacy of Community law, but instead the usual principle that the later law prevails.

235. Australia also suggests that there is a conflict between Regulation 2081/92 and the unfair competition laws of the Member States.[190] But it fails to provide any evidence of such conflict. In the EC, like in most countries, unfair competition laws complement the legislation on specific intellectual property rights, by providing supplementary protection.[191] Thus, for example, the Community Trademark Regulation contains a declaratory provision clarifying expressly that it applies without prejudice to the laws on unfair competition of the Member States.[192] The same is true of the Trademark Directive and of Regulation 2081/92.

236. For its part, the United States suggests that Article 2(1) of Regulation 2081/92 would exclude the application of the Directives on labelling and misleading advertising.[193] The United States has misunderstood the purpose of Article 2(1), which is to make clear that Members States cannot adopt or maintain their own national systems for protecting *specifically* geographical indications. For example, they cannot create or maintain a register of

---

[189] Australia's SWS, para. 146.

[190] Australia's SWS, para. 171.

[191] See e.g. Article 1(2) of WIPO's *Model Provisions on Protection Against Unfair Competition* (Exhibit AUS-9), which stipulates that those provisions "shall apply independently of, and in addition to, any legislative provisions protecting ... trademarks ... and other intellectual property subject matter". The comment to this Article reads as follows in pertinent part:

> Paragraph (2) makes it clear that the availability of ... trademark ... protection does not preclude the application of the provisions against unfair competition.... The protection against unfair competition then constitutes a kind of supplementary protection, additional to the protection of specific intellectual property subject matter...

[192] Cf. Article 14.2:

> This Regulation shall not prevent actions concerning a Community trademark being brought under the law of the member States relating in particular to civil liability and unfair competition.

[193] US SWS, para. 216.

geographical indications of their own. The Directives on labelling and misleading advertising, however, do not protect geographical indications *qua* geographical indications. They provide protection against any misleading trade description, including any misleading use of indications of source or provenance, regardless of whether they qualify as geographical indications.

VII. REGULATION 2081/92 IS CONSISTENT WITH OBLIGATIONS UNDER THE TBT AGREEMENT

237. Australia has raised two claims under the TBT Agreement:

- that Article (12)(2) of Regulation 2081/92 is incompatible with Article 2.1 of the TBT Agreement (Claim 37);
- and that Articles 4 and 10 of Regulation 2081/92 are incompatible with Article 2.2 of the TBT Agreement (Claim 38).[194]

238. As to the substance of these claims, the EC has already shown that Article (12)(2) of Regulation 2081/92 does not involve any discrimination between goods. As regards the requirement of inspection structures, the EC has also shown that these are indispensable for the attainment of the objectives of Regulation 2081/92. Accordingly, they cannot be considered as unnecessarily trade-restrictive.

239. However, for these questions even to arise under Article 2 TBT Agreement, Australia has to show that the relevant provisions of Regulation 2081/92 are a technical regulation. Australia's claims do not even meet this threshold test.

A. Article (12)(2) of Regulation 2081/92 is not a technical regulation

240. First of all, as regards Article (12)(2), the core issue is that this provision does not lay down any product characteristics for identifiable products.

241. Australia has not contested that the requirement in Article (12)(2) does not apply to all products covered by the Regulation, but only to a specific class of protected names, namely homonyms.[195] However, Australia argues that it is sufficient that the product be "identifiable".[196] It is certainly true that a product need not be *explicitly* identified in the document.[197] However, the product should at least be identifiable on the basis of the document itself. This is not the case here: as long as no application has been made for the registration of protected homonymous names, it is simply not knowable to which products this requirement will apply.

---

194 Australia's FWS, para. 249 et seq.
195 Australia's SWS, para. 191.
196 Australia's SWS, para. 192.
197 Appellate Body Report, *EC – Asbestos*, para. 70.

242. Second, Article (12)(2) does not *lay down* any product characteristics or labelling requirements. It merely provides that as a condition for the registration of a geographical indication, the indication of the country of origin is necessary. The specific labelling requirements will then be contained, in accordance with Article 4 (2) (h) of the Regulation, in the product specifications. Accordingly, Article (12)(2) is not a technical regulation, but simply a condition for the registration and acquisition of an intellectual property right.

243. Finally, the requirement to indicate the country of origin is also not a labelling requirement as it relates to a "product, process or production method". Contrary to the view of Australia, "origin" is a concept different from "product". Even though the origin can confer certain characteristics on a product, origin as such is not a "product characteristic". For this reason, an origin marking requirement does not fall under the definition of a technical regulation.

244. This interpretation is also required by the need for a harmonious interpretation of the WTO Agreements, which the Appellate Body has repeatedly recognised, and to which the EC has already referred above.[198] Article IX:1 GATT contains specific disciplines on origin marking, which exclude, as Australia has recognised, a national treatment obligation. If origin marking requirements nevertheless fell under Article 2.1 TBT Agreement, the specific rule in Article IX:1 would be devoid of its practical scope.

245. In response to the EC's reference to Article IX:1 GATT, Australia has invoked the general interpretative note to Annex 1 A to the WTO Agreement, and has argued that in case of a conflict, the TBT Agreement should prevail over the GATT.[199] However, the EC does not argue that there is a conflict. Rather, the EC argues that Article 2.1 TBT Agreement and Article IX:1 GATT should be interpreted in such a way as to give meaning to both of them. The natural result of such a harmonious interpretation is that, in line with the wording of the definition of a technical regulation, origin marking requirements do not fall under Article 2.1 TBT Agreement. The EC notes that otherwise, Australia's and the US's own country of origin marking requirements for imported goods would be in violation of Article 2.1 TBT Agreement (cf. Exhibits EC-66 to EC-68).

B. Articles 4 and 10 of Regulation 2081/92 are not a technical regulation

246. With respect to the requirement of inspection structures laid down in Articles 4 and 10 of the Regulation, the problem is similarly that these do not lay down product characteristics. Already in its previous submissions, the EC has explained that a requirement of inspection structures would, if anything, have to be regarded as a conformity assessment procedure.[200]

247. In its second submission, Australia has not provided any convincing arguments in response. Australia's only new argument has been that inspection

[198] Above para. 36.
[199] Australia's SWS, para. 213.
[200] EC SWS, para. 256.

structures might be regarded as "related processes".[201] However, this manifestly wrong. Point 1 of Annex 1 to the TBT Agreement refers to "product characteristics or their related processes". Accordingly, the processes must be "related" to the product characteristics, as would be the case for production processes and methods. If Australia's interpretation were correct, in contrast, then all conformity assessment procedures would automatically also become technical regulations. This would lead to a systematic overlap between the provisions of the TBT Agreement governing technical regulations and those governing conformity assessment procedures.

248. Accordingly, none of the provisions attacked by Australia can be considered a technical regulation. Australia's claims under the TBT Agreement should accordingly be rejected.

VIII. CONCLUSION

249. For the above reasons, the EC requests the Panel not to consider any claims not within its terms of reference, and to reject all other claims of the complainants.

*

* *

Thank you for your attention. This concludes our statement. We look forward to answering any questions that the Panel may wish to ask.

---

201 Australia's SWS, para. 202.

ANNEX B-7

REPLIES BY THE EUROPEAN COMMUNITIES TO QUESTIONS POSED BY THE PANEL FOLLOWING THE SECOND SUBSTANTIVE MEETING

(26 August 2004)

TABLE OF WTO AND GATT CASES REFERRED TO IN THE RESPONSES

Short Title	**Full Case Title and Citation**
Canada – Pharmaceutical Patents	Panel Report, *Canada – Patent Protection of Pharmaceutical Products*, WT/DS114/R, adopted 7 April 2000, DSR 2000;V, 2295.
EC – Asbestos	Appellate Body Report, *European Communities – Measures Affecting Asbestos and Asbestos-Containing Products*, WT/DS135/AB/R, adopted 5 April 2001
EEC – Regulation on Imports of Parts and Components	EEC – *Regulation on Imports of Parts and Components*, Report by the Panel adopted on 16 May 1990, L/6657 – 37S/132
Korea – Various Measures on Beef	Appellate Body Report, *Korea – Measures Affecting Imports of Fresh, Chilled and Frozen Beef*, WT/DS161/AB/R, WT/DS169/AB/R, adopted 10 January 2001
US – Section 110(5) Copyright Act	Panel Report, *United States – Section 110(5) of the US Copyright Act*, WT/DS160/R,adopted 27 July 2000, DSR 2000;VIII, 3769

GLOSSARY

Commission, EC Commission	Commission of the European Communities
Committee	Committee of representatives of the Member States referred to in Article 15 of Council Regulation 2081/92
Community Trademark Regulation	Council Regulation (EC) No 40/94, of 20 December 1993, on the Community Trademark, as amended
Council, EC Council	Council of the European Union
Court of Justice, European Courtof Justice	Court of Justice of the European Communities
DSU	Understanding on Rules and Procedures Governing the Settlement of Disputes
EC	European Communities
GATT	General Agreement on Tariffs and Trade 1994
FOS	First Oral Statement
FWS	First Written Submission
GI	Geographical indication
Member States, EC Member States	Member States of the European Union
Official Journal	Official Journal of the European Union
Paris Convention	Stockholm Act of the Paris Convention for the protection of Industrial property, of 14 July 1967
Regulation 2081/92, Regulation	Council Regulation (EEC) No 2081/92 of 14 July 1992 on the protection of geographical indications and designations of origin for agricultural products and foodstuffs, as amended on the date of establishment of the Panel
SCM Agreement, SCM	Agreement on Subsidies and Countervailing Duties
Trademarks Directive	First Council Directive 89/104, of 20 December, on the Community Trademark, as amended
TBT Agreement, TBT	Agreement on Technical Barriers to Trade
TRIPS Agreement, TRIPS	Agreement on Trade-Related Aspects of Intellectual Property Rights
US	United States
WTO Agreement	Marrakesh Agreement Establishing the World Trade Organization

Question 94

The Panel takes note that, in the EC's view, the specific conditions contained in Article 12(1) of Regulation (EC) No. 2081/92 do not apply to WTO Members because the introductory phrase "[w]ithout prejudice to international agreements" ensures that the WTO agreements prevail where there is a conflict with the Regulation (EC rebuttal, para. 55). Which precise EC obligations under the WTO agreements would be prejudiced by the application of those specific conditions to other WTO Members? In particular:

(a) would the EC's obligations under Article III:4 of GATT 1994 be prejudiced?

1. Yes.

(b) would the EC's obligations under Article 3.1 of the TRIPS Agreement be prejudiced? If not, please explain the relevance of your reference to the fact that the TRIPS Agreement obliges WTO Members to provide protection to GIs in accordance with Section 3 of Part II and the general provisions and basic principles of the TRIPS Agreement (EC first written submission, paras. 65-66).

2. No. As the EC has already explained, Regulation 2081/92 does not involve any discrimination between nationals.[1]

3. The fact that WTO Members are obliged under the TRIPS Agreement to provide protection to geographical indications is relevant because it means that it is not justified to apply conditions of reciprocity and equivalence to other WTO Members as a precondition for the protection of geographical indications. Should another WTO Member not provide adequate protection to geographical indications, then the appropriate response, in accordance with Article 23.1 of the DSU, would be recourse to dispute settlement under the DSU.

Question 95

Can the EC provide the Panel with any official statement by the Commission or any other EC institution, that the application of conditions of reciprocity and equivalence, such as those under Article 12(1) of Regulation (EC) No. 2081/92, would be inconsistent with the EC's obligations under international agreements, in particular, the WTO Agreement?

4. The EC can refer the Panel to the statement in the TRIPS Council it made on 16 June 2004, and to which it has already referred in response to the Panel's Question No. 16.[2] This EC statement is also reflected in the minutes of the TRIPS Council, which are attached as Exhibit EC-83.[3]

---

[1] EC FWS, paras. 110–111; SWS, para. 53 et seq.; EC SOS, para. 17 et seq.

[2] EC Response to Panel's Question 16, para. 39.

[3] IP/C/M/44, 19 July 2004 (para. 62–63). This should alleviate the concerns expressed by Australia "that there may not even be an official record of the EC's statement" (Australia's SWS, footnote 29).

5. Second, the EC can refer the Panel to the 2nd edition of the Guide to Regulation 2081/92, which the EC has provided as Exhibit EC-64. This guide was prepared by the Commission as guidance to the implementation of Regulation 2081/92, and is the most detailed and authoritative document available. The EC notes that the United States has also variously referred to this guide in support of its submissions before the Panel.[4]

6. Finally, the statements made on behalf of the EC before the Panel in the present proceedings are also official statements of the EC, and confirm that the EC does not apply conditions of reciprocity and equivalence.

Question 96

The EC has provided a revised Guide to Regulation (EC) No. 2081/92, dated August 2004 (Exhibit EC-64). Was this new version prepared in connection with this Panel proceeding? How is it relevant to the Panel's work if the Commission assumes no liability for its contents (see its cover page)? A new paragraph in the introduction (page 5) indicates that "the Commission reserves the right to amend procedures" and indicates the possibility of further possible revisions. Does this mean that the Guide could be changed back to the old version?

7. The revised edition was prepared in response to the increased interest from other WTO Members in the registration of geographical indications under Regulation 2081/92. This increased interest from other WTO countries has made it desirable to include a specific section in the guide providing guidance to interested governments and applicants. The guide was not prepared in connection with the Panel proceedings. However, the EC does not exclude that the increased interest is partially caused by awareness on the part of other WTO Members of the ongoing Panel proceedings.

8. The note on the cover page, according to which "the Commission does not assume any liability for its contents", is a standard liability disclaimer, which can be found in numerous similar publications.[5] The intention of this disclaimer is to ensure that the extra-contractual liability of the Community cannot be invoked as regards the contents of the guide. However, it is clear that the guide, like similar such publications, is prepared with utmost care, and that its contents are highly relevant for the application and interpretation of Regulation 2081/92 by all EC institutions.

9. In fact, according to the constant case law of the European Court of Justice, where an institution has adopted rules which are not legally binding, it may nevertheless not depart from such rules without giving the reasons which have led it to do so. Otherwise, the institution would infringe the principles of equality of treatment or the protection of legitimate expectations.[6]

---

[4] US FOS, para. 53; US SWS, para. 155.

[5] For examples for such disclaimers, see Exhibit EC-84 and Exhibit EC-85.

[6] Case 148/73, *Louwage*, [1974] ECR 81, para. 12 (Exhibit EC-86); Case T-15/89, *Chemie Linz*, [1992] ECR II-1275, para. 53 (Exhibit EC-87).

10. The final paragraph of the introduction to the guide merely states that in the light of administrative need and experience in managing applications, the Commission may modify certain practical aspects of the guide. Similarly, the Commission may also have to modify the guide if the rules contained in the basic legislative texts, and in particular Regulation 2081/92, are amended. In contrast, the Commission could not amend the guide in a way contrary to the basic legislative acts applicable.

11. There is therefore no conceivable reason why the Commission should change the Guide back to the old version. Moreover, since Regulation 2081/92 does in any event allow the registration of geographical indications from other WTO Members, such a change would not affect the possibility of such registrations under Regulation 2081/92.

Question 97

The Panel takes note of the EC's responses to Panel questions nos. 16 and 17 and the EC's rebuttal, paras. 79-86 Please explain in detail how the Commission's interpretation that Article 12(1) of Regulation (EC) No. 2081/92 does not apply to WTO Members is consistent with the statements in the EC responses in the TRIPS Council review of legislation to question No. 4 posed by New Zealand and the follow-up question posed by India on page 24 in IP/Q2/EEC/1 (cited in Australia's rebuttal, para. 33, fn. 23).

12. In response to the question posed by New Zealand, the EC gave the following response in the above-mentioned document:[7]

> As for the protection of geographical indications of WTO Members, it is necessary to distinguish the following situations:
>
> 1. The protection pursuant to Article 22 of the TRIPS Agreement, which is guaranteed by the Member States' application of Council Directive 79/112/EEC concerning labelling (prohibition to mislead the public). In the event of a problem relating to a geographical indication of a WTO Member, the EC Member States must also ensure the possibility for the operators concerned to take legal action in their courts.
>
> 2. The ex officio protection pursuant to the above-mentioned Regulation 2081/92, for which either:
>
> – the procedure followed by Community producers as outlined above must be followed, in accordance with the principle of national treatment; or
>
> – a bilateral agreement should be concluded as envisaged in Article 12, when the system of protection is equivalent to the Community regime.

13. The EC considers that this response is fully compatible with its submissions in the present proceedings. As regards protection under

---

[7] IP/Q2/EEC1, p. 4.

Regulation 2081/92, the EC's response distinguishes two possible alternatives for the protection of geographical indications of WTO Members: either the normal procedure for registration to be followed on a product-specific basis, or the conclusion of a bilateral agreement where the system of protection is equivalent to the Community regime. The reference to a bilateral agreement was clearly mentioned as an alternative, not as the only possibility for the protection of geographical indications from WTO Members.

14. In response to the Question from India, the EC confirmed essentially the same, namely that bilateral agreements were an alternative, not the only route to protection of geographical indications from other WTO Members under Regulation 2081/92:[8]

> It is important to stress that, in general, conditions provided in Article 12 of Regulation 2081/92/EEC are only required when a bilateral agreement is concluded between the EC and a WTO Member. This means that it only occurs when two parties voluntarily wish higher level of protection ("ex officio") than this provided under the TRIPS Agreement. So, this is not a compulsory condition but another option that can be used when systems are equivalent, in particular conditions under Article 4 (specifications) and Article 10 (inspection).

15. In response to the follow-up questions from India, which concerned particularly the requirement of inspection structures, the EC once again confirmed that there were no conditions of equivalence or reciprocity, but that the EC simply applied the conditions for registration contained in Regulation 2081/92 on a non-discriminatory basis:[9]

> (b) The inspection of the conformity for the products whose geographical name has been registered as a protected designation of origin (PDO) or a protected geographical indication (PGI) is essential to ensure the credibility of the system for the consumers. This is an essential element of the Regulation. In order to obtain the same protection (Article 13 of the Regulation), if it must be complied with by the producers established in the EC, it must also be complied with by the third country nationals, to avoid discrimination.
>
> (c) Article 12 of Council Regulation 2081/92/EEC provides for the same protection in respect of products from third countries which meet those requirements. Therefore, nationals from other WTO Members are afforded treatment "no less favourable" than Community nationals, as required by Article 3 of the TRIPS Agreement.
>
> (d) Under Council Regulation 2081/92/EEC, the advantage of registration is available to the nationals of all WTO Members

---

8 IP/Q2/EEC1, p. 23.
9 IP/Q2/EEC1, p. 24.

without any distinction. Accordingly, Council Regulation 2081/92/EEC is fully consistent with the requirements of Article 4 of the TRIPS Agreement.

16. In conclusion, the EC considers that the above statements are fully consistent with its submissions in the present proceedings.

Question 98

Is it the EC's submission that the conditions in Article 12(1) of Regulation (EC) No. 2081/92 do not apply to WTO Members so that:

(a) WTO Member nationals may obtain GIs for areas located in all countries; or

17. No. The conditions for the registration of geographical indications in Regulation 2081/92 do not depend on nationality. Inversely, nationality as such does not confer the right to register geographical indications in any particular country.

(b) persons from all countries may obtain GIs for areas located in all WTO Members?

18. Yes. Since the registration of geographical indications under Regulation 2081/92 does not depend on nationality, registration of a geographical indication in another WTO Member may be obtained by any group or person that complies with the requirements of Article 5 (1) and (2) of Regulation 2081/92,[10] regardless of nationality. Similarly, regardless of nationality, any person may use a geographical indication from another WTO Member protected under Regulation 2081/92, provided that the products are in accordance with the product specifications.

Question 99

The EC has referred to other Community legal acts in relation to the meaning of the phrase "without prejudice to international agreements" (EC rebuttal, paras. 62-66). Please also refer to Regulation (EC) No. 2082/92 on certificates of specific character for agricultural products and foodstuffs, which was adopted with the Regulation at issue in this dispute. To what international agreements does the phrase "[w]ithout prejudice to international agreements" refer as used in Article 16 of that Regulation?

19. As in the case of Article 12(1) of Regulation 2081/92,[11] the phrase "without prejudice to international agreements" used in Article 16 of Regulation 2082/92 refers to any international agreement concluded by the EC, including both multilateral and bilateral agreements. In the case of Regulation 2082/92, such agreements would include in particular the GATT.

---

[10] On these requirements, and notably on the fact that they do not involve a requirement of nationality, see already EC Response to Panel's Question No. 22.

[11] EC SWS, para. 68.

Question 100

In Regulation (EC) No. 753/2002 on wine (set out in Exhibit US-35), Articles 34-36 refer to "third countries", apparently to refer to both WTO and non-WTO Members. It expressly states wherever a "third country" is limited to, or excludes, WTO Members. Why was Regulation (EC) No. 2081/92 drafted in such a way that the meaning of "third country" in Articles 12 through 12d is not clearer each time it was used? Does the use of "WTO Member" together with "third country" in certain instances in Articles 12 through 12d of Regulation (EC) No. 2081/92 not suggest that the term "third country" excludes WTO Members in those articles?

20. Regulation 753/2002 and Regulation 2081/92 are separate legal acts and were drafted at different times. The fact that there may be differences in terminology or legal drafting between Community legislative acts is an inevitable result of complex legislative procedures, and is not something that is peculiar to the EC.

21. As concerns the drafting of Regulation 2081/92, it should be recalled that several of its provisions were also drafted at different points in time. In particular, Articles 12a to 12d were inserted only in 2003. The fact that they did not use the "without prejudice language" but instead distinguished specifically between WTO Members and other third countries may be due to the heightened awareness of the concerns of WTO Members at that time. However, this does not mean that the "without prejudice" language which was included in Article 12(1) in 1992 should be ignored and deprived of its useful meaning.[12]

Question 101

The Panel takes note of the parties' respective views on the meaning of "nationals" under the TRIPS Agreement and the Paris Convention. Without prejudice to those views, please explain in detail which nationals should be compared for the purposes of the TRIPS national treatment obligations, based on the text of the agreement.

Please refer to the quadrant in the third party submission of Chinese Taipei (para. 9). Both the EC and the US compare an EC national with rights to a GI located in the EC. On the US view, that national should be compared with a US national with rights to a GI located in the US. But on the EC view, that national should be compared with a US national with rights to a GI located in the EC. Would it be appropriate instead to compare all EC nationals with rights to GIs who might wish to register them under Regulation (EC) No. 2081/92, wherever the geographical areas are located, and compare them with all US nationals with rights to GIs who might wish to register them under the Regulation, wherever the geographical areas are located?

More generally, is there a principle in the TRIPS Agreement that all nationals of one WTO Member with rights to a particular category of intellectual property, such as GIs, should be compared with all nationals of other WTO Members with

[12] See also EC Responses to Panel's Questions 8 and 9.

rights to the same category of intellectual property, unless the text of the agreement indicates that with respect to particular types of products or other sub-categories, they require particular treatment?

22. The EC does not consider that the present case requires *any* comparison between nationals.

23. As the EC has already explained, Regulation 2081/92 does not contain any discrimination on the basis of nationality. For this reason, the quadrant prepared by Chinese Taipei in its third party submission is not pertinent. There are no two "columns" depending on the nationality of the applicant or producer. The only relevant element to which the Regulation refers is the location of the area to which the geographical indication is related. Accordingly, the present case may require a comparison in the treatment of goods originating in the EC, in the US, or in Australia. It does not require a comparison between nationals.

Question 102

Is it safe to assume that persons resident or established in one country to produce agricultural products or foodstuffs will be considered "nationals" of that country for the purposes of TRIPS? Why is it, or is it not, safe to assume that applicants for GIs under Regulation (EC) No. 2081/92 are "nationals" of the country where their GI is located, for the purposes of TRIPS?

24. It is not safe to assume that persons resident or established in one country to produce agricultural products or foodstuffs will be considered "nationals" of that country for the purposes of TRIPS. As the EC has already set out, the TRIPS Agreement, and in particular Article 3.1 thereof, uses the term "national". It requires national treatment as between nationals, not between "domiciliaries", "persons resident or established", or "products".[13]

25. Moreover, the EC sees no basis for the assumption apparently made by the US[14] that somehow, the definition of "national" might be different when agricultural products are concerned. Agricultural products are also products with an identifiable origin, which is not linked to the nationality of the producer.[15] Like any other product, agricultural products are subject to the disciplines of the GATT. The same also applies for foodstuffs.

26. In contrast, the TRIPS Agreement does not contain any different definition of the term "national" for agricultural products. The EC can therefore not agree that different disciplines should apply under the TRIPS Agreement to intellectual property rights depending on whether they relate to agricultural products, foodstuffs, or to other products.

---

[13] EC FWS, para. 104 et seq.; SWS, para. 28 et seq.; SOS, para. 17 et seq.

[14] US SOS, para. 14.

[15] Cf. also Article 2 of the Agreement on Agriculture, which defines the term "agricultural product" for the purposes of that agreement.

Question 103

The Panel takes note that the EC does not exclude entirely that "under certain circumstances, measures which are neutral on their face may nonetheless constitute less favourable treatment of foreign nationals" and that the EC believes that national treatment under TRIPS should not overlap with GATT 1994 (EC response to Panel question No. 29, paras. 71 and 74). What other considerations are relevant to the assessment of de facto discrimination under TRIPS? What is the relevance, if any, of the fact that the TRIPS Agreement does not contain a general exceptions provision analogous to Article XX of GATT 1994?

27. So far, Article 3.1 TRIPS Agreement has never been applied on a *de facto* basis. In particular, unlike under Article III:4 GATT, there is no accepted definition of what constitutes "less favourable treatment" of nationals with regard to the protection of intellectual property rights.

28. Under Article III:4 GATT, it is accepted that "treatment no less favourable" means "according *conditions of competition* no less favourable to the imported product than to the like domestic product".[16] However, in the view of the EC, this definition is not easily transposable to Article 3.1 TRIPS.

29. First, it cannot be assumed that nationals necessarily "compete" with respect to the protection of intellectual property rights. For instance, Article 3.1 TRIPS would require that the conditions for the protection of a patent for a pharmaceutical product of a foreign national are no less favourable than the conditions for the protection of a patent for an appliance to be fitted on a motor vehicle of a domestic national. However, it does not appear that the domestic and the foreign national are in any kind of "competitive relationship". Similarly, their products are not "like products", and are therefore also not in any relationship of competition.

30. Second, it should be noted that the objective of national treatment under the GATT and the TRIPS Agreement is not identical. According to Article III:1 GATT, the overarching objective of GATT national treatment is to prevent that internal measures are applied so as "to afford protection to domestic production". As the Appellate Body has stated in *EC – Asbestos*, this objective also inspires the interpretation of Article III:4 GATT.[17]

31. It cannot be assumed that this same objective also underlies Article 3.1 TRIPS Agreement. Rather, the objectives of TRIPS national treatment would seem to be related to the first paragraph of the Preamble to the TRIPS Agreement, which refers to the desire "to reduce distortions and impediments to international trade, and taking into account the need to promote effective and adequate protection of intellectual property rights, and to ensure that measures and procedures to enforce intellectual property rights do not themselves become barriers to legitimate trade".

---

16 Appellate Body Report, *Korea – Various Measures on Beef*, para. 229 (emphasis original).

17 Appellate Body Report, *EC – Asbestos*, para. 94.

32. In the view of the EC, the complainants have made no effort to show in which way Regulation 2081/92 discriminate between nationals. Instead, they have simply referred to alleged discriminations on the basis of the area to which the geographical area is related, i.e. on the basis of the origin of the good.[18] However, whereas the origin of the good may be a relevant starting point for examining whether the conditions of competition between domestic and foreign goods are altered to the detriment of foreign goods, it is not a relevant starting point for examining whether there is discrimination between nationals.

33. In the view of the EC, the Panel should therefore not simply transpose the jurisprudence on *de facto* discrimination under Article III:4 GATT to Article 3.1 TRIPS Agreement. Rather, the definition of less favourable treatment of nationals in the context of Article 3.1 TRIPS Agreement would have to be based on the wording and context of the provision, including the broader objectives of the TRIPS Agreement.

34. In the view of the EC, there is no need for the Panel to address this complex question in the present dispute. However, if the Panel wishes to address the issue of *de facto* discrimination under the TRIPS Agreement, it should also take into account the fact that both the TRIPS and the GATT are an integral part of the WTO Agreements, and the need for a harmonious interpretation between the two. As the EC has already set out, this means that the Panel should not interpret TRIPS national treatment in such a way as to create an unnecessary potential for conflict with the GATT.[19]

35. This potential for conflict is particularly evident with respect to Article XX of the GATT. As the EC has already said, it consider that a number of the challenged aspects of Regulation 2081/92, if they were held to constitute less favourable treatment, would nonetheless be justified by Article XX(d) GATT. The complainants have contested the EC's submissions in this respect, but they have not contested that Article XX(d) GATT is a possible defense to their claims under the GATT. However, they have not indicated what the relevance of Article XX GATT is with respect to their analogous claims under the TRIPS.

36. In the view of the EC, it would not be in line with a harmonious interpretation that a *de facto* application of the TRIPS Agreement would render inapplicable defenses which are available to otherwise entirely identical claims under the GATT. Therefore, should the Panel consider that Regulation 2081/92 involves *de facto* discrimination, the Panel would have to resolve the issue of what is the relevance of Article XX(d) GATT with respect to those claims under the TRIPS Agreement.[20]

---

[18] Cf. most recently US SOS, para. 7 et seq.

[19] See EC SOS, para. 36–37.

[20] See EC SOS, para. 37.

Question 104

Please provide your interpretation of the term "separate customs territory" as used in footnote 1 to Article 1.3 of the TRIPS Agreement in accordance with the customary rules of treaty interpretation. What relevance can be drawn from the fact that the same term is used in Article XXVI of GATT 1994?

37. In accordance with the customary rules of treaty interpretation as reflected in Article 31 of the Vienna Convention on the Law of Treaties, the term "separate customs territory" in footnote 1 to Article 1.3 of the TRIPS Agreement must be interpreted in accordance with the ordinary meaning to be given to the terms of the treaty in its context and in the light of its object and purpose.

38. The term "customs territory" is defined in Article XXIV.2 of the GATT to mean "any territory with respect to which separate tariffs or other regulation of commerce are maintained for a substantial part of the trade of such territory with other territories". There is no doubt that the EC, like the US or Australia, has a "customs territory" within the meaning of Article XXIV.2 of the GATT.

39. However, footnote 1 to Article 1.3 of the TRIPS Agreement does not just refer to "customs territories", but to "*separate* customs territories". The term "separate" is an essential part of the expression used, and must be given meaning. The adjective "separate" is defined as "separated, solitary, secluded, detached, set apart, not incorporated or joined".[21] In other words, the "separate customs territory" must be "separated" from something else.

40. However, it cannot be sufficient for it simply to be "separate" from the customs territory of other Members, since otherwise, any "customs territory" would also be a "separate customs territory". Rather, a separate customs territory is only a territory which otherwise constitutes part of another territory, and in particular another state, or for which another state has international responsibility. Accordingly, the term "separate customs territories" applies to territories such as Hong Kong, Macao, Chinese Taipei, or certain overseas dependencies of a number of WTO Members.[22]

41. This interpretation is also confirmed by the objective of footnote 1. Separate customs territories which are a part of another state frequently may not have a concept of "nationality" which could be applied for the purposes of the TRIPS Agreement. The definition in footnote 1 therefore serves as a substitute for the definition of "national" in such cases. This definition is not relevant to the EC, which has a nationality.[23]

42. The EC's interpretation is also confirmed by the context of the provision, and notably by the use of the term "separate customs territory" in the GATT. As the Panel has rightly pointed out, Article XXVI (5) (a) GATT refers to "other territories for which [a Member] has international responsibility, except such separate customs territories as it shall notify [...]". In a similar sense, Article XXXIII also refers to "a government acting on behalf of a separate

[21] The New Shorter Oxford English Dictionary, vol. 2, 1993, p. 2779.
[22] EC SOS, para. 23.
[23] EC SWS, para. 27; SOS, para. 23. See also EC response to the following question.

customs territory". It follows clearly that "separate customs territories" are territories for which another State has international responsibility, be it because they are part of its territory, or because they are in some other way dependent on it.

43. It is clear from these considerations that the EC cannot be considered a "separate customs territory". The EC has a customs territory which includes the territory of all its Member States. However, there is no other State which is responsible in international law for the EC, nor is the EC part of any other State. Accordingly, the EC cannot be said to be any more of a "separate customs territory" than the US or Australia.

Question 105

The Panel takes note of the EC's view that it is not a separate customs territory Member of the WTO within the meaning of footnote 1 to Article 1.3 of the TRIPS Agreement (EC rebuttal, para. 35).

> *(a) Which natural persons does the EC consider EC nationals for the purposes of TRIPS? Are they also nationals of EC member States?*

44. Article 17 (1) of the EC Treaty establishes the Citizenship of the Union, and provides that "every person holding the nationality of a Member States shall be a citizen of the Union". Accordingly, any person which is a national of a Member State is a national of the EC.

> *(b) Which legal persons does the EC consider EC nationals for the purposes of TRIPS? Are they also nationals of EC member States?* ***EC***

45. The nationality of legal persons in international law and in domestic law is a highly complex question.[24] Like the domestic law of most other WTO Members, EC law does not contain a specific definition of nationality for legal persons. However, Article 17 (1) of the EC Treaty is relevant by analogy. Accordingly, any legal person which is considered a national under the laws of a Member States would also be an EC national.

46. However, like the law of most other WTO Members, the law of the Member States may not contain a general definition of nationality of legal persons, but rather define nationality only for certain specific purposes. Moreover, the criteria used by Member States in this context may vary, and include criteria such as the law of incorporation, or the seat of the company, the nationality of shareholders, or a combination of such criteria.[25]

47. Moreover, it should be noted that where the nationality of legal persons is relevant for the application of Community law, Community law itself may define the relevant criteria. An example for this is Article 48 (2) of the EC Treaty, which provides that for the purposes of the freedom of establishment "companies

---

[24] As background on this issue, see A.A. Fatourous, *National Legal Persons in International Law*, Encyclopaedia of Public International, vol. 3, p. 495–501 (1997) (Exhibit EC-88).

[25] Cf. the overview in A.A. Fatourous, *National Legal Persons in International Law*, Encyclopaedia of Public International, vol. 3, p. 495–496 (1997) (Exhibit EC-88).

and firms formed in accordance with the law of a Member States and having their registered office, central administration or principal place of business within the Community shall, for the purposes of this Chapter, be treated in the same way as natural persons who are nationals of Member States". However, no such definition exists for the purposes of the application of Regulation 2081/92, since nationality is not a relevant element for the application of that Regulation.

48. Moreover, the EC would like to remark that the difficulty of establishing criteria for the nationality of legal persons cannot be an excuse for substituting other definitions, such as residence or establishment, for nationality, where nationality is in fact irrelevant for the purposes of the measure in question.

Question 106

What are the nationalities of the applicants for GIs registered under Regulation (EC) No. 2081/92? Have there been any applicants who were not nationals of the EC member State in which the relevant GI was located? Please supply details of any that were not, and the relevant GIs. To the extent that you are aware of the nationality of persons other than the applicants who use a GI in accordance with its registration, please supply the same information.

49. At the outset, the EC would like to clarify that the notion of "applicant" is of limited relevance in the context of the present dispute. According to Article 5 (1) of Regulation 2081/92, a group, or under certain conditions a natural person,[26] may apply for the registration of a geographical indication. However, the applicant is not identical with the rightholder. Since a geographical indication is a collective right, any person producing in accordance with the product specifications may use the geographical indication. The conditions for applicants are a procedural modality of the application process. They do not imply that the applicant becomes a rightholder.

50. As the EC has already said, Regulation 2081/92 does not contain any requirement as to the nationality of the applicant.[27] More importantly still, Regulation 2081/92 does not contain any requirement as regards the nationality of persons who use a protected name. Any person producing in accordance with the product specifications, regardless of nationality, may use the protected name.

51. Since nationality is not a relevant criterion under Regulation 2081/92, the EC does not request any information on the nationality of applicants or producers when an application for the registration is submitted. Similarly, the EC does not monitor the nationality of the producers of a product using a geographical indication.

52. Moreover, the EC would like to recall that the burden of proof for showing that Regulation 2081/92 involves discrimination on the basis of nationality is on the complainants, and not on the EC.

53. For these reasons, the EC is not able, and should not be expected to be able, to give detailed information about the nationality of producers of products

---

26 These conditions are set out in Article 1 of Commission Regulation 2037/93 (Exhibit COMP-2).

27 See EC Response to Panel's Question No. 22.

using names protected under Regulation 2081/92. In fact, such information is not any more available to the EC than it is to the United States and Australia.

54. Without prejudice to these remarks, and beyond the examples of non-EC producers already referred to in previous EC submissions,[28] the EC can refer the Panel to at least two examples where a producer of a product using a protected name comes from a different Member State than the one where the geographical area is located:

- Lactalis, a French-based dairy group, owns Locatelli and Invernizzi, which produce among others Gorgonzola and Grana Padano (Exhibit EC-62).
- Stella Artois, a Belgian Brewery, used to produce "Kölsch" beer, a protected name for beer from the Cologne area in Germany (Exhibit EC-89).

Question 107

The Panel takes note of the examples of foreigners and foreign companies which have invested in Europe (EC rebuttal, para. 46 and Exhibits EC-36 to EC-39; EC second oral statement, para. 28 and Exhibits EC-61 to EC-63). Is the Larsen firm a French company? Have Suntory Limited, E & J Gallo and the Robert Mondavi family formed subsidiaries, joint ventures or other entities under the laws of France and Italy to invest in those wine estates? Did Sara Lee, Kraft Foods and Nestlé purchase companies formed under the law of an EC member State?

The Panel takes note that the EC argues that the possibility that these foreign nationals formed legal persons under the laws of an EC member State is not attributable to Regulation (EC) No. 2081/92 (EC second oral statement, para. 30). Is it appropriate to exclude such other factors from an examination of the WTO-consistency of the Regulation? Does the EC submit that the Panel should "pierce the corporate veil" and refer to ownership and control to determine nationality for the purposes of TRIPS?

55. It appears from the information available on the website of Larsen Cognac that today, Larsen Cognac is a Société anonyme incorporated under French law. From the information contained in Exhibit EC-61, it appears that Al Ponte Prosciutti, an Italian limited liability company, was purchased by Sara Lee Personal Products S.p.A., an Italian cooperation. It also appears that Al Ponte Prosciutti is controlled by Aoste Holding, SA, a French Cooperation, which in turn was purchased by Sara Lee Charcuterie SA, a French cooperation belonging to the Sara Lee Group. The EC does not have specific information on the ownership situation in the other cases.

56. In the view of the EC, the measure at issue is exclusively Regulation 2081/92, which does not involve any discrimination on the basis of nationality. If, for practical considerations related for instance to taxation or labour law, a person producing in conformity with a product specification

[28] EC SOS, para. 28.

chooses to set up a legal entity in the area where the geographical indication is located, this is not related to Regulation 2081/92.

57. It is simply a practical consequence of the fact that products have to be produced in accordance with the product specifications, which may require that an important part of the production process takes place in the geographical area concerned. If the submission of the complainants were correct, then any discrimination on the basis of the origin of goods would *de facto* also always be a discrimination between nationals. The EC does not consider that such an interpretation would be an appropriate interpretation of the national treatment provisions of the TRIPS and the GATT.

58. Finally, the EC does not submit that the Panel should "pierce the corporate veil" and refer to ownership and control to determine the nationality for the purposes of the TRIPS. In the view of the EC, the nationality of the legal person involved, if and where relevant, should be determined on the basis of the municipal law of the Member concerned.[29]

Question 110

Does the EC contest that, to the extent that Regulation (EC) No. 2081/92 provides GI protection for EC nationals and is a law affecting EC products, GI protection for other WTO Member nationals and imported products solely through other laws, such as labelling and unfair competition, would be less favourable treatment?

59. No. However, as regards nationals, rather than products, the EC would like to recall that Regulation 2081/92 does not provide protection on the basis of nationality.

Question 111

Does the EC contest that national treatment and MFN obligations under TRIPS apply to TRIPS-plus protection, and apply to Regulation (EC) No. 2081/92 even to the extent that it does not merely implement the EC's obligations under Article 22?

60. The EC does not contest that national treatment and MFN obligations under TRIPS applies to more extensive protection granted in respect to intellectual property rights addressed in the TRIPS Agreement. However, the EC contests that Regulation 2081/92 involves discrimination on the basis of nationality.

Question 112

The Panel takes note that the Commission has not recognized any country under Article 12(3) of Regulation (EC) No. 2081/92 (EC response to Panel question No. 10, para. 22). Is the Commission obliged to recognize any country that satisfies the conditions set out in Article 12(1)?

---

[29] Cf. also EC Response to Panel's Question No. 105.

61. If the conditions of Article 12(1) are fulfilled, the Commission will normally recognise the country in question. However, Article 12(1) does not create any legal "obligation" as against the third country. This follows from the wording "this Regulation may apply" in Article 12(1) of Regulation 2081/92. Moreover, the EC would like to recall that the conditions of Article 12(1) do not apply to WTO Members.

Question 113

The EC argues that there must be a substantive difference between two provisions governing the registration of GIs in order for one to entail less favourable treatment (EC second oral statement, para. 40). What is a "substantive" difference in this sense? Does the EC allege that there is a de minimis standard for less favourable treatment under TRIPS or GATT 1994? Is a simple difference in language insufficient to establish different treatment?

62. For the purposes of Article III:4 GATT, it follows from the case law of the Appellate Body that a "substantive difference of treatment" is a difference in treatment which modifies the conditions of competition to the disadvantage of imported goods.[30]

63. As the EC has also explained, the definition of "less favourable treatment" for the purposes of Article 3.1 TRIPS is less clear, and cannot be assumed to be identical with that of Article III:4 GATT.[31] However, it would appear that in order to constitute a violation of Article 3.1 TRIPS, a measure would have to modify the conditions regarding the protection of intellectual property rights within the meaning of the TRIPS to the detriment of foreign nationals.

64. The EC does not believe that there is a *de minimis* standard for less favourable treatment under the GATT or under the TRIPS Agreement. However, as the Appellate Body has held, a formal difference in language, which does not modify the conditions of competition, cannot be held to constitute less favourable treatment under Article III:4 GATT.[32] Similarly, a simple difference in language which does not modify the conditions for the protection of intellectual property could not be held to constitute less favourable treatment under Article 3.1 TRIPS. This is not the application of a *de minimis* standard, but simply the application of the requirements of Article III:4 GATT and Article 3.1 TRIPS.

Question 114

With respect to registration applications under Article 12a(2) of Regulation (EC) No. 2081/92, a third country must verify that the requirements of the Regulation are satisfied before it transmits the application:

---

[30] Appellate Body Report, *Korea – Various Measures on Beef*, para. 229. Cf. also above, para. 28.

[31] Cf. above para. 28 et seq.

[32] Appellate Body, *Korea – Various Measures on Beef*, para. 137; cf. on this also EC SOS, para. 39 et seq.

(a) *to what extent is this designed to confirm the protection of the GI in its country of origin in accordance with Article 24.9 of the TRIPS Agreement, and to what extent does it respond to other objectives?*

65. The verification envisaged in Article 12a(2) of Regulation is intended to confirm that the requirements of the Regulation for the registration of the geographical indication are fulfilled. This means in particular that the application must contain a product specification in accordance with Article 4(2) of the Regulation. As can be seen from Article 4(2)(a) to (f), the details contained in the product specification permit to confirm that the name for which protection is sought corresponds to the definition of a geographical indication in Article 2 of Regulation 2081/92. Moreover, Article 12a(2)(b) of the Regulation also requires the third country to verify that the inspection structures required by Article 10 are established.

66. In addition, Article 12a(2)(a) of Regulation 2081/92 requires also "a description of the legal provisions and the usage and the usage on the basis of which the designation of origin or the geographical indication is protected or established in the country". The purpose of this requirement is to ensure, in accordance with Article 24.9 TRIPS Agreement, that the geographical indication for which protection is sought in the EC is also protected in its country of origin.

(b) *is this additional to the requirement that a registration application transmitted to the Commission must be accompanied by a description of the matters set out in Article 12a(2)(a)?*

67. The protection in the country of origin is a requirement for the registration of geographical indications from third countries, which is in accordance with Article 24.9 TRIPS Agreement. As regards geographical indications from within the EC, for which protection is obtained in accordance with Regulation 2081/92, this requirement can by definition not apply.

68. However, it should also be noted that the requirement that the geographical indication is protected in its country of origin, and the other conditions of the Regulation, are closely related and will tend to overlap. If a geographical indication is protected in its country of origin, this means that according to the country of origin, the geographical indication falls under the definition of Article 22.1 TRIPS, i.e. identifies goods as originating in the territory of a Member, or a region or locality in that territory, where a given quality, reputation, or other characteristics are essentially attributable to its geographical origin. Accordingly, if a geographical indication is protected in the country of origin, this should normally also facilitate the examination of whether the name fulfils the conditions for protection under Regulation 2081/92.

(c) *Does the Commission also examine whether the application satisfies the conditions for protection under Article 12b(1)(a)? How is this examination different from the verification by the third country?*

69. When deciding on the registration of a geographical indication from a third country, the Commission must verify whether the conditions for the

registration set out in Regulation 2081/92 are met. However, in making this evaluation, the Commission will rely on the factual assessment provided by the country of origin. In fact, only on the basis of this information can the Commission verify whether the conditions for registration are fulfilled.

70. As regards the requirement that the geographical indications must be protected or established in its country of origin, this question regards the law of a third country. The Commission will therefore have to rely on the assessment provided by the third country.

Question 115

With respect to objections under Article 12b(2)(a) of Regulation (EC) No. 2081/92, what is an objection that "comes from a WTO Member"? With respect to objections under Article 12d(1) of the Regulation, what is the meaning of a person who "is from a WTO Member"? Do they both refer to the place of residence or establishment of the person who wishes to object? Must objections under both provisions be sent to the country in which the person resides or is established?

71. In both Article 12b(2)(a) and in Article 12(d)(1), a person that "is from a WTO Member country" is a person resident or established in the WTO Member country.

72. In both cases, objections must be sent to the country in which the person resides or is established. In the case of Article 12b(2)(a), this follows from the reference to Article 12d.

Question 116

To the extent that certain responsibilities under Articles 12a and 12d(1) of Regulation (EC) No. 2081/92 are borne by non-EC WTO Members:

> *(a) how is the EC satisfied that every other WTO Member has the authorization to carry them out? (Please refer to Brazil's response to Panel third party question No. 1) (EC second oral statement, paras. 72-77).*

73. The EC does not consider that any specific "authorization" is needed to carry out the responsibilities in Articles 12a and 12d(1).

74. As regards the confirmation that the geographical indication is protected or established in its country of origin required by Article 12a(2)(a) of Regulation 2081/92, the EC would like to recall that a) all WTO Members are obliged to provide protection to geographical indications in accordance with Article 22 TRIPS Agreement, and b) that the EC is not obliged to provide protection to geographical indications not protected in their country of origin, in accordance with Article 24.9 TRIPS Agreement. Accordingly, any WTO Member should be able to state whether it protects a geographical indication for which protection is sought in the EC. A WTO Member can therefore not argue that it does not have "authority" to state whether a geographical indication is

protected in its territory, and at the same time claim that this geographical indication should be protected in the EC.

75. As regards the verification of the further requirements in Article 12a(2)(a), and notably the verification of the product specifications, this is a primarily factual verification carried out at the request of the applicant. The EC does not see why a specific "authorization" would be required for this purpose. Moreover, the EC would like to remark that the requirements of the product specifications closely reflect the requirements of Article 22.1 TRIPS Agreement. Since any WTO Member is obliged protection of geographical indications as defined in Article 22.1 TRIPS, it cannot be argued that a WTO Member "has no authority" to carry out such examinations.

76. As regards finally the transmission of the statement of objections required by Article 12d(1), this is, as the US has itself acknowledged,[33] a "purely ministerial act" of a kind routinely carried out by governments in many contexts.[34] The EC does not see why a specific "authorization" would be needed.

> *(b) if other WTO Member governments lack authorization to carry them out, can they be carried out by the EC instead?*

77. No. The EC cannot make findings as to whether a geographical indication is protected under the law of a third country. Second, as regards the other requirements of Regulation 2081/92, these relate to a geographical area located in a third country, and may involve inspections and verifications in the third country. The EC does not consider that it could carry out such inspections verifications in a third country without the consent of that country. Moreover, as the EC has also explained, the verifications require intimate knowledge of the conditions in the geographical area concerned, which the EC does not have.[35]

> *(c) to what extent does the EC itself accord no less favourable treatment to the nationals of other Members, and to what extent do other WTO Members share the implementation of that obligation? Can a Member delegate the implementation of WTO obligations to other Members with or without their prior consent?*

78. As the EC has explained in response to subquestion (a) and (b), where the registration of a geographical indication from another WTO Member is sought in the EC, that WTO Member must cooperate with the EC in two respects:

- it must enable the EC to evaluate whether the geographical indication is in accordance with the requirements of the Regulation, which reflect Article 22.1 TRIPS Agreement;
- it must confirm that the geographical indication is protected or established in its territory.

79. If the third country does not cooperate with the EC on these aspects, then the registration cannot be carried out. In this case, the failure to register would not be attributable to an act of the EC, but to the failure of the country of origin

33 US Response to Panel's Question No. 38, para. 74.

34 Cf. the examples given in EC Response to Panel's Question No. 37.

35 See EC Response to Panel's Question No. 33, para. 81.

of the geographical indication to assume those tasks which fall within its sphere of responsibility. To this extent, it can indeed be said that with respect to the registration of geographical indications abroad, the country of origin and the country of registration share obligations.

80. The EC does not consider that it can delegate the implementation of WTO obligations to other Members without their prior consent. However, the EC considers that it can require the cooperation of other WTO Members where this is indispensable for the proper implementation of provisions of the WTO agreements, such as Article 22.1, 22.2, and 24.9 TRIPS Agreement.

> *(d) to what extent has the EC accorded certain treatment to the nationals of other WTO Members rather than to the governments of those other WTO Members?*

81. Regulation 2081/92 does not accord any treatment to nationals, but to products. It also does not accord any treatment to governments. Rather, whether a government assumes its responsibilities with respect to the registration of a geographical indication relating to its territory can only be ascertained with respect to the specific application, not with respect to the third government overall.

Question 117

The Panel takes note of the EC's response to Panel question No. 8 concerning the meaning of "third country" and seeks clarification as to whether "third country" as used in Article 12(2) of Regulation (EC) No. 2081/92, includes WTO Members. If so, why does the "without prejudice" clause in Article 12(1) form part of the context of Articles 12(1) and (3) but not Article 12(2)? If not, where does the Regulation cover identical GIs from the EC and other WTO Members?

82. The reference to names "of a third country" refers to any name which has been protected under the Regulation, or for which protection is sought. Therefore, it can include names both from WTO Members and from other third countries recognized in accordance with Article 12(3).

83. The "without prejudice" clause in Article 12(1) is relevant for Article 12(3) because Article 12(3) sets out the procedure for establishing whether the conditions in Article 12(1) are met. Article 12(2) has no such specific link with Article 12(1). The fact that it is included in Article 12, and not for instance in Article 12a, is simply due to the fact that it was already contained in the original version of Regulation 2081/92.

Question 118

The Panel takes note that, in Australia's view, the identical GI labelling requirement would not be inconsistent with Article 2.1 of the TBT Agreement if it was applied to both EC and imported products according to date of registration, not origin. (Australia's response to Panel question No. 53). Even if Article 12(2) does not apply to EC products as well as imported products, does the Commission have the discretion to apply the same requirement according to the date of registration to EC products under Article 6(6) in order to ensure that the identical labelling requirement is applied to the later GI irrespective of the origin of the products?

84. Yes. As the EC has already set out, where the identical names are from different countries, the clear distinction in practice would normally require the indication of the country of origin.[36]

Question 119

What is the difference, if any, in the meaning of the word "homonymous" as used in Article 6(6) of Regulation (EC) No. 2081/92 and "identical" as used in Article 12(2)? Why does the EC consider that homonyms are covered by the word "identical" in Article 12(2) (EC response to Panel question No. 43)?

85. There is no difference. "Homonym" is defined as "a person or thing having the same name as another, a namesake".[37] In other words, "identical name" is a synonymous expression for "homonym".

86. Moreover, the French and the Spanish version of Regulation 2081/92 both use the same expression ("dénomination homonyme"/"denominación homónima") in both Articles 6(6) and 12(2) of Regulation 2081/92.

Question 120

The Panel takes note of Australia's confirmation that the only less favourable treatment under the identical GIs labelling requirement is relabelling costs (Australia's response to Panel question No. 52). Would imported products have to be relabelled? Would existing marks of origin satisfy this requirement? What does "clearly and visibly indicated" mean?

87. Imported products would not necessarily have to be relabeled. It the country of origin is already clearly and visibly indicated on the label, then this will be sufficient. Existing marks of origin may therefore be sufficient to the extent that the country of origin is clearly and visibly indicated. To the extent that the country of origin is not indicated, the affixation of an additional label clearly and visibly indicating the country of origin would also be sufficient.

88. What "clearly and visibly indicated" means must be evaluated in each specific case from the point of view of a normal consumer. The country of origin will be clearly and visibly indicated if a normally attentive consumer can easily notice the indication, and will therefore not be induced in error as to the origin of the product concerned.

Question 122

Please refer to the phrase "labelling requirements as they apply to a product" as used in the definition of "technical regulation" in Annex 1.1 of the TBT Agreement.

---

36 EC FWS, para. 479.
37 The New Shorter Oxford English Dictionary, vol. 1, 1993, p. 1254.

(a) *The EC argues that the "origin of a product is different from the product itself" (EC response to Panel question No. 50). However, as the EC acknowledges, the origin of a product may confer specific characteristics on it. This is consistent with the definitions of designation of origin and geographical indication in Article 2 of Regulation (EC) No. 2081/92, which provide that "the quality or characteristics of the product ... are essentially or exclusively due to a particular geographical environment ..." and that the product "possesses a specific quality, reputation or other characteristics attributable to that geographical origin ...". How then is the origin of a product entitled to bear a registered GI different from the product itself?*

89. The origin of a product is the place where the product originates. It can be a country, or a region or place in a country. The origin of a product is therefore different from the product itself.

90. Moreover, the origin of a product is also not necessarily linked to product characteristics. Where the origin does confer specific characteristics, then this may justify the protection of a geographical indication, as foreseen in the TRIPS Agreement. However, there are many cases, particularly in the case of industrial products, where the origin as such does not confer any characteristics on the product.

91. The concept of "origin" of a product is also the subject of regulation outside the TBT Agreement. Qualifying the origin of a product as a product characteristic within the meaning of the definition of a technical regulation in Point 1 of Annex 1 to the TBT Agreement would therefore risk creating unnecessary overlap and conflict between the TBT Agreement and other covered agreements.

92. One example is origin marking, which is already regulated in Article IX GATT. Another example are geographical indications, which are dealt with in the TRIPS Agreement. A third example would be Article XI:1 of the GATT, which prohibits quantitative restrictions on imports, including import bans on foreign products. If origin were a product characteristic, then an import ban could be interpreted as a technical regulation laying down that products must be of domestic origin. However, the EC sees no justification for applying Article 2.1 or 2.2 TBT Agreement to import bans, when such restrictions are already satisfactorily dealt with in the GATT.

93. Finally, the Agreement on Rules of Origin must also be mentioned in this context. According to Article 1.2 of the Agreement on Rules of Origin, the Agreement defines rules of origin in particular with respect to numerous provisions of the GATT, including explicitly Article IX GATT on marks of origin. In contrast, no mention is made of the TBT Agreement. If the TBT Agreement applied to marks of origin, however, then it would be hard to explain why Article 1.2 of the Agreement on Rules of Origin only mentions Article IX of the GATT, but not the TBT Agreement.

(b) *What is the meaning of the words "as they apply to" as used in this part of the definition? Do they refer to the application of labelling requirements to the characteristics of a product, or to the product itself, or both?*

94. The second sentence of Point 1 of Annex 1 to the TBT Agreement refers to "marking or labeling requirements as they apply to a product, process or production method". The EC would remark that a mark or a label cannot be applied to a process or production method as such. Rather, it would appear that the process and production method would be the content of the labeling requirement. Accordingly, it seems to the EC that the words "as they apply to" are meant to refer to the application of labeling requirements to characteristics of a product, process or production method.

Question 123

Does the requirement to display a country of origin on a label under Article 12(2) of Regulation (EC) No. 2081/92 constitute a mark of origin covered by Article IX of GATT 1994?

95. Yes.[38]

Question 124

The definition of "technical regulation" in Annex 1.1 of the TBT Agreement expressly encompasses "marking or labelling requirements as they apply to a product, process or production method". Are marks of origin and labels of origin covered by Article IX of GATT 1994 excluded from the scope of the TBT Agreement? Why did the negotiators not explicitly carve them out of its scope? Can a line be drawn between marks of origin that fall under the TBT Agreement and those that do not? What are the systemic consequences for marks of origin if they all fall within the scope of the TBT Agreement?

96. As the EC has already explained in response to the Panel's Question 122, origin marking requirements are not a technical regulation within the meaning of the TBT Agreement, and therefore do not fall within the scope of the TBT Agreement.

97. There was no need for the drafters of the TBT Agreement to specifically exclude origin marks from the scope of the agreement if the negotiators considered that origin marking did not fall under the definition of a technical regulation.

98. In the view of the EC, it is not possible to distinguish origin marks which fall under the TBT Agreement and such which do not. The US has suggested that Article IX:1 GATT might cover only "general origin marking requirements", but not origin marking requirements covering only specific products.[39] As the EC has already explained, there no textual basis for such a distinction in Article IX:1

---

[38] As to the US argument to the contrary, see EC SOS, para. 128 and below para. 98.

[39] US SWS, para. 77.

GATT.[40] Similarly, there is also no basis for this distinction in the definition of a technical regulation in Point 1 of Annex 1 to the TBT Agreement, which does not distinguish as to whether a technical regulation relates to many products or only to a few. Moreover, as the EC has also said, there is simply no logic to the proposition that an origin marking maybe imposed on all imported products, but not just on some.

99. As regards the systemic consequences of the complainants' interpretation, if marks of origin fell under the TBT Agreement, this would mean that any such marking requirements which apply only to imported products would be incompatible with Article 2.1 of the TBT Agreement. As a consequence, Article XI:1 GATT, which exempts origin marking from national treatment obligations would be obsolete. Similarly, origin marking requirements would be subject to Article 2.2 TBT Agreement, which would make the specific provisions of Article IX:2 to IX:6 GATT largely redundant.

Question 125

To what extent would any less favourable treatment under Article 2.1 of the TBT Agreement have to be determined in light of the regulatory objective a Member is trying to pursue under Article 2.2?

100. As evidenced by the 6th paragraph of the Preamble to the TBT Agreement, the TBT Agreement does not prejudice the right of WTO Members to pursue legitimate regulatory goals. However, frequently, the pursuit of such regulatory goals may make it necessary to discriminate between products even if consumers consider them as like, for instance on account of environmental hazards that they pose.

101. Therefore, the EC considers that the legitimate regulatory objectives of the Member concerned must be taken into account in the application of both Article 2.1 and 2.2 TBT Agreement. Alternatively, the Panel would have to consider whether Article XX of the GATT is applicable within the context of the TBT Agreement.

Question 126

With respect to Article 10(3) of Regulation (EC) No. 2081/92:

(a) the first indent sets out certain requirements for designated inspection authorities and/or approved private bodies. Do these apply to all countries whose GIs are protected under the Regulation, including non-EC member States?

102. Yes.

(b) the fifth indent appears to refer only to EC member States and third countries recognized pursuant to Article 12(3). Where does the Regulation refer to the applicable standard for WTO Members

[40] EC SOS, para. 128.

not recognized pursuant to Article 12(3), whose requirements private bodies must fulfil for approval purposes?

103. As the EC has set out earlier, the reference to the procedure in Article 12(3) is relevant only where the conditions of Article 12(1) are applicable.[41] Accordingly, the last subparagraph of Article 10(3) of Regulation 2081/92 applies also to WTO Members.

(c) the fifth indent refers to "[t]he equivalent standard or the applicable version of the equivalent standard". What equivalent standard has been established for GIs for areas located in WTO Members which do not satisfy the conditions of equivalence and reciprocity in Article 12(1)? What are the criteria for establishing that standard? Is it a matter of determining what is "equivalent" to standard EN 45011? Or is it a matter of determining what standard would fulfil the objectives of the Regulation in the light of each third country's own circumstances and conditions?

104. No standard has been established so far. Therefore, as long as no specific standard has been established, compliance with any equivalent standard to standard EN 45011 is sufficient. In its earlier submissions, the EC has referred to ISO Standard 65:1996 as such an equivalent standard.[42]

105. The EC would like to note that the situation is the same for EC Member States. Although the fourth subparagraph also provides a legal basis for establishing "the standard or the applicable version of standard EN 45011", no such standard or version has so far been established. In the absence of any decision on the basis of the fourth subparagraph of Article 10 (3) of Regulation 2081/92, standard EN 45011 continues to be applied.

Question 127

Article 12a(2)(b) requires a declaration by a third country government that the structures provided for in Article 10 are established on its territory. Article 10(2) refers to inspection authorities and/or private bodies approved for that person by the Member State and Article 10(3) provides that where they outsource they continue to be responsible vis-à-vis the Member State for all inspections. What is the exact nature of the role that third country governments must play in the creation and maintenance of the inspection structures that are called for under Article 10?

106. When a Member State or a third country approve an inspection structure, they must ascertain that the inspection structure is capable of fulfilling its functions in accordance with Article 10 (1), and that it meets the requirements of Article 10 (3) of the Regulation. Moreover, the Member State or the third country is also responsible for ensuring that the inspection body, as long as it is approved to carry out inspections, continues to comply with the requirements of Article 10 of the Regulation. How exactly the Member State or third country

---

[41] EC Response to Panel's Question No. 8; EC SOS, para. 48.

[42] EC FWS, para. 54 and Exhibit EC-3.

carries out this continued monitoring, i.e. through occasional on-the-spot checks, audits, or reporting requirements, is for each Member State or third country to decide.

Question 131

Which EC Directives govern conformity assessment to EC technical regulations in the goods area? To what extent do those Directives require foreign governmental involvement in the designation/approval of conformity assessment bodies, when mutual recognition agreements in the conformity assessment area do not already exist?

107. EC Directives governing conformity assessment to EC technical regulations in the goods area are extremely numerous, so that no exhaustive list can be given.

108. However, Council Decision 93/465/EEC concerning the modules for the various phases of the conformity assessment procedures and the rules for the affixing and use of the CE conformity marking, which are intended to be used in the technical harmonization directives (Exhibit EC-90) defines certain general principles for EC conformity assessment relevant in the present context. In particular, Point A (k) of the Annex to Decision 93/465 provides as follows:

> for the purposes of operating the modules, Member States must notify on their own responsibility *bodies under their jurisdiction* which they have chosen from the technically competent bodies complying with the requirements of the directives. This responsibility involves the obligation for the Member States to ensure that the notified bodies permanently have the technical qualifications required by the directives and that the latter keep their competent national authorities informed of the performance of their tasks. Where a Member State withdraws its notification of a body, it must take appropriate steps to ensure that the dossiers are processed by another notified body to ensure continuity;

109. Since conformity assessment bodies must be under the jurisdiction of the Member State, they must be located on the territory of that Member State. The reason for this rule is that only with respect to bodies under its jurisdiction can the Member States effectively ensure that the body properly exercises its functions. In principle, a Member State can therefore not designate a conformity assessment body located in a third country. Accordingly, the question of third country governmental involvement does not pose itself.

110. It should also be noted that the TBT Agreement explicitly foresees the possibility of Members to apply conformity assessment procedures to imported products. No provision of the TBT Agreement obliges Members to simply accept conformity assessment carried out by bodies of another Member. In fact, Article 6.1 TBT Agreement obliges Member to accept conformity assessment in other Members only under specific conditions, in particular if they are satisfied that procedures offer an assurance of conformity with applicable technical regulations or standards equivalent to their own procedures. Article 6.1 TBT

Agreement moreover recognises that prior consultations may be necessary to arrive at a mutually satisfactory understanding, and Article 6.2 encourages Members to enter into negotiations for the mutual recognition of conformity assessment procedures.

111. In addition, Article 6.4 TBT Agreement "encourages" Members to permit participation of conformity assessment bodies located in the territories of other Members in their conformity assessment procedures. However, it is clear from the word "encourage" that there is no legal obligation in the TBT Agreement to permit such participation. The reason for this is that the participation of a conformity assessment requires that certain guarantees for the technical competence and capacity of the conformity assessment to be fulfilled, and that fulfilment of these criteria may be difficult to guarantee for a body located in a third country, in particular in the absence of cooperation of the government of that country.

112. The EC notes that its practice in this respect is not unique. For instance, United States regulations foresee that the United States Federal Communications commission may designate telecommunication certification bodies to approve telecommunications equipment. According to 47 CFR 68.160 (b), the Federal Communications Commission shall designate such bodies located *in the United States* (Exhibit EC-91).[43] According to 47 CFR 68.160 (c), bodies outside the United States shall be permitted to authorize equipment only "in accordance with the terms of an effective bilateral or multilateral recognition agreement or arrangement to which the United States is a party" (Exhibit EC-91).

113. It is before this background that the EC, the US and Australia have concluded mutual recognition agreements under which they agree to recognize the results of conformity assessment carried out by bodies designated by the other party.[44] On this basis, numerous conformity assessment bodies have been recognized under the Sectoral Annexes to the EC-US and EC-Australia MRAs.[45]

114. As a consequence, bodies designated by the United States and Australia can carry out conformity assessment with respect to the EC's standards, and vice versa. Accordingly, such bodies are in exactly the same situation as inspection bodies approved by the United States or Australia to carry out inspections under Regulation 2081/92. The EC considers it odd that the complainants consider themselves disadvantaged by the possibility to approve inspection structures for the purposes of Regulation 2081/92, when this possibility to directly designate conformity assessment bodies for the covered sectors was in fact the main objective of the mutual recognition agreements between the parties.

---

[43] It appears that indeed all telecommunication certification bodies designated under this provision are located in the US (Exhibit EC-92).

[44] Cf. Exhibits EC-23 and EC-24. Telecommunications terminal equipment is one of the sectors covered by these agreements.

[45] Lists of approved conformity assessment bodies are available under http://europa.eu.int/comm/enterprise/international/indexb1.htm#listsapprovedcabs.

Question 132

The Panel takes note of the EC's examples of flexibility in the design of inspections structures (EC rebuttal, para. 104 and Exhibit EC-48). Do these examples all relate to the nature of the inspecting authority? Who determines what constitutes an appropriate inspection for each product, and on the basis of what criteria?

115. The examples given relate to the nature of the inspection body, i.e. whether this body is public or private, local, regional, or national, focusing only on geographical indications or not, commercial or non-profit.

116. Regulation 2081/92 does not define what constitutes an appropriate inspection for each product. Accordingly, it is in principle for each designated inspection structure to define the concrete modalities of inspections for the products in question, for instance with respect to the place, time, frequency, and other modalities of the inspections. In accordance with Article 10(1) of the Regulation, the basic criterion is that the inspections must effectively ensure that product bearing a protected name comply with the products specifications.

Question 133

The Panel takes note that Australia argues that the product specification requirements set out in Article 4(2) of Regulation (EC) No. 2081/92 include "product characteristics", in particular subparagraphs (b) and (e). (Australia's rebuttal, paras. 197 and 204) If the inspection structures are designed to ensure that the product specifications under Article 4 of the Regulation are fulfilled, how can they be a technical regulation and not a conformity assessment procedure?

117. In the view of the EC, they cannot be both a technical regulation and a conformity assessment procedure.[46]

Question 134

The Panel takes note of the EC's response to Panel question No. 61, in particular regarding the Panel's terms of reference. However, does the EC contest that a "conformity assessment procedure" within the meaning of the TBT Agreement assesses conformity with a "technical regulation" or "standard" within the meaning of the TBT Agreement? If not, then can the EC complete its analysis and explain whether the inspection structures of Regulation (EC) No. 2081/92 assess conformity with each individual product specification referred to in Article 4 of the Regulation for a registered name, and that those specifications therefore would constitute a "technical regulation" within the meaning of the TBT Agreement?

118. The EC does not contest that a conformity assessment procedure assesses conformity with a technical regulation or a standard as defined in Point 3 of Annex 1 to the TBT Agreement.

---

[46] EC SWS, para. 404 et seq.; EC SOS, para. 246 et seq.

119. However, since Australia has not made any claim under the provision of the TBT Agreement concerning inspection structures, the EC does not consider that the Panel needs to decide whether the inspection structures are indeed conformity assessment procedures or not. Since Australia has brought its claims exclusively under Article 2 TBT Agreement, the essential question which the Panel needs to decide is whether these structures by themselves are a technical regulation. According to Point 1 of Annex 1 to the TBT Agreement, this in turn depends on whether they lay down product characteristics. The EC has raised the aspect of conformity assessment merely to illustrate its argument that structures which "ensure conformity" with requirements regarding product characteristics (whatever their legal quality may be) are not "laying down product characteristics".

120. For this reason, the EC also does not consider that this Panel should examine the question of whether the product specifications are a technical regulation, a standard, or something else. Australia has not formulated any claim regarding the specifications for any particular product or name under the TBT Agreement. Accordingly, the question whether the product specifications can be considered a technical regulation, or a standard, is outside the scope of the present Panel.

121. In addition, the EC would note that this question is highly complicated and involves complex issues regarding the relationship between the TRIPS Agreement and the TBT Agreement. Moreover, such issues could arise not just in respect to geographical indications, but also to patents, designs, copyrights, plant variety rights, or other intellectual property rights which involve the definition of product characteristics.

Question 135

The EC invokes Article XX(d) of GATT 1994 as a defence to the national treatment and MFN claims with respect to third country governments' verification and transmittal of applications, the identical GIs labelling requirement and inspection structures requirement. The EC alleges that these requirements are "necessary" to secure compliance with Regulation (EC) No. 2081/92 or to attain the legitimate objectives of the Regulation (EC rebuttal, paras. 228-242, paras. 263-265; EC second oral statement, paras. 132-135):

(a) what is the "measure" necessary to secure compliance with laws or regulations within the meaning of Article XX(d) in each case? What are the laws and regulations with which each one secures compliance? Are the "measures" separate from the laws or regulations?

122. The "measure necessary to secure compliance with laws and regulations" are the provisions of Regulation 2081/92 which foresee the requirements of inspection structures, the verification and transmission of applications for the registration of geographical indications by the government of the country of origin, and the indication of the country of origin for homonymous geographical indications. The "laws and regulations" with which compliance is secured within

the meaning of Article XX(d) of GATT are equally provisions of Regulation 2081/92. It should be noted that Article XX(d) does not exclude that the "measures necessary to secure compliance" and the "laws and regulations" may be part of the same legal act.

(b) *can a measure that secures compliance with the "objectives" of a regulation, rather than a regulation itself, satisfy Article XX(d)?*

123. Article XX(d) GATT refers to measures necessary to "secure compliance with laws and regulations". Accordingly, the measure to be justified must secure compliance with the provisions of the law or regulation in question.[47] However, the objectives of a regulation may be relevant for establishing the meaning of the provisions with which compliance is secured.

(c) *in what sense does each of these measures "secure compliance" with laws or regulations? Are they enforcement mechanisms?*

124. According to Article 4(1) of Regulation 2081/92, to be eligible to use a protected designation of origin or a protected geographical indication, an agricultural product or foodstuff *must comply with a product specification*. Article 8 of Regulation 2081/92 provides that the indications "protected designation of origin", "protected geographical indication" or equivalent indications *may appear only on agricultural products and foodstuffs that comply with the Regulation*. Accordingly, both provisions contain clear obligations with which compliance must be secured.

125. According to Article 4(2)(g), the product specifications must contain details of the inspection structures foreseen in Article 10 of the Regulation. In accordance with Article 10 (3), the function of inspection structures is to ensure that "agricultural products and foodstuffs bearing a protected name meet the requirements laid down in the specifications". Accordingly, the function of inspection structures is to secure compliance with the requirement in Article 4(1) that products bearing a protected name must comply with a product specification. Similarly, the requirement of inspections structures also secures compliance with the requirement in Article 8 of the Regulation that the indications "protected designation of origin", "protected geographical indication" or equivalent indications may appear only on agricultural products and foodstuffs that comply with the Regulation.

126. In accordance with Article 12a(2) of the Regulation, the verification (and incidentally also the transmission) of the application by the government of the country of origin of the geographical indication serves the purpose of establishing whether the requirements of the Regulation for the registration of geographical indications are satisfied. Among these requirements are that the indication in question corresponds to the definition of a geographical indication in Article 2 of the Regulation, that the product specifications comply with Article 4(2) of the Regulation, that the geographical indication is protected or established in its country of origin, and that the required inspection structures are

---

[47] Cf. GATT Panel Report, *EEC – Regulation on Imports of Parts and Components*, paras. 5.17-5.18.

established. Accordingly, the verification of the application by the government of country of origin of the geographical indication secures compliance with the requirement in Article 8 of the Regulation that the indications "protected designation of origin", "protected geographical indication" or equivalent indications may appear only on agricultural products and foodstuffs that comply with the Regulation.

127. According to the first subparagraph of Article 12(2), if a protected name of a third country is identical to a Community protected name, registration shall be granted with due regard for local and traditional usage and the practical risks of confusion. According to the second subparagraph, use of such names shall only be authorised if the country of origin of the product is clearly and visibly indicated on the label. In this way, the second subparagraph secures compliance with the first. At the same time, the second subparagraph of Article 12(2) also secures compliance with the requirement in Article 8 of the Regulation that the indications "protected designation of origin", "protected geographical indication" or equivalent indications may appear only on agricultural products and foodstuffs that comply with the Regulation.

128. The EC is not entirely sure what is understood by "enforcement mechanisms". If enforcement mechanisms are understood as mechanisms which secure compliance with the regulation *ex post*, i.e. after the registration of a particular geographical indication has taken place, then the inspection structures would qualify as "enforcement mechanisms", but possibly not the verification and transmission of applications for the registration of geographical indications by the government of the country of origin, and the indication of the country of origin for homonymous geographical indications.

129. However, the EC notes that Article XX(d) GATT does not speak of "enforcement mechanisms", but of "measures necessary to ensure compliance", including those relating to "the protection of patents, trade marks and copyrights, and the prevention of deceptive practices". There is no indication in Article XX(d) GATT that only "*ex post*" enforcement could qualify under Article XX(d) GATT. Rather, measures which secure compliance at other stages, for instance through appropriate safeguards in the registration process, may also be regarded as measures to "secure compliance". Accordingly, the verification and transmission of applications for the registration of geographical indications by the government of the country of origin, and the indication of the country of origin for homonymous geographical indications should also be regarded as "measures necessary to secure compliance" within the meaning of Article XX(d) GATT.

(d) how are the laws and regulations with which each measure secures compliance not inconsistent with the GATT 1994?

130. Regulation 2081/92 is a measure which provides protection to geographical indications. It implements Section 3 of Part II of the TRIPS Agreement, which obliges WTO Members to provide protection to geographical indications. It does so in providing, in accordance with Article 1.1 of the TRIPS Agreement, a higher degree of protection than that required by Article 22 TRIPS

Agreement. Accordingly, Regulation 2081/29 is a measure which is not inconsistent with the GATT 1994.

Question 136

With respect to the issue whether the measures are necessary to secure compliance, and without prejudice to the WTO-consistency of any alternative measures:

> *(a) is the requirement that a third country government verify applications "necessary" to secure compliance in cases where an applicant itself is able to prove that a GI is protected in its country of origin, for example, by submitting an authenticated copy of a registration certificate?*

131. As the EC has set out above in Response to the Panel's Question 114, the verification to be carried out by the third country government does not only concern the question whether the geographical indication is protected in its country of origin, but also whether the other requirements for the registration of the geographical indication are fulfilled, namely whether the name complies with the definition of a geographical indication, whether the product specifications are in accordance with Article 4 (2) of the Regulation, and whether the necessary inspection structures are established.

132. As the EC has said in its previous submissions,[48] the verification of these conditions requires knowledge of local factors specific to the territory of the country of origin of the geographical indication, which typically only the country of origin will have. Moreover, the verification may also require on-site checks and verifications in the territory of the country of origin, which the EC could not carry out without the express consent of the country of origin. Accordingly, the verification of applications by the country of origin is necessary to secure compliance with the Regulation already for these aspects.

133. As regards the requirement that the geographical indication is protected in the country of origin, a certificate of registration of the geographical indication authenticated by the country of origin of the indication would normally provide sufficient evidence that the indication is protected in its country of origin. However, the EC considers that this question is hypothetical in the context of the present case. Many WTO Members, and in particular the United States and Australia, do not have specific registration systems for the protection of geographical indications. Therefore, the submission of an authenticated certificate of registration does not appear to be an option for a US or Australian geographical indication.

134. The EC would also like to recall that according to the Appellate Body, the evaluation of whether a measure is "necessary" within the meaning of Article XX(d) GATT requires "a process of weighing and balancing a series of factors which prominently include the contribution made by the compliance measure to the enforcement of the law or regulation at issue, the importance of

---

[48] EC Response to Panel's Question No. 33; EC SWS, para. 124 et seq.

the common interests or values protected by that law or regulation, and the accompanying impact of the law or regulation on imports or exports".[49] In the case of a country which does have a dedicated registration system for the protection of geographical indications, the preparation of an authenticated certificate would not pose any difficulties. Similarly, the transmission of this certificate together with the other documents required by Article 12a(2) would not seem burdensome. Accordingly, the impact on exports of this requirement in Article 12a(2) should be extremely small.

(b) is the requirement that a third country government verify applications "necessary" to secure compliance in cases where the third country has no registration system for GIs or where determinations that a GI is protected under unfair competition laws are only made by the judicial branch of government after litigation?

135. Yes. In fact, the requirement of verification by the country of origin is particularly necessary in this case. The EC appreciates that in the absence of a specific registration system, the evaluation of whether a geographical indication is protected in its country of origin may be more difficult. However, this does not create an exemption from Article 24.9 TRIPS, according to which there is no obligation to protect geographical indications which are not protected in their country of origin. Moreover, the question whether the geographical indication is protected in the country of origin remains a question of the law of the third country. Accordingly, the absence of a specific registration system makes the involvement of the country of origin more necessary, not less.

136. The United States has claimed that "the US government does not have any specialized knowledge or expertise that would render it better qualified than the right holder, or indeed, the EC".[50] As the EC has already explained, the EC does not find this argument credible.[51] The United States and Australia cannot claim protection of geographical indications which are not protected in their country.

137. The question which branch of government in the United States or Australia is responsible for the protection of geographical indications is not relevant. Under Article 24.9 TRIPS Agreement, the United States and Australia as WTO Members cannot claim protection for geographical indications which are not protected in their country. This is entirely independent of which branch of government assures this protection in the US and Australia. It is for the United States and Australia to decide which branch of government will be entitled to establish whether a geographical indication is protected in their country in accordance with Article 24.9 TRIPS Agreement.

138. The EC would also remark that if the US or Australian executive branch did not have authority, within the US or Australian legal system, to make such

---

[49] Appellate Body Report, *Korea – Various Measures on Beef*, para. 164.
[50] US SWS, para. 73.
[51] EC SWS, para. 134; EC SOS, para. 76.

findings, the EC hardly sees how the EU institutions could be expected to make them.

> *(c)* *is the requirement that a third country government transmit applications "necessary" to secure compliance in cases where an applicant itself is able to send an application to the Commission?*

139. The transmission of the application is an integral part of the application process, which reflects the necessary involvement of the government of the country of origin in the verification of the application. By transmitting the application, the government of the country of origin certifies that it deems the requirements of Article 12a(2) to be fulfilled. For this reason, the EC submits that the requirement that the application should be transmitted by the country of origin should not be considered in isolation, but in the context of the application and verification process.

140. The United States has also indicated that it considered that the transmission of applications or objections was a "purely ministerial act" which as such would not pose particular difficulties.[52] In the process of weighing and balancing as required by the Appellate Body in the context of Article XX(d) GATT, it therefore would not appear that the requirement that the application be transmitted by the country of origin could be regarded as having a significant impact on imports.

141. The EC also notes that in its second oral statement, Australia has indicated that the EC could "ask for the cooperation of another WTO Member after an application has been lodged should such cooperation be necessary to assess an application".[53] As the EC has set out above, cooperation between the country of origin and the country of registration *is* necessary. What remains therefore of the Australian submission seems to be that rather than asking for the cooperation before the application is filed, the EC should ask for it *after* it is filed. However, this is purely an issue of timing and sequencing of the application process. The EC does not see why it should make a difference whether the necessary cooperation occurs before the application is filed, or after.

> *(d)* *why does a third country government need to verify whether the person objecting is resident or established in the third country? Why does the Commission need consult with the third country if the statement of objection is admissible? (EC response to Panel question No. 34).*

142. First, the EC would like to note that the complainants have formulated their claims regarding the right of objection only under the TRIPS Agreement, not under the GATT.

143. Second, as the United States has indicated, the transmission of applications or objections is a "purely ministerial act" which as such would not pose particular difficulties.[54] This is why the EC has submitted that the

---

[52] US Response to Panel's Question No. 38, para. 74.
[53] Australia's SOS, para. 68.
[54] US Response to Panel's Question No. 38, para. 74.

transmission of applications by the government of the country of origin cannot be regarded as constituting less favorable treatment.[55]

144. Finally, as the EC has also indicated in response to subquestion c) above, in a process of weighing and balancing as required by Article XX(d) GATT, the pure transmission of an objection does not have any significant impact on trade in goods. Accordingly, should the Panel consider that Article XX(d) GATT is available as a defense to the complainants' claims under the TRIPS, it should find that the measure is necessary within the meaning of Article XX(d) GATT.

> *(e) is the identical GIs labelling requirement "necessary" to secure compliance in cases where there is already a clear distinction in practice in the usual presentation of the relevant products without clearly and visibly displaying the country of origin?*

145. Article 12(2) is based on the assumption that the protected names are homonyms. In such a situation, if the two homonyms are from different countries, the indication of the country appears as the most obvious distinguishing element. Accordingly, the EC considers it unlikely that an equivalent clear distinction could be achieved without the indication of the country of origin.

> *(f) is the requirement that a third country government designate inspection authorities "necessary" to secure compliance in cases where the Commission could designate them in third countries (see US second oral statement, para. 53)?*

146. The EC could not simply designate an inspection body in a third country. As the EC has explained, the designation of an inspection body may require on-site inspections and audits. Similarly, such on-site inspections and audits are also necessary at periodic intervals for the continued monitoring of the inspection body. The EC does not consider that it could carry out such inspections and audits without the agreement of the country in which the body is located.

147. In this context, the EC would like to note that certain provisions in the covered agreements give WTO Members under certain conditions the right to carry out inspections in the territory of another WTO Member. This is the case for instance for Article 6.7 AD Agreement and Article 12.6 CVD Agreement. Even here, the inspection may only be carried out, however, in accordance with the provisions of the annexes to these agreements, and if the importing Member does not object. Similar provisions implying a right to conduct investigations in another WTO Member can also be found in Article 6.3 of the SPS Agreement and in Point 2 of Annex C to the SPS Agreement.

148. However, similar provisions do not apply in the present case. The EC can therefore not simply assume that it may carry out such inspections in respect of inspection bodies for geographical indications in a third country. The designation by the third country is therefore necessary also out of respect for the territorial sovereignty of the third country.

---

[55] EC SWS, para. 158.

149. This is also fully compatible with the practice of the parties in the field of conformity assessment, as explained by the EC in response to the Panel's Question No. 127. Accordingly, the designation of the inspection body by the country of origin is necessary within the meaning of Article XX(d) GATT.

> *(g)* *is the requirement that a third country government declare that inspection structures are established on its territory "necessary" to secure compliance in cases where an applicant could arrange for independent inspection structures to be put in place in respect of a specific product (see US second oral statement, para. 53)?*

150. As the EC has explained, inspection bodies can be public or private.[56] However, as the EC has also explained, inspection bodies are required by Article 10 (3) to offer adequate guarantees of objectivity and impartiality with respect to producers or processors.[57]

151. This reflects the fact that independently of whether they are public or private, inspection bodies fulfill a function both towards producers and to consumers. This is why the Regulation requires that inspection bodies, even if private, must be responsible to the public authorities of the territory in which they are located. Only through some form of public oversight can it be ensured that the inspection body will at all times carry out its functions duly and appropriately in accordance with the requirements of the Regulation. This is also necessary to secure equal treatment between EC and third country geographical indications, which have to comply with the same requirements.

152. Accordingly, the declaration by the government in which the inspection body is located is necessary to secure compliance with the Regulation.

> *(h)* *how is the requirement that a private inspection body continues to be responsible vis-à-vis a third country government "necessary" to secure compliance in cases where the EC could conduct its own inspections of foreign GIs (see US second oral statement, para. 53)?*

153. The EC cannot itself conduct inspections of foreign geographical indications. First of all, the EC does not itself have inspection bodies. Rather, for EC geographical indications, inspections bodies are carried out through a multitude of public or private bodies in the individual Member States.[58] Second, the carrying out of inspections typically requires a presence in or near the geographical area to which the indication is related. Finally, the EC would remark that according to Article 10(7) of Regulation 2081/92, the cost of inspections must be borne by the producers using the protected name. Accordingly, if the EC carried out such inspections for foreign geographical indications, this would result in less favourable treatment for EC geographical indications.

---

56 EC SWS, para. 103.
57 EC SOS, para. 64.
58 Cf. EC SWS, para. 104 and Exhibit EC-48.

(f) *how is the requirement that the inspection authorities and/or private bodies have permanently at their disposal staff and resources necessary to ensure that all products bearing GIs comply with the product specifications in their registrations? (see Australia's rebuttal submission, para. 217).*

154. At the outset, the EC would like to clarify that this requirement does not apply to "*all* products bearing GIs". First, a particular inspection structure is only responsible, and its staff need must be determined with regard to, the specific product for which it has been designated. Second, there is no requirements that an inspection structure must examine "all" products in a physical sense. Rather, it is up to the inspection structure to decide the place, time and frequency of inspections. Obviously, such inspections may involve sampling or random checks.[59]

155. As regards the requirement to an inspection body must "permanently" have staff and resources at its disposal, Australia has argued that this may not be necessary in certain cases, for instance where there is a particular harvest season. Although this is not the rule for most protected products, the EC does not exclude that there might be products for which the entire production process is confined to a part of the year, and for which therefore the need for inspections arises only or primarily during that time of the year. In this case, Regulation 2081/92 does not require unnecessary levels of staff to be maintained throughout the year. In fact, since it is presumably not economic to establish and wind down an inspection body every year, in such a case it would be reasonable to entrust the function of inspections to a body which also carries out tasks other than inspections under Regulation 2081/92. In its second submission, the EC has pointed to the existence of private firms which can carry out such tasks.[60]

Question 137

The Panel takes note of the EC's view that Article 14(3) of Regulation (EC) No. 2081/92 allows its authorities to refuse or invalidate the registration of any confusing GIs (EC first written submission, para. 286; EC rebuttal, para. 270). The complainants do not agree (US second written submission, para. 166 and Australia's second written submission, para. 109). The following examples have been referred to in this proceeding:

(a) *BAYERISCHES BIER and BAVARIA and HØKER BAJER?*

(b) *BUDEJOVICKÉ PIVO and BUDWEISER?*

(c) *GORGONZOLA and CAMBOZOLA?*

Could these GIs be used in accordance with their registrations in a way that results in a likelihood of confusion with the respective trademark(s)?

156. At the outset, the EC would note that, of the three "examples", only the first one is relevant to this dispute.

---

[59] Cf. above Response to Panels' Question No. 132.

[60] EC SWS para. 107 and Exhibits EC-49 and EC-50.

157. The EC would recall, once again, that the names "Budějovické pivo", "Českobudějovické pivo" and "Budějovický měšt'anský var" were registered several months after the date of the requests for the establishment of this Panel and are, therefore, outside the Panel's terms of reference.[61] In any event, the EC understands that the United States does not argue that any of those names gives rise to a likelihood of confusion with the name "Budweiser". The US concerns appear to be limited to the use of some translations of those names to other languages.

158. In the Cambozola case[62], the right holders of the geographical indication "Gorgonzola" alleged that the use of the trademark "Cambozola" engendered one of the situations mentioned in Article 13(1) of Regulation 2081/92.[63] To the best of the EC's knowledge, the owner of the trademark "Cambozola" never claimed that the use of the geographical indication "Gorgonzola" gave rise to a likelihood of confusion with its trademark or that the registration of the geographical indication Gorgonzola should have been refused in accordance with Article 14(3) of Regulation 2081/92. The two issues are different and should not be confused.

159. In principle, a name which has been found not to be confusing *per se* following the assessment required by Article 14(3) should not give rise to confusion when used subsequently. The EC would submit that, in practice, this may happen only where the registered name is used together with other signs (whether verbal or figurative), or as part of a combination of signs. If those other signs, or the combination thereof, are themselves the subject of trademark rights, the trademark owner retains the right to prevent their use in a confusing manner. Even if they are not covered by trademark rights, the confusing use of those other signs, or of the combination including the geographical indication, could still be prevented under the laws on unfair competition or on misleading labelling or advertising.

160. The United States has argued that, in practice, a name registered as a geographical indication, even if not confusing *per se*, could be confusing when used in translation.[64] But, as already explained by the EC, the registration does no cover translations.

161. The United States also has argued that a name registered as a geographical indication which is not confusing *per se* may be confusing when used "as a trademark".[65] By this, apparently, the United States means that the use of a geographical indication may be confusing if displayed in a prominent way, or at least more prominently than the trademark. As explained by the EC, this reflects pre-conceived notions regarding the respective uses of trademarks and geographical indications which assume a priority of trademarks over geographical indications. The EC does not share those notions, which have no

---

[61] EC FWS, paras. 21-25.

[62] Case C-87/97, *Consorzio per la tutela del frommagio Gorgonzola v Käserai Champignon Hofmeister GmbH & Co Kg,* [1999] ECR I-1301 (Exhibit EC-32).

[63] EC Response to the Panel's Question No. 66.

[64] US SWS, para. 134.

[65] US SWS, para. 133.

basis in the TRIPS Agreement. In making the assessment required by Article 14(3) of Regulation 2081/92, the EC authorities will assume that the geographical indication will be used in what the United States calls "trademark-like" fashion. Accordingly, the EC authorities will refuse a proposed geographical indication it if is anticipated that, when used in what the United States calls "trademark-like fashion", it will result in a likelihood of confusion with an earlier trademark.

162. Finally, the United States has argued that the use of a registered geographical indication may be confusing when the registered name is deformed, mutilated or otherwise manipulated so as to imitate a trademark.[66] However, as already explained by the EC, a court could consider that, in such case, the used sign is different from the registered name.[67]

163. As noted by the EC, the complainants are requesting the EC to provide a remedy against the confusing use of a registered geographical indications which many Members do not provide with respect to the infringement of a registered trademark by a latter registered trademark. Indeed, as discussed below, in many Members the use of registered trademark is deemed not to be an infringement of an earlier trademark, subject to the possibility to invalidate the registration of the latter trademark on the grounds that it is confusing. (See below the response to Question 139). Upholding the complainants' claims would have necessarily the implication that the trademark laws of those Members are also in violation of Article 16.1 TRIPS.

Question 138

What is the meaning of the phrase "[w]ith due regard to Community law" in Article 14(2) of Regulation (EC) No. 2081/92? Which aspects of "Community law" are relevant?

164. The phrase "with due regard to Community law" clarifies that the right to use the trademark conferred by Article 14(2) of Regulation 2081/92 is not unqualified, but must be exercised in accordance with all other applicable provisions of EC law. Those provisions include not only the Community Trademark Regulation and the Trademark Directive but also, for example, the laws on labeling and unfair competition or the antitrust laws.

What is the meaning of the phrase "shall not affect [Regulation No. 2081/92] ... and in particular Article 14 thereof" in Article 142 of Regulation (EC) No. 40/94 on the Community trade mark?

165. It means that the relationship between Community trademarks and geographical indications registered under Regulation 2081/92 is controlled by the latter, and in particular by Article 14.

---

[66] US FOS, para. 54.
[67] EC SWS, para. 302.

Question 139

The Panel takes note of the EC's view that the owner of a trademark may not prevent the right holders of a registered GI from using the registered name on the grounds that such name is confusing (EC second oral statement, para. 181). Please confirm that as long as a GI remains registered and is used in accordance with its registration, a trademark owner may not enforce his trademark rights against that use either under the Regulation on the Community trademark or the national trademark laws of the member States.

166. The EC can confirm that a trademark owner cannot prevent the holders of a registered geographical indication from using the name or names registered under Regulation 2081/92 on the grounds that the use of such name or names is confusing *per se* with an earlier trademark.

167. As explained, however, this does not mean that the right holders of a geographical indication have an unqualified right to use the registered name in any conceivable manner. First, the right to use the registered name does not confer a right to use other names not covered by the registration, or to use the registered name together with other signs or as part of a combination of signs. Furthermore, the registered name must be used in accordance with other generally applicable laws, including in particular with the laws on labeling, misleading advertising and unfair competition.

What legal provisions prevent the trademark owners exercising their rights against persons using a GI in accordance with its registration?

168. Regulation 2081/92 does not contain any provision which prohibits expressly the trademark owners from exercising their rights with respect to a registered geographical indication. However, the protection provided by Regulation 2081/92 would become meaningless if a trademark owner could prevent the use of the registered name by the right holders of a geographical indication on the grounds that the use of such name is confusing *per se* with an earlier trademark.

169. The registration of a name under Regulation 2081/92 establishes a legal presumption that the use of that name as a geographical indication does not give rise *per se* to a likelihood of confusion with an earlier trademark, because otherwise the registration should have been refused in accordance with Article 14(3). In order to be able to exercise its trademark rights, the trademark owner must rebut first that legal presumption by invalidating the registration of the geographical indication.

170. The EC would note that, by the same token, under the trademarks laws of many Members, the use of a registered trademark is deemed not to constitute an infringement of an earlier trademark, subject to the possibility to invalidate the latter trademark on those grounds.[68]

---

[68] For example, Section 19 of *Canada*'s Trade Marks Law (Exhibit EC-93) provides that:

> the registration of a trade-mark in respect of any wares or services, unless shown to be invalid, gives to the owner of the trade-mark the exclusive right to the use throughout Canada of the trade-mark in respect of those wares or services.

Question 140

Under what provision of Regulation (EC) No. 2081/92 does the registration of a GI give the right holder a positive right to use the GI?

171. Regulation 2081/92 does not include any provision which confers expressly a positive right to use the registered name. But that right is implicit in several provisions, for example:

- Article 4(1), which provides that:

  ... to be eligible to use a protected designation (PDO) or a protected geographical indication (PGI) an agricultural product or foodstuff must comply with a specification.

- Article 8, which provides that:

  The indications PDO, PGI or equivalent traditional national indications may appear only on agricultural products and foodstuffs that comply with this Regulation.

- Article 13(1)(a), which states that registered names shall be protected against

---

Section 20 (1) (Exhibit EC-93) goes on to provide that the right of the owner of a registered trade-mark to its exclusive use is not deemed to be infringed by a person "entitled to its use under this Act".

Section 19(2) of *Hong Kong*'s Trade Marks Ordinance (Exhibit EC-94) provides that:

A registered trademark is not infringed by the use of another registered trademark in relation to goods or services for which the latter is registered (but see section 53(9) for the effect of a declaration of invalidity of registration).

Section 30(2) of *India*'s Trade Marks Act (Exhibit EC-95) provides that:

A registered trademark is not infringed where-... (e) the use of a registered trade mark, being one of two or more registered under this Act which are identical or nearly resemble each other, in exercise of the right to use that trade mark given by registration under this Act.

Section 93 of *New Zealand*'s Trade Marks Act 2002 (Exhibit EC-96) provides that:

A registered trade mark is not infringed by the use of another registered trademark in relation to any goods or services for which that other trademark is registered.

Section 28 of *Singapore*'s Trade Marks Act (Exhibit EC-97) provides that:

... a registered trademark is not infringed by the use of another registered trademark in relation to goods or services for which the latter is registered.

Section 34(2) of *South Africa*'s Trade Marks Act (Exhibit EC-98) provides that:

A registered trade mark is not infringed by - .... (g) the use of any identical or confusingly or deceptively similar trade mark which is registered.

Section 11(1) of the *United Kingdom*'s Trade Marks Act 1994 (Exhibit US-50) provides that:

A trademark is not infringed by the use of another registered trademark in relation to goods or services for which the latter is registered (but see section 47(6))(effect of declaration of invalidity of registration).

Finally, Section 122 of *Australia*'s Trade Marks Act 1995 (Exhibit EC-7) provides that:

In spite of section 120, a person does not infringe a registered trade mark when: [...] (e) the person exercises a right to use a trade mark given to the person under this Act.

> any direct or indirect commercial use of a name registered in respect of products not covered by the registration ...

172. Moreover, once again, if the right holders of a geographical indication did not have a positive right to use the name, the protection provided under the Regulation against other uses would be meaningless.

How is that right delimited? Does it include translations of the protected term?

173. The positive right to use a registered geographical indication extends to the name or names that have been entered into the "Register of protected designations of origin and protected geographical indications". The registered name or names are specified in the annex to the regulation providing for the registration of each name and are added to the annex to Regulation 2400/96[69], in the case of applications under Article 6, or the annex to Regulation 1107/96[70], in the case of applications under former Article 17.

174. The registered name must be used in accordance with the approved specifications, including the labeling details.

175. Subject to any restrictions provided in the specifications, the registered name may be used together with other signs (verbal or figurative) or as part of a combination of signs. But the registration under Regulation 2081/92 does not confer a positive right to use any such other signs or combination of signs. To the extent that those signs or combinations of signs are the same as, or confusingly similar to, a sign covered by a trademark right, the trademark owner is entitled to prevent their use. Even when they are not covered by trademarks rights, their use may be prevented under the laws on labeling, advertising or unfair competition.

176. The positive right extends only to the linguistic versions that have been entered into the register. Thus, for example, Commission Regulation (EC) No 865/2003 provided for the registration of both the Spanish name "Cítricos Valencianos" and the Catalan name "Citrics Valencians".[71]

For example, what uses do the registrations of the four cheese GIs referred to in Exhibit US-52 permit?

177. The EC is providing herewith the approved specifications for the four products concerned (Exhibits EC-99, EC-100, EC-101, EC-102).

178. As regards labeling details, the specifications provide the following:

- *Bitto:* the product must be marketed with a distinguishing mark consisting of the designation of origin with the accompanying logo. The trademark and the logo are reproduced in an annex to the Italian decree recognizing the geographical indication.
- *Tomme de Savoie:* the specifications state the following:

---

[69] Exhibit COMP-4 a.

[70] Exhibit COMP-3 a.

[71] Exhibit COMP-4bi.

L'identification du produit, conformément aux Réglements Techniques " Tomme de Savoie" 78 RA 01 et 89 RA 01 est realisé:

– Par un étiquetage en conformité avec la réglementation générale francaise et européenne.

– Par un étiquetage propre au "Label Regional Savoie"

* soit une vignette reproduisant le sigle de la Marque Savoie [reproduced in the specifications] + sigle I.G.P

* *soit sur l'étiquette commerciale de l'enterprise*

– impression rouge sur fond blanc de l'appellation " TOMME DE SAVOIE "

– % de MG

– le logo de la "Marque Collective Savoie" + sigle I.G.P.

– la mention de l'Organisme Certificateur.

- *Esrom:* the label must contain the mention "Esrom (45 + or 60 +)" followed by the mention "Beskyttet Oprindelses-Betignese" or "BOB" [PDO in Danish] in all Community official languages.
- *Bra:* the product must be marketed with the label of the relevant manufacturers' consortium.

How far does that positive right extend before it can be challenged under labelling and misleading advertising laws?

179. It is difficult to define *a priori* which particular uses of a registered geographical indication may violate the provisions of the Directives on labelling and misleading advertising and/or the laws on unfair competition. This question requires necessarily a case-by-case analysis and cannot be responded in the abstract. Nevertheless, the EC will attempt to set out here below some indications.

180. The use of a geographical indication in what the United States calls "trademark- like fashion" is not sufficient to consider that it is inconsistent with those laws. Indeed, the United States appears to consider that a geographical indication is used "as a trademark" whenever it is displayed prominently, or at least more prominently than the trademark. The EC does not share this view, which assumes that trademarks enjoy priority over geographical indications. As explained, EC consumers are familiar with the use of geographical indications for foodstuffs, value them as much as trademarks, if not more, and expect them to be used in ways which the United States would like to reserve for trademarks. EC consumers are unlikely to mistake a geographical indication for foodstuff for a trademark simply because it is displayed in the label in relatively big sized letters or in attractive colours or typography.

181. On the other hand, if the holder of a geographical indication which has a right to use a certain name (say "Bayerisches Bier") were to use it in a manner which imitates the label or the packaging of the products of a trademark ("Bavaria"), this could be considered as a breach of the laws on labelling and unfair competition, even if the constituent elements of the label or the packaging, other than the trademark itself, were not covered by any intellectual property rights.

182. To mention but another example, the laws on labelling and unfair competition could be violated if the name of the geographical indication were used together with other signs or statements that suggested or indicated that the geographical indication is in fact the trademark of a producer, rather than a geographical indication. For example, if the geographical indication were used under, or close to, the terms "produced by". Or if it were used together with a sign (e.g. a Dutch flag or emblem, a map of The Netherlands, or a Dutch windmill) which suggested that the product is of the origin generally associated with the products of a co-existing trademark, rather than with that indicated by the geographical indication.

Question 141

What is the legal basis for an action to invalidate a registration under Regulation (EC) No. 2081/92 on the grounds of confusion with a trademark?

183. Article 14(3) of Regulation 2081/92.

Is there any basis for an action to invalidate a GI registration in Regulation (EC) No. 40/94 on the Community trade mark?

184. No.

Question 142

The Panel takes note of the EC's view that the owner of a concurrent trademark could challenge a decision to register a GI inconsistently with Article 14(3) of Regulation (EC) No. 2081/92 even after the GI has been formally registered (EC response to Panel question No. 67; EC rebuttal paras. 270 and 296). If a trademark owner applied to invalidate a GI registration under Article 14(3):

(a) is this a precondition to a trademark infringement action?

185. As explained[72], the trademark owner may raise the invalidity of the registration of the geographical indication in accordance with the procedure laid down in Article 234 of the EC Treaty in the context of a trademark infringement action brought before a court of a Member State.

(b) is there any time-limit on such an invalidation action?

186. Applications in annulment under Article 230 of the EC Treaty must be filed within a two-month time limit. The possibility to raise the invalidity of the registration of the geographical indication under Article 234 of the EC Treaty is not subject to any time limit.

[72] EC SOS, para. 178.

(c) is this possibility available where the GI is registered pursuant to an Act of Accession or otherwise without the normal application procedures?

187. So-called "fast track" registrations made pursuant to a request under former Article 17 of Regulation 2081/92 can be annulled pursuant to an action brought in accordance with Article 230 of the EC Treaty or invalidated in accordance with Article 234 of the EC Treaty under the same conditions as the registrations made pursuant to an ordinary application under Article 6 of Regulation 2081/92.

188. Contrary to what has been suggested by the United States, the registration of a geographical indication pursuant to an Act of Accession is not a frequent occurrence. In fact, of the more than 600 registrations, only one has been made pursuant to an Act of Accession: that of the names "Budějovické pivo", "Českobudějovické pivo" and "Budějovický měšťanský var". As explained, this registration is not within the terms of reference of the Panel.[73] This registration is unique also in that it provides that it applies "without prejudice to any beer trademark or other rights existing in the European Union on the date of accession".

(d) how would such an application for invalidation relate to the cancellation procedure in Article 11a of the Regulation? Are the grounds for cancellation in Article 11a exhaustive?

189. The cancellation procedure presupposes that the registration is valid and produces effects *ex nunc*. The grounds for cancellation mentioned in Articles11 and 11a are exhaustive.

Question 143

The Panel takes note that the Council Decision to register BAYERISCHES BIER as a GI states that "[i]n view of the facts and information available, it was, however, considered that registration of [that name] was not liable to mislead the consumer as to the true identity of the product" (Exhibit EC-9, para. (3), cited in EC rebuttal, para. 287). Please detail what were the facts and information to which the Council referred in that Decision and how they were evaluated so that the Panel can see how the criteria in Article 14(3) were applied in that case.

190. The Council's decision took account of the submissions made by the interested parties and by some Member States, as well as of the discussions which took place within the Committee.

191. The main facts taken into consideration were: the similarity of the signs; the similarity of the products, having regard to the production methods and organoleptic properties; the date of registration of the trademark; the recognition of the trademark in the different Member States, having regard in particular to

[73] EC FWS, paras. 21-25.

the level of exports; and the labeling practices of the trademark and the proposed geographical indication.

192. In essence, it was concluded that, although the products were similar, the signs were not sufficiently similar to mislead the public, having regard to the degree of recognition of the trademark in the different Member States.

Question 144

The Panel takes note that Commission Regulation (EC) No. 1107/96 (set out in Exhibit COMP-3a), which effected the registration of many individual GIs, recites Article 14(2) and (3) of Regulation (EC) No. 2081/92. How were Article 14(2) and (3) taken into account in the registration of those GIs?

193. As already explained, Article 14(2) is not applied by the registering authority (see EC response to Question 66). It is for the courts to decide whether a trademark falls within one of the situations mentioned in Article 13(1) and, if so, whether the trademark is entitled to co-exist in accordance with Article 14(2) or should be invalidated or revoked in accordance with the Trademark Directive and the Community Trademark Directive.

194. Regulation 1107/96 provides for the registration of names notified by the Member States in accordance under former Article 17 of Regulation 2081/92. In the context of that procedure, the EC authorities conducted the assessment provided in Article 14(3) where, because of the concerns raised directly by interested parties or by the Member States, they became aware of the existence of a potentially conflicting trademark.

195. The recital mentioned in the question is an implicit reference to the Bayerische Bier case. Because of the concerns raised by the owners of the trademarks at issue and by some Member States, the EC institutions could not reach a decision with respect to that name as of the time of the adoption of Regulation 1107/96. Therefore, that name continued to be protected at national level in accordance with the second paragraph of Article 1 of Regulation 1107/96.

Question 145

Please refer to Article 24.5 of the TRIPS Agreement and comment on the suggestion that:

> *(a)* *the phrase "shall not prejudice eligibility for or the validity of the registration of a trademark" merely creates an exception to the obligations in Articles 22.3 and 23.2 to refuse or invalidate the registration of trademarks; and*
>
> *(b)* *the phrase "shall not prejudice ... the right to use a trademark" merely creates an exception to the obligations in Articles 22.2 and 23.1 to provide the legal means to prevent certain uses and does not create any positive right.*

196. Article 24.5 is not a "mere exception" to the obligations stipulated in the provisions of Section 3 of Part II of the TRIPS Agreement mentioned in the

question. The suggestion made in the question is mistaken in two fundamental respects.

197. *First*, Article 24.5 applies with respect to "any measures adopted to implement this section", and not just with respect to the provisions cited in the question. In accordance with Article 1.1 TRIPS, Members may implement more extensive protection of geographical indications than is required by the provisions of Section 3 of Part II cited in the question, provided that such protection does not contravene other provisions of the TRIPS Agreement. Any such additional protection is subject to the rule contained in Article 24.5, just like the minimum protection required by the provisions of Section 3 of Part II cited in the question

198. *Second*, Article 24.5 is drafted in mandatory terms, unlike the genuine exceptions in Articles 24.4, 24.6, 24.7 and 24.8. As a result, by limiting the obligations to protect geographical indications in Articles 22 and 23, Article 24.5 imposes simultaneously upon Members correlative obligations with respect to the protection of trademarks that go beyond those provided in Section 2 of Part II.

199. The following two examples may illustrate this:

- assume that a Member's trademark law provides that a trademark including or consisting of a geographical indication shall not be registered or, if registered, shall be invalidated.[74] This goes beyond the obligation stipulated in Article 22.3. Nevertheless, there is nothing in Section 2 of Part II and, more specifically, in Article 15.2, which would prevent a Member from enacting such additional protection of geographical indications. Yet, if a trademark has been registered, or applied for, before either of the two dates mentioned in Article 24.5, the Member in question would be prohibited by virtue of Article 24.5 from invalidating that trademark on the ground that such trademark is identical or similar to a geographical indication. This obligation not to invalidate certain trademarks does not result from Section 2 of Part II, or from Article 22.3, but exclusively from Article 24.5.
- assume that a Member's trademark law prohibits the use of any trademark acquired by use which is identical or similar to a subsequently recognized geographical indication. This prohibition goes beyond the obligation provided in Article 22.2. Nevertheless, it would be fully consistent with Section 2 of Part II, which provides for the "possibility"[75] to grant trademark rights on the basis of use, but imposes no obligation to do so. Therefore, Members are free to grant, limit or withdraw such rights at will.

[74] The example is not hypothetical. In practice, many Members prohibit the registration of trademarks including or consisting of geographical indications. For example, Section 61 of Australia's Trade Marks Act 1995 (Exhibit EC-103) allows to oppose the registration of a sign that contains or consists of a geographical indication.

[75] Cf. Article 16.1 of the TRIPS Agreement.

> Yet, if the rights to the trademark in question had been acquired before either of the dates mentioned in Article 24.5, the Member concerned would be prevented from prohibiting the use of that trademark by virtue of Article 24.5. Again, this obligation does no result from Section 2 of Part II, or from Article 22.2, but exclusively from Article 24.5.

200. As shown by the above two examples, Article 24.5 imposes self-standing obligations with respect to the protection of trademarks that go beyond the obligations provided in Section 2 of Part II. Therefore, it would be manifestly incorrect to characterize Article 24.5 as a "mere exception" to the obligations provided in other provisions of Section 3. "Exceptions" exempt from an obligation stipulated in another provision.[76] They do not impose positive obligations by themselves.

201. For the above reasons, Article 24.5 is not an "exception". Rather, Article 24.5 lays down a positive rule which defines in a comprehensive manner the boundary between the protection that Members *must* (in accordance with Articles 22 and 23) or *may* (in accordance with Article 1.1) afford to geographical indications and the protection which Members *must* (in accordance with Section 2 of Part II) or *may* (in accordance with Article 1.1) provide to the sub-category of "grandfathered" trademarks, as defined in Article 24.5. That rule stipulates rights and obligations which are different from, and apply in place of, those provided in Section 2, including in Article 16.1, and elsewhere in Section 3, with respect to other trademarks.

202. The special rule for grandfathered trademarks established in Article 24.5 purports to establish a compromise between the protection of trademarks and the protection of geographical indications and must be interpreted in the light of that objective. On the one hand, Article 24.5 limits the Members' right under Section 2 of Part II to refuse and invalidate the registration of a trademark on the grounds that it is identical or similar to a geographical indication. At the same time, however, Article 24.5 limits the obligations that would normally follow from the registration of one such trademark under Article 16.1, by providing that the trademark owner shall have "the right to use the trademark", but not the right to prevent the use of the trademark by the right holders of the geographical indication. This limitation, however, does not represent a real restriction of the protection of trademarks provided in Article 16.1, because it applies only within the limits of the additional protection provided in Article 24.5 with respect to "grandfathered" trademarks, which goes beyond that required by Section 2 of Part II.

Question 146

The Panel takes note of the respective views of the EC and US on simultaneous exercise of rights with respect to use (EC rebuttal, para. 309 and US rebuttal, para. 119). Without prejudice to the EC's views on Article 24.5, would there be any practical conflict between the rights to prevent certain uses conferred under

---

[76] See US SWS, para. 171.

Articles 16.1 and 22.2 of TRIPS? Under what circumstances is it impossible for, simultaneously:

(a) *a trademark owner to prevent uses of a sign where such use would result in a likelihood of confusion (under Article 16.1), and*

(b) *a right holder in a GI to prevent uses of an indication that are misleading with respect to the geographical origin of the product or which constitute unfair competition (under Article 22.2) except on the basis that the trademark is identical with, or similar to, the GI (under Article 24.5)?*

203. The EC has not argued that there is a "conflict" between the rights conferred by Article 16.1 and by Article 22.2 (or 23.1) because it is "impossible" to exercise both of them simultaneously.

204. Rather, the EC has noted that the simultaneous exercise of those two rights would lead to a situation where neither the trademark owner nor the right holders of the geographical indications could use the sign which is the subject matter of their respective right.

205. Although neither Article 16.1 nor Article 22.2 (or Article 23.1) confer expressly a positive right to use a trademark or to use a geographical indication, respectively, that right is implicit in the protection conferred by those provisions. The right to exclude others from using a sign, whether as a trademark or as a geographical indication, would be meaningless unless the holders of that right were entitled to use the sign themselves.

206. The simultaneous exercise of the rights conferred by Articles 16.1 and 22.2 (and 23.1) would prevent both rights from fulfilling the purpose for which they are granted and deprive them of their *raison d'être*, which is to ensure that the right holder can enjoy the right to use the sign exclusively. By doing so, the simultaneous exercise of Articles 16.1 and 22.2 gives rise to a genuine "conflict" in substance, if not in the form. That "conflict" is resolved by Article 22.3 (and 23.2), which provides for the invalidation of the trademark, thereby effectively giving priority to the geographical indication. This "rule of conflict", however, does not apply to "grandfathered trademarks", as defined in Article 24.5, which are subject to a different rule, as explained in the response to the preceding question.

Question 147

Article 24.5 as finally agreed contains the phrase "measures adopted to implement this Section shall not prejudice eligibility for or the validity of the registration of a trademark, or the right to use a trademark". Please comment on the suggestion that during the Uruguay Round negotiations there was a disagreement as to whether the predecessor to this provision in the Brussels Draft should be made permissive rather than mandatory, and that the choice of this language was part of an effort to reach agreement on the issue of the mandatory / permissive nature of the provision.

207. As suggested in the question, some participants in the negotiations were of the view that Article 24.5, like the other exceptions included in Article 24, should be permissive, rather than mandatory. Among other reasons, because a "mandatory exception" would have the anomalous result of imposing upon Members obligations with respect to the protection of trademarks that go beyond those agreed as part of Section 2 of Part II.

208. Also, as suggested in the question, the wording of Article 24.5 embodies a compromise. The EC and other participants agreed to make the "exception" mandatory on the understanding that the trademark owners would have "the right to use the trademark", as specified expressly in Article 24.5, but not the right to exclude the use of the trademark by the right holders of the geographical indication.

Question 148

What is the meaning of the phrase "where such use would result in a likelihood of confusion" as used in Article 16.1 of the TRIPS Agreement?

209. The phrase "where such use would result in a likelihood of confusion" must be read in the context of Article 15.1. The purpose of a trademark is to distinguish the products of a given undertaking from those of other undertakings. Accordingly, there is a "likelihood of confusion" where the use of a sign gives rise to a likelihood that the public will not be able to distinguish the products of the owner of the registered trademark from the products of other undertakings bearing the sign in question.

How should such likelihood of confusion be assessed?

210. The TRIPS Agreement does not provide any specific guidance to assess the likelihood of confusion. In practice, most Members use similar criteria.

211. Canada's trademark law, which is one of the few to specify the criteria to assess the likelihood of confusion, provides that[77]

> In determining whether trade-marks or trade names are confusing, the court or the Registrar, as the case may be, shall have regard to all the surrounding circumstances including
>
> (a) the inherent distinctiveness of the trade-marks or trade names and *the extent to which they have become known*;
>
> (b) *the length of time the trade-marks or trade-names have been in use*;
>
> (c) the nature of the wares, services or business;
>
> (d) the nature of the trade; and
>
> (e) the degree of resemblance between the trade-marks or trade names in appearance or sound or in the ideas suggested by them.

212. The tenth recital of the EC's Trademark Directive says that the appreciation of likelihood of confusion

[77] Section 6(5) of Canada's Trade-marks Act (Exhibit EC-73). Emphases added.

depends on numerous elements and, in particular, on the recognition of the trade mark on the market, of the association which can be made with the used or registered sign, of the degree of similarity between the trade mark and the sign and between the goods or services identified.

213. Interpreting Article 4(1)(b) of the Trademark Directive, which is the equivalent of Article 16.1, the ECJ has held that[78]

> The likelihood of confusion on the part of the public ... must be appreciated globally, taking into account all factors relevant to the circumstances of the case ...
>
> A global assessment of the likelihood of confusion implies some interdependence between the relevant factors, and in particular a similarity between the trademarks and between these goods or services. Accordingly, a lesser degree of similarity between these goods or services may be offset by a greater degree of similarity between the marks, and vice-versa ...
>
> Furthermore, ... the more distinctive the earlier mark, the greater the risk of confusion ... Since protection of a trademark depends, in accordance with Article 4.1(b) of the Directive, on there being a likelihood of confusion, marks with a highly distinctive character, either *per se* or because of the *reputation* they possess in the market, enjoy broader protection than marks with a less distinctive character.

214. In the United States, the courts have considered that the following factors may be relevant for a determination of likelihood of confusion:[79]

> (1) The similarity or dissimilarity of the marks in their entireties as to appearance, sound, connotation and commercial impression.
>
> (2) The similarity or dissimilarity of and nature of the goods or services as described in an application or registration or in connection with which a prior mark is in use.
>
> (3) The similarity or dissimilarity of established, likely-to-continue trade channels.
>
> (4) The conditions under which and buyers to whom sales are made, i.e. "impulse" vs. careful, sophisticated purchasing.
>
> (5) *The fame of the prior mark (sales, advertising, length of use).*
>
> (6) The number and nature of similar marks in use on similar goods.

---

[78] Case C-39/97, *Canon Kabushiki Kaisha v Metro Goldwyn-Mayer Inc.*, [1998] ECR I-5507, para. 16 *et seq*. (Exhibit EC-71). Emphases added.

[79] *E.I. Du Pont De Nemours & Co., Application of*, 476 F. 2d 1357 (Cust. & Pat. App. 1973), 26 (Exhibit EC-73). Emphases added.

(7) The nature and extent of any actual confusion.

(8) *The length of time during and conditions under which there has been concurrent use without evidence of actual confusion.*

(9) The variety of goods on which a mark is or is not used (house mark, "family" mark, product mark).

(10) The market interface between applicant and the owner of a prior mark:

(a) a mere "consent" to register or use.

(b) agreement provisions designed to preclude confusion, i.e. limitations on continued use of the marks by each party.

(c) assignment of mark, application, registration and good will of the related business.

(d) laches and estoppel attributable to owner of prior mark and indicative of lack of confusion.

(11) The extent to which applicant has a right to exclude others from use of its mark on its goods.

(12) The extent of potential confusion, i.e., whether *de minimis* or substantial.

(13) Any other established fact probative of the effect of use.

How does the assessment differ from that under Article 14(3) of Regulation (EC) No. 2081/92?

215. The assessment made by the EC authorities under Article 14(3) is analogous to the assessment carried out by the EC trademark authorities in order to establish whether the use of a later trademark will give rise to likelihood of confusion with an earlier trademark. When applying Article 14(3), the registering authorities, or the courts, as applicable, must take into account all relevant factors, including in particular the similarity of goods and signs. As explained, length of use, reputation and renown are mentioned expressly in Article 14(3) because geographical indications, when used as trademarks, are primarily descriptive and non-distinctive.

In particular:

(a) how should the likelihood of confusion, and the liability to mislead the consumer, be assessed with respect to a mark to which rights have not been acquired on the basis of use?

216. In principle, the criteria for assessing likelihood of confusion/liability to mislead are the same irrespective of whether the earlier trademark has been acquired through registration or through use.

(b) as of what time should the likelihood of confusion, and the liability to mislead the consumer, be assessed?

217. The "likelihood of confusion" is assessed as of the time of registration of the later trademark and/or at the time of the infringement, depending on the type

of procedure in the framework of which it is alleged and of the peculiarities of each legal system for the protection of trademarks.

218. The "liability to mislead" for purposes of Article 14(3) is assessed as of the time of the registration of the geographical indication. But if a trademark owner raises the invalidity of the registration subsequently, it could rely on any relevant intervening circumstances, such as, for example, cases of actual confusion, in order to show that the initial assessment was flawed.

> *(c) are the trademark's reputation and renown and the length of time it has been used necessarily relevant to both analyses?*

219. Yes, these criteria are relevant in all cases. However, this is not saying that they will have the same weight in all cases. As emphasized by the European Court of Justice, the criteria for assessing the likelihood of confusion are "interdependent".[80] In general, the more similar the signs, the less important will be these criteria. On the other hand, the "weaker" (i.e. the less inherently distinctive) the trademark, the more important will become these criteria. Terms which qualify, or which may reasonably qualify as geographical indications, are primarily descriptive and non-distinctive as trademarks. Indeed, the registration of those terms as trademarks should be permitted only to the extent that they have acquired distinctiveness through use. For that reason, the public is unlikely to confuse a geographical indication with a trademark consisting of that geographical indication if the trademark has never been used and enjoys no recognition.

220. For example, assume that the name Australia, which Australia claims is a geographical indication for wine, had been registered in the EC as a trademark for wine, but that such trademark had never been used. The EC public would be unlikely to mistake wine bearing the geographical indication "Australia" for wine of the totally unknown trademark "Australia", despite the identity of the names.

Question 149

What are the differences between "confusion" and "misleads" as used in Articles 16.1 and 22.2 of the TRIPS Agreement, respectively? Do they have any bearing on the misleading standard under Article 14(3) of Regulation (EC) No. 2081/92?

221. The meaning of the term "mislead" in TRIPS Article 22.2 (and 22.3) does not prejudge of the meaning of the term "misleading" in Article 14(3) in Regulation 2081/92.

222. In the first place, Article 14(3) must be interpreted in the context of Regulation 2081/92, including in particular Articles 7(4) and 7(5)(b), and in accordance with the rules and principles of interpretation of EC law.

223. Moreover, Article 14(3) of Regulation 2081/92 and Article 22.2 (and 22.3) TRIPS is concerned each with a different issue. The purpose of Article 14(3) is to prevent the use of a geographical indication where it may

---

[80] Case C-39/97, *Canon Kabushiki Kaisha v Metro Goldwyn-Mayer Inc.*, [1998] ECR I-5507, para. 16 *et seq*. (Exhibit EC-71).

cause an error with respect to the "identity of the product". In other words, to avoid that the public confuses the products bearing the geographical indication with the products of a given undertaking bearing an earlier trademark. This is the same type of error addressed by Article 16.1 TRIPS. In contrast, Articles 22.2 and 22.3 address the situation where the use of a sign in connection with a product may cause an error as to the geographical origin of that product.

224. Even assuming that Article 22.2 TRIPS were relevant for the interpretation of Article 14(3), from the mere fact that TRIPS Article 16.1 and Article 22.2 (and 22.3) use different terminology, it does not follow that they purport to establish substantially different standards, let alone that Article 22.2 (and 22.3) imposes a more rigorous standard, contrary to what is asserted by Australia.

225. As acknowledged by Australia, one of the ordinary meanings of "misleading" is "confusing".[81] That the two terms may be used interchangeably in ordinary speech, as well as in the specific context of trademark law is illustrated, for example, by the following passage of WIPO's Trademark Manual, which explains the notion of "likelihood of confusion" by saying that[82]

> A trademark is confusingly similar to a prior trademark if it is used for similar goods and so closely resembles the prior mark that there is a likelihood of consumers being *misled* as to the origin of the goods.

226. Australia argues that a misleading use is a use "which *positively* provokes an error".[83] However, Australia does not explain what it means by "positively". Articles 22.2 and 22.3 do not require an "intent" to mislead on the part of the infringer. As made clear by Article 22.3, all that is required is that the use be "of such a nature as to" mislead, i.e. objectively capable of causing an error.

227. The use of different terms in Article 16.1 and in Article 22.2 (and 22.3) reflects the fact that they are concerned each with a different type of error. Article 16.1 addresses the situation where the use of *two* similar signs for similar goods by *two* different undertakings has the consequence that the public cannot distinguish between the *two* signs and makes the error of mistaking the goods of one of the undertakings for those of the other. In contrast, Articles 22.2 and 22.3 address the situation where the use of *one* sign in connection with *one* product leads the public to make an error with respect to the geographical origin of *that* product. The term "confusion" would not be appropriate to describe the type of error addressed in Articles 22.2 and 22.3, because that error does not involve the impossibility of distinguishing between two signs for goods of two different undertakings.

---

[81] Australia's SWS, para. 104.

[82] WIPO, *Introduction to Trademark Law and Practice, The Basic Concepts, a WIPO Training Manual*, Geneva 1993, para. 6.2.2 (Exhibit EC-108). Emphasis added.

[83] Australia's SWS, para. 104.

Question 151

Please comment on the suggestion that Article 24.3 of the TRIPS Agreement was inserted in the draft text in November 1991 to make it clear that the exceptions provisions in Section 3 of Part II could not be used as a justification for diminishing a Member's pre-existing protection of GIs.

228. Assuming that the suggestion made in the question were correct, and assuming further that the complainants' interpretation of Article 24.5 were also correct, Article 24.5 would be one of the "exceptions provisions in Section 3". Accordingly, Members could not rely upon Article 24.5 as a "justification" to diminish the re-existing protection of geographical indications.

Question 152

If a Member is obliged to diminish the pre-existing protection of GIs in order to allow trademark owners to exercise their rights under Article 16.1 as against GIs, does that obligation not arise under Article 16.1 rather than "[i]n implementing this Section", as used in Article 24.3?

229. No. On the complainants' own interpretation of Article 24.5, the obligation to diminish protection would arise from the obligation imposed by Article 24.5 and not from Article 16.1. But for Article 24.5, Members would be entitled to invalidate and prohibit the use of "grandfathered" trademarks, as defined in Article 24.5, on the basis that they are identical or similar to a geographical indication, just like they are entitled to refuse or invalidate other trademarks on those grounds.

Question 153

Without prejudice to the EC's view that a GI confusingly similar to a trademark will not be registered, if one were registered nevertheless, in what way would this exception be "limited"? In particular, could the rights of the GI owner be limited in such a way as to minimize the likelihood of confusion?

230. The exception is "limited" because it allows the use of the registered name only in relation to goods that originate in the area designated by the geographical indication and which, furthermore, comply will all the relevant requirements provided in the approved specifications. The trademark owner retains the right to prevent the use of the name by *any* person in relation to *any* goods which originate in a different geographical area or which do not comply with the specifications.

231. As explained by the EC[84], the potential universe of uses covered by the exception claimed by the EC is narrower than the potential universe of uses of other descriptive terms, such as an indication of source which does not qualify as a geographical indication or a term used to describe a product characteristic. Yet, both Australia and the United States appear to concede that the use of those terms would qualify for an exception under Article 17.

[84] EC SWS, para. 338. EC SOS, paras. 213-218.

232. Article 17 contains no requirement to the effect that the "likelihood of confusion" must be "minimized". Indeed, such a requirement would pre-empt the balancing of conflicting interests required by the second condition of Article 17. If the term "limited" required to confine the likelihood of confusion to the strictly necessary, it would be unnecessary to "take account", as a separate condition, of the interests of the trademark owner and of third parties.

233. In any event, the exception claimed by the EC limits the likelihood of confusion in two different ways.

234. First, even if the complainants' reading of Article 14(3) were correct and that provision did not prevent the registration of all geographical indications that give rise to a likelihood of confusion with an earlier trademark, it would remain that Article 14(3) would prevent registration in those cases where the likelihood of confusion would be greater, because of the recognition enjoyed by the trademark.

235. Second, the use of the geographical indication is subject to the requirements of Directive 2000/13 on the labelling, presentation and advertising of foodstuffs[85], and in particular to Article 2(1)(a), which provides that "the labelling and methods used must not be such as could mislead the purchaser to a material degree". This applies *inter alia* with respect to any misleading statements concerning the producer or the brand of the goods.

236. Moreover, Article 3(1) of Directive 2000/13 requires that labels must state among other things:

> (7) the name, or business name and address of the manufacturer or packager, or of a seller established within the Community ...
>
> (8) particulars of the place of origin or provenance where failure to give such particulars might mislead the consumer as to the true origin or provenance of the foodstuff.

237. The requirement to state these particulars in the label limits the risk that the geographical indication may be mistaken for the brand name of the products.[86]

238. In addition, the use of registered geographical indications is subject to Directive 84/450 on misleading advertising.[87]

---

[85] Exhibit EC-30.

[86] In *Sociedad Anónima Viña Santa Rita v. U.S. Dept. of the Treasury*, 193 F. Supp. 2d 6 (D.D.C 2001) (Exhibit EC-48), the ATF argued, and the court accepted, that:

> ... the fact that domestic products are required to indicate name and address of the bottler or packer minimizes the likelihood of confusion between a "Santa Rita Hills" wine and a product of Santa Rita in Chile or any other place.

[87] Exhibit EC-31. Article 2(2) defines misleading advertising as:

> any advertising which in any way, including presentation, deceives or is likely to deceive the person to whom it is addressed or whom it reaches and which, by reason of its deceptive nature, is likely to affect their economic behaviour or which, for those reasons, injures or is likely to injure a competitor.

239. Finally, the use of registered geographical indications is subject to the unfair competition laws of the Member States, including both specific legislation and/or case law based on general tort law. One of the aspects typically covered by such laws is the imitation of labels and packaging in cases where it cannot be addressed as a trademark infringement.[88]

240. The requirement to use the registered geographical indications in accordance with the Directives on labeling and on misleading advertising and with the laws on unfair competition is equivalent to and, in practice, achieves the same effect as the requirements usually stipulated in the exceptions provided in the trademark laws of many Members with respect to the use of descriptive terms, including those used to indicate geographical origin. For example:

- Section 122(1)(b)(i) of *Australia*'s Trade Marks Act 1995[89] provides that a person does not infringe a registered trademark when

  > The person uses a sign in good faith to indicate the ... geographical origin ... of the goods ...

- Section 19(3) of *Hong Kong*'s Trade Marks Ordinance[90] provides that:

  > A registered trade mark is not infringed by - ....(c) the use of signs which serve to designate the ... geographical origin ... of goods ... provided the use is in accordance with honest practices in industrial or commercial matters.

- Section 95 of *New Zealand*'s Trade Marks Act 2002[91] provides that

  > A person does not infringe a registered trademark if, in accordance with honest practices in industrial or commercial matters, the persons uses -.... c) a sign to indicate – (i) ... the geographical origin...

- Section 28 of *Singapore*'s Trade Marks Act[92] provides that:

  > ... a person does not infringe a registered trade mark when: ...(b) he uses a sign to indicate (i) the ... geographical origin ... of goods or services ... and such use is in accordance with honest practices in industrial or commercial matters.

- Section 34(1) of *South Africa*'s Trade Marks Act[93] provides that:

  > A registered trade mark is not infringed by ... (b) the use by any person of any *bona fide* description or indication of the ... geographical origin ... of his

---

[88] See WIPO's *Introduction to Trademark Law & Practice, the Basic Concepts, a WIPO Training Manual*, Geneva 1993, 2nd Edition, pp. 97-100. (Exhibit EC-82).
[89] Exhibit EC-7.
[90] Exhibit EC-94.
[91] Exhibit EC-80.
[92] Exhibit EC-97.
[93] Exhibit EC-98.

> goods ... [p]rovided that the use contemplated in paragraph (b).... is consistent with fair practice.

- Section 30(2) of *India*'s Trade Marks Act 1999[94] provides that:

  > A registered trademark is not infringed where – (a) the use in relation to goods ... indicates the ... geographical origin ....

- Section 26(1) of *Japan*'s Trademark Law[95] provides that:

  > The effects of the trademark right shall not extend to the following trademarks ... (i) trademarks indicating, in a common way, the ... origin [of] of the designated goods or goods similar thereto ...

- Section 38 of *Romania*'s Trade Marks Act[96] provides that:

  > The owner of a mark may not request that other persons be prohibited from using in the course of trade ... (b) indications concerning ... geographical origin .... with the proviso that [they] are used in accordance with honest practice.

- Section 6 of *Iceland*'s Trade Marks Act[97] provides that:

  > Provided that the use is in accordance with honest business practice, the proprietor of a trade mark may not prohibit others from using in trade or business; .... 2. descriptions of ... [the] ... origin ... of the goods or services.

241. The above exceptions provide no requirements for using an indication of origin in co-existence with a registered trademark other than that such use must be "in good faith" or in accordance with "honest", "fair" or "proper" business or trade practices or "in a common way" and, therefore, would have to be deemed inconsistent with Article 17 if the complainants' narrow reading of that provision were upheld by the Panel.

242. The EC's own Trademark Directive[98] provides that:

> The trademark shall not entitle the proprietor to prohibit a third party from using, in the course of trade, ... (b) indications concerning the... geographical origin...of goods ... provided he uses them in accordance with honest practices in industrial or commercial matters.

243. Similarly, Article 12(b) of the Community Trademark Regulation provides that:

> The trademark shall not entitle the proprietor to prohibit a third party from using, in the course of trade, ... (b) indications

94 Exhibit EC-95.
95 Exhibit EC-104.
96 Exhibit EC-105.
97 Exhibit EC-106.
98 Cf. Article 6.1(b).

> concerning the ... geographical origin ... of goods ... provided he uses them in accordance with honest practices in industrial or commercial matters.[99]

244. It follows that, even if trademark owners were permitted to enforce their rights under the Trademark Directive or the Community Trademark Directive with respect to the confusing use of a registered geographical indication, as demanded by the complainants, the trademark owners could still not prevent such use if it is "in accordance with honest practices in industrial or commercial matters".

Question 154

What, specifically, are "the legitimate interests of the owner of the trademark and of third parties" within the meaning of Article 17?

245. Trademark owners have an interest in preserving the economic "value" of their rights.[100] That value is a function of the recognition enjoyed by the trademark, which in turn is related to the length of use and the reputation/renown acquired as a result. A trademark which has never been used or which is virtually unknown has little intrinsic value and could be easily replaced without significant prejudice to the owner.

246. The "legitimate interest" of the trademark owner must not be equated with the full enjoyment of the exclusivity rights granted by Article 16.1. There are circumstances in which the exercise of those rights may not be "legitimate", having regard to the purposes for which trademark rights are granted and/or having regard to the legitimate interests of other parties.

247. Thus, in *Canada – Pharmaceutical Patents*, the Panel rejected an argument to the effect that the patent owner had a "legitimate interest" in "the full enjoyment of its patent rights". The Panel noted, among other things that[101]

> ... a definition equating "legitimate interests" with legal interests makes no sense at all when applied to the final phrase of Article 30 referring to the "legitimate interests" of third parties. Third parties are by definition parties who have no legal right at all in being able to perform the tasks excluded by Article 28 patent rights. An exceptions clause permitting them to take account of such third party legal interests would be permitting them to take account of nothing. And third, reading the third condition as further protection of legal rights would render it essentially redundant in light of the very similar protection of legal rights in the first condition of Article 30 ("limited exception").

248. The panel went on to conclude that:[102]

---

[99] See the Judgement of the ECJ of 7 January 2004 in the Case C-100/02, *Gerolsteiner Brunnen GmbH & Co. v. Putsch GmbH*, which illustrates the application of Article 6(1)(b) of the Trademark Direcxtive with respect to geographical indications (Exhibit EC-107).

[100] Panel Report, *United States – Section 110(5)*, para. 6.227.

[101] Panel Report, *Canada – Pharmaceutical Products*, para. 7.68.

> To make sense of the term legitimate interests in this context, the term must be defined in the way that is often used in legal discourse – as a normative claim calling for protection of interests that are justifiable in the sense that they are supported by relevant public policies or other social norms.

249. The "legitimate interests of third parties" include the commercial interest of other parties that produce or sell goods originating in a certain area to which a given reputation or characteristic is associated in using the term which designates that area in order to describe their products. As explained in the US Restatement of Unfair Competition[103]

> That a watch is Swiss, that a wine is from California, that maple syrup is from Vermont, or that a dress has been designed in New York or Paris, are facts in which consumers are interested and which sellers therefore wish to disclose in a prominent manner.

250. The "legitimate interests of third parties" include also the interest of consumers in being informed about the geographical origin and the product characteristics associated to that origin. As noted by WIPO,[104]

> The legal recognition and protection of indications of source and appellations of origin are in the general interest. They convey very important information to consumers on the geographical origin of goods and services and, indirectly, on their inherent quality and characteristics. Therefore, if properly used, geographical indications can help the public in its purchasing decisions and frequently exercise a strong influence thereon.

251. The fact that the use of a geographical indication may give rise to some degree of *likelihood* of confusion does not necessarily mean that it is incapable of performing this important informative function. In particular, where the finding of likelihood of confusion is based on the presumption provided in Article 16.1, or where the geographical indication enjoys more recognition than the trademark.

How can legitimate interests be taken into account under Article 17 where they conflict with other relevant interests?

252. Article 17 calls for a balancing of the different interests in conflict. Members enjoy a wide margin of discretion in making such a balancing. Indeed, all that is required by Article 17 is that Members "take account of" the different interests at issue. Furthermore, Article 17 puts on an equal level all the interests involved. In contrast, Articles 26.2 and 30 distinguish between the interests of the right holder, which must not be "unreasonably prejudiced", and the interests of third parties, which must simply be "taken into account".

---

102 Panel Report, *Canada – Pharmaceutical Products*, para. 7.69.

103 *Restatement (Third) of Unfair Competition*, para. 14 cmt. D (1995). Cited in In *Sociedad Anónima Viña Santa Rita v. U.S. Dept. of the Treasury*, 193 F. Supp. 2d 6 (D.D.C 2001) (Exhibit EC-48).

104 WIPO (Ed.) *Introduction to Intellectual Property, Theory and Practice*, Geneva 1997, para. 1.55. (Exhibit EC-109).

253. In balancing the interests of the trademark owners and other parties in the case at hand, the following considerations are relevant and have been taken into account by the EC:

- trademarks are much easier to create than geographical indications. Trademarks can be acquired almost instantaneously, simply by an "intent to use" or by the mere lodging of an application with a registration system. In contrast, the creation of a geographical indication requires to establish first a "link" between the name and certain product characteristics, which may require years. Indeed, as is often the case in the EC, such link is the result of centuries of tradition. For this reason, the strict application of the first-in-time rule would privilege trademark owners and be inequitable to the holders of a geographical indication;
- trademarks are arbitrary, with the consequence that there is a virtually unlimited choice of trademarks. By choosing deliberately a geographical name as a trademark, an undertaking accepts the risk that the same sign may be used concurrently as a geographical indication. In contrast, geographical indications are "necessary" in the sense that the range of names used to designate a certain geographical is limited *a priori* by well established usage. Right holders of geographical indications may not easily change the name given by the public to the geographical area where they are located. For that reason, it is much more difficult to find an alternative geographical indication than it is to find an alternative trademark;
- geographical indications are collective rights, the use of which is available to any person who produces or sells goods which have the origin designated by the geographical indication and meet the relevant specifications. It would be inequitable to deprive that collectivity from the right to use a geographical indication for the exclusive benefit of an individual trademark owner, who may or may not have contributed to the development of the geographical indication, simply because he happened to register that name first as a trademark;
- geographical indications serve to inform consumers that the product originates in a certain area and has certain characteristics linked to that origin. In contrast, trademarks only guarantee the identity of the undertaking that markets the product. Thus, in addition to having a commercial function, geographical indications serve a public interest, which deserves additional protection.

254. Having regard to the above considerations, EC law allows in principle the use of a geographical indication in co-existence with earlier trademarks. Nevertheless, in order to take account of the legitimate interests of the trademark owners, such use is subject to the following restrictions:

- first, even on the complainants' interpretation of Article 14(3) of Regulation 2081/92, that provision would prevent the registration of geographical indications in those circumstances where the trademark owner would suffer a more significant economic prejudice, because of the reputation acquired by the trademark. As mentioned, a trademark which has not been used, or which is hardly known, has little intrinsic value and could be easily replaced with a more distinctive sign. In those circumstances, co-existence does not cause an unreasonable prejudice to the trademark owner;

- second, again, even if the complainants' reading of Article 14(3) were correct and that provision did not prevent the registration of all geographical indications that give rise to a likelihood of confusion with an earlier trademark, it would remain that Article 14(3) would prevent the registration in those cases where the likelihood of confusion would be greater, because of the recognition enjoyed by the trademark;
- third, as explained above, the Directives on labelling and misleading advertising and the laws on unfair competition ensure that geographical indications are used in a fair and honest manner, thereby reducing the likelihood of confusion and the ensuing prejudice to the interests of the trademark owner.

Question 156

Why do the requirements in Article 17 differ from those in Articles 13, 26.2 and 30 of the TRIPS Agreement? How should their interpretation reflect those differences?

255. The differences between the conditions of Article 17 and those of the other provisions cited in the question reflect, among other things, the different function of each type of intellectual property right, the nature and the extent of the obligations imposed by the TRIPS Agreement with respect to each of them, and the previous practice of Members in granting exceptions.

256. More specifically, and without purporting to be exhaustive, the EC would point to the following differences:

- unlike patents, copyrights or the rights over industrial designs, trademark rights do not reward an invention or a creative effort. Rather, they are an instrument of fair competition;[105]
- unlike inventions, artistic works or industrial designs, trademarks do not have to be novel or original, but merely distinctive. Trademarks are relatively easy to conceive and to register. For the same reason, trademarks have little intrinsic value. Whatever value

---

[105] WIPO has noted that, in the case of trademarks,

> ... the aspect of intellectual creations –although existent- is less prominent, but what counts here is that the object of industrial property typically consists of signs transmitting information to consumers, in particular as regards products and services offered on the market, and that protection is directed against unauthorized use of such signs which is likely to mislead consumers, and misleading practices in general.

WIPO (Ed.) *Introduction to Intellectual Property, Theory and Practice*, Geneva 1997, para. 1.9. (Exhibit EC-110).

they may have is a function of their recognition by the public and is acquired through use;

- unlike patents, copyrights or industrial designs, which all have a limited duration, trademarks may have an indefinite validity, or at least may be renewed without any limitation. This makes it more necessary to allow for exceptions, so as to avoid permanent monopolies;
- the WIPO conventions do not guarantee the exclusivity of trademarks. The TRIPS Agreement is the first multilateral agreement to recognize such right. It is only natural that the participants wished to reserve for themselves a wider discretion in granting exceptions with respect to trademarks than with respect to other intellectual property rights where international harmonization was more advanced;
- prior to the TRIPS Agreement, the trademark laws of most Members provided relatively broad exceptions, including in particular with respect to the use of descriptive terms.[106] The wording used in other exceptions clauses would not have accommodated many of the existing "descriptive terms" exceptions.

257. Irrespective of the reasons, it is beyond dispute that the requirements of Article 17 are substantially less stringent than those of the other provisions cited in the question. Alone among all the exceptions clauses, Article 17 does not require that the exceptions "do not prejudice unreasonably" the legitimate interests of the right holder, but merely that those interests be taken into account. Likewise, alone among all the exceptions provisions, Article 17 does not require that the exceptions "do not unreasonably conflict with a normal exploitation of the patent".[107] These differences must be given meaning. It would be contrary to the drafters' intention and to basic rules of treaty interpretation if these differences were ignored and Article 17 were interpreted as imposing, in practice, the same requirements as the other exceptions clauses.

Question 159

May protection for designations of origin and geographical indications now be afforded in the EC only within the framework laid down by Regulation (EC) No. 2081/92?

258. No. Regulation 2081/92 and the other measures mentioned by the EC in its first submission apply cumulatively. The other measures afford protection to any indication of source, including those that qualify as designations of origin or geographical indications under Regulation 2081/92.

---

[106] See the examples cited above in the response to Question No. 155.

[107] At the second meeting with the Panel, Australia seemed to argue that trademarks are not "exploited" but "used". Even so, this would not explain why Article 17 does not prescribe that the exceptions shall not "unreasonably conflict with the normal *use* of the trademark".

To what extent does the EC implement its obligations under Article 22.2 of the TRIPS Agreement through Regulation (EC) No. 2081/92 and to what extent through other measures (see EC first written submission, paras. 433 and 434)?

259. As explained, Regulation 2081/92 and the other measures apply cumulatively. The other measures afford protection to all indications of source, including all geographical indications as defined in Article 22.1 of the TRIPS Agreement. Regulation 2081/92 provides additional protection to those geographical indications that qualify as designations of origin or geographical indications within the meaning of that Regulation.

Are the other measures cited by the EC alone sufficient to fulfil its obligations under Article 22.2?

260. Yes. The EC refers to the responses provided by the EC and its Member States, as part of the review under Article 24.2 of the TRIPS Agreement, which have been submitted by the EC as Exhibit EC-29.

261. The EC understands that the complainants do not contest that the other measures cited by the EC are sufficient to fulfill the EC's obligations under Article 22.2. Indeed, they could hardly do so since the complainants purport to implement their obligations under Article 22.2 through the application of similar measures.

262. Instead, the United States appears to argue, mistakenly, that Regulation 2081/92 excludes the application of the other measures to designations of origin and geographical indications as defined in that Regulation.[108]

263. In turn, as far as the EC understands, Australia's claim under Article 22.2 is that the additional protection afforded to the registered geographical indications under Article 13(1) of Regulation 2081/92 (or the subsequent use thereof made by the holders of a geographical indication) could be an "act of unfair competition" within the meaning of Article 22.2, against which EC law provides no remedy, and not that the other measures cited by the EC are not sufficient to protect geographical indications that have not been registered under Regulation 2081/92.

Question 160

To what extent does the EC implement its obligations under Article 22.2 of the TRIPS Agreement through Regulation (EC) No. 2081/92 and to what extent through other measures?

264. See above the response to Question 159.

Does the EC believe that the complainants should prove a negative, i.e. that no legal means required under Article 22.2 are available? Can a respondent simply argue that other measures, outside the Panel's terms of reference, fulfil an obligation, without proof of how those other measures fulfil that obligation?

---

[108] See EC SOS, para. 236.

265. The complainants were well aware of the existence of the other measures cited by the EC in its first submission. Indeed, those measures had been identified in the response of the EC and its Member States in the review under Article 24.2 TRIPS among the means provided by them to comply with Article 22.2 TRIPS. Had the complainants been of the view that those measures are not sufficient to comply with Article 22.2, they could and should have mentioned them in their panel requests. A complaining party should not be allowed to shift the burden of proof to the respondent simply by asserting that the respondent provides no means to comply with Article 22.2, or by deliberately omitting to mention some of the means which the respondent has previously identified under the relevant WTO procedures among those implementing its obligations under Article 22.2.

266. In any event, assuming that the other measures in question were within the Panel's terms of reference, and assuming further that the complainants' mere assertion that the EC does not provide the necessary means to comply with Article 22.2 were sufficient to establish a *prima facie* case, the EC submits that the explanations provided by the EC in its previous submissions to the Panel, as well as in the responses of the EC and its Member States to the review under Article 24.2, which are part of the EC's submissions, would be sufficient to rebut that *prima facie* case.

267. It would then be for the complainants to make specific claims (or arguments) in order to show why the other measures identified by the EC are not consistent with Article 22.2, despite the explanations provided by the EC. The complainants, however, have not made any such claim or argument. The EC cannot be reasonably expected to identify and formulate each and every conceivable claim and arguments to the effect that its own measures fail to comply with Article 22.2 and then rebut them.

Question 163

The Panel takes note of Australia's and the EC's respective views on the applicability of Article 70.1 of the TRIPS Agreement to individual GI registrations (Australia's response to Panel question No. 90; EC rebuttal, para. 202). On 31 December 1995, at what stage of the procedure under the former Article 15 were the GIs later registered under Article 17? Did any individual GIs registered under Article 6 have an objection period that expired prior to 1 January 1996?

268. The draft regulation to register a first list of names under the simplified procedure under Article 17 was distributed to the Member States in the 7th meeting of the regulatory committee on 22 September 1995 and was discussed at every meeting until the end of 1995, the last of which was the 11th meeting (22 November 1995). The vote took place on 19 January 1996 and the matter was transferred to the Council later on.

269. Logically, if an objection procedure is provided for, then the decision-making process regarding the registration, including the consultation of the regulatory committee, cannot take place before the period for objections has

expired. This is also the case under the normal procedure provided for in Article 6 and 7 of Regulation 2081/92. Accordingly, by the time the file was referred to the regulatory committee, the time at which an objection procedure should have been foreseen, had it indeed been necessary, had passed.

270. The EC notes that in its second oral statement, Australia continues to insist that the relevant point in time is the registration of the geographical indications under the simplified procedure.[109] However, Australia forgets that it has brought a claim under the national treatment provisions of the TRIPS Agreement. In Australia's submission, the EC has violated its national treatment obligations by *not providing* for a possibility for objections. Accordingly, the alleged violation stems not from the *act* of registering the indications in question, but from the *omission* to provide a right of objection. However, this omission clearly occurred before 1 January 1996, i.e. the date of application of the TRIPS Agreement to the EC.

271. Moreover, the EC would like to recall that as a matter of fact, no objection procedure applied under the simplified procedure regardless of whether EC residents or foreign residents were involved.[110] There was therefore no violation of national treatment. Accordingly, the question "at which time" the national treatment violation may have occurred has a rather speculative character.

272. No application under Article 6 of Regulation 2081/92 had a period of objections which expired prior to 1 January 1996.

Question 164

In what way are the objectives and principles set out in Articles 7 and 8 of the TRIPS Agreement, and the considerations recited in the first paragraph of its preamble, relevant to the interpretation of the provisions of that agreement at issue in this dispute?

273. Regulation 2081/92 protects products which have a special quality, reputation, or other characteristics attributable to their geographical origin. As can be seen from Article 2 of the Regulation 2081/29, these characteristics must be due to a particular geographical environment with its inherent natural and human facts, which also may include traditional knowledge, processes, and working methods. Whereas Regulation 2081/92 does not primarily focus on technological innovation as referred to in Article 7 of the TRIPS Agreement, the human factor may include some such elements. Overall, however, Article 7 seems to be of limited relevance for the present case.

274. As stated in the Preamble to Regulation 2081/92, the production of agricultural products and foodstuffs has a vital role for the Community economy. The protection of geographical indications in Regulation 2081/92 is important for the development of this sector by encouraging diversification into high-value production. Accordingly, Regulation 2081/92 is a measure which promotes the

---

[109] Australia's SOS, para. 78.

[110] EC FWS, para. 91 et seq.

public interest in a sector of vital importance to the EC's socio-economic and technological development as referred to in Article 8.1 TRIPS Agreement, and which is consistent with the provisions of the Agreement.

275. The considerations recited in the first paragraph of the Preamble to the TRIPS Agreement are relevant for interpreting the provisions of the TRIPS Agreement in accordance with the customary rules of interpretation of international law.[111]

[111] Cf. also above, Response to Panel's Question No. 103, para. 31.

ANNEX B-8

REPLIES BY THE EUROPEAN COMMUNITIES TO QUESTIONS POSED BY AUSTRALIA FOLLOWING THE SECOND SUBSTANTIVE MEETING

Question 1

Can the EC provide any official statement predating its first written submission that expressly states that names of geographical areas located in WTO Members could be registered under regulation 2081?92 without satisfying its equivalence and reciprocity conditions?

1. The EC refers Australia to the EC's responses to the Panel's questions Nos. 16 and 95.

Question 2

The decision of the Court of First Instance in the "Canard" judgement held that Regulation 2081/92 "does not establish specific procedural safeguards for individuals", and for that reason a person who has made an objection against a proposed regulation "is not individually concerned by the contested [registration] within the meaning of the fourth paragraph of Article 230 of the EC Treaty.

In this light, can the EC say that a trademark holder will certainly be able to commence procedures under Article 230 of the EC Treaty to contest the registration of a GI under Regulation 2081/92.

2. The fourth paragraph of Article 230 of the EC treaty provides that

> Any natural or legal person may, under the same conditions, institute proceedings against a decision addressed to that person or against a decision which, although in the form of a regulation or a decision addressed to another person, is of direct and individual concern to the former

3. The decision to register a geographical indication under Regulation 2081/92 takes the form of a Council or Commission regulation. Accordingly, a trademark holder will be able to bring an action in annulment under Article 230 against the registration of a geographical indication if he can show that the registration, although in the form of a regulation, is of direct and individual concern to him.

4. According to well-established case law of the European Court of Justice[1],

> a provision which by virtue of its nature and scope is of legislative nature, may be of individual concern to natural or legal persons where it affects them by reason of certain attributes which are

---

[1] See e.g. Case T-215/00, *SCEA La Conqueste v. Commission*, [2001] ECR II-181, para. 34 (Exhibit COMP-12).

> peculiar to them or by reason of circumstances in which they are differentiated from all other persons and by virtue of those factors distinguishes them individually just as in the case of the addressee of a decision …

5. *One* of the situations in which regulations have been found to be of individual concern to an economic operator is where the regulation has been adopted pursuant to a procedure that affords certain procedural safeguards specifically to that operator.[2] For example, the ECJ held in the *Timex* case that regulations imposing anti-dumping measures may be challenged under Article 230 by the person who filed the complaint.[3] Subsequently, the ECJ has recognised standing to the investigated producers or exporters[4] and to their related importers[5], but not, in principle, to the independent importers.[6]

6. However, contrary to what appears to be Australia's understanding, the situation described in the above paragraph is not the only situation where an economic operator may be found to be individually concerned for the purposes of Article 230. In particular, the ECJ has held that a regulation may be of individual concern to an operator where it adversely affects that operator's *specific* rights. Thus, in the *Codorniu* case[7], the ECJ held that the applicant had standing to challenge a regulation concerning the use of a designation for sparkling wine ("crémant"), because as a result it was prevented from using a graphic mark which it had registered and used for a long time before the adoption of the contested regulation, so that it was distinguished from all the other economic operators.

7. In the *La Conqueste* case[8], the applicant was a producer of *canard à foie gras* of the area designated by the geographical indication who had objected to the specifications approved by the Commission. The applicant argued that the application was admissible on *two* different grounds: first, referring to the *Codorniu* judgement, because the measures affected adversely his specific rights; and second, referring to the *Timex* case law, because Regulation 2081/92 afforded him certain procedural guarantees.

8. The Court of First Instance rejected both arguments and held the application inadmissible. First, the court distinguished, on the facts, the situation of the applicant from the situation in *Codorniu*.[9] Second, the court held that,

---

2 This case law originated in Case 191/82 *EEC Seed Crushers' and Oil Processors' Federation (Fediol) v. Commission* [1983] ECR 2913, which concerned a complaint under the EC Basic Anti-subsidy Regulation.

3 Case 264/82, *Timex v. Council and Commission* [1985] ECR 849 (Exhibit EC-112).

4 See e.g. Case C-156/87 *Gestetner Holdings plc v. Council and Commission* [1990] ECR I-781.

5 See e.g. Case T-164/94 *Ferchimex SA v. Council* [1995] ECR II-2681.

6 See e.g. Case 205/87 *Nuova Cream Srl v. Commission* [1987] ECR 4427.

7 Case C-309/89, *Codorniu v. Council* [1194] ECR I-1853 (Exhibit EC-111).

8 Case T-215/00, *SCEA La Conqueste v. Commission*, [2001] ECR II-181 (Exhibit COMP-12).

9 *Ibid.*, para. 28.

unlike the EC Basic Anti-dumping Regulation, Regulation 2081/92 does not establish specific procedural safeguards, at Community level, for individuals.[10]

9. The court's finding that Regulation 2081/92 does not establish specific *procedural* safeguards, at Community level, for individuals would prevent a trademark holder from invoking the *Timex* case law in order to establish that it is individually concerned. However, this does not mean necessarily that a trademark holder will never be able to show that it is individually concerned. In particular, a trademark holder could seek to rely on the *Codorniu* case law. Whether or not a trademark holder will be able to show that the registration of a givc geographical indication affects adversely its "specific" *substantive* trademark rights will depend upon the factual circumstances of each case.

Question 3

Will a trademark holder, even if he or she can not show direct and individual concern and/or even if he or she does not commence proceedings within 2 months of the decision being made, certainly be able to take advantage of the procedure for obtaining a preliminary opinion under Article 234 of the EC Treaty to have the ECJ review the validity of the registration of a GI under regulation 2081/92.

10. The fact that an operator is not individually and directly concerned by a Community regulation is *never* an obstacle for raising the invalidity of that measure in accordance with the procedure provided in Article 234 of the EC Treaty.

11. Contrary to what has been said by the United States[11], there is no general rule to the effect that if a person could have brought a direct action under Article 230, but fails to do so within the two month time limit, it is precluded from raising the invalidity of the measure under Article 234.

12. The case law cited by the United States[12] applies only in very specific situations where the applicant is "fully aware of [the measure] and of the fact that it could *without any doubt* have challenged it under Article [230]".[13]

13. So far, the ECJ has found that these conditions were present in a case involving the beneficiary of a state aid[14] and a in a case concerning a related

---

[10] *Ibid.*, para. 47. Australia's question misquotes the paragraph of the judgement which it cites by omitting the crucial words "at Community level".

[11] US SOS, para. 78.

[12] *Ibid.*

[13] Case C-188/92, *TWD Textielwerke Deggendorf v. Bundesrepublik Deutschland* [1994], ECR, I-833, point 24 [emphasis added] (Exhibit US-78).

[14] Case C-188/92, *TWD Textielwerke Deggendorf v. Bundesrepublik Deutschland* [1994], ECR, I-833 (Exhibit US-78).

The ECJ took pains to distinguish this case from a previous case (Case 216/82, *Universität Hamburg v. Hauptzollamt Hamburg-Kehrwieder*, [1983] ECR 2771). The ECJ noted that in that case the ECJ had declared the request for a preliminary ruling admissible on the grounds that (*Ibid.* at para. 23, emphasis added):

> the rejection of the application by national authority was the only measure directly addressed to the person concerned of which it had been necessarily informed in

importer in an anti-dumping investigation.[15] In both cases, there was well-established and clear case law recognising generally the standing of any individual in the same procedural position as the applicant to bring a direct action under Article 230.[16]

14. In contrast, as explained in the response to the previous question, whether or not a trademark holder will have standing to bring an action under Article 230 against a regulation registering a geographical indication will depend on the appreciation of the particular circumstances of each case by the court, something which cannot be predicted in advance "without any doubt" by the trademark holder.

15. Moreover, the concern expressed by the United States is that a registered geographical indication which is not confusing *per se* may be used in a confusing manner after the two month time limit.[17] However, since in that case the circumstances that could, arguably, justify a finding of individual concern for the purposes of Article 230 would not have been present during the two month period, the applicant could not have been "fully aware" during that period that it could "without any doubt" bring a direct action.

16. As a final remark, it should be noted that the Court of Justice has stressed repeatedly the principle that all Community legal acts must be subject to effective judicial review:[18]

> 29. ... individuals are entitled to effective judicial protection of the rights they derive from the Community legal order, and the right to such protection is one of the general principles of law stemming from the constitutional traditions of the member States. That right has also been enshrined in Articles 6 and 13 of the [European Convention on Human Rights] ...
>
> 30. By Articles 230 EC and 241 EC, on the one hand, and by Articles 234, on the other, the Treaty has established a complete system of legal remedies and procedures designed to ensure review of the legality of acts of the institutions and has entrusted such review to the Community Courts. Under that system, where natural or legal persons cannot, by reason of the conditions for admissibility laid down in the fourth paragraph of Article 230 EC, directly challenge Community measures of general application,

good time and *which it could challenge in the courts without encountering any difficulty in demonstrating its interest in bringing proceedings*.

[15] Case C-239/99, *Nachi Europe GmbH v. Hauptzollamt Krefeld* [2001] ECR I-1197, para. 37 (Exhibit US-78).

The court emphasised that the applicant "could *undoubtedly* have sought its annulment under Article 230 of the EC Treaty" (*Ibid.*, para. 370) [emphasis added].

[16] As regards the standing of a complainant in an anti-dumping proceeding, see above the Timex case. As regards the standing of the beneficiary of a state aid, see Case C-730/79 *Philip Morris v. Commission* [1980] ECR 2671.

[17] US SOS, para. 78.

[18] Judgement of the European Court of Justice of 1 April 2004, Case C-263/02, *Commission v. Jégo-Quéré & Cie. SA* [not published yet in the ECR] (Exhibit EC-113).

they are able, depending on the case, either indirectly to plead the invalidity of such acts before the Community Courts under Article 241 EC or to do so before the national courts and ask them, since they have no jurisdiction themselves to declare those measures invalid, to make a reference to the Court of Justice for a preliminary ruling on validity....

31. Thus it is for the Member States to establish a system of legal remedies and procedures which ensure respect for the right to effective judicial protection ....

32. In that context, in accordance with the principle of sincere cooperation laid down in Article 10 EC, national courts are required, so far as possible, to interpret and apply national procedural rules governing the exercise of rights of action in a way that enables natural and legal persons to challenge before the courts the legality of any decision or other national measure relative to the application to them of a Community act of general application, by pleading the invalidity of such an act.

ANNEX B-9

COMMENTS OF THE EUROPEAN COMMUNITIES TO AUSTRALIA'S AND THE UNITED STATES' REPLIES TO QUESTIONS POSED BY THE PANEL FOLLOWING THE SECOND SUBSTANTIVE MEETING

(2 September 2004)

1. In its present submission, the EC provides its comments on the responses of the complainants to the Questions of the Panel after the second substantive meeting. Given the advanced stage of the proceedings, the EC will, in the present submission, focus on arguments which are made for the first time in the responses of the complainants. The fact that the EC does not comment on a particular response does not imply that the EC agrees with the response. To the extent that the complainants reiterate arguments to which the EC has already responded in earlier submissions, the EC refers to its earlier submissions.

Question 101

2. As the EC has already stated in its response to Question 101, the EC considers that the quadrant provided in the third party submission of Chinese Taipei is not pertinent, since Regulation 2081/92 does not involve any discrimination on the basis of nationality.

3. In their responses, the complainants are relying on this quadrant to demonstrate that the EC measure involves discrimination between nationals. However, the arguments of the complainants have no basis in the text of Regulation 2081/92, and in addition are logically inconsistent. For ease of reference, the table in question is reproduced below:

GI: EC National: EC 1	GI: Non-EC National: EC 3
2 GI: EC National: Non-EC	4 GI: Non-EC National: Non-EC

4. An examination of whether the EC measure violates the national treatment obligation of Article 3.1 TRIPS would require a comparison of the treatment it accords to domestic nationals and to foreign nationals. Logically, the comparison of treatment should therefore take place between quadrants 1 and 2, and between quadrants 3 and 4. In the case of Regulation 2081/92, this examination would confirm that there is no difference in treatment on the grounds of nationality. This is why the EC has submitted that the only relevant

comparison is between the treatment accorded to domestic geographical indications, and to foreign geographical indications.[1]

5. Interestingly, in their responses, the complainants do not allege any difference in treatment between quadrants 1 and 2, or between quadrants 3 and 4. The complainants do not attempt to show, either, that there is any difference between quadrants 1 and 3, or between quadrants 2 and 4. Rather, they argue that the comparison should take place between *quadrants 1 and 4*.[2] In support of this view, the United States claims that quadrant 1 is the sole "benchmark", against which *both* quadrants 2 and 4 should be measured. As for quadrant 3, the US argues that "it does not matter whether some EC nationals (...) are also treated less favourably than the EC nationals in quadrant 1".[3]

6. In the view of the EC, these arguments simply disregard the content of Regulation 2081/92. The EC has pointed out repeatedly that Regulation 2081/92 treats EC and foreign nationals exactly alike as regards the protection of geographical indications relating to areas in the EC. Similarly, the EC has pointed out that Regulation 2081/92 treats EC and foreign nationals exactly alike as regards the registration of geographical indications relating to areas outside the EC. The complainants cannot respond to this by arguing that the treatment accorded by Regulation 2081/92 in quadrants 2 and 3 should simply be ignored. Such an approach to the interpretation of Regulation 2081/92 would clearly be incompatible with Article 11 of the DSU, which requires an objective assessment of the facts.

7. The EC also finds the complainants' arguments logically inconsistent. If the complainants accept that the quadrant prepared by Chinese Taipei constitutes a correct description of the possible constellations for comparison of favourable treatment of nationals and goods in respect of geographical indications, then the complainants must accept this analytical tool in its entirety. They cannot simply ignore half of the possible constellations and base their argument purely on a comparison of those constellations which suit them. Such a selective reasoning does not do justice to the national treatment obligations of the TRIPS Agreement.

Question 102

8. In its response to Question No. 102, the United States argues that "it is not critical for the Panel to make a factual assumption that all persons producing GI products in a country are nationals of that country". The United States goes on to argue that "[i]ndeed, it is undisputed that the EC GI Regulation on its face provides for different treatment of persons depending on which quadrant set out in response to question 101 they fall in".[4]

---

[1] EC Response to Panel's Question No. 101, para. 23.

[2] US Response to Panel's Question No. 101, para. 2; Australia's Response to Panel's Question No. 101, para. 2.

[3] US Response to Panel's Question No. 101, para. 4.

[4] US Response to Panel's Question No. 102, para. 9.

9. Already these premises are false. The EC does not see how the US can submit that the Panel should make a finding that Regulation 2081/92 involves discrimination between nationals and at the same time claim that the Panel need not come to any conclusion on whether in fact there is any link between nationality and the protection of geographical indications under Regulation 2081/92.

10. The EC is also astonished that the US would claim that "it is undisputed" that Regulation 2081/92 provides for different treatment of persons "depending on which quadrant set out in response to question 101 they fall in". As the EC has repeatedly confirmed, Regulation 2081/92 treats EC and foreign nationals exactly alike as regards the protection of geographical indications relating to areas in the EC. Similarly, the EC has pointed out that Regulation 2081/92 treats EC and foreign nationals exactly alike as regards the registration of geographical indications relating to areas outside the EC. Accordingly, the treatment accorded by quadrant 1 is the same as that accorded by quadrant 2, and the treatment accorded by quadrant 3 is the same as that accorded by quadrant 4.

11. In its further attempts to show that there is discrimination on the basis of nationality, the United states argues that "in order to produce agricultural foodstuffs in accordance with the product specifications for a protected name, persons "will be established in that area" and "will have to set up a legal person under the laws of the country in which they are established".[5] The US goes on to argue that "it will generally follow that those established [...] are nationals of that Member" and that this "also generally follows as a practical matter".[6]

12. In the view of the EC, these US arguments are mere speculation without any supporting proof. Regulation 2081/92 does not require any form of establishment, nor does it require the setting up of legal persons. Similarly, even where a natural or legal person is resident or established in a particular country, this does not mean it becomes a national of that country.

13. The EC notes also that the United States has not provided the Panel with any information as to what legal persons it considers to be its nationals. In this context, the EC would refer to the definition of "enterprises of a Party" in the North American Free Trade Agreement (NAFTA), which reads as follows: "enterprise of a Party means an enterprise constituted or organized under the law of a Party".[7] It is interesting to note that NAFTA, to which the US is a party, does not in fact define the nationality of enterprises on the basis of establishment.[8]

14. It seems to the EC that the complainants are attempting to impose a definition of nationality on the EC which has no basis in the EC measure in

5 US Response to Panel's Question No. 102, para. 10.

6 US Response to Panel's Question No. 102, para. 12.

7 NAFTA Article 201.1 (Exhibit EC-111).

8 Another relevant example would be Article XXVIII (m) (i) of the GATT, which defines a "juridical person of another Member "as a juridical person which is "constituted or otherwise organized under the law of that other Member, and is engaged in substantive business operations in the territory of that Member or any other Member".

question, does not reflect the national treatment provisions of the TRIPS Agreement, and runs counter to international practice.

15. The EC notes that the United States also points out that "US agricultural land is held almost exclusively by US nationals".[9] The EC does not consider this statement relevant for the present case, nor does it wish to speculate on why the percentage of foreign ownership in the US might be so low. The EC notes also that the United States has not shown that the same is also true for EC agricultural land. Finally, the United States has not shown that there is no foreign ownership in the food-producing sector, which is equally concerned by Regulation 2081/92.

Question 103

16. In its response to the Panel's questions, the EC has emphasized that Article 3.1 TRIPS requires that the conditions for the acquisition of intellectual property rights are modified to the detriment of foreign nationals.[10] The EC has also shown that the interpretation of TRIPS national treatment is a complex question, which cannot simply be resolved by transposing the jurisprudence under Article III:4 GATT to the TRIPS Agreement.[11]

17. In their response, the complainants make very little effort to interpret the specific terms of Article 3.1 TRIPS Agreement. Rather, the United States repeats its argument according to which "there is a close connection between geographical indications, geographic regions, and the persons established in those regions".[12] The EC is unsure what exactly the United States means by "close connection", and what is the relevance of this "close connection" for the purposes of TRIPS national treatment.

18. Whatever the precise meaning the US attaches to these terms, it seems to the EC that with the same justification it could be argued that there is a "close connection" between the place where any product is produced and the persons who produce it. However, the EC does not think that this can mean that any person producing a product must therefore necessarily have the nationality of the place where the product is produced. Otherwise, any discrimination on the basis of the origin of a product would also be discrimination on the basis of nationality.

19. In its response, the United States has attempted to dismiss the examples of foreign involvement by characterizing them as examples of "EC nationals with some non-EC connections". This response misses the point of the EC's examples. First, the EC's examples show clearly that Regulation 2081/92 contains no legal obstacle to foreign nationals taking advantage of EC geographical indications. Second, that they may do so, "as a practical matter" and for reasons unrelated to Regulation 2081/92, by setting up a legal entity under EC law or by acquiring such an entity, does not show that Regulation 2081/92 involves discrimination on the basis of nationality. Finally, the EC finds it misleading to characterize

[9] US Response to Panel's Question No. 102, para. 12.
[10] EC Response to Panel's Question No. 113, para. 63.
[11] EC Response to Panel's Question No. 103, para. 27.
[12] US Response to Panel's Question No. 103, para. 16 (3).

cases where a US multinational acquires 100% of an EC producer of protected products as a case of an EC national with "some non-EC connections".

20. As regards the relevance of Article XX GATT, the complainants argue that this provision is not applicable in the context of the TRIPS Agreement, and that the non-inclusion of a similar provision in the TRIPS Agreement is deliberate.[13] However, the complainants fail to acknowledge that the limitation of TRIPS national treatment to *nationals* is equally deliberate. Moreover, the fact that the TRIPS Agreement contains not provision corresponding to Article XX GATT must be seen before the background that the TRIPS Agreement, and TRIPS national treatment in particular, is concerned primarily with nationals, not with the treatment of goods. The complainant's expansive interpretation of TRIPS national treatment has the effect of rendering ineffective defenses which would otherwise be available under Article XX GATT. The EC considers such an interpretation incompatible with the principles of a harmonious interpretation of the WTO Agreements.

Question 104

21. In its response to Question No 104, the United States persists in arguing that the EC is a "separate customs territory" within the meaning of footnote 1 to Article 1.3 of the TRIPS Agreement.

22. In support of its argument, the US is referring to Article XII:1 of the WTO Agreement, according to which "any State or separate customs territory possessing full autonomy in the conduct of its external commercial relations" may accede to this Agreement. In the submission of the United States, this provision proves that there are two categories of WTO Members, namely States and separate customs territories; therefore, in the view of the United States, since the EC is not a State, it must be a separate customs territory.[14]

23. This view is incorrect. Article XII:1 WTO Agreement does not apply to the EC. Rather, as the United States notes itself, the EC became an Original Member of the WTO under Article XI:1 WTO Agreement, which provides for the Membership of the "contracting parties to the GATT 1947 [...] and the European Communities".[15] In other words, the WTO Agreement refers to the EC neither as a state *nor* as a separate customs territory, but instead refers to it individually as a specific case.

24. The US has attempted to explain this drafting by arguing that "the EC could be identified by name as the sole original WTO Member that was not a GATT contracting party".[16] However, the US fails to explain why such a specific reference to the EC was then not made in footnote 1 to Article 1.3 of the TRIPS Agreement, if indeed the intention had been that this footnote should apply to the EC.

---

[13] US Response to Panel's Question No. 103, para. 18; Australia's Response to Panel's Question No. 103, paras. 13-14.

[14] US Response to Panels' Question No. 104, paras. 24-27.

[15] US Response to Panel's Question No. 104, para. 28.

[16] EC Response to Panel's Question No. 104, para. 28.

25. In fact, it is noted that there are also other provisions which refer specifically to the EC. For instance, Article IX:1 WTO Agreement defines the voting rights of the European Communities. This shows that where a specific provision was necessary to take account of the specific nature of the EC, a specific provision was included. The fact that no such provision concerning the EC was included in the TRIPS Agreement means that the general provisions applicable to all Members should apply to the EC.

26. It should also be noted that the US interpretation would deprive the word "separate" in the expression "separate customs territory" of its useful purpose. As the US has acknowledged, "separateness" is an intrinsic feature of a "customs territory".[17] However, by arguing that the EC is a "separate customs territory Member of the WTO", the US is effectively removing the word "separate" from the definition in footnote 1. In fact, if the US interpretation were correct, the United States, Australia, or in fact all other WTO would also have to be considered a "separate customs territory Member of the WTO".

27. The US has also argued that footnote 1 should apply to the EC because the EC "has no nationals".[18] As the EC has already explained in response to Panel's Question No. 105, this is patently wrong. Moreover, as the EC has also explained, the fact that the definition of nationality for legal persons is a complex question does not mean that the EC "has no nationals". In this context, it is also useful to refer to Brownlie's International Law, which fully confirms the EC's view:[19]

> The attribution of legal persons (personnes morales) to a particular state for the purpose of applying a rule of domestic or international law is commonly based upon the concept of nationality. The borrowing of a concept developed in relation to individuals as awkward in some respects but is now well established. *A major point of distinction is the absence of legislative provisions in municipal law systems which create a national status for corporations*: domestic nationality laws do not concern themselves with corporations. The consequences of this are twofold. First, *the nationality must be derived either from the fact of incorporation*, i.e. creation as a legal person, within the given system of domestic law, *or from various links including the centre of administration (siège social) and the national basis of ownership and control*. Secondly, *the content of the nationality tends to depend on the context of the particular rule of law involved*: nationality appears more as a functional attribution or tracing and less as a formal and general status of the kind relating to individuals.

28. The US has also referred to the drafting history of the TRIPS Agreement. In particular, the United States has noted that an earlier version of footnote one

---

17 US Response to Panel's Question No. 104, para. 23.

18 US Response to Panel's Question No. 104, para. 33.

19 Ian Brownlie, *Principles of Public International Law*, 5th edition (1998), p. 425–426 (Exhibit EC-112). Emphases added.

referred specifically to Hong Kong.[20] This footnote, which was contained in the Brussels draft of the TRIPS Agreement, read as follows:[21]

> When the term "national" is used in this Agreement, it shall be deemed, in the case of Hong Kong, to mean persons, natural or legal, who are domiciled or who have a real and effective industrial or commercial establishment in Hong Kong.

29. The only significant different between this version and the final version of footnote 1 is that the reference to "Hong Kong" has been replaced by a reference to a "separate customs territory Member of the WTO". In other words, the specific reference to Hong Kong was replaced by a generic reference to the category of Member to which Hong Kong belongs. The drafting history therefore confirms the EC's submission that footnote 1 was intended to cover cases of territories such as for instance Hong Kong or Macao, but not the EC.

30. In addition, the US also refers to an "Informal Note by the Secretariat" dated 7 December 1992. Unfortunately, the US does not provide a copy of this "Informal Note", which is not available to the EC, as an Exhibit. Accordingly, the EC cannot comment on the US arguments in this respect. The EC requests the United States to provide a copy of the informal note to the Panel and the other Parties. Moreover, the EC should be given an occasion to comment on the note once it has been provided by the United States. As long as the EC has not had an occasion to comment, the Panel should not take into account the arguments made by the US in respect of the informal note of 7 December 1992.

31. Australia, for its part, has referred to the fact that competence for the matters covered by the TRIPS Agreement is shared between the EC and its Member States, and has argued that for this reason, "there may be occasions in relation to matters covered by the TRIPS Agreement when the customs territories of its Member States may be distinct from the customs territory of the EC itself".[22] This is entirely wrong. The fact that competence for matters falling under the TRIPS Agreement is shared between the EC and its Member States is due to the fact that the TRIPS Agreement also concerns the harmonisation of intellectual property law.[23] The fact that certain areas of intellectual property law may not be harmonised within the EC has nothing to do with the customs territory of the EC. The EC has exclusive competence for trade in goods, and it has only one customs territory; this also applies for the purposes of the TRIPS Agreement.[24]

---

[20] US Response to Panel's Question No. 104, para 34.

[21] Cf. Daniel Gervais, *The TRIPS Agreement: Drafting History and Analysis*, 2nd edition (2003), para. 2.15.

[22] Australia's Response to Panel's Question No. 104, para. 16.

[23] See Opinion 1/94, *Accession to the WTO*, [1994] ECR I-5389, para. 58 (Exhibit Aus-13).

[24] This is confirmed in Opinion 1/94, *Accession to the WTO*, [1994] ECR I-5389, para. 55 (Exhibit Aus-13), where the Court of Justice confirmed that the provisions of the TRIPS Agreement on the enforcement of intellectual property rights at the border, which are carried out by the customs authorities, fall under exclusive Community competence for the commercial policy.

Question 108

32. The EC fails to see the relevance of the discussion of the ECJ's case law concerning Article 13(1) of Regulation 2081/92 included in Australia's response to this question, given that Australia confirms that it is not making any claim under GATT Article III:4 to the effect that Article 13(1) provides less favourable treatment to imported products.[25]

33. In view of the above, the EC does not consider it necessary to address all the errors made in Australia's response. The EC would like, nevertheless, to correct Australia's mistaken reading of the findings of the ECJ in the Case C-66/00, *Dante Bigi*[26] (which Australia calls the "Parmesan judgement").

34. Australia says that the use of the word "parmesan" is banned in the EC "on the basis that the ECJ found 'it is far from clear that the designation 'Parmesan' has become generic'" in that case.[27] This is incorrect. The question whether the term "parmesan" is generic was not before the ECJ and was not decided in that case. The Italian court had raised a number of questions regarding the interpretation of Regulation 2081/92, but not the question whether "parmesan" was a generic term. The German Government, which intervened as a third party, raised the preliminary objection that the reference was not admissible because the questions put by the Italian court were not relevant, given that in any event "parmesan" was a generic term which could not be protected under Regulation 2081/92.

35. The ECJ first recalled that, in principle, it is for the national courts to decide whether the reference to the ECJ is necessary:[28]

> It is settled case-law that, in the context of the cooperation between the Court of Justice and the national courts established by Article 234 EC, it is solely for the national court before which the dispute has been brought, and which must assume responsibility for the subsequent judicial decision, to determine in the light of the particular circumstances of the case both the need for a preliminary ruling in order to enable it to deliver judgment and the relevance of the questions which it submits to the Court. Consequently, where the questions submitted by the national court concern the interpretation of Community law, the Court of Justice is, in principle, bound to give a ruling (see, for example, Case C-415/93 Bosman [1995] ECR I-4921, paragraph 59).

36. The ECJ then went on to recall that, in exceptional cases, the ECJ may refuse to rule on a question referred by a national court where it is obvious that the question is unrelated to the dispute before that court:[29]

---

[25] Australia's Response to Panel's Question No. 18, para. 27.

[26] Exhibit AUS-16.

[27] Australia's Response to Panel's Question No. 18, para. 26.

[28] Exhibit AUS-16, para. 18.

[29] Exhibit AUS-16, para. 19.

> However, the Court has also stated that, in exceptional circumstances, it can examine the conditions in which the case was referred to it by the national court, in order to assess whether it has jurisdiction. The Court may refuse to rule on a question referred for a preliminary ruling by a national court only where it is quite obvious that the interpretation of Community law that is sought bears no relation to the actual facts of the main action or its purpose, where the problem is hypothetical, or where the Court does not have before it the factual or legal material necessary to give a useful answer to the questions submitted to it (see, for example, Case C-390/99 Canal Satélite Digital [2002] I-607, paragraph 19).

37. The German Government had argued that the questions raised by the Italian court were irrelevant because "parmesan" was in any event generic, with the consequence that Regulation 2081/92 was inapplicable. The ECJ, nevertheless, concluded that it was far from clear that "parmesan" was generic and, therefore, the questions raised by the Italian court were not so obviously irrelevant as to be inadmissible:[30]

> However, in the present case it is far from clear that the designation parmesan has become generic. It is contended by all the governments which have submitted written observations in this case, apart from the German Government and, to a certain extent, the Austrian Government, and by the Commission that the French designation parmesan is the correct translation of the PDO Parmigiano Reggiano.
>
> Against that background it cannot be argued that it is clear that the questions raised by the referring court are covered by one of the situations listed in the case-law cited at paragraph 19 of this judgment. It follows that the reference for a preliminary ruling is admissible.

38. In sum, in the *Dante Bigi* Case, the ECJ was not asked to rule, and did not rule, on the question whether the term "parmesan" is generic. The ECJ considered that question only in order to resolve a preliminary procedural objection to the effect that *other* questions raised by the Italian court were obviously irrelevant and inadmissible.

39. As noted by Australia[31], the EC Commission is of the view that "parmesan" is not a generic term. Germany, however, takes a different view. For that reason, the EC Commission has brought infringement proceedings under Article 226 of the EC Treaty against Germany. It will be for the ECJ, in the context of those proceedings, to decide whether or not "parmesan" is a generic term. The EC fails to see what is so intrinsically objectionable about the fact that the application of Article 13(1) of Regulation 2081/92 to a particular set of facts

---

[30] Exhibit AUS-16, paras. 20-21.

[31] Australia's Response to Panel's Question No. 108, para. 21.

may give rise to doubts and that different interested parties may take different views, with the consequence that it is necessary for the courts to resolve the disagreement. Or is it that in Australia the federal government and the states never disagree about the interpretation of federal law?

40. Contrary to what Australia says at paragraph 23, Article 13(1) of Regulation 2081/92 does not prejudge the question of whether "the owner of a registered trademark would be able to prevent confusingly similar or identical use of a sign for similar or identical goods". Australia confuses two different issues: the scope of the *negative* right of the holders of a registered geographical indication to prevent certain uses, which is defined in Article 13(1), and the scope of the *positive* right to use a registered geographical indication, which is circumscribed to the registered sign (see below the comments to Australia's response to Question 137).

41. Australia concludes this response by saying that:

> the uncertainties created by the practical operation of Article 13.1 of Regulation No. 2081/92 and its application in situations involving generic terms partially inform Australia's claims concerning Articles 22.2 and Paris Articles 10*bis*(1) and 10*ter*(1) in respect of the registration of an EC-defined GI. Australia has not been able to identify any means within the EC's legal order why which a legitimately interested person –whether natural or legal, or a national of the EC or of another WTO Member – is assured of access to a court empowered to consider substantively an act of unfair competition contrary to honest practices in industrial or commercial matters, including in international trade, in respect of the registration of an EC-defined GI.

42. The EC would note, first of all, that the above passage appears to contradict Australia's response to Question No. 161, where Australia explains that the "EC measure" is inconsistent with Paris Article 10*bis*(1), because it "diminishes the legal protection of trademarks". The EC fails to see the connection between Australia's concerns about the use of generic terms and the protection of trademarks.

43. Second, the EC has provided a thorough rebuttal to Australia's suggestion to the effect that the registration of a name which is not generic in the EC but may be generic in "international trade" may be an "act of unfair competition".[32] Australia has not responded to the EC's arguments. Instead, at the second meeting with the Panel, Australia denied that it was making such a claim [33]

> Australia has not said that registration of a term as an EC-defined GI in territory A could be deemed misleading simply because the term has become generic in territory B

44. Australia then reformulated its claim as follows:[34]

---

[32] EC SWS, paras. 381-393.
[33] Australia's SOS, para. 82.
[34] Australia's SOS, para. 85.

> What is clear, however, is that the EC has an obligation to provide the legal means by which interested parties can seek to test such issues in relation to the registration of an EC-defined GI.

45. This amounts to saying that a Member may not adopt any legislation or regulations that specify which types of uses may or may not be deemed an "act of unfair competition", but instead must leave *exclusively* to the courts to define what constitutes an "act of unfair competition". The EC disagrees with that proposition, which is manifestly contrary to the fundamental principle enshrined in the last sentence of Article 1.1 TRIPS. Article 22.2 does not impose an obligation to provide means to "test" any conceivable allegations of "unfair competition", no matter how frivolous. Rather, Article 22.2 requires to provide the means to prevent uses that constitute genuine "acts of unfair competition". If a use is not an "act of unfair competition", there is no obligation to provide any means to prevent it. Accordingly, in order to establish a violation of Article 22.2, the plaintiff must establish, first, that a certain type of use would constitute an "act of unfair competition" within the meaning of Paris Article 10*bis*(1) and, second, that the respondent does not provide the necessary means to prevent that type of uses.

46. Finally, the EC has clarified repeatedly that, in any event, Regulation 2081/92 does not exclude the application of the Directives on labelling and misleading advertising and of the laws on unfair competition of the Member States with respect to the use of registered geographical indications. Australia seems to concede that those Directives and laws are sufficient to comply with TRIPS Article 22.2 and Paris Articles 10*bis*(1) and 10*ter*(1) with respect to the use of non-registered geographical indications. At the very least, Australia has submitted no argument or evidence to the effect that the provisions of those Directives and laws in question are not sufficient *per se* to comply with those provisions. Since, contrary to Australia's mistaken assumption, the same Directives and laws apply also with respect to the use of registered geographical indications, Australia's concerns are unfounded. Yet, apparently, Australia takes the view that, in respect of registered geographical indications, the EC should replace those Directives and laws by an EC Regulation. However, there is no obligation under the TRIPS Agreement to provide the required protection at any given territorial level. Australia's claims represent an unfounded and unacceptable attempt to interfere with the constitutional allocation of powers between the EC and its Member States.

Question 112

47. The EC notes that in its response to the Panel's Question, the United States appears to argue that Article 12(3) contains a legal obligation towards the third country concerned.[35] As the EC has explained in its response, this is not the

[35] US Response to Panel's Question No. 112, para. 45.

case.[36] The EC notes that its view is shared by Australia, which offers an interpretation contrary to that of the United States.[37]

Question 120

48. In its response to the Panel's Question No. 120, the United States argues that the requirement to indicate the country of origin for homonymous geographical indications "is not simply a labelling cost issue", but that the labelling requirement "is in the nature of a qualifier that detracts from the value of the GI", implying that the foreign GI "is something other than a 'true' GI".[38]

49. At the outset, the EC notes that these arguments of the United States are contradictory with those of Australia, which has clearly stated that it does not allege that Article 12(2) of Regulation 2081/92 entails less favourable treatment other than with regard to labelling costs.[39]

50. In addition, the US response is without any basis in Regulation 2081/92. Article 12(2) of the Regulation requires simply that in the case of two homonymous names from the EC and from a third country, the country of origin be indicated for the name which is registered later. As the EC has already explained, the objective of this rule is to inform the consumer about the true origin of the product concerned.[40] In the case of two homonymous geographical indications, this is an entirely legitimate policy objective. The truthful indication of the country of origin does not in any way detract from the value of the geographical indication, nor is there any implication in the requirement of Article 12(2) that the geographical indication to which the requirement is applied is somehow "of a different stature" or "something other than a true GI".

51. Finally, the US is also incorrect to argue "the EC-based GI will be known purely by that GI, while the non-EC product's homonymous GI will be qualified by a country of origin".[41] As the EC has already explained repeatedly, the labelling requirement of Article 12(2) will apply to whichever of the names is registered later, regardless of whether this is the EC or the foreign name.[42]

Question 123

52. In its response to Question No. 123, the United States persists in its argument that Article 12(2) of Regulation 2081/92 is "not a general country of origin marking requirement", but is "above and beyond any other general country of origin marking requirement that may apply to all agricultural products and foodstuffs".[43]

---

36 EC Response to Panel's Question No. 112, para. 61.
37 Australia's Response to Panel's Question No. 112, para. 33 – 34.
38 US Response to Panel's Question No. 120, para. 47.
39 Australia's Response to Panel's Question No. 52.
40 See EC Response to Panel's Question No. 54, para. 126.
41 US Response to Panel's Question No. 120, para. 47.
42 See most recently EC SOS, para. 145.
43 US Response to Panel's Question No. 123, para. 48.

53. As the EC has already explained in its responses, there is simply no basis for arguing that Article IX GATT applies only to "general" origin marking requirements, but not to an origin marking requirement such as the one contained in Article 12(2).[44]

54. The full absurdity of the US argument becomes apparent when considering once again the United States' own practice as regards origin marking. Under US law, "every article of foreign origin [...] imported into the United States shall be marked in a conspicuous place as legibly, indelibly, and permanently as the nature of the article will permit in such manner as to indicated to an ultimate purchaser in the United States the English name of the country of origin of the article".[45]

55. It is fair to say that this origin marking requirement of the United States for imported products is, if anything, more restrictive and burdensome than the EC requirement contained in Article 12(2) of Regulation 2081/92. The fact that the United States, like Australia, applies this discriminatory country of origin marking to *all* products rather then just to some can hardly be a mitigating factor. It seems therefore that if the United States were right, and Article 12(2) constituted a violation of national treatment obligations, then the origin marking requirements of the United States and Australia are also in violation of national treatment obligations.

56. The United States has also claimed that the EC has not argued that "any existing origin marking requirements in the EC" would meet the requirement of Article 12(2) of Regulation 2081/92.[46] This argument is besides the point. Since the EC does not have country of origin marking requirements, requirements "in the EC" are obviously not relevant. However, as the EC has already said, it is very well possible that marks of origin affixed pursuant to the requirements of other countries, such as the United States, might fulfil the requirements of Article 12(2) of the Regulation.[47]

57. In any event, the main point of the EC is that the United States has for many years, presumably because it considered that national treatment obligations do not apply to country of origin marking requirements, applied discriminatory marking requirements. The US claim is therefore in stark contrast with the United States' own practice, and the Panel should not disregard this fact in evaluating the US claim.

58. In addition, the EC would also draw the attention of the Panel to the logical conclusion of the United States argument: if really Article IX:1 GATT covered only "general", but not product-specific marking requirements, the EC could easily remedy any eventual finding of a violation by introducing a general

---

[44] EC Response to Panel's Question No. 124, para. 98.

[45] 19 US 1304 (a) (Exhibit EC-113). Exhibit EC-66, which the EC provided earlier, contains only an indirect reference to this provision; for ease of reference of the Panel, the EC also provides the immediate source.

[46] US Response to Panel's Question No. 122, para. 47; US Response to Panel's Question No. 123, para. 48.

[47] EC Response to Panel's Question No. 120, para. 87.

origin marking requirement similar to the one of the United States and Australia. In other words, Article IX:1 GATT would encourage the adoption of more rather than less restrictive requirements. This is hardly an interpretation in line with the objectives of the GATT.

Question 124

59. In its Response to Question No. 124, the United States argues that the US claim "does not present the systemic questions posed in the Panel's question". As the EC has just explained, this US view is based on a highly artificial and self-serving interpretation of Article IX:1 GATT. Accordingly, the United States' attempts to isolate its claim regarding Article 12(2) of Regulation 2081/92 from the general question of origin marking must fail.

60. In addition, the United States argues that the requirement of Article 12(2) to indicate the country of origin "is all the more confusing since geographical indications by their very nature concern indicating the particular geographical origin of products". The truthful indication of the country of origin gives the consumer more information, rather than less. The EC does therefore not see how the truthful indication of the country of origin, in which the geographical area is located, could be confusing for the consumer. Moreover, if the US arguments were correct, then the application of the US country or origin marking requirements to EC products bearing a name protected under Regulation 2081/92 would equally have to be regarded as confusing for the consumer, and as detracting from the value of the geographical indication.

Question 128

61. In their responses to the Panel's Question No. 128, both the United States and Australia fail to explain why they consider the requirement of government involvement in the approval of inspection structures problematic. Since they have no satisfactory answer to this question, they instead choose to mischaracterise the requirements of Regulation 2081/92 by arguing that the Regulation imposes "a requirement on sovereign WTO Members to put in place certain inspection structures dictated by the EC",[48] or involves the "imposition of EC-mandate inspection structures on other WTO Members".[49]

62. As the EC has already explained a number of times, the requirement of inspection structures is applied and evaluated purely with respect to the specific product for which protection is sought.[50] Accordingly, contrary to the arguments of the United States and Australia, it is not "equivalence by another name". Regulation 2081/92 does not concern the question of how the complainants protect geographical indications within their own territory, and in particular whether they require the existence of inspection structures for this purpose or not. The objective of the Regulation is purely to ensure that in order to be

[48] US Response to Panel's Question No. 128, para. 53.

[49] Australia's Response to Panel's Question No. 128, para. 51.

[50] EC SOS, para. 54 et seq.; EC SWS, para. 96 et seq.

protected in the EC, geographical indications from third countries fulfil the same conditions as geographical indications from the EC.

63. As the EC has explained, since the inspection bodies will be located on the territory of the country of origin of the geographical indication, an involvement of the home country of the geographical indication is indispensable for the designation and continued monitoring of such inspection structures.[51] As the EC has also said, this possibility to have inspection bodies approved by their home country should in fact constitute an advantage rather than a disadvantage for applicants and producers from the US or Australia.[52]

64. In its response, the United States is contesting this argument by claiming that the EC "does not allow the United States to make its own determination as to the sufficiency of the inspection structures".[53] This is misleading. Article 12a (2) (b) of Regulation 2081/92 requires a declaration by the country of origin "that the structures provided for in Article 10 are established on its territory". Obviously, the Community institution responsible for deciding on an application for protection under Regulation 2081/92 must make sure that all the requirements of the Regulation are met. However, as the EC has already said, in doing so, the Community institutions will have to rely to a considerable extent on the information provided by the country of origin.[54] Contrary to the US' suggestion, the declaration of the country of origin is therefore of considerable importance, and will be given due weight by the Community institutions in the registration process.

Question 130

65. The EC notes that in their responses, the US and Australia fail to identify any aspect of the requirement of inspection structures beyond the involvement of their governments that they consider objectionable.[55] Accordingly, the EC understands that the claims of the United States and Australia are therefore now limited to the requirement of government involvement in the designation of inspection structures.

Question 137

US Response

66. The United States complains that it "does not have access to the product specifications for any of the GIs cited by the Panel". This complaint is unwarranted.[56] The specifications of any registered geographical indication,

---

[51] EC Response to Panel's Question No. 136, para. 146.

[52] EC Response to Panel's Question No. 131, para. 114.

[53] US Response to Panel's Question No. 128, para. 57.

[54] EC Response to Panel's Question No. 114, para. 69.

[55] US Response to Panel's Question No. 130, para. 62; Australia's Response to Panel's Question No. 130, para. 53.

[56] US Response to Panel's Question No. 137, para 65.

including those mentioned in the question, can be obtained upon request from the EC Commission or from the competent authorities of the Member States.

67. With respect to the argument made at paragraph 67, the terms used by the EC are "not very qualified". The EC used those terms in order to make clear that whether a "used" sign is the same or different from the sign covered by the registration can only be decided on a case-by-case basis. The EC does not see how the complainants could disagree with this.

68. With respect to the issue of translations[57], the EC has explained repeatedly that the registration confers a positive right to use the registered name, to the exclusion of any other sign. A "translation" is not necessarily a different sign, something which appears to be overlooked by the United States. For example, the translation of the name "Gorgonzola" into Spanish, English and French is in all cases "Gorgonzola". For that reason, it would be not be correct to say that the registered term cannot be used in "translation". Moreover, in some cases a registration may cover different linguistic versions (e.g. "Cítricos Valencianos" and "Citrics Valencians").[58] For those reasons, the relevant issue is not whether the registration allows the use of a name "in translation", but rather whether it gives a positive right to use a different sign, a question which has been answered by the EC in an unequivocal manner.

69. As explained by the EC in its response to Questions 2 and 3 from Australia, the assertion made by the United States in footnote 38 is based on a misunderstanding of the relevant EC law.

70. At paragraph 69 the United States asserts that:

> Under Article 16.1, rather than seeking rejection or cancellation of a GI registration on an EC wide basis, the owner of an identical or similar valid trademark registered in the EC is entitled to prevent particular "uses" of the GI that confuse consumers in that state.

71. The EC submits that, in accordance with the last sentence of Article 1.1 TRIPS, it is for each Member to decide whether or not the sign should be invalidated first. As explained by the EC[59], in many Members the owner of a registered trademark cannot be prevented from using it, even where it results in a likelihood of confusion with an earlier trademark, unless the registration is invalidated first. The interpretation advanced by the United States would imply that the trademark laws of all those Members are inconsistent with Article 16.1 TRIPS.

72. At paragraph 70, the United States refers to a decision of a South African court, according to which the use of the trademark "Budějovické Budvar" would give rise to a likelihood of confusion with the trademarks "Budweiser" and "Bud". In the first place, the EC recalls, once again, that the registration of the names "Budějovické pivo", "Českobudějovické pivo" and "Budějovický

57 US Response to Panel's Question No. 137, para. 68.
58 See EC Response to Panel's Question No. 140, para. 176.
59 See EC Response to Panel's Question No. 138, para. 170.

měšťanský" is not before this Panel[60], as well as the fact that such registration is unique in that it is the only registration under Regulation 2081/92 which is subject to the proviso that it applies "without prejudice to any beer trademark or other rights existing in the Eureopean Union as of the date of accession". Moreover, the names "Budějovické Budvar" and "Bud" are not among the names registered under Regulation 2081/92. In any event, as stressed by the United States elsewhere, a determination of likelihood of confusion must take account of "the consumers' perception in a given territory".[61]

73. The United States also refers[62] to a decision of an Italian court enjoining a Czech producer of beer from using the names "Bud" and "Budweiser" because they give rise to a likelihood of confusion with the trademarks "Budweiser" and "Bud". However, once again, the names "Bud" and "Budweiser" are not among those registered under Regulation 2081/92.

74. Moreover, the EC understands that the decision of the South African court was adopted in response to an application for the registration of a trademark by the Czech producer and not in the context of infringement proceedings involving two registered trademarks. Therefore, it is totally irrelevant in connection with the issue raised in the Panel's question, which is whether a validly registered sign which is not confusing *per se* may, nevertheless, be used subsequently in a confusing manner. Similarly, the EC understands that the Italian case involves the infringement of a registered trademark by a non-registered trademark and is, therefore, irrelevant for the same reasons.

75. Finally, the EC would note the United States is misleadingly selective when citing examples of "likelihood of confusion" involving the trademarks "Bud" and "Budweiser". The Panel should be aware that the courts of other countries, including, for example, Australia and New Zealand, have found that there was no likelihood of confusion between the names which it cites in its response.[63]

Australia's Response

76. Australia says that[64]

> Even within the Member States where the trademarks "Bavaria", "Hoker Bajer" and "Budweiser" are registered, the protection afforded by Regulation No. 2081 – in particular Article 13.1 – makes clear that the owner of a registered trademark would not be able to prevent confusingly similar or identical use of a sign or identical goods …

---

60 EC FWS, paras. 21-25.
61 US Response to Panel's Question No. 137, para. 64.
62 US Response to Panel's Question No. 137, para. 70.
63 See Exhibit EC-114 and Exhibit EC-115.
64 Australia's Response to Panel's Question No. 137, para. 59.

77. Australia is confusing two different issues. Article 13(1) of Regulation 2081/92 defines the scope of the *negative* right of the right holders of a registered geographical indication to prevent certain uses, including as trademarks. It does not prejudice the answer to the distinct and previous question of whether the registration of a geographical indication must be refused in accordance with Article 14(3). Nor does it prejudge the answer to the distinct question of what is the scope of the *positive* right to use a geographical indication[65], and more specifically of whether that right includes the right to use a geographical indication in a manner that is contrary to the labelling Directive and the laws on unfair competition.

78. Australia also says that:[66]

> Even where those trademarks are not registered in other EC Member States, each could still enjoy a reputation in the territories of those other States –particularly in adjoining States- which the EC-defined GI right holders could exploit through confusingly similar use of translations of the EC-defined GIs. The EC has not explained how, in such situations, the owners of those trademarks would be assured of the rights of a registered trademark owner to initiate infringement action, or of the standing to initiate legal action under other legal provisions, such as labelling, misleading advertising or unfair competition laws.

79. The relevance of this argument in the context of Australia's claims is unclear to the EC. As emphasised by Australia throughout these proceedings, trademark rights are territorial. The registration of a trademark in Member State A confers no exclusive rights in Member State B, just like the registration of a trademark in the United States confers no exclusive rights in Australia (subject to what is provided in Article 16.2 TRIPS, which Australia has not invoked in this dispute). Indeed, it is precisely for that reason that the EC institutions adopted the Regulation creating the Community Trademark.

80. On the other hand, the EC can confirm, once again, that there is nothing that prevents the owner of a trademark registered in Member State A from bringing an action in Member State B against the use of a geographical indication in a manner which is contrary to the Directive on labelling or to the unfair competition laws of Member State B, even if the trademark concerned is not registered in Member State B.

Question 145

81. The EC notes that the responses of the United States and Australia are contradictory and irreconcilable. While the United States persists in the mistaken theory that Article 24.5 is an "exception" to Articles 22 and 23[67], Australia

---

[65] By the same token, the fact that a registered trademark confers the *negative* right to prevent the use of confusingly similar signs does not mean that the owner of the trademark has a *positive* right to use the confusingly similar signs himself.

[66] Australia's Response to Panel's Question No. 137, para. 59.

[67] US Response to Panel's Question No. 145, para. 72.

agrees with the EC that Article 24.5 is not a "mere exception"[68] and that it creates "positive rights".[69] Further, Australia agrees with the EC that Article 24.5 "defines the boundary between a Member's right to implement measures relating to TRIPS-defined GIs and its obligation to afford protection to pre-existing trademarks".[70] Nevertheless, Australia, fails to draw the appropriate conclusion from this.

82. If, as Australia and the EC agree, Article 24.5 is not an "exception" but rather defines the "boundary" between the right to implement protection for geographical indications and the obligation to protect grandfathered trademarks, it would follow that a Member which acts consistently with its rights and obligations under Article 24.5 could not violate Article 16.1. Yet, both Australia and the United States have made a point of not raising any claim, even in the alternative, to the effect that Article 14(2) of Regulation 2081/92 is inconsistent with Article 24.5. Their claims concerning the issue of co-existence are based on Article 16.1 exclusively.

83. The EC, therefore, submits that, if the Panel agrees with the definition of the relationship between Articles 24.5 and Article 16.1 put forward by Australia and the EC, it should reject the complainants' claim under Article 16.1 with respect to the issue of co-existence, without it being necessary for the Panel to consider whether Article 14(2) of Regulation 2081/92 is inconsistent with Article 24.5, given that the complainants have not submitted any claim to that effect.

84. The United States takes advantage of the response to this question in order to elaborate upon its interpretation of the phrase "shall not prejudice ... the validity of the registration".[71] As explained by the EC, the United States fails to distinguish between the "validity" of the registration and the exercise of the rights conferred by the registration. Moreover, the US interpretation would render duplicative and superfluous the reference to "the right to use a trademark". That right is the most fundamental right of the owner of any trademark, whether or not it is registered. If the drafters of Article 24.5 specified that the measures to implement protection of geographical indications shall not prejudice the right to use a trademark, but not the right to exclude others from using the trademark, it is because they did not intend to limit the Members' right to do so. The US interpretation reads an obligation to preserve the right to exclude others, where Article 24.5 provides none.

85. Furthermore, the US interpretation is clearly contradicted by the Spanish and the French versions of Article 24.5, which read as follows:[72]

> Cuando una marca de fábrica o de comercio haya sido solicitada o registrada de buena fe, o cuando los derechos a una marca de

---

[68] Australia's Response to Panel's Question No. 145, para. 61.

[69] *Ibid.*

[70] *Ibid.*

[71] US Response to Panel's Question No. 145, para. 74.

[72] Emphases added.

fábrica o de comercio se hayan adquirido mediante su uso de buena fe:

a) antes de la fecha de aplicación de estas disposiciones en ese Miembro, según lo establecido en la Parte VI; o

b) antes de que la indicación geográfica estuviera protegida en su país de origen;

las medidas adoptadas para aplicar esta Sección no **prejuzgarán** la posibilidad de registro ni la validez del registro de una marca de fábrica o de comercio, ni el derecho a hacer uso de dicha marca, por el motivo de que ésta es idéntica o similar a una indicación geográfica.

Dans les cas où une marque de fabrique ou de commerce a été déposée ou enregistrée de bonne foi, ou dans les cas où les droits à une marque de fabrique ou de commerce ont été acquis par un usage de bonne foi:

a) avant la date d'application des présentes dispositions dans ce Membre telle qu'elle est définie dans la Partie VI, ou

b) avant que l'indication géographique ne soit protégée dans son pays d'origine,

les mesures adoptées pour mettre en oeuvre la présente section ne **préjugeront** pas la recevabilité ou la validité de l'enregistrement d'une marque de fabrique ou de commerce, ou le droit de faire usage d'une marque de fabrique ou de commerce, au motif que cette marque est identique ou similaire à une indication géographique.

86. The Spanish term "prejuzgarán" and the French term "préjugeront" do not have the ordinary meaning which the United States attributes to the English word "prejudice", i.e. to cause "injury, damage, harm".[73] The dictionary definition of "prejuzgar"is "juzgar de las cosas antes del tiempo oportuno, o sin tener de ellas cabal conocimiento". [74]

87. In turn, the dictionary definition of "préjuger"[75] is

I. 1. *Vx ou littér.* porter un jugement prématuré sur (qqch.). *Je ne veux point préjuger la question.* – Prévoir au moyen des indices dont on dispose. *Autant qu'on peut le préjuger; a ce qu'on peut préjuger.* 2 *Dr.* prendre un décision provisoire sur (qqch.) en laissant prévoir le jugement définitif.

88. The above definitions are similar to one of the ordinary meanings of the English term "prejudice", which is to "judge beforehand".[76]

---

73 US Response to Panel's Question No. 76, para. 99.

74 Diccionario de la Real Academia Española, 20th Edition, 1984.

75 Le Nouveau Petit Robert, 1993.

76 The New Shorter Oxford English Dictionary, Ed. Lesley Brown, Clarendon Press, Oxford 1993.

89. Article 24.5 may be contrasted with other provisions of the TRIPS Agreement, such as Articles 13, 16.1, 26.2 or 30 where the English term "prejudice" has been rendered as "perjuicio" in the Spanish version and as "préjudice" in the French one. Unlike the terms "prejuzgar" and "préjuger" those terms mean "harm, injury, damage". This difference confirms that the terms "prejuzgarán" and "préjugeront" were chosen deliberately in order to convey a different meaning from that which the United States attributes to the English term "prejudice".

90. The French and the Spanish versions of Article 24.5 make it clear that, contrary to the US view, the phrase "shall not prejudice ... the validity of the registration" does not mean that a Member is prevented from taking any measure that may affect negatively the exercise of the rights conferred by the registration. Instead, it means that Members cannot invalidate the trademark merely on the basis that it is identical or similar to a geographical indication, *without prejudice* to the possibility to invalidate it on other grounds, such as that the trademark is not distinctive or is deemed misleading for other reasons. By the same token, the phrase "shall not prejudice ... the right to use the trademark" means that Members may not deny the right to use a trademark on the basis that it is the same or similar as a geographical indication, without prejudice to the possibility to do so on other grounds (e.g. because it would result in a likelihood of confusion with an earlier trademark).

Question 148

91. The United States persists in obfuscating unnecessarily the discussion by confusing two issues which are clearly distinct under the TRIPS Agreement and under the trademark laws of both the United States and the EC.

92. The fact that Article 16.3 TRIPS and the anti-dilution provisions of the EC Trademark Directive and the Community Trademark Regulation afford additional protection to trademarks which enjoy reputation does not mean that reputation is irrelevant in order to establish a likelihood of confusion between signs for similar goods. The EC has shown that this is an uncontroversial proposition under both EC law and US law.[77]

93. The United States mischaracterizes the EC position. The EC has not said that a finding of likelihood of confusion for the purposes of Article 16.1 TRIPS requires *always* a finding that the earlier trademark enjoys reputation, regardless of the inherent "strength" (distinctiveness) of the trademark. Rather the EC has noted the following:

- first, terms which are, or which may reasonably qualify, as geographical indications for a certain product are "descriptive" terms and, hence, primarily "non-distinctive". As such, they may be validly registered only to the extent that they have acquired distinctiveness (secondary meaning).

---

[77] EC SOS, paras. 166-169.

- second, the "strength" or degree of distinctiveness of a trademark (whether inherent or acquired) is a relevant criterion for assessing the "likelihood of confusion";
- third, length of use, reputation and renown are the basic criteria for measuring the degree of acquired distinctiveness of a trademark. Therefore, those criteria are particularly relevant when assessing the likelihood of confusion with trademarks which are primarily non-distinctive because they consist of descriptive terms, such as a geographical indication.

94. For the above reasons, Article 14(3) of Regulation 2081/92 directs expressly the authorities to consider length of use, reputation and renown. But this does not mean that other criteria are irrelevant. Nor that the criteria mentioned in Article 14(3) are necessarily dispositive. As explained by the EC[78], if Article 14(3) does not mention the similarity of signs and goods is because such criteria are necessarily relevant for any determination of likelihood of confusion. Indeed, as also explained by the EC[79], the criteria mentioned in Article 14(3) could not be meaningfully applied without taken into account the similarity of goods and signs.

95. For the above reasons, the decisions of the OHIM, of the ECJ and of Member State courts cited by the United States[80] are irrelevant. Indeed, as far as the EC can see, none of them concerns a situation involving a situation which can be considered as similar to that addressed by Article 14(3) of Regulation 2081/92, i.e. a situation requiring the assessment of the likelihood of confusion between a geographical indication or another descriptive sign and a registered trademark which consists of such sign.

Question 149

96. The EC notes that the United States appears to concede[81] that Article 22.2 TRIPS is not relevant for the interpretation of Article 14(3) of Regulation 2081/92, given that Article 14(3) does not purport to implement that provision, but instead Article 16.1 TRIPS.

97. The United States, nevertheless, goes on to argue that:[82]

> The word "mislead" appears to be used throughout the EC GI Regulation in the sense of affirmatively leading the public to believe something about the product that this is not true …

98. Similarly, Australia contends that:[83]

> the word "misleading" is used throughout the Regulation – in Articles 3.2, 6.6, 13.1(c), 13.1(d) and 14.3 – in the sense of an

78 EC Response to Panel's Question No. 68.
79 *Ibid.*
80 US Response to Panel's Question No. 148, para. 98.
81 US Response to Panel's Question No. 149, para. 102.
82 Australia's Response to Panel's Question No. 149, para. 104.
83 Australia's Response to Panel's Question No. 149, para. 77.

action which positively provokes an error on the part of the consumer.

99. However, neither Australia nor the United States explain what they mean by "positively" or "affirmatively", respectively. Nor do they explain how the text of the provisions which they cite support that conclusion.

100. Both Australia and the United States contend that the French version of the provisions which they cite would confirm their reading. But they limit themselves to copy the text of those provisions, without explaining how it supports their interpretation.[84] As explained by the EC[85], one of the ordinary meanings of the Spanish term "error", and of its equivalents in other romance languages (e.g. "erreur", "errore") is "confusión" ("confusion", "confusione"). The complainants do not address this argument.

101. The complainants' assertions fall short of a proper contextual interpretation. They limit themselves to note the obvious fact that different terms are used in different provisions, but make not attempt to read them in a coherent manner.

102. As explained by the EC, Article 14(3) of Regulation 2081/912 must be read together with Articles 7(4) and 7(5)(b)[86]. Article 7(4) allows trademark owners to object to the registration of a proposed name *inter alia* on the grounds that the registration would give rise to the situation described in Article 14(3). Article 7(5)(b) then provides that the authorities must resolve that objection having regard to the "likelihood of confusion". It would give rise to an internal contradiction within the Regulation if the standard for deciding an objection under Article 7(5)(b) were different from and more rigorous than the standard of Article 14(3).

103. Additional guidance is provided by Article 13(1)(d), which provides that registered names shall be protected against "any other practice liable to mislead the public as to the true origin of the product". The term "other" implies that the practices previously described in letters a) b) and c) are also "liable to mislead". Yet, those letters do not provide for a more rigorous standard than that of "likelihood of confusion" within the meaning of Article 16.1 TRIPS, but rather the opposite.

Question 150

104. In answering this question the United States concedes that the exceptions provided in Article 6.1(b) of the Trademark Directive and Article 12(b) of the Community Trademark Directive are consistent with Article 17 TRIPS. Indeed, the United States could hardly contest this given that many other Members have similar exceptions in their statute books.[87]

---

84 US Response to Panel's Question No. 149, para. 104 and Australia's Response to Panel's Question No. 149, para. 78.

85 EC SOS, para. 162.

86 See also the equivalent provisions in Articles 12b(3), 12d(2) and 12d(3).

87 See EC Response to Panel's Question No. 153, para. 240.

105. Yet, as explained by the EC[88], the requirement to use a registered geographical indication in accordance with the Directives on labelling and misleading advertising and with the laws on unfair competition is equivalent to the condition that they must be used "in accordance with honest practices in industrial or commercial matters".

106. Thus, in definitive, what the United States appears to consider objectionable is the mere fact that the limitations on the use of a registered geographical indication are not provided in the EC's trademarks laws but instead in different legal instruments. However, neither Article 16.1 TRIPS nor any other provision of the TRIPS Agreement contains any requirement to that effect. To the contrary, Article 1.1 provides that "Members shall be free to determine the appropriate method of implementing the provisions of this Agreement within their own legal system and practice".

Question 151

107. The United States says that it agrees with the proposition made in the question that "Article 24.3 is an exception to Part II, Section 3".[89]

108. The EC does not read the suggestion made in the question as meaning that Article 24.3 is an "exception", but rather the opposite. As the EC understands it, the suggestion made in the question is that the obligation provided in Article 24.3 applies only with respect to the "exceptions" provided in *other* paragraphs of Article 24. If Article 24.3 were also an "exception", it could not impose upon Members the obligation not to rely upon those exceptions as a justification for diminishing pre-existing protection.

Question 154

109. The EC takes issue with the US suggestion[90] that the "legitimate interests" of consumers are necessarily the same as those of the trademark owner. Consumers, and in particular the EC consumers of foodstuffs, are often more interested in being informed about the origin of the products, and the characteristics associated thereto, than about the identity of the undertaking which is the source of the goods, in particular where that undertaking has no special reputation.[91]

110. In this connection, it is important to recall that, even if the complainants' narrow interpretation of Article 14(3) of Regulation 2081/92 were correct, that

---

88 EC Response to Panel's Question No. 153, paras. 242-244.

89 US Response to Panel's Question No. 151, para. 108.

90 US Response to Panel's Question 154, paras. 113 and 119.

91 While US consumers may not be as familiar yet with geographical indications, there is a growing awareness. For example, as explained by the EC, the State of California has enacted legislation which prohibits the use of *any* trademark including or consisting of a recognised geographical indication for wine, including earlier trademarks grandfathered by Article 25.4, and regardless of whether they are subject to invalidation as being misleading. This statute, which has been recently upheld by California's Supreme Court (Exhibit EC-81) purports to protect not only the interests of the wine makers concerned but also those of the Californian consumers. This suggests that the State of California does not agree with the views expressed by the USTR in this dispute.

provision would prevent the registration of a geographical indication where it leads to confusion with a trademark that has been used for a certain period of time and enjoys some reputation or renown. Thus, on the complainants' own interpretation of Article 14(3), Article 14(2) would provide for the co-existence of geographical indications only with trademarks that have been used for a short period of time and/or enjoy little reputation/renown, if at all.

111. Both complainants attempt to read into the conditions of Article 17 a narrow "necessity" test, whereby the use of indications of origin would be permitted only to the extent strictly necessary to inform consumers about the origin of the products.[92]

112. This interpretation is not supported by the text of Article 17. All that is required by Article 17 is that the exception be "limited" and that the interests of the trademark owner and of third parties be "taken into account". Reading the condition that the exception must be "limited" as imposing a strict "necessity" test would pre-empt the balancing of interests provided in the second condition of Article 17. In turn, the condition to "take account of the legitimate interests of the trademark owner and third parties" does not establish any hierarchy between the relevant interests and affords a margin of discretion to Members in order to find a proper balance between them.

113. Moreover, the "necessity" test advanced by the complainants would render irrelevant the exception provided in Article 17 with respect to the fair use of descriptive terms. The holders of a geographical indication have a legitimate interest in informing consumers about the origin of their products, and the characteristics associated thereto, in a manner which can be easily recognised by the public. One could, of course, argue that all that is "necessary" in order to inform consumers that a product is of a certain geographical indication is to mention it in small print at the bottom of a back label, somewhere between the ingredients list and the expiry date. That use, however, would not give rise to a "likelihood of confusion" and would not need to be justified under Article 17. The exception provided in Article 17 with respect to the "fair use" of descriptive terms only becomes necessary to extent that geographical indications are used in what the United States calls misleadingly "trademark-like" fashion.

114. Finally, as shown by the EC, the "necessity" test devised by the complainants cannot be reconciled with the terms of the exceptions clauses included in the trademark laws of a large number of Members, which do not require that the use be "necessary", but instead that it be "in good faith", or in accordance with "honest", "fair" or "proper" business or trade practices.[93]

115. By way of conclusion, the Unites States asserts that:[94]

> Under the EC's interpretation of TRIPS Article 17, all uses of a registered GI are automatically entitled to the "fair use" exception,

[92] See e.g. US Response to Panel's Question No. 154, paras 119-120; Australia's Response to Panel's Question No. 154, para. 84.

[93] EC Response to Panel's Question No. 153, para. 240.

[94] EC Response to Panel's Question No. 154, para. 120.

> no matter what the facts of particular case at hand (i.e. whether the use is fair, the term is descriptive, or the legitimate interests of the trademark owner are considered) by simple virtue of registration alone.

116. This is a gross mischaracterization of the EC's position:

- first, the EC does not claim an exception with respect to terms that are not "descriptive". The EC argues that geographical indications, like all other indications of source, are *per se* descriptive terms;
- second, the EC has explained that the interests of the trademark owners are taken into account in several ways.[95] The United States does not address the EC's arguments in its response.
- third, the EC has explained that registered geographical indications must be used in accordance with the requirements of the Directives on labelling and misleading advertising and the laws on unfair competition. This reduces the likelihood of confusion and ensures that the use of the geographical indications is "fair".[96] Again, the US does not address this argument in its response.

Question 155

117. The EC agrees with both complainants that "trademarks are not merely descriptive and cannot be considered 'descriptive terms' within the meaning of Article 17."[97]

118. As pointed out by Australia[98], the reason why trademarks are not "descriptive" is that, in accordance with Article 15.1 TRIPS, they must be "distinctive", i.e. they must be capable of distinguishing the products of *one* undertaking from those of other undertakings. A "descriptive" term is inherently not "distinctive" and, therefore, incapable of being a trademark. A geographical term (except where it is fanciful because it cannot be reasonably associated to the products concerned) is primarily descriptive of the origin of the products and, hence, non-distinctive. For that reason, geographical terms are generally not registrable as trademarks, unless they have acquired distinctiveness through use.

119. Having explained correctly that trademarks are not "descriptive" terms because they must be "distinctive" within the meaning of Article 15.1 TRIPS, Australia goes on to assert that[99]

> In the same way, and for the same reasons, use of a GI cannot be said to be merely use of an indication of source within the meaning of the Paris Convention or to be use of a descriptive term within the meaning of TRIPS Article 17.

---

95 EC Response to Panel's Question No. 154, para. 254.

96 See e.g. EC Response to Panel's Question No. 153, paras. 234-244.

97 See e.g. US Response to Panel's Question No. 155, para. 123; US Response to Panel's Question No. 156, para. 130; and Australia's Response to Panel's Question No. 155, para. 92.

98 Australia's Response to Panel's Question No. 155, para. 89.

99 Australia's Response to Panel's Question No. 155, para. 92.

120. This is incorrect. The analysis made by Australia with respect to trademarks cannot be extrapolated to geographical indications. Australia disregards that there is a fundamental difference between trademarks and geographical indications. Unlike trademarks, geographical indications are not "distinctive" within the meaning of Article 15.1, because they do not serve to distinguish the products of *one* undertaking from those of other undertakings. Rather, the purpose of a geographical indication is to identify the geographical area in which a product originates, where certain characteristics are associated to that origin, regardless of the undertaking which produces or markets that product.

121. Australia is also wrong when it says that geographical indications are not indications of source within the meaning of the Paris Convention.[100] Geographical indications are a subset of indications of source. The name "Australia" is always an indication of source, regardless of whether it may qualify as well as a geographical indication with respect to certain products, as claimed by Australia outside these proceedings. Commenting upon Article 1(2) of the Paris Convention, Bodenhausen says that[101]

> Appellations of origin are now considered to be a *species* of the *genus* 'indications of source', characterized by their relationship with quality or characteristics derived from the source.

122. Geographical indications differ from simple indications of source in that, in addition to describing the origin of the products, they describe certain product characteristics that are attributable to that origin. But this does not make them "distinctive" within the meaning of Article 15.1.

123. Australia also says that "if geographical indications were purely descriptive there would not be any need –or indeed any basis- for an intellectual property right".[102] The EC does not understand this argument, which appears to be based on the erroneous notion that intellectual property rights must necessarily be owned by individuals. As explained, descriptive terms cannot be the subject of trademark rights because trademarks must be "distinctive". On the other hand, there is no reason why a descriptive term cannot be the subject of other intellectual property rights owned collectively by all the producers of goods conforming to the relevant description. Indeed, Article 1(2) of the Paris Convention provides expressly that "the protection of industrial property has as its object", among other things, "indications of source", which Australia does not dispute are "purely descriptive".

124. Finally, even if geographical indications were not "descriptive terms" within the meaning of Article 17, the complainants have not given any good reason why fair use of a geographical indication should not qualify for an exception under Article 17. The exception provided in Article 17 with respect to the fair use of descriptive terms is just an example. The potential universe of uses

---

[100] Australia's Response to Panel's Question No. 157, para. 92.

[101] G.H.C. Bodenhausen, *Guide to the Application of the Paris Convention for the Protection of Industrial Property*, BIRPI Geneva 1968, p. 23.

[102] Australia's Response to Panel's Question No. 157.

of an indication of source is not more "limited" than that of a geographical indication. And the interest in using a geographical indication is no less "legitimate" than the interest in using an indication of source. Nor is there any reason why the use of a geographical indication should be more confusing *per se* or more prejudicial to the interests of the trademark owner. Australia has said that it is "reasonable and fair for people to be able to say ... 'made in Australia'".[103] The EC agrees. The EC would add, however, that it is reasonable and fair for people to be able to say that their products are made in Australia, irrespective of whether "Australia" is an indication of source or a geographical indication for the goods concerned (as Australia claims with respect to wine, for example). It would be absurd if only the producers of goods originating in an area which qualifies as a geographical indication were prevented from indicating the origin of their goods.

Question 156

125. The United States makes a remarkable argument to the effect that the exception provided in Article 17 is narrower than the exceptions in Articles 13, 26.3 and 30 because it is subject to *less* conditions.

126. Even more remarkable is the US argument to the effect that the "take account" standard of Article 17 is in fact more protective of the interests of the right holder than the "unreasonably prejudice" standard of Articles 13, 26.3 and 30, even though Articles 26.3 and 30 distinguish expressly between the two standards and reserve the "take account" standard for the interests of third parties.

127. In essence, the United States argues that Article 17 does not include the "normal exploitation" and the "unreasonable prejudice" conditions because any limitation of the exclusive rights of the trademark owner would necessarily fail to meet those conditions.[104] However, from the fact that Article 17 does not include those conditions it cannot be inferred that it purports to provide even stricter standards which are not reflected in the wording of the text. Rather, the logical inference is that the drafters mean to provide for more lenient standards.

128. The United States confuses the "legitimate interests" of the trademark owner with the full enjoyment of its legal rights, despite the clear distinction drawn by the Panel in *Canada – Pharmaceutical Patents*.[105]

129. Moreover, even where legal rights rather than legitimate interests are taken into account, the co-existence of a trademark with another trademark or with a geographical indication is far from being so "abnormal" or "unreasonable" as the United States pretends. It is envisaged by several provisions of Sections 2 and 3 of Part III, even where it may lead to some confusion. For example:

- Article 16.1 provides for the co-existence of registered trademarks with existing prior rights;

---

[103] Australia's Response to Panel's Question No. 154, para. 86.
[104] US Response to Panel's Question No. 156, para. 130.
[105] Panel Report, *Canada – Pharmaceutical Patents*, paras. 7-68-7.69.

- Article 23.2 allows co-existence of a geographical indication for wines or spirits and a trademark consisting or including such geographical indication if used for wines and spirits originating in the area to which the geographical indication relates. *A priori*, the risk that consumers may confuse that geographical indication with the trademark may be the same as when the products covered by the trademark do not originate in that area. Nevertheless, co-existence is allowed because it does not mislead consumers as to the true geographical origin of the products;
- co-existence may arise as well from Article 24.3, when the protection of geographical indications existing before the date of entry into force of the WTO Agreement provided for such co-existence;
- co-existence is envisaged also by Article 24.4, which provides that a Member may allow "continued and similar" use of a geographical indication[106] for wines or spirits of another Member by its nationals or domiciliaries who have used it before 1 April 1994 in good faith or for at least 10 years preceding that date, regardless of whether this gives rise to confusion with the products of the other Member that are entitled to use that geographical indication.

130. Finally, there is nothing in the TRIPS Agreement that prevents Members from providing for the co-existence of non-registered trademarks and other trademarks, including latter registered trademarks, or geographical indications. In particular, as conceded by Australia, Article 24.5 allows co-existence with respect to non-registered grandfathered trademarks even on the complainants' reading of that provision.

Question 157

131. Contrary to the US assertions,[107] it is simply not true that the EC has left "unspecified" the other measures which it applies in order to comply with Article 22.2 TRIPS, in addition to Regulation 2081/92. The EC mentioned those measures in its first written submission.[108] Furthermore, the EC referred the Panel and the other parties to the responses of the EC and of its Member States to the review under Article 24.2 TRIPS, where those measures were further specified and explained. The EC has provided as Exhibit EC-22 copies of those responses, which must therefore be deemed part of the EC's submissions to the Panel.

132. The EC noted in its first written submission that the complainants were well aware of the existence of those other measures, as well as of the EC's position that those measures implement its obligations under Article 22.2. The

[106] The EC recalls that the United States has argued that Article 24.4 applies also with respect to the use of geographical indications as trademarks, including trademarks which are not grandfathered by virtue of Article 24.5.

[107] US Response to Panel's Question No. 157, para. 134.

[108] See EC FWS, para. 434.

complainants have not denied this. Yet, neither of them mentioned those measures in their panel requests. Furthermore, even after the EC confirmed in the course of these proceedings that, as explained in its responses to the review under Article 24.2 TRIPS, it applies other measures in order to implement Article 22.2, the United States and Australia failed to submit any argument or evidence in order to show that, contrary to what is explained in the responses, those measures are not sufficient to comply with Article 22.2.

133. The US suggestion[109] that the EC declined to provide information requested by the Panel is also untrue. At the first meeting with the Panel, the EC confirmed its willingness to provide any information requested by the Panel. The EC, nevertheless, pointed out that in makings its requests for information the Panel should be careful not to shift the burden on proof from the complainants to the EC. This was a legitimate concern which the EC believes the Panel has properly taken into account in formulating its questions to the parties.

[109] US Response to Panel's Question No. 157, para. 134.

ANNEX B-10

COMMENTS OF THE EUROPEAN COMMUNITIES ON THE REPLY OF THE INTERNATIONAL BUREAU OF WIPO TO THE PANEL'S LETTER OF 9 JULY 2004

(28 September 2004)

The EC is referring to your letter of 14 September 2004, in which you are requesting comments on the factual information provided by the International Bureau of WIPO.

The EC notes that in its letter to WIPO, the Panel requested information in particular as regards the meaning of the term "national" in Article 2 of the Paris Convention.

In the view of the EC, the drafting materials of the Paris Convention provided by the International Bureau of WIPO confirm the view which the EC has expressed throughout the proceedings, namely that the word "national" is a distinct term which cannot be equated with persons "domiciled or established" in the territory of a particular member.[1]

In particular, the EC notes that until the Act of the Hague, 1925, Article 2 of the Paris Convention referred to "subjects or citizens", instead of nationals. The terms "subject or citizen" clearly refer to a specific status conferred on persons under the law of the State in question. The terms "subjects or citizens" were subsequently replaced by the single expression "nationals" (French: ressortissants) for reasons of simplification.[2] There was clearly no intention to enlarge the meaning of "nationals" to all persons domiciled or established in the territory of a party.

The same is also demonstrated by the drafting history of Article 3 of the Paris Convention. In the Materials of the Paris Conference of 1880, it is clarified " que la Convention sera applicable, *non pas à tous les étrangers*, sans distinction, mais à ceux qui seraient domiciliés ou établis dans l'un des Etats de l'Union ". It follows clearly from this that a person which does not possess the nationality of a Member is not a "national" of that Member only because it is domiciled or established on the territory of the Member.

---

[1] Cf. EC Second Oral Statement, paras. 20–21.

[2] Cf. for instance the discussions in the Actes de la conférence de Paris de 1880, neuvième séance, p. 125.

Accordingly, the drafting history of Articles 2 and 3 of the Paris Convention illustrate that contrary to the views of the complainants, "nationality" is a different concept from domicile or establishment. In the view of the EC, the same also applies for the similarly worded provision of Article 3(1) of the TRIPS Agreement.

The EC would like to thank the Panel for this occasion to comment on the information provided by WIPO.

ANNEX C

ARGUMENTS OF THE THIRD PARTIES

TABLE OF CONTENTS

Page

1. This Annex reflects the arguments made by third parties. It has been prepared by the Panel based on the written submissions, oral statements and responses to questions received from the third parties.

A. Argentina

1. Introduction

2. Argentina has a general systemic interest in the proper implementation and interpretation by WTO Members of the rights provided for in the TRIPS Agreement. However, as a major agro-exporter, Argentina also has a specific interest in the proper implementation of multilateral rules, to ensure that they are not implemented in such a way as to constitute or become obstacles to food trade. Firstly, Argentina wishes to make it quite clear that it does not object to the European Communities having, nor does it consider that the European Communities does not have, a legitimate right to develop or maintain a unified geographical indication registration and protection system in its territory. Neither does Argentina question the system chosen by the European Communities to establish such protection, given that the TRIPS Agreement itself authorizes Members to implement the Agreement within their own legal system and practice. Nonetheless, Argentina does agree with the complainants' comments on the importance of Members providing protection, in accordance with the TRIPS

Agreement, for both trademarks and geographical indications, without either one being to the detriment of the other.

2. *The EC Regulation in the light of the TRIPS Agreement*

(a) The concept of a geographical indication

3. The definition given in Article 2 of the EC Regulation differs from that established in Article 22 of the TRIPS Agreement. Article 2(1) of the EC Regulation protects designations of origin and geographical indications of agricultural products and foodstuffs. Article 2(2) establishes two concepts for ensuring such protection, namely, "designations of origin" and "geographical indications". Argentina believes that there is a substantial difference between the definition laid down in Article 22 of the TRIPS Agreement and that established in Article 2.2(a) and (b) of the EC Regulation, namely the requirement that production and/or processing and/or preparation take place in the defined geographical area. Additionally, the EC Regulation in turn includes in Article 2(3) a sub-classification pursuant to which "[c]ertain traditional geographical or non-geographical names designating an agricultural product or a foodstuff originating in a region or a specific place, which fulfil the conditions referred to in the second indent of paragraph 2(a) shall also be considered as designations of origin." In this regard, Argentina draws attention to the fact that, in the case of "traditional names", the EC Regulation affords the possibility of protection being granted to non-geographical names, in stark contrast to the practice of WTO Members and the spirit of the TRIPS Agreement. This tendency of the European Communities to provide for protection other than that envisaged by the TRIPS Agreement is reinforced by Article 2(4) of the EC Regulation, according to which, under certain circumstances, certain geographical designations shall be treated as designations of origin where the raw materials of the products concerned come from a geographical area larger than or different from the processing area.

4. Argentina points out that, under Article 2(2) of the EC Regulation, protection is extended by allowing a degree of independence in the concept of a geographical indication from a geographical area (Article 2(3)), and by including certain raw materials from a geographical area larger than or different from the processing area, subject to three restrictions (Article 2(4)). Argentina is of the opinion that this is inconsistent with Article 22 of the TRIPS Agreement.

(b) Coexistence of protection systems

5. One protection system may not prevail at the expense of or to the detriment of the other, given that this would create a conflict of predominance between Sections 2 (Trademarks) and 3 (Geographical indications), both of which are found in Part II of the TRIPS Agreement. However, the obligations set out in these two sections are not mutually exclusive: each category must be granted the degree of protection conferred by the provisions of the Agreement. In other words, Members must ensure that protection is afforded both to

trademarks, under Article 16.1, and to geographical indications, under Article 22.2, without, in so doing, undermining in any way the protection granted under the other Article. By providing for the coexistence of a trademark with a geographical indication or designation of origin and making such coexistence conditional upon a given temporal relationship, the EC Regulation violates Article 16.1 of the TRIPS Agreement (which provides for the exclusive right to use a trademark, so the possibility of coexistence restricts the right of the owner of the trademark), Article 22.3 (which neither provides for coexistence, nor establishes a specific cut-off date, as is the case of the EC Regulation), and Article 24.4 (which provides for a critical time different from the cut-off date established in the Regulation).

6. Article 24.5, in addition to establishing a different cut-off date from that laid down in the Regulation, prejudices eligibility for and the validity of the registration of a trademark, and the right to use a trademark, on the basis that such a trademark is identical with, or similar to a geographical indication. Moreover, Article 24.5 does not provide for the possibility of restricting the right of a trademark owner, as is the case in the Regulation, which provides for coexistence. Strictly speaking, it is Article 24.5 which determines the confines of the alternatives available to WTO Members with regard to the application of measures related to the protection of geographical indications and their interrelation with trademarks.

(c) The registration procedure is inconsistent with the TRIPS Agreement

7. Argentina considers it important that particular reference be made to the registration procedure established in the Regulation in the light of the obligations laid down in the TRIPS Agreement. To this end, there follows an objective description of each of the various steps involved, together with comments on their inconsistency with the TRIPS Agreement, as deemed appropriate.

(i) Application for registration / Compliance with specifications

8. Article 4 of the Regulation provides that "to be eligible to use" a protected designation of origin (PDO) or a protected geographical indication (PGI), an agricultural product or foodstuff must "*comply with a specification*". In this respect, the Regulation gives rise to great uncertainty, given that, while it sets forth a series of nine elements – Article 4.2(a), (b), (c), (d), (e), (f), (g), (h) and (i) – with which compliance is mandatory, it is precisely subparagraph (i) which allows for the possibility of other requirements being "*laid down by Community and/or national provisions*". Such uncertainty is related to the familiarity with or identification of the relevant Community and/or national provisions in order to comply with the registration requirement, and the means for complying with the requirement laid down in subparagraph (i), bearing in mind the above-mentioned difficulty in identifying pertinent legislation. Knowledge of Community and/or national legislation is obviously even more complicated for a foreign applicant.

9. Furthermore, by mentioning "Community and/or national provisions" without stating whether this refers to regulations specifically related to the protection of geographical indications, the said provision expands yet further the legislative universe with which a potential applicant must comply and could act as a market-access restriction on a product applying for effective protection by means of a PGI / PDO. That is to say that, while the requirements of subparagraphs (a) to (h) are binding upon applicants, this does not mean that the list of requirements is exhaustive, given that, by virtue of subparagraph (i), it can be extended by means of a series of conditions which can be provided for in Community and/or national legislation and compliance with which is also – in principle – mandatory. It should be recalled at this point that, pursuant to Article 12 of the Regulation, the third country shall be able to give guarantees identical or equivalent to those referred to in Article 4, extending it to the requirement laid down in Article 10.

10. Argentina also makes a further comment on requirements relating to Article 4(h), which refers to the inspection structure(s) provided for in Article 10. The question here is what the criteria for identifying these inspection structures would be in the case of a foreign applicant. It should be noted that, for a foreign applicant and with regard to this stage, Article 12 provides that "the third country concerned has inspection arrangements (...) equivalent to those laid down in this Regulation." This creates an obstacle which is altogether immune to any decision by a foreign natural or legal person to "accept" the Article 4 requirement, given that the decision to create the inspection bodies referred to in Article 10 is restricted to State level. Provision is not made for inspection structures in all third countries and, even supposing that they were provided for, such structures could fail to meet the equivalence requirement under Articles 10 and 12 of the Regulation.

(ii) Application for registration at the national level (of a member State) / Transitional protection at the national level

11. Pursuant to Article 5(4) of the Regulation, applications shall be sent to the member State in which the geographical area is located. The member State is then responsible for checking that the application is "justified" and, "if it considers that it satisfies the requirements of this Regulation", it forwards the application, including the product specification and other documents on which it has based its decision, to the Commission. That member State may then grant transitional protection at the national level. Such protection ceases when protection is granted at Community level. Furthermore, it is incumbent on the member State to consult another member State or a third country if the application concerns a name designating a border geographical area or a traditional name connected to that area, regardless of whether it is situated in another member State or in a third country.

(iii) Role of the Commission / Examination of applications / Publication of applications/Objections

12. At this stage, it falls to the Commission to conduct, within a period of six months, a formal investigation to verify whether the registration application includes all the particulars provided for in Article 4. The Commission shall inform the member State of its findings and publish the registration applications and their filing dates. The purpose of publication is to permit the notification of statements of objection. Three possibilities exist, (a) No statement of objections is notified and the name is entered in the Register of Protected Designations of Origin and Protected Geographical Indications, as published in the Official Journal of the European Communities; (b) there are objections to the registration – Article 7 – within six months of the date of publication in the Official Journal of the European Communities; and (c) the Commission concludes that the geographical indication does not qualify for protection and decides not to proceed with publication. The Commission may in all cases request the opinion of the Committee on Designations of Origin and Geographical Indications – Article 15 – prior to publication.

(iv) Amendment of a specification

13. Article 9 authorizes any member State to request the amendment of a specification to take account of developments in scientific and technical knowledge or to redefine the geographical area.

(v) Failure to comply with specifications / Right of complaint / Intervention of the Commission / Cancellation of registration

14. Any member State may submit that a condition laid down in the product specification has not been met – pursuant to Article 11 – by making its submission to the member State concerned. The member State concerned shall examine the complaint and inform the other member State of its findings and of any measures taken. The Commission will have to intervene in the event of repeated irregularities. If the member States concerned fail to come to an agreement and file a duly substantiated application, the Commission will examine the application by consulting the member States concerned and, where appropriate, having consulted the specific committee and considering it pertinent, will take the necessary steps, including cancellation of the registration. Article 11*bis* establishes the cases in which the registration may be cancelled.

15. To sum up, Argentina emphasizes the uncertainty with regard to: (a) the possible implementation of these provisions in the case of non-Community countries, and (b) their consistency with the characterization of intellectual property rights in the TRIPS Agreement, by requiring that States manage the registration of geographical indications instead of their legitimate owners, persons under private law (not to mention what appears yet more serious: the covert subordination, established by the Regulation, of governments of non-

member states vis-à-vis EC institutions). Therefore, and contrary to the assertions of the European Communities, the EC Regulation does indeed make a distinction on the basis of nationality. Evidence for this are the provisions under Articles 5, 6, 7 and 10.

16. In short, the reciprocity and equivalence requirements laid down in Council Regulation (EEC) No. 2081/92 are inconsistent with the national treatment clause in Article 3 of the TRIPS Agreement.

(d) Applicability of equivalence and reciprocity criteria to WTO Members

17. Argentina observes the European Communities' attempt to reduce the entire issue raised by the complainants to a mere question of the interpretation of the relevant Community legislation. To this end, Argentina submits a brief interpretation to demonstrate that the Regulation provides for a method inconsistent with the European Communities' obligations in the WTO in the light of the TRIPS Agreement. In Argentina's opinion, the explanation by the European Communities in its first written submission of the application of reciprocity and equivalence criteria is not convincing. Had the intention been to make a distinction not only between EC member States and non-Community countries but also, as the European Communities maintains, between WTO Members and third countries, the distinction could have been made more explicitly. However, even a simple amendment to that effect would not resolve the substantive issues previously raised regarding the application of this regulation to non-Community countries, given that the only registration and objection procedures provided for are through the intermediary of member States and that the requirements are laid down for the establishment of inspection structures which are not binding on any country other than EC member States. The requirements mentioned above clearly deviate from the national treatment obligation in Article 3 of the TRIPS Agreement.

3. Points raised in response to the Panel's questions

18. Argentina is not aware of any group or person ever having filed with its authorities either an application for or an objection to a registration pursuant to the EC Regulation. As to the question whether Argentina would be willing or able to transmit such applications, without prejudice to its willingness to cooperate in any procedural aspect involving the transmission of an application for registration, on behalf of any domestic group or person, that eventually the Government of Argentina could hypothetically show at any point in time, Argentina would like the Panel to note that, as a non-EC member, it has never delegated any sovereign right to the supranational institutions of the European Union. Hence, there would be no legal obligation for the Argentine State to fulfil any requirement imposed by the EC legislation, even less in a case like the one in question, which involves a private right, as established in the preamble of the TRIPS Agreement. Argentina's legislation allows direct access by GI applicants to the national authority irrespective of nationality.

19. Argentina's domestic law establishes the exceptions to trademark rights provided for in Article 17 of the TRIPS Agreement, under the conditions and with the scope provided therein. Argentina is not aware of any GIs registered under the EC Regulation that are identical or confusingly similar to Community protected trademarks owned by nationals of Argentina. It notes, however, that this should not be interpreted as saying that this would never happen, as the EC Regulation provides for the possibility of broadening the applicability of the Regulation, by making products which are not currently included in the list of products covered by this Regulation, subject to it in the future.

20. Argentina believes that there is – in principle – no conflict between Articles 16.1 and 22.3 of TRIPS Agreement. However, given the broad discretion given by the TRIPS Agreement to the Members in implementing its provisions (Article 1.1 of the TRIPS Agreement), such a conflict could arise as a consequence of the way a Member chooses to implement it. In other words, there is no contradiction arising from the textual reading of either provision, but for those that could eventually arise during, or as a consequence of its implementation.

21. Argentina is of the view that the EC Regulation is challengeable under the TRIPS Agreement, due its mandatory nature.

B. Brazil

1. Introduction

22. Brazil has a systemic interest in the matter subject to this dispute. Brazil has no geographical indications ("GIs") as yet registered in the EC under the procedure set out in the measure at issue, but private parties in the country have demonstrated increasing awareness of the implications stemming from the development of a culture fostering the registration of Brazilian GIs, both in Brazil and elsewhere.

2. Reciprocity and equivalence requirements in the registration of, and objection to, a GI

23. Both Australia and the United States claim that Article 12(1) of the EC Regulation fails to comply with the national treatment obligation provided for by Article 3 of the TRIPS Agreement and Article III:4 of GATT 1994 since, in order to benefit from the Regulation, it requires that WTO Members meet certain conditions, such as reciprocity and equivalence. Brazil supports this understanding. In fact, the requirements set forth in Article 12(1) of the EC Regulation, despite assertions to the contrary by the European Communities, clearly establish "extra hurdles" for WTO Members. The several requirements spread throughout Article 12 create a bias against third countries and violate national treatment obligations. As a matter of fact, these inconsistent requirements pervade most of the Regulation and taint its practical operation to the detriment of other WTO Members. In a nutshell, and as abundantly argued by the complainants and other third parties, WTO Members, before they can

apply for protection under Article 12(1), must adopt an internal system for GI protection that guarantees equivalence to the EC Regulation and that must also provide reciprocity to "corresponding" EC products. These requirements, if they do not amount to something close to "extra-territoriality", certainly collide with the essence of the national treatment obligations enshrined in Article III of GATT 1994 and Article 3.1 of the TRIPS Agreement.

24. As graphically shown by New Zealand in the exhibits to its submission, nationals from WTO Members are at a disadvantage with regard to EC nationals. The GATT and WTO underlying principle of national treatment would be completely voided of any meaning if it were made conditional on requirements of reciprocity and adoption of equivalent legislation. The European Communities in its first submission argues that the proviso in Article 12(1) – "without prejudice to international agreements" – excludes WTO Members from the scope and requirements of Article 12. Brazil welcomes this novel and official interpretation by the European Communities to the effect that "international agreements" include the WTO agreements and that consequentially Articles 12(1) and 12(3) of the Regulation do not apply to WTO Members. Irrespective, however, of this interpretation by the Commission, which would not necessarily withstand scrutiny by a judicial body, it would seem unlikely that provisions in the EC Regulation that refer to "third countries" would have been drafted only with a handful of non-WTO Members in mind. Furthermore, the utilization of the terms "third countries" and "Community" in Article 12(2) suggests that, in this opposition, "third countries" mean all those countries which are not EC member States. If, on any account, one were to accept the EC's arguments about the proviso, i.e. that it excludes WTO Members, it could, *a contrario senso*, indicate a recognition by the European Communities that the reciprocity and equivalence requirements in Article 12 violate national treatment obligations in the GATT 1994 and TRIPS Agreement. Brazil takes note, however, of the use in the Regulation of the terms "WTO members" and "third countries" in Articles 12b(2)(a) and (b) and 12d(1), something that could indicate that third countries are confined to those non-WTO Members. Therefore, Brazil is of the view that the language of Article 12(1) should clearly specify that WTO Members are exempt from offering reciprocity and equivalence in order to be in compliance with the national treatment obligation.

25. As regards the issue of objection procedures to registration of GIs, Brazil is equally concerned with the fact that the procedures, set forth in Article 12d(1), can be subject to the same inconsistent requirements of reciprocity and equivalence applicable to the registration procedure as explained above.

3. Aspects of the registration and objection procedures for GIs

26. Brazil also calls the attention of the Panel to two specific procedural aspects of both the registration and the objection procedures as stated in Articles 12a(1) and (2) and 12d(1), which appear to be inconsistent with the agreed multilateral rules.

27. These provisions require that WTO Members "pre-approve" the application for registration of geographical areas located in their territories before they forward it to the European Commission. WTO Member national authorities must first analyse and deem that the requirements of the EC Regulation are satisfied. Brazil opines that, if this requirement applies to WTO Members, it is in striking violation of the national treatment obligation under Article 3 of the TRIPS Agreement and Article III:4 of GATT 1994. The inconsistencies appear to be twofold: first, that an additional national procedure is introduced, whereas in the EC, the application sent to an EC member State by an EC applicant is tantamount to a mere formality (Article 5(5) of the Regulation); second, and most disturbing, the analysis by the national authority in the WTO Member must be undertaken according to the EC Regulation, and not to its own domestic rules – Article 12a(2) of the Regulation. In this situation, assuming that the State concerned will likely have its own standards to assess the adequacy of the application *vis-à-vis* the EC Regulation, it is only fair to assume that more often than not, the Commission, in its turn, will not deem appropriate the evaluation carried out by the WTO Member, which could then lead to further procedural delays. Thus, a more balanced treatment of the issue would be to grant applicants from WTO Members direct access to the Commission for registration purposes. This direct access by the applicant to the national authority, irrespective of nationality, is provided, for example, by the Brazilian legislation. In sum, even if in formal terms the treatment given to applications from EC member States and WTO Members is similar, the effects that are produced by such procedure are clearly different and detrimental to interested parties located in the latter.

28. Article 12d(1) of Regulation 2081/92 requires that, whenever a natural or legal person from a WTO Member wishes to object to the registration of a geographical indication submitted by an EC member State, it should do so by sending a duly substantiated statement to the country in which it resides. Brazil is of the opinion that this requirement establishes an "unnecessarily complicated or costly" procedure concerning the enforcement of intellectual property rights, in breach of Article 41.2 of the TRIPS Agreement. Brazil sees no "necessity" that would justify preventing private parties from addressing their objections directly to the European Commission. Many countries, like Brazil, have domestic legislations that allow for direct access by foreigners in order to object to registration procedures. The EC has not provided convincing reasons to deny interested parties direct access to the EC bodies. If, according to its Article 12d(2), the Regulation already determines that the "Commission shall examine the admissibility of objections", Brazil fails to see the need for requiring prior submission of the objection to the WTO Member in which the objector resides or is established.

4. Remarks on the coexistence of trademarks and GIs

29. While Brazil recognizes that both trademarks and GIs are "signs" that represent products or services, one cannot overlook the fact that geographical

indications that are identical to trademarks are likely to create confusion and, consequently, may affect the value of trademarks. Brazil recalls that Article 16.1 of the TRIPS Agreement protects the owner of a registered trademark from the use by third parties of identical or similar signs for goods or services identical or similar to those in respect of which the trademark is registered, where such use would result in a likelihood of confusion. Therefore, what seems clear is that the protection the TRIPS Agreement mandates countries to offer to owners of trademark comprehends the use of any sign (and not only that of a trademark) that might cause confusion. In Brazil's view, Article 16.1 of the TRIPS Agreement deals with trademarks in general, and not only with those referred to in the narrow terms of Article 14(3) of the Regulation, which establishes that a geographical indication shall not be registered where, "in the light of a trademark's reputation and renown and the length of time it has been used, registration is liable to mislead the consumer as to the true identity of the product".

30. Despite a theoretical hypothesis of coexistence between a trademark and a geographical indication in terms of Articles 24.5 and 16.1 of the TRIPS Agreement, when read in conjunction, Brazil believes that without disregarding the peculiar features surrounding the use of a geographical indication and the need to protect it, one must not do so at the expense of both the trademark owners and the consumers. Otherwise, the commercial value of a trademark may be undermined, which runs contrary to the "exclusive rights" of a trademark owner provided for in Article 16.1 of the TRIPS Agreement. It should also be noted that pursuant to Article 16.1, in cases of the use of an identical sign for identical goods or services, "a likelihood of confusion shall be presumed". Regulation 2081/92 does not have any provision incorporating such a presumption. Brazil does not agree with the EC's argument that there was no need to "reproduce explicitly" this presumption, on the grounds that it would suffice that domestic law grants the registering authority or to the courts the adequate level of discretion to apply this provision. Brazil submits that even if domestic law incorporated the presumption in each EC member State, this would not mean automatically that Community-level registration, regulated by Regulation 2081/92, would have also provided for its incorporation. Therefore, the European measure would still remain inconsistent with the TRIPS Agreement.

31. Brazil also highlights another possible imbalance between the protection of EC nationals and WTO Member nationals as regards the effective use of the protection mechanism of Article 22.3 of the TRIPS Agreement in that, through the use of the EC Regulation, the EC national would much more rapidly and efficiently protect a GI to the detriment of a previous registered trademark, than would a WTO Member national be in a position to defend trademark owner rights *vis-à-vis* the application for registration of a new GI.

5. *Points raised in response to the Panel's questions*

32. Brazil is not aware of any group or person ever having filed with its authorities either an application for, or an objection to, a registration pursuant to the EC Regulation. As to the question whether Brazil would be willing or able to transmit such applications, it states that, the issue here is not simply a matter of mechanistic, bureaucratic "transmittal" of applications. Article 12a(2) of the EC Regulation requires from authorities of third countries a thorough analysis of the applications in light of that Regulation before transmitting them to the Commission. Brazil also recalls that there is no legal provision in Brazilian law establishing the need for Government intervention in the registration of GIs in foreign countries. Moreover, the Brazilian authorities would be devoid of legal competence to perform the analysis of the application as required by the EC Regulation, especially in light of the principle of legality, enshrined in Article 37 of the Brazilian Constitution.

33. Brazil calls the Panel's attention to the existence of the Patent Cooperation Treaty ("PCT"). This Agreement imposes that requests for international search and preliminary examination of private parties' patent applications be transmitted to the Office of the PCT by national governments. The European Communities, through Regulation 2081/92 – rather than through an internationally agreed mechanism – seeks to impose unilaterally its own rules and parameters on all other countries, something which would amount to extra-territoriality. Harmonization of rules or standards on intellectual property rights can only be obtained through multilateral or bilateral cooperation agreements. The European Communities' stance, if taken *ad absurdum*, could allow a situation where other countries would also issue their own strict legislation and procedures and would request that all other countries analyse applications for registration in accordance with those unilaterally-fixed rules.

34. Brazil understands that the interpretation of "nationals" as used in Articles 1.3 (including its footnote 1), 3.1 and 4 of the TRIPS Agreement and Article 2 of the Paris Convention, depends on how a national legal system defines the "nationality" of a legal person. Due to particular features pertaining to geographical indications – which are necessarily bound to a given territorial basis – it is reasonable to assume that the legal person holding the right over their use, will be a group or association established in the territory of the Member in which the GI is located, without prejudice to the provision of Article 2(2) of the Paris Convention. This is tantamount to saying that the geographical area from which a geographical indication originates determines the nationality of the interested parties seeking to register it and that the parties applying for registration of non-EC GIs will most likely be legal persons that are "nationals" of non-EC countries. The European Communities concedes that Regulation 2081/92 provides for different treatment regarding "geographical areas".[1] Thus, in most cases, discriminating between geographical areas is equivalent to discriminating between nationals. In other words, the area in which a

[1] European Communities' first written submission, para. 125.

geographical indication is located is actually linked to the nationality of the applicant.

35. Brazil agrees that the words "country of the Union" in Article 2(1) of the Paris Convention (1967), as incorporated in the TRIPS Agreement by its Article 2.1, should be read *mutatis mutandis* to refer to "WTO Member". This reasoning is in accordance with the understanding of the Appellate Body in *US – Section 211 Appropriations Act.*[2]

36. Brazil's views on the relationship between the national treatment obligation under the TRIPS Agreement and GATT 1994 are threefold. First, Brazil notes that on a theoretical level not all "different treatment" amounts to "less favourable treatment". Second, Brazil understands that a less-favourable-treatment-situation in violation to national treatment obligation arises where a measure "modifie[s] the conditions of competition in the market to the detriment of imported products", which appears to be the case with reference to the EC Regulation at issue. Third, as the Appellate Body stated in *US – Section 211 Appropriations Act*, "[t]he Panel was correct in concluding that, as the language of Article 3.1 of the TRIPS Agreement, in particular, is similar to that of Article III:4 of the GATT 1994, the jurisprudence on Article III:4 of the GATT 1994 may be useful in interpreting the national treatment obligation in the TRIPS Agreement".[3]

37. Brazil is not aware of any GIs registered under the EC Regulation that are identical or confusingly similar to Community protected trademarks owned by Brazilian nationals.

38. Brazils recalls that previous WTO panels and Appellate Body reports have considered that there is a presumption against conflict in public international law, and it quotes two panel reports in this regard.[4] If it can be assumed that there is a presumption against conflicts between international legal instruments, one can also reasonably expect that the same presumption applies to apparent conflicts within the same agreement. Therefore, in addressing the issue of the conflict between Articles 16.1 and 22.3 of the TRIPS Agreement, Brazil submits that Article 22.3 imposes two tests in order to allow a trademark registration to be refused or invalidated. In turn, Article 16.1 grants the trademark owner the exclusive right to prevent third parties from using identical or similar signs for goods or services which are identical or similar to those in respect of which the trademark is registered, where such use would result in a likelihood of confusion. The protection of the distinctiveness of the trademark is thus contingent upon the likelihood of confusion brought about by signs which are identical or similar. One should consider that, without disregarding the peculiar features surrounding the use of a geographical indication and the need to protect it, this must not be done at the expense of both the trademark owners and the consumers. In other words, it means that the approach to the issue should be

---

2 Appellate Body Report on *US – Section 211 Appropriations Act*, para. 238.

3 *Ibid.*, para. 242.

4 Panel Report on *Indonesia – Autos*, para. 14.28 and fn. 649; and Panel Report on *Turkey – Textiles*, para. 9.92.

carried out taking due account of the fact that: a) geographical indications do not *a priori* prevail over registered trademarks; and b) other factors must be borne in mind when deciding whether to allow either the coexistence between trademarks and geographical indications or the predominance of one over the other, such as, for instance, the length of time a given trademark has been used.

39. Brazil's Industrial Property Law (Article 132) sets out exceptions to the exclusive right of a trademark owner. Accordingly, a trademark owner cannot: (a) prohibit retailers or distributors from utilizing distinctive signs pertaining to their businesses along with a product trademark for marketing purposes; (b) prohibit parts manufacturers from utilizing a trademark in order to indicate the product destination, provided fair competition practices are met; and (c) prohibit the mentioning of a trademark in a speech, scientific or literary work or in whatever sort of publication, as long as deprived of commercial meaning and without prejudice to its distinctive character.

40. Brazil notes that in *US – Section 211 Appropriations Act*, a dispute dealing with the interpretation of several TRIPS provisions, the Appellate Body confirmed the Panel's view in *US – 1916 Act* and stated that "a distinction should be made between legislation that mandates WTO-inconsistent behaviour, and legislation that gives rise to executive authority that can be exercised with discretion".[5] On the other hand, the Appellate Body in *US – Corrosion-Resistant Steel Sunset Review*, did not express a view on whether the mandatory/discretionary distinction is a legally appropriate analytical tool for panels to use. It observed that "as with any such analytical tool, the import of the mandatory/discretionary distinction may vary from case to case. For this reason, we also wish to caution against the application of this distinction in a mechanistic fashion".[6] Thus, while the distinction can certainly be applied under the TRIPS Agreement, as a jurisprudential construction, it must be used with caution (*cum granum salis*). Brazil also remarks that the mandatory/discretionary distinction is always centred on a specific measure taken by a Member. As to the issue of "omissions" or "failures" to take certain required actions, Brazil is of the opinion, firstly, that an omission can also be considered a violation of a provision and, secondly, that, by definition, the "mandatory/discretionary" distinction cannot be applicable to instances of failure to take action, i.e. an omission, for there would be no concrete legislation issued by a Member upon which the distinction could focus.

C. Canada

1. Introduction

41. Canada has a systemic interest in the interpretation of the national treatment obligations of WTO Members under the TRIPS Agreement, specifically as these apply to the implementation of intellectual property rights for the protection of geographical indications.

---

5 Appellate Body Report on *US – Section 211 Appropriations Act*, para. 259.

6 Appellate Body Report on *US – Corrosion-Resistant Steel Sunset Review*, para. 93.

42. Canada focuses its views mainly on two issues related to national treatment obligations under the TRIPS Agreement as they are interpreted and applied in the present case. These are:

- the degree to which Articles 2.1 and 3.1 of the TRIPS Agreement prevent a WTO Member from requiring *reciprocity and equivalence* when protecting the intellectual property rights of nationals of other WTO Members, including whether or not such reciprocity and equivalence is in fact required by the EC Regulation; and
- the implications of the reference to *nationals* in Articles 2.1 and 3.1 of the TRIPS Agreement, in particular the degree to which such references permit WTO Members to discriminate in a manner not directly based on *nationality* when protecting intellectual property rights.

2. Reciprocity and equivalence requirements of the EC Regulation

43. The national treatment obligations under the TRIPS Agreement prevent the European Communities from requiring reciprocal and equivalent protection in non-EC WTO Members as a condition for protection in the European Communities of geographical indications originating in the territory of those WTO Members. The national treatment obligations of WTO Members with regard to the protection of intellectual property are contained in two separate provisions of the TRIPS Agreement. First, the earlier national treatment obligations of the Paris Convention are incorporated by reference into Article 2.1 of the TRIPS Agreement. Second, national treatment applies in the TRIPS Agreement more broadly by virtue of the requirement in Article 3.1 that a WTO Member "accord to the nationals of other Members treatment no less favourable than it accords to its own nationals with regard to the protection of intellectual property". These obligations mean that any intellectual property right provided by a WTO Member within its territory must be made available to nationals of all other WTO Members, without regard to the conditions of substantive protection available in those WTO Members. Requiring reciprocal and equivalent treatment – that is, conditioning the protection of rights of foreign nationals in the domestic jurisdiction on equivalent protection being afforded to domestic nationals in the foreign jurisdiction – runs precisely counter to national treatment obligations.

44. All parties to the present case substantially agree on the fundamental importance of the national treatment obligations under the TRIPS Agreement. The main issues of contention are: (i) whether the EC Regulation treats geographical indications originating outside the European Communities less favourably than geographical indications originating within the European Communities; (ii) and whether this less favourable treatment applies also to geographical indications originating in the territory of other WTO Members.

45. The European Communities submits that a significant feature of the EC Regulation is the provision of separate procedures for the registration, and

objection to registration, of geographical indications originating from an area *within* the European Communities (in Articles 5, 6 and 7) and the parallel procedures set out for the registration, and objection to registration, of geographical indications originating from areas *outside* the European Communities (in Articles 12, 12a, 12b, 12c and 12d). While the two separate procedures in the EC Regulation do exhibit certain similarities, a significant difference is that Article 12 provides that the EC Regulation "may" apply to geographical indications originating from the territory of a third country but only if that third country meets certain conditions. One of these conditions is the requirement in Article 12(1) that "the third country concerned is prepared to provide protection *equivalent to that available in the Community* to corresponding agricultural products [or] foodstuffs coming from the Community." Article 12(3) further requires the European Commission to examine the national legislation of the third country to certify that it satisfies the "equivalence conditions" specified in Article 12(1).

46. In other words, applicants for intellectual property protection in the European Communities of geographical indications originating in third countries that do not meet the conditions in Article 12(1) are automatically disqualified from eligibility for such protection simply on the basis of the absence of equivalent protection in their home jurisdiction. This requirement imposes a condition on applicants for geographical indications originating outside the European Communities that does not exist for applicants for geographical indications originating within the European Communities. The EC Regulation therefore accords less favourable treatment to geographical indications from outside European Communities than it accords to geographical indications from within the European Communities. The European Communities in fact admits that Article 12 of the EC Regulation requires reciprocity and equivalence for registration for protection in the European Communities of geographical indications originating from outside the European Communities (see, e.g., recital 9 of EC Regulation No. 692/2003, which says that "[t]he protection provided by registration under Regulation (EEC) No 2081/92 is open to third countries' names by reciprocity and under equivalence conditions as provided for in Article 12 of that Regulation"). If these *de jure* discriminatory provisions were to apply to WTO Members, they would violate the European Communities' national treatment obligations under the TRIPS Agreement.

47. The European Communities contends in its first written submission that the reciprocity and equivalence requirements contained in Articles 12(1) and (3) simply do not apply to WTO Members since these countries already must provide adequate protection for geographical indications by virtue of their obligations under the TRIPS Agreement. To justify this interpretation of Article 12, the European Communities points to the reference in Article 12(1) to "[w]ithout prejudice to international agreements", arguing that this clause preserves the rights of WTO Members to access the EC registration system on a national treatment basis. Heartening as this contention is in principle, when read in the context of Articles 12a, 12b and 12d, Article 12 cannot support the interpretation advanced by the European Communities. The ambiguous reference

to "international agreements" in Article 12 is simply insufficient to counter the clear wording of Articles 12, 12a, 12b, and 12d, which, when taken together suggest an interpretation opposite to that offered by the European Communities.

48. First, if the European Communities' interpretation of Article 12(1) and (3) were to be accepted, there would not appear to be an alternative legal basis for an applicant with a geographical indication originating from the territory of a non-EC WTO Member to commence an application for registration in the European Communities. The EC Regulation is drafted in such a way that the only starting point for third countries, WTO Members as well as non-Members, is Article 12 (additionally to Canada it remains unclear why the European Communities argues that these sub-articles operate in this manner whereas Article 12(2) does not). The European Communities response is that the relevant starting point for WTO Members is Article 12a, suggesting that these countries pass immediately to the procedures provided for in that article for registration of geographical indications from third countries. While Article 12a is the operative paragraph governing the *transmission* of an application to the European Communities, this provision does not appear to operate in the manner suggested by the European Communities. Article 12a(1) of the EC Regulation provides that "*[i]n the case provided for in Article 12(3)* ... a group or a natural or legal person ... shall send a registration application to the authorities in the country in which the geographical area is located" [emphasis added]. The underlined portion of that provision suggests that this procedure is only available in the case of those third countries that have already qualified according to the procedure laid out in Article 12(3), which requires meeting the conditions specified in Article 12(1). Even Article 12a(2), which governs the actual transmission of the applications from the third country to the European Communities, depends on the country first being identified by the procedure in 12a(1). Therefore, Article 12a does not provide an independent basis for a geographical indication originating from a non-EC WTO Member to be registered in the European Communities.

49. Second, the European Communities refers to distinctions made in Articles 12b(2)(a) and (b) (objections to registrations of geographical indications originating from areas outside the European Communities) and 12d(1) (objections to registrations of geographical indications originating within the EC). Those provisions distinguish between a "WTO Member" on the one hand and, respectively, "a third country meeting the equivalence conditions of Article 12(3)" and "a third country recognized under the procedure provided for in Article 12(3)". The European Communities' argument seems to be that the distinction in these latter provisions implies the existence of a distinction between WTO Members and third countries for the purposes of Article 12(1) and (3). However, the European Communities' own argument on a separate but related point supports precisely the opposite conclusion. Specifically, with respect to Article 12d(1) the European Communities argues that the reference to 12(3) only applies to "third countries other than WTO Members". The European Communities continues: "[O]therwise, the specific reference to WTO members [in 12d(1)] would be meaningless." Using the European Communities' own logic, if the *presence* of the reference to "WTO Members" in the context of

Article 12b and 12d *meaningfully* suggests differential application of those provisions between WTO Members and other third countries, then the *absence* of a reference to "WTO Members" in the context of Article 12 and 12a must *meaningfully* suggest no differential application of those provisions between WTO Members and other third countries.

50. Thus, notwithstanding the contrary interpretation offered by the European Communities, the clear wording of Article 12 and 12a means that those provisions apply equally to WTO Members and other third countries. The only way for "a group or a natural or legal person" from a WTO Member to apply for registration for a non EC-based geographical indication is for the WTO Member from which the indication originates to qualify according to the "equivalence conditions" of Article 12(1) and 12(3). Moreover, in the September 2002 meeting of the Council for TRIPS, the European Communities provided its views on the application of national treatment in the context of registration systems for geographical indications saying that "[t]he EC believes that registration systems should be primarily aimed at the identification of domestic GIs".[7] Later in the same intervention, the European Communities continued: "[I]t seems to us that the logical conclusion is to *limit the registration system to domestic GIs* and protect foreign GIs via other means". In light of these statements, there is no doubt about the European Communities' intention that Article 12 applies to WTO Members.

3. *National treatment of "nationals" of WTO Members under the TRIPS Agreement*

51. The reference to *nationals* in the TRIPS Agreement cannot be interpreted so narrowly as to render that term meaningless when it comes to national treatment with regard to the protection of intellectual property rights. This is most importantly the case in the context of the protection of geographical indications, which are tied more closely to the territories from which they originate than to the nationality of the rights holders. The European Communities acknowledges the important, and deliberate, emphasis in the TRIPS Agreement on *nationals*, as opposed to the focus on *products* under the GATT. Since minimum standards for intellectual property protection is about conferring rights, it necessarily follows that *natural and legal persons* are the holders of these rights, and that as a result WTO non-discrimination obligations generally apply as between the *nationals* who hold these rights. However, having acknowledged these important features of the TRIPS Agreement, the European Communities fails to fully appreciate their implications.

52. Specifically, the European Communities submits that even if the two parallel procedures in the EC Regulation operate differently (which the European Communities does not admit), the separate procedures do not distinguish between *nationals*, but simply distinguish between *geographical areas*, that is, geographic indications originating from areas within the European Communities,

[7] See the minutes of that meeting in document IP/C/M/37/Add.1, at p. 80.

as opposed to geographic indications originating from areas outside the European Communities. The European Communities claims that "[w]hether the area to which a geographic indication is related is located inside the European Communities or outside is in no way linked to the question of the nationality of the producers or the product concerned". This statement misinterprets the nature of intellectual property rights generally and the nature of protection of geographical indications specifically. The European Communities ignores the full meaning of Article 3.1 of the TRIPS Agreement, in particular by downplaying the *de facto* effect on nationals of a measure that the European Communities itself admits discriminates on the basis of national territories. The European Communities further underestimates the degree to which Article 3.1 applies to more than just the nationality of a national from a WTO Member, but also to the full availability and scope of the rights sought.

4. *De Facto discrimination according to nationality*

53. The European Communities claims that Articles 5 and 6 operate without distinction as between nationals when it comes to geographical indications originating from within the European Communities, and that Articles 12 and 12a operate in a similarly non-discriminatory fashion when it comes to geographical indications originating from outside the European Communities. This claim ignores the simple and incontestable reality that EC nationals are likely to register for protection of geographical indications originating from within the European Communities, whereas non-EC nationals are likely to register for protection of geographical indications originating from outside of the European Communities. The distinction between geographical areas is illusory if the effect of the EC Regulation is to *de facto* prevent nationals from non-EC WTO Members from registering for protection of the geographical indications from their own territories.

54. As the United States has argued, the principles developed in the context of national treatment with respect to goods are instructive. In particular, in assessing whether the EC Regulation *de facto* affords more favourable treatment to EC nationals than it does to non-EC nationals, this Panel needs to look beyond the literal provisions of the EC Regulation, and examine objectively the structure and overall application of the Regulation, including the underlying criteria used to allow registration of a geographical indication.[8] The structure of the EC Regulation clearly provides two different procedures for the registration of geographical indications. The sole criterion used in determining which procedure an application for registration shall follow is *geographical area*, with the only difference being whether or not the geographical area is within the boundaries of the European Communities. This choice of the boundaries of the European Communities as the only criterion raises significant concerns about the neutrality of the provisions as to the nationality of the applicants. This is particularly the case for geographical indications that, by definition, are tied to the production of

---

[8] Appellate Body Report on *Japan – Alcoholic Beverages II*, DSR 1996:I, at 120.

goods originating in the area identified by the geographical indication and, by extension, producers in that area. Given this explicit requirement that physical production of the associated good take place in the same area as indicated by the geographical indication, an applicant for a geographical indication that refers to an area within the European Communities will, in all probability, be a national of an EC member State. Conversely, an applicant for a geographical indication referring to an area in a third country will, in all probability, be a national of that third country. As a result, despite the apparently neutral application of the EC Regulation regarding nationality, it is clear that the procedure set aside for geographical indications originating within the European Communities (Articles 5 and 6) *de facto* serves EC nationals, whereas the procedure set aside for geographical indications originating outside the European Communities (Article 12 and 12a) *de facto* serves nationals of third countries, including nationals of other WTO Members.

55. The European Communities claims that caution must be exercised in finding that the EC Regulation provides *de facto* less favourable support to non-EC nationals, citing the Panel report in *Indonesia – Autos*.[9] The Panel in that case failed to find discrimination between nationals on the grounds that the Indonesian National Car Programme (which forced applicants to the programme to choose between the mark of the local programme and their global marks) applied equally to Indonesians and foreigners. The Panel found no discrimination between nationals on the basis that both nationals and non-nationals faced the same choice.[10] That is not the case here. The EC Regulation does not require all applicants to choose between registering a foreign geographical indication (or global mark) and an EC-based geographical indication. Rather, the EC Regulation requires all applicants to choose between registering an EC-based geographical indication and not registering a geographical indication at all. Applicants of non-EC nationality are, by definition, not likely to be registering an EC-based geographical indication.

56. The European Communities further cites with favour the finding of that same Panel regarding the application of TRIPS Agreement national treatment obligations to matters not directly related to equal treatment of *nationals*. The Panel found that it would be unreasonable to use the national treatment obligations in relation to intellectual property rights to challenge domestic support measures not involving intellectual property rights, on the grounds that such measures could have the *de facto* effect of giving an advantage to domestic nationals.[11] Once again, that is not the case here. Invoking national treatment concerns against an EC system that *de facto* favours EC nationals, as does the EC Regulation, is not about challenging a non-intellectual property support measure to enforce equal treatment of nationals with regard to intellectual property rights. On the contrary, it is precisely about challenging the operation of an intellectual property measure in order to enforce equal treatment of nationals

---

9 Panel Report on *Indonesia – Autos,* paras. 14.271 and 14.273.

10 Panel Report on *Indonesia – Autos*, para. 14.271.

11 Panel Report on *Indonesia – Autos*, para. 14.273.

with regard to that *same* intellectual property measure. The findings of the Panel in *Indonesia – Autos* have no bearing on this case.

5. *De jure discrimination according on nationality*

57. The EC Regulation *de facto* discriminates between EC nationals and non-EC nationals in a manner that violates the national treatment obligations contained in Articles 2.1 and 3.1 of the TRIPS Agreement.

58. Canada submits that the EC Regulation discriminates between nationals of WTO Members as a matter of legal construction. Consider further the example of an inventor seeking patent protection for her invention. In all but the rarest of cases, an invention is also independent of the location of production and the location of eventual patent protection. Further, an inventor could be a natural person with nationality in her country of origin, or an inventor could be a legal person whose nationality, so to speak, will be in the country in which it has such legal personality. In either case, when patent protection is sought in Europe, the nationality of the inventor is usually retained. It is therefore equally important that European patent law not deny the inventor a patent over the invention because of nationality, and of course it cannot.

59. Contrast those two scenarios with the case of an applicant for protection of a geographical indication. First, unlike copyrighted works or patented inventions, which are independent of the location of their creation, geographical indications are by definition tied to the particular location that they represent. Second, determining the nationality of the rights holder of a geographical indication is a different matter than it is for the creator of a copyrighted work or a patented invention. In the specific case of the EC Regulation, the rights holder will only in exceptional cases be a natural person or even an individual producer. Rather, the rights holder will generally be a group or association of local producers, established for the purpose of marketing their similar products, and it is these groups that subsequently authorize individual producers to use the geographical indication. Since these groups are the "interested parties" referred to in provisions on geographical indications in the TRIPS Agreement, it is the nationality of these groups that is relevant for the purposes of national treatment, and not the nationality of individual producers. The nationality of these groups or associations will invariably be in the jurisdiction in which they operate.

60. Combining these two features of geographical indications – a group of local producers (by design) registering a local indication (by definition) – virtually guarantees that the *nationality* of the rights holder will be in the country from which the geographical indication originates. In other words, the geographical area from which a geographical indication originates *determines* the nationality of the interested parties seeking to register it. For example, if a Canadian farmer establishes operations in Belgium to produce a product to be marketed with a geographical indication from Belgium, that farmer's nationality will not alter the Belgian nationality of the local group that is the registered rights holder of the geographical indication. As a result, despite the apparently neutral application of the EC Regulation regarding nationality, it is clear that the

procedures set aside for geographical indications originating within the European Communities *de jure* serve EC nationals, whereas the procedures set aside for geographical indications originating outside the European Communities *de jure* serve nationals of third countries. Therefore, by discriminating according to geographical area, the parallel procedures in the EC Regulation not only discriminate between nationals of WTO Members as a matter of simple probabilities, they discriminate between nationals of WTO Members as a matter of legal construction.

61. This problem is best illustrated with reference to other branches of intellectual property rights. Consider, for example, an author claiming protection under copyright for a work such as a book. The book can be written anywhere in the world, so the act of creation is independent of the location of production and the location of eventual copyright protection. Further, the author is likely to be a natural person with citizenship in his country of origin, and if he seeks protection in Europe for the book, he is likely to retain his nationality. It is important then that European copyright law not deny him copyright in the book because of his nationality, and of course it cannot.

6. National treatment applies to geographical area

62. While the prohibition on discrimination between *nationals* in the TRIPS Agreement is fundamentally different from the prohibition on discrimination between *products* that is central to national treatment under the GATT, it is possible, as the European Communities has done in its submission, to make too much of that distinction. The reference to nationals in the TRIPS Agreement cannot be divorced from its context in a trade agreement under the WTO. It cannot, for example, be reduced to a source of a general right to be free from discrimination on the basis of nationality (in the sense of citizenship) in the laws and practices of domestic institutions. The European Communities appears to be suggesting that as long as *nationality* is not specifically cited by a WTO Member as the reason for refusing the registration of an intellectual property right, that WTO Member would not be in violation of its national treatment obligations. If Article 3.1 of the TRIPS Agreement referred only to nationality, the European Communities argument might have some merit. However, the TRIPS Agreement provides national treatment to *nationals* "with regard to the protection of intellectual property" and not simply their nationality. "Protection" is further defined in footnote 3 to include "matters affecting the *availability*, acquisition, *scope*, maintenance and enforcement of intellectual property rights as well as those matters affecting the use of intellectual property rights specifically addressed in this Agreement" [emphasis added]. The European Communities notes that non-EC nationals are eligible to *acquire*, without discrimination, intellectual property rights under Articles 5 and 6 of the EC Regulation, as long as the geographical indication for which protection is sought originates within the European Communities. However, the protection of intellectual property rights in geographical indications involves more than just *acquisition*; it also involves, *inter alia*, the *availability* and *scope* of those rights. The full scope of

the requirement to provide national treatment to *nationals* of all WTO Members is not restricted to the *nationality* of the party seeking registration, but extends to all facets of the protection of rights. By the European Communities' own admission, Articles 5 and 6 of the EC Regulation limit the *availability* and *scope* of protection available to a non-EC national to rights in geographical indications originating in a narrowly defined geographical area (i.e. within the European Communities). To avail themselves of the full scope of rights over geographical indications, non-EC nationals must turn to Articles 12 and 12a, an avenue that is closed off for nationals of all but a few WTO Members. The requirement to provide national treatment under the TRIPS Agreement to nationals therefore extends beyond the mere nationality of the applicant, and applies to the availability and scope of the rights for which registration is sought. By providing more favourable treatment to geographical indications from a narrow geographical area, the EC Regulation violates Articles 2.1 and 3.1 of the TRIPS Agreement.

63. Canada requests this Panel to find that EC Regulation 2081/92 violates the European Communities' national treatment obligations contained in Articles 2.1 and 3.1 of the TRIPS Agreement. In particular this Panel should find that the EC Regulation *de jure* accords less favourable treatment to geographical indications originating from outside the European Communities than it does to those originating within the territory of the European Communities, and further that, contrary to the European Communities' interpretation of its own Regulation, this less favourable treatment applies to WTO Members. This Panel should further find that the European Communities may not rely on an artificial distinction between nationality and geographical area to mask what is otherwise *de facto* less favourable treatment in the EC Regulation of non-EC nationals than EC nationals, both with regard to the fact that geographical indications originating from outside the European Communities are sought by non-EC nationals and vice versa, and with regard to the fact that the scope of protection against discrimination in the case of geographical indications extends to include geographical area.

7. *The relationship between WTO Members, the EC, EC member States and nationals*

64. The EC Regulation, and the European Communities' first written submission in defence of that regulation, confuse the respective rights and responsibilities of these various actors, and as a result improperly imposes burdens on nationals of WTO Members in the name of equal treatment. The TRIPS Agreement requires WTO Members to implement in their domestic laws minimum standards concerning the protection of what are ultimately private rights. WTO Members are also required to ensure that these domestic private rights regimes – whether based on the minimum standards or reflecting more extensive protection – are equally accessible to nationals from other WTO Members. These requirements establish a direct relationship between WTO Members and foreign nationals, a relationship that is independent of any

involvement of the government of the foreign nationals. The European Communities disregards this point completely when it claims that it "finds it remarkable that the United States would invoke its own unwillingness to cooperate in the registration process in order to demonstrate a national treatment violation on the part of the EC".[12] In fact, the United States would be entirely justified in invoking any unwillingness to cooperate in the registration process, because the United States is under no obligation to facilitate the acquisition of private rights by its nationals in the European Communities. That obligation falls exclusively on the European Communities. The European Communities cannot then require another WTO Member to assist it in fulfilling its obligation to protect the rights of foreign nationals, regardless of whether or not that assistance would be "burdensome".

65. The European Communities then takes the confusion a step farther by drawing EC member States into the equation. It is not Canada's place to interpret the internal EC rules governing the division of competence between the European Communities and its member States when it comes to the implementation of the TRIPS Agreement – and Canada will not do so here. Instead, Canada relies on the European Communities' own statements that: (i) it has adopted the EC Regulation on the basis of its own competence; (ii) the European Communities is an original Member of the WTO; (iii) it is irrelevant that the EC member States are also Members of the WTO; and (iv) the subject matter of the present dispute falls within the exclusive competence of the European Communities.[13] On the basis of these explanations provided by the European Communities, Canada concludes that the EC Regulation is the equivalent of a national measure, and that any functions carried out by EC member States for the purposes of implementing the EC Regulation are carried out as sub-national units of the European Communities. As a result, Canada is not surprised that the EC Regulation delegates certain functions to EC member States that it cannot delegate to the sovereign governments of third countries. Of particular note, Article 5(6) provides that "EC member States shall introduce the laws, regulations and administrative provisions necessary to comply with this Article." There is no equivalent provision in the sections that set out the procedures that apply to third country governments; nor could there be.

66. However, having established its exclusive competence over the registration of geographical indications within the European Communities, the European Communities then confuses its relationship toward sub-national units of the European Communities with its relationship toward sovereign WTO Members.[14] In particular, the European Communities seeks to defend the requirement that third country governments, including those of WTO Members, assist applicants to comply with the requirements of the EC Regulation. This position by the European Communities effectively equates the downward delegation of responsibility to sub-national units with the outward delegation of

[12] European Communities' first written submission, para. 130.
[13] European Communities' first written submission, paras. 253-255.
[14] European Communities' first written submission, para. 129.

responsibility to sovereign WTO Members. The European Communities apparently considers it "equal treatment" to require nationals of sovereign WTO Members to depend on the action of their governments (over which the European Communities has no authority) in the same way nationals of the European Communities depend on the action of their own governments (in circumstances where European Communities law requires that action). This is not equal treatment; it is less favourable treatment. The EC Regulation therefore imposes on WTO Members a requirement for reciprocal and equivalent treatment that is in violation of the national treatment obligations contained in Articles 2.1 and 3.1 of the TRIPS Agreement.

8. Points raised in response to Panel's questions

67. Canada interprets the term "nationals", based on the ordinary meaning of this term as used in various provisions of the TRIPS Agreement, to refer to those natural and legal persons that have certain kinds of legal status in a given WTO Member, either through citizenship, in the case of natural persons, or through place of incorporation, in the case of legal persons such as corporations or associations. As such, natural and legal persons will be "nationals" of a WTO Member when they acquire such legal status. Only in the case of separate customs territory Members of the WTO, and in the case of nationals of non-WTO-Members residing or operating in the territories of WTO Members, does domicile or commercial establishment become a relevant factor for determining whether a natural or legal person is eligible for treatment otherwise available to nationals of a WTO Member. This distinction is clear from the provisions of the TRIPS Agreement, and from related provisions in the Paris Convention (1967) and the Berne Convention (1971), incorporated by reference into the TRIPS Agreement. For instance, Article 1.3 of the TRIPS Agreement provides that nationals "shall be understood as those natural or legal persons that would meet the criteria for eligibility for protection provided for in the Paris Convention (1967) [and the] Rome Convention (1971)". Article 3 of the Paris Convention (1967) sets out how to treat nationals from countries that are not members of the Union, and in doing so makes an explicit distinction between natural or legal persons who are "nationals of countries outside the Union who are domiciled or who have real and effective industrial or commercial establishments" in a country of the Union, on the one hand, and "nationals" of a country of the Union on the other. Similarly, Article 3(2) of the Berne Convention (1971) makes an explicit distinction between authors who are "not nationals of one of the countries of the Union but who have their habitual residence" in a country of the Union on the one hand, and "nationals" of a country of the Union on the other. In both these cases, as a result of their domicile, habitual residence, or industrial or commercial establishment, natural or legal persons who are not otherwise nationals of a country of the respective Unions are *accorded treatment similar* to that accorded nationals of a country of one of the Unions. However, they *do not become nationals*, for the purposes of granting rights, of the country in which they reside. Therefore, as a result of the explicit reference to this distinction, the ordinary definition of "nationals" does not "necessarily include" natural persons

who are domiciled, and legal persons who have an industrial or commercial establishment in a WTO Member.

68. Canada believes that the words "country of the Union", used in Article 2(1) of the Paris Convention (1967) as incorporated in the TRIPS Agreement by its Article 2.1, should be read *mutatis mutandis* to refer to "WTO Members". The TRIPS Agreement incorporates by reference certain of the substantive provisions (Articles 1 through 12, and Article 19) of the Paris Convention (1967) such that the obligations contained in those provisions apply to WTO Members as if they were all members of the Paris Union. While WTO Members who are *not* a "country of the Union" have no rights under the Paris Convention *per se*, the TRIPS Agreement incorporates these provisions of the Paris Convention (1967) for *all* WTO Members such that the Paris Convention (1967) provisions become WTO provisions. Therefore, for the purpose of the operation of the provisions thus incorporated, the words "country of the Union" are the same as "WTO Members". For example, Article 3 of the Paris Convention operates such that it grants national treatment to certain natural and legal persons for the purposes of the operation of the Convention. As a result of incorporation into the TRIPS Agreement, that provision should be read as: "Nationals of Non-WTO Members who are domiciled or who have real and effective industrial or commercial establishments in the territory of a WTO Member shall be treated in the same manner as nationals of WTO Members."

69. Canada understands that, in traditional trade disciplines, which are generally prohibitions on trade-distorting discriminatory behaviour, a WTO Member may have a legal measure that is broad enough to be applied by domestic statutory authorities either consistently or inconsistently with that Member's international trade obligations. The question in such a case is whether the fact that the measure *could* be applied in a manner inconsistent with international trade law is sufficient to challenge the measure as such. In the case of intellectual property rights, the TRIPS Agreement establishes minimum standards of the protection. It *requires* WTO Members to implement domestic legislation that grants rights to private rights applicants as long as they meet the minimum criteria for eligibility established by the TRIPS Agreement. While a WTO Member has flexibility in deciding how to protect these rights, all Members must protect the same rights according to at least the minimum standards. Given that it is the specific rights that are prescribed by the TRIPS Agreement, once a Member has decided how it intends to grant those rights, the implementing measure cannot authorize the exercise of discretion other than in a manner consistent with the minimum standards. Otherwise, there would be no minimum standards for rights.

D. China

1. Introduction

70. China submits that a successful resolution of this dispute requires the removal of ambiguity in, and proper interpretation of, the following issues:

- applicability of Article 12 of the EC Regulation to non-EC WTO Members;
- verification and publication affecting non-EC WTO Members; and
- product specifications and inspection structures affecting non-EC WTO Members.

71. The provisions of the EC Regulation of particular concern to China are those relating to non-EC WTO Members. In this respect, ambiguities remain in the EC Regulation. Its frequent references to "third countries", "conditions for protection", etc., are without any express delineation as to whether certain provisions are applicable to a non-EC WTO Member or not. The interpretations and cross-references offered in the European Communities first written submission fail to remove these ambiguities.

2. *Applicability of Article 12 of the EC Regulation*

72. The European Communities' textual interpretation of Article 12, including the wording "[w]ithout prejudice to international agreements" is not accompanied by any evidentiary support, whether in terms of actual implementation or of judicial deliberation. Nor is there any regulatory language in the provisions to expressly exclude the applicability of these provisions to non-EC WTO Members. While paragraph (10) of the recitals speaks specifically of a right of objection granted to nationals of WTO Member countries on the basis of the "without prejudice" *chapeau*, the preamble of the EC Regulation's amendments does not expressly exclude WTO Members from the Article 12 applicability of the reciprocity and equivalence requirement to third countries. Had the drafters intended that Article 12 would not apply to non-EC WTO Members, a clause to that effect sitting next to the express reference to the right to object in the Preamble would have been inserted.

73. The European Communities itself admits that the EC Regulation *does* require that conditions be met in respect of "specific geographical indications from third countries" which, more likely than not, includes WTO Members, where it stated that it does require that the product specifications and inspection regimes with regard to specific GIs from third countries meet the conditions of Regulation 2081/92.[15]

74. Immediately after that paragraph, the European Communities continues to argue that, in the event that the above equivalence and reciprocity requirements with respect to product specification and inspection regime were challenged by the complainants in this case, it would not be inconsistent with Article 3.1 of the TRIPS Agreement and Article 2(1) of the Paris Convention.

75. The language of Article 12 does not support the European Communities' interpretation that it was not applicable to WTO Members. That interpretation requires steps in reasoning with precise attention to the WTO TRIPS Agreement. The "without prejudice" *chapeau* is too general to reflect such reasoning.

---

15 European Communities' first written submission, para. 118.

76. Putting aside the legitimacy of such specification and inspection issues, it is worth noting that the European Communities' reversion to demanding equivalence and reciprocity in respect of certain components of its GI protection regime is particularly significant. It further added complication to the proper interpretation of Article 12 as quoted above. By reintroducing the equivalence and reciprocity requirement for specifications and inspections in relation to specific GIs from WTO Members, the European Communities appears to admit that portions of Article 12, particularly in respect of the whole first indent and the first portion of the second indent of Article 12(1), apply to WTO Members, in contradiction to its earlier argument that the whole Article does not apply.

77. The language of Article 12 does not suggest a split in the applicability of, for example, the registration requirement versus the overall protection regime. The leading sentence "this Regulation may apply to an agricultural product or foodstuff from a third country provided that" appeared to suggest that the overall applicability of the whole Regulation would be available or withheld depending on whether equivalence would be met. The European Communities' split interpretation could only be understood easily if there were a separate set of provisions regarding applicability of this Article to non-EC WTO Members, or if WTO Members are expressly excluded from the definition of third countries in relation to specific indents of this Article.

3. *Verification and publication affecting non-EC WTO Members*

78. Other provisions pertaining to verification and publication in the EC Regulation did not appear to afford clarity. As the European Communities describes, verification and publication bifurcated to two "parallel" sections of the GI Regulation, Article 6 in relation to GIs from the European Communities, and Article 12b in relation to GIs from third countries. However, in the same portions of its first written submission, the European Communities avoids setting out in detail the different verification and publication procedures as they respectively apply to applications from EC member States and those from third countries, including WTO Members. A closer reading of the two articles reveals that, while parallel in form, they are not the same in substance. If no less favourable treatment is granted to GIs from WTO Members in comparison to those from EC member States, Article 6 should govern both EC member States and WTO Members, and non-WTO third countries should be governed by Article 12b.

79. Under Article 6, within six months of its receipt of an application transmitted from an EC member State, the EC Commission is required to verify and investigate whether the application contained all product specification requirements under Article 4. If the Commission finds "that the name qualifies for protection", publication for objection and ultimate registration would ensue; if the Commission concludes otherwise, the name is not published. Prior to publication, the Commission may request the opinion of a Committee composed of representatives of EC member States; in the event that the Commission differs with the Committee, or if the Committee delivers no opinion, the matter is

required to be submitted to the EC Council for final determination on the basis of qualified majority.

80. Article 12b, on the other hand, requires the EC Commission to verify and investigate "whether the registration request sent by the third country [including WTO Members] contains all the necessary elements", a wording different from "whether the application includes all the particulars provided in Article 4" in respect of applications from the European Communities. A transmission from WTO Members, together with non-WTO third countries, is treated as a "registration request" in contrast to an "application" from within EC member States. Such a difference in terminology, albeit slight, is significant as a scrutiny of whether the request contains "all the necessary elements" is wider and more intensive than a verification of whether the application includes all the particulars under Article 4. For verification by the Commission of requests from third countries, including WTO Members, Article 12b does not simply refer to Article 4 particulars. It appears to suggest that a third country, including a WTO Member in transmitting its request, has more to satisfy than a EC member State in transmitting an application. The suggestion is further borne out by the requirement under Article 12a(2) that the third country, including a WTO Member must "deem the requirement of this Regulation to be satisfied" before transmitting in contrast to the Article 5(5) requirement that a EC member State only has to "check that the application is justified".

81. Further indication of the difference and likely extra burden is the Article's reference to "conditions for protection". In place of the parallel requirement that the EC Commission shall make the determination of whether to publish or not based on whether a EC name "qualifies for protection" under Articles 6(2) and 6(5), Article 12b requires that the Commission make the determination of publication by analyzing whether a third country name, including a name from a WTO Member, "satisfies the conditions for protection".

82. The EC Regulation fails to define what "all the necessary elements" and what "the conditions for protection" are. Yet these requirements tend to lead WTO Members to look to the direction of the prior European Communities' insistence upon reciprocity and equivalence requirements, at least in respect of product specifications and inspection regimes.

83. Prior to publication of names from all third countries including WTO Members, the Commission may request the opinion of a Committee composed only of representatives of EC member States. In the event that the Commission differs with the Committee, or if the Committee delivers no opinion, the matter is then required to be submitted to the EC Council for final determination on the basis of qualified majority. This resolution of possible disputes on publication was again available to names from WTO Members, but the process does not invite WTO Members to participate.

4. Product specifications and inspection structures affecting non-EC WTO Members

84. Article 10 contains relatively detailed provisions with respect to the obligations on EC member States to establish inspection structures to ensure quality of EC GIs; the EC Regulation does not contain express parallel provisions for WTO Members in connection with their own GIs. The European Communities insists that its EC Regulation does require that the product specifications and inspection regimes with regard to specific geographical indications from third countries, presumably including WTO Members, meet the conditions of Regulation 2081/92.[16]

85. There is no express definition or cross-reference as to what these conditions are in relation to WTO Members. Article 12a(2) provides that a WTO Member must attach certain documents to its transmitted registration request. The EC Commission, pursuant to its verification and publication powers under Article 12b, determines whether the above attachment transmitted by the WTO Member satisfies the conditions of the EC Regulation. It is not clear that the above requirements are the only conditions for WTO Members to satisfy. Again, in possible cases of doubt, the EC Council would have the final power to make sure a determination, under Article 12b, without participation from other WTO Members.

86. In contrast, the parallel provision of Article 5(4) does not require EC member States to guarantee Article 10 inspection structures, as they are obligated to establish the structure pursuant to the requirements under the Article; nor are EC member States required to describe their domestic GI protection system. Subsequently, EC member States can expect a relatively simple prima facie verification process, involving only a review of whether the application contained all the particulars.

87. A further example of the European Communities' ambiguity under Article 10 is the silence on whether designated inspection authorities in non-EC WTO Members can be readily accepted by the EC Commission and how that acceptance relates to the particulars of its inspection structure which is to be reviewed by the Commission. Under Article 10(2), EC member States, while obligated to establish their respective inspection structures, can reasonably expect no objection by the Commission to accept their designated authorities. With respect to "approved inspection bodies" in third countries, the EC Regulation specifically requires that "third countries recognized pursuant to Article 12(3)" are to comply with "[t]he equivalent standard or the applicable version of the equivalent standard" "to be established or amended in accordance with the procedure laid down in Article 15", a procedure without representation from other third countries. Ambiguity exists as to whether WTO Members are required to comply with this requirement. Again, since the European Communities in its first written submission in interpreting Article 12 admits that WTO Members are required to meet the conditions of the GI Regulation in

---

16 *Ibid.*

respect of product specification and inspection structure, it appears that under the GI Regulation, WTO Members are required to establish "equivalent standard" for private inspection bodies and possibly for "designated inspection authorities".

88. No clarification as to what that equivalent standard is was available until the European Communities gave its first written submission. It provides no guidance as to what constituted equivalent standard for WTO Members. It refers to ISO/IEC Guide 65:1996, but only as "an example"[17], and it is also not clear whether that standard has passed the Commission's Article 15 procedure, as required under Article 10(3) of the Regulation below.

89. If the European Communities' interpretation that "third countries recognized pursuant to Article 12(3)" did not include WTO Members for the purpose of awarding right to object[18] is to be acceptable, the EC Regulation is again silent as to what the equivalent standard for private inspection bodies is for WTO Members except for the general statement made in its first written submission that it did require reciprocity and equivalence in respect of inspection structures, or it would be contradicting itself by implying that ISO/IEC Guide 65:1996 applies to WTO Members. Such a contradiction does not assist in the proper interpretation of the EC Regulation.

90. Notwithstanding the above inconsistency, the European Communities insists upon reciprocity and equivalence conditions, both in terms of product specifications and in particular inspection structure, whether appearing in the form of requisite attachments or the outright requirement for equivalence. WTO Members are required to have a prior established set of legal rules for the protection and inspection of GIs, including GIs from the European Communities, before they can expect to transmit registration requests from their nationals to the European Communities for EC GI protection. In making a transmission, no WTO Member would ignore the EC Regulation's "all the necessary elements" and "the conditions for protection" requirement set out by the European Communities under Article 12b(1) or the European Communities' express insistence upon equivalence in product specifications and inspection structures. The safest approach in order to have their respective registration request accepted for publication is to meet the European Communities' equivalence conditions.

91. In that respect, China believes that product specification and inspection structures are quintessential for the value and quality of GIs, just as the European Communities argued.[19] An overall GI protection system built upon reciprocal and equivalent product specification and inspection from WTO Members can hardly be described as reciprocity and equivalence, neutral for such WTO Members. In arguing that its reciprocity and equivalence conditioning would only be limited to these two components of its GI protection regime and not be applicable to its overall GI regulatory protection system, the European Communities is far from convincing. The essential link between product

17 European Communities' first written submission, para. 54.
18 European Communities' first written submission, para. 74.
19 European Communities' first written submission, paras. 48-55 and 121.

specification and inspection structure and the overall GI protection cannot be artificially separated.

5. *Other points raised in response to the Panel's questions*

92. China refers to the example of the Patent Cooperation Treaty ("PCT") as an international arrangement according to which national governments cooperate by acting as agents or intermediaries in the protection of private rights. To the best of China's knowledge, there is no other international arrangement established under the legislation of one of the parties to that arrangement. In the case of international arrangement established under PCT, application requirements and procedures are applied universally and equally among members. If an international arrangement in respect of protection of private rights is to be established under the legislation of one of the parties to the arrangement, such legislation or international arrangements, established thereunder, shall not impose extra burdens with respect to availability, acquisition, scope, maintenance and enforcement of private rights as well as those matters affecting the use of such private rights.

93. China understands that the term "nationals" as used in Article 1.3, including footnote 1, and Articles 3.1 and 4 of the TRIPS Agreement and Article 2 of the Paris Convention (1967) relates to national treatment in this dispute. In the context of protection of intellectual property rights, natural persons who were domiciled, or legal persons who had a real and effective industrial and commercial establishment in a specific member are required under the TRIPS Agreement and Paris Convention (1967) to be treated in the same manner as nationals of that Member. In this regard, China believes that "nationals" as used in Article 1.3, including footnote 1, and Articles 3.1 and 4 of the TRIPS Agreement and Article 2 of the Paris Convention (1967) covered both natural or legal persons holding the nationality of a certain Member of the TRIPS Agreement as well as natural persons who are domiciled, or legal persons who had a real and effective industrial and commercial establishment in that Member.

94. China does not consider that the words "country of the Union", in Article 2(1) of the Paris Convention (1967), as incorporated in the TRIPS Agreement by its Article 2.1, should be read *mutatis mutandis* to refer to "WTO Member" for the following reasons. First, the text of the two international agreements does not support such an inference. According to Article 1(1) of the Paris Convention (1967) the words "country of the Union" refer to a member state of the Paris Convention (1967). In contrast, "WTO Member" means a party to the Agreement Establishing the World Trade Organization. The Paris Convention and the Agreement Establishing the World Trade Organization are two international agreements among different member states. The TRIPS Agreement was one of the series of WTO agreements. The member states of each of these two international agreements promised to take on different obligations and are entitled to different rights under different international agreements of which they are member states. Although certain Articles of the Paris Convention are incorporated by Article 2.1 of the TRIPS Agreement, the

two agreements still remain separate and independent international agreements, and both are in force. The incorporation does not affect other existing obligations between other member states under TRIPS and the Paris Convention. Second, the factual member status does not allow such inference. In fact, there are more member states of the Paris Convention than of the WTO; while the Paris Convention has 160 member states, the WTO has 147 Members.

95. China considers that that different treatment of GIs under the EC Regulation would also amount to less favourable treatment of like products. It quotes the view of the Appellate Body in *Korea – Various Measures on Beef* that according "treatment no less favourable" means according conditions of competition no less favourable to the imported product than to the like domestic product and that this should be assessed by examining whether a measure modified the conditions of competition in the relevant market to the detriment of imported products.[20] Therefore, in the current case, if different treatment accorded to names by the EC Regulation is found to result in modification of the conditions of competition under which like products, imported products and EC like products, competed in the EC market to the disadvantage of imported products, then the different treatment granted to names would amount to less favourable treatment of like products. China therefore believes that evidence in respect of different treatment of names is relevant to a determination of less favourable treatment of like products.

96. China believes that measures that came into force after this Panel was established are within the terms of reference of this Panel. The complainants had specified the concerned amendments in their request for the establishment of a panel, and those contents accordingly have been properly included in the terms of reference of this panel. The European Communities claims that only measures in force at the time that the Panel was established are within the terms of reference of the Panel. However, there is no requirement in the DSU or in WTO dispute settlement practice for arguments that the Panel's jurisdiction is only limited to measures that had already come into force when the Panel was established. The European Communities does not provide any legal basis for its claim nor could it find support from the functions and the objective of the terms of reference, as explained by the Appellate Body in *Brazil – Desiccated Coconut*. The parties and third parties, therefore, were given sufficient information concerning the claims at issue in the dispute, and were allowed enough opportunity to respond to the complainant's case. It is irrelevant in this respect whether the concerned amendments came into effect before or after this Panel was established. Furthermore, following the European Communities' logic, when a measure was challenged before the DSB, once the respondent had replaced the challenged measure with an amendment before the Panel was established, and that new amendment came into force immediately after the establishment of the Panel, then the Panel would not be able to examine either the old measure or the amendment, because the challenged old measure no

[20] Appellate Body Report on *Korea – Various Measures on Beef*, para. 135.

longer had any effect by the time of the Panel's establishment, while the new amendment had not yet come into effect.

97. China considers that the mandatory/discretionary distinction in GATT and WTO jurisprudence fully applies under the TRIPS Agreement and that the nature of the concerned obligations under the TRIPS Agreement therefore shall not affect the application of the distinction. It is irrelevant whether the nature of some TRIPS obligations is to prohibit or to oblige Members to take certain actions in respect of the application of the mandatory/discretionary distinction. The nature of the concerned obligations under the TRIPS Agreement therefore shall not affect the application of the distinction. It is established under WTO law that a Member could challenge measures of another Member on a *per se* basis when those measures mandate, in certain circumstances, a violation of its WTO obligations. There is a considerable body of dispute settlement practice concerning the mandatory/discretionary distinction, or *per se* violation rule, as it is more commonly referred to. In the relevant panel and Appellate Body reports addressing the mandatory/discretionary distinction, nowhere is it stated that the nature of the concerned WTO obligations as distinguished by the Panel in this question shall affect the application of the distinction. Furthermore, certain obligations, (e.g. the national treatment principle under TRIPS), *inter alia*, on one hand, that oblige Members to take certain actions, are also prohibitions in nature on the other. The national treatment principle in Article 3.1 of the TRIPS Agreement, prohibits a Member according to the nationals of other Members treatment less favourable than that it accords to its own nationals. Therefore, from the text of this provision, it is clear that the nature of the national treatment principle is an obligation which both obliges each Member to accord to the nationals of other Members treatment no less favourable than that it accords to its own nationals, and prohibits Member from according to the nationals of other Members treatment less favourable than that it accords to its own nationals.

E. Colombia

1. Introduction

98. Colombia has a systemic interest in this dispute in that it attaches great importance to determining the scope of the obligations assumed by WTO Members under the TRIPS Agreement. As a country that has protected one of its main export products with a trademark, Colombia is interested in ensuring that WTO Member countries continue to be entitled to allow their nationals to decide whether they must choose one of the intellectual property protection instruments or whether they are in fact entitled to combine those instruments according to the specificities of the different markets.

2. Reciprocity and equivalence requirement

99. In response to the argument made by Australia and the United States with respect to the violation of the national treatment provisions for the registration of, or objection to, a geographical indication, the European Communities has

stated that the expression "without prejudice to international agreements" included in Article 12(1) and (3) of the EC Regulation ensures that the rights of WTO Members are preserved. According to the European Communities, the WTO membership of the country to which the applicant for registration belongs is a sufficient guarantee that there is protection of geographical indications.[21] If this is the correct interpretation of the legislation, Colombia thinks the Panel should recommend that the European Communities amend its legislation to ensure that the clause in question is given the scope and meaning that the European Communities attributes to it in its submission as such an interpretation cannot be drawn from a simple reading of the clause in its current version.

100. Even if Colombia were to accept, for the sake of discussion, that this is the scope of the clause with respect to international agreements, there is still a point that remains unclear, namely the way in which the third country would transmit the registration application under Article 12a(2). Indeed, Colombia wonders whether the country of origin of the applicant, being required in any case to describe the legal provisions protecting the said designation and the way in which its inspection structures operate, is not subject to a certification or equivalency process. In practice, Colombia sees this requirement as a condition involving an evaluation of protection systems in force in the country of origin of applicants for geographical indications. Consequently, Colombia sees protection as being clearly contingent on the evaluation of the applicant's system, and this is contrary to Article 1.1 of the TRIPS Agreement.

101. Colombia does not agree with the European Communities' argument that drawing a distinction between geographical areas or territories is not a violation of the national treatment principle. Any distinction that in any way identifies the geographical indications of the European Communities as opposed to the others would clearly result in a violation of national treatment commitments.

3. Relationship between trademarks and geographical indications

102. With respect to the relationship between trademarks and geographical indications, Colombia agrees with the argument that the TRIPS Agreement does not establish any supremacy of one instrument of protection over another. This does not mean, however, that the European Communities' regulations can simply ignore the right of the trademark owner under Article 16.1 of the TRIPS Agreement. To do so is a clear violation of the European Communities' WTO commitments.

F. India

1. Points raised in response to the Panel's questions

103. India is not aware of any group or person ever having filed with its authorities either an application for, or an objection to, a registration pursuant to

---

21 European Communities' first written submission, para. 66.

the EC Regulation. If such filing was to occur, India would be willing to transmit such an application to the European Communities. However, the question whether the Government would be able to do so would depend upon what the transmission entails, in particular whether it may involve any procedures or need for any infrastructure for which there may be capacity constraints. India allows direct access by GI applicants to its national authority irrespective of nationality. In respect of applicants who do not have a principal place of business in India, it is necessary to indicate an address for service in India. In case of applicants from other WTO Member countries, it is necessary to include a certificate by the Registry or competent authority of the Geographical Indications Office of the WTO Member country in the application for registration and it is necessary to include the particulars of the geographical indication, the country and date of filing of the first application in the WTO Member country and such other particulars as may be required by the Registrar.

104. India understands that the European Communities has stated that it does not provide less favourable treatment to geographical indications located in other WTO Members.[22] At the same time, it is not very clear to India from the European Communities' statement whether providing no less favourable treatment to nationals of other WTO Members along with providing less favourable treatment to geographical indications located outside the EC member States would satisfy the requirement of national treatment in Article 3.1 of the TRIPS Agreement. It is India's view that the only valid interpretation of the terms "treatment...with regard to the protection" in Article 3.1 is that "no less favourable treatment" to nationals of other WTO Members cannot be provided unless "no less favourable treatment" is also provided to the geographical indications applied for by them, whether located inside the EC member States or located in other WTO Members. The only deviations permitted are the procedural ones, such as those provided in Article 3.2, whereby additional requirement for judicial or administrative procedures can be imposed upon applicants of other WTO Member countries.

105. In India's view, the words "country of the Union" in Article 2(1) of the Paris Convention (1967) as incorporated in the TRIPS Agreement by its Article 2.1, should be read *mutatis mutandis* to refer to "WTO Member".

106. India is not aware of any GIs registered under the EC Regulation that are identical (or confusingly similar) to Community protected trademarks owned by Indian nationals.

107. India sees no apparent conflict between Articles 16.1 and 22.3 of the TRIPS Agreement. Article 16.1 deals with rights of a trademark owner against "third parties" in the context of use of identical or similar signs which may cause confusion. It also provides that these rights shall not prejudice any existing prior rights. Article 22.3 entitles WTO Members to refuse or invalidate the registration of a trademark which consists of or contains geographical indication with respect to the goods not in the territory indicated if such use is of a nature as to mislead

[22] European Communities' first written submission, para. 125.

the public as to the true place or origin. Any potential conflict would be avoided in India as provisions of Section 25 of the Geographical Indications of Goods (Registration and Protection) Act, 1999 of India provide for refusal or invalidation of registration of trademarks that contain or consist of geographical indications that may cause confusion.

108. Under Section 12 of India's Trade Marks Act of 1999, registration by more than one proprietor of trademarks which are identical or similar may be permitted in the case of honest concurrent use. However, GIs are not covered by that provision. Section 26 of India's Geographical Indications (Registration and Protection) Act of 1999 provides that where a trademark contains or consists of a geographical indication and has been applied for or registered in good faith under the law relating to trademarks or where rights to such trademark have been acquired through use in good faith either (a) before the commencement of the Act, or (b) before the date of filing of the application for registration of such geographical indication under the Act, nothing contained in the Act will prejudice the registrability or the validity of the registration of such trademark or the right to use such trademark on the ground that such trademark is identical with, or similar to, such geographical indication. India's Geographical Indication Act does not discriminate between GIs and trademarks of European Communities and non-EC countries.

G. Mexico

1. Introduction

109. Mexico presents arguments in support of its view that the EC Regulation is inconsistent with the TRIPS Agreement. It addresses the following points which it considers fundamental to this dispute:

- the national treatment obligation;
- the MFN treatment obligation;
- the protection of trademark rights under Articles 16.1 and 24.5 of the TRIPS Agreement; and
- cochineal: a product of Mexican origin.

2. National treatment

110. Like the complaining parties, Mexico submits that Article 12(1) of the Regulation violates the principle of national treatment in that it accords less favourable treatment to third countries than it accords to EC member countries. Under Article 12(1) of the Regulation, foreign countries cannot enjoy the same benefits as EC nationals with respect to the registration of geographical indications unless they meet certain conditions of reciprocity. The language of Article 12(1) of the Regulation is precise and unequivocal: a third country must "give guarantees identical or equivalent" in order to be able to receive the same protection as EC member countries; otherwise, nationals of other WTO Members cannot enjoy the protection accorded by the Regulation. This is clearly contrary

to the principle of national treatment contained in Article 3.1 of the TRIPS Agreement. Moreover, the Regulation violates the principle of national treatment by once again imposing conditions of reciprocity and preventing nationals of countries that are not EC members from submitting their objections with respect to applications for the registration of geographical indications directly to the European authorities. Indeed, Article 12d(1) of the Regulation stipulates that objections from WTO Member countries must be submitted first to the government of the country in question, which must then transmit the objection to the European Commission. In other words, unlike the EC member countries, WTO Member countries that do not belong to the European Communities bear the additional burden of first having to address themselves to their national authorities, and then having to delegate to those authorities the task of following up the objection process.

3. *MFN treatment*

111. The Regulation also represents an infringement of the principle of most-favoured-nation treatment established in Article 4 of the TRIPS Agreement. By limiting intellectual property protection exclusively to third countries that provide equivalent guarantees, the European Communities is denying equal treatment to non-EC member States. Article 12(1) of the Regulation provides for treatment that discriminates between third countries to the detriment of those which fail to comply with the reciprocity conditions laid down in the Regulation. In other words, the advantages, favours and privileges of the Regulation are available to certain third countries only, and are not accorded immediately and unconditionally to the nationals of all other WTO Members as stipulated in Article 4 of the TRIPS Agreement.

4. *Protection of trademark rights under Articles 16.1 and 24.5 of the TRIPS Agreement*

112. This dispute touches on the delicate subject of the relationship between trademarks and geographical indications. Indeed, these two forms of protection of intellectual property rights can easily become the subject of conflicts, since they can protect, albeit from different angles, one and the same product with the same distinctive sign. The TRIPS Agreement addresses, and tries to resolve, these possible confusions through Articles 16.1 and 24.5, which establish the rights of trademark and geographical indication owners. In this connection, Mexico notes that the Regulation violates at least two provisions of the TRIPS Agreement, namely Articles 24.5 and 16.1.

113. Article 14(1) of the Regulation clearly violates Article 24.5 of the TRIPS Agreement. Contrary to what is provided for in the TRIPS Agreement, this provision of the Regulation gives clear preference to geographical indications over trademarks that were registered subsequently. This priority for GIs takes as a time reference the day of registration or application of the trademark with the EC authorities and rejects the possibility of a trademark having previously been registered in a non-EC member country. The deliberate failure to recognize prior

registrations in third countries violates not only Article 24.5 of the TRIPS Agreement, but also Article 4 of the Paris Convention. In its written submission, the European Communities confirms its position by stating that the only relevant date for the purposes of Article 24.5 is the date of filing of the application before the national authorities, in this case before the EC authorities. This argument clearly does not justify a deviation from Article 24.5 of the TRIPS Agreement.

114. The exclusive right conferred by Article 16.1 is severely impaired by Article 14(2) of the Regulation, which permits coexistence between a previously registered trademark and a subsequent geographical indication. This means that in the European Communities, the fact that a trademark was registered prior to a subsequent geographical indication does not constitute an obstacle to invalidating the registration of the geographical indication. In its first written submission, the European Communities goes so far as stating that the TRIPS Agreement not only permits the coexistence of trademarks and geographical indications, but, in fact, requires such coexistence. In the same submission, the European Communities admits that coexistence of the two types of protection is not the perfect solution, but it is preferable to a rigid application of the "first-in-time" rule. Mexico considers these justifications to be insufficient. By acknowledging that the solution implemented under the Regulation may not be the perfect solution, the European Communities is recognizing the inconsistency of its legislation. Similarly, by ignoring the "first-in-time" approach, the European Communities is violating not only Article 24.5 of the TRIPS Agreement, but also a recognized general principle of law.

5. Cochineal: a product of Mexican origin

115. Mexico considers that "cochineal" should be removed from Annex II of the Regulation. Annexes I and II of the Regulation specifically mention the products falling within the scope of application of the Regulation. Article 1 of the Regulation establishes the relationship between Annexes I and II and the other provisions. The list of products in Annex II includes a product of Mexican origin, "cochineal" (*Coccus Cacti*), a small insect which lives on the nopal cactus, or Mexican cactus, and which produces an intense red colour used as textile dye and food colouring. The use of cochineal in Mexico dates back to the pre-colonial period. The Aztecs used this colouring matter for centuries before Hernán Cortés arrived in Mexico from Spain in 1519. The first export of the product to Spain took place in 1523, a few years after Cortés's invasion of Mexico. Subsequently, cochineal bugs were cultivated in parts of Spain in which the climate and conditions were similar to those of Mexico. Thus, cochineal is now also produced in Spain, specifically in the Canary Islands. Given that the product exists simultaneously in Mexico and the European Communities, registration of cochineal from Mexico in the European Communities would clearly be refused under the Regulation.

116. Mexico submits that, according to the definition of geographical indications in Article 22 of the TRIPS Agreement, the product in question must be of a quality, reputation or other characteristic essentially attributable to its

geographical origin. In the case of cochineal, a number of its characteristics can be attributed essentially to the territory of Mexico. The product's history demonstrates that, if there is a country to which the special qualities of cochineal can be attributed for the purposes of intellectual property protection, it is Mexico. Consequently, it would make no sense to register cochineal as a geographical indication in any territory which is not in Mexico. Hence, Mexico requests that the Panel rule that the inclusion of the product "cochineal" as eligible for protection as a geographical indication of the European Communities is illegal.

117. In response to a question from the Panel, Mexico explains that it considers cochineal a product classification which is capable of being registered as a geographical indication under the EC Regulation. The categories of "product classification" and "geographical indication" are not mutually exclusive. The EC Regulation is the "specific measure at issue". Since Annex II is part of such Regulation, it is clearly contained in the "specific measure at issue". Mexico is fully aware that this Panel has standard terms of reference and is, therefore, limited to examining the claims made by Australia and the United States. As a third party, Mexico does not intend to submit, and is not submitting, claims which are different from those raised by the parties. In fact, Mexico is only addressing some of these claims. In this respect, Mexico is providing arguments to support at least two of the three claims made by the parties, namely the violation of the principles of national treatment and MFN treatment and the violation of the TRIPS rules regarding the relationship between trademarks and geographical indications. Mexico brings cochineal as a real-world example of how the EC Regulation violates these rules and it simply intends to support the United States' and Australia's arguments in these respects. From Mexico's perspective, it is clear that Mexican producers of cochineal are required to go through specific procedures which EC nationals (national treatment) or countries which give equivalent guarantees to nationals of the European Communities (MFN treatment) are not. Furthermore, Mexico would observe that the Panel is fully entitled under Article 19.1, second sentence, of the DSU, to suggest ways in which a Member may implement the Panel's own recommendations and rulings. There is no requirement in the DSU that such a request has to be forwarded by a party to the case. In the past, panels have issued suggestions for Members to withdraw their measures which have been found to be WTO-inconsistent.[23] Given that Mexico's interest in cochineal is so specific, Mexico does not request that the Panel suggest that the European Communities repeal its legislation as a whole, but merely to solve Mexico's very specific problem in this way. If the Panel does not deem it appropriate to suggest specifically that the European Communities remove the name of cochineal from Annex II of the Regulation, Mexico would certainly obtain the same result if the Panel suggested that the European Communities comply with its recommendations and rulings by withdrawing the Regulation.

[23] Panel Report on *Guatemala – Cement I*, para. 9.6; and Panel Report on *US – Offset Act (Byrd Amendment)*, para. 8.6.

6. Points raised in response to the Panel's questions

118. Mexico is not aware of any group or person ever having filed with its authorities either an application for or an objection to a registration pursuant to the EC Regulation. As to the question whether Mexico would be willing or able to transmit such applications, according to Article 6.III of Mexico's Industrial Property Law (LPI), the Mexican Institute of Industrial Property (IMPI) is the administrative authority in charge of ensuring the protection of appellations of origin. The IMPI, acting through the Ministry of Foreign Affairs, would thus be empowered to request or, where appropriate, to transmit an application for registration of an appellation of origin to any international agency. The use of this procedure, including the submission of an application for registration of a Mexican appellation of origin under the EC Regulation will, however, depend on the findings made by this Panel. Mexico's LPI makes no distinction on the basis of nationality. According to its provisions, the owner of appellations of origin is the Mexican State and authorization to use them is issued by the IMPI to any natural person or legal entity that complies with the requirements and procedures in Articles 169-178 of the LPI.

119. Mexico submits that foreign GIs are protected under the TRIPS Agreement, the Lisbon Agreement for the Protection of Appellations of Origin and their International Registration, and treaties which Mexico has concluded with other countries. As established in the Paris Convention, the principles of national treatment and of assimilation to nationals imply that, with respect to industrial property, each member State is required to afford nationals of other member States the same treatment as that afforded to its own citizens without conditioning such treatment on reciprocity. Hence, nationals – i.e. both natural persons and legal entities – enjoy the industrial property rights granted by the member State without any requirement as to domicile or establishment. Pursuant to Article 2(3) of the Paris Convention, however, member States may apply the domicile requirement for the purpose of judicial or administrative procedures. Additionally, the fact that Article 2(1) of the Paris Convention is incorporated by reference in Article 2.1 of the TRIPS Agreement, means that WTO Members are required to comply with Articles 1 through 12 and Article 19 of the Paris Convention in respect of geographical indications as regulated in Part II of the Agreement.

120. Mexico is not aware of any GIs registered under the EC Regulation that are identical or confusingly similar to trademarks in the European Communities registered by Mexican nationals. Mexico also considers that Articles 16.1 and 22.3 of the TRIPS Agreement apply to different situations. Article 16.1 of the TRIPS Agreement deals with trademarks, and more specifically with the rights conferred on trademark owners and situations relating to existing prior rights and rights made available on the basis of use. Article 22.3 regulates the protection which WTO Members are required to provide for geographical indications and specifies the circumstances in which registration of a trademark which contains or consists of a geographical indication may be invalidated or refused.

121. Under Mexican law, and specifically the LPI, there are two situations in which registration of a mark is not effective against third parties, as well as exceptions to the use of a mark being classified as an administrative infringement. In the first instance, Article 92.I of the LPI specifies that the owner of a registered mark may not prevent a third party acting in good faith from using the same or a confusingly similar mark for the same or similar products or services, provided that such use is made in good faith and occurred prior to the date of filing the application for registration, or the date of first declared use of the mark. In the second instance, Article 213.X of the LPI provides that, in the case of comparative advertising, a third party may use a registered mark for the purpose of informing the public, provided that the comparison is not tendentious, false or exaggerated within the meaning of the Federal Consumer Protection Law. Application of these two scenarios to geographical indications is governed by the provisions of the TRIPS Agreement and other international instruments to which Mexico is party.

122. Mexico does not believe that previous panel decisions constitute binding jurisprudence for subsequent panel determinations, including previous decisions on the mandatory/discretionary distinction in GATT and WTO. In this sense, Mexico agrees with the statement by the Appellate Body[24] that panel reports bind the parties to the dispute but do not create definitive interpretations of the relevant provisions.

H. New zealand

1. Introduction

123. New Zealand has a significant systemic interest in ensuring that the WTO disciplines applicable to intellectual property rights are respected. These disciplines seek to ensure that such rights are adequately and effectively protected while also ensuring that the measures Members adopt to enforce these rights do not of themselves become barriers to legitimate trade. New Zealand has a significant interest in maintaining protection for the intellectual property rights of New Zealand producers who have invested in innovation and in the promotion of their products, and in ensuring that the market access and ability to brand New Zealand products is not precluded. As a major exporter of agricultural products and foodstuffs, New Zealand has an interest in ensuring that its producers are able to brand and promote their agricultural products in export markets, including the European Communities.

124. In the present case New Zealand brings forward arguments to support the claims of the complainants that the EC Regulation violates the European Communities WTO obligations. New Zealand focuses its arguments on the claims raised by the complainants under Articles 2.1, 3.1, 16.1 and 22.2 of the TRIPS Agreement and Article III:4 of GATT 1994. New Zealand also supports the arguments made by Australia that the EC Regulation is inconsistent with

---

24 Appellate Body Report on *Japan – Alcoholic Beverages II,* at pp 13-14.

Articles 2.1 and 2.2 of the TBT Agreement but, for the sake of brevity, does not address them in its submissions.

2. *The EC Regulation is inconsistent with national treatment obligations under the TRIPS Agreement and GATT 1994*

(a) Introduction

125. The national treatment obligation is "a cornerstone of the world trading system that is served by the WTO".[25] In the TRIPS Agreement, this obligation is incorporated into the legal framework for protection of intellectual property rights by way of Article 2.1 (which requires WTO Members to comply with, *inter alia*, Article 2(1) of the Paris Convention) and Article 3.1. By virtue of Article 2.1, the European Communities is obliged to provide nationals of other WTO Members with "the same protection" as its own nationals. Under Article 3.1, the European Communities is obliged to provide "treatment no less favourable than that it accords to its own nationals with regard to the protection of intellectual property". The European Communities is also obliged under Article III:4 of GATT 1994 to accord to imported products of the territory of any contracting party "treatment no less favourable than that accorded to like products of national origin in respect of all laws, regulations and requirements affecting their internal sale." The European Communities does not dispute that these national treatment obligations apply to the EC Regulation.

(b) Interpretation of the EC Regulation

126. The European Communities disputes as a factual matter the complainants' interpretation of Article 12(1) of the EC Regulation on which the national treatment violation arguments are based. The European Communities claims this interpretation "is based on a misunderstanding" of its Regulation.[26] The European Communities argues that Article 12(1) of Regulation 2081/92 clearly applies "without prejudice to international agreements". It goes on to state that such international agreements include the WTO Agreements, and for this reason "Article 12(1) and (3) of Regulation 2081/92 do not apply to WTO Members".[27] Rather, the European Communities continues, WTO Members are to follow the procedures set out in Article 12a and 12b of the EC Regulation. This novel interpretation of the European Communities does not withstand close scrutiny. First, it runs counter to the usual meaning of the phrase "without prejudice to international agreements". Second, it is inconsistent with the wording of the EC Regulation itself. Third, to New Zealand's knowledge, this is the first time that this interpretation has been raised by the European Communities, despite consultations being held on the interpretation of its Regulation.

---

[25] Appellate Body Report on *US – Section 211 Appropriations Act*, para. 241.

[26] European Communities' first written submission, para. 65.

[27] European Communities' first written submission, para. 66.

127. The European Communities interprets the phrase "without prejudice to international agreements" in a manner which acknowledges its obligations under the TRIPS Agreement.[28] It appears to New Zealand that the European Communities is effectively admitting that requiring nationals of WTO Members to follow the procedures set out in Article 12(1) and 12(3) of the EC Regulation would be contrary to its WTO obligations. However, in New Zealand's view there are sufficient internal inconsistencies between the European Communities' novel interpretation and the wording of the EC Regulation to doubt whether any reliance can be placed on this interpretation of the EC Regulation in the future. The European Communities notes the distinctions made in Articles 12(b)(2)(a) and (b) and Article 12d(1) between "WTO countries" and "third countries" in support of its interpretation. It also states that the procedure provided for in Article 12(3) does not apply to WTO Members. New Zealand notes, however, that Article 12a is prefaced with the phrase "[i]n the case provided for in Article 12(3)". If Article 12(3) does not apply to WTO Members then, based on the European Communities' own arguments, Article 12(a) would not apply to WTO Members. Taken to its logical conclusion, therefore, the European Communities' argument would mean that there is in fact no application procedure in the EC Regulation under which a national of a WTO Member could apply for GI protection. In that case the Panel must find that the European Communities is in breach of its national treatment obligations under the TRIPS Agreement and GATT 1994 by failing to provide a WTO-consistent application procedure for GI registration for WTO Members. New Zealand does not believe that the European Communities would agree with this consequence of its interpretation. New Zealand notes that this is the first time this interpretation has been raised, despite numerous consultations on the EC Regulation, including under the DSU. As the Appellate Body has indicated, all parties engaged in dispute settlement under the DSU should be fully forthcoming with respect to the facts, and consultations "do much to shape the substance and the scope of subsequent panel proceedings."[29]

128. Essentially, the European Communities' argument that Article 12(1) and 12(3) of the EC Regulation do not apply to WTO Members rests on the claim that the Regulation will indeed be interpreted in the manner the European Communities suggests, that is, in a WTO consistent manner. But the European Communities can offer no basis for assuring WTO Members that this will be so. The European Communities' position is even less credible where the interpretation that the European Communities puts forward is one that is not suggested by the ordinary meaning of the text of the EC Regulation. The alternative interpretation, and one which is consistent with the wording of the EC Regulation, is that adopted by the complainants, namely that Article 12(1) and (3) apply to WTO Members.

---

[28] European Communities' first written submission, para. 65.

[29] Appellate Body Report on *India – Patents (US)*, para. 94.

(c) Article 2.1 of the TRIPS Agreement (incorporating Article 2(1) of the Paris Convention) and Article 3.1 of the TRIPS Agreement

(i) The EC is obliged to provide no less favourable treatment to other WTO Member nationals than it does to EC nationals

129. Article 2.1 of the TRIPS Agreement requires WTO members to comply with, *inter alia*, Article 2(1) of the Paris Convention. The European Communities is therefore obliged to provide nationals of other WTO Members with "the same protection" as provided to foreign nationals. It is also required to accord to nationals of other WTO Members "treatment no less favourable than that it accords to its own nationals with regard to the protection of intellectual property" under Article 3.1 of the TRIPS Agreement. There are three essential components of the national treatment obligation under Articles 2.1 and 3.1 of the TRIPS Agreement. First, it is the treatment received by "nationals" that is key. Second, the standard for comparison with the treatment received by foreign nationals is the most favourable treatment received by domestic nationals. Third, foreign nationals must receive no less favourable treatment than that accorded to nationals.

130. The national treatment obligations in the TRIPS Agreement are owed to nationals, that is, natural or legal persons (see Article 1.3). In the context of the present case, this means that the standard for comparison is simply with EC nationals, since all EC nationals are potentially eligible to apply for GI registration under the EC Regulation.

131. In the present case, the European Communities has raised a creative but nevertheless erroneous interpretation of "nationals" in an attempt to claim that its conditions for registration and objections do not breach its national treatment obligations. In particular, the European Communities claims that "the conditions and procedures contained in Regulation 2081/92 for the registration of geographical indications do not depend on nationality".[30] New Zealand submits that this interpretation of the national treatment obligation as applying to persons of a particular "nationality" cannot be correct. The WTO Agreements are to be interpreted according to the ordinary meaning of the words in their context, and in light of their object and purpose (see Article 31(1) of the Vienna Convention on the Law of Treaties). In the context of the TRIPS Agreement the term "nationals" clearly has a geographical connotation. Support for this is gleaned from both the TRIPS Agreement and the Paris Convention (incorporated by reference into the TRIPS Agreement). Article 1.3 of the TRIPS Agreement provides that "[M]embers shall accord the treatment provided for in this Agreement to the nationals of other Members. In respect of the relevant intellectual property rights, the nationals of other Members shall be understood

---

[30] European Communities' first written submission, para. 123.

as those natural or legal persons *that would meet the criteria for eligibility for protection in the Paris Convention*" (emphasis added). One particular category of natural or legal persons that meet the criteria for eligibility for the same protection as nationals under the Paris Convention are those eligible under Article 3 [Same Treatment for Certain Categories of Persons as for Nationals of Countries of the Union] of the Paris Convention. This provides that "[n]ationals of countries outside the Union who are domiciled or who have real and effective industrial or commercial establishments in the territory of one of the countries of the Union *shall be treated in the same manner as nationals* of the countries of the Union" (emphasis added). The Paris Convention therefore includes not only a "nationality" element to the national treatment obligation, but also includes a "geographical" element relating to the person's place of domicile or establishment. This is further supported by footnote 1 to Article 1.3 of the TRIPS Agreement which also adopts a geographical element to the term "nationals" when used in the relation to separate customs territories.

132. In the geographical context of GIs, therefore, the term "nationals" includes not only natural or legal persons of a particular nationality, but also those who are domiciled or who have a real and effective industrial or commercial establishment in a particular WTO Member. Those legal or natural persons who are domiciled or have an establishment in the third country to which the GI relates are therefore "non-EC nationals" for the purpose of the national treatment obligation under the TRIPS Agreement. As a consequence of its erroneous interpretation of "nationals", the European Communities asserts that it is the area where the GI is located that determines which procedure under the EC Regulation applies in a given case, not the "nationality" of the producers of the product concerned. Therefore, it claims there is no breach of the national treatment obligations. If this argument were correct, it would mean that even if a Regulation provided that only EC GIs could be registered, there would be no violation of the national treatment obligation because in theory the nationals of any country could live in the European Communities and register their GIs. This would gut the TRIPS Agreement of the national treatment obligation with respect to GIs. In any case, the EC Regulation as drafted does not support the European Communities assertion. In particular, New Zealand submits that the plain meaning of the words "a group or a natural or legal person ... in a third country" in Article 12a of the EC Regulation is that all persons domiciled or with a real and effective industrial or commercial establishment outside of the European Communities are subject to the procedure in Article 12a of the EC Regulation (provided that the requirements of Article 12(3) have been met). So a person's location is indeed relevant to which application process applies. The EC Regulation, therefore, adopts two different registration procedures – one for EC nationals in respect of GIs located in the EC; and one for nationals "in a third country". The European Communities is obliged by its national treatment obligations to provide a no less favourable application process for nationals "in a third country" than it does for EC nationals.

133. New Zealand supports the complainants arguments that a WTO Member cannot require reciprocity of a higher standard of treatment than that required by

the TRIPS Agreement before the right to that higher standard accrues under national treatment. To do otherwise would in effect result in a WTO Member being able secure concessions that it was unable achieve at the negotiating table.

134. In determining whether a particular measure violates the national treatment obligation, a first line of inquiry is whether there is a difference in treatment in the applicable laws. A difference in applicable law, by itself, is not sufficient to constitute a breach of national treatment.[31] It must be demonstrated that "less favourable treatment" or some disadvantage accruing to the foreign national as a consequence of the difference in treatment has occurred.[32] In terms of what may amount to a disadvantage, the Appellate Body has found that subjecting foreigners to additional procedures constitutes a breach of national treatment. The Appellate Body in *US – Section 211 Appropriations Act* concluded that "even the *possibility* that non-United States successors-in-interest face two hurdles is *inherently less favourable* than the undisputed fact that United States successors-in-interest face only one".[33] Thus an "extra hurdle" faced by foreigners constitutes "less favourable treatment" under Article 3.1 of the TRIPS Agreement. Further, whether or not "less favourable treatment" is accorded to nationals should be assessed "by examining whether a measure modifies the *conditions of competition* in the relevant market".[34] In other words, treatment no less favourable in Article III:4 of GATT 1994 calls for "effective equality of opportunities".[35]

(ii) Registration procedure provides less favourable treatment to WTO Member nationals

135. The complainants have demonstrated that nationals from WTO Members are subject to different registration procedures from those applying to EC nationals. New Zealand has summarized the differences between the registration processes applicable to the European Communities and WTO Member applications.[36] The particular difference at issue between the two registration procedures is the requirements of equivalence and reciprocity in Article 12(1) of the EC Regulation (this argument takes as its premise the fact that Article 12(1) and 12(3) of the EC Regulation apply to WTO Members.). Further, while the requirement to submit all applications through government applies equally to applications from the European Communities and WTO Member nationals, its effect is to disadvantage nationals from WTO Members.

136. New Zealand submits that the effects of the differences in registration process mean that, at worst, the benefits of registration are entirely unavailable to producers from countries outside the European Communities. Indeed,

[31] See the GATT Panel Report on *US – Section 337,* cited by the Appellate Body in *US – Section 211 Appropriations Act*, at para. 261.

[32] See the Appellate Body Report on *Korea – Various Measures on Beef*, at para. 135.

[33] Appellate Body Report on *US – Section 211 Appropriations Act,* para. 265.

[34] Appellate Body Report on *Korea – Various Measures on Beef,* para. 137.

[35] GATT Panel Report on *US – Section 337*, para. 5.11.

[36] See Exhibit NZ-1 reproduced at the end of this Annex.

New Zealand is not aware of any successful registration applications from nationals from WTO Members made under the process set out in the EC Regulation, whereas there have been more than 600 successful applications for registration of EC GIs. At best, WTO Member nationals are subject to "extra hurdles" and are as a consequence, disadvantaged under the EC Regulation when compared to EC nationals. An "extra hurdle" exists for WTO Member nationals if WTO Members are required to comply with the equivalence and reciprocity requirements in the EC Regulation. The complainants have shown that before a WTO Member national is eligible to apply for protection under Article 12(1) of EC Regulation, the country of origin of that national must grant *reciprocal* treatment for EC GIs under an *equivalent* system.

137. Not only are these requirements for reciprocity and equivalence a breach in and of themselves of the national treatment obligations, but they also mean that WTO Member nationals do not have the same opportunities to protect their GIs through registration as do EC nationals. In such case, an individual's right to apply for registration under the EC Regulation is conditioned on factors over which the applicant has no control, in other words, whether the applicant's government applies reciprocal and equivalent treatment. New Zealand notes that applications for registration under the EC Regulation are to be submitted by governments, rather than by individuals (Articles 5(5) and 12a(2) of the EC Regulation). The European Communities claims that the "rules relating to the registration of such geographical indications from outside the EC ... closely parallel the provisions applicable to geographical indications from inside the EC".[37] It is worth recalling, however, that a breach of national treatment may arise from the application of formally identical laws.[38] New Zealand argues that in this case "formally identical legal provisions" (or closely parallel legal provisions) in the EC Regulation do indeed result in less favourable treatment for WTO Member nationals. EC nationals have an enforceable right that applications that satisfy the requirements of the regulation are forwarded to the Commission. This right exists by virtue of Article 5(6) of the EC Regulation. Thus, for an EC national, submission via their member State government becomes essentially a formality. Failure to submit an application may be judiciable according to the member States' applicable national laws. WTO Member nationals have no such enforceable right to ensure that submission occurs. Thus, WTO Member nationals face significant "extra hurdles" in order to obtain protection for their GIs under the EC Regulation and are thus accorded less favourable treatment than an EC national. Furthermore, the Panel should find that the European Communities is in breach of its national treatment obligations by conditioning the receipt of intellectual property protection on provision of reciprocal equivalent treatment.

138. For producers able to register a GI under the EC Regulation, registration grants certain advantages, including: (i) being able to protect GIs from certain conduct set out in Article 13(1) of the EC Regulation; (ii) being able to prevent

37 European Communities' first written submission, para. 62.

38 See the GATT Panel Report on *US – Section 337*, para. 5.11.

the GI term from becoming generic under Article 13(3) of the EC Regulation; (iii) being able to obtain such protection of GIs on a Community wide basis; and (iv) according to the EC Regulation's preamble, being able to secure higher incomes as a result of "a growing demand for agricultural products or foodstuffs with an identifiable geographical origin". Accordingly, not being able to register GIs under the EC Regulation results in commercial disadvantage for WTO Member nationals. They are unable to obtain the same level of protection on a Community-wide level as EC nationals and are unable to "secure higher incomes", as claimed by the European Communities to be a consequence of their GI protection. Thus the conditions of competition faced by WTO Member nationals are modified by the operation of the EC Regulation. As a consequence, the EC Regulation effectively operates as a barrier to trade.

(iii) Objections procedure provides less favourable treatment to WTO Member nationals

139. As stated in its preamble, the EC Regulation also provides an objection procedure to enable "any person individually and directly concerned in a member State to exercise his rights by notifying the Commission of his opposition". The objection procedure can potentially result in an application for registration but not for a proceeding. Consequently, not having the right to object is a loss of a valuable right in the arsenal of a producer to protect his or her commercial interests or intellectual property rights. The complainants have demonstrated that nationals from WTO countries are subject to different objection processes from EC nationals. New Zealand has summarized and compared the applicable objection procedures.[39] The process for objections from WTO nationals suffers from the same shortcomings as the process for registrations: namely, objections are subject to reciprocity and equivalence requirements and must be submitted through governments.

140. The European Communities has, however, asserted that the requirements for reciprocity and equivalence do not apply to WTO Members and thus are not preconditions for the admissibility of objections from WTO Members. In particular, the European Communities has argued that "[t]he phrase [in Article 12d(1) 'recognised under the procedure provided for in Article 12(3)' only refers to third countries other than WTO Members".[40] As has been indicated earlier, New Zealand finds the above argument unconvincing. Such an intention (to refer to third countries other than WTO Members) is not clear from the language of the EC Regulation. The fact that the rest of the EC Regulation and, in particular, the application procedure under Articles 12 and 12a, fail to explicitly distinguish between WTO Members and third countries suggests that there is in fact no such distinction. The distinction could have been made clear in Article 12d(1) by inserting a comma or words in the phrase to make it apparent that the procedures provided for in Article 12(3) apply only to third countries and

[39] See Exhibit NZ-2 reproduced at the end of this Annex.
[40] European Communities' first written submission para. 74.

not to WTO Members. However, no such distinction is apparent from the face of the EC Regulation. Therefore the conclusion must be drawn that the EC Regulation requires both WTO Members and third countries to be recognized under the Article 12(3). New Zealand submits that the complainants' interpretation of Article 12d(1) is the correct interpretation. WTO Members are required by the EC Regulation to provide equivalent and reciprocal treatment as a precondition to the initiation of the objection procedure by their nationals. Accordingly, the objection procedure breaches the European Communities' national treatment obligations for the same reasons that the registration procedure does. The effect of the differences in objection processes means that, at best, WTO Member nationals are disadvantaged under the EC Regulation when compared to EC nationals. At worst, the benefits of the right to object are entirely unavailable to producers from countries outside the European Communities. As a result, the European Communities has in place a system that virtually guarantees no objections will be received from WTO Member nationals to applications for the registration of EC GIs.

(d) GATT 1994

(i) The EC Regulation is inconsistent with Article III:4

141. New Zealand considers that the complainants have demonstrated that all three elements constituting a violation of Article III:4 of GATT 1994 have been satisfied.[41] First, the European Communities agrees that the EC Regulation is a measure affecting the internal sale of products. Second, the European Communities appears not to raise concerns about whether the products at issue must be "like products." New Zealand notes, in any case, that the United States is correct that for measures of general application the issue is whether the measure makes distinctions between products based solely on origin, rather than whether particular traded products are "like". It follows that the only issue under debate is whether the EC Regulation confers "less favourable treatment" on imported products. As the phrase "less favourable treatment" is the same as that used in Article 3.1 of the TRIPS Agreement, all arguments raised by New Zealand under Articles 2.1 and 3.1 of the TRIPS Agreement apply equally to Article III:4 of GATT 1994 and demonstrate that the EC Regulation also breaches Article III:4 of GATT 1994.

(ii) The EC Regulation cannot be justified under Article XX(d)

142. The European Communities has also claimed that the measure is justified under Article XX(d) of GATT 1994. In particular, the European Communities claims that "the requirements at issue are *necessary* in order to ensure that only those products which conform to the definition of geographical indications contained in Article 2(2) of Regulation 2081/92, which is itself fully consistent

[41] See the Appellate Body Report on *Korea – Various Measures on Beef*, para. 133.

with GATT 1994, benefit from the protection afforded to geographical indications by Regulation 2081/92" (emphasis added).[42] New Zealand agrees with the United States that the European Communities' claim cannot be sustained. Whether a measure is "necessary" is assessed against the high standard of whether the measure is the "least-trade restrictive" option available to the party. Hence, if another WTO-consistent alternative can be employed, then a measure will not be justified under Article XX(d).

143. The European Communities claims that it is necessary for all applications to be submitted through government "to ensure that only those products which confirm to the definition of geographical indications contained in Article 2(2) of the EC Regulation … benefit from the protection afforded to geographical indications". Given that the European Communities itself conducts a six-month investigation into precisely the issue of whether the products conform to the definition of a GI (that is, as set out in the product specification required under Article 4 of the EC Regulation), New Zealand submits that it is not necessary for applications to be passed through a government filter. The European Communities provides no claim with respect to the necessity of reciprocity and equivalence requirements imposed on non-EC products. Further, this claim does not apply to objection procedures, which are also transmitted through governments. New Zealand therefore submits that the EC Regulation cannot be justified on the basis of Article XX(d) of GATT 1994. The Panel should find that the EC Regulation violates Article III:4 of GATT 1994 as well as Articles 2.1 and 3.1 of the TRIPS Agreement.

3. *The EC Regulation is inconsistent with Article 22.2 of the TRIPS Agreement*

144. Article 22.2 of the TRIPS Agreement provides a negative right, or a right to prevent certain actions, rather than a positive right, such as a right to authorize use. Consequently, it is an important legal right for "interested parties" to ensure appropriate use of geographical indications. The complainants have demonstrated that the European Communities has failed to provide this right to nationals of WTO Members by requiring reciprocity and equivalence as preconditions to admissibility of registration applications and objections, and by requiring that all applications be submitted through government. New Zealand raises three points to support the complainants' views.

145. First, New Zealand submits that the phrase "legal means" is used to indicate any laws, rules and regulations through which redress for misleading uses and acts of unfair competition "in respect of geographical indications" can be obtained. Various models of legal means are envisaged under Article 22.2 of the TRIPS Agreement, consistent with the principle that WTO Members are free to determine the most appropriate method of implementation within their own legal system and practices (see Article 1.1 of the TRIPS Agreement). For GI users, registration of their GI under the EC Regulation provides the legal means

---

[42] European Communities' first written submission, para. 226.

to prevent a range of uses, including misleading uses and acts of unfair competition under Article 22.2 (see Article 13(1) of the EC Regulation). Once a GI has been registered under the EC Regulation, persons affected by use of that GI have extremely limited options to challenge the use of that registered GI. Indeed, they have no such options under the EC Regulation itself for only repeated failure to comply with the product specification or a request for cancellation by the natural or legal person or group authorized to seek cancellation may result in the registration being cancelled. Thus the right to object to an application for registration of a GI prior to registration occurring is a crucial aspect of the legal means that the European Communities must provide under Article 22.2 of the TRIPS Agreement.

146. Second, New Zealand submits that "interested parties" is a broad term. "Interested" is defined as meaning "having an interest, share, or concern, in something; affected, involved".[43] "Parties" encompasses any legal or natural person, or group of legal or natural persons. In the context of the TRIPS Agreement, "interested parties" has a broad meaning and includes persons with an interest in, or affected by, a GI. The term "interested parties" can be contrasted with specific terms used in other provisions which confer rights on particular groups of people. For example, when setting out the particular rights accruing to persons that have registered a trademark, Article 16.1 of the TRIPS Agreement refers specifically to "the owner of a registered trademark". Likewise, Section 1 of Part II of the TRIPS Agreement refers to "authors" in Article 11, "right holders" in Article 13, and "performers" and "producers of phonograms" in Article 14. The European Communities claims that Article 22.2 "cannot be invoked by a trademark right holder in order to prevent the use of a geographical indication which supposedly infringes its trademark right".[44] This assertion reveals the European Communities' particular bias toward systems of GI protection analogous to its registration model. It fails to acknowledge that WTO Members implement their obligations on GIs under the TRIPS Agreement in a variety of ways, including for example through collective and certification trademarks. Some trademark owners clearly do have a concern or are affected by use of geographical indications. A trademark holder can, and should in particular circumstances, be able to defend use of a trademark under Article 22.2 of the TRIPS Agreement. The European Communities' narrow interpretation of the phrase "interested parties" in Article 22.2 of the TRIPS Agreement cannot be justified.

147. Third, New Zealand submits that the obligation in Article 22.2 to provide a legal means to prevent misleading uses or acts of unfair competition must be read together with the other provisions of the TRIPS Agreement, including in particular the national treatment obligations in Articles 2.1 and 3.1 of the TRIPS Agreement. Thus the European Communities is obliged to provide "the same protection" or "the same legal means" to WTO nationals as it does to EC nationals. The European Communities has argued that there are other means of

---

[43] *The New Shorter Oxford English Dictionary*, (4th edition, 1993), Vol. 1, p.1393.

[44] European Communities' first written submission, para. 412.

preventing the acts mentioned in Article 22.2 of the TRIPS Agreement available in the European Communities. However, in failing to provide the opportunity for WTO nationals to register under the EC Regulation at the centre of the present dispute, the European Communities fails to provide the same legal means to WTO nationals as it has to the more than 600 GI users in the European Communities that have had their GIs registered.

4. The EC Regulation is inconsistent with Article 16.1 of the TRIPS Agreement

148. The European Communities is obliged under Article 16.1 of the TRIPS Agreement to give owners of registered trademarks the "exclusive right" to prevent confusing uses of similar or identical signs by "all third parties". This right recognises the utility of trademarks to their owners as marketing tools. While Article 16.1 of the TRIPS Agreement provides an "exclusive right" to registered trademark owners, this is not an *absolute* right to prevent all use of the sign by other parties. The right is subject to certain limitations explicitly set out in the TRIPS Agreement in the same way that the rights to GI protection in Articles 22.2 and 22.3 are also explicitly limited by the terms of Articles 22 and 24 of the TRIPS Agreement. In any given case, for example, a registered trademark owner bringing an infringement claim against a GI user might not succeed under the requirements of Article 16.1 of the TRIPS Agreement. The trademark owner may fail to prove that the GI is identical or similar to the trademark; or that the use of the sign is in respect of goods that are identical or similar; or that use of the GI would result in a likelihood of confusion. Alternatively, the GI user may successfully argue in defence that the trademark misleads the public as to the true place of origin of the goods and should therefore be invalidated under the national law implementing Article 22.3 of the TRIPS Agreement. Article 16.1 does, however, guarantee the entitlement of a trademark owner, whether a national of the European Communities or another WTO Member, to a "day in court" to argue his or her rights against *all* third parties.

(a) Relationship between Articles 16.1 and 22.2 of the TRIPS Agreement

149. New Zealand agrees with the observations of Australia and the United States regarding the relationship between Articles 16.1 and 22.2 of the TRIPS Agreement. Despite appearances of a conflict between the two rights on the face of both provisions due to the "exclusivity" of the rights they both accord, there is a presumption of consistency between international obligations.[45] Further, any exception to an obligation must be explicit in the text of an Agreement.[46] The rights in Articles 16.1 and 22.2 of the TRIPS Agreement must therefore be balanced – each must be read to the fullest extent permissible under the text of

[45] See the Panel Report on *Indonesia – Autos,* para. 14.28.
[46] See the Appellate Body Report on *EC – Sardines*, paras. 201-208.

the relevant provisions without conflicting with the other right. In other words, the protection of one right cannot be enhanced at the expense of the other. Where the negotiators intended a conflict between two rights to be resolved by compromising this exclusivity, they specifically provided for this in the TRIPS Agreement. Article 24.5 of the TRIPS Agreement is one example of this. In all other cases, upholding the rights granted in both Article 16.1 for trademarks and Article 22.2 for geographical indications is required. To the extent that the EC Regulation compromises the exclusive rights guaranteed to registered trademark owners in ways not foreseen by the TRIPS Agreement, it is inconsistent with Article 16.1 of the TRIPS Agreement.

(b) The EC Regulation is inconsistent with Article 16.1 of the TRIPS Agreement

150. New Zealand agrees with the complainants that the EC Regulation violates Article 16.1 of the TRIPS Agreement. New Zealand addresses three aspects of the EC Regulation in particular that violate Article 16.1 of the TRIPS Agreement, namely Articles 14(2), 14(3) and 7(4) of the EC Regulation.

151. Article 14(2) of the EC Regulation provides that use of a prior registered trademark that engenders one of the situations prevented by Article 13 of the EC Regulation "may continue notwithstanding the registration" of a GI. The effect of this provision is that under the EC Regulation a registered trademark and a registered GI can "co-exist" despite the existence of a likelihood of confusion between the two. The United States is correct in pointing out that under Article 14(2) of the EC Regulation the best that the owner of a valid prior registered trademark can hope for is the ability to continue using his or her trademark, but without the ability to exclude all others from using a confusingly identical or similar GI. In effect, Article 14(2) of the EC Regulation excludes registered GI users from the scope of the group of "all parties" against whom the owner of a prior registered trademark owner should be entitled under Article 16.1 of the TRIPS Agreement to defend the trademark. This is inconsistent with the exclusive rights of the trademark owner under Article 16.1 of the TRIPS Agreement.

152. Article 14(3) of the EC Regulation provides for an exception to the presumption of coexistence of prior registered trademarks and registered GIs in Article 14(2) of the EC Regulation, taking into account the "reputation, renown and the length of time trademark has been in use". However, just as there is no basis for coexistence under Article 14(3), there is no basis in Article 16.1 of the TRIPS Agreement for conditioning a prior registered trademark owner's right to prevent misleading use on such factors. New Zealand agrees with the United States that the exclusive right in Article 16.1 to prevent confusing use is not limited to owners of trademarks that are longstanding, renowned or reputable. Rather, it is an exclusive right that must be provided to all owners of valid prior registered trademarks, irrespective of how long the trademark has been used, or its reputation and renown.

153. Article 7(4) of the EC Regulation provides the criteria by which the admissibility of a statement of objection to an application for registration of a GI is judged. The criteria in Article 7(4) of the EC Regulation apply to objections from nationals of the European Communities, as well as from nationals of WTO members by virtue of Article 12d(2) of the EC Regulation. One such criterion of admissibility is if the objection "shows that the proposed registration of a name would *jeopardise the existence* of an entirely or partly identical name or of a mark..." (Article 7(4) of the EC Regulation). If the proposed GI registration is identical to the prior registered trademark, however, under Article 16.1 of the TRIPS Agreement there is a presumption of confusion and the trademark owner should have the right to prevent the use of the GI. Consequently, New Zealand agrees with the arguments by Australia that the EC Regulation breaches Article 16.1 of the TRIPS Agreement because the owner of the registered trademark may not be able to successfully object to a proposed GI even if its use would constitute use of an identical or similar sign that would result in a likelihood of confusion.

(i) Article 24.5 of the TRIPS Agreement does not permit "coexistence"

154. The European Communities relies on Article 24.5 of the TRIPS Agreement as envisaging coexistence of GIs and earlier trademarks. The European Communities adopts a flawed interpretation as the basis for its argument that coexistence of GIs and earlier trademarks is envisaged under Article 24.5 of the TRIPS Agreement. It argues that Article 24.5 distinguishes the "right to use" a trademark, which may not be prejudiced, from the right to prevent others from using the trademark sign, which may be prejudiced. New Zealand submits that this interpretation is incorrect for two reasons.

155. First, the purpose of Article 24.5 is to prevent the implementation of new forms of intellectual property resulting from the negotiations of the TRIPS Agreement from prejudicing rights to intellectual property legitimately acquired prior to the entry into force of the TRIPS Agreement. Trademark owners who had registered a trademark or acquired rights to a trademark through use had the rights both to use and to prevent others from using their trademarks prior to the entry into force of the TRIPS Agreement. New Zealand contends that the TRIPS Agreement was not intended to detrimentally affect the private rights of individuals by removing trademark owners' entitlement to prevent all third parties from using their trademark where its existence pre-dated the TRIPS Agreement.

156. Second, Article 24.5 covers trademark rights acquired by registration as well as trademark rights acquired by use. The rights protected under Article 24.5 are dealt with separately. Thus "where a trademark has been applied for or registered in good faith" GI protection measures "shall not prejudice eligibility for or the validity of the registration of a trademark". And "where rights to a trademark have been acquired through use in good faith" GI protection measures "shall not prejudice the right to use a trademark".

157. The European Communities' reading of Article 24.5 confuses the two concepts of registration and use. It suggests that registered trademarks retain the right to use as well as rights to the continued eligibility for or validity of registration. If this reading were correct, the corollary would also be true, namely that trademark rights acquired by use would continue to be eligible for registration, despite the owner not having submitted an application for registration prior to the entry into force of the TRIPS Agreement. As the purpose of Article 24.5 is to protect private rights existing immediately prior to the entry into force of the TRIPS Agreement, it is clear that it was not intended that unregistered trademark owners would gain the right to registration through use, despite having failed to safeguard their rights through registration prior to the entry into force of the TRIPS Agreement. Thus New Zealand agrees with the complainants that Article 24.5 of the TRIPS Agreement does not permit coexistence of "grandfathered" trademarks and GI registrations.

(ii) The EC is not required to maintain coexistence on the basis of Article 24.3 of the TRIPS Agreement

158. The European Communities goes on to argue that, irrespective of whether coexistence of geographical indications is consistent with Article 24.5, it is required to maintain coexistence under Article 24.3 of the TRIPS Agreement. The purpose of this Article appears to be the same as Article 24.5, namely to prevent the entry into force of the TRIPS Agreement from detrimentally affecting the private rights of individuals. However, despite the EC Regulation having entered into force on 14 July 1993, the first registration of a geographical indication under the regulation did not occur until after the entry into force of the TRIPS Agreement on 1 January 1995. So while the EC Regulation provided for coexistence prior to the entry into force of the TRIPS Agreement, in fact the EC Regulation conferred no rights to individuals at that time. In any case, New Zealand submits that the phrase "[i]n implementing this Section" that prefaces Article 24.3 does not justify a breach of other sections of the TRIPS Agreement, including Section 2 on trademarks.

(iii) Coexistence is not a limited exception under Article 17 of the TRIPS Agreement

159. The European Communities also argues in the alternative that coexistence is justified as a "limited exception to the rights conferred by a trademark" under Article 17 of the TRIPS Agreement. In New Zealand's view the exclusion of an entire group of producers from the parties which a registered trademark owner has the right to prevent from using an identical or similar mark in confusing manner is not a "*limited* exception". Rather, it is a major exception to the rights granted to a registered trademark owner.

5. *Points raised in response to the Panel's questions*

160. New Zealand has not received any registration applications or objections to registrations pursuant to the EC Regulation from persons or groups in its territory. New Zealand notes that its Government and potential New Zealand applicants and objectors understood the EC Regulation to mean that no applications or objections would be accepted or considered by the European Communities without New Zealand meeting the reciprocity and equivalence requirements. As to the question of what would be New Zealand's position if such filing was to occur, New Zealand notes that this is a hypothetical question and it is difficult to answer in the abstract. Despite no formal procedure for the transmission of applications for registration or objections to registration under the EC Regulation existing in New Zealand, New Zealand would consider any registration or objection submitted to New Zealand authorities on a case-by-case basis. In any event, the issue before the Panel is the consistency of the EC Regulation with the WTO Agreements, not whether other WTO Members would comply with the requirements of a WTO-inconsistent measure.

161. New Zealand provides the legal means for the protection of geographical indications, as required by Article 22 of the TRIPS Agreement, through its trademarks legislation (including collective trademarks and certification trademarks), and through consumer protection law (Fair Trading Act, common law tort of passing off). These legal means are available to all interested parties irrespective of nationality. A geographical indication (that meets the requirements for registration) may be registered as a trademark through applying, including via the internet, directly to the Intellectual Property Office of New Zealand. An interested party may also apply directly to the Intellectual Property Office to oppose or seek invalidation of the registration of a trademark. For geographical indications other than those registered as trademarks, nationals of any country may take action in New Zealand courts to enforce their rights under the Fair Trading Act 1986, and the common law tort of "passing off". The New Zealand Parliament has enacted a Geographical Indications Act, but this is not in force.

162. New Zealand submits that, by virtue of Article 2.1 of the TRIPS Agreement, all WTO Members must comply with Article 2(1) of the Paris Convention. All WTO Members are therefore "countries of the Union" for the purposes of that Article of the Paris Convention as incorporated in the TRIPS Agreement.

163. New Zealand submits that Article 22.1 of the TRIPS Agreement defines geographical indications as indications that "identify a good as originating in the territory of a Member, or a region or locality in that territory, where a given quality, reputation or other characteristic of the good is essentially attributable to its geographical origin". By definition, therefore, a geographical indication must relate to a particular good. As a consequence, the indication and the good are inextricably linked. The EC Regulation claims that commercial benefits are conferred on goods or products bearing a registered geographical indication. In other words, it claims that the conditions of sale are positively affected by the

products bearing registered geographical indications. As a result of the different treatment accorded to EC nationals and nationals of WTO Members, only products bearing a registered EC geographical indication have the opportunity to obtain any commercial benefits which are claimed by the European Communities to ensue from protection under the EC Regulation. The foreign like product does not have this opportunity and therefore receives less favourable treatment. New Zealand considers that evidence of disadvantages accorded to foreigners in applying for and objecting to protection of particular geographical indications is relevant to whether like products receive less favourable treatment.

164. Under New Zealand's trademark legislation, a trademark (including a geographical indication for which registration as a trademark has been sought) that would otherwise be considered identical or similar to a registered trademark may be registered if: (i) the owner of the registered trademark consents to the registration of the later filed trademark; or (ii) the Commissioner of Trade Marks (or Court) considers that a case of honest concurrent use exists or other special circumstances exist, which makes it proper for the trademark to be registered. In making such a determination, the Commissioner of Trade Marks (or Court) will have regard to, *inter alia*, whether confusion is likely to occur, the degree of that confusion, and whether any confusion has in fact been proved. A registered trademark may be used for the purpose of comparative advertising provided that the mark is used in accordance with honest practices in industrial or commercial matters. Use of a sign (including a geographical indication) will not amount to infringement of a registered trademark if, in accordance with honest practices in industrial or commercial matters, the sign is used to indicate, *inter alia*, a person's name, place of business, or the kind, quality, geographical origin or other characteristic of the goods or services. If the use of the trademark is misleading or is likely to cause confusion then its use is unlikely to be considered "in accordance with honest practices"

165. In New Zealand, the concurrent use of geographical indications with prior trademarks would not be permitted where this would result in a breach of the Trade Marks Act, the Fair Trading Act or the common law tort of "passing off". Confusion is relevant to all three causes of action. Infringement proceedings may be taken under the Trade Marks Act (section 89) for use of a sign that is identical or similar to a registered trademark where such use would be likely to deceive or confuse (note, however that there is a presumption of infringement under the Trade Marks Act where a mark that is identical to a registered trademark is used in respect of identical goods). The Fair Trading Act (section 9) prohibits conduct in trade that is deceptive or misleading or likely to deceive or mislead, while passing off is aimed at preventing misrepresentation that can result from use of a confusingly similar mark. A geographical indication could not be protected as a registered trademark if its use would be likely to deceive or cause confusion, particularly with a prior registered mark (sections 17 and 25 of the Trade Marks Act).

166. New Zealand believes that the mandatory/discretionary distinction has limited application under the TRIPS Agreement. As indicated by the Appellate Body in *US – Section 211 Appropriations Act*, the characterization of legislation

as mandatory or discretionary is not the only relevant inquiry for a panel.[47] Nor should a finding that the legislation is discretionary be conclusive as to whether a State has complied with WTO rules. In particular, the "extra hurdles" in the EC Regulation that disadvantage foreigners and breach national treatment apply regardless of whether or not that legislation is deemed "discretionary". Further, the granting of intellectual property rights necessarily involves the exercise of discretion, as does for example the initiation of anti-dumping investigations. The objectives of the TRIPS Agreement would be undermined if the European Communities can be excused from its TRIPS obligations on the basis that its implementing legislation is discretionary. New Zealand notes that obligations prohibiting certain action and obligations requiring certain action, whether in the TRIPS Agreement or in other WTO Agreements, are all binding and mandatory obligations upon WTO Members. Accordingly, New Zealand cannot see that WTO jurisprudence on the mandatory/discretionary distinction should apply differently depending on whether the obligations prohibit certain action, or require certain action.

I. Separate Customs Territory of Taiwan, Penghu, Kinmen and Matsu

1. Introduction

167. The Separate Customs Territory of Taiwan, Penghu, Kinmen and Matsu (hereinafter referred to as "Chinese Taipei") has a trade and systemic interest in the proper interpretation of the TRIPS Agreement, specifically, the national treatment requirements contained in the TRIPS Agreement and Paris Convention, the MFN requirement contained in the TRIPS Agreement, and in the relationship between geographical indications ("GIs") and trademarks.

2. National treatment

168. National treatment is a long-standing and fundamental obligation in the multilateral trading system. The European Communities completely ignores the fact that the protection of intellectual property plays a part in the national treatment provisions. By citing the specific paragraph in the Panel Report of *Indonesia – Autos* cautioning against reading extraneous obligations into a provision, the European Communities also seems to suggest that the protection of intellectual property rights is not in fact an objective of the TRIPS Agreement, and that one should not read the protection of intellectual property into Article 3.1 of the TRIPS Agreement. The drafters of Article 3.1 of the TRIPS Agreement and Article 2(1) of the Paris Convention recognize that, in the context of the protection of intellectual property, nationals and the intellectual property rights they hold cannot be divorced from each other. Conceptually, to grant national treatment to nationals who are not holders of intellectual property rights would be illogical. Similarly, intellectual property rights by themselves

[47] See the Appellate Body Report on *US – Section 211 Appropriations Act*, para. 260.

cannot enforce the requirement of national treatment without their attendant holder-nationals. The two national treatment provisions would simply be incomprehensible if the protection of intellectual property were taken out of the equation. Furthermore, Article 3.1 of the TRIPS Agreement and Article 2(1) of the Paris Convention do not specify the origin of the intellectual property being held by the "nationals". The focus of the national treatment provisions is on the nationals who have an intellectual property to register or the rights to enforce, not on the origin of the actual intellectual property. Be it domestic nationals holding domestic intellectual property rights, domestic nationals holding foreign intellectual property rights, foreign nationals holding domestic intellectual property rights, or foreign nationals holding foreign intellectual property rights, national treatment applies in all scenarios in the same manner.

169. In order to demonstrate how the TRIPS Agreement and Paris Convention national treatment obligations apply in this case, Chinese Taipei presents the following chart:

GI EC National EC 1	GI Non EC National EC 3
2 GI EC National Non EC	4 GI Non EC National Non EC

170. The four quadrants represent the four possible scenarios. The European Communities, focusing only on nationals in its interpretation, is essentially arguing that it can establish a separate set of rules for and discriminate against non-EC GIs as it wishes. To the European Communities, quadrants 1 and 2 are completely independent from quadrants 3 and 4. As long as the national in quadrant 2 is treated no less favourably than the national in quadrant 1, and the national in quadrant 4 is treated no less favourably than the national in quadrant 3, the national treatment obligation, according to the European Communities, is satisfied. However, as already presented above, there exists two linked elements in the TRIPS Agreement and Paris Convention national treatment obligations, and the four quadrants need to be examined as a whole. This means that quadrants 2, 3, and 4 all cannot be treated less favourably than quadrant 1. Therefore, the Panel should examine, whether the EC Regulation results in any one of the quadrants 2, 3, or 4 being treated less favourably than quadrant 1. If even one of the quadrants is treated less favourably, the EC Regulation would be inconsistent with the national treatment obligations. Chinese Taipei agrees with the submissions of the United States and Australia in their analyses of how Article 12 of EC Regulation results in less favourable treatment being afforded to non-EC nationals. Since the scenarios in quadrant 2 and 3 in practice happen infrequently, it would suffice to examine only the consistency of the EC Regulation with regard to the scenario under quadrant 4. By applying the same

arguments the two complainants made with regard to EC Regulation Article 12, the Panel would be able to see a blatant violation in the scenario represented by quadrant 4.

171. Chinese Taipei also agrees with the United States and Australia that Article 12.1 of the EC Regulation constitutes conditions on WTO Members in exchange for the recognition of GIs from non-EC sources. Such conditions violate Article 3.1 of the TRIPS Agreement and Article 2(1) of the Paris Convention. The European Communities conditions the protection of GIs, an explicit obligation under Article 22 of the TRIPS Agreement, on reciprocity and equivalence. Such requirements do not exist in Part II Section 3 of the TRIPS Agreement which deals with GIs nor anywhere else in the TRIPS Agreement as preconditions to implementing an explicit TRIPS Agreement obligation. Furthermore, Article 12.3 of the EC Regulation provides that, "[t]he Commission shall examine, at the request of the country concerned...whether a third country satisfies the equivalence conditions and offers guarantees within the meaning of paragraph 1 as a result of its national legislation". Therefore, even if a WTO Member deems its GI specifications, inspection arrangements, the right to object and protection of EC GIs to be equivalent, the European Communities still holds the final say on whether the equivalence conditions have been met. The European Communities has yet to give an indication as to what it considers to constitute "equivalence", but the existence of this requirement to gain approval from the Commission suggests that the standard for equivalence is high.

172. In essence, the European Communities is requiring other WTO Members to adopt a system of GI protection substantially similar to, if not the same as, the European Communities and be prepared to accept automatically all EC GIs. By requiring the reciprocity and equivalency conditions, the European Communities ignores the fact that the second sentence of Article 1.1 of the TRIPS Agreement provides that, "Members shall be free to determine the appropriate method of implementing the provisions of this Agreement within their own legal system and practice", and that Article 22 of the TRIPS Agreement does not specify any particular "legal means" for the protection of GIs. In this connection, Chinese Taipei agrees with the United States that the TRIPS Agreement recognizes more than one acceptable GI protection system. Moreover, reciprocity and equivalency may be better addressed in the context of bilateral or multilateral negotiations, should the European Communities wish to do so. But they cannot constitute conditions on the implementation of an explicit TRIPS Agreement obligation to provide national treatment to foreign producers with regard to intellectual property. Additionally, if a Member such as the European Communities believes that another Member is not granting the proper protection to GIs as stipulated in the TRIPS Agreement, the recourse is the WTO dispute settlement, not the denial of national treatment. As it is, these reciprocity and equivalence conditions are simply extra hurdles to be fulfilled by WTO Members before producers with GIs from their territories can gain protection from the European Communities. These extra hurdles constitute an additional burden on non-EC nationals seeking to register, and enforce non-EC GIs within the European Communities as compared to the requirements on EC nationals. Thus, the EC

Regulation violates the national treatment provisions pursuant to Article 3.1 of the TRIPS Agreement and the Article 2(1) of the Paris Convention.

3. *MFN treatment*

173. Chinese Taipei also shares the view of the United States and Australia that, just as the EC Regulation violates the national treatment obligation under the TRIPS Agreement, the measure also violates the TRIPS Agreement MFN obligation. It should be noted, in light of the arguments presented above on national treatment, that the MFN obligation with regard to nationals should be viewed with respect to the protection of intellectual property, from the perspective of nationals holding intellectual property rights. Similarly, as with TRIPS and Paris Convention national treatment obligations, Article 4 cannot be interpreted as an obligation on nationals alone.

174. The chart presented in the context of national treatment above can be slightly modified to be applied here:

GI approved National approved 1	GI not approved National approved 3
2 GI approved National not approved	4 GI not approved National not approved

175. The above chart sets out how the MFN treatment comparison should be made. With regard to the protection of intellectual property, the MFN treatment in essence requires the Member in question to grant equal treatment to the nationals of all other Members. Therefore, the basic premise of this quadrant is that both the GI and the national are non-EC in origin (Chinese Taipei takes no position with regard to the issue raised by the complainants that the individual members of the European Communities who are also Members of the WTO should be viewed as separate non-EC Members of the WTO under MFN treatment). The term "national" in the table is used in the same manner as the word "nationals" in Article 4 of the TRIPS Agreement, but with the above premise in mind. The terms "approved" and "not approved" relate to the approval scheme in Articles 12(1) and 12(3) of the EC Regulation under which a third country GI may be protected within the European Communities after determination by the EC Commission that the "equivalence conditions" have been satisfied. "Approved" thus means that the GI or national originated from a WTO Member which has been deemed by the EC Commission to have satisfied the conditions set out in Article 12(1). On the other hand, "not approved" means that the GI or national originated from a WTO Member which has not been deemed by the EC Commission to have satisfied the conditions set out in the

Article 12(1). The GI and the national may have different origins, hence the existence of quadrants 2 and 3.

176. Under the MFN treatment, the scenarios under quadrants 2, 3, and 4 must all receive the same treatment from European Communities as the treatment received by quadrant 1, or else the European Communities has violated the obligation. Having granted full protection under the EC Regulation to the nationals of an approved WTO Member holding GIs originating from the territories of that member, the European Communities cannot deny the same "advantage, favour, privilege or immunity" to the nationals of other WTO Members holding GIs originating from other territories. But this is exactly what EC Regulation does. Once again, quadrant 4 shows where the EC Regulation most blatantly violates the MFN treatment obligation.

4. *Relationship between GIs and trademarks in the TRIPS Agreement*

177. Unlike other types of intellectual property such as patents and copyrights, which tend to be independent concepts and manifest themselves in different forms, trademarks and GIs are closely related. The purpose of both is to inform consumers about the source and indirectly the quality of the product. Because of this purpose, GIs and trademarks can and tend to manifest themselves in similar forms, i.e., as prominent and distinguishing signs. The close relationship between GIs and trademarks and the possible overlap in their physical manifestations and protection are recognized in the TRIPS Agreement. Articles 22.3, 23.2 and 24.5 directly address the relationship between GIs and trademarks. The rights are derived from the need to prevent consumers from being misled about the qualities of the product, and thus the provision in Article 16.1 for trademarks and Article 22.2 for GIs spelling out the extent of the rights.

178. However, the text of these two TRIPS provisions must be given their full scope in a manner that would not cause conflict. This is consistent with the established principle of international treaty interpretation, which requires that the "interpretation must give meaning and effect to all the terms of a treaty". Furthermore, "[a]n interpreter is not free to adopt a meaning that would result in whole clauses or paragraphs of a treaty to redundancy or inutility".[48] An interpretation or implementation of these two provisions that creates conflict would inevitably render one of the provisions inutile. Thus, the Panel in *Indonesia – Autos* concluded that, "in public international law there is a presumption against conflict".[49] However, the EC Regulation creates precisely such a conflict by allowing a later registered GI to be used alongside a prior trademark, even when such use has the potential of resulting in the likelihood of confusion on the part of the consumer. Thus, Article 14(2) of the Regulation negates the right of trademark owners contained in Article 16.1 of the TRIPS Agreement. Likewise, under Article 14(3) of the EC Regulation, a potential GI is

[48] Appellate Body Report on *US – Gasoline*, DSR 1996:I, at 21.

[49] Panel Report on *Indonesia – Autos*, para. 14.28.

only prevented from being registered if the trademark fulfils the conditions of reputation, renown, and length of time, the provision negates the right granted to trademark owners pursuant to Article 16.1 of the TRIPS Agreement. The result of the EC Regulation is the creation of a hierarchy between GIs and trademarks, when the two are equal under the TRIPS Agreement. GIs within the European Communities have a superior status than trademarks, and the protection of GIs is granted at the expense of trademarks. Such a hierarchy is simply not contemplated in the TRIPS Agreement.

5. *Points raised in response to Panel's questions*

179. Chinese Taipei is not aware of any group or person ever having filed with its authorities either an application for, or an objection to, a registration pursuant to the EC Regulation. In any case, it does not believe that whether its Government is able and/or willing to transmit to the European Communities an application from persons interested in a GI or objection has any bearing on the issues in this dispute. Even if its Government is able and/or willing, the fact remains, that the TRIPS Agreement does not contain any obligation for Members to comply with an internal regulation of the European Communities. The European Communities is free to require its member States to do so, but to require WTO Members to transmit applications for registration or objections to registration when no such obligation exists in the TRIPS Agreement would be to create an additional hurdle for non-EC nationals who wish to register their GIs within the European Communities, thus violating Article 3.1 of the TRIPS Agreement and Article 2 of the Paris Convention.

180. Chinese Taipei's legislation protects trademarks and collective marks of foreign nationals in the same manner as that of domestic nationals, and nothing in its legislation prevents foreign nationals with a potential GI from applying for the registration of a trademark or collective mark.

181. Chinese Taipei believes that footnote 1 of the TRIPS Agreement is meant to apply the term "nationals" to separate customs territory Members of the WTO. The first clause of the footnote makes the application of the definition to the entire Agreement clear with the words "in this Agreement". The definition therefore applies to the European Communities, as a separate customs territory, with regard to Articles 3.1 and 4 of the TRIPS Agreement. There is no logical reason to believe that the term "nationals" in Article 2 of the Paris Convention should be interpreted any differently from the TRIPS Agreement, with respect to the European Communities. It is established jurisprudence that Articles 1 through 12 and Article 19 of the Paris Convention are incorporated into the TRIPS Agreement. Article 3 of the TRIPS Agreement, which is the parallel provision to Article 2 of Paris Convention, makes explicit reference to the applicability of the exceptions in the Paris Convention. If key terms such as "nationals" are interpreted differently in the TRIPS Agreement and the Paris Convention, incorporation and direct applicability of certain provisions would be difficult, if not impossible. Therefore, unless there is an explicit reason to believe

otherwise, the term "nationals" in Article 2 of the Paris Convention should be interpreted in the same manner as in the TRIPS Agreement.

182. Chinese Taipei understands that Articles 16.1 and 22.3 of the TRIPS Agreement do not, and should not be, interpreted to conflict. The established principle of international treaty interpretation requires that any interpretation shall give meaning and effect to all terms of a treaty. An interpretation that creates a conflict between two provisions would inevitably render one of the provisions inutile. The third sentence of Article 16.1 states that, "the rights described above shall not prejudice any existing prior rights". Therefore, the "exclusive right" granted to trademarks under Article 16.1 is dependent upon existing prior rights. Similarly, and in a parallel manner, the rights obtained pursuant to GI protection are curtailed by Article 24.5, where the right of a prior trademark owner, which is exclusive, is guaranteed. The combination of Articles 16.1, 22.3 and 24.5 establishes a protection scheme where a prior existing right, be it under trademark or GI, bars any later requests to register trademarks or GIs that would confuse or mislead the public. The EC Regulation creates a conflict between the protection of trademarks and GIs, when no such conflict exists, by disregarding the exclusive right of prior trademarks owners and favouring the right of GI owners. Such a hierarchy is not contemplated by the TRIPS Agreement.

EXHIBIT NZ-1

APPLICATION PROCESS FOR THE REGISTRATION OF A GEOGRAPHICAL INDICATION UNDER EC REGULATION 2081/92[1]

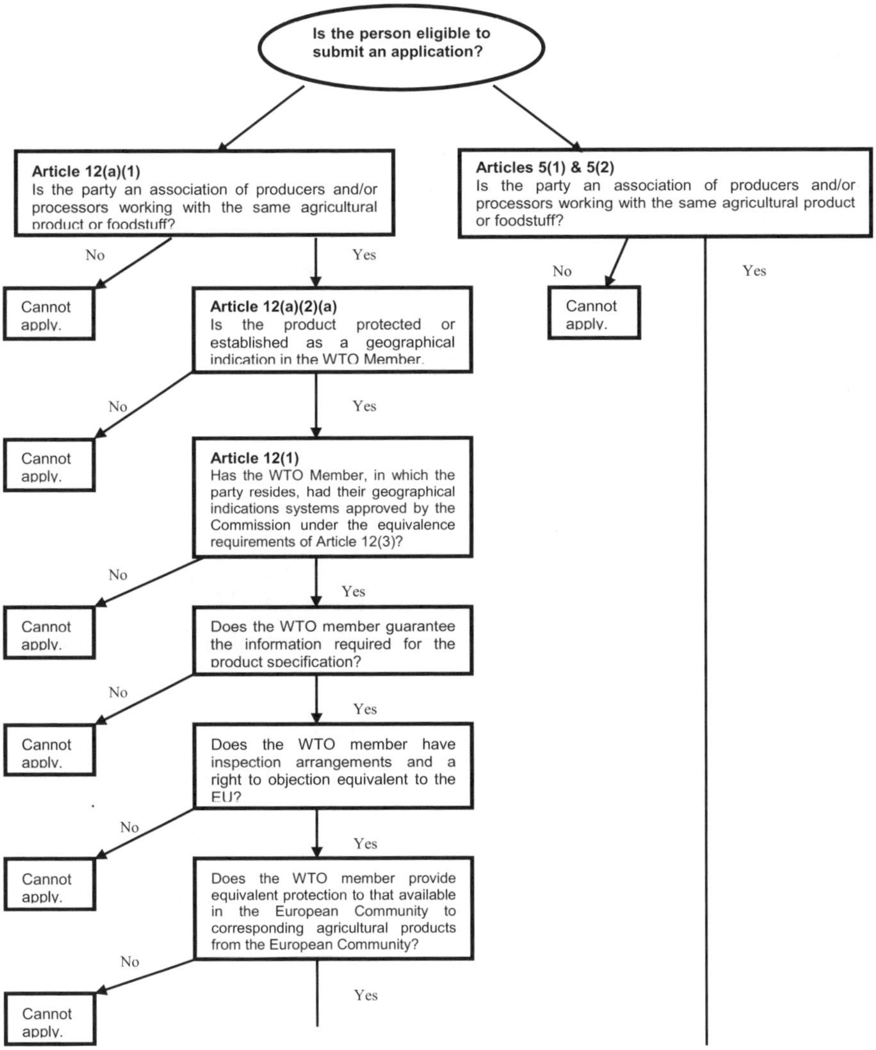

[1] Note this flow-chart excludes procedures relating to homonymous names and the procedures applicable to third countries that are not WTO Members.

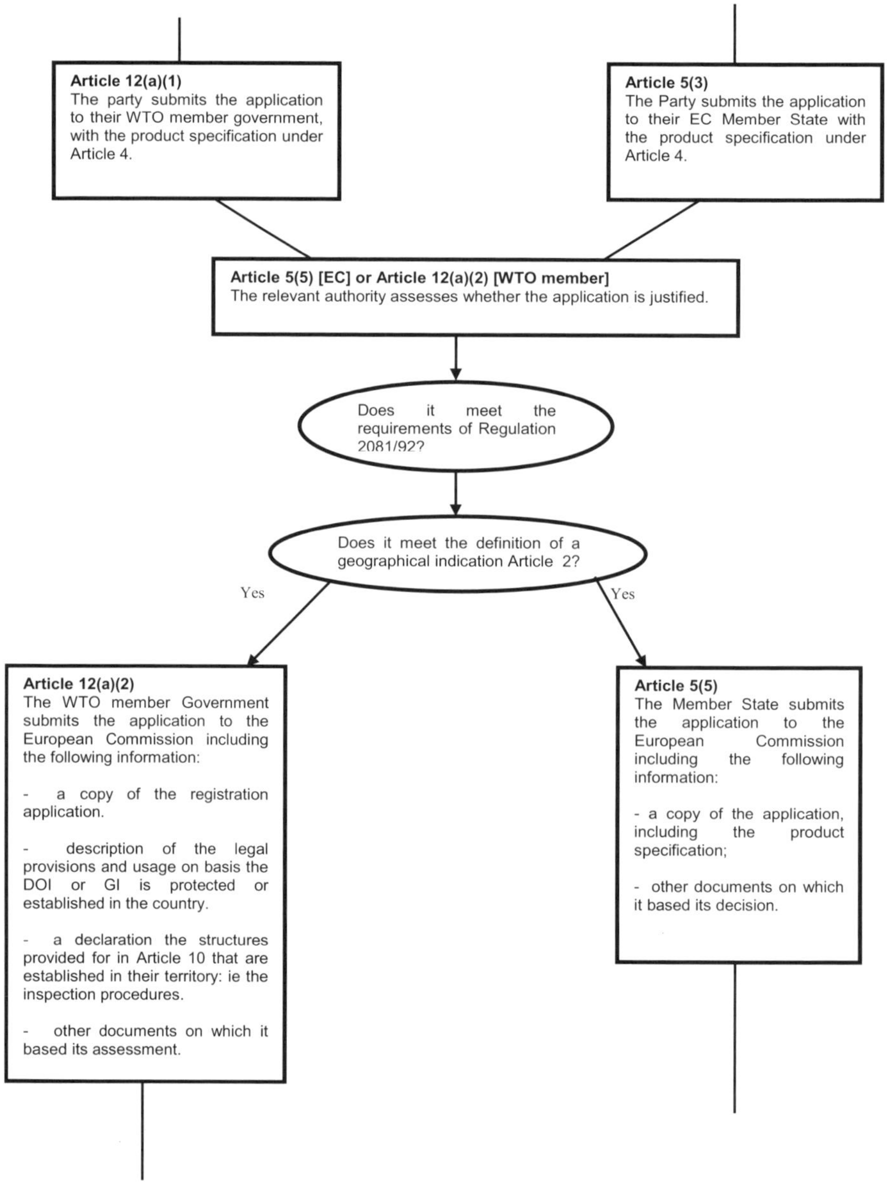
Article 12(a)(1)
The party submits the application to their WTO member government, with the product specification under Article 4.
Article 5(3)
The Party submits the application to their EC Member State with the product specification under Article 4.
Article 5(5) [EC] or Article 12(a)(2) [WTO member]
The relevant authority assesses whether the application is justified.
Does it meet the requirements of Regulation 2081/92?
Does it meet the definition of a geographical indication Article 2?
Yes
Yes
Article 12(a)(2)
The WTO member Government submits the application to the European Commission including the following information:
- a copy of the registration application.
- description of the legal provisions and usage on basis the DOI or GI is protected or established in the country.
- a declaration the structures provided for in Article 10 that are established in their territory: ie the inspection procedures.
- other documents on which it based its assessment.
Article 5(5)
The Member State submits the application to the European Commission including the following information:
- a copy of the application, including the product specification;
- other documents on which it based its decision.

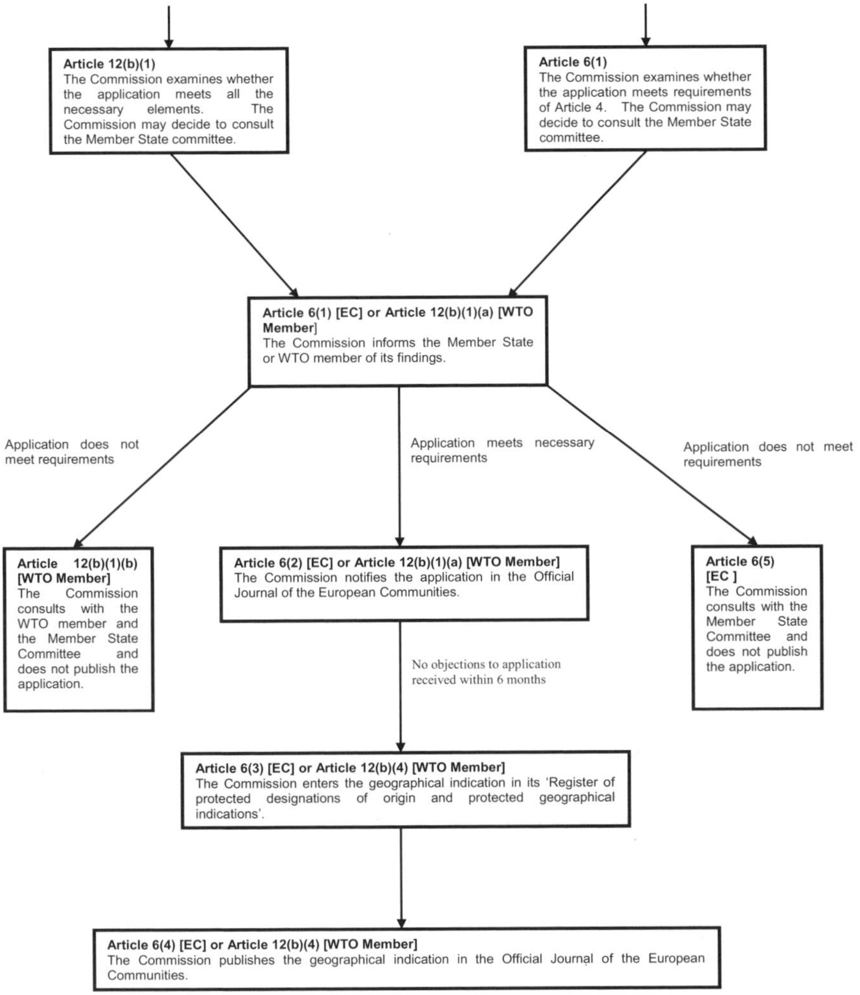
Article 12(b)(1)
The Commission examines whether the application meets all the necessary elements. The Commission may decide to consult the Member State committee.
Article 6(1)
The Commission examines whether the application meets requirements of Article 4. The Commission may decide to consult the Member State committee.
Article 6(1) [EC] or Article 12(b)(1)(a) [WTO Member]
The Commission informs the Member State or WTO member of its findings.
Application does not meet requirements
Application meets necessary requirements
Application does not meet requirements
Article 12(b)(1)(b) [WTO Member]
The Commission consults with the WTO member and the Member State Committee and does not publish the application.
Article 6(2) [EC] or Article 12(b)(1)(a) [WTO Member]
The Commission notifies the application in the Official Journal of the European Communities.
Article 6(5) [EC]
The Commission consults with the Member State Committee and does not publish the application.
No objections to application received within 6 months
Article 6(3) [EC] or Article 12(b)(4) [WTO Member]
The Commission enters the geographical indication in its 'Register of protected designations of origin and protected geographical indications'.
Article 6(4) [EC] or Article 12(b)(4) [WTO Member]
The Commission publishes the geographical indication in the Official Journal of the European Communities.

EXHIBIT NZ-2

OBJECTION PROCESS DURING THE REGISTRATION OF A GEOGRAPHICAL INDICATION UNDER EC REGULATION 2081/92[2]

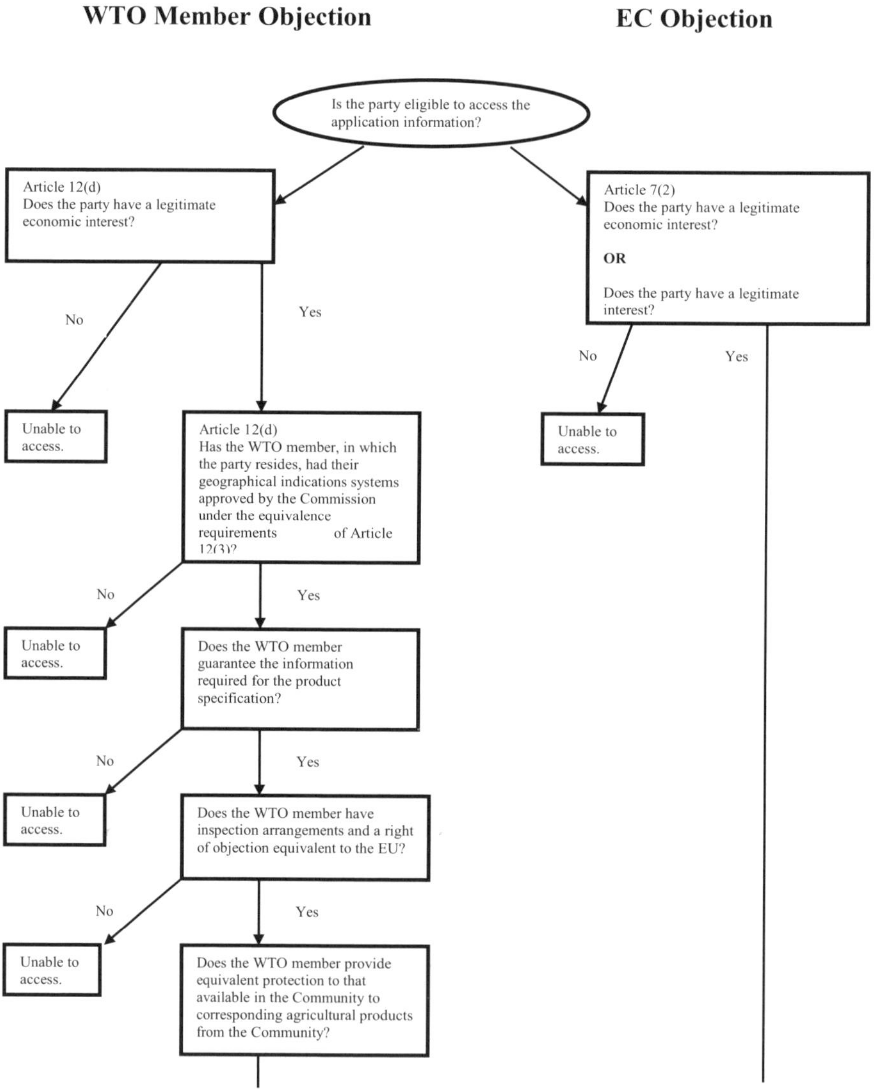

[2] Note, this flow-chart excludes homonymous names and the procedures for third countries that are not WTO Members.

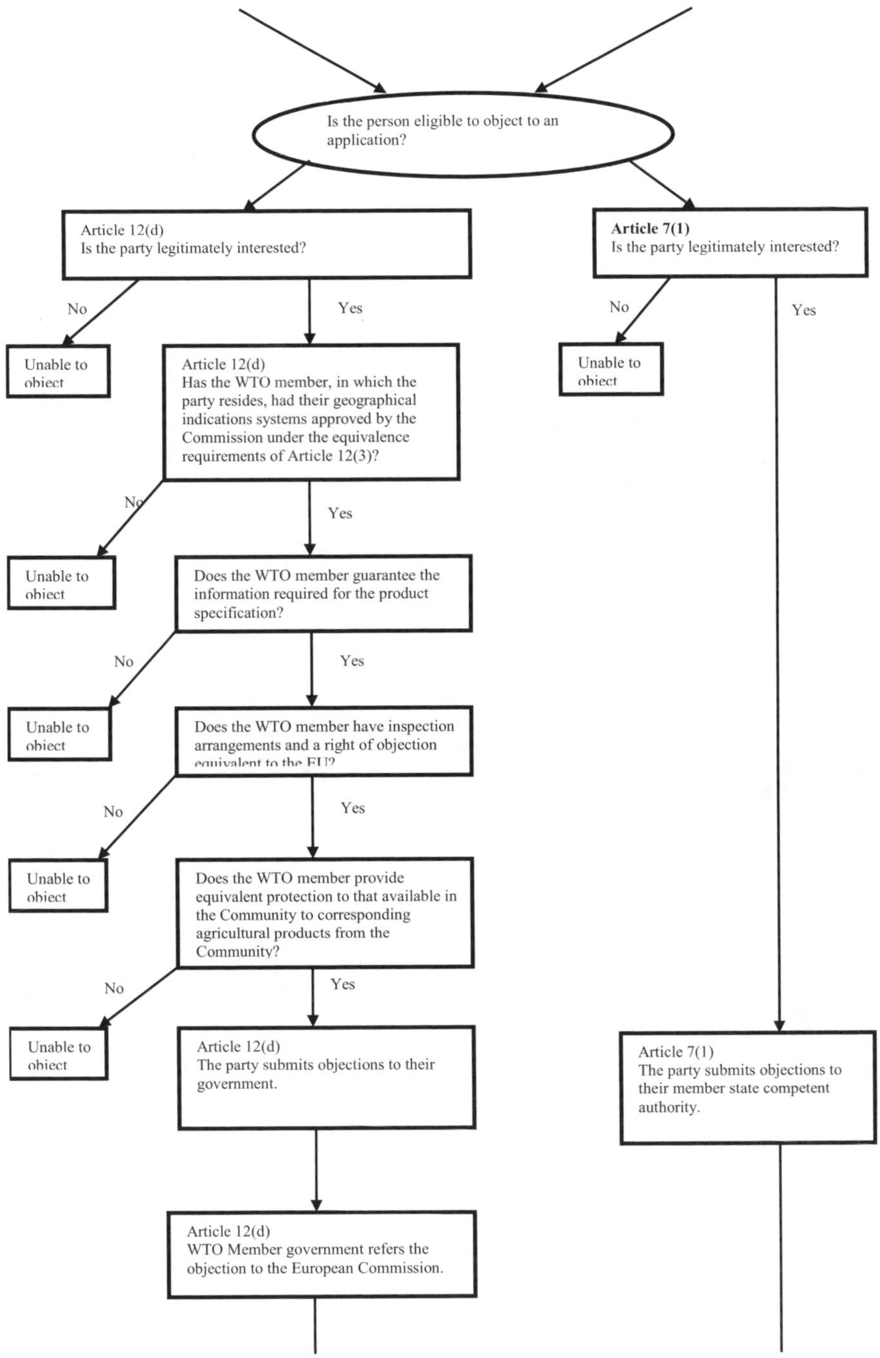
Is the person eligible to object to an application?
Article 12(d)
Is the party legitimately interested?
Article 7(1)
Is the party legitimately interested?
No
Yes
No
Yes
Unable to object
Article 12(d)
Has the WTO member, in which the party resides, had their geographical indications systems approved by the Commission under the equivalence requirements of Article 12(3)?
Unable to object
No
Yes
Unable to object
Does the WTO member guarantee the information required for the product specification?
No
Yes
Unable to object
Does the WTO member have inspection arrangements and a right of objection equivalent to the EU?
No
Yes
Unable to object
Does the WTO member provide equivalent protection to that available in the Community to corresponding agricultural products from the Community?
No
Yes
Unable to object
Article 12(d)
The party submits objections to their government.
Article 7(1)
The party submits objections to their member state competent authority.
Article 12(d)
WTO Member government refers the objection to the European Commission.

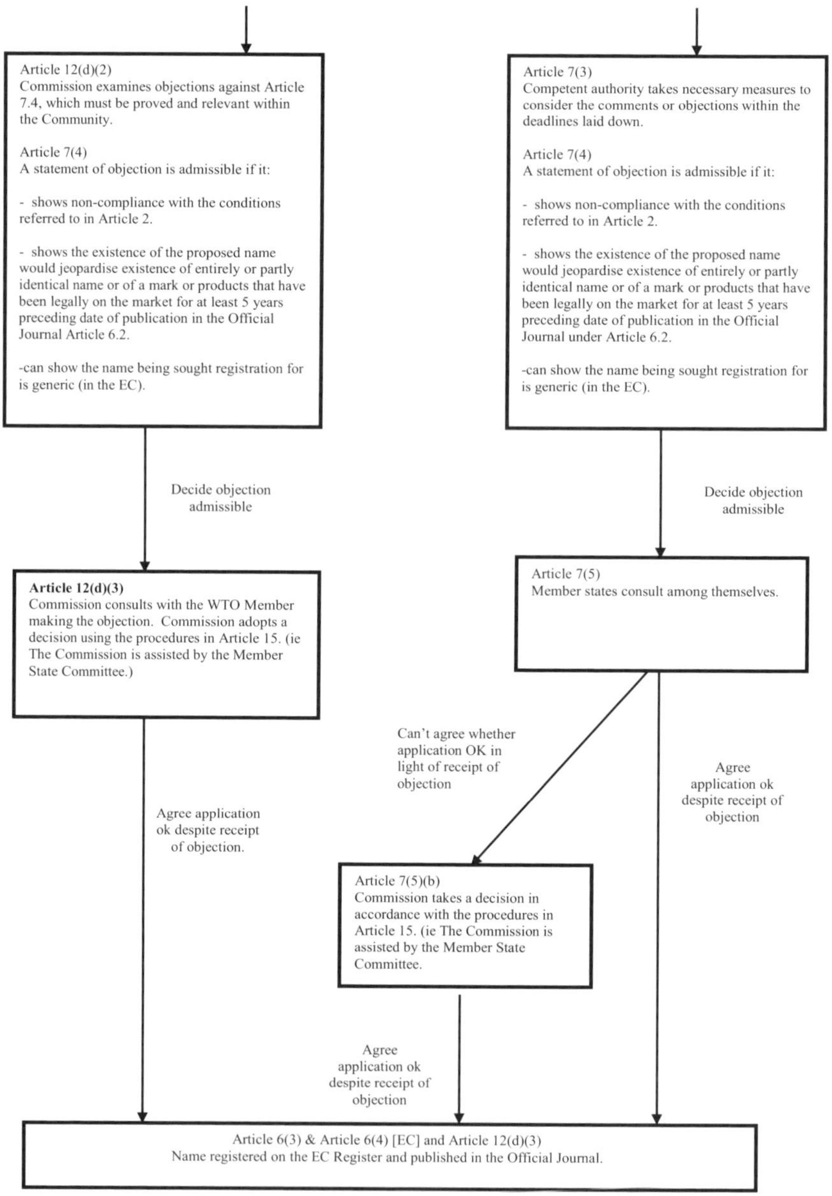
Article 12(d)(2)
Commission examines objections against Article 7.4, which must be proved and relevant within the Community.
Article 7(4)
A statement of objection is admissible if it:
- shows non-compliance with the conditions referred to in Article 2.
- shows the existence of the proposed name would jeopardise existence of entirely or partly identical name or of a mark or products that have been legally on the market for at least 5 years preceding date of publication in the Official Journal Article 6.2.
-can show the name being sought registration for is generic (in the EC).
Article 7(3)
Competent authority takes necessary measures to consider the comments or objections within the deadlines laid down.
Article 7(4)
A statement of objection is admissible if it:
- shows non-compliance with the conditions referred to in Article 2.
- shows the existence of the proposed name would jeopardise existence of entirely or partly identical name or of a mark or products that have been legally on the market for at least 5 years preceding date of publication in the Official Journal under Article 6.2.
-can show the name being sought registration for is generic (in the EC).
Decide objection admissible
Decide objection admissible
Article 12(d)(3)
Commission consults with the WTO Member making the objection. Commission adopts a decision using the procedures in Article 15. (ie The Commission is assisted by the Member State Committee.)
Article 7(5)
Member states consult among themselves.
Can't agree whether application OK in light of receipt of objection
Agree application ok despite receipt of objection
Agree application ok despite receipt of objection.
Article 7(5)(b)
Commission takes a decision in accordance with the procedures in Article 15. (ie The Commission is assisted by the Member State Committee.
Agree application ok despite receipt of objection
Article 6(3) & Article 6(4) [EC] and Article 12(d)(3)
Name registered on the EC Register and published in the Official Journal.

ANNEXES D

MISCELLANEOUS

ANNEX D-1

WORLD TRADE ORGANIZATION

WT/DS290/18
19 August 2003

(03-4315)

Original: English

EUROPEAN COMMUNITIES – PROTECTION OF TRADEMARKS AND GEOGRAPHICAL INDICATIONS FOR AGRICULTURAL PRODUCTS AND FOODSTUFFS

Request for the Establishment of a Panel by Australia

The following communication, dated 18 August 2003, from the Permanent Mission of Australia to the Chairman of the Dispute Settlement Body, is circulated pursuant to Article 6.2 of the DSU.

My authorities have instructed me to request the establishment of a panel on behalf of Australia.

On 17 April 2003, Australia requested consultations with the European Communities (EC) pursuant to Article 4 of the *Understanding on Rules and Procedures Governing the Settlement of Disputes* (DSU), Article XXII of the *General Agreement on Tariffs and Trade 1994* (GATT 1994), Article 64 of the *Agreement on Trade-Related Aspects of Intellectual Property Rights* (TRIPS Agreement) and Article 14 of the *Agreement on Technical Barriers to Trade* (TBT Agreement) concerning the protection of trademarks and the registration and protection of geographical indications for foodstuffs and agricultural products in the EC. The request was circulated to Members on 23 April 2003 in document WT/DS290/1. Consultations were held on 27 May 2003 but did not lead to a resolution of the dispute.

Consequently, Australia requests that a panel be established pursuant to Articles 4.7 and 6 of the DSU, Article XXIII:2 of GATT 1994, Article 64 of the TRIPS Agreement and Article 14 of the TBT Agreement.

The measure at issue is Council Regulation (EEC) No. 2081/92 of 14 July 1992 *on the protection of geographical indications and designations of origin for agricultural products and foodstuffs*, any amendments thereto (including Council Regulation (EC) No. 692/2003 of 8 April 2003, published in the *Official Journal of the European Union* No. L99 of 17 April 2003), and related implementing and enforcement measures ("the EC measure"). The EC measure lays down and implements rules on the protection of designations of origin and geographical indications for agricultural products and foodstuffs, excluding wines and spirits.

Australia is of the view that the EC measure:

- diminishes the legal protection for trademarks under the TRIPS Agreement, contrary to Articles 1, 2 (incorporating by reference Articles 6*quinques*(B), 10, 10*bis* and 10*ter* of the Paris Convention (1967)), 16, 20, 24.5, 41 and/or 42 of the TRIPS Agreement;
- does not accord immediately and unconditionally to the nationals and/or products of each WTO Member any advantage, favour privilege or immunity granted to the nationals of any other WTO Member, contrary to Articles 1 and 4 of the TRIPS Agreement and/or Article I:1 of GATT 1994;
- does not accord to nationals and/or products of each WTO Member treatment no less favourable than that it accords to its own nationals and/or like products of national origin, contrary to Articles 1, 2 (incorporating by reference Article 2 of the Paris Convention (1967)) and 3.1 of the TRIPS Agreement and/or Article III:4 of GATT 1994;
- does not provide the legal means for interested parties to prevent misleading use of a geographical indication and/or to prevent any use of a geographical indication which constitutes an act of unfair competition within the meaning of Article 10*bis* of the Paris Convention (1967), contrary to Articles 1 and 22.2 of the TRIPS Agreement;
- is not applied in a transparent manner, contrary to Articles 1, and 63.1 and 63.3 of the TRIPS Agreement;
- is a technical regulation within the meaning of Annex 1 to the TBT Agreement, does not accord to products imported from the territory of any WTO Member treatment no less favourable than that accorded to like products of national origin and/or to like products originating in any other country, and/or has been prepared, adopted and/or applied with the effect of creating unnecessary obstacles to trade, being more trade-restrictive than necessary to fulfil a legitimate objective, taking account of the risks non-fulfilment would create, contrary to Articles 2.1 and 2.2 of the TBT Agreement;

and that, as a consequence of the EC measure's inconsistency with the abovementioned provisions of the TRIPS Agreement, GATT 1994 and/or the TBT Agreement, the EC is not in conformity with its obligations:

- under Article 65.1 of the TRIPS Agreement to apply the provisions of that Agreement, as the period of one year following the date of entry into force of the WTO Agreement has expired; and/or
- under Article XVI.4 of the *Marrakesh Agreement Establishing the World Trade Organization*, to ensure the conformity of its laws, regulations and administrative procedures with its obligation as provided in the annexed Agreements.

Australia requests the establishment of a panel with terms of reference in accordance with Article 7.1 of the DSU.

I would be grateful if you would place this item on the agenda for the next DSB meeting scheduled for 29 August 2003.

ANNEX D-2

LETTER DATED 9 JULY 2004 FROM THE PANEL TO THE INTERNATIONAL BUREAU OF WIPO

At its meeting on 2 October 2003, the WTO Dispute Settlement Body established the Panel on European Communities – Protection of Trademarks and Geographical Indications for Agricultural Products and Foodstuffs pursuant to the requests by the United States in document WT/DS174/20 and Australia in document WT/DS290/18 (please see the attached documents), in accordance with Article 9 of the Dispute Settlement Understanding. On 23 February 2004, a Panel was composed to examine this complaint (please see the attached document with a dual symbol WT/DS174/21 and WT/DS290/19).

A number of provisions of the Paris Convention have been raised in these proceedings as relevant to the interpretation of the European Communities' obligations under the TRIPS Agreement. Given that the International Bureau of WIPO is responsible for the administration of that Convention, the purpose of this letter is to request, on behalf of the panel, the assistance of the International Bureau of WIPO in the form of any factual information available to it relevant to the interpretation of the provisions in question, in particular as reflected in the materials of diplomatic conferences, subsequent developments in the framework of the Paris Union or other work under the auspices of the WIPO as well as, to the extent available to the International Bureau, on the state practice of the Paris Union members.

The specific provisions of the Paris Convention in regard to which the panel would seek this assistance at this stage are:

– Article 2 of the Stockholm Act of 1967 of the Paris Convention, in particular as regards:

  (a) the national treatment obligation contained in that provision; and

  (b) the intended meaning of the term "national" used therein.

– Any other provisions, of relevance to the categories of intellectual property at issue in this dispute, which set out criteria for the eligibility of natural or legal persons for protection under the Paris Convention (1967).

The Panel may, at a later stage, wish to seek from the International Bureau further such information on other provisions of the Paris Convention (1967) that have been referred to by the parties to the dispute.

It would facilitate the work of the Panel if such information could be made available by Thursday, 29 July 2004.

ANNEX D-3

REPLY FROM THE INTERNATIONAL BUREAU OF WIPO TO THE PANEL'S LETTER DATED 9 JULY 2004, RECEIVED BY THE PANEL AND THE WTO SECRETARIAT ON 14 SEPTEMBER 2004

I refer to your letter of July 9, 2004, addressed to the Director General of the World Intellectual Property Organization (WIPO), relating to the Panel established by the WTO Dispute Settlement Body to examine two ongoing disputes on the basis of the matter referred to in WTO documents WT/DS174/20 and WT/DS290/18.

In response to your request, please find attached a note with five annexes prepared by the International Bureau.

On behalf of WIPO, I wish to reiterate our readiness to provide any further assistance.

LIST OF MATERIALS FROM DIPLOMATIC CONFERENCES ADOPTING, REVISING AND AMENDING ARTICLES 2 AND 3 OF THE PARIS CONVENTION FOR THE PROTECTION OF INDUSTRIAL PROPERTY (1967)

General

This note contains a list of the materials that the International Bureau of the World Intellectual Property Organization (WIPO) has compiled following a request for assistance as contained in a letter, dated July 9, 2004, received from Mr. Miguel Rodríguez Mendoza, Chairman of the Panel on European Communities – Protection of Trademarks and Geographical Indications for Agricultural Products and Foodstuffs established by the WTO Dispute Settlement Body.

The Panel has sought the assistance of the International Bureau of WIPO, at this stage, in respect of Article 2 of the Paris Convention for the Protection of Industrial Property (Stockholm Act of 1967) and any other provisions, of relevance to the categories of intellectual property at issue in this dispute, which set out criteria for the eligibility of natural or legal persons for protection under the Paris Convention requesting, as indicated in the letter in question, "the assistance of the International Bureau in the form of any factual information available to it relevant to the interpretation of the provisions in question, in particular as reflected in the materials of diplomatic conferences, subsequent developments in the framework of the Paris Union or other work under the auspices of the WIPO as well as, to the extent available to the International Bureau, on the state practice of the Paris Union members."

The Panel's request would, at this stage, appear to concern:

(i) the national treatment obligation contained in Article 2 of the Paris Convention and the intended meaning of the term "national" used therein; and

(ii) the criteria for determining the eligibility of natural or legal persons to enjoy protection under the Paris Convention.

The materials compiled by the International Bureau in respect of these two items and listed below are confined to Articles 2 and 3 of the Paris Convention. Article 2 refers to what is generally referred to as the "national treatment" obligation. Article 3 provides for the assimilation of certain persons with "nationals" of the Paris Union. Both articles apply generally to all categories of industrial property under the Paris Convention.

The International Bureau understands that the Panel's request for information does not extend to the question of a person's "eligibility" under any specific provision of the Paris Convention resulting from compliance with the particular requirements specified by such provision in addition to the qualification of that person under Articles 2 and 3.

The materials compiled include excerpts from the Official Records of the various Diplomatic Conferences which adopted, amended or revised the provisions currently contained in Articles 2 and 3 of the Paris Convention (Stockholm Act of 1967). These provisions were last changed at the Revision Conference held at The Hague in 1925, and have not been amended since.

The official records of the diplomatic conferences, from which the excerpts listed below have been extracted, are only available in the French language. The English translations of the successive versions of Articles 2 and 3 as included in the abovementioned Acts of the Paris Convention have been prepared by the International Bureau of WIPO and are also attached.

1. Excerpts from the Records of the Paris Diplomatic Conference (1880/1883)

A. Conférence internationale pour la protection de la propriété intellectuelle (1880)

General

Pages 11 to 24 (*Procès-verbal de la première séance*)

Pages 25 to 41 (*Procès-verbal de la deuxième séance)*

Article 2

Pages 42 to 47 (*Procès-verbal de la troisième séance*)

Articles 2 and 3

Pages 123 to 132 (*Procès-verbal de la neuvième séance*)

Article 3

Pages 137 to 138, 147 to 150 (*Procès-verbal de la dixième séance*)

Pages 161 to 167 (*Séance de clôture, Projet de convention et Protocole de clôture)*

B. Conférence internationale pour la protection de la propriété intellectuelle (1883)

General

Pages 3, 51 to 62 (*Convention et Protocole de clôture)*

2. *Excerpts from the Records of the Brussels Revision Conference (1897/1900)*

Article 2

Pages 89 and 95 to 97 (*Proposition présentée par l'Administration des États-Unis*)

Pages 143 to 144 (*Première annexe au procès-verbal de la Réunion préparatoire du 1er décembre 1897 – Tableau général des propositions, contre-propositions et amendements soumis à la conférence)*

Articles 2 and 3

Pages 163 and 164 (*Proposition présentée par la Délégation française au cours de la réunion préparatoire du 1er décembre 1897*)

Pages 185, 187, 188 (*Procès-verbal de la deuxième séance – 4 décembre 1897)*

Pages 195 to 200 (*Procès-verbal de la troisième séance – 6 décembre 1897)*

Pages 309 to 311 *(Procès-verbal de la neuvième séance – 13 décembre 1897)*

Page 341 (*Premier protocole final - 14 décembre 1897)*

General

Pages 407, 410 to 412 *(Acte additionel du 14 décembre 1900 modifiant la Convention du 20 novembre 1883 ainsi que le Protocole de clôture y annexé)*

3. *Excerpts from the Records of the Washington Revision Conference (1911)*

Article 2

Pages 42 to 44 and 53 *(Exposé des motifs et propositions préparé par le Bureau international; II. Personnes protégées et étendue de la protection; Juridiction)*

Pages 58 and 59 *(Avant-projet d'une Convention pour la protection de la propriété industrielle)*

Articles 2 and 3

Pages 94, 105, 106, 109 and 110 *(Propositions, contre-propositions et observations présentées par diverses administrations: 2. Administration de la France; 3. Administration de la Grande-Bretagne; 4. Administration des Pays-Bas)*

Pages 183 to 187 *(Procès-verbal de la réunion préparatoire, première annexe: Tableau général des propositions, contre-propositions et amendements soumis à la Conférence)*

Pages 223 and 224 *(Procès-verbal de la réunion préparatoire, deuxième annexe: Propositions présentées au cours de la réunion préparatoire)*

Page 226 *(Procès-verbal de la réunion préparatoire, troisième annexe: Nouvelle rédaction pour les articles 1, 2, 5 à 9, 11, et 16 de l'avant-projet)*

Pages 245 to 247 *(Procès-verbal de la troisième séance)*

Pages 269 to 271 *(Premier rapport présenté au nom de la sous-commission chargée d'examiner les articles 1 et 2 de la Convention)*

Pages 306, 307, 310 to 312 *(Rapport présenté à la commission plénière)*

Page 331 *(Actes adoptés par la Conférence)*

4. *Excerpts from the Records of the Hague Revision Conference (1925)*

Article 2

Pages 222 to 225 (*Exposé des motifs et propositions; II Principes fondamentaux de la Convention*)

Page 267 (*Avant-projet de la Convention de Paris révisée pour la protection de la propriété industrielle; Texte unique révisé*)

Page 333 (*Propositions, contre-propositions et observations*)

Page 413 to 415 (*Rapport de la première sous-commission*)

Page 517 (*Rapport de la commission générale à la conférence*)

Pages 536 to 537 (*Rapport de la commission de rédaction*)

Page 572 (*Procès-verbal de la deuxième séance plénière*)

Article 3

This provision was not discussed at the Hague Revision Conference.

5. *English translations of Articles 2 and 3 as contained in the 1883, 1900, 1911 and 1925 Acts of the Paris Convention*